◀ NE⊙S ▶

N ew – In the NEOS guides emphasis is placed on the discovery and enjoyment of a new destination through meeting the people, tasting the food and absorbing the exotic atmosphere. In addition to recommendations on which sights to see, we give details on the most suitable places to stay and eat, on what to look out for in traditional markets and where to go in search of the hidden character of the region, its crafts and its dancing rhythms. For those keen to explore places on foot, we provide guidelines and useful addresses in order to help organise walks to suit all tastes.

E xpert – The NEOS guides are written by people who have travelled in the country and researched the sites before recommending them by the allocation of stars. Accommodation and restaurants are similarly recommended by a 🛏 on the grounds of quality and value for money. Cartographers have drawn easy-to-use maps with clearly marked itineraries, as well as detailed plans of towns, archaeological sites and large museums.

(•) pen to all cultures, the NEOS guides provide an insight into the daily lives of the local people. In a world that is becoming ever more accessible, it is vital that religious practices, regional etiquette, traditional customs and languages be understood and respected by all travellers. Equipped with this knowledge, visitors can seek to share and enjoy with confidence the best of the local cuisine, musical harmonies and the skills involved in the production of arts and crafts.

S ensitive to the atmosphere and heritage of a foreign land, the NEOS guides encourage travellers to see, hear, smell and feel a country, through words and images. Take inspiration from the enthusiasm of our experienced travel writers and make this a journey full of discovery and enchantment.

B. Pérousse/MICHELIN

Practical information   92

GREECE

Official name: Hellenic Republic
Area: 131 944km^2
Population: 10.6 million
Capital: Athens (Athína)
Currency: euro (formerly drachma)

Setting the scene

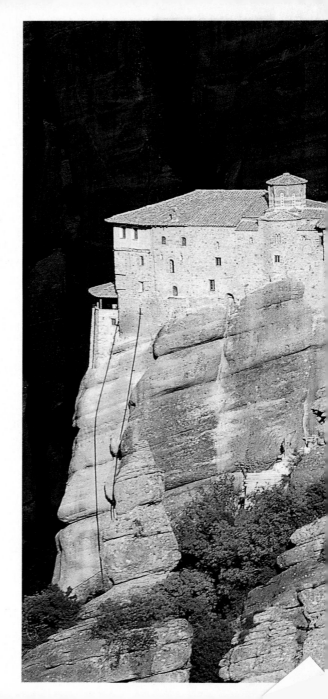

The Roussánou
Monastery,
between heaven
and earth
(Metéora, Thessaly)

BETWEEN MOUNTAIN AND SEA

With a surface area of nearly 132 000km², Greece is a small country, a little over half the size of the United Kingdom. However, its exceptional geographical location in the heart of the Mediterranean Sea, its hospitable climate and historical reputation make it one of the top destinations for holidaymakers, drawing archaeology enthusiasts and sun-seekers alike. The jagged contours of Greece form the southern extremity of the great Balkan Peninsula with a particularly fragmented relief. If you look at a map of Greece, you will immediately be struck by the fact that there are mountains everywhere, covering almost 80% of the country and even extending to the islands. The mountains are mostly part of the **Dinaric Alps**, a range which rises far to the north, then crosses Croatia, Bosnia and Herzegovina, Montenegro and Albania. However, although many of the summits in Greece exceed 2 000m, the legendary **Mt Olympus**, the highest of them all, peaks at only 2 917m. On the other hand, some massifs do stand out on account of abrupt changes of level and dramatically steep slopes. Consequently, very little room remains for the rare **plains** in Greece, which are to be found mainly in the north (Thessaly, Thrace and Macedonia). But although the mountains stand proudly for all to admire, it is the sea which seems to cast an irresistible spell upon visitors, who are drawn to it as if by the call of the Sirens. We are referring here, of course, to the **Aegean Sea**. For, despite the extensive western coastlines facing the Ionian Sea and the Sea of Crete in the middle of the Mediterranean, when the Greeks talk of the sea, they are almost invariably thinking of the Aegean and its countless islands. Even the country's loss of the territories in Asia Minor did little to undermine the feeling that the sea is Greek to the core, since all of the islands bordering the Turkish coast except for two were annexed by Greece over a century ago.

A land in constant movement

The rather unusual landscape of Greece can be explained by two great tectonic phenomena. First of all, at the beginning of the Tertiary Period, a movement of the earth's crust gave birth to the **eastern Hellenidic ranges**. This structural mass of limestone with its regular folds forms the spine of Greece, with the peaks of the **Epirus**, **Pindus**, and **Peloponnese** ranges and the **mountain ridge of Crete** running from north to south. Erosion then set to work, carving out a karstic landscape sprinkled with caves, plateaux and inland basins, such as peaceful Arcadia in the heart of the Peloponnese. The history of eastern Greece and the Aegean Islands (except for Crete) is somewhat different: they are connected to an ancient primary substratum which fragmented, causing both **subsidence**, allowing the Aegean Sea to flood in, and **upthrusts**, of which the most striking remains are Mt Olympus in the north of Thessaly, **Pelion**, in the south-east of the same region, and above all the **Aegean Islands**.

As for the great arc of the Hellenic islands, its curvature can be attributed to the African plate moving under the European plate: the friction between these two titans is the cause of the **earthquakes** and **volcanic activity** which have been going on in the Aegean since time immemorial, in particular around the island of Santoríni, home of the legend of Atlantis.

The heart of Greece

Like a giant four-fingered hand, the **Peloponnese Peninsula** marks the southern tip of mainland Greece, a strange appendage linked to Attica by the Isthmus of Corinth and separated from the north by the narrow gulf of the same name. This peninsula became an island upon the construction of the **Corinth Canal** (1882-93), a two-millennia-old project which was finally completed at the end of the 19C. The Peloponnese, where some of the most famous ancient sites are to be found, is an extremely mountainous area with three peninsulas extending from its southern end.

Backed by farmland, most of its large towns stand near the coast on the plains of **Elis** to the west, **Achaia** and **Corinthía** to the north, **Messinía** and **Lakonía** to the south, and **Argolis** to the east. The only exception to this rule is the town of Trípoli, which is set in the heart of the pasturelands of **Arcadia**.

Further south, the rugged **Taíyetos** mountain range culminates in the **Máni Peninsula**, an arid landscape dotted with astonishing villages of tall square towers. The population in these villages is dwindling, and indeed some have been completely abandoned, because, despite the region's attractiveness to tourists, it provides a difficult living environment.

To the north of the Peloponnese lies **central Greece**, the heart of the country, which stretches down into the famous **Attica Peninsula**, forever dominated by the imposing city of Athens. Bounded by the peaks of **Mt Parnes**, **Mt Pentelikon** and **Mt Hymettus**, the vast urban centre of Athens, which has been the capital city since 1834, today boasts a population of over 3 million, almost one third of the country's total population.

Running parallel to the coastline of Attica and Boeotia is the island of **Euboea**, separated from the mainland by a narrow channel. This very mountainous island stretches out in a long ridge with sheer eastern slopes that offer no natural harbour on the Aegean. The island compensates for this handicap by turning more towards the mainland and making the most of its proximity to the capital.

The two vast and fertile plains of **Boeotia**, watered by the Kifisós and Asopós rivers, extend to the north of Attica. It was from their wealth that the ancient city of Thebes drew its strength to become the main city of the Boeotian League. Today, however, this old rival of Sparta and Athens is no more than a small commercial town of no great importance.

To the west, the mountains once again stake their claim, marking the boundary with **Phocis** and some of the most significant places in Greek mythology, including **Mt Parnassus** (2 457m), which was home to Apollo and his nine Muses. Its slopes are today the privileged domain of hikers and skiers, but also of the countless tourists who come to explore the illustrious oracular shrine at **Delphi**, dedicated to Apollo.

The border country

The peaks of Phocis mark the beginning of the imposing **Pindus Chain** which, from north to south, isolates **Epirus** from the rest of the country. With rainfall levels much higher than the national average, the Pindus range, culminating in **Mt Smólikas** (2 637m), is cloaked in thick coniferous forests which make access to the hinterland difficult. These wooded mountains moreover served for a long time as a natural barrier against the advance of the Ottomans. They are now mainly inhabited by wolves, bears and a whole range of wildlife which, for a number of years now, has been able to flourish undisturbed in the two large **national parks** north of **Ioánnina**. To the west of this wall of rock, a few small plains with market gardens and orchards are scattered around the **Gulf of Árta** (to the south). Further northwards, a thin strip of coast heads up to the Albanian border, leading to the majestic site of **Párga**, with its coves, clear blue water and sandy beaches. Not far from here, on the once marshy **Acherón** estuary, is where the ancients situated the Gates of Hell, from where Charon ferried the souls of the deceased to the realm of Hades (*see page 48*).

Fertile plains

East of the Pindus, **Thessaly** presents a different aspect of the country. This is Greece's main agricultural region, stretching out in an immense plain, surrounded on all sides by the highest mountains. To the south, Timfristós and Óthris, to the west the impenetrable Pindus Chain, to the north, **Mt Olympus**, the country's highest peak and realm of the gods, without forgetting, to the east, Óssa and Pelion, which the Giants of mythology wanted to pile on top of each other to compete with their divine neighbours. Irrigated by the **River Piniós** and its numerous tributaries, the fertile lands of the Thessalian plain are ideal for cultivating cereals and raising cattle. In a curious contrast with the surrounding plain and Pindus massif, the **Metéora**, huge pillars of rock created by erosion, stand like sugar loaves set down by some eccentric god. Perched on their summits are several Byzantine monasteries dating back to the 14C and 15C.

To the north of Thessaly, between Olympus and Óssa, the narrow Vale of Tempe leads up to **Macedonia**, birthplace of **Philip II** and of his son **Alexander the Great**. Here the mountains give way to alluvial valleys, all of them agricultural basins. Cotton fields extend over the plain, which is fed by the Axiós and Aliákmonas rivers and culminates in a marshy delta.

Further westwards, the foothills of **Mt Vérmio** are covered in vineyards and fruit trees, while to the east lies the great port of **Thessaloníki** (Salonika), the second largest city in Greece. Thessaloníki guards the entrance to **Chalcidice**, a broad three-pronged fork covered in forests, which juts out into the sea. Although the sandy beaches of Sithonía and Kassándra attract many a holidaymaker, the **Mt Athos Peninsula** is a land apart, timeless territory of the biggest monastic city in Europe, which is more than ten centuries old and off-limits to women.

Beyond Thessaloníki, eastern Macedonia's fields of **cotton** and especially tobacco, provide a foretaste of the landscapes of **Thrace**. Fragmented by the southern reaches of the **Rhodope Mountains**, which lie mainly in Bulgaria, the Thracian plains are also bathed in the reddish-brown colour of the **tobacco** leaves which are left to dry on long wooden pikes. Near the border with Turkey, which is separated from Thrace by the **River Évros**, the region takes on an oriental flavour: mosques, bazaars and women in headscarves are to be seen in the villages, and Turkish can already be heard in the streets.

"Thálassa", or the Greek islands

No fewer than 437 islands, over 150 of which are inhabited, are scattered all around Greece, like pearls that have fallen from a broken necklace, with Crete being lost near the shores of the African continent. And this is without counting the islets, reefs, plain old rocks, or Scylla and Charybdis.

The most Greek sea of all, the **Aegean** boasts the greatest number of these islands, including the sun-drenched archipelago of the **Cyclades**, a favoured travellers' destination. It is a strange sight to see these almost bare and arid islands whose population increases tenfold in summer. Here you will be dazzled by the colours: the clear blue of the sea, the brilliant white of the houses and the ochre of the bare hills.

Just as mountainous, the "twelve islands" of the remote **Dodecanese** are barely any greener. Only **Kos** and prestigious **Rhodes** enjoy a more gentle climate, with sufficiently fertile land and enough rainfall to produce fruit and cereals.

The **north-eastern islands**, even closer to the Turkish coast, are blessed with a more lush vegetation. The island of **Sámos** even has expanses of dense pine forests and the flourishing Mediterranean scrubland known as garrigue.

Heading southwards, **Crete**, the last frontier before Egypt, is the largest and most populated of the Greek islands. Here, the land is fertile, producing an abundance of cereals, fruit, vegetables, vines and olives. But it is also just as mountainous as the rest of Greece, consisting of a long rocky ridge culminating in **Mt Ida** (2 456m), into which erosion has carved numerous basins, cirques and caves steeped in legend.

On the western side, the seven **Ionian Islands** hug the Greek coastline, facing Italy. Long occupied by the Venetians, they reflect a curious but attractive mixture of Hellenic and Latin influences. Although these islands have been hit by earthquakes many times throughout the centuries, they differ from the Aegean Islands in that they have a much higher population, more profuse vegetation and a greater capacity to accommodate tourists.

A land of sunshine

For the most part, Greece has a **typically Mediterranean climate** with mild wet winters and hot dry summers. There are, however, considerable differences between the regions, mainly due to variations in altitude and latitude. In the north, in **Thrace** and especially in **Macedonia**, the temperatures are more bearable in summer, but the winters can sometimes be extremely harsh, with temperatures dropping to minus 20°C in eastern Macedonia. On the other hand, winter is practically non-existent in the south of the **Peloponnese**, and particularly in **Crete**, which even has some banana groves.

In autumn and winter, the **Ionian Islands** and **western coasts** suffer heavy rainfall which turns into snow on the higher ground, while the east of the country is protected by the mountain chain in the centre. Thus

H. Choimet/MICHELIN

Bougainvillaea, flowers of the islands

Corfu has an average annual rainfall three times greater than that of Athens.

But with the sunshine comes the drought. Raging through most of the country in summer, it often causes fires, fanned by the **meltem**, a hot dry wind which blows across the Aegean from May to September.

Flora...

With over 6 000 plant varieties, Greece boasts a particularly rich and colourful flora. The mountainsides and the humid lands of Epirus are carpeted in **forests** of Aleppo pines, holm oaks, Greek firs, chestnut and beech trees. Below an altitude of 800m, the forests give way to a varied **maquis**, a scrubland vegetation of lentisk, carob, cistus, myrtle, heather, oleander and juniper, whose combined fragrances infuse the air with a balmy and delicious scent.

The arid regions of the south and the Cyclades are mostly covered in a sort of low-lying garrigue called **phrygana**, which is just as fragrant. The omnipresent **olive trees** dominate the Greek countryside, painting the landscapes with their soft grey-green colour, so typical of the Mediterranean countries. In addition to **orange** and **lemon trees, vineyards** can still be found in many places, where grapes are cultivated both for eating (notably producing the famous currants) and for **wine**.

... and fauna

Although perhaps not quite as abundant, the wildlife in Greece does spring a few surprises. A great variety of **birds** live, reproduce or make a stop on their long migratory journeys in the marshy deltas and other wetlands here: **geese**, **ducks** and **cormorants** cross paths with huge **white pelicans** and **Dalmatian pelicans**, and also with **white storks**, whose large nests can often be seen crowning church domes in Thessaly. **Birds of prey** reign over the higher reaches: various vultures and falcons, as well as the extremely rare **greater spotted eagle**, are to be seen gliding through the air before swooping down on their prey.

A few **brown bears**, lynx, wolves and wild cats inhabit the dense forests of Epirus, home of the Víkos-Aoós and Pindus nature reserves. Much greater numbers of **wild boar** roam the forests in search of berries, while various species of **lizard** live among the rocks. In Crete, the odd **chameleon** can be found hiding among the leaves.

Flora and fauna

Five millennia of history

Dates	Events	Places
6000-3000	Neolithic Period	*Seyklo, Dimini*
3200-1900	Cycladic civilisation	*Cyclades*

The Bronze Age in Crete (3000-800 BC)

Dates	Events	Places
3000-2000	Early Minoan. Early Bronze Age	
2000-1570	Middle Minoan. First palaces.	*Knossós*
	Linear A script	
1570-1150	Late Minoan. Disappearance of the Minoan civilisation on the mainland	
2500-2000	Early Helladic. Early Bronze Age	
2000-1600	Middle Helladic. Arrival of the Achaeans	
1600-1100	Late Helladic. Mycenaean civilisation.	*Mycenae, Árgos*
	Linear B script	
Circa 1100	Dorian invasions. Colonisation of Asia Minor by the Ionian Greeks	
1100-800	The "Dark Age"	

Antiquity (8C BC – 395 AD)

Dates	Events	Places
8C	Homer writes the *Iliad* and the *Odyssey*. *Pólis* civilisation. Greek alphabet	
776	Creation of the Olympic Games	
735-734	Beginning of the colonisation of Italy and Sicily	*Náxos, Syracuse*
734-680	Lelantine War	
680-660	Colonisation of the Black Sea	*Byzantium*
655-585	Tyranny of Cypselus and Periander	*Corinth*
595-586	First Sacred War to gain control of Delphi	
546-510	Tyranny of Peisistratus and his sons	*Athens*
546	The Persians led by Cyrus impose their sovereignty upon the Ionian Greeks	
499	Beginning of the Persian Wars. Revolt of the Ionian Greeks	*Sardis*
490	Battle of Marathon	
480-479	Battles of Thermopylae, Salamis and Plataea	
449	Peace of Callias	
460-429	The "Age of Pericles". Peloponnesian War. Athens is conquered by Sparta	*Athens*
338	Battle of Chaeronea. Philip II of Macedon conquers Greece	
334-323	Alexander the Great builds his Empire	
197	Battle of Cynoscephalae. Roman occupation of Greece	
27 BC	Greece becomes the Roman province of Achaia	
330 AD	Constantinople becomes capital of the Empire	

The Byzantine Period (395-1453 AD)

Dates	Events	Places
395	Beginning of the Byzantine Empire. Invasion by Alaric and the Visigoths	
467	Invasion by Gaiseric and the Vandals	
476	End of the Roman Empire in the West	
7C	Slav and Avar invasions	
1054	East-West Schism	

1204	Capture of Constantinople by the Crusaders. Founding of the Latin Empire
1261	Michael VIII Paleologus recaptures Constantinople
1402	The Mongol Tamerlane defeats the Ottomans *Ankara*
1453	Mehmet II and the Ottomans capture Constantinople

The Ottoman Period (1453-1830 AD)

1521-66	Reign of Süleyman the Magnificent
1522	Rhodes captured by Süleyman
1571	Conquest of Cyprus
1669	The Venetians lose their last base in Crete *Candia (Haniá)*
1770	Revolt in the Peloponnese. Turkish repression
1797	Napoleon takes the Ionian Islands
1798	Execution of Rígas Pheraíos
1821	Beginning of the revolt in Greece
1825	Intervention of the troops of the viceroy of Egypt, Mehmet Ali
1827	Egyptian-Turkish fleet defeated by a combined Russian-British-French fleet *Navarino*
1829	Signing of the Treaty of Adrianople

Modern times

1830	Treaty of London
1831	Kapodístrias assassinated
1832-62	Reign of Otto I of Bavaria
1863-1913	Reign of George I
1878	Congress of Berlin on the Balkans
1897	Defeat of Greek soldiers in Macedonia and Crete
1912	First Balkan War
1913	Second Balkan War
1919-20	Treaties of Neuilly and Sèvres, considerable territorial gains
1922	Mustafa Kemal's victory over the Greeks. Asia Minor and western Thrace become Turkish. Exodus of the population
1924-35	Unsuccessful attempt at a republic
1936-41	Dictatorship of General Metaxás
1941-44	German, Italian and Bulgarian occupation
1946-49	Civil War, victory of anti-Communist forces
1947	Restitution of the Dodecanese Islands
1951	Greece joins NATO
1967-74	Colonels' junta
1974	Turkish invasion of Cyprus
1981	Greece joins the EEC
1992-94	Crisis with the new Republic of Macedonia
1995	Kostis Stephanopoulos, ex-member of Karamanlís' party, elected President
1997	Election of the Socialist Kóstas Simítis, representative of the PASOK movement
February 2000	Re-election of the Conservative Kostis Stephanopoulos by the Chamber of Deputies
April 2000	Re-election of the Socialist Kóstas Simítis by popular vote
1 January 2001	Greece enters the European Monetary Union

Five millennia of history

THE CRADLE OF EUROPE

Like Egypt and a handful of other countries, Greece has the distinction of being profoundly marked by one period in its history. The exceptional appeal of Antiquity and the Hellenic civilisation should not, however, be allowed to outshine two millennia of history set in the heart of the Macedonian, Roman, Byzantine and Ottoman empires, which witnessed a succession of legendary characters such as Alexander the Great, Emperor Constantine, and Süleyman the Magnificent of Turkey.

The history of Greece is that of a country which, at the price of stubborn and often heroic resistance, managed to regain its freedom and independence and take a firm foothold in Europe and the modern age.

The dawn of history
(5000-1200 BC)

Traces of human life dating back to the Neolithic Period have been found at the sites of Sesklo and Dimini in Thessaly, and the remains of a very ancient settlement from the 5th millennium BC have also been found in the Cyclades. The discovery in Argolis (in the east of the Peloponnese) of 13 000-year-old tools made of obsidian from the island of Mílos, revealed that the islanders, as well as being experienced sailors, entertained relations with the mainland.

The Cyclades, or a civilisation of idols

At the end of the 4th millennium BC, a veritable civilisation began to flourish in the Cyclades. Traces of its influence have been found as far afield as Portugal and the mouth of the Danube. Originally, the island settlements were built mainly along the coast, but the threat of piracy subsequently encouraged the islanders to take refuge in fortified villages in the higher reaches. Very little remains of these little cities, and it is the necropolises that have yielded the most information to archaeologists. Indeed, these generally mass graves contained a great many objects: crockery, jewellery, statuettes, but above all the famous marble "idols" (*see page 34*) with their very modern forms, which have become the symbol of this original civilisation. Soon, however, the rise of the Minoan civilisation in Crete swept the Cyclades up in its path, and another page of history was turned.

From labyrinths to fortified cities

It was not until the Bronze Age that two great so-called palace civilisations began to develop. The earliest one, which was discovered in 1900 by **Sir Arthur Evans'** excavations on the site of Knossós, originated in Crete. It was named the **Minoan civilisation** after the legendary King of Crete, **Minos**, who is thought to have lived in the palace of Knossós. The Minoan civilisation really began to make its mark in 2200 BC, when the foundations of the first palaces were laid at Knossós, Phaistos and Mália. Veritable autonomous urban complexes, they contained shrines, shops, craftsmen's workshops and houses. These "palace-cities" contained a very hierarchical society, where the arts flourished and business prospered, with trade relations being established with the Cyclades, Syria, Egypt and the western coast of Asia Minor.

However, for some reason which is still a mystery – perhaps a volcanic eruption on Santoríni, an earthquake or invasions – this brilliant civilisation suddenly disappeared between 1450 and 1375 BC. It was superseded by another palace civilisation, this time developing on mainland Greece, the **Mycenaean civilisation**. Born from the mingling of the local populations with the **Achaeans**, a seafaring people who had arrived from the north at the beginning of the 2nd millennium BC, it flourished towards 1600 BC around palatial centres such as Mycenae, Árgos and Tírintha in Argolis, and Pílos in Messinía. This warlike society, discovered by the German archaeologist **Heinrich Schliemann** between 1870 and 1890, constitutes the historical basis of all of the legends linked to the heroic age and the Homeric Trojan War, Upon contact with the Minoan civilisation, it gained **syllabic script** (known as Linear B), derived from Cretan script (Linear A), which the British architect **Michael Ventris** deciphered in 1952.

However, around 1200 BC, most of the palace-cities were destroyed, and the Mycenaean world in turn disappeared, for reasons which also remain unclear. Some speak of internal conflicts, caused purely by the bellicose nature of the Mycenaean people; others prefer the theory of an external cause, a new wave of invasions by an Indo-European people, the **Dorians**. Legend has it that they caused the Ionians of Attica and the island of Euboea to flee to the western coast of Asia Minor where they founded the **first Ionian cities**. Whatever the real reason, the fall of the Mycenaean civilisation marks a major turning point in the history of Greece. Not only were the main sites abandoned, but their script also disappeared, not to come to light again until three centuries later with the Phoenicians. However, after slowly maturing during this Dark Age (12C-9C BC) a new and totally transformed Greek society was to see the light of day in the 8C BC.

Antiquity, or the Greece of legend
(8C BC-4C AD)

The golden age of the "pólis"
Gradually, a new social organisation emerged, the *pólis*, a **city state** consisting of an urban centre and the surrounding farmland. The *pólis* inhabitants formed a rigidly structured civic community harking back to distant ancestors, often mythical founders of the city. With the abandonment of the palaces, the real power subsequently passed to the aristocracy (*basileís*) in a large majority of cases, and the citizens regularly gathered together for ceremonies of their shared cults, in particular to worship the **god of the pólis.**

Bearing witness to its power, the *pólis* began to spread abroad: from the late 8C to the early 6C BC, Chalcis, Corinth, Megara, Miletus and many other cities set up **colonies** in Sicily (Syracuse, Catania), in southern Italy (Cumae, Tarentum) and in the south of

The frescoes of Firá (Santoríni),
an exceptional portrait of life in the Cyclades around 1500 BC

Gaul (Alalia in Corsica, Massalia / Marseille), up to the periphery of the Propontis (Byzantium) and the Black Sea, via the islands and promontories of Thrace and Macedonia.

Organised warfare

Judging by the success of the great pan-Hellenic sanctuaries of Olympia, Delos and Delphi, one may be forgiven for thinking that perfect harmony reigned between the cities. But this was far from the truth; conflicts were rife. However, the face of war was changing: at the end of the 8C BC, the Lelantine War between Chalcis and Eretria was probably the last Homeric-type war, ie a ritualised combat where the

Inter-city games

Created in 776 BC, the Olympic Games gave the city states the opportunity to measure each other's strength peacefully, through sports. In the stadium of Olympia, in the palestra or gymnasium, the winners of running races, pentathlons, wrestling sports and chariot races (quadriga) were awarded prizes and honours, their victories reflecting glory onto their "pólis". This highly political prestige, however, did not come without danger. On one notable occasion, the sons of Peisistratus, taking offence at the third quadriga victory of Cimon of Athens (528 BC), and in fear of losing their power, did not hesitate to have him assassinated.

use of arrows was not allowed and during which the champions fell one by one. In the 7C BC, a veritable military formation, the **hoplite phalanx**, appeared and continued to be used until the 2C BC. It consisted of several closed ranks of soldiers, the *hoplites*, advancing together, each equipped with greaves, breastplate and helmet made of bronze, a heavy shield of wood also set in bronze, a spear and short sword.

From tyranny to democracy

Sparta was the hoplite city par excellence. With its power extending over the whole of the Peloponnese, its constitution spread far and wide, sweeping away in its path the **tyrants** who had been dominating the surrounding cities from the mid-7C BC. These despots (Cypselus in Corinth, **Peisistratus** and his sons in Athens, Orthagoras and Cleisthenes in Sicyon) took advantage of popular discontent to seize power unlawfully from the ruling aristocracy. Although they were often overthrown after one or two generations on account of their authoritarianism, the success of these tyrants highlighted the necessity for **democratic reform**. After the first measures taken by the legislator Solon early in the 6C BC, it was Cleisthenes, in 508 BC, and **Pericles**, around 450 BC, who eventually ensured the rule of democracy in Athens. This democracy was, however, very relative, concerning only 8% of the citizens.

The Persian Wars

Since 546 BC, the Persians had been imposing their sovereignty over the Greek cities of Ionia in Asia Minor. In 499 BC, at the instigation of Aristagoras, the tyrant of Miletus, these cities revolted and burnt down Sardis, with the aid of Athens and Eretria. The revolt ended in 494 BC following a naval defeat and the sacking of Miletus. Three years later, the Persian **Darius** decided to take revenge, demanding earth and water from the Greeks as a symbol of submission. Of the big cities, only Athens and Sparta –

The battle of the champions

Around 546 BC a rather curious battle was fought between Sparta and Árgos, a combination of old-style – or Homeric – war and hoplite combat. In the long conflict between the two cities, 300 Spartans confronted 300 Argives. When the fighting was over, one single Spartan survivor found himself facing two Argives, who proclaimed victory and promptly fled... causing the Spartans to claim that victory was in fact theirs.

which were allies for a time – refused to accept the Persian claims and, in 490 BC, Darius suffered a bitter defeat at the hands of the Athenians on the now famous Marathon plain.

In 480 BC, it was Sparta's turn to provide the heroes. This time it was **Xerxes**, the great new King of Persia, who was planning to subjugate the Greeks. With a considerable army and a fleet of over 600 ships, he won a crushing victory over the Spartans at **Thermopylae**. But the heroism of **Leonidas** and his 300 men, who sacrificed their lives to slow the advance of the Persians, has gone down in history. Shortly afterwards, the great sea battle of **Salamis** dashed Xerxes' hopes completely. The Persian ships were overwhelmed by the Greek fleet under the command of the skilful Athenian strategist, **Themistocles**. This victory was confirmed on land the following year at the battle of **Plataea**.

The Classical Period

It was only the alliance between Sparta and Athens which enabled Xerxes' army to be vanquished.

The first Marathon

After landing at Eretria, the Persian army was preparing to go into battle on the Marathon plain. Warned by a trained runner, Pheidippides, who ran over 200km in 36hr (almost five times the distance of a modern marathon), the Spartans proffered the excuse of a religious festival for arriving when the battle was over. The 10 000 Athenians under the command of Miltiades therefore had to do without the Spartans, but with the help of 1 000 Plataeans, they managed to rout the enemy, forcing them to flee back to their ships. The Persians lost over 6 000 men, the Athenians only 192. This victory was the pride of Athens for generations to come, and, for a long time, there was considered to be no greater honour than to have been part of it.

However, this alliance was against nature. In 478 BC, Sparta had preferred to relinquish command of the fleet to the Athenians rather than share it. So in order to complete the liberation of the entire territory of Greece, Athens created the **Delian League**, which, in 466 BC, won the Battle of the Eurymedon before signing the **Peace of Callias** in 449 BC with Persia. Athenian hegemony was at its peak: at the head of an extremely powerful fleet, the city controlled the Aegean Sea and trade, and asserted its domination over the allied cities. After being sacked by the Persians in 480 BC, Athens had rebuilt its fortifications, which were linked to the port of Piraeus by two "Long Walls" of protection. Ambitious work was begun on the Acropolis, and with the enlightened cultural politics of **Pericles** (460-429 BC), Athens became the centre of Greece: this was the age of Sophocles, Euripides, the Sophists and **Socrates**.

This domination, however, riled and angered the other Greek cities which valued their freedom, particularly Athens' great rival, Sparta. Conflict was inevitable and came in 431 BC, when Sparta leapt to the defence of Corinth, which had taken a stand against Athens. Alliances were formed and soon the whole of Greece was in the grip of the Peloponnesian War. Athens managed to stand firm until the Peace of Nicias (421 BC), despite a terrible plague which killed almost one third of the city's population. Peace was, however, short-lived, and the failure of the expedition against Sicily (415-413 BC), undertaken on the advice of **Alcibiades**, marked a reversal of fortune from which Athens was never to recover. Despite a few resounding victories over the following years, the Athenian fleet suffered a disastrous defeat at the hands of the Spartan general, **Lysander**, in 405 BC. In 404 BC, Athens was forced to capitulate.

After a short period of calm, hostilities resumed and the next half-century witnessed successive attempts by Sparta, Athens and Thebes to gain hegemony over Greece. Signalling a serious decline in nationalism, these cities didn't hesitate to call on Persia to achieve their aims. The previously defeated Persia was quick to take advantage of the situation to seek revenge, imposing its authority when the peace treaties were signed.

Sparta, the anti-Athens

A Dorian city, proud of its constitution which saved it from tyranny, Sparta was the archetypal hoplite State. The originality of the Spartan system lay in its dual monarchy: two kings from two families both claiming to be descendants of Heracles, with their power being supervised and counterbalanced by five ephors elected for one year. With its sights set mainly on war, the city also became a refuge for all the oligarchs of Greece.

Alcibiades: portrait of an opportunist

Born into a great Athenian family, raised by Pericles, and a friend of Socrates, Alcibiades was handsome, rich, eloquent and intelligent. His flamboyance made him a magnet to women and men alike, he spent lavishly, and dazzled all and sundry with the success of his racing stables. A demagogue, he flattered the pride of the Athenians and secured the expedition against Sicily. However, his escapades also earned him many enemies. Accused of irreverence to the gods, he fled to Sparta where he did not hesitate to betray his birthplace by revealing Athens' weak points and sealing an alliance with Persia. However, kept at arm's length by the Spartans, Alcibiades betrayed them in turn, finally managing by way of intrigue, disavowals and clever speeches to return to Athens as a saviour. But not for long. He was stripped of all credit following the defeat of the Athenian fleet at the Battle of Notium (406 BC). He was removed from office, and his judicious advice to proceed with caution before the battle of 405 BC against Lysander was greeted with contempt. Following Athens' defeat, he took refuge in Phrygia, where the Spartans had him assassinated.

Victorious – but Macedonian – Hellenism

Ironically, the new outburst of Hellenism in the face of Persian influence came from a region that the Greeks considered to be practically barbaric. But Macedonia had become united very early on, and had since then been unfailingly philhellenic. Under the command of **Philip II** (359-336 BC), it took the Macedonian army less than 20 years to conquer Greece, taking advantage of the division between the cities and the endless indecision of Athens. When resistance was finally organised, the allies were easily overcome by the Macedonian phalanxes equipped with sarissas (5 to 7m-long spears) at the Battle of Chaeronea in 338 BC. Victorious, Philip founded the **League of Corinth** in order to guarantee the freedom of the Greek cities and to fight Persia.

When Philip was assassinated in 336 BC, his son **Alexander III the Great** pursued his dream and managed to achieve the tremendous conquest of the Persian Empire (334-323 BC). However, on his death in 323 BC, the young Macedonian Empire was already breaking up and being divided between his generals – including the founder of the **Seleucid** dynasty – and Greece found itself placed under the protectorate of the kings of Macedonia. Its attempts to regain its freedom were unsuccessful in spite of the recurrent conflicts between Alexander's successors.

A Roman province

After subjugating the Aetolians in 217 BC, Philip V sought to take control of the Adriatic and decided to support **Hannibal** in his campaign against Rome. Unfortunately, the Carthaginian was defeated, and the Romans waged two successive campaigns in Greece, culminating in their victory at **Cynoscephalae** in 197 BC. The following year, the consul, Flaminius, undertook to guarantee the freedom of the Greek cities. However, unsuccessful attacks led by the Seleucid King Antiochus III (192 BC), then the Macedonian King Perseus (168 BC), and in particular a rebellion by the Achaean League (headed by Corinth and severely quelled in 146 BC), tolled the knell of any hopes of independence.

Thereafter, the fate of Greece was inextricably linked to that of Rome. After claiming victory over Antony and Cleopatra at **Actium** (31 BC), Augustus annexed all of the Hellenic lands and turned Greece into the Roman **Province of Achaia** (27 BC). Greek civilisation nevertheless retained a great deal of prestige in the eyes of the Romans: the Romans demonstrated greater tolerance here in matters of both politics and religion than elsewhere in the Empire. Cities such as Ephesus, Alexandria and Athens were thus able to perpetuate the intellectual and cultural aura of Hellenism.

Byzantine Greece (395-1453 AD)

From the 3C AD, the Roman Empire suffered successive waves of barbarian invasions, which were to destroy its unity. The Eastern Empire was under particular threat and required the almost permanent presence of the emperor at the frontier (the **limes**).

A first step towards division was taken in 325, when Constantine ordered a city to be founded on the walls of what had formerly been Byzantium. This city was named after him – **Constantinople** – and he proclaimed it the new capital of the Empire (330). The Empire was effectively divided in 395 upon the death of Theodosius I, who shared the territory between his two sons, Honorius and Arcadius. And so Arcadius inherited control of the Eastern Empire, which at that time included the Balkans, Asia Minor, Syria, Palestine, northern Mesopotamia and Egypt in addition to Greece.

Alaric, or the Visigoth tornado
In an attempt to neutralise Alaric, Emperor Theodosius' successor, Arcadius, appointed him "master of the soldiers" in Illyricum and gave him Epirus. But this was all in vain: the Visigoth seized the opportunity to invade Italy and sow panic throughout the West (401-402). Driven back a first time by General Stilicho, he returned to Italy and sacked Rome in 410 but died before being able to invade Sicily.

A land under constant threat

In Greece at this time, the traces of the sea expeditions of the Goths, Heruli and Scythians in the second half of the 3C had begun to fade away, and only the terrible **earthquake** of 21 July 365 disturbed a period of relative peace that was to last for over a century. Under the reign of Theodosius, **Christianity** became the State religion, pagan cults were banned and the Olympic Games abolished. Despite the preaching of St Paul, paganism remained very much alive in Greece. This resistance to State Christianity was perhaps not unrelated to the passivity of the imperial troops when Alaric's **Visigoths** invaded Macedonia, then Thessaly and Achaia in 395.

Thereafter followed an increasing number of invasions. Arriving from Africa, the **Vandals**, led by Gaiseric, pillaged Rome then ravaged Greece (467) but did not stay for long. Conversely, the successive and occasionally simultaneous invasions of the **Slavs and Avars**, beginning in the late 6C, brought about extensive and long-lasting demographic change. On the one hand, a considerable number of Greeks were forced to flee the Peloponnese, and on the other, a steadily increasing number of Slavs were settling all over Greece, to such an extent that Byzantium had to resort to force to impose its authority over the region (783 and 805).

A cause for even greater concern, while the **Muslims** occupied Crete in the 9C and 10C, mainland Greece was facing invasions by the **Bulgars** led by Simeon and Samuel (late 10C), as well as the threat of the **Normans** of Sicily (late 11C). In the face of these regular challenges to its existence, the Byzantine Empire buckled but did not break. At least not under the blows of a known enemy. In one of the paradoxes of history, it was to yield to the Christians who had come from the West to lend assistance against the Turks.

The betrayal of the Crusaders

At the bidding of the French Pope, Urban II (1095), a tremendous spiritual impetus drove Western Christianity towards Jerusalem, which had been in Muslim hands since the 7C. The Byzantine emperors had indeed requested this intervention in the hopes of obtaining a reserve of men placed under their orders to help them

Byzantium, a Christian Empire
(fresco from Mt Athos)

B. Kaufmann/MICHELIN

reclaim land which was historically theirs. However, unaware of these reasons, the European noblemen who had embarked on the Crusade kept all of the land taken from the Seljuq Turks for themselves, organising it according to the feudal system. **Latin States** began to flourish: the Kingdom of Jerusalem, the County of Edessa, the County of Tripoli and the Principality of Antioch, whose existence was to further poison relations between Byzantines and Westerners, already considerably damaged by the religious issues which had led to the Schism of 1054.

Moreover, in Constantinople the growing number of Latin merchants, Venetians in particular, was stirring up jealousy and rancour, eventually leading to a sinister pogrom in 1182. Although Greece was little affected by the first three Crusades, it was directly involved in the fourth (1202-04), a *Chronicle* of which was written shortly afterwards by the marshal of Champagne, **Geoffroi de Villehardouin**. This Crusade was, in fact, to cause the fall of the Byzantine Empire. The original aim of the Crusaders was to attack the Muslim Empire in Egypt. However, when the knights were unable to pay for the Venetian ships which were to ferry them across the Mediterranean, they paid off their debt by carrying out the wishes of the Doge of Venice. And so, ignoring the bans and excommunications of Pope Innocent III, the Crusaders headed for Constantinople on the pretext of restoring the overthrown emperor, Isaac Angelus, and his son, Alexius IV, to the throne. After a first intervention in the capital which went smoothly, a second one, caused by friction with the Byzantine aristocracy, ended in the mass pillaging of the city and the creation of the **Latin Empire** in 1204.

The Franks in Greece

In truth, the Latin Empire of Constantinople pales in comparison with its predecessor. The unity which had been the strength of the Byzantine Empire was unable to withstand the diverging ambitions and infighting among the Crusaders. When the spoils were shared out, the Venetians took half of the capital, most of the Aegean Islands and a large number of strongholds in mainland Greece. Although **Baldwin of Flanders** could pride himself on being the first emperor of the Latin Empire, he had direct control only in the city of Constantinople and the surrounding regions, Thrace and Asia Minor. Elsewhere, he had to allow the main Crusade leaders to create their fiefs, following the purest feudal tradition. Boniface of Montferrat, who had led the Crusade, inherited the Kingdom of Thessaloníki. The Peloponnese, renamed **Principality of Morea** (or of Achaia), fell to Guillaume de Champlitte from Champagne. Through various vassals, the principality itself controlled a certain number of fiefs, including the powerful Duchy of Athens.

The Latin conquest of 1204 split the Byzantine Empire into four States: the Latin Empire of the East, the Byzantine Empires of Nicaea and Trebizond and, in Greece, the Byzantine Despotate of Epirus. The struggle between the Latins and the Byzantines thus commenced, barely delayed by a Bulgar invasion in Thrace. In 1224, the Byzantine Despotate of Epirus took possession of the Kingdom of Thessaloníki. At this time, the Franks were mainly concentrated in the Principality of Morea. Having fallen into the hands of the **Villehardouin** family, Morea gradually became suffused with French influence. In 1236, Geoffroi II Villehardouin saved the Latin emperor, Baldwin II, who was under siege in Constantinople, thereby asserting the strength of his principality. However, his successor, Guillaume de Villehardouin, bowed down before the *basileus* of Nicaea, the emperor **Michael VIII Paleologus**, thus sealing the fate of Constantinople (1261).

Death of an empire

The fall of the capital and the restoration of the Byzantine Empire did not immediately rid Greece of the Latins. Guillaume de Villehardouin was set free shortly after the siege in exchange for four important fortresses in the Peloponnese, including the one at **Mistra**, which became the bridgehead of the Byzantine re-conquest in Morea. By accepting these conditions, however, Guillaume himself opened the floodgates to

A chivalrous defeat
A rather curious family matter prefaced the fall of the Latin Empire. In 1259, the despot of Epirus, Michael Angelus Ducas and the basileus of Nicaea, Michael VIII Paleologus, both Byzantine, were fighting over Macedonia. After obtaining the aid of his son-in-law, Guillaume de Villehardouin, the despot of Epirus suddenly refused to do battle, leaving the Latins of Morea to fight alone for something that did not concern them. Although the Frankish knights knew that they were powerless against their much stronger adversary, they refused with dignity to abandon their foot soldiers. This was a chivalrous act, but with grave consequences: the absence of these men, defeated and taken captive, was decisive in the capture of Constantinople.

the evil that was to sweep through his fief. He tried to stem the tide by accepting the suzerainty of Charles I of Anjou, King of Sicily and brother of St Louis, but neither Anjou nor, subsequently, Navarre were able to prevent Byzantium from gradually subjugating the entire principality (1428).

Nevertheless, the restored Byzantine Empire was but a shadow of its former self. It was unable to put up any resistance to the invasion of Thessaly and Epirus by the **Serbian Empire** under Stefan IX Dusan (1331-55). Then, after defeating the Serbs at the Battle of Kosovo Polje in 1389, the **Osmanli Turks** proved even more dangerous. Arriving from Bithynia in Asia Minor, where they were rapidly shaking off Seljuq domination, they advanced into Europe, taking possession of Thessaly, pillaging Morea (1394) and steadily marching on towards Constantinople. Their surprise defeat at the hands of the Mongols under the command of **Tamerlane** in Ankara in 1402 was but a temporary setback. The Byzantine emperors made repeated appeals to the West, but to no avail. On 29 May 1453, Constantinople fell to the Ottomans under Sultan **Mehmet II** (1451-81). One by one, the last Latin and Byzantine strongholds crumbled. Only the Venetians put up any real resistance and delayed the advance of the Ottomans, but despite their efforts, Rhodes and the Dodecanese Islands were conquered in 1522, Chios in 1566 and Cyprus in 1571. Crete, the Venetians' last bastion in Greece, capitulated in turn in 1669.

Ottoman Greece
(1453-1830)

Consensual occupation
Under Ottoman occupation, the Greek Christians, like all of the non-Muslim communities (*rayás*), were tolerated but considered inferior. They took particular exception not only to being more heavily taxed than the Muslims, but also to the fact that young Christians were being arbitrarily recruited to serve in the sultan's personal guard, the Janissaries.

21 December 1522:
Süleyman I at the walls of Rhodes
(16C manuscript, Bibliothèque
Nationale de Paris)

AKG Paris

However, although the intellectual elites had fled to Italy en masse upon the announcement of the fall of Constantinople, the weight of Ottoman rule on the Greek population should not be exaggerated. By comparison with the authoritarian and oppressive government of the Venetians in the Aegean Islands and in Crete, the Ottoman sultan showed great indulgence towards the non-Muslim population, leaving local administration up to the Greeks and demonstrating a broad

The Janissaries, Christian soldiers

Originally made up of prisoners of war, this elite corps later gleaned its recruits from the Empire's Christian communities, converting children to Islam and training them in the arts of war. Although the method of recruitment was distressing, being chosen to become a future Janissary was often the only way for a large part of the Christian community to forge a career in the Ottoman administration. In the 17C, commissions in the Janissary corps (from the Turkish "yeni çeri", meaning "new troop") became hereditary, and corruption became rife as the soldiers began to act in their own interests. Extremely close to the seat of power, they eventually came to be a threat to the sultan, who ordered that the corps be totally disbanded in 1826 by having all of its members killed.

religious tolerance. Thus, far from banning the Orthodox clergy, the sultan confirmed the prerogatives of the Patriarch of Constantinople and even made him the representative of all the Christians in the Ottoman Empire and the guarantor of their loyalty (*see also the chapter on "Religion", page 66*). The attitude of the Church was certainly rather ambiguous: although it was thanks to the Church that Greek language and culture were able to survive, the patriarchs were constantly encouraging the faithful to consider the Ottomans as their protectors and condemning any movement of insubordination.

The slow awakening of nationalism

Up until the 17C, the "Sublime Porte" (government of the Ottoman Empire) experienced a strong period of expansion, marked by the reign of **Süleyman the Magnificent** (1521-66). However, the subsequent decline of the Empire coincided with the emergence of a revival of Greek nationalism. Resistance to the Turkish occupation began with the growing success of the **klephts**, bands of robbers from the mountains who harassed the Ottomans. Indeed, the *armatoles*, Greek militiamen trained by the Turks to keep the klephts under control, often ended up joining forces with those whom they were supposed to be fighting!

However, there was to be no widespread national uprising in Greece until the 18C. On the contrary, taking advantage of the Muslims' reversal of fortune, some Greeks, mainly from the Phanar district in Constantinople (Istanbul), gradually infiltrated the wheels of the Empire, managing to obtain key positions in the sultan's entourage. These **Phanariotes** first of all helped themselves to the highest ecclesiastical magistratures and to an increasing part of the trade carried out by the Sublime Porte. Their extensive knowledge of European affairs soon led them to take charge of the diplomatic affairs of the Ottoman Empire and to secure certain offices, such as those of dragoman (official interpreter) of the Sublime Porte, dragoman of the fleet, or governor of the provinces of Moldavia and Walachia.

However, in spite of this infiltration of the Ottoman institutions, the idea of a revolution began to gain ground and came to fruition in 1770 when a revolt spread through the Peloponnese, emboldened by the promise of support from Catherine II of Russia. Yet, at the first sign of a setback, the small Russian fleet quickly turned tail, abandoning the Greeks to Turkish repression. But it did not stop there: the quest for freedom was encouraged by the rapid decline of the Ottoman Empire and also by the propagation of ideas from the French Revolution, and by the secession of the pasha of Epirus, Ali Pasha Tepelenë. In 1797, **Napoleon** took possession of the Ionian Islands. After falling into the hands of the Russians (1799-1800), then back to the French (1807-14) and lastly occupied by the British (1814-64), these islands embodied a refuge and hope for all of the Greek revolutionaries.

AKG Paris

The War of Independence: a philhellene camp
(painting by von Heideck, 1835, Karlsruhe)

In the early 19C, the elites who were fighting for the cause of independence tried to gain support in European circles. In Vienna, the poet **Rígas Pheraíos** thus founded a secret society (hetaireia) militating for an independent and multi-racial Greece. His activism, however, unsettled the Austrian authorities, who arrested him and handed him over to the Turks. His execution in 1798 turned him into a martyr and soon other secret societies were also springing up around Europe, in Paris, Athens and particularly in Odessa.

The road to independence
Fomented with the support of Russia under **Alexander I**, on the initiative of his close Greek advisors, Alexander Ypsilántis and Ioánnis Kapodístrias – also eminent members of the hetaireia of Odessa – the rebellion took shape in Moldavia and Walachia but rapidly failed (1821). But that was not the end of it: shock waves from the revolutionary movement spread throughout Greece. The Patriarch of Patras, **Germanós**, signalled the start of the revolt on 25 March 1821. Within a few months, klephts, armatoles and all the opponents of the occupation had driven the Turks out of the Peloponnese, central Greece and most of the Aegean Islands.

After this initial success, internal conflicts caused the revolution to grind to a halt, giving the sultan an opportunity to organise a counter-attack. Despite the intense feeling stirred up in intellectual circles in Europe, especially among the Romantics, the major powers did not intervene, in the name of the principle of the Holy Alliance, which gave priority to the maintenance of the status quo in Europe over becoming involved in national affairs. Only a few took a personal stand in favour of the Greek revolution, among them **Lord Byron**, who died at Missolonghi. In order to quell the rebellion once and for all, Sultan Mahmoud II called upon the viceroy of Egypt, **Mehmet Ali**, for assistance (1825). Led by the viceroy's son, **Ibrahim**, the Turko-Egyptian troops crushed the insurgents in Crete before reaching the mainland, where, after much bloodshed, they took the positions held by the Greeks.

The heroic defence put up by the insurgents, led by **Geórgios Karaïskákis** and **Theódoros Kolokotrónis**, and the massacre of tens of thousands of Christians, finally forced the European governments to react. Russia, Great Britain and France

27

offered to mediate, exhorting the Sultan to grant the Greek territories an autonomous status under Ottoman sovereignty. Mahmoud II could not accept this, but his army was no longer in a position to resist, and the Turko-Egyptian fleet suffered a severe defeat at Navarino Bay (1827). While French troops were landing in the Peloponnese, the Russians were threatening Istanbul, forcing the Ottomans to sign the **Treaty of Adrianople** (1829) which established the autonomy of Greece. Elected president of the Republic in 1827, the authoritarian **Ioánnis Kapodístrias**, however, suffered from his reputation as a Russian agent and from an increasing difference of opinions with the leading citizens. His assassination in 1831 was the prelude to the application of the **Treaty of London**, which officially recognised the independence of Greece and established an absolute monarchy guaranteed by the contracting powers.

The Greek State

Greece under the Bavarian Otto I

Greece had gained its independence, but a great deal of frustration remained, so far removed did the new State turn out to be from the aspirations of the revolutionaries. Far from encompassing all the historic lands of Hellenism, the kingdom was limited to the Peloponnese, the south of central Greece and a certain number of islands close to the mainland: in all, barely 800 000 people gathered together in an impoverished, essentially agricultural and war-ravaged State. It is not difficult to understand, therefore, how the great Hellenistic project, the desire to bring all the lands that were historically or ethnically Greek together under one single nation, became the main axiom of Greek claims. The contracting powers had also chosen a Bavarian sovereign. Young **Otto**, who was still a minor when he came to the throne, caused further upset among his subjects by entrusting key positions in the government and army to his Bavarian compatriots. In 1843, a bloodless coup d'état compelled the monarch to promulgate a constitution adopted by the National Assembly. Bringing no major changes, this period of constitutional monarchy was marked in particular by great ministerial instability and the growing discontent of the population. Another coup d'état in October 1862 brought Otto's reign to an end, causing him to go into exile.

The first successes of Greek irredentism

This time it was Great Britain whose influence was predominantly felt in the choice of the new dynasty of **George I**, youngest son of the King of Denmark, and also in allowing the return of the Ionian Islands. This time, the king no longer had absolute control, and the Government had to be supported by a **Parliament**, elected by universal suffrage. On a national level, the last quarter of the 19C, marked by the personality of the liberal prime minister Kharílaos Trikoúpis, coincided with a period of intense development: population growth, land reform (1871), and the cutting of the Isthmus of Corinth by the construction of the **Corinth Canal** (1882-93).

After the **Congress of Berlin** (1878) on the Balkans question, the Ottomans were pressured by the major powers into giving up Thessaly and southern Epirus (1881). The Greeks' nationalist claims, however, remained largely unsatisfied and now had to withstand the territorial ambitions of the Bulgars and Serbs. So when **Crete** rebelled against the Turkish occupation (1897), the Greek authorities didn't hesitate to send in troops to support the rebels and even extended the conflict to Macedonia. But all in vain: in both cases, the Ottomans crushed their opponents, who were saved only by the mediation of Great Britain.

This defeat merely served to exacerbate Greek irredentism. When **Elefthérios Venizélos** of Crete proclaimed the island's unification with Greece (1908), the Government preferred to take no concrete action, despite popular pressure. But the following year, the **Goudi coup**, a rebellion staged by a group of radical officers, forced the King to call on Venizélos to form a government. The latter immediately made clear his determination to unite all Greek lands within one single nation and entered into an alliance with Serbia, Montenegro and Bulgaria to free the Balkans from Ottoman rule. Having emerged victorious from the **First Balkan War** (1912-13), the allied Christian countries argued over the partition of Macedonia at the London Conference. This caused Bulgaria to launch the **Second Balkan War** against Greece and Serbia, but, after suffering a rapid defeat, it was forced to sign the **Treaty of Bucharest** (August 1913). Greece gained a considerable amount of territory from both conflicts: Crete, southern Epirus, southern Macedonia and most of the islands in the Aegean Sea, except for the Dodecanese, which remained under Italian rule.

A time of disillusionment

The outcome of the First World War allowed Greece to grow even more, satisfying practically all of the nationalists' hopes, despite the fact that Greece had only decided to side with the Allies late in the day. Succeeding his father George I, who had been assassinated in Thessaloníki in 1913, the new king, **Constantine I**, brother-in-law of the German Kaiser Wilhelm II, seemed to favour the Central European powers. Forced to resign by the King on account of his attempts to align with the Allies, the prime minister, Venizélos, formed a counter-government in September 1916 in Thessaloníki, which also served as a base for Allied operations from 1915 to 1918. Meanwhile, French naval fusiliers landed and overcame Constantine, who soon abdicated in favour of his second son Alexander I. Under the **Treaties of Neuilly** (1919) and **Sèvres** (1920), Greece gained western and eastern Thrace, the islands of Imbros and Ténedos, and a large part of the Aegean provinces of Asia Minor around Smyrna (Izmir) came under its administration.

However, Greek irredentism had now reached its limits. When the Turks under the leadership of **Mustafa Kemal** (Atatürk) refused to accept the Treaty of Sèvres, Venizélos decided to invade Anatolia. But the situation at home soon took a dramatic turn: the conflict cost the prime minister his office, and a plebiscite placed Constantine I back on the throne, left vacant following Alexander's sudden death. The Germanophiles' return to power immediately left the country without any support from abroad. Repeated military failures ensued. After two years of fighting, Mustafa Kemal managed to drive the Greeks out of Anatolia, and a second treaty (**Lausanne**, 1923) restored full Turkish sovereignty over all of Asia Minor, eastern Thrace, Smyrna, Trebizond, Erzurum and the Dardanelles. This heralded a mass **exchange of populations** between Turkey and Greece: 1.5 million Greeks from Asia Minor crossed paths with 500 000 Turks from Greece.

From World War to civil war

The crushing military defeat, the exodus of the Greeks from Turkey and economic difficulties were to cause the successive abdications of Constantine I (October 1922), and of his son George II (December 1923). The **Republic** which was proclaimed in March 1924 was unable to stem the tide of discontent and become firmly established.

Wracked by political and financial crises, it disappeared with the more or less tacit consent of the Republicans. And so, in March 1935, the monarchy was restored and George II reclaimed his throne. With his backing, General **Metaxás** set up a dictatorship along the lines of Italian fascism. However, despite the convergences with Mussolini's regime, the territorial ambitions of Il Duce caused Athens to side with the

Decisive action

It was in Greece that the outcome of the Second World War began to take shape. By inflicting such a crushing and unexpected defeat on the Italian troops, the Greek army humiliated the Italian leader, Mussolini, who was forced to watch the Führer's soldiers come to the aid of his men. But more importantly, in order to come to the aid of the Italians, Hitler had to postpone his Russian campaign, Operation "Barbarossa", until June. This two-month delay may have prevented the Wehrmacht from reaching Moscow before the terrible winter of 1941-42, resulting in Hitler's first failure.

Allies. Although numbering twice as many, the Italian troops suffered a bitter defeat in 1940, forcing Hitler to send his army to their aid. In a blitzkrieg, the Wehrmacht swept through the Balkans and marched into Greece on 6 April 1941. Aided by a British force, the Greeks put up fierce resistance, which even impressed the German high command, but were unable to prevent the invasion or the partition of the country into three occupied zones: Italian, German and Bulgarian.

With the King and government in exile in Cairo, resistance against the occupier back home was organised around two large movements using guerrilla tactics. However, at the end of the war, the increasing friction between the monarchist EDES movement and the Communist EAM movement, which ceased to recognise the legality of the government in exile, turned into civil war (1946-49), the first embodiment of the **Cold War**. With the support of Yugoslavia and the USSR, the Communists, led by **General Márkos**, began to gain ground, but defeat became inevitable when the United States came to the aid of the lawful government and relations were broken off between Tito and Stalin.

Democracy lost...

Under **Paul I** (1947-64), Greece, which had been given the Dodecanese Islands in 1947 and joined NATO in 1951, was in theory governed by moderate right-wing governments, but was in reality controlled by parallel extreme right-wing forces. When **Geórgios Papandréou**, who came to power in 1963 at the head of the Centre Union, proposed democratic reforms, he struck fear into these hidden forces and was rapidly asked to resign by the young King Constantine II (1965). This heralded a period of political crisis, resulting in the coup d'état of 21 April 1967 and the beginning of the **colonels' junta**. After a failed counter-coup attempt, Constantine II was forced to take exile in Rome. The military junta, led by Colonel **Papadópoulos**, set up an authoritarian and repressive government which alienated the people and attracted international disapproval, with the exception of the United States. In response to popular discontent and student demonstrations (1972-73), the regime applied martial law and created special courts.

...and found

Neither the proclamation of the Republic (July 1973) nor the replacement of Colonel Papadópoulos by General Ghizíkis could shake off this political deadlock. The Cyprus question was to serve as an epilogue to the colonels' junta. The junta's failed attempt to assassinate the President of Cyprus and the reaction of the Turks, who invaded 40% of the north of the island, led Ghizíkis to hand government over to the former right-wing prime minister, **Karamanlís** (July 1974). Shortly afterwards, a referendum confirmed the monarchy's replacement by the Republic, and a new constitution was promulgated in 1975. In 1981, the socialist party, **PASOK** (an evocative acronym meaning "cleaned up"), took over the reins of government under the leadership of **Andréas Papandréou**, marking the beginning of political alternation. In the same year, Greece joined the EEC. However, relations with neighbouring countries still remained turbulent; in the 1990s, not only did Greece have to contend with the recurrent conflict with Turkey, but it also came into conflict with **Albania** over control of northern Epirus and was faced with refusal by the Greeks to accept the name and flag of the new Republic of Macedonia.

GREECE TODAY
A YOUNG REPUBLIC

It is difficult to establish exactly when the Greek Republic came into being: it was proclaimed in 1973, but the colonels' junta did not come to an end until July 1974 and the new Constitution was only adopted in 1975. Despite its relative newness, the Republic with its tried and tested institutions now seems to have taken a firm foothold among the Greek population.

The **president of the Republic** is elected for five years by a two-thirds majority of Parliament. He is also head of the armed forces and appoints the prime minister, although this is purely a matter of form since the office automatically falls to the leader of the party with the majority of votes in Parliament. Moreover, he does not have actual executive power, which belongs to the **prime minister**. The latter heads a government which is collectively accountable to **Parliament**, an assembly composed of 300 members elected for four years and which holds full legislative power. Furthermore, the Constitution of 1975 guarantees freedom of religion, even though it paradoxically recognises the primacy of the Orthodox Christian religion.

At an administrative level, Greece is divided into **nine large regions**, which stems more from historical reality than from a desire to decentralise power. At the level below, **prefects** represent the government in each of the 52 districts or **nomí**. Lastly, both the municipalities with over 200 000 inhabitants (*demes*) and those with over 500 inhabitants (*municipes*) have a mayor and council, elected every four years by universal suffrage.

A bipartite political context

Two large parties have monopolised the political scene from the beginning of the Republic. The left-wing Pan-Hellenic Socialist Movement, **PASOK**, which was founded in 1974 and has long been dominated by the personality of Andréas Papandréou, is well represented in rural areas and presents itself as a nationalist party, opposed to Social-Democratic and Communist policies. Its main aims concern the promotion of greater social justice and it stands against the influence of the major powers. The right of the political spectrum is dominated by Konstantinos Karamanlís' **New Democracy** party. Taking up where his National Radical Union left off before the junta, this party is pursuing the development of liberal policies in a European context. Other than these two influential parties, only the Communist party **(KKE)**, which is firmly rooted in working-class milieus, has enough support to be regularly represented in Parliament. Rather less successful, its "little brother", the **KKE Interior**, advocates reform and European integration.

For some years, a **left-wing ecological** coalition, Synaspismos, has managed to obtain a few seats. The same cannot be said of the **National Front**, however; the extreme right has never managed to become a serious contender in the political life of the nation.

An economy on the move

Greece's membership of the **EEC** was decided in 1979 and became effective in 1981. Although previously not in favour of such a step, once PASOK came to power in 1981 under the leadership of Andréas Papandréou, it no longer questioned the participation of Greece in the construction of Europe. The Community's poorest country clearly had everything to gain by joining the European Union.

But despite progress made, the Greek economy is still trailing behind the European average. However, for some years now, the socialist government of **Kóstas Simítis** has been following a stringent budgetary and monetary policy and a privatisation

Greece today

programme, which have unquestionably caused the economy to move forward but have also produced an upsurge of discontent in the process. Thanks to this policy, the rate of inflation has fallen below 5%, the annual growth rate is bordering on 4%, and the country – originally refused entry into the economic and monetary union because of failure to satisfy the convergence criteria defined by the **Treaty of Maastricht** – has now gained entry into the euro zone. On the flipside of the coin, 10% of the population are unemployed, even though the Greeks' purchasing power has increased considerably and now stands at US$12 500 per capita per year.

Agriculture and industry

Despite these encouraging results, much effort remains to be made in various economic areas. The **agricultural sector** still sustains almost 20% of the working population, with a production whose market value does not exceed 13% of the GDP. Although modern farming methods are gradually spreading, Greece still remains a country of smallholdings, with an average area of 4ha per inhabitant.

It is nevertheless to agriculture that **industry** owes a large part of its vitality, through the processing of agricultural products. **Construction** companies are the other major-league players in industry.

The country's **mining resources** are limited. **Lignite** extracted mainly in Ptolemaís fuels some thermal electric power plants, and there is an **oilfield** near the island of Thassos, but these are insufficient to meet the country's energy needs. Greece still has a little **nickel**, **zinc** and **magnesium**, but its greatest resource is **bauxite**, which is extracted from Mt Parnassus by the Pechiney group and used in the production of aluminium.

Three essential blessings

The imbalance between the requirements of the population and the current economic performance of Greece lie at the root of a large deficit in its trade balance. The fact that the European Union absorbs almost half of the products exported by Greece and provides two-thirds of its imports bears witness to its successful integration into Europe. Fortunately, the trade deficit is partly offset by profits from the merchant navy, by income sent by Greeks who have emigrated abroad – 5.5 million strong, the Greek diaspora is indeed a significant factor (*see page 57*) – but above all, by revenue drawn from tourism. The combination of sun, sea, islands and the prestigious vestiges of Antiquity attracts almost 10 million tourists every year, which is as much as the country's entire population, and brings almost 4 billion dollars into the country.

An area in which Greece could probably make savings is in its rather onerous defence budget; with expenditure equal to 4.6% of its GDP in 1999, this is by far the highest rate of all the NATO countries.

Although Greek society is still archaic in many ways, progress has undeniably been made. The State notably plays quite a remarkable role in **education**, devoting a considerable amount of its budget to the development of public schools throughout the country and also to maintaining a high level of further education. A growing network of private schools is also flourishing alongside the public system.

A nation of shipowners

In their day, the turbulent lives of the extremely rich shipowners Onássis and Níarchos, brothers-in-law and rivals, provided many a story for magazines the world over. Aristotle Onássis' love affairs with Maria Callas and Jackie Kennedy are legendary, and wild rumours still circulate about the suspicious circumstances of the deaths of his daughter, Christina, and the first wife of Stávros Níarchos. But alongside these great shipowners, who were also great patrons of the arts in the purest Greek tradition, is a myriad of other, more unassuming individuals, who hold a few shares in one or more ships and contribute, in their own way, towards endowing this little country with one of the world's most powerful merchant fleets. However, in recent years, this fleet has been sailing more often than not under flags of convenience.

A small and unevenly spread population

With a little under 11 million inhabitants, Greece is small in comparison with other European countries. With a population density of around 80 inhabitants per square kilometre, ie three times less than in Germany or the United Kingdom, it even seems to be rather underpopulated. But it is difficult to make any real comparison, considering the country's extremely mountainous landscape.

The proportion of the population living in urban areas stands at almost 60%, which is a little lower than in the major developed countries; it is nevertheless quite considerable for a country with such a deep-rooted rural tradition. Over the last fifteen years, the mountains of the Peloponnese and the Pindus have witnessed a population exodus, as have many of the islands. But the gaps are being filled by immigrants from the Eastern European countries who have been flooding into Greece in successive waves since the fall of the Soviet empire.

With the main destination of the initial **rural exodus** being the capital city, **Greater Athens** is now home to over 3 million people, ie almost one third of the country's total population, although in 1821 the city was nothing more than a little town with 5 000 inhabitants.

Uneven urbanisation

The influx of so many people within such a short period of time was bound to create problems. Some have been or are in the process of being solved, in particular the tricky question of supplying the capital with water, which has been solved by impounding the waters from Mt Parnassus. The saturation of Athens airport, which had been a problem for many years, has been eased by the recent inauguration of a new airport in Spáta, built with the aid of European subsidies. However, the air in Athens is still unbreathable on very hot days on account of the very high level of **air pollution**, in spite of the alternating traffic system set up by the municipal authorities.

Trailing far behind Athens, the Macedonian city of **Thessaloníki** has 700 000 inhabitants, while the country's third largest city, **Patras** (Peloponnese), has only 100 000. This uneven population distribution means that the centres of production are concentrated around Athens, and, more broadly speaking, along the Athens-Thessaloníki and Athens-Patras routes. Population figures are on the rise in these areas, but the growth rate remains relatively low, at +0.3%.

Platía Omónia, in the heart of modern Athens

ART AND ARCHITECTURE

Whether it be monuments with lofty columns still standing proudly on some rocky spur, or vestiges unearthed by archaeologists after centuries of oblivion, Greece yields a seemingly endless supply of relics from its illustrious artistic past, which are always a moving sight to behold. The art of Ancient Greece, above all, which already fascinated the Romans so long ago, obviously has its own special place. However, this chapter would be incomplete without a mention of the Byzantine, Latin and Ottoman civilisations which also left their imprint in Greece, allowing new artistic trends to flourish in a reflection of the strength of their culture.

See also the lexicon and architectural plates at the end of this chapter.

The Bronze Age, or the art of the first palaces

As early as the Bronze Age, the city states of the two great Minoan and Mycenaean civilisations demonstrated an already highly-developed mastery of architecture and original artistic characteristics.

The Cretan palaces

Veritable cities with a highly complex layout, the Cretan palaces of **Phaistos**, **Mália** and **Knossós** contained places of worship, shops, workshops for various different trades, and royal apartments. Set around a vast central courtyard – a prelude, perhaps, to the Greek agora – they spread over several levels (as many as five floors in Knossós), linked by countless passageways and staircases, which breathe life into the legend of the **labyrinth**.

Sweeping **frescoes** decorated the walls of the royal apartments, reception rooms and those devoted to worship in a powerful display of naturalism. They depicted dolphins, floral friezes, bouquets of reeds, and acrobats dancing on the backs of bulls, all enhanced by the most iridescent colours. In time, Minoan painting nevertheless began to focus increasingly on the representation of the human being, full-size figures or delicate faces, such as the charming *Parisienne* at the Herakleion Museum. This taste for realism paved the way for **relief painting**, murals with a low stucco relief which made the subjects even more life-like.

However, it was in the **minor arts** of **metalwork**, ceramics and marquetry that the Cretans excelled, as evidenced by the countless pieces of jewellery, figurines and everyday objects discovered in the royal necropolis of Mália. **Ceramic art** included magnificent jars and giant *pithoi* on which, after the dense geometric patterns, a whole world of sea creatures danced freely, with octopi, seaweed and fish undulating in red lines on the ochre of the terracotta.

The Mycenaean cities: colossal undertakings

The Mycenaeans left little in the way of pictorial evidence, excelling more in the art of **fortification**, which undoubtedly betrays a more bellicose temperament. Unlike the Cretans, they built their cities on elevated sites protected by strong **Cyclopean**

Cycladic art and idols

The brilliant civilisation which flourished at the end of the 3rd millennium BC in the Cyclades left behind a great deal of artistic evidence. This included painted and engraved ceramics, jewellery, elaborate weapons, but, above all, astonishing marble statuettes, the famous Cycladic idols, whose function still remains shrouded in mystery. They mainly represent women, their arms crossed over their naked bodies, with oval, flat and perfectly smooth heads and only a nose protruding. Some less common statuettes depict musicians, flautists or harpists sitting cross-legged. These truly remarkable and surprisingly modern works of art with their perfect proportions, bold curves and an acute sense of stylisation, influenced many 20C artists, starting with the Cubists.

walls composed of enormous perfectly-pointed blocks of stone, some weighing several tonnes. The best example of these colossal constructions – better still than Mycenae – is the city of **Tírintha** in Argolis.

However, their warlike character did not prevent the Mycenaeans from developing a highly refined **funerary art**, in particular in **metalwork**, as demonstrated by the fabulous treasure found in the nineteen royal tombs discovered in 1876 by the archaeologist Heinrich Schliemann *(see page 18)* at the site of **Mycenae**. It included gold masks, hundreds of filigree gold plates, diadems, bracelets, rings, gold-plated silver sceptres with rock-crystal handles and damascened daggers. An extraordinary wealth providing a stark contrast with the extreme material poverty that followed the disappearance of the Mycenaean civilisation.

Ancient architecture

At the end of the Dark Age, the glorious Mycenaean civilisation fell into oblivion. Gradually a new society emerged in which each man belonged to a **city**. The importance of this civic community explains why Greek architecture lost interest in private houses and began to focus more on public buildings. However, at the height of the Archaic Period, the **agora** – public meeting place – was still nothing but a vast esplanade with no buildings; the first elements of civic architecture, **temples**, did not start to appear until the second half of the 8C BC. Indeed, until the 6C BC, the shrines devoted to the gods differed little in the way of architecture from residential buildings. A clay model of the Temple of Hera in Árgos (Peloponnese) shows the main characteristics: a large rectangular room **(megaron)** covered by a two-sided roof, with a small porch projecting at the front supported by two columns. Possibilities for innovation were still limited, however, by the materials used: clay, wood and stone blocks.

Cycladic purity: an idol from Páros (Musée du Louvre, Paris)

H. Lewandowski/RMN

The birth of monumentality

A first step towards monumental architecture was taken at the Temple of Hera in Sámos at the turning point of the 8C and 7C BC, when the room devoted to the deity (the **cella**) was surrounded by a gallery supported by wooden columns **(peristyle)**. There was now a clear distinction between the houses of men and those of gods. But it was only when they began to use carved stone, particularly marble, that the Greeks were able to give free rein to their creative genius. Thus, in the 6C BC the first monumental structures appeared.

Two opposing styles immediately developed. In mainland Greece, the rather geometric **Doric style** obeyed rules of strictness and sobriety, with columns having plain capitals and no bases. In Asia Minor, the more decorative and lighter aspect of the **Ionic style** allowed architects greater freedom. Unlike the Doric order, the columns rested on moulded bases and the capitals boasted twin volutes.

The Temple of Artemis in **Corfu** was the earliest stone temple to be discovered and dates back to around 580 BC. Subsequent works were built on an ever-increasing scale. The Temple of Artemis in **Ephesus** - one of the Seven Wonders of the Ancient World – was 50m wide by 100m long, like Temple "G" at **Selinus**. The possibilities of these gargantuan undertakings were soon exhausted, and they also proved extremely costly. Such was the case of the gigantic **Temple of Olympian Zeus** in Athens *(see page 149)*: begun by the Peisistratids and continued by their successors, it was not completed until six centuries later by the Roman emperor Hadrian.

Ancient architecture

The Age of Pericles, or the golden age

The association of the sculptor **Phidias** and the architect **Ictinus** for the construction of the **Parthenon** in Athens (447-432 BC) marked the beginning of a new phase: the temple's originality lay not in its sheer size, but in the perfection of its proportions, the widening of the cella by the reduction of the lateral galleries, and in the refinement of the decoration. At the beginning of the 4C BC, in the **Temple of Athena Alea** in Tegea (south of Árgos, Peloponnese), the architect and sculptor, **Scopas**, accentuated this trend of embellishing the interior spaces by getting rid of the lateral columns and imposing the even more decorative **Corinthian order** with its curled acanthus leaves and volutes on the capital. But it is probably the very elaborate decoration of the **treasuries** which most clearly reveals the full extent of the Greeks' artistic talent. These little religious buildings dotted the Sacred Ways of the great pan-Hellenic sanctuaries – **Olympia**, **Delos** and, of course, **Delphi.** Built by a victorious city or a grateful family, they served simply as depositories for offerings. Enjoying greater freedom than they did with the temples, the artists decorated them with exquisite mouldings, paintings, carved friezes and caryatids, giving free rein to their imagination.

Religion and prestige

The great wave of temple building that marked the 6C cannot be explained by technical progress alone or by a new religious fervour. At this time, the ruling tyrants had directed the spirit of competition ("agon") among the Greeks towards a sort of architectural rivalry. Indeed, the Greek cities were embellished under the tyrants' rule in an ostentatious display of their power and wealth, which also bestowed glory on the person commissioning the work. The aristocrats were quick to catch on and pursued this prestigious public patronage. When fire damaged the famous Temple of Apollo at Delphi, it was the Alcmaeonid family, in exile from Athens, who obtained the right to rebuild it. And, to make sure that they would not be forgotten, they added a pediment made from the finest Parian marble.

The original theatre

Created for ceremonies of the cult of Dionysus, the Greek theatre ("théatron" is "a place of seeing") originally consisted of an area of beaten earth surrounded by wooden tiers. The chorus and dancers performed in the central area, where an altar to the god took pride of place. However, the theatre very soon stepped beyond these strictly religious bounds and also became a stage for the performance of tragedies. It became very popular in the 5C BC, but it was not until the following century that the first stone structures appeared, including the famous Epidaurus theatre, a perfect example of its kind. The tiers were now arranged in a semicircle ("cavea") backing onto a hillside, and, in the orchestra, the altar was moved so as not to stand in the way of the chorus. As drama evolved, the chorus began to interact with the actors. The "skene", a simple wooden structure (later made of stone) serving both as the wings and a backdrop, then acquired a "proskénion", a narrow platform projecting to the fore. It was subsequently replaced by a wider "skene", gradually gaining in depth to become the large stage of modern-day theatres.

The spirit of Hellenism

Important changes took place in the 4C BC which were to leave an indelible mark on Greek architecture. Already in the 5C BC, **Hippodamus of Miletus** had begun to change the face of city planning in Greece by using a grid plan separating business and residential districts. Initially applied to Miletus (Asia Minor) and to Piraeus, the **Hippodamian plan** did not become widespread until much later on, when the conquests of Alexander the Great led to the building of many new cities. Among the great architectural innovations of the time was the increase in **ramparts** built around cities, **porticoes** (stoae) surrounding sanctuaries and agorae – pleasant shaded galleries with colonnades housing shops and offices – as well as the emergence and rapid success of the **theatre**.

The Hellenistic Age was to witness a veritable revolution in ways of thinking. The centre of Hellenism shifted outside Greece and rivalries between the independent Greek kingdoms were expressed not only in the political arena but also in an **ostentatious architecture** made to serve royal ends. The greatest artists set to work for the rich sovereigns of Asia Minor, Syria and Egypt, where they developed a monumental art encompassing oriental techniques. Some of the most renowned Greek architects and sculptors were thus to embellish Halicarnassus (Bodrum), the residence of the Persian satrap (governor) Mausolus; they built a monumental tomb for him there, the famous **Mausoleum**, which is also one of the Seven Wonders of the World.

But this great new development was not limited to sovereigns alone; it also reached into private homes, which had, up until that time, been deliberately austere. **Alcibiades** *(see sidebar page 22)* caused yet another great stir in the 5C BC by hiring Agatharcus to decorate his house. Indeed, the decline of civic sense in the 4C BC corresponded to a new desire of the wealthy to display their personal success. And where better to start than at home? Henceforth, luxuriously decorated, vast and beautiful houses were to be seen adorning the business districts and areas where the high-ranking officials lived in Alexandria, Pergamon and elsewhere.

Ancient sculpture

The 7C BC marked the arrival of great Greek sculpture, inspired by Egyptian models, with one of the favourite themes of **Archaic statuary**, the kouros and the kore. They served a religious function and were placed in sanctuaries as an offering to the deity, and were also to be found adorning tombs to honour the memory of the deceased. As a result, they comply with strict conventions of representation. Carved from marble, limestone (*poros*) or bronze, the **kouros** represents a naked young man, standing with his left foot forward, his arms stretched down close to his sides, his fists clenched. In the second half of the 7C BC, the kouroi reached colossal proportions, before returning to a more human scale in the 6C BC. Their female counterpart, the **kore**, depicts a young girl, standing with her feet together, one arm stretched down by her side and the other crossed over her chest. Even more of a prisoner of the stone, the figure looks more like a pillar than a human body, the anatomy being suggested only by the movement of the drapery of the ceremonial robe.

Hygeia, Goddess of Health
(National Archaeological
Museum, Athens)

The Classical Age, or the liberation of the body

After a so-called "Severe" transitional period, illustrated by the marvellous **Charioteer of Delphi**, the Classical Age gradually freed itself from the rigidity of the kouros model. In the 5C BC – the **High Classical Period** – Athens enjoyed absolute supremacy over the Greek world, attracting most of the great artists. Among them, the sculptor **Phidias**, whose figures displayed a flexibility, movement and majesty never seen before. Creator of the chryselephantine statue (made of ivory and gold) of the Olympian Zeus, which no longer exists but was, in its time, considered to be one of the Seven Wonders of the World, Phidias also decorated the Parthenon, creating in particular the wonderful **frieze of the Panathenaea**, which can now be seen in London and Paris.

T.A.P.

Another supremely talented sculptor, **Polyclitus**, emerged in Árgos. He created a canon of proportions according to which the total height of the body should be equal to seven times that of the head. Only Roman copies of his works survive, including the famous bronze **Doryphorus**, depicting a naked spear bearer.

In the **Late Classical Period** (4C BC), the Athenian **Praxiteles** departed from the hieratic style of the preceding period, injecting his works with a more natural and graceful quality: he was particularly adept at sculpting nude, sensual female bodies and carving his male subjects in languid poses.

The figures sculpted by **Scopas of Páros** were more expressive and tormented, triggering a movement towards realism which gathered great momentum in the Hellenistic Period. Subsequently, **Lysippus** of Sicyon produced many portraits of his protector, Alexander the Great, as well as bronze statues that had more slender forms than those of Polyclitus. Lysippus effectively created a new canon which held that the body equalled eight times the height of the head. His pupil, **Chares of Lindos**, adopted this model for his gigantic bronze statue of Helios (the Sun), the famous **Colossus of Rhodes**. This giant, over 30m high, another of the Seven Wonders of the World, sadly did not survive the earthquake of 227 BC intact.

Greek vases, painting's living memory

Of the bright colours which once enhanced the architecture of the great monuments of Ancient Greece almost every trace has disappeared, worn away by time. Some beautifully decorated ceramics have however survived, to give us some idea of the evolution of painting as an autonomous art. Here again, the Dark Age swept away Mycenaean knowledge and, in the 9C BC, the decoration of vases was again reduced to simple bands of **geometric designs** around the body. Human and animal figures began to appear in the next century, although still in very schematic form: a circle was used to symbolise a man's head and a triangle his body. The main centre of geometrical ceramic production was in Attica, and particularly in **Athens**, with the most famous of them being the great funerary amphorae of the **Dipylon Master**.

Black figures...

In the second half of the 8C BC, increasing contact with the Near East revolutionised this art. **Corinth** became a flourishing centre of production, inspired by **oriental models**. The geometrical motifs now gave way to palms, rosettes, lotus flowers, and lions, panthers and sphinxes. The black-figure technique moreover allowed the subjects to be depicted with much greater expression and realism: the figures were painted in black on the orange-red terracotta surface and the details were incised with a burin; white or red strokes were then added to emphasise the contours of the bodies. The famous **Chigi vase**, dating from around 650 BC, provides an unrivalled example of the possibilities afforded by this technique, with several friezes showing various scenes from ancient life and mythology, including a combat between hoplite soldiers accompanied by flute players, a lion hunt, a procession on horseback and the Judgement of Paris.

"Opus tessellatum"

Probably invented by the Sumerians, the earliest known mosaics, discovered in Mesopotamia, date back to the end of the 4th millennium BC. They consisted of small coloured cones of clay on a bitumen or cement base arranged in all sorts of patterns serving to decorate temple and palace façades. The art of mosaic was perfected in the Hellenistic Period, with the development of pavements made of pebbles and in particular of tesserae – small cubes of coloured stone, ceramic or glass paste – which were used to ornament temples and the homes of the wealthy. But it was the Romans who really turned it into a fine art, most notably in the Imperial Age when all buildings, public and private alike, were decorated with mosaics. This was when this art form reached its heights, with tiny tesserae as small as 4mm^2, yielding blends similar to painting. Byzantine artists also subsequently excelled in this art.

Art and architecture

... and red figures

In the 6C BC, Attica in turn became the main production centre of black-figure pottery. Besides the inevitable scenes from mythology, the subjects mainly revolved around scenes from aristocratic life. Around 525 BC, the black-figure technique gradually gave way to the so-called red-figure technique: here, the outlines were painted in black, as was the background, but the figures were left in the red colour of the clay and the incision technique no longer used. The treatment of forms and faces in painting and sculpture developed along parallel paths: emotional expression intensified and bodies were revealed. **Polygnotus of Thasos** (5C BC) was a pioneer in this field and is also said to be the originator of the **notion of spatial depth** in painting, by placing his characters in settings composed of several planes.

As vase painting ran out of steam towards the end of the Classical Period, **wall painting** began to make an appearance. Like sculpture, it was to serve royal ends, and the painter **Apelles** made numerous portraits of Alexander the Great, depicting him as a conqueror and later as a god.

Byzantine architecture, or the art of Christianity

Greece seemed to lose its artistic vitality when it fell under foreign domination. Henceforth, the only outlet for the talents of the Greeks lay in religious – Christian – architecture, where they were able to express original ideas in architectural design. But even then, a few centuries passed before they were really able to develop a style of their own, because initially (4C-6C AD) **basilica type** churches inspired by secular Roman architecture predominated.

In the 6C, the **dome**, already much appreciated in Rome, started to become the main element around which **Byzantine churches** were built. They became smaller in size, and gradually the **Greek-cross plan** took over: at the crossing of the transept, the dome rises from a drum adorned with windows, itself resting on four barrel vaults producing a cross with four arms of equal length. More often than not, this was contained within a square through the addition of side aisles and apses; this type of plan is known as a **cross-in-square**.

Particularly well suited to this new architectural style, magnificent mosaic decorations depicted various scenes from the Gospels according to a well-defined **liturgical arrangement**: **Christ Pantocrator** in the dome, the **Virgin Theotókos** in the apse, scenes from the Life of Christ or the Virgin placed according to the feast days of the year in the nave or narthex. The **Dafní Monastery** (11C) in Attica thus contains a remarkable collection of mosaics enhanced with gold.

Óssios Loukás: the golden age of Byzantine mosaics (here: the Washing of the Feet)

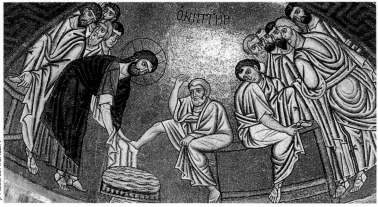

Lastly, a rather curious but interesting combination of earlier architectural styles emerged in **Mistra**: a basilical plan at ground level, with a Greek-cross plan above (Afendikó Church, at the Vrondohíon Monastery).

In the last great innovation of the Byzantine Period, the mosaics gradually gave way to **frescoes**, which, although they followed the exact same codes of representation as the mosaics, proved to be much less costly.

Modern times

Between Ottomans and Venetians

After the Turkish conquest, purely Greek art practically disappeared for four centuries. Mosques, Turkish baths, bazaars and caravanserais were soon to be seen dotting the Greek countryside. Great admirers of Byzantine churches, the Ottomans transformed the most beautiful of them into **mosques**. Besides adapting the Christian sanctuaries to the rites of Islam, the Turkish architects gave expression to their talent in a few grand creations, but most of the mosques in Greece were still relatively modest structures, consisting of a simple prayer room.

Under Ottoman domination, Christian art managed to persevere only on Mt Athos and in the Venetian enclaves of Crete and the Ionian Islands. Indeed the influence of **Venice** was very much in evidence here, particularly in **military architecture**; the Venetians built numerous fortified citadels in Corfu, Zacynthus and Cephalonia, and especially in **Crete**, which continued to hold out against Turkish assaults. The entrances to many of these strongholds are still guarded by **lions of St Mark**, the official symbol of Venice.

As for civil architecture, it inherited elegant **loggias**, such as the one in Herakleion which now houses the town hall, or the one in Réthimnon which has been turned into a library. And, of course, there are the **fountains** – symbol of the prosperity of those in power – whose refinement matches those of the Turks.

Venice also left its imprint on religious architecture, particularly in **painting**: the icons produced by some Greek artists, such as **Damaskinós**, reflect a skilful combination of Byzantine rigour and the sensual inspiration and more realistic forms of the Venetians. The most famous of these painters, Doménikos Theotokópoulos, is better known under the name of **El Greco** (1541-1614). After training in Crete, he moved to Spain where he gave expression to the full range of his talent alongside local and Italian masters. After Crete was captured by the Ottomans in 1669, many artists, such as **E Tzanès** (1610-90), settled in the Ionian Islands where they formed what is usually known as the **"Ionian School"**.

Neo-Classicism, or the revival of Antiquity

The defeat of the Ottomans and the liberation of Greece in 1821 brought with them an overwhelming thirst for artistic renewal. Everywhere, the signs of Turkish domination were wiped out, submerged by a feverish desire to once again bring to the fore the monuments of Antiquity – proud symbols of the identity and prestige of Greece – and to re-endow the cities of the young nation with an authentic Greekness.

Already very fashionable in Western Europe, the **neo-Classical style** was therefore quickly adopted in Greece. Introduced by foreign artists, first of all Bavarian (following in the wake of King Otto), this trend, which was largely inspired by Antiquity, seemed to be the natural choice for the (re)construction of public buildings. **Athens** led this revival, with its University, National Library and Academy *(see page 151)*.

Modern painting and sculpture

Some painters, such as **Nikifóros Lytrás**, left to study in Munich, but all forms of artistic expression were still influenced by academism in the 19C. It was not until the turn of the century that the new artistic trends from Western Europe began to catch on in Greece, undoubtedly first introduced by the painter **Konstandínos Parthénis**, who was the first to take an interest in **Impressionism** and **Fauvism**.

Konstandínos Dimitriádis led the way in the field of sculpture, drawing inspiration from Rodin. Soon to follow suit were the expressionist painter **Giórgos Bouziánis**, the cubist **Níkos Ghíka** and the surrealist **Níkos Engonópoulos**. This modernist trend, however, did not win everybody over to its cause. A strong **traditionalist movement**, firmly rooted in the country's Hellenic, Byzantine and popular culture, persisted under the leadership of the painter **Spýros Vassilíou** and the architect **D Pikiónis**.

These traditionalist and modernist styles continued in the post-Second World War period; the painter **Yánnis Morális**, intent on rediscovering and respecting the roots of Greek culture, embodied the former, while some of his contemporaries sought to explore the new artistic trends of the Western world. Among them, the painters **Aléxandros Kontópoulos** and **Yánnis Spyrópoulos** became involved in abstract art. However, representational art soon made a graceful comeback under the aegis of the painter **Jánnis Ghaítis** and the sculptor **Giórgos Giorgiádis**. In a sign of the times, Greek artists were beginning to settle abroad and obtain international recognition. **Jánnis Kounéllis** rose to the fore in Italy in the Arte Povera movement, and Panayiotis Vassilakis, better known as **Tákis**, has worked in Paris for almost half a century. Specialising in technological art, his work explores the effects of magnetism, sounds and light, and the artist has gained a certain reputation with his "electromagnetic sculptures", "light art" and "musical sculptures".

ARCHITECTURE OF ANTIQUITY

THE TEMPLE

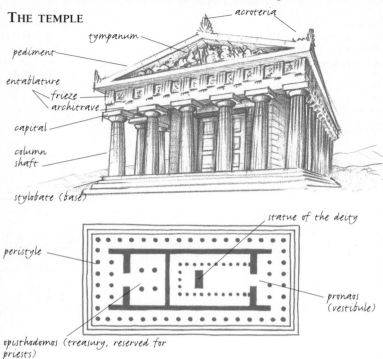

acroteria

tympanum

pediment

entablature

frieze

architrave

capital

column
shaft

stylobate (base)

statue of the deity

peristyle

pronaos
(vestibule)

opisthodomos (treasury, reserved for
priests)

THREE CLASSICAL ORDERS

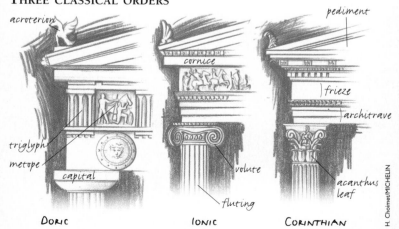

acroterion

pediment

cornice

frieze

architrave

triglyph

metope

capital

volute

acanthus
leaf

fluting

DORIC

IONIC

CORINTHIAN

H. Choimet/MICHELIN

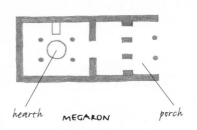

hearth MEGARON porch

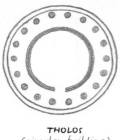

THOLOS
(circular building)

THE THEATRE

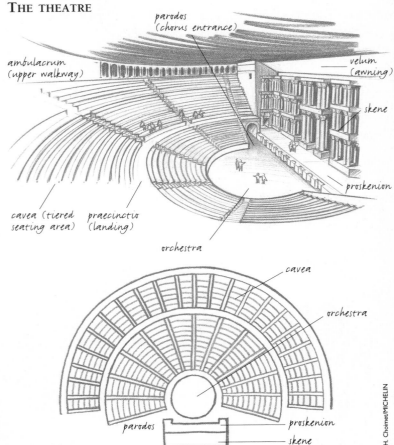

parodos
(chorus entrance)

ambulacrum
(upper walkway)

velum
(awning)

skene

proskenion

cavea (tiered
seating area)

praecinctio
(landing)

orchestra

cavea

orchestra

parodos

proskenion

skene

H. Choimet/MICHELIN

43

BYZANTINE CHURCH

dome rising above transept crossing

drum

east end (choir + apse)

nave

transept

narthex

GREEK-CROSS PLAN

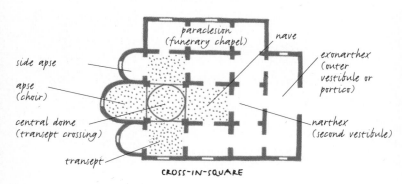

paraclesion (funerary chapel)

nave

side apse

exonarthex (outer vestibule or portico)

apse (choir)

central dome (transept crossing)

narthex (second vestibule)

transept

CROSS-IN-SQUARE

DOMES

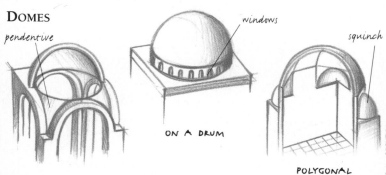

pendentive

windows

squinch

ON PENDENTIVES

ON A DRUM

POLYGONAL ON SQUINCHES

H. Choimet/MICHELIN

Antiquity and general terms

Acanthus	Plant whose scalloped leaves served as a model for the decoration of the Corinthian capital.
Acropolis	The upper town of Greek cities, serving as a citadel and a place of worship.
Agora	An open space in Greek cities, used as a market place and political centre.
Altar	In a sanctuary, a small stone structure in the open usually in front of a temple, where offerings to the deity were placed.
Amphora	Two-handled vase used to store and transport oil and wine.
Anastylosis	Reconstruction of a ruined building using the fragments of the original.
Bond	Method of laying stones in a building (*opus* in Latin).
Bouleuterion	In Greece, the state council building (the council was known as the "boule"). It was a sort of small covered theatre, set in the agora and could also be used as an odeon.
Caryatid	A female statue used as a column.
Cella	The main body of a temple, usually housing the statue of the deity.
Dipteral	Term describing a monument with a double peristyle.
Exedra	Semicircular room containing a stone bench. Also more broadly denotes any apse or niche opening out to a larger space.
Gymnasium	Sports complex in Ancient Greece, comprising open-air grounds and various buildings: changing rooms, palaestrae, anointing rooms, etc.
Hexastyle	Describes a building with six frontal columns.
Hypostyle	A temple or palace with a roof supported by columns ("stylos" means "column" in Greek).
Lekythos	A small vase with a long, cylindrical body and a narrow neck, used for funerary offerings.
Megaron	From the Greek meaning "large room". An abode dating from the Neolithic Period and Bronze Age, with a porch and vestibule opening into a rectangular room with a central hearth. Greek temples were based on this plan.
Metope	A rectangular space, sometimes carved, between two triglyphs (*see this term*) in a Doric frieze.
Mosaic	Assemblage of multicoloured tesserae, used to decorate the walls and pavements of buildings in Ancient Greece and subsequently in the Byzantine Period.
Nymphaeum	A small shrine dedicated to the Nymphs, built around a natural spring or fountain.
Octastyle	Describes a building with eight frontal columns.
Odeon	A small, usually covered theatre, used for concerts and lectures.
Oinochoe	A broad-bodied jug, with a vertical handle, used for pouring wine into goblets.
Opisthodomos	In a Greek temple, a room where offerings were laid out (treasury).
Order	Style of architecture defined by the decoration of the capital and entablature.
Palaestra	An exercise ground, set apart from or contained within a gymnasium, surrounded by a portico leading to changing rooms, washrooms, etc.
Peripteral	A term describing a monument surrounded by a single row of columns.
Peristyle	A gallery or colonnaded portico surrounding a temple or courtyard.
Pithos	Large jar, usually set in the ground, used for storing grain.
Portico	Covered gallery supported by a colonnade (*stoa* in Greek).
Proedria	In a theatre, a row of honour reserved for high-ranking citizens (the proedri).
Pronaos	Vestibule of a Greek temple, leading to the cella.
Propylaeum	Monumental entrance to an important public building, sanctuary, sacred precinct, generally in the form of a large porch.

Art and architecture

Prostyle	A term describing a temple which has freestanding frontal columns.
Prytaneion	Seat of the Prytaneis, Greek city officials who were in charge of convening the boule (see "bouleuterion").
Stadium	Long open space mainly for running, but also used for wrestling, jumping and discus and javelin throwing. Approximately 180-190m long, the stadium was lined on three sides by earthen, wooden or stone terraces. The main remaining stadia are at Delphi and Olympia. A stadium was also a unit of length.
Stoa	See "portico".
Stucco	Plaster (gypsum) used in wall and ceiling decoration.
Temenos	A sacred enclosure around a sanctuary, where the faithful gathered. Sacred esplanade of an acropolis.
Tessera	Small cube of stone or glass used in the making of mosaics.
Tholos	Circular building with a conical roof or dome, for worship or funerary purposes.
Triglyph	Projecting rectangular part in a Doric frieze, with three carved vertical channels, between two metopes.

Byzantine Period

Ambo	In Christian basilicas, a raised stone stand for the reading of the Gospels.
Aniconic	Without figurative images.
Apse	In a church, semicircular chapel at the end of the choir.
Archivolt	Continuous moulding ornamenting the extrados (outer face) of an arch.
Basilica	Civil building with three aisles used by the Romans as a court of justice or meeting place. Name given to the first Christian churches built according to this plan.
Bema	The raised part of an Eastern church, usually in front of the apse, containing the altar and the bishop's throne.
Chancel	Low balustrade in front of the choir in a church.
Diaconicon	The sacristy in Byzantine churches where the deacons kept their vessels and vestments.
Diptych	Two painted or carved panels hinged together.
Exonarthex	External vestibule preceding the narthex in some Byzantine churches.
Fresco	From the Italian "a fresco", painting on "fresh" plaster. The paintings in the first Byzantine churches were executed directly onto the stone, only partially covering the walls. The fresco technique, which provided a surface smoother than the wall and allowed a better reproduction of the colours, meant that artists could cover all of the church walls.
Iconostasis	A screen decorated with icons separating the nave from the choir in Eastern churches.
Narthex	Covered porch or vestibule in a church where penitents and catechumens assembled before they were baptised.
Pendentive	Triangular concave space between the four arches supporting a dome, enabling the transition from square to circular.
Post-Byzantine style	Synthesis between the traditional Byzantine iconography and the Italian manner which appeared in several Cretan monasteries during the 16C.
Prothesis	Sacristy located to the left of the apse, near the diaconicon, where bread and wine were prepared for consecration.
Synthronon	Tiered benches following the semicircular shape of the apse, reserved for the clergy in Byzantine churches.
Transept	Transversal separation of the nave and choir, forming the arms of the cross. Not all churches have a transept.
Triptych	A work comprising three painted or carved panels, whose outer sections can be folded over the central section.

GREEK MYTHOLOGY

We are all familiar with Greek mythology, that vast compilation of narratives and legends about the gods and heroes of Antiquity which has become such a part of our shared culture. It has provided an endlessly fascinating source of inspiration for the greatest authors, from Homer to James Joyce, Euripides to Mary Shelley, Virgil to Cocteau. However, although many episodes of mythology remain etched in our memory, they often give the impression of being a rather disjointed and obscure collection, because either we have forgotten or were never aware of the "links" which would allow us to appreciate their unity and complexity. Because mythology has a meaning. A wealth of meanings, in fact. Hidden behind the countless characters and multitude of situations lies a whole world of symbols, an amazing reflection of historical events, philosophical thoughts and timeless proverbs.

Of this vast, variable and almost boundless "compilation", we shall simply try to lay out the principles and trace the outline, in the knowledge that the poets of ancient times produced a myriad variations – sometimes quite considerable – each having their own version of the love affairs or tribulations of a certain god or hero.

The birth of gods and man

The origin of the universe, first of all, is a matter of myths per se: **theogonic** myths recount the origin of the gods, while **cosmogonic** myths deal with the creation of the world and mankind.

The pre-Olympian deities

In the beginning there was **Chaos**, shortly followed by **Gaea** (the Earth) then **Eros** (Love). Alone, Gaea produced **Uranus** (Heaven), then the Mountains, the Nymphs and the barren Sea.

Uranus and his mother Gaea ruled the world together, and together gave birth to the second divine generation, the **Ouranides**. These included the **twelve Titans**, six boys and six girls, then the three **Cyclopes** and lastly the three **Hecatoncheires** (Hundred-Handed).

However, Uranus hated his offspring and imprisoned them in the depths of the Earth, in Tartarus. This eventually led to his downfall: Gaea could not bear such treatment being inflicted upon her children and started plotting with **Cronus**, the last-born of the Titans. With the aid of his brothers and sisters, who held down their father, the young Titan cut off Uranus' testicles. However, in the process, some of his seed spilt onto Gaea, who soon gave birth to the **Erinyes**, goddesses of vengeance, the **Giants** and the **Meliads** (Nymphs of the ash-trees). According to some authors, **Aphrodite**, the goddess of love, was also born as a result of this occurrence, after some sperm became mixed with foam from the Sea.

Cronus then began to rule in his father's place and married his sister Rhea with whom he planned to continue the family line. However, when a terrible prediction informed him that one day he would be dethroned by one of his children, he did not think twice about swallowing them as soon as they were born. Hestia, Demeter, Hera, Hades and Poseidon thus passed directly from their mother's belly into their father's. However, as in the previous generation, the danger was to come from the last-born of his children. **Zeus** managed to escape the sad fate of his brothers and sisters thanks to his mother, Rhea, who hid her newborn in a cave in Crete before tricking Cronus into swallowing a stone wrapped in swaddling clothes. When he reached adulthood, Zeus set his brothers and sisters free and, from the top of Mt Olympus, began to wage battle with them against Cronus and the Titans, who had taken refuge on Mt Óthris. This **Battle of the Titans** lasted for ten years until the Olympians finally claimed victory, aided by the Cyclopes and the Hecatoncheires, but resulted in no deaths, since it was fought between immortals.

But before finally becoming rulers of the world, the gods of Olympus still had to tackle the **Giants** (gigantomachia), whom they overcame thanks to the arrows of the mortal **Heracles**. Zeus then had to endure a long and merciless struggle with the terrifying monster, **Typhon**.

The birth of man

According to **Hesiod**, the first humans – all male – were directly produced by Gaea. They had a happy and carefree existence alongside the gods, fearing not even death, which took them by surprise in their sleep. This perfect harmony was disturbed by **Prometheus**, a descendant of the Titan Iapetus: during a banquet, he was caught favouring men over the gods when sharing out the meat of an ox. Annoyed by such trickery, Zeus decided to deprive man of fire. But Prometheus once again dared to defy the omnipotent god by stealing fire and returning it to man. The wrath of Zeus knew no bounds: Prometheus was chained to the summit of Caucasus and his immortal liver endlessly devoured by an eagle.

And in order to punish mankind, Zeus created woman, "an evil to men, with a nature to do evil". Endowed with a different quality by each of the Olympian gods, **Pandora**, "the gift of all the gods", was thus offered to Epimetheus, Prometheus' brother. Once on Earth, Pandora discovered a strange jar and, unable to contain her curiosity, opened it, allowing all the evils of the world to escape and leaving hope alone inside. And so mankind was punished.

The main gods of Olympus

High up in the mists of Olympus, the main deities convened in a "Council of the Gods", made up of twelve members. The actual members, however, vary according to the author and time of writing, with the only constant being that Zeus and his five brothers and sisters were definitely part of it.

Following their victory over the Titans, Cronus' three sons divided the world between them. **Zeus** took Heaven and quickly gained pre-eminence over his brothers. As master of the universe – although subject to Destiny – he was the protector of families and cities, and was devoted to ensuring the rule of justice and equity. Wisest of the wise, he is often depicted enthroned in limbo on Olympus, sporting

a large beard, with a sceptre in one hand and a thunderbolt in the other. His notorious weakness, however, was his great appetite for women (and incidentally for men). Thus, in addition to his official wives, the goddesses Metis, Themis, Eurynome, Mnemosyne and **Hera**, he had many affairs with both goddesses and mortals, with whom he had a vast divine progeny.

Zeus' brother, **Poseidon**, ruled over the seas, although he was also able to make the Earth tremble. His palace was hidden in the ocean depths, which he occasionally left, riding on a sumptuous chariot, trident in hand and accompanied by a cortege of sea monsters (Tritons).

Hades, Zeus' second brother, inherited the underworld and the kingdom of the dead. Wearing a helmet that made him invisible, he kidnapped **Persephone**, the daughter of Zeus and Demeter, then married her.

The powerful bronze Poseidon of Artemision (National Archaeological Museum, Athens)

Hestia, goddess of the domestic hearth and of the public hearth of the Prytaneis *(see Prytaneion page 46)*, was the eldest of Zeus' three sisters. Despite the advances made by Poseidon and Apollo, she remained a virgin and never left Olympus.

Zeus' sister **Demeter** had no such scruples and had an affair with him. Goddess of agriculture, and wheat in particular, she left the harvests to rot out of grief when Hades stole her daughter Persephone away. She eventually managed to arrange for Persephone to live with her for six months of the year, from the first growth of spring until sowing time in September.

Zeus' legitimate and permanent wife, **Hera**, vehemently detested all of her unfaithful husband's lovers and their offspring. So it is entirely natural that she should be the deity of marriage, protectress of conjugal fidelity and mothers. She was also goddess of vegetation.

Eight other gods and goddesses, all children of Zeus possessing outstanding powers and influence, can also lay claim to a place in the "Council of the Gods". The eternally young and handsome **Apollo** is a complex deity, with many strings to his bow: god of poetry, music and song, he led the chorus of the Muses and played the **lyre**. Protector of fields and herds, he was blessed with healing powers but could also spread epidemics with his bow. But despite his great beauty, he had an unhappy love life.

Athena mourning
(Acropolis Museum, Athens)

Hephaestus, lame since the day Zeus threw him off the top of Olympus, was married to Aphrodite, who betrayed him with Ares. The crippled god took his revenge by laying a trap for the two lovers and exposing them to the view of all the gods. God of **smiths** and of metalwork, he created Pandora, the first woman, on the orders of Zeus.

The antithesis of **Ares** — the rough, brutal and cruel god of war who was intensely disliked by the Greeks — **Athena** was perceived as a warrior goddess full of good counsel. She was also the protectress of cities, women's work and peace, despite her appearance: iconography shows her emerging fully armed from Zeus' head, wearing a helmet, carrying a lance on one arm and her father's shield on the other. This shield (or her breastplate) bears the head of **Medusa** (one of the **Gorgons**) with its tresses of snakes. The head of this terrible creature, who turned to stone anyone who met her gaze, was given to Athena by Perseus.

Armed with a bow and arrow like her twin brother Apollo, **Artemis** had no qualms about killing anyone outright if they offended her. She spent the rest of her time hunting with her dogs. Although an eternal virgin, she personified fertility, a quality which she shared with the goddess of love and beauty, **Aphrodite**, who was said to have had countless lovers, including the handsome **Adonis**. In order to make sure that Paris would name her the most beautiful goddess rather than Hera or Athena,

T.A.P.

she immediately promised him the hand of the fair Helen, thus causing the Trojan War (*see below*). God of wine, ecstasy and fertility, **Dionysus** set out to conquer the East on a chariot drawn by panthers, with a kantharos full of wine in his hand and a cortege of daemons, including **Bacchants** and **Satyrs**. With his winged sandals, **Hermes** was the messenger of the gods, and carried the **caduceus** (herald's staff). Inventor of the lyre and panpipes (or syrinx, the shepherds' pipe), he was also portrayed as the god of travellers, trade, shepherds and sport, and his cunning spirit also made him the protector of thieves!

The great legendary cycles

A tireless labourer

Six of Heracles' Labours were performed in the north of the Peloponnese: the hero choked the reputedly invincible Nemean lion with his bare hands before using its skin as a coat. Then he used a sling to kill the man-eating birds of the Stymphalian lake. South of Árgos, he cut off the nine heads of the Hydra of Lerna. Next, he ran the ferocious wild boar of Mt Erymanthus to ground, after hunting it for months. It took him a year to capture the hind of Cerynea, which moved faster than air, but just one day to clean the stables of Augeas by diverting two nearby rivers. The other Labours consisted of capturing a mad bull in Crete, taming man-eating horses in Thrace, killing a three-bodied and three-headed king near the Strait of Gibraltar, capturing Cerberus, the hound that guarded the gates of Hell, and taking, in turn, the golden girdle of the Queen of the Amazons and the golden apples from the Hesperides' garden.

Alongside the myths lies a whole catalogue of cycles composed of countless stories portraying heroes, gods and incredible monsters, their unity being formed by one of the characters or their descendants. Here are some of the most well known:

The adventures of Heracles

Son of Zeus and the mortal Alcmene, half god, half man, Heracles was endowed with extraordinary strength and performed a multitude of brilliant feats, conducting as many love affairs. Despised by Hera, Zeus' legitimate wife, he was provoked into killing his own children in a fit of madness sent by the goddess. To atone for these murders,

he was ordered to carry out **Twelve Labours**, which he accomplished in the same number of years. Heracles performed several other feats before meeting his death after putting on a poisoned coat. However, the gods allowed him into Olympus, where he became immortal. And so justice was done.

Jason and the Argonauts, or the quest for the Golden Fleece

Upon the death of his royal father, the young Jason's throne was usurped by his uncle Pelias. The latter agreed to return it to him on condition that his nephew bring him the Golden Fleece which was kept in Colchis on the Black Sea by King Aeetes. Pelias knew this was an impossible task, but Jason was not to be discouraged and set sail on board the **Argo**, a mighty ship built by Argos, a man with several pairs of eyes. Accompanied by his fifty **Argonauts** - including Heracles, the twins **Castor and Pollux**, and the musician **Orpheus** – he was to face many incredible ordeals throughout his voyage. He was aided not only by the precious powers of his companions, but also by the beautiful sorceress **Medea**, Aeetes' own daughter, whom he fell in love with and married. It was thanks to her powers that Jason was eventually able to secure the precious fleece.

Theseus and the Minotaur

The great Athenian hero, Theseus, son of the King of Athens, **Aegeus**, accomplished feats similar to those of his contemporary Heracles. One of these, his fight with the **Minotaur**, is particularly famous. Son of Minos, King of Crete, this monster – half man, half bull – lived in his father's palace, a labyrinth designed by the brilliant architect **Daedalus**. Every nine years, Minos demanded that Athens, which he had just subjugated, send him seven young men and seven young women to be fed to the creature. Theseus volunteered to go and, when he arrived in Crete, managed to kill the beast. Thanks to the thread given to him by **Ariadne**, Minos' own daughter who had fallen in love with him, Theseus was able to find his way out of the labyrinth and return to Athens. But as he neared the shores of Attica where his father was watching for his return, he forgot to raise the white sails in a sign of victory. Believing his son to be dead, Aegeus threw himself from the top of the cliffs of the Acropolis.

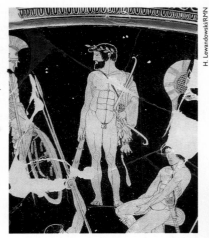

H. Lewandowski/RMN

The cycle of the Theban legends

A model labourer: Heracles (5C BC, Musée du Louvre)

This cycle traces the history of the origins of the city of **Thebes**, which was founded by **King Cadmus** on the spot where, as predicted by Apollo, a heifer collapsed from exhaustion. After a long reign, the elderly Cadmus passed his throne down to his descendants, **Laius** and his wife **Jocasta**. With them began one of the most famous and tragic episodes of the Theban legends, that of their son Œdipus. After being abandoned at birth, as a young man he unwittingly fulfilled the terrible prediction of the **Delphic oracle** by killing his father and marrying his mother. It was during this episode that he rid the city of the **Sphinx**, a monster – half lion, half woman – which was devouring all the passers-by who were unable to solve the riddle it put to them.

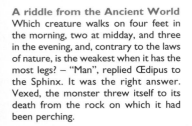

A riddle from the Ancient World
Which creature walks on four feet in the morning, two at midday, and three in the evening, and, contrary to the laws of nature, is the weakest when it has the most legs? – "Man", replied Œdipus to the Sphinx. It was the right answer. Vexed, the monster threw itself to its death from the rock on which it had been perching.

The Theban cycle came to an end shortly thereafter with the quarrel between Œdipus' two sons, Eteocles and Polyneices, who killed each other, then with the tragic end of their sister, **Antigone**, who was immured alive for trying to give Polyneices a symbolic burial. The following generation was to witness the destruction of Thebes by the Argives.

The Trojan War

Made famous by Homer, the story begins with Hera, Athena and Aphrodite assembling on Mt Ida in Crete where, under the auspices of the goddess of discord, a competition was to take place to choose the most beautiful goddess. The prize – a golden apple – was to be handed to the winner by the handsome **Paris**, the youngest son of **Priam**, the King of Troy. However, perfidious Aphrodite bribed the young man into choosing her by promising him the love of the most beautiful mortal, **Helen**, the wife of **King Menelaus**. Paris took her at her word and kidnapped the young woman, whom he brought back to Troy, thus causing war to break out.

On one side, the Achaeans, led by **Agamemnon**, King of Mycenae and ally of Menelaus. On the other, the Trojans, aided by **Aeneas**, Aphrodite's son. The siege lasted nine years. Homer's account, the *Iliad*, actually recounts only one of the last episodes, that of the famous **Trojan horse**. Since the Trojans were holding out, Agamemnon decided to play a trick, offering Priam a magnificent wooden horse in which he was hiding with his best men, **Achilles**, **Odysseus** and **Ajax**. The horse entered the city, the enemy along with it, and Troy fell at last.

Homer also relates the quarrel that took place between Agamemnon and Achilles before the horse made its appearance, and the heroic deaths of the warriors Patroclus and Hector, then Achilles, who was wounded in the heel – his only vulnerable point – by a poisoned arrow.

The return of Odysseus

Back from Troy, Odysseus set off for his kingdom, the Ionian island of Ithaca. During this ten-year voyage, which is related in the *Odyssey*, the hero encountered innumerable dangers: **Giants**, the sorceress **Circe**, the treacherously sweet song of the **Sirens**, as well as the monsters **Scylla** and **Charybdis**, not to mention the **cyclops Polyphemus**, son of Poseidon, whose murder brought the wrath of the god of the Sea down upon Odysseus and his companions. After finally returning to Ithaca twenty years after he had left, the warrior was recognised by his wife, the faithful **Penelope**, because he was the only one able to string his bow and shoot a single arrow through twelve axes standing in a row.

These legendary cycles are as exciting as they are numerous. You are sure to come across many others on your travels, such as the tragic fate of the Atreids who haunt the ruins of Mycenae, and you will find them in the relevant sections of this guide.

From Greek to Latin

Greek name	Latin equivalent		
Aphrodite	Venus	Hephaestus	Vulcan
Apollo or Phoibos	Apollo or Phoebus	Hera	Juno
Ares	Mars	Heracles	Hercules
Artemis	Diana	Hermes	Mercury
Asklepios	Aesculapius	Hestia	Vesta
Athena	Minerva	Erinyes	Furiae
Cronus	Saturn	Leto	Latona
Demeter	Ceres	Persephone	Proserpina
Dionysus	Bacchus	Poseidon	Neptune
Eros	Cupid	Rhea	Cybele
Hades	Pluto	Zeus	Jupiter

Bellerophon and Pegasus; red-figure kantharos (National Archaeological Museum, Athens)

The great legendary cycles

Meeting the people

The kafenío, or
the art of relaxation

A HOMOGENEOUS NATION

"Where do you come from? Which village? Which family?" these questions are frequently asked when Greeks first meet. Solidarity and a willingness to help each other often best define relations between compatriots. This is because regionalism has always been synonymous with cultural and social identity since well before the notion of national identity began to develop under the yoke of Ottoman rule. Despite the country's small size, the regional disparities of modern Greece are quite considerable: Epirus has a distinct Balkan flavour, and a fisherman from Santoríni has very little in common with a wealthy shipowner from Athens living on European time. Nevertheless, the 10.7 million inhabitants of Greece have managed to form a homogeneous nation, built up over the centuries around the **language** and the **Orthodox Church**.

National colours

Although Greeks acknowledge the same flag – five blue bands and four white, with the white cross of the Greek Orthodox Church in one corner – they don't all agree on the meaning of its colours. For most people, the blue represents the sky and the sea, and the white the struggle for independence. For others with more poetic leanings, the blue bands symbolise sea and the white ones its foam. But the religious maintain that the blue is the colour of wisdom, the white representing the purity of the soul.

The origins of the Greek world

To be Greek is to be the living memory of the country's wealth of history: the grandeur of Ancient Greece, the splendour of the Byzantine Period, the suffering of the Ottoman invasion and the pride of present-day Greece, which is busily trying to catch up with the rest of Europe while preserving and honouring a certain ideology of the past.

The first Greeks: the Hellenes

The Hellenes, a group encompassing various Indo-European peoples considered to be the first Greeks, first appeared in the 2nd millennium BC. After 2000 BC, the early inhabitants of the Hellenic Peninsula, the **Pelasgi**, were forced to flee as the **Ionians** advanced. The latter were followed by the **Achaeans**, mariners from the north who mixed with the local populations and gave birth to the Mycenaean civilisation (*see page 18*). This civilisation was to disappear, in turn, around 1200 BC in the face of the **Dorian** invasion. It was this last Indo-European wave which drove the Greeks towards the western shores of Asia Minor (Aeolis, Ionia, Doris), bringing them into contact with the eastern civilisations.

Settlers from abroad

After 395 AD, the history of Greece merges with that of the Byzantine Empire, the heir to Rome and Hellenism. Further invasions beginning in the late 6C brought about considerable demographic change. While many Greeks were forced to flee the Peloponnese, **Slavs** began to settle throughout the territory. They were followed by the **Vlachs** (or **Aromani**), an Indo-European people who originated from a region corresponding to what is now Romania, and who still inhabit the mountains of Epirus, Thessaly and Macedonia.

Then came the **Arab** occupation of Crete in the 9C and 10C, the arrival of the **Gypsies** in the 9C, the **Bulgar** incursions (late 10C) in mainland Greece, and the attempted conquests of the **Normans** of Sicily (late 11C). Very early in the 13C, the Greek islands fell into the hands of the **Venetians**, whose presence still persists in the small Catholic communities of the Cyclades. Lastly, the capture of Constantinople by the **Ottomans** in 1453 was to have an important impact on demographic makeup, particularly in the north.

It is also important to note the presence of a small **Jewish community**, consisting mainly of the descendants of Jews driven out of Spain and Portugal in the 15C, who were taken in by the Ottomans. Of the 80 000 Jews living in Greece in 1940 (50 000 of them in Thessaloníki), 62 500 were deported by the Nazis during the Second World War.

The Greeks and the world

The Greeks have a very revealing expression which helps to better understand the link that binds them to their homeland, which they call the "centre of the world": when Greeks set out to travel abroad, they say "I'm going outside" *("exoterikó")*, in other words, they are leaving their home to venture into the intrinsically hostile unknown; 400 years of Ottoman occupation have deeply marked the collective sub-conscious. Moreover, a feeling of latent insecurity – Greece still feels itself surrounded by enemies – continues to affect its relations with other countries.

The Greek diaspora

Greece's historical importance and geographical location have encouraged its inhabitants to venture beyond their borders. Overpopulation and poverty in the early 20C generated a strong wave of emigration between 1906 and 1915, when over 250 000 Greeks (out of a total population of 3 million) took the road to exile. An estimated 5.5 million Greeks now live abroad in Egypt, Central Europe, around the Black Sea, in the Middle East – regions where Greek communities settled in very ancient times – and particularly in the **United States**, where there are currently thought to be over 3 million of them. **Michael Dukakis**, the Democratic candidate in the 1988 American presidential elections (running against George Bush), is a good example of the Greeks' successful integration on the other side of the Atlantic. In recent times, emigrants have headed for other industrialised countries such as Canada, Australia, South Africa and Germany.

Status of minorities

A Greek citizen is an individual who practises the Orthodox religion (mention of religion has only just been removed from identity cards) and speaks Greek, which is the case of 97% of those living on Greek territory. However, within its present borders, which were stabilised after the Second World War, the country unites Greeks from all sorts of backgrounds, some of them from populations who have been moved at some point in their history.

The largest minorities include nationals from the border countries who are no longer in their own homeland for historical, economic or political reasons. Under the 1923 **Treaty of Lausanne** *(see page 29)*, 500 000 Muslims left for Turkey and 1.5 million Greeks flooded in from Asia Minor where there had been a Greek presence for thousands of years. However, approximately 60 000 **Turks** managed to avoid this painful exchange of population and still live in Greece, while Istanbul has only a very small Greek community.

Greece also has some 120 000 **Pomaks**, Bulgarian-speaking Muslims who live mainly in western Thrace, **Macedonians** in northern Greek Macedonia, and **Albanians** from Epirus who remained in Greece when the borders were being mapped out, hence the presence of Orthodox Christians in Albania, which is at the root of the strained relations between the two countries.

From 1975, Greece became a country of immigration as thousands of Poles, Filipinos, Kurds, Romanians, Iraqis, Pakistanis, Ethiopians, Egyptians, people from the former Yugoslavia and particularly from the countries of the old **Soviet Union** began to flood into the country looking for work. An estimated 7% of the Greek population are therefore immigrants, including a large proportion of "illegals". The State eyes these minorities with suspicion and officially recognises only one of them, the Muslims of Turkish origin, in accordance with the Treaty of Lausanne.

DAILY LIFE

At the dawn of the third millennium, Greece is keen to renew its image and take its place in the modern world. The prospect of holding the Olympic Games of 2004 in particular has transformed the capital city into a huge building site, injecting life into many projects which had long remained on the backburner. Athens is getting a makeover: it is polishing up and restoring its ancient relics, extending its metro, renovating and developing its road network, working to reduce pollution and creating pedestrian zones. In short, it is making every effort to be worthy of its future guests, who will be coming from all over the world and from the Europe of tomorrow, to which it now also belongs.

This metamorphosis is, however, only visible in the cities. The mountains and islands of rural Greece are still largely unaffected by this technological revolution, and the rural exodus *(see page 33)* is only serving to widen the gap between town and country. While Internet cafés are mushrooming in cities all over the country, some mountain folk still communicate with their neighbours in the next village by using an elaborate whistling code. But mobile phones have made their appearance here too...

Family portraits

In Kifissiá, an upmarket district of Athens

Nícos Papadópoulos lives with his wife Hélena and their two children in an elegant neo-Classical house in Kifissiá, an upmarket district in the north of the capital. Nícos and Hélena met when they were very young. Their respective fathers had shared business and financial interests, and the marriage of their children served to strengthen their partnership. Since then, Nícos has taken over as manager of his father's company. Hélena, who has never worked, spends her spare time shopping and making every effort to be the "perfect woman", with frequent trips to the hairdresser and beautician. In the evening, the couple like to meet up with friends at a restaurant or in the chic *bouzoúkia (see sidebar page 76)* of the capital.

Their children, Geórgos and Anastasía, attend one of the best private schools in Athens, reserved for the children of the capital's "upper crust". They are taught in both Greek and English and are studying for an international baccalaureate which will allow them to go to university abroad. Lessons begin at 8am and the children are back home at around 3.30pm, where a copious lunch prepared by the maid awaits them. They spend the rest of the afternoon at the **frondistírio**, a private institute which fills the gaps of both public and private teaching.

In Trípoli, a small town in the heart of the Peloponnese

Theódoros and Dímitra call each other *Papoú* and *Yayá*, like all of the grandfathers and grandmothers of Greece. They left their mountain village after their wedding to live in Trípoli, the nearest town. There, Theódoros found a job and a better environment in which to raise their two children in the way they wanted. Now a retired post office worker, he has a modest pension and devotes his spare time to the upkeep of the church in the village where he grew up, which gives him the opportunity to chat with lifelong friends. He also grows vines, which produce a pleasant rosé wine. Dímitra has never worked, but during the civil war she did much to help the locals and is still actively involved in the life of the community. She still finds time to take care of her kitchen garden, diligently watering it each morning before the council cuts off the public water supply, which it does every day until the evening.

In Heliópolis, a working class district of Athens

Danáï, 20 years old, and Vassilis, 28, are engaged to be married. Vassilis has opened a computer shop with two of his school friends, tapping a rapidly expanding market. As for Danáï, she is busy with the wedding preparations under the watchful eye of her mother. The big day will, of course, begin with the church ceremony, and then it will be party time. But first of all, she must take care of the *"príka"*, the dowry: like all brides-to-be in Greece, Danáï must provide her husband with a furnished apartment where the couple will, at last, be able to live together. And since Danáï doesn't know how to cook, it is her mother, who lives on the floor below, who will take care of the cooking and the education of her future grandchildren. While waiting for their new life to begin, the two lovebirds often go out together in the evening. After an early-evening siesta, they will join their friends in a café or nightclub, unless the *paréa* (group of friends) prefers to go to a taverna, as is often the case at the weekend.

In Shinoússa, an island lost in the middle of the Cyclades

In winter, Shinoússa has only 90 inhabitants, who all live in the village. In the low season, there are fewer connections by boat and the inhabitants have to rely on community spirit to cope with the isolation and hardship of winter. At the primary school, all of the children are taught together in one class by one single teacher. The oldest ones have to go and live with their cousins on the neighbouring island of Náxos in order to attend the secondary school. But with the holidays comes the time for family reunions: the children, along with all the

What's in a name?
During your travels, you may be surprised to find yourself constantly coming across the same first names – Níkos, Geórgos, Kóstas, etc. It is traditional in Greece for boys to be given the same name as their grandfather, which means that first names skip a generation but always reappear. The same goes for girls although, unlike for boys, some exceptions are tolerated on condition, however, that the name comes from the Orthodox calendar.

other family members living far away, return to live on the island, and the population multiplies by ten. The first tourists herald the return of summer and, along with it, a radical change in atmosphere: the solidarity and conviviality of the islanders gives way to competition, a necessity of business. But this is just until the summer holidays come to an end, when the island becomes tranquil once again.

Slices of life

At the "laïkí", the market

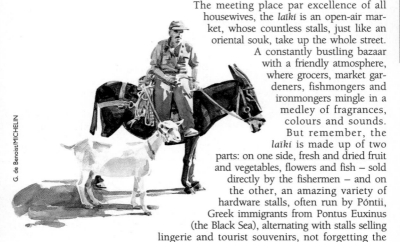

The meeting place par excellence of all housewives, the *laïkí* is an open-air market, whose countless stalls, just like an oriental souk, take up the whole street. A constantly bustling bazaar with a friendly atmosphere, where grocers, market gardeners, fishmongers and ironmongers mingle in a medley of fragrances, colours and sounds. But remember, the *laïkí* is made up of two parts: on one side, fresh and dried fruit and vegetables, flowers and fish – sold directly by the fishermen – and on the other, an amazing variety of hardware stalls, often run by Póntii, Greek immigrants from Pontus Euxinus (the Black Sea), alternating with stalls selling lingerie and tourist souvenirs, not forgetting the

G. de Benoist/MICHELIN

Yássas (Cheers!)

Africans with their alarm clocks, watches and radios. The *laïki* are mainly frequented by Greek women, who love to meet up there and share their opinions on the latest fashions or the quality of the tomatoes, for which they never tire of bargaining.

At the "kafenío": coffee and komboloï

Women at the *laïki*, men at the *kafenío*. Impregnable bastion of the gentlemen – moustaches trimmed and caps firmly in place – every self-respecting kafenío must possess a television set, placed high on an oilcloth-covered shelf so that it can be seen by all. The Greeks go there at any time of day, for no particular reason, with the events of the day and the activity in the streets providing endless topics of conversation. Sitting in front of a Greek coffee or glass of ouzo (always served with a large glass of water), they discuss the TV news and football, criticise the latest law passed by Parliament, enthuse about the stock market, or chat, just as seriously, about donkeys and goats. Some play cards or **távli**, a very traditional board game (similar to backgammon) inherited from the Byzantines; others sit alone on the terrace watching the world go by, lacing their *komboloï* through their fingers. And so they pass the time peacefully until dinner time, when they all go home to enjoy the culinary delights prepared by their wives or mothers.

The picture would be incomplete without a mention of the **komboloï**, a curious "rosary" which all of these men, regardless of age and social background, hold in their hands and click through their fingers at their own pace. Some women have also taken to doing this – the actress Melína Mercoúri was one notable example – but in their case, it is considered to be more of a feminist statement. The first traces of this object date back to prehistory, to the famous caves of Altamira in Spain. They were originally made of animal knucklebones, the number and quality of which corresponded to its owner's rank within the tribe. A symbol of power among wise men, then gradually becoming considered as sacred through the centuries, they had various functions. In Greece, the *komboloï* have no religious significance, a rare thing in this country. Of plastic or precious materials and threaded, one by one, through the fingers all day long, the beads are of mainly sentimental value, tinged with a certain sensuality. But this does not prevent the inhabitants of some country areas from also attributing to the *komboloï* the power to ward off the "evil eye".

A buzzing night-life

Like almost everywhere else around the Mediterranean, night-life in Greece is long and lively. It gets going around 11pm and carries on until dawn. Every night of the week, the night-clubs and *bouzoúkia* (see page 76) are full to bursting, the former attracting mainly young people, and the latter a greater mix of generations. People go to bouzoúkia to listen to their favourite singers, throw them flowers and get into the swing by dancing on the tables, if not joining them on stage! Then, of course, there are the restaurants, where *parées* (groups of friends) like to meet up, but not before 11pm.

At the most touristy sites and beaches in the high season (in Greece, summer begins at Easter and finishes in October), the nights come alive with the noise and lights of all these bustling places where the holidaymakers party together until the early hours of the morning. Which means that you'll find the biggest traffic

The Greeks rarely entertain at home, preferring to meet up with their friends elsewhere. Although the "laïkí" is assiduously frequented by housewives, and the "kafenío" by married or retired men, the street remains the most popular meeting place: influenced by Western fashion, cafés and fast-food outlets are very popular with the younger generation, who meet up with their "parées" there.

jams – cars and backfiring two-wheelers – between 9pm and 4am. So if you're hoping to sleep peacefully, make sure you avoid rooms which give on to the street!

At school

Whether public or private, all Greek schools are obliged by law to teach Orthodox theology, and at the beginning of every month, the parish priest comes to say a prayer to the schoolchildren.

School is compulsory between the ages of 6 and 15 and the school day has a minimum of five hours of lessons. However, insufficient funding means that many public establishments are unable to provide a fuller education and since there are not enough of them to educate all of the children, the State has imposed a system of half-day sharing of premises: the pupils go to school either in the morning or in the afternoon, so the establishment is fully occupied all day long. Likewise, schoolbooks are often terribly out of date, with some schools still using editions which are 30 years old. This explains why it is not uncommon to find words of warning in some history books advising children to "be wary of foreigners in general, and Turks in particular"!

The wealthiest families therefore often choose to send their children to private school, where they receive a fuller education, which includes learning several foreign languages and sports. But this remains a very expensive privilege, with some monthly instalments costing more than the equivalent of the Greek minimum wage.

Religion, part of everyday life

As the State religion (*see the chapter on this subject page 66*), Orthodox Christianity touches every aspect of Greek life and dictates a good many customs. At birth, for example, children are given a provisional name – *Baby* for boys, *Béba* for girls – until their baptism, when their godfathers give them their proper name, which, for the boys, is traditionally their grandfather's.

Every event, whether private or public, has to receive the **ayasmó**, the inevitable blessing of the Church. Depending on the occasion, it is the Orthodox priest or the archbishop who officiates (in return for payment, of course): the prelate to bless the election of a new president of the Republic or the forming of a new Parliament, the priest for the purchase of a house, a car or the opening of a shop.

As a mark of devotion to God, the **sign of the cross** - which contrary to the Catholic practice goes from right to left – is made on every occasion: children do it every morning at school before entering the classroom, and when passing a holy place it should be made three times.

Officially recognised by the State, **weddings at the Orthodox Church** suffice in themselves and couples are not required to go to the registry office as well. The number of registry office weddings, which are uncommon and unpopular, is estimated at less than 3%. Indeed, to many Greeks, a refusal to comply with religious traditions reminds them of Communism and civil war, the dark memory of which still lurks at the back of peoples' minds.

Family ceremonies

The Greeks certainly know how to party, and weddings and baptisms bring family and friends together in the most festive atmosphere. If, during your travels, you come across such an occasion in a village, don't hesitate to join in: you will certainly be made to feel welcome, and these moments of joyful celebration are sure to leave you some wonderful memories.

Baptism (váptisi)

The sacrament of baptism marks the entry of the faithful into the fold of the Church, and is the occasion on which the child is given its first name, chosen by its godfather (*O Nonós*) and godmother (*I Noná*). Holding the baby in their arms, they undress it and cover it all over with holy (olive) oil, before handing the child over to the priest, who then immerses it totally in water in a large tub three times in succession. The child is then dried and given **new clothes** which have never been worn before, so that it can enter life with "a new body, new spirit... and new clothes" – this special notion of "newness" is very important to Orthodox Christians. After this, the child is placed back in the arms of its godparents, who walk around the altar with it three times. Lastly, the priest cuts a **lock of hair** from the child, the first offering to God by the new member of the flock, in thanks for its consecration.

Marriage (gámos)

The wedding ceremony is an even more colourful affair than a baptism. At the church, the congregation is free to move around during the liturgy, so family and friends greet one another, and introductions, hugs and congratulations abound as gleeful children run around in all directions. On this occasion, the congregation is exceptionally allowed to approach the altar on the other side of the iconostasis in order to follow the event more closely. Standing just behind the future husband and wife, the witnesses each hold a **crown of flowers** (*Stephánia*) above their heads, as a symbol of purity. Then all four of them walk around the altar three times under a shower of rice and flower petals as the cheers of the guests echo throughout the church. When they finally leave the church, the newlyweds and their respective families are congratulated by one and all with the words *"Na zíssete"* (long may you live), while the witnesses are wished *"Pánda áxios"* (be always worthy). Incidentally, divorce and remarriage are accepted by the Orthodox Church.

Funerals (kidía)

The death of a loved one is obviously also an important time. In the villages, it is customary for the corpse of the deceased to be laid out at his or her home until the funeral so that everyone – family members and villagers – can go and pay their last respects. For the religious ceremony, the coffin is set down at the centre of the church surrounded by the deceased's family who, in some regions, still wear the black armbands of mourning. The Orthodox priest talks about the life of the deceased and of their being called to God while awaiting the resurrection of body and spirit. On leaving the church, the family hands out slices of cake which are supposed to ease the pain. The funeral cortege then forms to accompany the coffin to the cemetery. After the burial, the mourners gather around a copious meal served with wine, brandy and coffee. Finally, forty days later, one last mass is celebrated in memory of the deceased, the *Mnimósyno*.

Family spirit... and women of today

Shaped by long centuries of Ottoman (Muslim) culture and a strict Orthodox tradition, the status of women in Greece still remains bound by many family customs and ancient social conventions.

But times are changing. In the villages, although the oldest grandmothers, bowed by hard work, still wear headscarves and dress in black from head to toe, their grand-daughters are wearing makeup with tight T-shirts and trousers and hanging out at the cafés in town with their groups of friends. These two facets of Greek women symbolise the paradox of present-day society: a sincere attachment to tradition on the one hand, and a fierce desire to move into a new era, on the other.

Since 1952 when Greek women were finally given the right to vote (in Turkey it was in 1923), many laws have been introduced which have changed the status of women. Abortion has been legalised, divorce has rapidly become widespread and Greek women now have the right to keep their maiden name after marriage. On the other hand, although the **dowry** which the wife was supposed to give her husband has been officially abolished, the tradition has remained alive and it is still done for brides to provide their husbands with furnished accommodation as a wedding present.

In fact, most families continue to live together under the same roof, with parents and children dividing the storeys between them, and it is customary for parents to build or buy a house with as many apartments as they have daughters. This social convention has naturally caused a **very strong family bond** to develop, in which help from the parents plays a fundamental part. Furthermore, grandmothers still raise their grandchildren and are in charge of cooking for the entire household, with their daughters dropping in every day to pick up the dishes they prepare.

Far from disappearing, this family tradition is actually very well suited to the lives of women today. Women are now staking a claim to very different lives from those of their mothers and grandmothers, according more importance to building a career than a family. As a result, more and more women aim to have only one child or two at the very most, and head into the cities in search of greater social and personal fulfilment.

Family spirit

A short break at the kafenío between masses

V. Voutsas/ON LOCATION

SOCIAL ETIQUETTE

Greece welcomes over 8 million visitors every year, a source of profit which certainly warrants special attention from the inhabitants. But beyond such business consider-ations, the Greeks have a real sense of hospitality, remaining true to the tradition which holds that a traveller should be welcomed like a guest. This idea is reflected in the double meaning of the word *xenos*, which means both "foreigner" and "guest". As soon as you arrive, you will appreciate the spontaneity with which the Greeks welcome you, eager to help make your stay easier in any way they can or to give you directions using whatever foreign words they know. In return, remember to thank them with a warm *"Evharistó polí"*, and you will see in their smiles the genuine pleasure they take in being able to give you a helping hand.

A strong temperament
Like all true Mediterranean peoples, the Greeks have a **passionate** temperament and a fierce individuality, and are quickly carried away by their feelings. This character trait comes to the fore in all circumstances whenever personal or professional issues are at stake. They will fall into each other's arms and frantically embrace, just as they will argue and lecture each other at the slightest disagreement, gesticulating wildly. As you walk through a square, past a market stall or restaurant, you may even become unwittingly involved in such a spirited conversation yourself. Neighbours and passers-by will also join in to mediate or give their opinion before the altercation ends in front of a glass of ouzo to the accolades of a crowd satisfied with the show. You may be rather surprised by this excess of gestures and decibels, at times almost theatrical, but it is rarely of any great consequence.

The Greeks are **fervent patriots** and extremely proud of their roots, culture and land – hardly surprising for a people forced to endure four centuries of foreign dom-ination. Thus they also care a great deal about what travellers think of their country.

How to mix with the locals

A wish for every occasion
Popular tradition holds that people should wish each other all sorts of good things not only when a major occasion arises, but also throughout the day, the seasons, and with the passing of time. For the Greeks, this is actually a way of keeping the "evil eye" at bay (*see page 73*). So there is a saying for every occasion, and you are sure to please if you can slip one in at the right time. Here are a few examples:
- *Na sas zíssi* on the birth of a child, which literally means "may he (or she) live long",
- an ill person should be wished a *Perastiká*, a good recovery,
- for expectant mothers, one hopes for a *Kalí eleftheria*, literally a "good freedom",
- on the patron saint's day, the whole family is wished *Hrónia pollá*, which means "many years", the equivalent of our "many happy returns".

Wishes are also exchanged at the beginning of every season, month and week:
- *Kaló himóna*: have a good winter,
- *Kaló kalokaíri*: have a good summer,
- *Kaló mína*: have a good month,
- *Kalí evdhomáda*: have a good week.

And of course every day starts with a lively *Hérete!*, lasting until the end of the after-noon when it gives way to the customary *Kalispéra* (have a good evening), then to the bedtime greeting *Kalí níhta*.

Lastly, if you want to flatter a friend, congratulate a child or shower a newborn baby with praise, it is customary to finish with an emphatic *Ftoussou*, a magic formula which protects the loved one from the "evil eye".

Sign language

- If, in answer to a question, your interlocutors throw their head back, raising their chin, it means no. However, if they incline their head slightly to the side, they are saying yes.
- You can clap your hands to attract a waiter's attention in a restaurant without being considered rude.
- Be warned: raising your hand with your five fingers spread (palm facing forward) is considered an insult.

Do's and don'ts

As in all countries, it is good form to adapt your behaviour to suit the occasion. Being a religious people, the Greeks like visitors to respect their **holy places**: it is highly improper to enter while eating, and visitors must be suitably attired. Many monasteries and churches will allow women and girls to enter only if they are wearing below-the-knee skirts or dresses and their shoulders are covered. Likewise, men may be required to wear long trousers, heat wave or not!

In the country, or in regions where few tourists venture, the inhabitants may appear reserved or even distant. Each village effectively has its own customs and traditions, and the arrival of visitors in these peaceful and unchanging micro-societies can cause them to become particularly withdrawn. So if you want to **take photographs** of someone, be sure to ask their permission first with a smile.

If you are invited to a **family home**, you will soon discover that they don't stand on ceremony. In particular, at mealtimes, where the servings are often very copious, don't feel that you have to finish what is on your plate. These large servings are a counter-reaction to all the deprivation of the dark years and the lady of the house will not be offended, merely surprised by your "small appetite".

Lastly, when you meet people, remember to avoid certain **sensitive subjects** which are likely to put a damper on the atmosphere. Be sure, in particular, to avoid any comparison with or even reference to **the Turks**. Resentment against Turkey, which is still being fuelled by the Cypriot question, remains very much in the hearts of the Greeks, despite the efforts of the Foreign Minister, Papandréou. A more conciliatory approach, however, appears to have emerged since the earthquake of summer 1999, which hit both countries in succession and resulted in spontaneous offers of mutual aid from Ankara and Athens.

It is also advisable to avoid raising any discussion about the events in **Kosovo**, since the Greeks, who are pro-Serb, very clearly opposed the attitude of the West, and the United States in particular.

In any event, although the Greeks love to discuss politics among themselves, they prefer to broach much lighter subjects with a *xenos* (foreigner) and laud the treasures of the "most beautiful country in the world".

RELIGION

Orthodox Christianity is the official religion of Greece and unites 97% of the population. Since there has been no separation between Church and State, the president of the Republic is sworn in on the Bible, every public event unfailingly takes place in the presence of a representative of the Church, and the compulsory reference to religion on the national identity card – the only country in the whole of Europe to do this – has only recently been abolished. It is also important to remember that, in the early 19C, the clergy took an active part in the fight for independence which brought four centuries of Ottoman domination to an end. All in all, the Orthodox religion plays a major role in the national consciousness and is a fundamental part of Greek identity. If you're in any doubt, just attend one of the big religious festivals which dot the calendar and you will experience all the fervour of the Greek people at first hand *(see page 70)*.

Orthodox Christianity, a State religion

The Great East-West Schism

At first united by their genesis and doctrine, the paths of **Orthodox Christianity** and **Catholicism** began to diverge in the 5C, eventually resulting in the greatest schism in the history of Christianity. This rupture became official in July 1054 with the definitive separation of the Western Latin Church and the Eastern Church. Two worlds drew apart, and Byzantium, proclaiming itself the sole heir to Rome, became the new symbol of Hellenism. The main causes of the Great Schism – which are as numerous as they are complex – resulted, very basically, from two different readings of the Trinity or **"filioque"** (Latin, meaning "and from the son"): for the Catholics, the Holy Spirit came, in effect, from the Father and from the Son, while for Orthodox Christians, it came from the Father alone.

There is also the fundamental question of **language**: loyal to Rome, the Catholics held mass in Latin, while the Orthodox Christians, heirs to the Byzantine tradition, used ancient Greek with a vocabulary which yields a different interpretation of the Apostles' teachings.

Caught in a stranglehold between two Churches (although still mainly under Roman rule at the time), the Greek cities hesitated between East and West. Shaken by historical events, Greece wavered in its religious convictions for a long time, with the successive waves of invaders serving only to add to the confusion, first of all with the arrival of Arabic Islam in the 7C, then the intrusion of the Latins and Mongols in the 13C, followed by four centuries of Turkish Islam beginning in the 15C.

A Christian enclave in a Muslim land

"Better the Ottoman turban than the Latin mitre" was the Patriarch of Constantinople's reaction when the Pope offered to send his soldiers to stave off Mehmet II's army, which was already standing at the gates of the city (1453). In one of the paradoxes of history, the Turks actually worked in favour of Orthodox Christianity gaining supremacy in Greece: under the aegis of the Patriarchate of Constantinople, they turned the conquered land into a **millet**, a community administered by the Orthodox Church, thus imposing Orthodox Christianity as the religion of Greece. The sultan's strategy was a clever one, allowing him to undermine the Pope's authority in the country while waiting for the last embers of Byzantium to die down in turn.

This privilege naturally meant that heavy tributes had to be paid to the Ottoman crown. What was initially considered to be a victory of Hellenic thinking over the Turkish occupant was gradually revealed as a compromise. And so, as the years of occupation turned into centuries, Orthodox Christians gradually turned their backs

An ecumenical century?

It was not until the 20C that a dialogue was struck up again between the Catholic and Orthodox Churches. First in Jerusalem in 1964, then in 1967, when Pope Paul VI met the Patriarch of Constantinople, Athenagoras I. The first tangible signs of a reconciliation at last began to appear after centuries of cold opposition. The separation of Church and State is another recurring debate in Greece and a constant source of concern to the Orthodox Christians, since the Church has always played an important part in the country's affairs. on the Patriarch of Constantinople, in favour of the parish priests, who were more in touch with the people and their expectations. The capture of Constantinople by the Turks served only to consummate the split. The millet system thus disappeared at the end of the 18C when the Greek bourgeoisie was casting off the political yoke of the Patriarchate, leaving it with nothing more than an ecumenical role. Today, only the Dodecanese and Crete – which joined Greece much later on – and Mt Athos still depend, at least in theory, on Constantinople.

The heir to the Byzantine Church

It was the Church of **Byzantine rite** which gave itself the epithet of "Orthodox", ie "conform to doctrine". It represents the faith of the Fathers of the Church and considers itself to be the loyal heir to the writings of the Apostles. Although the Orthodox Church acknowledges the Pope, it does not consider him to be St Peter's successor, but merely a bishop.

The **Holy Synod** is the governing body of the Orthodox Church: the ecumenical patriarchate, the archdioceses and dioceses, and the parishes.

Despite being autonomous entities, the **patriarchates** all recognise the honorary primacy of the Patriarchate of **Constantinople**, the great historical patriarchates being those of Rome, Antioch (Antakya), Jerusalem, Aleppo and Alexandria.

The Greek Orthodox Church is independent. Since 1835 it has been an **autocephalous church**, governed by its own head bishops, having split away from the Patriarchate of Constantinople. Thus demonstrating a certain spiritual independence, it aims to be less of an institution and more the expression of a united and holy church, present even in the country's smallest villages and in touch with the people. This choice is reflected in various media initiatives, so it is not at all unusual to see the Patriarch of Athens on television commenting on current affairs in social-oriented statements.

In a remarkable departure from the Catholics, the Orthodox Church allows certain low-ranking secular priests to marry. **Orthodox priests** are therefore entirely at liberty to start a family and frequent the same places as any other citizen. So don't be surprised if you come across one of these honourable defenders of the Byzantine faith – long black *rasa* and grey beard under the inevitable *kalimavci* – wandering around a supermarket or sitting in a *kafenio*, talking away on his mobile phone!

The icons, or images of the Kingdom of God

Another significant feature of Orthodox Christianity is the importance accorded to

Mt Athos, sanctuary of the Byzantine faith

Spiritual and intellectual bastion of the purest Orthodox Christianity, the community of Mt Athos has, since the 10C, been the closed domain of hermits and monks living according to a tradition of strict discipline introduced by St Athanasius the Athonite. Although many pilgrims manage to gain entry to these monasteries, members of the fair sex are never to be seen there, since Athonite rules forbid any form of female presence – animal or human – on their territory. Since 1926, Mt Athos has had an autonomous administrative status, placed under both the canonic jurisdiction of the Patriarch of Constantinople and the political protectorate of the Greek government. In the 16C there were around 15 000 monks on Mt Athos but there are now only 1 500.

F. Guiziou/HEMISPHERES

The iconostasis: splendour and mystery of the Byzantine church

images (icons) evoking the Kingdom of God, and the profound and mystical intensity of the liturgical vocabulary. In the churches, a high screen covered in icons – the **iconostasis** – separates the nave from the sanctuary, isolating the officiating Orthodox priest from the worshippers during consecration (the central doors are opened and closed according to the different stages of the ceremony), creating an atmosphere shrouded in mystery. The word **mystery** is also used by Orthodox Christians to describe what other Churches call sacraments (baptism, marriage, etc). In the Orthodox religion, the images of the saints play a very special part. However, contrary to the thinking of the iconoclasts of the 7C-8C, these icons are not in themselves objects of worship linked to idolatrous practices, but symbolic images devoid of any realism, which comply with strict conventions established right from the outset. Each character can thus be recognised by its attributes, the colour of the clothes and so forth, thereby creating a visual language that allows everyone, literate or not, to identify the saint to whom they are praying.

A holy icon
After the iconoclastic crisis which caused the loss of thousands of masterpieces from the world of art, it was the Empress Theodora who, on 11 March 843, reinstated the icons and their role in Byzantine churches. Since then, this date has been celebrated each year in all of the Orthodox parishes in Greece. The revered icon of the Virgin Mary on the island of Tínos attracts thousands of pilgrims, especially on the Day of the Assumption. According to tradition, this icon was the work of St Luke himself and is also said to possess miraculous powers, as evidenced by the countless crutches piled up in a corner of the church.

Religious minorities

In Greece, the religious minorities are gathered together under the high patronage of the Orthodox Church. In practice, this means that for the renovation or construction of a church, mosque or synagogue, for example, they have to obtain permission from the relevant Orthodox bishop.

Catholics

The Greek Catholic community numbers approximately 45 000, but despite this relatively low figure, it has encountered strong resistance from the Orthodox Church. Although the archbishoprics of Corfu, Thessaloníki and Tínos have been officially recognised by the Greek State, this is still not the case of the archbishopric of Athens, founded in 1880, ie almost 60 years after the War of Independence.

The same distance exists in civic affairs: marriages between Catholics are recognised by the Greek State, but matters are complicated when the husband and wife do not share the same faith. In the event of a "mixed" marriage, Catholics recognise and tolerate the Orthodox party and accept the union without any particular requirements. But there is no reciprocity, and the Orthodox Church only acknowledges the marriage if it is celebrated within its fold. The future husband and wife are, however, free to hold a Catholic wedding beforehand.

Furthermore, in order to avoid conflicts between the followers of different faiths during Lent or feast periods, Greek Catholics have agreed to celebrate Easter according to the Julian calendar, like the Orthodox Christians.

Muslims

The Muslims of Greece are still living with the memory of the dramatic and difficult **exodus** which followed the end of the First World War. Once independence was proclaimed, the Greeks immediately set about eradicating every trace of Ottoman domination from their territory. The last bastion of Islam in the country, **Thrace** (north-east Greece) is today home to 120 000 Muslims, and the region's cities are still dotted with minarets.

This minority has acquired a special position and status within the Greek State and is even represented in Parliament by two elected authorities, guaranteeing the Muslims a certain number of rights and provisions. This presence at government level enables, among other things, the national recognition of Koranic schools (medrese), the official teaching of Turkish, and the integration of Muslim students into Greek universities. Thrace is divided into three prefectures and governed by a **mufti**, an elected administrator in charge of religious affairs and the administration of the Islamic clergy of the region.

Jews

Greece has experienced several waves of Jewish immigration, the first one as long ago as very early Antiquity when merchants left Israel c 2300 BC to set up trading posts around the peninsula. Since they spoke Greek, they had no difficulty in mixing with the local populations, who subsequently began to call them **Romaniotes**, ie Jews of Greco-Roman origin.

In the 15C, a large **Sephardic** community found refuge in Greece after being driven out of Spain by the Inquisition in 1492. They were followed five years later by Jews from Portugal, then from Central Europe and southern Italy. The community thus increased extensively, bringing a know-how and culture that the Ottoman occupiers were quick to put to use, seeing it as a providential instrument to reduce Christian opposition. And so the Turks granted the Sephardic Jews a number of privileges (the Romaniote Jews were considered to be less "educated", more boorish), and for several centuries helped this community to settle in Greece. The Second World War, however, decimated this community in the most tragic fashion. Originally numbering 77 000 individuals, the Jewish community, which is mainly based in Macedonia, has been reduced to a mere 5 000.

TRADITIONAL FESTIVALS

Since religion is firmly imprinted in daily life, dictating many cultural and social customs, most of the major festivals in Greece correspond to the liturgical calendar. However, while certain celebrations are steeped in a pious atmosphere of purely Orthodox contemplation, particularly in the islands and villages, other occasions combine the holy and the profane – hovering somewhere between a mass and a village fête – in a mixture of deep piety and pagan rituals, the undying legacy of ancient times. This provides the Greeks with a multitude of opportunities to celebrate life and the seasons with their all-consuming and ever-colourful fervour.

Let the festivities begin...

The most ecumenical festival of all is, of course, **New Year's Day**, but this does not stop people from going to church on this day too. In the evening of 31 December, the whole household gathers together around the traditional *Vassilópita* **(St Basil's Cake)**, which contains a gold medal or coin. As the twelve strokes of midnight ring out, the head of the family cuts the cake with great solemnity, following a very specific ritual: after cutting it into four – in the sign of the cross – he then cuts it into as many pieces as there are guests, not forgetting to leave a piece for God and for absent friends and to set aside other pieces to ensure the protection of the home, for good luck or to make a wish come true. Once the cake has been handed out, the person who finds the hidden coin or medal will have good luck and happiness in the coming year.

The major dates in the liturgical calendar

All Greeks, be they devoutly religious or sceptic, celebrate the main religious occasions. This is because, beyond their liturgical bases, these festivals also have a national dimension which unites the whole population, Orthodox Christianity being part of the cement which bound the Greek nation together after it was freed from the yoke of Islam under the Ottomans.

In 1923, the church officially adopted the **Gregorian calendar**, with the exception of Easter, which is still celebrated according to the **Julian calendar**.

• **Epiphany**, 6 January, commemorates the baptism of Jesus in the River Jordan, with a blessing of the waters. After the church service, the Orthodox priest traditionally throws a cross into the sea, which the local boys race in to retrieve.

• The three weeks before the beginning of Lent (the period of fasting leading up to Easter) is a very festive time, when adults and children alike parade around the streets in **carnival** (or **Lent Announcement**) costumes. This respite in the heart of winter gives each town an opportunity to organise its own festivities, and Patras, for example, is renowned for its superb parades of decorated floats.

• Forty days before Easter, **Clean Monday** (Katharí deftéra) marks the beginning of Lent, a period of partial fasting during which several types of food are forbidden (mainly meat and milk, but also some fatty foods), and the skies are filled with fluttering kites.

• During **Holy Week**, various events herald the Resurrection, the most important one being Good Friday, with the procession of **epitáphios,** large liturgical cloths representing the shroud of Jesus on which he is depicted surrounded by weeping angels. They are covered in flowers, marking the arrival of spring, and in some villages, photographs of those who passed away during the previous year are also attached to them. Every church has its *epitáphion,* which is carried on high through the streets of the town, followed by a crowd of worshippers holding lighted candles in their hands. The most spectacular epitáphios are in Athens and in the churches of Kifissiá, Corfu and the island of Mýkonos.

• Much more so than Christmas, **Easter** is the main festival of the year, and is a time of great celebration throughout Greece. As well as being a religious festival, it is also an exaltation of spring. The celebrations begin on the morning of Easter Saturday and reach their high

One single flame for one single god
Each year at Easter, the same small flame passes throughout almost the entire country. It is flown over from Jerusalem, landing in Greece on Easter Saturday, ready to light all the candles in the country.

point at midnight when, after a long mass, the Orthodox priest emerges from the church holding a lighted candle to announce the resurrection of Christ: *"Christós Anésti!"*. The crowd awaits him on the square, each person holding an unlit candle. The priest then lights one of the candles with his flame and, within minutes, the square is alight with a myriad of small flickering flames, while the bells ring out long and loud. Back home again, the head of the family draws the sign of the cross with the smoke from his candle on the embrasure of the front door (this is also customary when blessing a new house). Everybody can then sit down for **Easter dinner**, with, on the menu, soup made with the intestines of milk-fed lambs, and roast meat and potatoes, all much appreciated by the guests after the long period of Lent. At the end of the meal, eggs painted red (symbolising the blood of Christ) are handed around and broken with one's neighbour. At dawn the next day, the master of the house lights the fire under the Easter lamb and *kokorétsi*, brochettes of tripe. Throughout the day and well into the following night, relatives and friends come to eat and drink to the resurrection of Christ. A communal meal is usually also organised in the village square to give everybody the chance to celebrate Easter properly, regardless of social standing.

• 15 August is the feast of the **Assumption**, commemorating the ascent of the Virgin Mary (*Panagía*, the "All-Holy") into heaven after she fell asleep for the last time (Dormition). Celebrations are held by all the churches and many pilgrimages take place in the towns and villages, in particular on the island of Tínos.

• The last major festival of the year is **Christmas**, celebrating the birth of Christ. In Greece, it is not celebrated to the same extent as in the rest of Europe since the Orthodox faith attaches much greater importance to the symbol of the resurrection. Children traditionally go carol-singing from house to house.

National festivals...

In addition to the religious festivals, the Greeks celebrate two historic dates, which are of the utmost importance for this nation of patriots: **25 March**, commemorating the beginning of the Greek War of Independence, and **28 October** or "No! day" ("*Óchi* day"), in remembrance of the rejection of the Italian ultimatum in 1940.

These two commemorative festivals are celebrated in a similar way. Every town or village organises its **parréllassi** (parade) of all the important local figures. Soldiers, representatives of the Church in ceremonial dress, local dignitaries, the best students and sports club members march by to the sound of the brass band. In a moderately nationalistic speech, the mayor usually recalls the heroism of the Greeks, who emerged victorious from these episodes of history, and the national flag can once again be seen flying in every public place.

"Panigíri", or festivals every day
In Greece, saints' days are celebrated with even greater enthusiasm than birthdays. These are the panigíri, and the most important are celebrated in style, such as that of the patron saint of Greece, St George (Ágios Geórgios), whose name is one of the most common in the country (along with Ioánnis, Constantínos and Eléni – or John, Constantine and Helen). On this occasion, travelling salesmen – often gypsies – and tradesmen set up shop at the numerous fairs which are held throughout the country. The villagers flock there to rummage through the displays and make their purchases in preparation for winter, buying hardware, tools, animals, hi-fis, records, clothes, household linen, toys, trinkets, and much else besides. Musicians from the surrounding areas come to play and encourage the locals to dance a few steps.

In Greece, where the month of May can always be counted on to keep its promises of sunshine, **Labour Day** is also the **Flower Festival**. On 1 May, city-dwellers go out to picnic in the countryside, and in the villages, garlands of flowers adorn the front doors.

... and regional festivals

In summer (July and August) numerous **wine festivals** are scattered throughout the mainland and in the islands, but the dates and venues can vary from year to year. In a lively atmosphere, revellers can sample as much of the year's wine as they like and dance until dawn. The most popular festivals are at **Loubarda** in Agía Marína (near Cape Soúnion), **Dafní** (near Athens), Piraeus and all over **Crete**.

Another more unusual celebration, the **Anastenariá** (from the word *"anastenázo"*, meaning "to groan"), takes place on 21 May in **Macedonia** and **Thrace** in commemoration of a particular event – the rescue of icons from a burning church in the 13C – which has been stigmatised by the Church. Certain villagers (men or women) bearing icons, dance barefoot on burning coals groaning loudly to evoke the panic caused by the incident.

Still in northern Greece, some villages have taken the original step of instituting the equivalent of a **"Women's Day"** on 8 January. To celebrate this **gynaecocracy** (gynaikokratía), men and women swap roles for a day, giving the ladies free rein to spend the day on the café terraces while their dearly beloved stay home to do the housework.

Village festivities: a traditional wedding in Arkasa, Kárpathos

Traditional festivals

HUMOUR AND SUPERSTITION

The Greeks love to have fun, all the more so since the country's recent history did not really encourage this trend. So they are often to be found gathering together in *parées* (small groups of friends) around a drink or meal, telling the latest jokes or spreading, for better or for worse, the latest gossip. Although the Greeks willingly laugh at the expense of their peers, they are not overly fond of being the butt of other people's jokes themselves. So beware of teasing them about certain subjects – humour is not always compatible with national pride and self-esteem!

Karaghiózis, the Greek puppet show

Like the Indonesians and the Turks, the Greeks have their own **shadow theatre**. Using silhouettes cut out of painted leather and mounted on sticks, the stories are enacted before a lighted canvas. The comparison is not purely by chance, since the Javanese *Wayang kulit*, which was imported into Egypt by the Arabs, probably inspired the Turkish Karagöz from the 16C, then the Greek Karaghiózis. Others, however, maintain that Karagöz is of purely Turkish origin and dates back to the 14C. The two main heroes, Karagöz and Hacivat, were hired as workmen on the building site of a mosque in Bursa. However, the two cronies worked only half-heartedly, preferring to spend their time entertaining their fellow workers. To punish and make an example of them, Sultan Orhan had them hanged, but the townspeople missed them so much that a certain Seyh Küsteri came up with the idea of making puppets in their effigy, using them to perpetuate their stories. This, so it is said, is how the Turkish shadow theatre, and subsequently its Greek counterpart, were born. The Karaghiózis puppet is a **caricature of the Greek man in the street**. With his big "black eyes" – literal translation of the Turkish word *Karagöz* – his hunched back and his inordinately long arm, the hero of Greek shadow theatre is hideously ugly. The incarnation of the Evil One, a truly artful character, he is quick in repartee, with a ready wit and a consummate knack for storytelling and trickery in which he sometimes gets almost inextricably caught up himself. He is facetious, irreverent, sometimes generous, sometimes dishonest, but always patriotic and, above all, constantly famished. He has turned his hand at every trade, taken all sides, and meddled in every love affair and political or financial intrigue. His adventures are a joyful combination of history – especially Ottoman domination – everyday life and Greek mythology, with never a care for anachronism. The other protagonists represent various figures from late 19C Greece. The vain and garrulous Athenian is represented by **Morphonios** ("the Educated" in a pejorative sense), whose enormous head symbolises the intellectual. **Hadziavatis**, the Turk, is the double of Karaghiózis, his accomplice, often his victim, and always the butt of his jokes. Although the Karaghiózis shadow theatre seems to be dying out, the spirit of his character lives on a little in every Greek man who loves his country but detests the State, who respects knowledge but lampoons scholars and who can, on every occasion, make a mockery of the things he reveres the most.

Popular superstitions

The evil eye

The legacy of centuries of Ottoman invasion, the **mati** (literally the "eye") borders on the obsessive among the Greeks, who live in constant fear of becoming *mati-assmeni* (being hit by the evil eye). People suffering from flu, nausea or colds, in particular, often say that they are *matiassmeni*. And so, to ward off any malediction, everyone carries a small glass eye set in turquoise blue. They can be seen pinned onto clothes and babies' cradles, hanging around the necks of children and adults, inside houses, cars, shops and any other inhabited place. The "guardian angel" eye is said to provide protection against the treacherous and jealous spirits which lie dormant in all people.

Compliments should never be made to a child or newborn baby unless immediately followed by a **ftoussou**: this movement of the lips, which is actually rather like spitting, indicates that the praise is sincere and devoid of any feeling of hidden jealousy. In maternity wards, there are countless signs saying that it is forbidden to "ftoussou" on the infants, for reasons of hygiene!

If, in spite of these precautions, a person does fall under a spell, certain people "in the know" – often the grandparents – claim that they hold a miraculous formula which, with the aid of a glass of water and a drop of olive oil, will deliver the afflicted from the evil eye in an act of "purification" which can even be carried out by telephone.

Lacheío! Lacheío!

The Greeks like to gamble and are great believers in their good fortune. This spirit of speculation has resulted in a great proliferation of games involving chance and luck. In particular, "propó" and "loto" – ordinary or sports – "xistó" (scratch card), "lacheío" (numbered tickets), along with a multitude of variations. Every district in every town has a shop exclusively devoted to selling these lucky tickets and officially recording bets and lottery cards. They can also be bought from street vendors who walk around the streets shouting: "Lacheío! lacheío!".

A mixed blessing

In the country, the building of a house, factory or any other place for living or working, sometimes begins with a ceremony during which a cockerel's throat is cut. Under the watchful eye of the family, friends or workers, the Orthodox priest sacrifices the creature before giving it to the poor. In the towns, instead of this ritual, it is still customary to seal a gold or silver cross in the building's foundations.

Proskinitario, chapels of remembrance

On your travels, you are bound to notice the tiny chapels which stand at the side of roads, motorways or country lanes, often not far from a bend in the road. These remarkable little constructions are to give thanks to the Lord for an accident in which no-one was killed or, on the contrary, to honour the memory of the deceased. Enthroned inside is an icon of the patron saint, illuminated by a small oil lamp – often just a glass filled with olive oil – along with a few offerings and a bouquet of faded flowers cloaked in dust.

P. Texier/HOA QUI

MUSIC AND DANCE

A few friends, a glass of ouzo and high spirits are the basic ingredients of any impromptu party. The Greeks rarely pass up an opportunity to listen to music and dance a few steps of the *syrtáki*, *bálo* (in the islands) or *zeïbékiko*, which are popular with men and women of every generation.

From classical music to music of the classes

Very little is known about the music of Ancient Greece, other than that a prestigious operatic art existed in the 5C BC, mainly in the cities of Delphi, Sparta and Athens. Music subsequently seems to have rapidly fallen by the wayside, leaving the more potent force of poetry to take centre stage.

The revival of Greek music did not take place until the mid-19C, when two very different trends emerged; on the one hand, classical music mainly influenced by Italian works, and, on the other, popular **(laïkí musikí)** and folk **(dimotikí musikí)** music, which were closer to the lives and preoccupations of the people.

Classical music

The composer of the national anthem, **Nikólaos Mantzaros** (1795-1872), was the pioneer of the classical music movement which continued in the following generation under the leadership of Manólis Kalomíris – composer of the first Greek opera, *The Masterbuilder*, in 1915 – and Níkos Skalkottás.

Iánnis Xenákis (1922-2001) was undoubtedly the most innovative Greek musician of the 20C. Noted and recognised by his peers well beyond the borders of Greece, this trained mathematician and architect became an eminent composer of contemporary stochastic music, which applies probability theory and random variables to music. Mention should also be made of **Geórges Apérghis** (b 1945), who helped to introduce the "musical theatre" genre.

Rembétika: popular songs and music

In the late 19C, in the slums of Smyrna (now Izmir), Istanbul, Athens and Piraeus, a new form of music, *rembétika*, was beginning to emerge, and a whole social and political movement along with it. Often compared with blues music, *rembétika* flourished in the 1920s among the Greeks from Asia Minor and the country folk who had come to look for work in the cities. In this milieu of misfits, the musicians organised secret gatherings *(stéki)* to dance, play the music "of the poor townspeople" *(ipokosmos)*, smoke hookahs and throw plates. The *rembétis* (*rembétiko* singers) lived on the fringe of society, taking a certain pride in their non-conformism. But they were poets nonetheless, and their texts, which were often written in slang and railed against injustice, abuse and inequality, also recount stories involving drugs and women of loose morals. Although its roots were in Asia Minor, a truly Greek style of music began to emerge thanks to the work of musicians such as **Vassílis Tsitsánis** (1915-84). The movement spread very rapidly, despite – or perhaps because of – the contempt of the bourgeoisie, who preferred more Western styles of music. With the revival of nationalism in the post-war period, record companies took the opportunity to bring *rembétika* out of the shadows, turning it into a huge success.

But what would the lyrics of *rembétika* be without the **bouzoúki**? Originally known to the bourgeoisie as the "devil's instrument", the story goes that this mandolin was subsequently upstaged by the *baglamás*, a smaller version which could be hidden inside a coat!

The Greek music revival – Two renowned contemporary artists, **Míkis Theodorákis** (b 1925) and **Mános Hadzidákis** (1925-94), were intent on preserving and exploiting the musical legacy of Greece. The former, in addition to his commitment to politics which has made him a real living legend in his country, also composed scores for films such as *Z* and *Zorba the Greek*, which achieved great success abroad. Hadzidákis also worked in films and notably composed songs for Nana Mouskouri. Other talented contemporary singers include Yórgos Daláras, Háris Alexíou and Eleftheria Arvanitáki.

Folk music (dimotiki musiki)

Every town and village has its own brass band, which the Greeks rather ambitiously call "philharmonic orchestras". These formations are composed of musicians of all ages, who are mostly self-taught and perform at every festival.

The music and the instruments on which it is played vary from region to region, and even from one town to the next, but a certain unity can be found in the essence of the pieces. The *cantáta* (cantatas) of the Ionian Islands, for example, are love stories and local tales set to violin and guitar music, which resemble melodies from southern Italy, whereas the *miroloï* and *pípiza* variations in Epirus are more doleful, recalling the suffering of a people in exile.

Say it with flowers

The "bouzoúki" also gave its name to a type of night-club where, every evening, the popular musicians of the moment come to perform in front of an audience of people from every generation and social class. Although the musical background of these singers has little in common with the rembétika of the 1920s, the enthusiasm of the crowd is just as fervent. And the plates which the public used to throw as a sign of their appreciation have now been replaced by flowers.

Folk dancing

Every *rembétiko* or *dimotiki musiki* orchestration is accompanied by figures that are not governed by any choreographic rules as such, but rather by a tradition of harmony between the body, the mind and facial expression. This explains the regional variations which you may see in dances that are performed throughout the land. Among the most common is the **hassápiko** ("butchers' dance"), which dates back to the Byzantine era when it was performed by the butchers of Constantinople for their guild festival. A simplified and slower version of this dance, the **syrtáki**, was made famous the world over by the film *Zorba the Greek*, released in the 1960s. The **zeïbékiko** – a dance associated with *rembétika* – originated in Asia Minor. It was originally performed by a single dancer surrounded by an audience which would crouch and clap along in a very specific rhythm.

Others which are also worthy of mention are the **mandíli kalamatianó** ("handkerchief dance"), the wedding dance par excellence, and the **tsiftetéli**, named after the two-stringed violin which used to provide the accompaniment in times gone by. This belly-dance performed by women stems from ancient fertility rituals from Asia Minor.

Traditional instruments	
Baglamás	small bouzoúki (also found in Latin America)
Bouzoúki	long-necked mandolin with three or four pairs of strings
Daoúli	wooden cylinder with a taut skin membrane at each end
Défi	tambourine
Floyéra	a shepherd's flute made of reeds or wood
Gáida	bagpipes (mainland Greece)
Láouto (lagouto)	lute with four pairs of strings
Lýra	a three-stringed viol played with a bow
Miroloï	long rough-sounding flute
Oúti	short-necked lute
Pípiza	high-pitched oboe
Sandoúri	zither played by striking the strings
Toumbeléki	tambourine
Tsaboúna	bagpipes (Greek islands)
Zournás	oboe (often accompanied by the daoúli)

LITERATURE AND CINEMA

The legacy of Greek literature has shone out like a beacon since ancient times, providing a model for the Western world. Plato's philosophy, Sophocles' plays and Homer's epic poems have been passed down through the ages and civilisations. Their legendary heroes have not aged a bit and continue to haunt the modern world which they helped to shape: the Ulysses of James Joyce's novel walks the streets of Dublin in 1904, while the Ulysses brought to celluloid life by the Coen brothers, directors of the film *O Brother, Where Art Thou?*, lives in the United States of the late 20C. And these are just two examples of the countless adaptations of Homer's *Odyssey*. Three thousand years of literature have passed since this epic was written, and modern literature – free of the vast legacy of Ancient Greece, but enriched by it – is very much alive in Greece, as evidenced by the Nobel prizes awarded to two Greek poets Giórgos Seféris and Odysséus Elýtis.

Birth of a pleiad of styles

Ancient Greek literature covers a very long period, stretching from the *Iliad* and the *Odyssey* (9C-8C BC) to the fall of the Byzantine Empire (1453). The most beautiful pages in its history were written during the Age of Pericles (5C BC), after which it fell into gradual decline under Roman domination. With the arrival of Christianity, Byzantium closed the academies, marking its end. A certain neo-Classicism did continue to exist as Byzantine literature developed, but as soon as the Gospels were written in Greek, a new Gnostic form of Greek "literature" began to emerge. Until the 3C, the Christian doctrine was conveyed in this language, before Latin began to prevail as the language for religious works and the teaching of the Christian faith throughout the Mediterranean basin.

The Iliad and the Odyssey: the origin of Greek literature

The earliest known expression of Greek literature dates back to the 9C or 8C BC, when **Homer** wrote his two **epic poems**, the *Iliad*, which relates the last episodes of the Trojan War (Ilion), and the *Odyssey*, which narrates Odysseus' (Ulysses) long journey back to Ithaca. These major works, which in all likelihood were based on a longstanding oral tradition, tackle the founding myths, depicting the origins and fate of the Greek people under the supervision of the gods *(see page 50)*.

At around the same time, a farmer by the name of **Hesiod** penned a prose work, the *Works and Days*, in which he promoted his vision of how life in the countryside should be lived. He is also credited with writing the *Theogony*, a document of great importance since it was the first to address the issue of the origins of the world and the genealogy of the gods. Of the numerous authors who followed in the footsteps of these pioneers, many were to fall into oblivion, but others, such as **Sappho**, the famous poetess of Lesbos, carved their names in stone.

Aesop's fables

The very existence of Aesop (6C BC) is still shrouded in mystery. According to some, he was a Greek slave from Thrace, whose spirit and perspicacity earned him his freedom. Subsequently gaining popularity at the court of King Croesus, this supremely gifted fabulist went on to achieve great literary success. However, one day he accused the priests of the oracle of Delphi of plundering the worshippers' offerings. Not one of his better ideas, this denunciation was to cost him his life and he was condemned to death in 564 BC. The 350 fables which are attributed to him today, provided a great source of inspiration for the 17C French author, Jean de la Fontaine.

The success of the theatre

In the 5C BC, the theatre really began to come into its own and amphitheatres were filling with a growing number of spectators *(see page 36)*. Of religious origin, this

An undying art: a performance at the Odeon of Herodes Atticus, Athens

literary genre is associated with the cult of Dionysus. Indeed, theatres were generally to be found near the temple devoted to the god, where certain rites were carried out during performances. To compose their masterly tragedies, **Aeschylus**, **Sophocles** and **Euripides** delved into mythology, depicting human nature in all of its excesses, with incest, parricide or madness taking pride of place in their plays. **Aristophanes**, for his part, became a master in the art of comedy, never hesitating to combine clever puns or vulgar farces with philosophical thought.

Making History

Thanks to the great traveller **Herodotus** of Halicarnassus, nicknamed the "Father of History", the 5C witnessed the birth of a new literary genre concerned with recording factual events and sticking as closely as possible to the truth. History, with a capital H, was born. **Thucydides** was one of the greatest of these ancient historians and is particularly renowned for his political analysis of the Peloponnesian War, which was supported by various eyewitness accounts.

The invention of philosophy

In the cities, as the art of oratory began to generate cohesion at meetings, the role of the word took on increasing importance. The collective nature of decisions – specific to cities – effectively led to a certain "publicity" of knowledge which could no longer be confined to discussion between those in the know, but must, on the contrary, be disclosed and explained. Although philosophy is a tradition in Greece, it was not until the 4C BC that it really began to make its mark.

Through dialogue, **Socrates** (470-399 BC) endeavoured to lay bare the falsehoods distorting public opinion, refute politicians' claims and reveal their ignorance. This midwife's son, an expert in the art of maieutics (eliciting new ideas from people who had not been aware of them), left no written documents, but his teachings were passed down through the generations thanks to his disciple, **Plato** (428-347 BC). Plato devoted part of his work to the memory of his master, using the same analysis to denounce the violence, immorality, injustice and disorder which were gradually

The father of geographers

It was in Nyssa (Turkey) that the Greek geographer Strabo (64 BC-circa 22 AD) studied history and geography. With his diploma in his toga pocket, he set to work on two voluminous essays, "Historical Sketches" and "Geography" (only the latter is still extant). Little known during his lifetime, his work was rediscovered during the Renaissance and was of great interest to Leonardo da Vinci. Although two thousand years old, Strabo's "Geography" with its reflections on the origins of peoples, the history of empires and, above all, man's relationship with his natural environment, is still a remarkably relevant work which merits greater attention.

taking hold of the cities. Plato subsequently became the master of the philosopher and scholar **Aristotle** (384-322 BC), whose philosophical and scientific thinking were to greatly influence the Western world, particularly in the field of logic. Other philosophers, representing various schools of thought (Stoicism and Epicureanism, to name but a few), succeeded them, but very few of their writings have survived the passage of time.

The quest for Greek identity

Modern Greece steadfastly celebrates its mythology and classical literature with numerous summer festivals held in ancient theatres. But the country is not content to rest on its laurels. Influenced by literary trends similar to those which have spread through Europe since the 15C, Greece has also managed to cultivate its own individuality, producing a generation of modern, internationally renowned writers.

Greek literature during the Ottoman Empire

In the 10C, the characters of a modern Greek literature began to emerge with the great cycle of epic-style folk ballads celebrating the exploits of **Digenis Akritas Basileios**, the legendary hero of the Byzantine Empire's struggle against the Arabs on the Euphrates frontier. This new form of literature really began to flourish with the fall of the Byzantine Empire in 1453, when several styles emerged, varying from one region to another in the wake of the Ottomans' advance.

Some islands which were spared the Turkish invasion for longer than the mainland (until 1669 in Crete, for example), were effectively able to demonstrate a certain originality in their literary creations. The Dodecanese, Chios, Cyprus, Crete and the Ionian Islands became important centres of island literature, greatly influenced by Western occupiers, such as the Venetians or the Genoese. **Vitzéntzos Kornáros** of Crete is thus remembered as the author of the epic poem *Erotókritos*, the last large-scale work before the Ottoman invasion.

On the mainland, however, the arrival of the Turks put a considerable damper on literary creation, causing many scholars to emigrate to the West from the 15C onwards. The scholars from **Phanar** (a quarter of Constantinople) in the late 17C, were thus to be the last representatives of Hellenism on Turkish soil.

It was not until the 19C that a veritable revival of Greek literature was brought about by the Greek Enlightenment movement, whose most famous representative was **Koraïs** who studied and lived in France, and the Ionian school, influenced by Italy.

The emancipation of Greek literature

After the Greek War of Independence, the Turks withdrew from the peninsula, leaving behind a traumatised people in search of a national identity. This mass disorientation did not spare the novelists either who, badly in need of inspiration, turned either towards the West with its Enlightenment and modernity, or to the Christian East, land of the Byzantine tradition.

During the dispute over language *(see page 82)* which was stirring up Greek society at the time, divisions in society were reflected in the balancing act between classicism and progressivism. Falling between the popular and the scholarly language, *katharévoussa* was chosen as a compromise between the classical form and modern usage advocated by **Adamántios Koraïs** (1748-1833). The defence of the common vernacular was taken by poets such as **Dhionísios Solomós** (1798-1857), who is considered to be the first poet of modern Greece. The leader of the **Ionian School** (or Heptanesian School), he stood in opposition to the **Athenian School**, which favoured extreme romanticism, before turning to symbolism. In the late 19C, the intellectuals decided to use Demotic in their works, one of the most staunch "demoticists" being **Yánnis Psicháris** (1854-1929), whose narrative *My Journey* was partly a manifesto against a language that was too scholarly and elitist.

Pastures new

After the "Great Catastrophe" of 1922 *(see page 29)*, which sketched out the geographical outline of modern Greece, writers were plunged into an era of total defeatism. Greek literature was pulled out of this painful and pessimistic period by the **1930s generation**, which decided to drop the linguistic controversy and focus on the substance, propelling Greece into the world of modern literature. This new wave brought with it such prestigious authors as the 1963 Nobel prize-winner, **Giórgos Seféris** (1900-71), who opened the way to surrealism, and the 1979 Nobel prize-winner, **Odysséus Elýtis** (1911-96), one of the leading poets of this new narrative technique, which gathered a good many writers in its train. Mention should also be made of the poet **Constantine Caváfy** (1863-1933), a Greek from Alexandria who represents the Hellenism of the famous Greek centres of the late 19C. Greek literature was subsequently taken far beyond the country's borders by **Vassílis Vassilikós** (b 1934), author of *Z*, and **Níkos Kazantzákis** (1883-1957) who penned *Zorba the Greek* and *The Last Temptation of Christ*, works which, oddly enough, gained a better reception abroad than in Greece.

Cinema

Heavily influenced by popular Italian comedies and burlesque theatre, Greek cinema really began to come into its own in 1949 at the end of the civil war.

The 1950s, marked by Italian neo-Realism, were dominated by two great directors: **Michális Cacoyánnis**, who made the comedy *Windfall in Athens*, then *Stella* – his biggest film, starring **Melína Mercoúri** – and **Níkos Koúndouros** with *Magic City* and *The Ogre of Athens*. But it was not until the following decade that one could really start talking about a "golden age" of the cinema: encouraged by relative political stability, the studios were able to boost production. This was the era of the light comedies starring Alíki Vouyouklláli, Lámbros Konstandáras and Georgía Vassiliádou, which are still today the very epitome of insouciance.

The emergence of "auteur" films

With the arrival of television in people's homes and the creation of the first national Greek television channel (ERT), the public began to turn their backs on the cinema in favour of the small screen. In the 1970s, with the dictatorship in full swing, the commercial cinema was plunged into its first big crisis. The new directors were indulging a more introspective, rather obscure, genre, while most cinemagoers were looking for escapism. This yawning gap between the cinema and its public eventually led to the studios' collapse.

The fall of the colonels' junta in 1974 coincided with the beginning of the **new Greek cinema**, headed by **Theódoros (Theo) Angelópoulos**. This director's long film career was studded with international awards, including the Golden Lion at the Venice Film Festival for *Alexander the Great* (1980), the award for the best screenplay in Cannes for *Voyage to Cythera* (1984), the Silver Lion at the Venice Film Festival for *Landscape in the Mist* (1988), the Grand Jury Prize at the Cannes Film Festival for *Ulysses' Gaze* (1995) and lastly the *Palme d'Or* at Cannes for *Eternity and a Day* (1998).

Return to a wider public

With the spectacular development of video clubs in the 1980s, the **Greek Film Centre**, which was the only investor at that time, became caught in the stranglehold of its increased politicisation, and dragged the auteur movement down with it in its fall. In 1989, the private television channels (Antenna and Mega) burst onto the scene, tolling the knell of Greek cinema. In the face of European and Hollywood productions, the few Greek films which were still being screened fell by the wayside. It was not until the middle of the 1990s that the Greek Film Centre changed its position, agreeing to give financial backing to commercial films with more Western-style screenplays, more in tune with cinemagoers' expectations. For its part, Parliament passed a law subjecting television channels to a fee to subsidise film production. The new generation of producers is now striving to give a fresh lease of life to Greek cinema by making films with greater public appeal, as you will see if you take a trip to the **Thessaloníki Film Festival** in October, where the year's films are presented.

Open-air cinemas

A summer tradition and THE place to go to start your evening out, open-air cinemas show the previous winter's hits in a friendly atmosphere. The screen looms above an area filled with tables and chairs, where spectators can have a drink while watching the film, which always has an interval.

"Never on Sunday"

CAT'S Collection

MELINA MERCOURI
Grand Prix d'interprétation au Festival de Cannes
JULES DASSIN dans **Jamais le Dimanche** avec GEORGES FOUNDAS · TITOS VANDIS
Musique de MANOS HADJIDAKIS
Directeur de la Photographie JACQUES NATTEAU
Scénario et mise en scène de JULES DASSIN
Une Production MELINAFILM Distribuée par LES ARTISTES ASSOCIÉS

VISA N° 7242

LANGUAGE

Despite the long centuries of Turkish occupation, the Greeks managed to preserve their language, the symbol of national identity. Around 97% of the country's inhabitants speak Greek, while the minorities still use their mother tongue, which means that Turkish, Albanian, Bulgarian, Romany, etc, are also spoken in certain areas *(see page 56)*. So, Modern Greek is spoken throughout the land by over 10 million people, and in Cyprus by 500 000. Not forgetting the vast Greek diaspora, 5.5 million people living in countless communities spread all over the world. Moreover, the Greeks pride themselves on being able to travel without having to learn another language, since they are always sure to meet one of their compatriots wherever they go. *Also see the glossary page 113.*

The road to Modern Greek

A vector of Greek philosophical and scientific thought, language of the Gospels and the Church, and also the official language of the Byzantine Empire, Ancient Greek testifies to the exceptional influence of one of the greatest civilisations of the planet. Suffice it to say that its modernisation was no mean feat...

The birth of Greek

After having gradually imposed their Indo-European language in Greece during the latter half of the 2nd millennium BC, the Hellenes, who came from the North, soon borrowed the script of the **Phoenicians**, who had also settled in the Mediterranean area. In all likelihood, the adaptation of the Phoenician alphabet for use by the Greeks around the 8C BC resulted in the Greek alphabet such as we know it. This borrowing was coupled with a revolutionary innovation, **vowels**, which the Greeks substituted for certain Phoenician consonants for which they had no equivalent sounds in their language.

A bitter linguistic controversy

The gap gradually began to widen between **classical Greek** and the **common vernacular**, *koiné*, which was mostly based on the dialect of Attica and incorporated words of foreign – mainly Turkish – origin. When the sensitive issue of the future national language arose in the late 18C, right in the middle of the turmoil caused by the independence movement, this marked the beginning of a long dispute which was to rage between classicists and modernists over the next two centuries, and which has still not been resolved.

In fact, this linguistic controversy was merely one facet of a much wider debate concerning the position and prestige of the nation: the decision to continue or to break away from classical Greece.

For the *Phanariótes*, the administrative nobility of the 18C (originally established in the Greek quarter of Phanar, in Constantinople), maintaining classical Greek guaranteed them control of the cultural and political life of the country, in particular over the bourgeoisie and the working classes. It wasn't until the early 19C that the intellectuals took up the issue, launching a pitched battle between the partisans of a pure language and those of a "vulgar" language.

Following the War of Independence, the solution advocated by **Adamántios Koraïs** (1743-1833), leader of the Greek Enlightenment, won out and a clever compromise between the classical form and modern usage, **Katharevusa** (*katharos* meaning pure) was born. Although it was adopted as the official language of the country, it remained alien to the people, who continued to use **Demotic** (demotikí) (*démos* meaning people), the popular language of oral tradition. Demotic was supported by authors such as **Dhionísios Solomós** (1798-1857), who is regarded as the first great poet of modern Greece and who, incidentally, wrote the national anthem.

In the late 19C, rebelling against this scholarly and elitist language, some intellectuals again decided to use *demotikí* rather than *katharévoussa* in their works of literature. At the heart of an increasingly political conflict, the supporters of Demotic fiercely opposed the conservatism of the *katharévoussa* partisans. Notable examples of subsequent champions of popular culture include poets such as **Giórgos Seféris** (1900-71) and **Odysséus Elýtis** (1911-96), both winners of the Nobel Prize for literature.

Modern Greek: a simplified language

In the end, it was the colonels' junta which took *katharévoussa* down with it when it fell in 1974. In order to emphasise the break with the previous regime, Karamanlís' government decreed Demotic to be the official language. However, its linguistic simplifications are still the subject of many a debate: from one ministry to the next, between the Ministry of Education and the highways department (in charge of road signs), for example, discussion still continues on whether to use the *y* or the *i*, and whether or not to keep the *h*, and so on.

Be that as it may, while Ancient Greek had five genders, Modern Greek has only three: masculine, feminine and neuter. Demotic has also passed through various stages of development, the most remarkable undoubtedly being the "ee-ification", consisting of replacing the pronunciation of numerous vowels or diphthongs from Ancient Greek by an "ee" sound.

Give-and-take

With its considerable linguistic heritage, Greek vocabulary reveals a highly complex system of declensions and syntax as well as myriad possibilities for creating neologisms. Over the centuries it has also been further enriched by numerous foreign influences.

Contributions from abroad...

Although Greek vocabulary forms the basis of the theological, philosophical, scientific and technical terminology of the West, it itself contains a certain number of words borrowed from various invaders – the most obvious being words of Turkish origin – and from foreign languages, especially French, the language of a society which enjoyed great prestige in the late 19C and early 20C. Influences from nearby Italy and the English-speaking world can also be detected.

...and vice versa

In addition to Latin (which gave us *vice versa*), Greek constitutes one of the main bases of many languages, including English, to which it has given innumerable prefixes. Here are just a few of the most common: *micro* (small) has given us the microscope, microwave and micrometry, *megalo* (big) megalopolis, megalomania, megahertz, and *kiclos* (round) has mutated into cycle, cyclic, cyclone, etc.

Likewise, Greek has provided us with a whole catalogue of suffixes, including *logia* and *logos* (theory, speech), which are used to designate all of our sciences (geology, biology, etc), *graphein* (to write) giving us the telegraph, *philos* (friend) anglophile, and its opposite, *phobia* (fear) xenophobia, claustrophobia, etc.

Countless English words thus stem from Ancient Greek in an endless combination of prefixes and suffixes. Other words derive from a whole word, including all medical terms: paediatrician (*pediatros*) comes from the word *pediá* (children), gynaecologist (*gynekológos*) from *gynéka* (woman), and podiatrist (*podólogos*) from *pódia* (feet), to name but a few.

Foreign flavours

Many English and French words which have passed into the Greek language belong to specific areas. Greek football terminology, for example, has borrowed several words from English, such as "máts" (match), "fáoul" (foul), "off-sáit" (offside), "kórner" (corner), "jkól" (goal). And many a French word has, unsurprisingly, slipped into the field of gastronomy, for example, millefeuilles, gratins, "volovène" (vol au vent), "quislorène" (quiche lorraine) and "bessamél" (bechamel).

Language

THE GREEKS AT HOME

From the islands to the mainland, Greece contains a great variety of housing ranging from drystone dwellings to big bourgeois homes with neo-Classical façades, and small fishermen's cottages tucked away at the foot of rugged hillsides. This diversity can be explained by the country's contrasting geography, which embraces all kinds of different environments: mountains, sea and agricultural plains, with varying amounts of rainfall and sunshine. Although the archetype of the Cyclades – those charming white houses with blue shutters which make such beautiful postcards – is so emblematic of Greece, the architecture on the mainland is undoubtedly a better reflection of the country's cultural legacy, with its combination of Byzantine and Ottoman traditions. But the differences have been levelled out in recent times, with breeze-blocks and concrete becoming sadly ever more commonplace throughout the country, like everywhere else in the Mediterranean.

In the cities

Shortly after stepping off the plane at Athens airport and hopping into a bus for the city, visitors are plunged into the capital's notorious traffic jams. The kilometres of teeming avenues are lined with unattractive six- or seven-storey apartment buildings all sporting concrete balconies covered in flowers which hide the flaking paint. Below, the ground-floor "arcades" house shops, offices, banks and cafés. This rather grim architecture has sadly shaped the face of present-day Athens.

Reinforced concrete...

Until the early 1950s, detached houses still largely dominated the urban landscape of the Greek metropolis, except for the centre. However, the following decade witnessed the propagation of reinforced concrete, and a uniform type of structure built in a slapdash manner began to spread chaotically throughout the country like a plague.

In addition to constant **demographic pressure**, it was the pressing necessity of establishing an urban infrastructure which led to this unbridled transformation of Athens. After the war, a law was passed under which anyone who owned a house or piece of land could hand it over to an entrepreneur for the construction of an apartment building, gaining some of the apartments in exchange. This led to many of the historic quarters being destroyed by a combination of anarchic initiatives and public decisions, in a total lack of concern for preserving the national heritage. Over the last twenty years, however, new regulations have been introduced to protect and restore the surviving old traditional or neo-Classical houses.

But concrete has also started creeping into some of the villages and, in recent years, an increasing number of arson attacks in the countryside, ridding the land of its vegetation, have left the way open to property developers.

Unfinished business

In Greece, building is a must. Although less prevalent than before, the tradition which holds that parents should build a house for their daughters as a dowry still stands. Consequently, wherever you go, you are sure to come across houses or buildings cast in concrete, terraces one atop the other with their iron skeletons poking out. Not one village in Greece has been spared these unfinished constructions, which are constantly awaiting the unlikely addition of an extra storey. This phenomenon has been encouraged by two laws. The first one stipulates that an illegal construction can be torn down only if the offender is caught in the act. However, given that controls are carried out only during the day, many sections of wall are raised during the night and are still wet at dawn. The second law states that as long as a construction has not been roofed and the iron rods are still exposed, the owner cannot be taxed. Between aesthetics and taxes, most Greeks make the same choice.

...and bourgeois houses of yesteryear

But rest assured, the 19C charm of the towns and villages has not totally disappeared. A few shining examples of the urban architecture from the age of King Otto still remain in Athens and in the **hóra** (capitals) of the islands. Torchbearer of the Hellenic revival and reclaimed independence, European neo-Classicism rapidly found a home in Greece. Embodying the new trend of optimism after four centuries of Ottoman occupation, so-called **neo-Hellenic architecture** aimed to resuscitate the golden age of Ancient Greece. This trend was reflected in a mushrooming of opulent villas, imposing one- or two-storey houses with façades which followed the broad outlines of Ancient architecture but were also influenced by the Italian Renaissance and, in particular, 17C French classicism: on the ground floor, Doric columns and pilasters stand against walls or jut out to frame the **porch**, and the first floor is decorated with Ionic columns between the bays containing **high windows**. A small **balcony** enhances the central bay window beneath a broad tiled roof set off by acroteria and antefixae. During the golden years of the merchant navy, the wealthiest shipowners of the islands even went so far as to erect small pediments decorated with bas-reliefs or statues of chimeras.

Behind these elegant façades, prosperous members of the middle class live Western-style in vast, high-ceilinged and well-lit rooms decorated with wainscoting, paintings and period furniture. The kitchen is on the ground floor and several small out-buildings stand nearby.

The same style of construction can also be found in the towns, where various **apartment buildings** boast equally elaborate façades.

However, this neo-Classical architecture was used mainly for the great public monuments and the private residences of the wealthy. Alongside these bourgeois homes, families forced into exile from Asia Minor in 1922 and country folk coming to the towns to look for work hurriedly built much more modest houses, urban versions of their country homes with whitewashed walls of stone blocks or rendering. They usually consisted of one single room on the ground floor serving as a kitchen, dining room and living room, with, depending on the family's means, two bedrooms on the first floor.

Rural homes

With their ochre roughcast or whitewashed walls, and terrace or Roman-tiled timbered roofs, rural homes of the past were mainly built according to principles of functionality, depending on the climate and activity. Although modern conveniences – electricity, telephones and running water – are now widespread, those age-old houses that have managed to survive earthquakes and have not been abandoned for more modern constructions, are still extremely rustic. Here you will find the traditional **living room**, with perhaps another storey, covered by a **roof adapted to the climate**: a flat terrace roof in the sun-drenched islands, a four-sided roof in the regions with higher rainfall or snow, as in the north of the country.

The "archontiká" or house of prosperity

Reflecting commercial prosperity and a mixture of influences, the "archontiká" are the residences of the local dignitaries. Typical examples of these opulent one- or two-storey mansions are to be found on the island of Hydra with its great families of shipowners. Under a roof of tiles or flat stone slabs, the stone or roughcast walls are studded with narrow windows fitted with leaded glass panes which filter the light even more. Above the stone-built ground floor, the upper floor made of wood and daub juts out in an overhang to form a sort of loggia (*hagiátsi* or *xostego*), thus creating a more spacious interior, the **sarái** or reception room. A bench resembling a Turkish sofa skirts the room and the walls and floor are swathed in warm fabrics and carpets. Decorated with carved and painted motifs whose refinement reflects the wealth of the household, the ceiling (*tavani*) is the main ornament of the room. Many of these beautiful buildings influenced by Ottoman architecture are still to be found in the towns and villages of **Macedonia**, Thessaly and **Epirus** (Ioánnina, Métsovo), some of them complete with garden.

A Greek's house is his castle

In regions which were often subject to attack by pirates or other foreign invasions, **pirgóspito** (from *pirgos*, meaning "tower") began to appear. These large austere drystone buildings in the shape of round or square towers with narrow loophole-type windows, rise several storeys high like watchtowers, heirs to the Hellenistic towers. The **Máni Peninsula**, in particular, in the south of the Peloponnese, abounds with these tower houses, most of them built in the 15C, which make the villages look like medieval citadels. The towers were built by local noblemen and

G. de Benoist/MICHELIN

Siesta time

provided a place of refuge for the villagers in times of conflict – which was frequent – with their neighbours. The living quarters proper occupied the first floor, while the ground floor was used as a stable and barn. Various outhouses were attached to the main building, the whole ensemble of buildings being protected by a surrounding wall.

Island life

In the Aegean Sea

The small whitewashed cube-shaped houses which are so typical of the Greek islands look as if they have been painted with sunshine. They generally spread out over two or three split levels, following as closely as possibly the lie of the land, which is often uneven. The overall impression is one of a picturesque chaos of cell-like structures lining a maze of narrow streets. In the Cyclades, this seeming disorder does, however, comply with a well-defined **defence plan**, whereby houses are set as close as possible to each other in order to form a sort of rampart. For the same reason, doors and windows mainly open towards the interior of the village and are small in size, thus allowing the houses to remain cool inside. The villages are usually laid out around one single narrow street paved with cobbles or large paving stones, which winds its way to the main square.

On account of the climate and lack of wood in these arid islands, flat roofs are more common than pitched ones, but the indoor ceilings are vaulted, since this makes them more resistant to earth tremors. The islands have one particularly distinctive feature: the furniture is built into the structure of the houses. A **stone bench** skirts the walls, and the seats, beds and couches, which are all whitewashed, are likewise an extension of the walls or floor. This traditional heritage which makes the islands so charming, is fortunately very well adapted to the new anti-seismic standards and to the ever-increasing demands of the hotel trade, thereby ensuring its preservation.

Italian influences

Influenced by nearby Italy, the **Ionian Islands** boast luxurious mansions with impressively elaborate façades, the **palazzi**, directly inspired by Venetian palaces. These elegant homes respect a very precise architectural symmetry, both as regards the façade, in iridescent pastel shades of yellow, orange or ochre, and the internal layout. Many ordinary houses also look more Italian than Greek.

Other islands steeped in an Italian atmosphere include **Rhodes**, which reflects a happy combination of Venetian and Ottoman influences, and **Crete**, most notably in Haniá, where houses with overhanging upper storeys alternate with the flat façades of the Venetian palazzi subtly enhanced by Ancient Greek and Renaissance motifs.

Krokalia

In the islands – the Cyclades in particular but also the Dodecanese (Rhodes) – many houses still have beautiful "krokalia" paving, arrangements of black and white pebbles used to decorate both the outdoor courtyards and the floors of the rooms inside. They come in a variety of geometrical, aquatic or animal designs, not forgetting the "méandros", a sort of decorative frieze passed down from Antiquity which symbolises the continuity of life.

GREEK CUISINE

It will come as no surprise that, in such an old melting pot as Greece (*see page 56*), the cuisine has been flavoured by the many peoples who formed or passed through the country. But it remains, above all, a **cuisine of the sun**, full of the flavour of olives, resin and honey.

"Horiátiki", or the national salad

The proper name for what is commonly known as a "Greek salad" is **horiátiki** (or choriatiki) meaning "the rustic". This national dish, full of authentic flavours, contains all the basic ingredients from a Greek village: delicious sun-ripened tomatoes mixed with slices of firm cucumber and red onion, all covered by a slice of feta and seasoned with oregano, a few olives and a dash of olive oil from Kalamáta. A very simple but inimitable combination.

Meze galore

Mezé are served at the *mezedopolío* and *ouzerí* (ouzo bar). This Turkish word designates an infinite variety of hot or cold side-dishes made with meat, fish, cheese or vegetables. They range from the very simple – a few olives with a slice of feta – to the more complicated, such as stuffed mushrooms in wine

> **Ancient Greek gourmets**
> The notion of gastronomy, of course, dates back to Ancient Greece. The Athenian philosophers, great thinkers that they were, were also experienced gourmets who were already glorifying "pleasant living". In the 5C BC, cooking competitions were even organised with large prizes – often pecuniary – being handed out to the winners. The Athenian cook, Archestratus, caused a stir with his delicious oven-baked fish wrapped in a fig leaf. This exquisitely simple recipe served merely to confirm the ancient proverb that the mark of a good cook ("archimágeiras") lies in the way he cooks fish.

sauce, and are served with white wine, beer, ouzo or rakí. Although some ouzo bars offer only around twenty kinds of meze and could almost be mistaken for kafenía, others have around one hundred on the menu. There are far too many to mention, there being probably as many *mezé* as there are cicadas, but here are a few to whet your appetite: **saganáki**, fried or flambéd cheese, courgette and aubergine fritters (*melidzánes*), which can be seasoned with **skordaliá**, a garlic and potato purée, and **dolmádes** and **dolmadhákia**, dainty pâtés of meat and rice wrapped in vine or cabbage leaves, which can be eaten hot or cold.

If you're more than a little peckish, you may prefer a few of the more filling **keftédes**, fried meat or vegetable balls. The island of Santoríni has developed its own version of this recipe, **tomatokeftédes**, tomato and melted cheese balls.

The Greeks are also great fans of **pulse** salads: haricot beans (*fassólia*) or lentils (*fakés*), mixed with slices of onion, parsley and a hint of olive oil.

Grilled meats...

For a quick snack, there is nothing better than a little **gíros**, Greek counterpart of the Turkish *döner kebap*, lamb roasted on a vertical spit from which thin slices are cut as it cooks. You may, nevertheless, prefer the **souvlákia**, small brochettes of pork or chicken which line the refrigerated displays of all the tavernas. Gíros and souvlákia are served in a *pita* filled with tomatoes, onion and *tzatzíki*, covered by a generous sprinkling of paprika. Or you could allow yourself to be tempted by a traditional **tirópita** or **spanakópita**, tasty pasties, one stuffed with cheese, the other with spinach.

The tavernas have all sorts of grilled or roast meats on the menu – lamb, pork, beef, poultry and even goat – which are generally served with potatoes, the most common vegetable in Greek cuisine. And if you are partial to a lamb chop, you are sure to appreciate the **païdhákïa**, which are served by the kilo!

The gíros, or the oriental-style roast
Turkish folklore has it that in the late 19C a man named Iskender (Alexander) had the novel idea of placing lamb's meat vertically on a spit to roast it. And so the famous "döner", or "gíros" in Greek, was born (literally meaning "which constantly revolves").

A few **traditional family dishes** have now become regular restaurant fare, such as the world-famous **moussaká**, a gratin of aubergines and minced meat in tomato sauce covered with bechamel. But you may not be as familiar with **kokinistó kréas**, a highly flavoured stew (the islands of Sífnos and Tínos in the Cyclades are renowned for their meat specialities, among others), or **pastíchio**, a gratin of macaroni in tomato sauce with a generous covering of bechamel. These dishes can all be found on the menus of certain tavernas, but they may well disappoint gourmets in the more touristy areas, since they are frequently swimming in oil and have been reheated once too often...

...and fish

Surrounded by 15 000km of coastline, Greece has access to a wide variety of fish and seafood. The fishermen, who mainly come from the islands, sell their catch directly to the restaurateurs, so the products are very fresh. If you are a connoisseur, you can ask to choose your fish straight from the refrigerators in the kitchen; otherwise, ask the chef what he recommends. A few delicious suggestions to try: fried or grilled **barboúni** (red mullet), and the exquisite **grouper** (*sforos*), which is fished not far from the shore. You could also try the **sole** (*glóssa*), which, although it generally comes from fish farms, is a true delight, or common bream (*fagrí*) and bream (*sférida*). And there is always the **octopus** (*octapódi*) and squid, which you will see everywhere hanging from hooks in the tavernas. Fished from the coastal reefs, they are served grilled, perhaps with a dash of olive oil, or marinated in white wine.

Oriental sweetmeats

Waiting for the octopi to dry

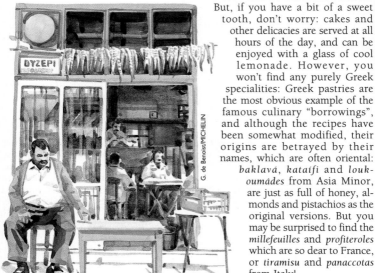

G. de Benoist/MICHELIN

Greek meals do not include dessert. But, if you have a bit of a sweet tooth, don't worry: cakes and other delicacies are served at all hours of the day, and can be enjoyed with a glass of cool lemonade. However, you won't find any purely Greek specialities: Greek pastries are the most obvious example of the famous culinary "borrowings", and although the recipes have been somewhat modified, their origins are betrayed by their names, which are often oriental: *baklavá*, *kataífi* and *loukoumádes* from Asia Minor, are just as full of honey, almonds and pistachios as the original versions. But you may be surprised to find the *millefeuilles* and *profiteroles* which are so dear to France, or *tiramisu* and *panaccotas* from Italy!

Pines and wines

In Plato's famous *Symposium*, Socrates talks of the importance of the pleasure of the palate, devoting a large place to **wine**. Indeed, the sunshine and the shade of the pine trees are encapsulated in the aroma of **retsína**, which is made with pine resin. However, it can be an acquired taste and you may prefer the wines with more classical flavours. Greece and its islands produce a wide variety of pleasant red and white wines, some of which deserve a mention. Among the whites, **mandinia** from Arcadia and **roditis** from the island of Límnos are two very flavourful wines. The wines of **Santoríni** are also renowned for their special aroma, which is said to come from the island's volcanic soil.

The art of ouzo

A national emblem of Greece, the ouzerí is a veritable institution with its own set of rules, without which the ritual would lose its essence. First of all, there are no individual place settings on the tables and ouzo drinkers usually require at least two or three chairs to make themselves really comfortable – one to sit on, an elbow resting on the back of a second and a leg on the bars of a third. This all underscores a certain detachment with respect to the food, and facilitates cursory and nonchalant gestures. The varied meze must be served in small portions and chosen in order to maintain a balance between the taste of the ouzo and a blend of garlic, salt, vinegar and spice flavours. Lastly, this is no place for serious conversation or sharp comments; quips and anecdotes are much better suited to the ouzo atmosphere. Once comfortably ensconced, it is easy to while away the hours.

As for red wines, there are some very respectable **Cabernet Sauvignons**, both in the north of Greece and in the Peloponnese. More typically local wines, **agiorítiko** from Neméa and **xinómavro**, are also quite full-bodied.

And, of course, no trip to Greece could ever be complete without a small glass of **ouzo**, an aniseed-flavoured drink which originated from French pastis. Friends gather together to savour its delights at **ouzerí** (ouzo bars) – where else? – and pick at a delicious assortment of meze.

The taverna, or a taste of sunshine

A restaurant of the people... and of travellers, the *tavérna* is the ideal place to sample the local cuisine. Here you will find simple traditional dishes, and the service is usually fast. Each taverna, nevertheless, has its own specialities, depending on the chef's home region and savoir-faire. Consequently, some of them offer mainly fish and seafood (*psarotavérna*) while others specialise in grilled meats (*psistariá*). You will, however, find certain dishes wherever you go, even beyond the borders of Greece: what better to have with your aperitif than a spot of **taramosaláta**, a purée of fish eggs finely mixed with breadcrumbs, olive oil, lemon, garlic or onion, or **tzatzíki**, a creamy sauce made with yoghurt, garlic and cucumber. Not forgetting **melizanosaláta** (or "aubergine caviar") made with tender grilled and seasoned aubergine flesh.

The waiter will bring you the menu (*catálogos*), but it is often a good idea to ask him what is readily available. This way, he will be able to recommend the freshly made dishes of the day, avoiding products that require defrosting. And don't be shy to go into the kitchen to make your choice directly from the pans or traditional refrigerated displays where all the goods are laid out. Allowing yourself to be guided by the various aromas is by far the best way of discovering specialities whose names you don't know.

HANDICRAFTS

Although the Greeks have no great crafts tradition, some tradesmen have managed to adapt certain typically regional creations to foreign tastes. Most of the items marked as "traditional", and intended exclusively for tourists, do not necessarily come from local craftsmen. But you may well be able to unearth some "authentic" objects in the villages off the beaten track.

Woodwork

Some islands, the **Northern Sporades** in particular, are renowned for their traditional furniture, which includes beds, sideboards, trunks *(kasséla)*, benches *(nissiótikos kanapés)*, dressers *(piatothíki)*, tables and chairs, painstakingly fashioned out of chestnut, fruit trees, oak or mahogany.

The Peloponnesian town of **Vitina** is known for its objects in walnut, cherry-wood or pine, ranging from hair slides to salad bowls, bread boards, cutlery and the ever-popular water pitchers.

Jewellery

In the 1950s, **Ilias Lalaounis** started a trend in jewellery-making by copying precious objects from Ancient Greece. A school and workshops were founded under his patronage to train craftsmen in the techniques of working with **gold**. These workshops still produce wonderful pieces inspired by the Minoan, Macedonian, classical Greek and Byzantine civilisations, and such pieces are now also produced by other jewellers. Although it is not always easy to differentiate between individually made and industrial productions, the difference in price is often a good indicator.

In tourist areas, shops offer a large selection of metalwork, jewellery and charms, often beautiful copies of ancient or modern pieces. Even if they were not made by a craftsman, the – often original – pieces of gold jewellery are good value for money, although still rather expensive. People on smaller budgets will have to settle for **silver** jewellery, which is a speciality of the town of Ioánnina.

Leather and fur

Leather products are produced mainly in northern Greece. A wide range of handbags, rucksacks and travel bags, sandals, leather flip-flops and belts are sold at reasonable prices in all tourist spots.

During your travels, you may be surprised by the rather impressive number of fur shops. The skin trade, which is encouraged by tourism, is particularly traditional in **Kastoriá**, Epirus.

Carpets and fabrics

Most carpets, which are in the Ottoman tradition, are woven mechanically in the numerous factories of the Thessaloníki region. But some fabrics from Crete, Delphi and Epirus merit special attention on account of their weave and designs – often with stripes or checks – which have remained unchanged for several generations.

In times gone by, young girls prepared their trousseau by embroidering **kendímata**, fabrics with colourful designs representing flowers, animals, seascapes or landscapes as well as scenes inspired by mythology. It is still possible to unearth some true masterpieces in a few rare villages off the usual tourist trail, for example in northern Greece or Kárpathos, one of the Dodecanese Islands.

Souvenir shops

As well as all the usual objects, you may want to bring back a **távli** (a board game of Ottoman origin), **flitzanáki** (small white porcelain coffee cups), **keramiká** (pot, pitcher or any other ceramic object from Sífnos, Rhodes and the neighbouring islands), **bouzoúki** *(see page 76)* or one of the famous **kombolói** *(see page 60)*.

Practical information

Newspapers,
souvenirs, stamps:
a períptero has
everything you need

BEFORE GOING

• Time difference

Greece is 2 hours ahead of Greenwich Mean Time (GMT) and 7 hours ahead of Eastern Standard Time (EST). The time is the same throughout the country, from the islands to the mainland.

• International dialling

Dial international + 30 + the number you wish to call without the first 0 of the area code.

For regional area codes, see page 102.

International information: if you are searching for a phone number in Greece, dial 32 12 for information (applicable throughout the country).

• When to go

Unless you are hoping to find a crowd, it is obviously preferable to avoid the summer months, particularly from mid-July to the end of August. The first 20 days of August are the busiest, as the Greeks, who for the most part spend their summer holidays in their own country, add to the already considerable number of foreign visitors. Accommodation is full and restaurants are overcrowded. As a result prices increase and the service given to guests a few weeks earlier becomes slack due to high demand. Everything from lodging to restaurants to rentals is therefore more difficult and more expensive. Also keep in mind that in August the wind (the *meltém*) sometimes blows violently across the Aegean Sea. While it may seem a refreshing change from the scorching heat, at the same time it makes the beaches much less enjoyable. If you plan to visit archaeological sites you will also want to avoid the high tourist season, if possible, when the museums and sites are jam-packed.

The month of June (as well as the end of May and the beginning of July) is THE ideal season to visit. You'll benefit from summer weather without the high temperatures or the violent winds and some of the spring colours can still be found. Accommodation is half price and it is not necessary to make reservations. Hoteliers are attentive and in a good mood at the beginning of the season.

September is also an auspicious month to visit. The first week of the month is still considered summer, even if the Greeks say *"Kaló himóna"* ("have a good winter"). September is a perfect time for anyone who likes warm water as the sea reaches its maximum temperature at this time. This mild autumn weather lasts until mid-November although many of the hotels and restaurants close at the end of October. Afterwards, the days become noticeably shorter and the rain from the storms revives the colour of the vegetation.

Although brief and intense, **spring** is a splendid season throughout Greece where all the colours are at their peak. The mountains, as well as the islands, are covered with gorgeous blossoms, however the sea is still a bit cool.

In **winter** the country has two contrasting faces. In the north and at high altitudes, thick snow blankets the countryside, while in the south and on the islands the sea tempers the winter weather. The average temperature is 11°C (52°F) in Athens and 12°C (54°F) in Herakleion in January. It is possible to ski on slopes two hours away by car from Athens and dine on the capital's outdoor terraces (warmly dressed, of course) on bright days.

• Packing list

Clothing

In the **summer**, plan to bring light clothing (cotton rather than synthetic) and don't forget a hat and **sunglasses**, essential everywhere in the country. If you are travelling in the spring, bring one or two light jumpers, as evenings can still be a bit cool depending on the region, and a raincoat for the north of Greece. In **winter**, be sure to bring your coat – a heavy one for the north and a lighter one for the south.

Before going

In summer, bring a light **windcheater** that you can roll up and stick in your bag. This is ideal for high altitude cold, especially if you plan to travel by bicycle or motorcycle (if you return after the sun sets, it can be quite chilly). It will also be useful when you're on a boat or when the meltem occurs. Don't forget that nights by the sea are quite cold, even in the middle of summer. If you plan to rough it, a sleeping bag or warm clothes are a must. Finally, if you visit **monasteries** and other sacred sites, women should plan to wear something to cover their legs. A skirt that is easy to put over shorts will do the trick.

• A trip for everyone

Travelling with children
You will have no trouble finding lodging if you are travelling as a family. Tourist rentals include many studios or furnished apartments equipped with small kitchens. They're often even more economical than two double rooms.

Travelling alone
A woman travelling on her own should fear nothing more than the legendary Greek *kamáki* (literally the "harpoon"). In other words, the Greeks may try to seduce you but they're not aggressive.

Disabled travellers
Unfortunately there is still little in the way of facilities catering for disabled persons outside Athens. You'll be able to count more on the kindness of the locals than on appropriate facilities.

• Address book

Tourist information
United Kingdom – 4 Conduit Street, London W1R ODJ, ☎ (020) 7734 5997, Fax (020) 7287 1369.
USA – Olympic Tower, 645 Fifth Avenue, New York, NY 10022, ☎ (212) 421 5777, Fax (212) 826 6940.
Canada – 1300 Bay Street, Toronto, Ontario, MSR 3K8, ☎ (416) 968 22 20, Fax (416) 968 65 33.
1233 rue de la Montagne, Suite 101, Montreal, Quebec, H3G 1Z2, ☎ (514) 871 15 35, Fax (514) 871 14 98.
Australia – 51-57 Pitt Street, Sydney, NSW 2000; PO Box R203 Royal Exchange NSW 2000 ☎ (2) 9241 1663 / 4 / 5 or 9252 1441, Fax (2) 9235 2174.

Cultural centres
The Hellenic Centre – 16-18 Paddington Street, Marylebone, London W1U 5AS, ☎ (020) 7487 5060, Fax (020) 7486 4254, www.helleniccentre.com
Hellenic American Union – Massalías 22, 10680 Athens 368-0000, www.hau.gr

Web sites
Surfers may find the following websites useful:
Greek Tourism Organisation: www.gnto.gr
Maritime schedules: www.gtpnet.com
Greek Cultural Heritage: www.culture.gr
Travel information: www.travelocity.com
Hellenic Resources Network: www.hri.org
Hellas: www.greece.org provides useful information about Greece and discusses Greek issues.

Embassies
United Kingdom – IA Holland Park, London W11 3TP, ☎ (020) 7229 3850, Fax (020) 7229 7221.
USA – 2221 Massachusetts Avenue NW, Washington, DC 20008, ☎ (202) 667 3169, 939 5800, Fax (202) 939 5824.
Canada – 76-80 MacLaren Street, Ottawa, Ontario, K2P 0K6, ☎ (613) 288 62 71, Fax (613) 238 56 76.

Australia – 9 Turrana Street, Yarralumla, Canberra 26000, ☎ (62) 733 158 / 733 011, Fax (62) 732 620.

● Modern Greek courses
Hellenic College of London – 67 Pont Street, London SW1X 0BD, UK, ☎ (020) 7581 5044, Fax (020) 7589 9055, www.ukstudies.gr
International Center for Language Studies, Inc (ICLS) – 727 15th Street NW, Suite 400, Washington, DC 20005-2168, USA, ☎ (202) 639 8800, english@icls.com

● Specialised bookshops
The Hellenic Bookservice – 91, Fortess Road, London NW5 1AG, UK, ☎ (020) 7267 9499, Fax (020) 7267 9498, hellenicbooks@btinternet.com, www.hellenicbookservice.com

● Formalities
ID, visas
For nationals of states belonging to the European Union, a passport (even one that has expired less than 5 years ago) or valid identity card is sufficient. Americans and Canadians must show a valid passport. For all other nationals, check the Greek consulate in your country for entry requirements.
Customs
Regulations with regards to imports (alcohol, cigarettes, etc.) are the same throughout the European Union. Cars are exempt from customs duties for up to 6 months. After that time, you must either take your vehicle out of the country or request temporary registration.
Health regulations
There are no particular health regulations governing entrance to Greece.
Vaccinations
No vaccinations are required.
Driving licence
If you plan to drive in Greece (either cars or motorcycles), UK citizens must have their national driving licence and proof of insurance. For US, Canadian and Australian nationals, an international driving licence is obligatory. *(See the section above on ID).*

● Local currency
Cash
The euro became the official currency of Greece in 2001. However, the Greek **drachma (Dr)** will remain in circulation during the changeover period until 2002. At the time of writing, €1 is worth approximately US$0.9 and Dr340.
Currency exchange
It's better to change your money once you arrive as commissions are lower. In the cities, there are many exchange offices. You can change money at the airport or post office, as well as in banks and hotels. Keep in mind that hotels will offer worse exchange rates.
Travellers' cheques
Use of travellers' cheques is still limited to the tourist areas and large cities. You can, however, change them easily in all the banks.
Bank cards
Cash dispensers (ATMs) for international bank cards are available in all cities, on most islands and at the main tourist sites. In some cases, banks will provide cash upon presentation of a bank card with an approximate 3% commission added on. Most large hotels accept payment by bank cards and an increasing number of establishments are starting to do so. On the other hand, this is not very common in small hotels or guesthouses.

• Spending money

Be it accommodation, food or shopping, life in Greece is not as cheap as it used to be. While the quality of **accommodation** has increased, so have the prices. Of course, rooms in local homes (with shared bathroom facilities) remain reasonably priced, but owners prefer to improve the level of comfort so they can raise their rates, and competition for reasonably priced lodging is very tough. Moreover, prices vary considerably depending on the period you visit; they practically double between low and high season depending on the place. In high season, a double room with private bath can rarely be negotiated for less than €23.

It's a different story with family-operated local **restaurants**. You can easily find little *tavérnas* that offer delicious meals at a modest price. *Souvláki* (around €1) is one nutritious solution and is well worth trying. If you travel during the warm season, you may also want to consider having a picnic; tomatoes, fruit from the markets, local cheese and freshly baked bread are good choices. This is still the cheapest way to eat and there are plenty of lovely places to enjoy these feasts.

Entrance to **archaeological sites** and small **museums** is usually around €1.50 or €7.50 for the most expensive. As far as **public transport** is concerned, buses are more reasonable than trains, which also serve fewer destinations, and ferries are a better deal than hydrofoils, which are double the price.

Hotels in **Athens** are slightly more expensive. You should plan to spend around €45 for a good quality room (although there are some decent ones for €30-38) and €7.50-15 is necessary for a good meal. You should therefore plan to spend around €68-75 per day including your transport costs and the obligatory bottle of water or soda to counter the scorching heat.

In short, with a daily budget of €60 per person (based on two people travelling together), you will have a very enjoyable holiday equipped with an economy rental car, without depriving yourself. For those on a tighter budget, €23-30 (based on double occupancy) will suffice if you travel by bus, dine on "souvláki" and "tirópita" (around €7.50 for both meals) and stay in small, modest hotels.

• Booking in advance

Advanced booking is necessary if you travel to tourist areas in high season on an average budget. Decent accommodation at standard rates is subject to tough competition. As soon as you arrive in Athens, reserve your next stop, and, if possible, ask the staff at your hotel to negotiate the deal in Greek. Before 15 July and after the end of August, there are fewer problems and you can arrive without advance notice.

• Travel / health insurance

Consider taking out repatriation insurance before leaving home if travelling independently. Many tour operators already include repatriation insurance in the price of your trip (be warned, this can be very expensive). Contact your local insurance company for information on obtaining this.

GETTING THERE

• By air

In the summer, be sure to book your flight at least 2 months in advance. The weight and the number of authorised bags vary according to the airline company and the class you select. As a general rule you can check in up to 20kg of luggage on regularly scheduled flights and 15kg on charter flights.

Scheduled flights

From the UK

British Airways – Waterside, PO Box 365, Harmondsworth UB7 OGB, ☏ (08457) 733377. Daily flights from various cities in the UK to Athens via London.

Cronus Airlines – Reservations, ☎ (020) 7580 3500, info@cronus.gr
Olympic Airways – 11 Conduit St, London W1R OLP, ☎ (0870) 6060460, Fax (020) 7629 9891, email@olympicairways.co.uk or at Heathrow Airport, Terminal 2, ☎ (020) 8745 7339 / 8759 5884, Fax (020) 8897 0279.

From the USA

Delta Air Lines – Hartsfield Atlanta International Airport, Atlanta, GA 30320, ☎ (1 800) 241 4141 or (404) 715 2600. Daily departures from New York's JFK to Athens.

Olympic Airways – Olympic Towers, 645 Fifth Ave, New York, NY 10022, ☎ (212) 735 0200, Fax (212) 735 0212.

Charter flights

Other companies have weekly charter flights from major cities. Obtain information from travel agencies or the Internet, and don't forget that some large companies provide charter rates on their regularly scheduled flights.

Lambda World – 350 Fifth Avenue, Suite 3304, New York, NY 10118, USA, ☎ (212) 439 5268, info@lambdaworld.com, has flights from NYC to Athens and Thessaloníki.

Avro – Wren Court, 17 London Road, Bromley, Kent BR1 1DE, UK, ☎ (020) 8695 4440, Fax (020) 8695 4004, reservations@avro.co.uk Flights from numerous cities in the UK to Athens, Corfu, and Herakleion.

Confirmation

To be on the safe side, confirm your return flight at least 48hr before departure.

Airport taxes

Airport departure tax in Greece has gone up to about €20. However, this is generally included in the price of your plane ticket.

• By train

Only those who really love to travel by train will want to choose this form of transport (travel time from London to Brindisi, Italy, takes more than 25hr). From there you still have to cross by ferry to Patras before climbing aboard a Greek train to your selected city. There are daily departures from London to Paris aboard the Eurostar (to the Gare du Nord). You must then change stations (Gare de Lyon) and take a night train to Milan or Turin. From there, you will connect to Brindisi. A combined ferry / train ticket is not available and you will need to reserve the crossing from Brindisi to Patras through a ferry company (see the section "By boat").

• By bus

Needless to say, this is also a very time-consuming way to travel (at least 55hr from London to Athens) but what an experience for those who have the time! The price war among airline companies, however, gives little reason to use this type of transport. Check that the connection (which operates only during the summer) is working.

• By car

A driving licence is sufficient for European Union nationals. You must, of course, provide documentation for your vehicle and be sure to verify that your insurance contract covers any damage incurred in Greece.

It's possible to travel to Greece by car passing through Eastern Europe (plan at least 5 days if travelling from London). However, the political instability in the Balkans may make crossing through certain states difficult if not impossible. A (long) detour via Hungary, Romania and Bulgaria is highly recommended. Contact the embassies of these countries for information on entry conditions. For a shorter trip, go via Italy instead and take the ferry *(see below)*.

• By boat

Book at least 2 months in advance during the summer, especially if you plan to bring your car.

Via Italy

Leave from an Italian port (Venice, Ancona, Bari, Brindisi or Trieste). To reserve a passage (for you and / or your vehicle), contact:

Paleologos SA – Odós 25 Avgoústou 5, 71202 Herakleion, Crete, ☎ (081) 346185 / 330598, Fax (081) 346208, www.greekislands.gr, info@greekislands.gr Provides reservations for all the main ferry lines connecting Italy to Greece

ANEK Lines – www.anek.gr, booking@anek.gr

Minoan Lines – www.minoan.gr, info@minoan.gr

Information on most of the ferry companies operating in Greece can be found at www.ferries.gr

Length of crossing

Travel time from Venice to Patras is approximately 36hr, 20hr between Ancona and Patras, and around 10hr for a connection from Brindisi or Bari to Patras.

• Package deals

Generalists

Anemone House – 109 Myddleton Road, London N22 8NE, UK, ☎ (020) 8889 9207, Fax (020) 8889 1127, holidays@anemone.co.uk

Odysseys Unlimited – 85 Main Street, Suite 101, Watertown, MA 02472, USA, ☎ (888) 370 6765 or (781) 370 3600, Fax (781) 370 3699, corp@odysseys-unlimited. com Small group travel for 12-24 passengers.

Tourlite International – 120 Sylvan Ave, Englewood Cliffs, NJ 07632, USA, ☎ (800) 272 7600 or (201) 228 5280, Fax (201)228 5281, tourlite@tourlite.com

Greece specialists

Avenir Travel & Adventures – 2029 Sidewinder Drive, PO Box 2730, Park City, UT 84060, USA, ☎ (1 800) 367 3230 or (435) 649 2495, Fax (435) 649 1192, info@AvenirTravel.com

Destination Greece – 195 West Como Avenue, Columbus, OH 43202, USA, ☎ and Fax (614) 261 8444, Operations@DestinationGreece.com

Intersky Holidays – 407 Green Lanes, London N4 1EY, UK, ☎ (020) 8341 9999, Fax (020) 8341 1153, Info@InterSkyHolidays.co.uk

Sunvil Holidays – Sunvil House, Upper Square, Old Isleworth, Middlesex TW7 7BJ, UK, ☎ (020) 8568 4499 / 8232 9797, Fax (020) 8568 8330, greece@sunvil.co.uk

Tourcom – 53 Condict St, Jersey City, NJ 07306, USA, ☎ (888) 868 7266 or (201) 395 9401, Fax (201) 395 9403, tour@tourcom.com

Ya'll Tours USA, Inc – 4711 SW Huber Street, Portland, OR 97219, USA, ☎ (1 800) 644 1595 or (503) 977 3758, Fax (503) 977 3765, inquire@greecetraveltours.com

Getting there

Cultural trips
Educational Tours & Cruises – 94 Prescott St, Medford, MA 02155-3750, USA, ☎ (800) 275 4109, Fax (718) 396 3096, edtours@aol.com

OPA Tours Greece – 137 Genoa Street, Suite B, Arcadia, CA 91006, USA, ☎ and Fax (800) 672 7155, opatours@aol.com

Westminster Classic Tours, Ltd – Suite 120, 266 Banbury Road, Summertown, Oxford OX2 7DL, UK, ☎ (01865) 728565, Fax (01865) 728575, info@wct99.com

Adventure trips
Country Walkers – PO Box 180, Waterbury, VT 05676, USA, ☎ and Fax (802) 244 5661, ☎ (888) 886 4075, info@countrywalkers.com Walking tours of Crete and the Peloponnese.

ExperienceGreece – 4595 Westmore, Montreal, QC H4B 2A1, Canada, ☎ (888) 317 8622 or (514) 489 2722, Fax (450) 451 3358, contactus@experiencegreece.com Provides walking tours in Greece.

ExperiencePlus! Specialty Tours, Inc – 415 Mason Ct #1, Fort Collins, CO 80524, USA, ☎ (800) 685 4565, Fax (970) 484 8489, tours@ExperiencePlus.com Bicycle and walking tours.

THE BASICS

• Address book
Tourist information
All of the tourist centres, regardless of their size, have their own tourist information office. These usually provide good documentation and have competent staff to help you. Don't hesitate to visit them. If there is no tourist information office available, local travel agencies often provide the same services (accommodation, transportation, etc). **Greek National Tourism Organisation (EOT)**, open 9am-7pm, Saturday 10am-3pm; closed Sunday. Odós Amerikís 4 (near Sýndagma), ☎ (01) 331 05 61 / 2 / 5. Lots of information is available here, not only on Athens but also on all types of transport in Greece (including schedules and rates) to the islands, Attica, the Peloponnese or the north of the country. The staff are often overworked but very friendly.

Embassies and consulates
United Kingdom – Odós Ploutárchou 1, 106 75 Athens, ☎ (01) 727 2600, Fax (01) 727 2720, info@athens.mail.fco.gov.uk

United States – Leofóros Vassilíssis Sofías 91, 101 60 Athens, ☎ (01) 721 2951

Canada – Odós Ioánnou Gennadíou 4, 115 21 Athens, ☎ (01) 727 3400, Fax (01) 727 3480

Australia – Odós Dimitríou Soútsou 37, Ambelókipi 11521, Athens ☎ (01) 645 0404, Fax (01) 646 6595, ausembgr@hol.gr

• Opening and closing times
Government offices, public offices (post office and telephone) and banks are closed in the afternoon.

Banks
Banks are open Monday to Friday 8am-1.30 or 2pm. They are closed Saturdays and on public holidays. Staff will serve customers who have arrived before the doors close, so if you are in a queue, be patient. Be sure to take a ticket to await your turn.

Post offices
Post offices are generally open Monday to Friday from 7.30am-2pm. In main post offices you will also need to take a number before you queue up.

OTE (telephone) offices

OTE offices are open from 8am-2pm, with the exception of some of the Athens offices: Odós Stadíou 15, which is open daily around the clock and Odós Athinás 50, open 24hr a day during the week and from 7am-10pm on Saturday and Sunday.

Shops

In the cities, shops are open Monday, Wednesday and Saturday from 8 or 9am-3pm (on Saturday, supermarkets stay open until around 6pm), and Tuesday, Thursday and Friday from 8am-8pm. Some shops (particularly grocery stores) close for one to two hours in the afternoon. On Sundays, bakeries and stores selling wines, spirits, soda, ice cream, etc, are open, some of them until about 8pm.

Kiosks

A mainstay in Greek daily life, kiosks, or **períptero**, never really close; or rather, there is always at least one open in every neighbourhood. In addition to buying their main product, tobacco (in Greece, smokers never lack anything), you can buy newspapers, cold drinks, and snacks. Most kiosks also sell emergency items, such as aspirin, stamps and envelopes, film, condoms, shampoo and thousands of other useful little things.

Restaurants

Opening hours vary depending on the restaurant, but they generally stay open and serve meals (whatever is left, of course) until late. Except in small, isolated hamlets with fewer than twenty houses, it's quite common to find a **psistariá** open nearby where you can sample souvláki, chips, a salad and a beer or a glass of retsína.

• Museums, monuments and archaeological sites

Opening times

Notable efforts have been made to standardise opening hours. Despite this, variations still remain, some of them logical (sites undergoing excavation must close earlier), others less so. As a general rule, in the summer, archaeological sites and museums open at approximately 8am and close at either 3pm or 7pm (earlier in winter). Monasteries and small art and folk museums keep variable hours; however, even if the opening times are indicated, they are not always respected.

Churches

Diocesan churches (where Orthodox priests celebrate the liturgy daily) are open in the morning and sometimes at the end of the afternoon. The more important ones stay open all day. On the other hand, private churches (the countless chapels scattered across the countryside and Greek towns) are closed more often. This is unfortunately also the case with historic churches and monasteries. The panigíri (religious or village festivals) often provide the chance to explore these buildings. You will, however, find small chapels open to passers-by (especially on the islands).

Entrance fees

Ticket prices range from €1.50-3 as a general rule. The large museums in Athens and the Acropolis are more expensive (€6). Student discounts are given at the larger sites and museums upon presentation of an international student identification card.

• Post offices

You'll easily recognise Greek post offices by their yellow sign with the word **ELTA** and a profile of the god Hermes. In addition to the standard-priced stamp, the Greek postal service offers an "express" rate, which is cheap and quick (a letter sent from the Sýndagma post office in Athens will arrive in London in 2 days for approximately €1.50). You can also buy stamps (gramatóssima) at the períptero (kiosk) for postcards. Money can be exchanged at the post office, however there are no public phones.

G. de Benoist/MICHELIN

Finally, you can receive all types of mail through poste restante upon proof of identification.

● Telephone (OTE)

Telephone booths are everywhere and you can get phone cards (*kárta tilephónou*) in any períptero. International phone calls from Greece can be quite costly. If you're planning to call overseas, make sure you have several phone cards or go to an OTE office to make the call. You can also make calls from the períptero.

International calls

To make an international call, dial **00 + country code + number** (without the first 0 of the area code). To call the UK, dial 00 44; for the US and Canada, 00 + 1; for Australia 00 + 61.

Local calls

Each district (be it a village, an island or a district) has its own area code (between parentheses) composed of 1 to 3 numbers preceded by a 0. For example, Athens (01), Thessaloníki (031), Réthimnon (0831), etc. The phone numbers themselves consist of between 5 and 7 digits according to the place. For a local call within the same region, you only need to dial the main number. If calling another region, first dial 0, followed by the code for that region (3 digits everywhere except Athens) and the number you want to call.

Mobile phone numbers are longer and their area code varies according to the operator, but all begin with 09. If you call these numbers from abroad, dial the international dialling code from your country + 30 for Greece + the number you are trying to call without the 0.

Useful numbers

For all OTE services, ☏ 134.

Telephone directory services, ☏ 131 (in Attica), ☏ 132 (in the rest of Greece)

International telegrams, ☏ 165.

International phone calls, ☏ 161.

To obtain international codes (in English), ☏ 169.

● Public holidays

1 January	New Year's Day.
6 January	**Epiphany**. Blessing of the sea. In every port, regardless of its size, young people dive into the water to recover the cross that is ceremoniously thrown in by the Orthodox priest.
Clean Monday	*Katharí deftéra*: 41 days before Orthodox Easter (dates vary), the first Monday of Lent. The *kouloúma* is celebrated in the countryside, weather permitting, and the menu consists of fish and seafood.
25 March	**Greek Independence Day and Annunciation**. A military parade in Athens and Thessaloníki and school parades all over Greece.
Easter	On Good Friday, all the churches prepare an *epitáphion* decorated with flowers, the symbol of Christ's shroud that the faithful follow in a procession. Celebrations for the Resurrection start Saturday at midnight with fireworks. On Sunday, traditional lamb from the spit is eaten.
1 May	**Labour Day.**
28 October	*Óchi* Day when Greeks said "No" and rejected the Italian ultimatum in 1940. Military parade.
25-26 December	Christmas.

GETTING AROUND

• By car

Car rentals

There are many car rental agencies, both local and international, in Athens and all over Greece. Some hotels and travel agencies also provide this service. Rates vary according to the place, season, number of days, and the type of vehicle. For example, a lower-range car rented in Athens at a major rental company costs around €55 a day. The same car will cost €68 in Mýkonos in August.

Road network

The quality of the roads is not bad but some of the **main roads** are not wide enough to handle the heavy traffic. On the hilly islands the main roads are often narrow and winding. You will often find yourself stuck behind a large truck with no chance of overtaking for miles. In this case, it's common for the emergency breakdown lane (when there is one) to become an extra lane for slower vehicles, while the regular lane is used for overtaking. As the railway network is not well developed, almost all travel is done by road. Motorways are multiplying on the mainland and very soon you should be able to travel from Patras to Thessaloníki via Athens exclusively by toll motorway.

Additionally, the country preserves countless **trails**, which are sometimes impassable without a four-wheel-drive vehicle.

Off the beaten track, road signs are often rudimentary and are only in Greek. You may therefore want to familiarise yourself with the Greek alphabet as soon as possible. Finally, on country roads and in villages, be careful of the sheep and goats, either in flocks or alone, which can hold up traffic.

Driving

While driving rules may be similar to those in other European countries, police patrols tend to be more infrequent.

Fuel

Fuel stations are scattered throughout the country, although these are a bit harder to find in the mountains and remote areas. Fuel tends to be a bit less expensive than in most European countries. Be aware that very few stations accept credit cards. There is no self-service in Greece and an attendant will pump the fuel for you.

Parking in town

There is no metered parking in the centre of Athens, and spaces are difficult to find during the day. If you park illegally, an officer will confiscate one of the licence plates to ensure that the offender comes to the police station to pay the fine.

Accidents

A report must be written up by a police officer in due form and you will need to obtain a copy. After this you will be able to repair your vehicle at a garage.

• By taxi

Taxis are yellow in Athens and grey or burgundy in the rest of the country.

• By train (OSE)

The railway network is not well developed but it is inexpensive. Trains run frequently and you can get to the main Greek cities easily from Athens. Some examples of rates and travel time (for **intercity trains**) are: Athens-Patras, 3hr30min, around €9; Athens-Náfplio, 3hr, around €6; Athens-Thessaloníki, 5hr30min (by express train), approximately €24. Be sure to make advance reservations if you want a seat on the train between Athens and Thessaloníki. Note that the two railway stations in Athens are now connected by the metro.

Two routes that are particularly picturesque: the line from Kalávrita (in the Peloponnese) by rack railway and the "aerial" route from Livadiá to Lamía which passes by impressive viaducts.

Getting around

• By bus

Bus services are well developed in Greece and are reliable (with numerous departures), inexpensive compared to trains, and generally faster as well. They more than make up for the lack of a comprehensive railway network. Bus lines connect Athens with the Ionian Islands (via boat) and this is the best means of exploring northern Greece. It is however inconvenient that the long-distance bus terminals in Athens (that go further than Attica) are more difficult to get to than the railway stations.

• By boat

All inhabited islands in Greece have a **ferry** service, however the frequency of crossings varies enormously. There are several departures daily for Páros and Santoríni but only one ferry a week for Koufoníssi. Overall, the Cyclades have a better service than the islands of the Dodecanese or the Sporades.

Keep in mind that the unexpected can always happen when travelling by sea. If there is a storm warning only the large ferries will operate. The most modern ones are equipped with stabilisers, however if you are prone to seasickness, you should plan to stay below deck. Although the Mediterranean is a landlocked sea, it nonetheless tosses boats around in a very unpleasant manner.

Hydrofoils are highly susceptible to wind and if you choose this form of transport, you may want to confirm that it will operate the evening before or the morning of your departure. Boats that are equally as fast but larger and more reliable during bad weather are now available: the **Highspeed** and **Seajet** (sometimes called **catamarans** because of their shape). These heavy boats with their enclosed and air-conditioned passenger space are more comparable to trains (or planes) than boats. Their main advantage is their speed which is practically double that of a classic ferry – but they are also double the price.

The large ports

The port at **Piraeus** (*see details in the "Making the most of Piraeus" section, page 166*) operates services to the islands of the Saronic Gulf, the Cyclades, the Dodecanese, Lesbos and Crete. The port at **Rafina** provides a service to the Cyclades and Euboea (Káristos and Marmári). The port at **Lávrio** serves the island of Kéa (Tziá). The port at **Patras** serves the Ionian Islands and Italy. The port at **Igoumenítsa** serves the islands of Corfu and Paxós as well as Italy. And the port at **Kilíni** serves the islands of Zacynthus (Zákinthos) and Cephalonia.

Rates

Tickets can be purchased at shipping agencies at the port or on-board ship. A ticket check is carried out systematically once the ship is at sea. There are several classes available on board; first class or sleeper berths are only worthwhile for trips of 10hr or more. Some sample rates (in economy class) are: Piraeus-Herakleion, around €21.50; Piraeus-Mýkonos, around €15; and Rafína-Ándros, approximately €7.50.

Information

The EOT office in Athens provides thorough information on these three means of transport (routeing, frequency of departures, hours) and even rates for the bus and train.

• Renting two-wheel vehicles

You can rent a two-wheel vehicle (up to a capacity of 125cc) upon presentation of your driving licence. The rental agencies rarely supply **helmets**, often considered superfluous in Greece, particularly in the summer. For your own safety, ask for one (even if you only get a relic from the 1970s) especially if you plan to travel on winding roads. The daily rate for a 50cc vehicle is approximately €11-15.

Be sure to specify if the length of rental time is for the day (from morning to evening) or for 24hr as rental agencies are sometimes evasive about this matter. Also quickly check the **state of your vehicle** (tyres, lights and the amount of fuel in the tank, as the gauges are often unreliable).

If there are two of you riding on the same vehicle, you may want to consider the traditional **papáki** (literally "little duck"). These are three-speed mopeds without a clutch and are thus named due to the noise they make when they slow down. While they are less glamorous than motor scooters, these rustic machines, often used in the Middle East and in Asia, are nonetheless solid, relatively powerful and hold the road well.

G. de Benoist/MICHELIN

They are also well suited to the dirt roads that are ubiquitous in Greece. The gears allow you to accelerate on hills and provide a good brake when going downhill – two appreciable assets. It's easy to learn how to manage the accelerator. Although you may feel intoxicated by the wind and the beauty of the countryside when riding your bike, don't forget that the sun burns just as much as it does on the beach, so be careful of sunburn. Headgear (especially a helmet) and a T-shirt are essential.

● **Domestic flights**

Olympic Airways no longer has a monopoly on domestic flights even if it remains the primary Greek company going to certain islands, such as Mýkonos, Santoríni, Páros, etc. Some small private companies also operate domestic services, and the proliferation of flights to Crete and Thessaloníki has lowered fares. Addresses in Athens:
Cronus Airlines, Odós Óthonos 10, ☎ (01) 33 15 502-4.
Aegean Airlines, Leofóros Vouliagménis 572, ☎ (01) 99 88 350.
Olympic Airways, Odós Filelínon 15, ☎ (01) 92 67 444.

● **Organised tours and excursions**

Greece has been a popular tourist destination for a long time now. You'll be able to find whatever you're looking for, from cruises to archaeological tours, resort holidays to all sorts of hikes and treks and any possible combination of these different components.

BED AND BOARD

Hotel provision in Greece is very well developed with lots of variety, ranging from deluxe hotels to small hotels to rooms to let. The quality of accommodation has also improved considerably and you will find it to be clean and comfortable no matter what category. On the other hand, it's not always that easy to track down hotels with charm; the 1960s and 70s produced a large number of concrete boxes. The current tendency, however, is to return to a more traditional architecture. This can either be authentic, when restoration or new construction is carried out with care using the old materials, or pseudo, particularly prevalent in the Cyclades, where walls are merely painted white and shutters blue and a few concrete arches are provided. This is nonetheless more pleasant than a standard rectangular block.

In short, good clean accommodation with that little extra touch is mostly to be found in the middle category. If you want to combine charm and comfort with reasonable rates, you should plan to come in the low season, in June or September, when these establishments offer reduced rates.

If you're travelling with family or friends, a worthwhile option is to rent a studio with a kitchenette. This type of lodging is widespread in Greece and can be a good alternative not only for its high quality (in comparison to rooms) but also for the price. Breakfast costs at least €4.50 daily and fewer meals in restaurants will more than compensate for the additional cost of this type of accommodation.

Rates

The rates mentioned in this guidebook are calculated on the basis of double occupancy in high season or the price of a studio apartment for two people. Be sure to bargain in low season or in less touristy areas, especially if you plan to stay for several days, as there is often a sliding scale.

• Various categories

Hotels

The Greek National Tourism Organisation **(EOT)** classifies hotels, studios and rooms into six categories: Deluxe, A, B, C, D, and E. These categories are determined by a set of criteria: the service provided, the facilities, the size of the rooms, their decor, available staff, etc. You will have to be the judge of the charm, the view, the quality of the furniture and additional services. For your information, we have listed below some daily rates based on double occupancy in high season, from the cheapest to the most expensive.

- E: €13-33
- D: €18-35
- C: €36-100
- B: €75-122
- A: €82-152
- Deluxe: €90 and up

These rates are not enforced. They vary from one establishment to another, according to the season and how touristy the site is. With this in mind, a new C category hotel can be more expensive than an old hotel that has a B ranking. D and E category hotels don't systematically include private bathrooms or breakfast. EOT classified lodgings have a small blue and yellow plaque and post their rates. They are itemised at local tourist information offices and travel agencies.

Rooms to let

The hotel categories don't apply to rooms to let, which are undeclared. On certain islands, the owners come to welcome the visitors at the port when the boats arrive. If this isn't the case, you can either telephone when you arrive (the reply will be in Greek or very rudimentary English) or just show up at the house which is the best means to judge the quality of the lodgings. Signs marked *Rooms* or *Domátia* will indicate where to go. You can also shop around; in Greek villages, a good number of the houses are almost always empty. To find this out, go to the *kafenío* (café) or the village bar and ask *"Psáhno dhomátio sto horió"* ("I'm looking for a room in the village"), after giving the respectful greeting *("Yá sas")*. Keep in mind however that you will not always find philanthropists. Make sure you set a budget and know that it's always easier to negotiate a lower rate for five nights than for two.

Camping

In principle, camping in the wild is forbidden but every island and tourist area has at least one campsite. All have relatively good facilities (mini-markets, bathrooms, etc.) and are often pleasantly shaded. A site for two people with shower costs about €12 per day.

Youth hostels

Youth hostels have never been particularly widespread in Greece, given the low rates charged by small hotels and for rooms to let.

Youth Hostel Association of Greece, Odós Dragatsaníou 4, Athens, ☎ (01) 32 34 107.

On the taverna terrace

• Eating out

There is no shortage of places to eat out and you can find something for every taste and budget. There are five broad categories of restaurants. For both standard cuisine or fish and seafood, **tavérnas** are popular restaurants that serve simple traditional Greek dishes that are inexpensive for the most part. **Ouzerís** (ouzo bars) and *mezedopolio* differ from tavernas by their menus, which offer meze (*see page 88*) rather than cooked or meat dishes. The term **psistariá** (literally "steakhouse") stands for small, inexpensive restaurants (with or without tables) where you can buy *souvlákia* (brochettes) and other grilled meats (chicken, lamb, etc), served with chips and sometimes a tomato salad. **Kafenía** are Greek cafés par excellence and also serve some meze to nibble on. You'll also find cafeterias which serve as cafes and provide breakfasts and some dishes. Naturally there are lots of multi-service establishments. As for **restaurants** (*estiatório* in Greek), you can find both Greek and international cuisine, and even elaborately prepared gourmet dishes. The decor and service are generally meticulous and prices are higher than elsewhere. Hotel restaurants – even well-established ones – are generally expensive and disappointing, particularly in Athens, with the exception of some famous gourmet restaurants.

Prices

Obviously prices vary according to the place and the menu. Keep in mind however that you will need to spend €7.50-11 per person for a decent meal in an ordinary taverna. Fish, on the other hand, is very expensive. Although Greece is surrounded by water, its resources of seafood are unfortunately diminishing rapidly and prices reflect this (around €30 per kilo for a top-category fish).

SPORTS AND PASTIMES

• Sports activities

Hiking

If you are a rambler, you will be in heaven. Greece is covered with paths, trails, unusual sites and nature parks (especially in the north of the country) which make for wonderful walking. Whether you're an avid hiker or simply enjoy a peaceful walk, there is something for everyone, particularly those who like to combine the outdoors, history and finding out about the local way of life.

In some areas and on some of the islands, the local tourist information office distributes more or less reliable maps of paths and trails. You'll find all the necessary information at tourist information centres in Athens or abroad for skiing, golf, horse riding (still undeveloped for tourism), hiking in the mountains, and caving (Greece has a large number of sites that already have their followers).

• The sea

Sailing

Boating indisputably offers one of the most pleasant ways of exploring the Greek coast and its numerous islands. This type of tourism is booming but today is encountering difficulties due to the insufficient mooring space in the ports and marinas. It is common to have long queues alongside the quay in the middle of August. Once again, it's better to travel in the spring, in June or September.

Addresses

Anemos Tours – 12-10 Astoria Park South, Long Island City, NY 11102-3704, USA, ☎ (718) 777 5050, Fax (718) 721 8043 or (520) 569 1479, info@anemos.net
Hellenic Professional Yacht Owners Association, Zéa Marina (Piraeus), Greece, ☎ (01) 45 26 335, 42 80 465, Fax (01) 45 26 335.
Minotaur Charters – 204 Altham Grove, Harlow, Essex CM20 2PW, ☎ (01279) 830478 (in the UK) or (0645) 92027 (in Greece), Fax (01279) 830478 (in the UK) or (0645) 92845 (in Greece), infor@minotaurcharters.com
Sailing Paradise – 59 Bark Ave, Central Islip, NY 11722, USA, ☎ (888) 864 SAIL(7245) or (631)342 0219, sparcom@sailingparadise.com

Scuba diving

Take advantage of your stay in Greece to learn how to scuba dive or to perfect your style. The depths of the Aegean or Mediterranean may not be as attractive as some of the warmer seas but it is always pleasant to come across sea turtles, dolphins and large groupers, or even the remains of an ancient wreck (which must absolutely be left alone). Local agencies have appropriate equipment and certified instructors available.
Eurodivers Club – Parikía (Punda), Páros Island, ☎ and Fax (0284) 92071, mobile (093) 233 6464, info@eurodivers.gr, www.eurodivers.gr
Vikings Yacht Cruises – 4321 Lakemoor Dr, Wilmington, NC 29405, USA, ☎ (800) 341 3030 or (910) 350 0100, Fax (910) 791 9400, cocco44a@prodigy.net or greek@gicc.net (in the USA) or ☎ (01) 8980 729 / 8949 279, Fax (01) 8940 952, vikings@vikings.gr (in Greece), www.vikings.gr

Surfing, windsurfing and water-skiing

On the islands and at beach resorts, those who thrive on big thrills will revel in the choices between windsurfing, water-skiing or even jet-skiing. The best surfing areas can be found on Páros (in the Cyclades). Avoid weighing yourself down with your own equipment. Local clubs rent it out, particularly on Páros, Mýkonos and Santoríni.

• Night-life

Summer cinemas

Enjoy the pleasure of an open-air cinema. Devout film lovers will, however, be somewhat discouraged – the sound is not very good quality, your neighbour may be nibbling loudly on a snack and there will be a 15min break in the middle of the film. Nonetheless it's an original way to see repeats of American and European blockbusters from the past year. (*See also page 80.*)

Bars and discos

Night-owls will find plenty of things to occupy the warm summer nights. Greeks certainly don't drink iced coffee until 10pm and go home to bed afterwards. In tourist areas, you will find all kinds of music. Keep in mind though that a club that plays techno can just as easily switch to Greek music at 4 or 5 in the morning if there is a local crowd. This is the opportunity to discover the *tsifteteli*, oriental-style melodies and dance set to contemporary music.

• Cultural activities

In addition to the large cultural summer festivals, particularly dance and theatre (in Athens, Epidaurus, Náfplio and Réthimnon), and big religious festivals like 15 August, each village celebrates its saints during the merry *panigíri*. You can get information on site but don't forget that the meal and the evening activities always take place the day before the actual holiday. During this time there is a commemorative mass. For more details, see the practical information in each section.

SHOPPING

• What's on offer

Culinary specialities

Epicureans will find all sorts of products to bring home so they can prolong their holiday with the tastes and aromas of the country. There is a wide choice ranging from honey from Kalamáta or Attica (thyme honey), fig or cherry jam, *amigdalotá* (a type of macaroon), *kourabiédes* (almond pastries), pistachios (a speciality of Égina), *halvá* (a type of sesame paste, sometimes stuffed with pistachios), *pastéli* (a honey and sesame macaroon), retsína from Attica, red wines from the Peloponnese or Thessaly, white wines from Santoríni, Léros, the Peloponnese and Thessaly, liqueur wines (muscatel from Sámos and Mavrodaphni), spirits (*Plomári* ouzo from Mitilíni, Lesbos, or rakí and tsípouro from Thessaloníki), not to mention olive oil from Crete.

Handicrafts

You'll find examples of some of the best and the worst items in the souvenir shops, from antique reproductions to T-shirts. At the same time, some handicrafts of good quality (sometimes rather expensive) are sold in all the big tourist centres today. These range from pottery and ceramics to carpets and hand-woven fabrics, knitted goods, embroidered clothing, **lace**, **embroidery**, bedspreads, wool carpets (originally from Aráhova or Thessaly), furs from Kastoriá, sponges from Kálimnos, and gold **jewellery**, both contemporary pieces and styles reproduced from Antiquity. Some jewellers, such as Lalaounis or Zolotas, are internationally renowned. You'll also find traditional silver jewellery from Ioánnina and Macedonia, carved wooden objects, **marble** and **onyx** sculptures, and reproductions of **icons** (especially in the monasteries).

Kritsá and Haniá are known for their Cretan **leather** boots, and the island of Skíros for its painted furniture. In Athens and on all the islands you'll find a large selection of leather sandals and handbags, popular in the 1970s, which are cheap but poor quality. Lastly, don't bypass the famous **kombolóï**, the beads that Greeks are constantly threading through their fingers and which can be found in all the shops.

• Bartering

Bartering is no longer commonly practised in Greece and you'll risk causing offence if you try it. Negotiating room rates, however, can lead to a pleasant discussion. You can also negotiate the price of your purchases in tourist shops, jewellery stores and silver and goldsmiths. Your margin of negotiation will be the equivalent of the item's VAT. On the other hand, in grocery stores and tavernas, this is completely inappropriate.

• Tax and payment

The ΦΠΑ (FPA), the Greek VAT, is always included in all marked prices. In Greece, payment by bank card is not always welcome, except in tourist areas, because this is proof of income that can be easily checked by the State and subject to tax. Shopkeepers prefer cash and they will be more likely to negotiate prices if you pay by this method. Bear in mind that shopkeepers must always give you a receipt whenever you make a purchase.

HEALTH AND SAFETY

• Precautions

There are no diseases in particular which you need to worry about in Greece, but beware of sunstroke. In the summer, especially on the islands, the sun is scorching and if you stay in it for too long, you'll risk getting burned, nausea, or a headache. If you plan to travel by bicycle or motorcycle, be sure to protect your shoulders, likewise if you're driving a convertible or walking, and remember to wear a hat. Also make sure you drink plenty of water.

Medical kit

You'll find everything you need in Greece, however you may want to bring a small medical first aid kit with you. Some essential items include aspirin, sunscreen (crucial in the summer), plasters, cotton balls, and antiseptic lotion for small cuts. Also remember to bring some mosquito repellent.

• Health

First aid

The small Greek hospitals are reliable but they are only equipped to handle minor illnesses. In the event of a serious problem, make sure you're transferred to Athens or repatriated (*see the section on "Travel / health insurance", page 97*).

Pharmacies

As Greeks are large consumers of medicine, you will find many pharmacies in Greece that sell all sorts of brand name pharmaceutical products. As in other countries, you will need a prescription for antibiotics.

Doctors

Most doctors (and pharmacists) speak a foreign language: English, French or Italian (many study in Italy). And there is almost always a doctor nearby.

Reimbursement

If you have health insurance at home, be sure to bring your insurance papers with you. Contact your local insurance company before leaving home for information on reimbursement procedures for medical or hospital services and medication in Greece.

• Emergencies

Dial 166 anywhere in Greece.

FROM A TO Z

• Antiques

Exporting antiques is strictly forbidden. No object over 100 years old may be taken out of Greece and you risk a heavy fine if you attempt it. Don't ever pick anything up from an archaeological site or when diving, be it a fragment of stone or pottery, even if it appears to be insignificant. The laws are very severe for this type of theft.

• Cigarettes

Smoking in public places or on public transport is prohibited. The Greeks respect the no-smoking laws concerning public transport, but elsewhere you will have to contend with smokers, who make up the majority of the Greek population.

• Drinking water

Water is fit to drink throughout the country. When it comes from natural springs (in the Peloponnese, northern Greece and on some islands), it is even delicious. On the other hand, arid islands like Santorini import water in tanks in the summer. Although it is fit for consumption, it doesn't taste very good.

• Electricity

Electricity is 220 volts in Greece.

• Laundry

You will find dry cleaners in the cities but very few self-service launderettes. Tourism has however caused some to open in tourist areas. Many hotels have their own laundry service and small hotels often provide a washing machine for their guests' use.

• Newspapers

Most of the main foreign newspapers are available the day after publication. If you don't want to miss any local or international current events while you're travelling, read the *Athens News,* printed in English and available in Athens and tourist areas.

• Photography

Unless you are partial to a special brand, you can buy film without any problem in Greece. You will, however, find print film more easily than slide film. Prices are also often cheaper than in many other countries. Make sure you check the expiry date and avoid purchasing film that has been displayed in the windows and exposed to the sun.

• Radio and television

Since the State's monopoly on television disappeared, numerous private channels have emerged. Most of them focus on political debates, society issues, game shows, variety shows, or Mexican and American series. In short, the usual programmes found on regular channels. **ERT** (one of the three public channels) is unanimously considered to be the best. In some hotels that provide satellite TV, you will be able to pick up the BBC and CNN.

• Safety

Athens and most of Greece are relatively peaceful. There are almost always lots of people out at night and this is your best guarantee for safety. Moreover, the State and shopkeepers are careful to preserve Greece's reputation with tourists. As a result, a lot of crime has been stamped out. Sometimes, however, the hordes of summer visitors still encourage a certain amount of moneygrubbing, but this is exceptional (and another good reason to avoid coming during the high season).

• Tipping / gratuities

No one will ever ask for a tip but this is no reason not to give one. As in other parts of Europe, it's common practice to leave something (usually about 10% of the bill) in cafés or restaurants. As far as taxi drivers are concerned, as a rule you should round up the balance to their advantage.

• Units of measurement

Greece follows the metric system.

Distances in this guide are given in kilometres. As a rule of thumb, one kilometre is five-eighths of a mile: 5 miles is therefore about 8 kilometres, 10 miles is about 16 kilometres and 20 miles is about 32 kilometres.
Consult the table below for other useful metric equivalents:

Degrees Celsius	35°	30°	25°	20°	15°	10°	5°	0°	-5°	-10°
Degrees Fahrenheit	95°	86°	77°	68°	59°	50°	41°	32°	23°	15°

1 centimetre (cm) = 0.4 inch
1 metre (m) = 3.3 feet
1 metre (m) = 1.09 yards
1 litre = 1.06 quart
1 litre = 0.22 gallon
1 kilogram (kg) = 2.2 pounds

• Weather

Weather reports are broadcast daily on television and in the newspapers. You won't need to understand Greek; you only need to look at the small suns illustrated on the map of the country! In the summer, climatic uncertainty focuses only on the possibility and the intensity of scorching heat and on the strength of the wind (important if you plan to take a boat out).

LOOK AND LEARN

• History and archaeology

BULFINCH Thomas, *Myths of Greece and Rome*, Viking Press, 1981.
DREWS Robert, *The Coming of the Greeks*, Princeton University Press, 1994. Through history, archaeology and linguistics, this scholar delves into the origin of the Greeks.
FINLEY Moses I, *The Ancient Greeks*, Viking Press, 1992.
HAMILTON Edith, *The Echo of Greece*, 1964 and *The Greek Way*, (reprint 1993), WW Norton & Company. The pre-eminent scholar of the classical world explores the Greek world and culture.
KITTO Humphrey Davy Findley, *The Greeks*, Penguin USA, 1991.
PEDLEY John Griffiths, *Greek Art and Archaeology*, Harry N Ambrams, 1997.
SEKUNDRA Nicholas, *The Spartans*, Osprey Publishing Co, 1999. Provides background on Greek warfare.
STEPHANIDES Menelaos, *The Gods of Olympus*, Sigma, 1999. A world renowned study of Greek mythology.
WOODHOUSE CM, *Modern Greece: A Short History*, Faber & Faber, 2000.

• People and culture

BLUNDELL Sue, *Women in Ancient Greece*, Harvard University Press, 1995.
KREMEZI Aglaia, *The Foods of Greece*, Stewart Tabori & Chang, 1999. This internationally renowned food expert shares 135 regional dishes from her homeland.

• Literature

BERNIERES Louis de, *Captain Corelli's Mandolin*, Vintage Books, 1995. This bestselling novel that sheds light on the history of Cephalonia has been made into a film (starring Nicholas Cage).
FOWLES John, *The Magus*, Modern Library, 1998. Originally published in 1965, this spellbinding novel forays into the adventures of a young Englishman caught in a game of psychological intrigue on a Greek island.
PAPANDREOU Nicholas C, *A Crowded Heart*, Picador USA, 1998. An autobiographical novel that blends politics, Greek culture and American influences.
PRESSFIELD Steven, *Gates of Fire*, Bantam Books, 1998. A suspenseful historical novel about the Spartan War and *Tides of War: A Novel of Alcibiades and the Peloponnesian War*, Doubleday Books, 2000.
RENAULT Mary, *The Mask of Apollo*, Vintage Books, 1988. Set in the 4C BC, this novel is a must for anyone interested in the history of theatre.
STORACE Patricia, *Dinner with Persephone*, Vintage Books, 1997. A penetrating exploration of the complexities of contemporary Greek life, history and identity.
VALTINOS Thanassis, *Data from the Decade of the Sixties: A Novel*. Northwestern University Press, 2000. A chronicle on the transformation of Greece in the 1960s.

• Travelogues

DURRELL Lawrence, *Prospero's Cell*, Marlowe & Co, 1996 (reprint). A memoir about Durrell's time spent on the island of Corfu.

FERMOR Patrick Leigh, *Mani*, Penguin, 1984.
KIZILOS Katherine, *The Olive Grove: Travels in Greece*, Lonely Plan
MILLER Henry, *Colussus of Maroussi*, WW Norton & Company, 198
of his travels in the 1930s and 40s, Miller depicts ancient and modern
flowing poetic style.

● **Films and documentaries**
DASSIN Jules, *Never on Sunday*, 1959. In Piraeus in the 1950s, a prostitute with a
big heart meets an American who is trying to understand Greek society. Dassin
directed Melína Mercoúri, his future wife, for the first time in this film.
CACOYÁNNIS Michális, *Stella*, 1955. The film that brought Melína Mercoúri to
stardom. A tender and tragic evocation of the poor neighbourhoods in post-war
Greece. *Electra*, 1962, and the famous *Zorba the Greek*, 1964, starring Anthony
Quinn and adapted from the novel by Kazantzákis, give two spectacular portraits of
the Greek soul.
COSTA-GAVRAS, *Z*, 1969. The film on the rise to power of the colonels' junta. A
political thriller inspired by the Lambrákis affair, a leftist member of parliament is
assassinated at the beginning of the junta (Z is the first letter of the verb *"zóo"* which
means "to live").
ANGELÓPOULOS Theo, *The Suspended Step of the Stork*, 1991, *Eternity and a
Day*, 1998. The recurrent themes of identity, boundaries and memory pervade the
films of Angelopoulos, the only world-famous Greek filmmaker.
GILBERT Lewis, *Shirley Valentine*, 1989. A British housewife embarks on a spontaneous holiday to the Greek islands that will change her life.

● **Music**
THEODORÁKIS Míkis, *His best popular songs, The very best of Theodorakis*.
Discover the mythical figure of Greek music.
Three aspects of Greek song:
ALEXÍOU Háris, Ψίθυροι ("Murmurs"), ARVANITÁKI Eleftería (Polygram) and
DALÁRAS Geórgos, *Kalós tous* (Mínos).
TITSÁNIS Vassílis, *Homage to Tsitsánis*. One of the great figures of rembétika.
REMBÉTIKA, Rembetica: Historic Urban Folk Songs from Greece (Rounder Records).
The Soul of Greece: 101 Strings (Madacy Records).
Folk music of Greece (Topic World records). Traditional music from the four
corners of the Greek world.

● **Maps**
MICHELIN, *Greece* (Map 980), 1/700 000.

GLOSSARY

● **Pronunciation**
Here's a glance at the Greek alphabet and its pronunciation.

A α   a
B β   v (van)
Γ γ   g (gate) before a consonant and the vowels a, o, and ou; y (yoghurt)
            when placed before the i sound (η, ι, υ, εε ι). The same rule follows
            for Georgos ("Yorgos"), because of the e.
Δ δ   th (the); transcribed by *d*.
E ε   e
Z ζ   z
H η   i
Θ θ   th (think)

	i
κ	k
Λ λ	l
M μ	m
N ν	n
Ξ ξ	x (taxi)
O o	o
Π π	p
P ρ	r
Σ ς	s
T τ	t
Υ υ	i
Φ φ	f
X x	kh (as in "loch")
Ψ ψ	the sound *ps*
Ω ω	o

Common expressions

Good morning	Kaliméra
Good evening	Kalispéra
Greeting (at any time of the day)	Hérete
Hi (good day, goodbye, see you later)	Yássou (informal term) or Yássas (formal or polite form)
Please	Sas parakaló
Thank you	Evharistó
Yes	Naí
No	Óhi
Excuse me	Signómi (pardon), Me sinhoríte (formal or polite form)
OK, all right	Endáxi
I don't understand	Den katalavéno
I don't speak Greek	Den miláo helliniká
Do you speak English?	Miláte angliká?
I would like	Tha íthella
There is	Ipárhi
There isn't	Den Ipárhi
Me / you (informal) / he / she / us / you (formal) / them	egó / essí / aftós / aftí / emís / essís / aftí

Basic conversation

How are you?	Ti kánete?
Where are you from?	Apo pou íssaste?
I am British / American	Íme ánglos / amerikános

Time

What time is it?	Ti óra íne?	hour	óra
it is 7 o'clock	Íne eftá	day	méra
yesterday	kthés	week	evdomáda
today	símera	Monday	deftéra
tomorrow	ávrio	Tuesday	tríti
morning	proí	Wednesday	tetárti
evening	vrádi	Thursday	pémti
early	norís	Friday	paraskeví
late	argá	Saturday	sávato
night	níhta	Sunday	kiriakí

Common adjectives

handsome / beautiful	oréo, ómorfo (person)	open	anigtó
expensive	akrivó	hot	zestó
inexpensive, cheap	ftinó	cold	krío
new	kainoúrio	good	oréo, kaló
old	pallió	bad	kakó
big	megálo	fast	grígoro
small	mikró	slow	argó
closed	klistó		

Colours

white	áspro, lefkó	black	mávro
blue	ble, galázios	red	kókino
yellow	kítrino	green	prássino

Finding your way

here	edó	road	drómos
there	ekí péra, ekí	tourist information	touristikó grafío,
north	vória (B)	office	grafío tou EOT
south	nótia (N)		(eótt)
east	anatoliká (A)	museum	moussío
west	ditiká (Δ)	church	eklissía
to the right	dexiá	hotel	xenodohío
to the left	aristerá	rooms	domátia
straight ahead	efthía	taverna	tavérna
where is?	Pou ínai?	restaurant	estiatório
village	horió	post office	tahidromío
What's the name	Pos to léne	entrance	íssodos
of this village?	aftó to horió?	exit	éxodos
square	platía	sea	thálassa
town centre	kéndro	lake	límni
street	odós	beach	paralía
avenue, boulevard	leofóros		

Transport

bus	leoforío (bus),	ticket	issitírio
	auto-car (luxury coach)	return ticket	issitírio mè epistrofí
car-ferry	karávi, plío,	car	aftokínito
	vapóri, féri	motorcycle	mihanáki
aeroplane	aeropláno	fuel station	venzinádiko
train	tréno	garage	synergío
bus station, stop	stássi	please fill	yémissé to
port	limáni	the tank up	
airport	aerodrómio		
railway station	stathmós trénon		

At the hotel

passport	diavatírio	toilet paper	hartí iyías
luggage	valítses	ladies	yinekón
room	domátio	gentlemen	andrón
single bed	monóklino	sheets	sendónia
double bed	díklino	towel	petséta

room	domátio mé bánio	blanket	kouvérta
with private bath		key	klidí
shower	dous	breakfast	proïnó
toilet, WC	toilétes	laundry	stegnokatharistírio

At the restaurant

table	trapézi	eat	tróo
menu	catálogo	drink	píno
salad	saláta	knife	mahéri
grilled	psitó	fork	piroúni
meat	kréas	salt	aláti
chicken	kotópoulo	pepper	pipéri
fish	psári	rice	rízi
dessert	gliká	sugar	záhari
a drink	potó	yoghurt	yaoúrti
mineral water	fissikó metalikó	milk	gála
	neró	egg	avgó
fruit juice	himó	olive	eliés
wine	krassí	soup	soúpa
tea	tsái	the bill, please	to logariasmó sas
coffee	kafé		parakaló
bread	psomí		

At the post office

stamp	gramatóssima
Do you have stamps?	Éhete gramatóssima?
envelope	fákelo
letter	gráma
package	déma
send	stéllno
telegram	tilegráfima
telephone card	kárta tilephónou

Shopping

How much is this?	Pósso káni? Pósso éhei?
It's too expensive	Ínai polí akrivó
It's very beautiful	Ínai polí oréo
money (change)	leftá
cigarettes	tsigára
credit card	pistotikí kárta
travellers' cheques	traveler's cheques

Emergencies

It doesn't work	den litouryí
Call the police	Páre tin astinomía
There was	Sinévike éna atíhima
an accident	
doctor	yiatró
hospital	nossokomío

Numbers

0	midén	30	triánda
1	éna	40	saránda
2	dío	50	penínda
3	tría	60	exínda
4	téssera	70	evdomínda
5	pénde	80	ogdónda
6	éxi	90	enenínda
7	eftá	100	ekató
8	októ	200	diakóssia
9	eniá	1000	híllia
10	déka	1 million	ekatomírio
20	íkossi		

• Non-verbal language or gestures

Whether or not you find it easy to speak Greek, communicating in gestures is always very useful. In a country where excess is the norm, gestures instantly translate the thoughts of the person you are speaking with as well as many nuances. It's therefore worthwhile to understand their meaning, especially when they are foreign to us. For example, to say "no", Greeks simply raise their head, or sometimes only their eyes, and lightly click their tongue. To say "yes" they lower their head and their eyes, sometimes recoiling slightly. These signs, which are barely perceptible to those who aren't used to them, are useful for repelling an aggressive salesperson or a taxi in search of passengers.

A light rotation of the hand translates into a gesture the onomatopoeia "po po po" which is the equivalent of "oh dear" or "goodness me" and signifies surprise. If the movement increases with the hand open, it becomes a matter of admiration. Greeks will be more than willing to give you information and if they can't help you out, they will hail a passer-by who will bend over backwards to help you.

Exploring Greece

The noble tholos
of Marmariá,
in Delphi

Cape Soúnion seen through the columns
of the Temple of Poseidon

B. Kaufmann/MICHELIN

ATTICA

Like an arrow pointing towards the sparkling circle of the Cyclades, the Attica Peninsula forms a narrow triangle stretching all the way to rocky **Cape Soúnion**, upon which stand the lofty columns of the Temple of Poseidon. On its western side it shields the busy waters of the Saronic Gulf, which leads to the Corinth Canal, the only gateway to the Gulf of Corinth and the country's outlying regions. Its eastern side faces the peaceful shores of Euboea, the second-largest island after Crete. This choice location between the mainland and the sea was the ideal place for the cradle of Greek civilisation to develop.

A fertile land with alternating plains and green valleys, Attica has a few mountains which relieve the monotony of its landscapes. To the south stands **Mt Hymettus (Imitós)** with its wooded slopes, while further to the north lies **Mt Parnes (Párnitha)** and to the east **Mt Pentelikon (Pendéli)**, where the marble for many of the masterpieces in ancient Athens came from. Their forests continue to supply the capital with oxygen – but for how much longer? They are like three huge rocks dropped there by the gods to shade the vineyards, especially those in the **Plain of Mesógia**, or "Midland", which produces the famous pine-scented retsína wine.

But nowadays the mountains themselves seem to be gradually disappearing, as if inundated by the flood of concrete from the Athens suburbs – a sprawling monster that reaches further inland every year. More industrial near Elefsína, they turn residential in Glifáda, a dreary new town dotted with shopping malls, rich houses and investment properties. The noise from the aircraft passing overhead is a thing of the past as Ellinikó Airport has been permanently replaced by Elefthérios Venizélos Airport, better equipped to accommodate tourists from around the world... as well as the thousands of spectators expected for the Olympic Games.

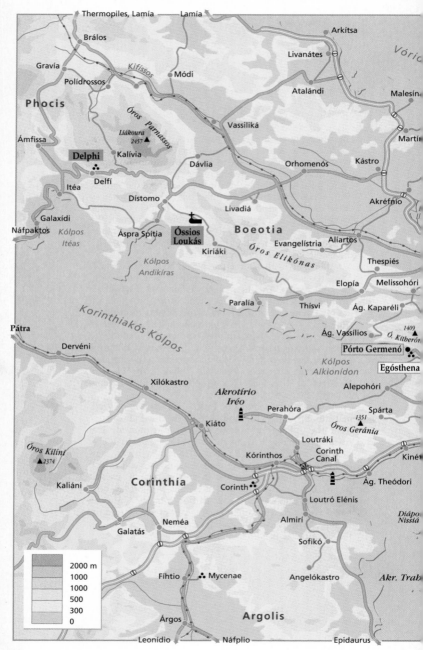

Thermopiles, Lamía — Lamía

Brálos

Arkítsa

Livanátes

Vório

Gravía

Kifíssos

Módi

Polídrossos

Atalándi

Malesín

Phocis

Óros Parnassós

Vassiliká

Martí

Ámfissa

Liákoura 2457

Kalívia

Dávlia

Orhomenós

Kástro

Delphi

Delfí

Akréfnio

Itéa

Dístomo

Livadiá

Galaxídi

Áspra Spítia

Óssios Loukás

Boeotia

Náfpaktos

Kólpos Itéas

Kiriáki

Evangelístria

Alíartos

Óros Elikónas

Thespiés

Kólpos Andikíras

Elopía

Melissohóri

Paralía

Thísvi

Ág. Kaparéli

Korinthiakós Kólpos

Ág. Vassílios

Ó. Kitherón 1409

Pátra

Dervéni

Pórto Germenó

Kólpos Alkionídon

Egósthena

Xilókastro

Akrotírio Iréo

Alepohóri

Perahóra

Spárta

Kiáto

Óros Geránia 1351

Óros Kilíni ▲2374

Loutráki

Corinth Canal

Kórinthos

Kiné

Kaliáni

Corinthía

Corinth

Ág. Theódori

Loutró Elénis

Diápo Nissiá

Neméa

Almirí

Galatás

Sofikó

2000 m
1000
1000
500
300
0

Fíhtio

Mycenae

Angelókastro

Akr. Trah

Árgos

Argolis

Leonídio

Náfplio

Epidaurus

122

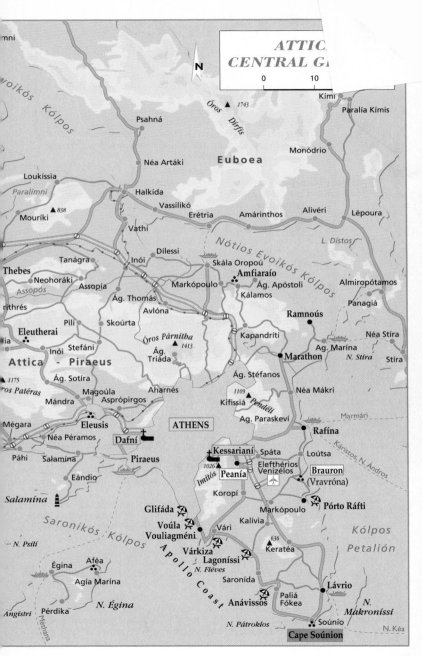

Óros Dírfis ▲ 1743

Kími

Paralía Kímis

Psahná

Néa Artáki   **Euboea**

Monódrio

Loukíssia

Paralímni

Halkída

Vassilikó   Alivéri   Lépoura

Mouríki ▲ 838

Erétria   Amárinthos

Vathí

L. Dístos

Dílessi   *Nótios Evoikós Kólpos*

Tanágra

Thebes   Inói

Skála Oropoú

Neohoráki

Assopós   Markópoulo   Amfiaraío

Assopía   Ág. Apóstoli   Almiropótamos

rithrés   Ág. Thomás   Kálamos

Ramnoús   Panagiá

Eleutherai   Avlóna

Píli   Skoúrta

lia   Óros Párnitha ▲ 1413   Kapandríti   Néa Stíra

Inói   Stefáni   Ág.   Ag. Marína

Attica - Piraeus   Triáda   *N. Stíra*   Stíra

Marathon

▲ 1175

os Patéras   Ág. Sotíra   Ág. Stéfanos

Aharnés   Néa Mákri

Magoúla   Asprópirgos

Mándra   1109 ▲   *Marmári*

Kifissiá   *Pendéli*

Mégara   **ATHENS**

Eleusis   Ag. Paraskeví   Rafína

Néa Péramos   **Kessarianí**   Spáta   *Kárstos, N. Andros*

Páhi   Salamína   Loútsa

Piraeus   1026 ▲   Eleanthérios

Eándio   **Peanía**   Venizélos   **Brauron**

Imitós   (Vravróna)

Salamína ♒   Koropí   Pórto Ráfti

Markópoulo   *Kólpos*

Glifáda   ✈   Kalívia   *Petalión*

Saronikós Kólpos   Vári

Voúla ✈

– N. Psilí   Vouliagméni   636 ▲

Várkiza   Keratéa

Égina   Aféa   Lagoníssi ✈

N. Fléves   *N.*

Agía Marína   Saronída   *Makroníssi*

Angístri Pérdika   *N. Égina*   Anávissos ✈   Paliá   Lávrio

Fókea

N. Pátroklos   Soúnio

N. Kéa

Cape Soúnion

ATHENS★★
(ATHÍNA)
Capital of the country and of the district of Attica
Michelin map 980 fold 30 – Plans on following pages
Pop 3 million – Very hot climate in summer, temperate in winter

Not to be missed
The Acropolis and Greek Agora.
Strolling through the streets of Pláka and Monastiráki.
The National Archaeological Museum, the Benáki Museum and the Museum of
Cycladic Art.

And remember...
Adapt your activities to the climate: visit outdoor sites in the morning;
have lunch around 2pm, then choose between a nap or an air-conditioned museum;
go for a stroll in the evening and have a late dinner.

Athens stretches across a wide basin dotted with steeply sloping hills along the shores of the Saronic Gulf. From the majestic promontory of the Acropolis, the modern city spreads for miles in every direction and now numbers over 3 million inhabitants – a third of the country's population! Moreover, the millions of visitors who come every year to admire its monuments may have somewhat conflicting feelings about it. Indeed, one never gets tired of contemplating the Acropolis, of strolling through the colourful Pláka district, or of exploring the origins of Western civilisation in an elegant marble statue. Likewise, what could be more delightful than enjoying the cool evening air on a taverna terrace or sipping a glass of ouzo in the sun? But one might also be tempted to flee this hectic modern metropolis with its noise and pollution.

So, when in Athens, do as the Athenians do. For those who are observant of the little things in everyday life, the city has a lot more to offer than a mere voyage back in time, no matter how fabulous it may be. It is a real odyssey taking you deep into the history of the Mediterranean and of the Balkans on the border between Europe and the Orient.

The city of Athena
The **Ionians** came from the North at the beginning of the 2nd millennium BC to settle in Attica, where their influence spread throughout the region. They founded the bustling city of Athens which gradually dominated the little principalities in the area during the Mycenaean Period (1600-1100 BC). Its solidly fortified acropolis was built in terraces and possessed a palace, placing it among the top three Mycenaean cities next to Tírintha and Mycenae itself.

Then history gets blurred with legend: the struggle between Poseidon and Athena for guardianship of the city ended in favour of the goddess. At the same time, Theseus went to the palace of Minos in Crete and slew the Minotaur. Both myths symbolise the victory of Attica (Athena's territory) over the Minoan world (of the sea). As for Theseus, he was personified by **Cecrops,** the first king of Athens, who established the Greeks' sovereignty and independence on the mainland.

In the 11C BC, however, the monarchy was undermined by the collapse of the Mycenaean world, giving way to an aristocratic government composed of the chiefs of the region's four biggest tribes. The new Attica born from this alliance was unified by the 6C BC. It was a feudal territory, but the archon **Solon,** followed by the tyrant **Peisistratus** and his sons, were to tone down its land-based, seigneurial character in favour of the new business elite. Athens began to really blossom, focusing its commercial and political ambitions on the entire Aegean area. This was the start of a

brilliant artistic flowering marked by the geometric style in ceram
the birth of monumental architecture, skilful urban planning (water
road maintenance), and dazzling religious activity (Panathenaic a.
Festivals). Through this wealth of innovations, Athens rose to the stature

The Golden Age – Athens reached its high point in the 5C BC with a ho
ical, artistic and intellectual achievements which established it as the
Western civilisation. After a popular revolt in 508 BC, **Cleisthenes** created a democratic system for the city, whose institutions were established by his successor, **Pericles**. Re-elected every year for thirty years (460-430 BC), Pericles surrounded himself with the greatest artists and scholars of his day. Their works reflect one of the most brilliant phases in Hellenic civilisation, an era known as the Age of Pericles, which they passed on to posterity.

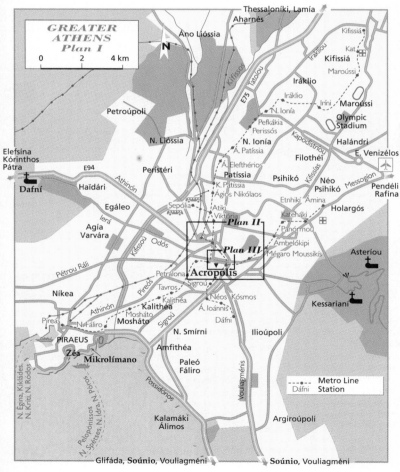

ATHENS
Plan II–Centre

0   200   400 m

N

Lárissa

Ioánnínon

Pétras

Pelopónissos

N. Metaxá

Liossíon

M. Vóda

Ipírou

Ahamón

Ioulíanou

Alkiviádou

Mármi

VÁTHI

3 Septemvríou

Platía Anexartissías

Árgous

Platánas

Deligiáni

Lénorman

Deligiáni

Palamidíou

Híou

Psarón

Akominátou

Soniérou

Mármi

Athínón

Kímonos

Monastiríou

Metaxourgío

Faviérou

Victor Hugo

Platía Karólou

Platía Karaïskáki

METAXOURGIÓ

Ag. Konstandínou

T

Omónia

Ahiléos

Platía Metaxourgíou

Kolonoú

Deligeórgi

Menándrou

Sokrátous

Omónia

Likoúrgou

Stadio

Spírou Pátsi

Konstandinoupóleos

Marathónos

Kolokinthoús

Keramíkou

(Pireós)

Genadíou

Sokrátous

Athinás

H

Pl. E. Andístass

Bours

Ierá Odós

Thermopíon

(Pireós)

Platía Eleftherías

Sofokléous

Evripídou

Central Market

Ag. Theódo

Persefónis

GÁZI

Keramikós Cemetery

Ag. Anargíron

San´

PSIRÍ

Athinás

Plan III

Dafní, Kórinthos

Tehnópoli M. Hantzidákis

Orféos

Ermoú Thissío

MONASTIRÁKI

Kapnikaréa

P. Tsaldári

THISSÍO

Thissío

Monastiráki

Cathedral

Iraklídon

Dimofóndos

Aktéou

Iraklídon

Apostólou Pávlou

Pireás

Ipothondídon

Melitéon

Observatory

Areopagus

ANAFIÓTIKA

Pnyx

ACROPOLIS

Kníðou

Thessaloníkis

Á. Dimítrios Lombadiáris

HOTELS	
Art Gallery	①
Athenian Inn	②
Athinea	③
Austria	④
Erechteion	⑤
Hera	⑥
Lycabette	⑦
Marble House	⑧
Orion-Dryádes	⑨
Tony's	⑩
Youth hostel	⑪

Wall of Themistocles

Prison of Socrates

MAKRIGIÁNI

Filopápos Theatre

P

Akrópo

Apolloníou

Filopápos Monument

Erethíou

Missralíotou

Hill of the Muses

T

Moussón

Drákou

Falírou

A. Sígrou

G. Kolokotróni

Panetolíou

Zahaítsa

Veíkou

Dimitrakopoúlou

KOUKÁKI

Pireás

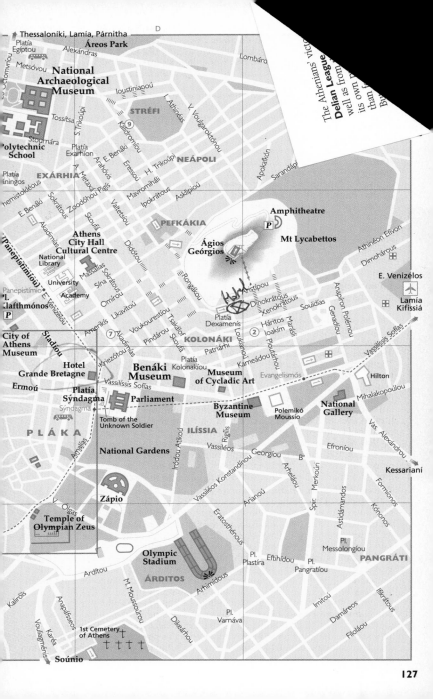

ry over the **Persians** (490-479 BC) put them at the head of the ɡ, an alliance which included all the cities from the Aegean Islands as the coast of Asia Minor. Under Pericles, Athens subjugated its allies for rofit within an economic and political framework that was more imperial ederal.

t this desire for hegemony over the Greek world was not to everyone's liking, and Athens soon earned the hostility of Sparta, Corinth and Euboea, leading to the Peloponnesian War (431-404 BC). **Sparta** won the war, triggering the political decline of Athens.

Yet despite this gradual decline, Athens remained the undisputed metropolis of Hellenic civilisation, whose new leaders, **Philip II of Macedon** and above all **Alexander the Great**, extended it all the way to the borders of Asia. Under **Lycurgus** – and thanks to the kings' favour towards the Hellenistic Orient – this civilisation experienced a great renewal between 350 BC and the late 2C BC marked by the construction of many monuments.

Athens regained its independence during a second golden age consolidated by the Roman victory over Macedonia (168 BC).

But this last gasp of prosperity was suddenly interrupted when the city was captured and sacked by **Sulla** (68 BC). Nevertheless, this *pax romana* enabled Greek culture to be disseminated on an unprecedented scale throughout the Mediterranean world, making Athens a kind of university city where part of the political, intellectual and artistic elite of the Roman Empire went to be educated.

An outlying town – Yet its decline was inevitable. After destruction in the barbarian invasions (the **Heruli** in 267 AD, the **Goths** in 396), the closing of the philosophy schools in the 5C AD and the transformation of pagan buildings into Christian basilicas put an end to over ten centuries of influence. Athens and Rome took a back seat to Constantinople as the Christian Hellenistic world moved back towards Eastern Europe, Asia Minor and the Middle East. Though still relatively densely populated, the Greek city was reduced to a small provincial town on the fringes of the Empire. The Byzantine churches and monasteries built after the expedition of Emperor Basil II to the Balkans (11C-12C) were the city's last sparkle before its long sleep, dramatically triggered by the **Saracen raid** in the late 12C.

From the 13C, Athens was passed from the Crusaders (1204-1311) to the Catalans (1311-87), then from the Florentines to the **Venetians** (1387-1456), before being handed over to the **Turks**, who settled on the Acropolis and its environs for four centuries (1456-1833). Just below the fortified town was a settlement of about 10 000 people, mostly Greeks and Albanians. When the ancient buildings weren't fortified or transformed for civil purposes, they were used as stone quarries for houses or as raw material for limekilns! In short, the city which European travellers passed through in the 18C was an unrecognisable place on its last legs.

The reign of Otto, or the awakening of modern Athens – The choice of Athens as the capital of the young Hellenic kingdom (*see page 28*) at the height of European neo-Classicism in 1834 signalled its revival. The challenge was a stimulus to the imaginations of the Greek and Bavarian architects charged with drawing up plans for the future new town. But not one of the numerous projects proposed was undertaken, and the city grew haphazardly. The urban fabric sprawled in an anarchic fashion, even gobbling up the archaeological area around the Acropolis. The government undertook some large-scale works, however, and even went so far as to periodically force people to leave their homes in order to inaugurate new streets, including wide avenues such as Alexándras and Sigroú (in the 1880s).

For want of any urban planning, a handful of architects – Kléanthis, Schaubert, the two **Hansen brothers**, **Ziller**, Boulanger, Kálkos and Kaftanzóglou – designed a number of neo-Classical structures, lining the straight avenues of the capital with imposing buildings with marble façades. Houses in a composite style blending elements of neo-Renaissance and Baroque were built for the upper classes in the area around Platía Sýndagma.

Sprawling growth – At the turn of the 19C and 20C, the population of Athens grew sharply – 453 000 inhabitants in 1928 compared to 110 000 in 1889. This phenomenon was due in particular to the massive arrival of **Greeks from Asia Minor** following the Treaty of Lausanne (1923), and prolonged after the Second World War by the huge **rural exodus**. Once distinctly separated from the capital by the countryside, the village of Maroússi to the north-west and Piraeus to the south-east were now connected by a continuous network of housing. In its colossal expansion, the urban area absorbed the two local rivers, the **Ílissos** and the **Kifisós**, which disappeared beneath boulevards.

Until the 1950s, however, space-consuming individual houses were still the dominant feature in the urban landscape of the Greek metropolis outside the city centre. But the following decade saw the spread of concrete constructions that were all identical with their superimposed apartments, graceless balconies and ground-floor galleries occupied by shops and cafés. This particularly dreary architecture has nevertheless shaped the face of the whole of present-day Athens.

In recent years, however, preparations for the 2004 Olympic Games have in turn disrupted the capital. In addition to large-scale work on the metro and the road network, the city centre has acquired new pedestrian areas such as the large, paved Odós Ermoú. And, in a historical twist, the famous archaeological area that Kléanthis and Schaubert wanted in 1833 is finally on the verge of being created...

Athens and its neighbourhoods

Upon arriving in Athens you will probably go through **Platía Sýndagma** (Plan II, D3), the city's nerve centre where banks, hotels and airline companies are lined up across from the Parliament. **Odós Ermoú** (Plan III, D2) cuts through the heart of the city, prolonging the square's central axis all the way to Piraeus. This great commercial thoroughfare is dotted with animated little squares and innumerable clothing shops. To the south-west, leading to the slopes of the Acropolis, is **Pláka**, the tourist area with a host of tavernas and souvenir shops in its old houses and winding alleyways. To the west near the **Greek Agora** lies **Monastiráki**, the old Turkish quarter that has preserved its atmosphere of a Balkan bazaar with its flea market. North of Sýndagma, the straight streets of **Kolonáki** hem in the wooded slopes of **Mount Lycabettos (Lykavitós)**. With its chic, trendy boutiques, this residential neighbourhood is an area frequented by the established local bourgeoisie and the intelligentsia. From Sýndagma, **Leofóros Stadíou** and **Leofóros Panepistimíou** feed into the north-west side of noisy **Platía Omónia** (Plan II, C2). Nearby stands the **National Archaeological Museum** in a part of Athens that has a neo-Classical feeling to it.

If you have only one day to spend in Athens:

The Acropolis and surrounding area. A walk through Pláka. The National Archaeological Museum. Have dinner in Exárhia or in Pláka.

If you have a minimum of four days in Athens:

1st day	**The Acropolis and surrounding area**. A walk on Filopápos Hill, the Pnyx. Dinner in Pláka.
2nd day	**Pláka**. The Byzantine churches, the City of Athens Centre for Popular Arts and Traditions, Anafiótika, the Kanelópoulos Museum, the Tower of the Winds, the Roman Forum, Monastiráki. Dinner in Psirí or Gázi.
3rd day	**In the heart of Athens**. The Greek Agora, Keramikós Cemetery, Psirí, Kendrikí Agorá (Central Market), the National Archaeological Museum. Dinner in Exárhia.
4th day	**Around Sýndagma**. Hadrian's Arch, the Temple of Olympian Zeus, the Stadium, the National Garden, Odós Ermoú, the Benáki Museum and the Museum of Cycladic Art. Cocktails on Mt Lycabettos, and dinner there or in Kolonáki or Dexaméni.

Athens

The Acropolis★★★ (Acrópoli)

Count on 2hr for your visit, more if you're feeling contemplative. Plan page 133.

There are two ways to go: from Pláka via the Perípatos, a long paved path that climbs up the north face of the Acropolis; the other access, via the rock's southern side, leaves from Odós Dionissíou Areopagítou where it intersects with Odós Apostólou. 8am-6.30pm. Entrance fee. The ticket includes the site and museum.

Even if you are just passing through Athens, do not miss the Acropolis. The site and the collection of monuments and treasures exhibited in the museum are indeed among the most prestigious bequeathed to us by Antiquity. Visit it preferably early in the morning before the sun and marble become scorching. And if the crowds are already there, remember that in olden times the celebrations honouring Athena drew just as many people.

Due to construction work that has closed off traffic on large sections of Odós Dionissíou Areopagítou, you must make a detour on Odós Kalispéri if you are coming from Sýndagma or Pláka. A huge project is underway to turn the Acropolis and its surroundings into an **archaeological park**, a pedestrian space incorporating the Stadium (to the east) and including the collections from the Acropolis Museum, which is currently closed. The area will be served by the future Makrigiáni metro station, which is also under construction. Large signs placed at each end of Odós Dionissíou Areopagítou give an idea of the project, which is scheduled to be finished for the Olympic Games.

As you walk towards the Acropolis, take a short detour first up to the **Areopagos** (Ários Págos) (Plan III, A3), a wide rocky promontory overlooking the Agora (*shortly before the entrance to the Acropolis, on the right alongside the Perípatos*). A bronze plaque at the foot of the boulder shows the way up via steps carved out of the rock (*be careful as the steps are rather steep and slippery*) and recalls that St Paul passed this way. It affords a splendid **view** of the site and the huge grey expanse of the city fading into the distant haze. The debris scattered on the ground spoils the ambience

The Athens Acropolis, the dawn of Western civilisation

a bit, but the lofty silhouette of the Acropolis makes you quickly forget the turpitude of modern life. Dedicated to Ares (the god of war), this hill (*págos*) gave its name to the oldest Council of Athens, the Areopagos, which was both a judicial tribunal and a political council at first and was later reduced to preserving customs and laws. It is said that the principle of a person's right to defence first arose within this assembly, and also that **St Paul** preached about the 'unknown god' here, converting one of its members, Dionysius, the future **St Dionysius the Areopagite** who was to become the first bishop of Athens.

A site to match the mightiest city in Greece

The Athens Acropolis, whose name means 'the city summit' (Lycabettos is higher, but it was outside the city limits at the time) is a huge stone vessel that seems to float above the plain, occupying an exceptional site. Its flat summit is nearly 300m long by 156m at its widest, forming a vast 3ha esplanade that overlooks the lower city from a height of 115m. It was an ideal site for the Acropolis of the most powerful city in Ancient Greece.

Before viewing the monuments, take time to contemplate the fabulous **panorama★★**. To the south-west (*with your back to the Parthenon*) it goes all the way to the **Saronic Gulf** (when the sky is clear enough), while to the south-east, to the north-east and to the north you can see, successively, **Mounts Hymettus (Imittós)**, **Pentelikon (Pentéli)** and **Parnes (Párnitha)**; not to mention **Filopápos Hill** (Plan II, B4) quite nearby (to the south-west), crowned with the monument of the same name.

Inside the **ramparts** (which date mainly from the 5C BC), a few vestiges go back to the Mycenaean Period (1400-1125 BC) but most of the visible monuments are from the great **Age of Pericles** (5C BC) of which they are a brilliant illustration. Admittedly, the air pollution, the earthquake in 1981 and clumsy measures taken in the past have altered their beauty and made it necessary to protect the stone and replace the remaining sculptures (*exhibited in the Acropolis Museum*) with copies. But the site has preserved all of its majesty, and indeed the inside of the Parthenon has been restored with Pentelic marble identical to the original.

Athens

In the footsteps of the Panathenaea

Now you can follow the path taken by the **Panathenaea** processions during which people went to the Acropolis to offer Athena the *peplos*, a tunic woven by young Athenian women. The ceremony, which took place every four years, heralded the end of a lavish festival of musical, athletic and equestrian contests dedicated to the city's tutelary goddess.

After a climb in the shade of the olive and pine trees, the procession reached the Propylaea via a series of ramps. The current path takes the little **Roman way** on the side overlooking on the left the pedestal of the **Agrippa Monument**★, an edifice that supported the statue of the Emperor Augustus' son-in-law, raised up on a bronze chariot (178 BC). At its base, a projecting platform affords a fine **view**★ of the surrounding area.

At the foot of the ramparts is an imposing wall topped by the slender columns of the Temple of Athena Nike. Opposite you are the steps of the Propylaea, while behind you lie the remains of the **Beulé Gate**★ (from the name of its discoverer, archaeologist **Ernest Beulé**), unearthed in 1852-53 under the Turkish bastion. Dating from the early 3C AD, this edifice with its two adjoining towers was probably built to reinforce the Acropolis' defences.

The Propylaea★★

Now walk up the marble steps of the Propylaea, protected by wooden planks. This monumental entrance was equal to the grandeur of Pericles' sumptuous acropolis. After the Parthenon had been completed (a wide opening was needed to let the slabs of marble through as it was being built), the architect **Mnesikles** got to work on the Propylaea in 437 BC. He was intent on finding a harmonious solution to the problems posed by differences in level while still facilitating the passage of the Panathenaea. Devoid of any sculpted decoration, the complex includes a central body flanked by two asymmetrical wings, wide pavilions which the bishops and dukes of Athens made into their residence from the 12C to the 15C.

The **central part**, a huge rectangle built in the form of a staircase, was preceded by a **portico** of which six Doric columns remain. Beyond that lay the **vestibule**, framed by two lateral naves separated by six Ionic columns. The left wing, or **Pinakotheke**, the largest, was first a banquet hall, then a painting gallery (thus its name). The much smaller **right wing** seems to have been built above all to re-establish a sense of symmetry, yet without detracting from the Temple of Athena Nike close by. At the end of the vestibule were **five doors**, the wider middle one being used by the Panathenaea procession. These doors led to a last portico analogous to the one at the (partly preserved) entrance, giving onto the Acropolis area.

Once past the Propylaea, you emerge onto the vast plateau of the **temenos**, and are immediately drawn towards the lofty silhouette of the Parthenon standing imposingly on the right. But in the days of Pericles, your gaze would have landed first of all on the colossal **statue of Athena Promachos**, an impressive 9m-high bronze female warrior standing in its centre. Created by Phidias, it commemorated the Athenian victories over the Persians.

The Parthenon★★★

The inside and immediate surroundings of the temple are not accessible. Nowadays visitors turn first of all to the Parthenon. And the majesty of this vision is no accident. Raised slightly and at an angle to the axis of the Propylaea, the temple offers you its best profile. But imagine this imposing façade with red, yellow and blue stripes! Indeed, buildings and statues were entirely painted; and the immaculate white marble to which the Renaissance and its taste for the ancient world accustomed us is only due to the wear and tear of time. Commissioned by Pericles, this temple to the glory of the goddess and her city was designed by the architect **Ictinus** under the direction of **Phidias**, who also supervised the making of the sculpted decorations. This jewel of Doric architecture – its yardstick, one could say – was apparently considered a masterpiece as soon as it was completed.

While the marble on the roof fell in the fire of 267, the monument preserved its columns, walls, roof and most of its internal spaces... until the Acropolis was bombarded by the Venetians in September 1687. Thus, the building was nearly intact when it was turned into a Byzantine church (the first one in the 6C). Afterwards, it became a cathedral under Frankish rule, then a mosque with a minaret adjoining the temple's south-west corner (some remains are still visible). At that time a large part of its sculpted decoration remained, until **Lord Elgin**, the British ambassador to Constantinople, removed the friezes between 1801 and 1803. The long job of restoration began as early as 1834, marked in particular by the difficult process of raising the columns, known as 'anastylosis', carried out by Greek archaeologists.

Built in Pentelic marble, the Parthenon stands on a thick **stylobate** (upper layer of the base), which itself lies on a limestone foundation. Almost none of the **sculptures**, **bas-reliefs** and **statues** that decorated the temple are visible on the site. You must go to the British Museum (whom Greece has been asking to return the friezes for years), to the Louvre and, closer by, to the Acropolis Interpretation Centre (*temporarily closed*), which has casts of nearly all of the building's statues. Use your imagination to reconstruct the Parthenon with the colours, bas-reliefs and gold that made it so beautiful.

Polychrome sculptures stood out against a blue background on the **pediments**. Phidias' genius consisted in using this highly constraining triangular space to his

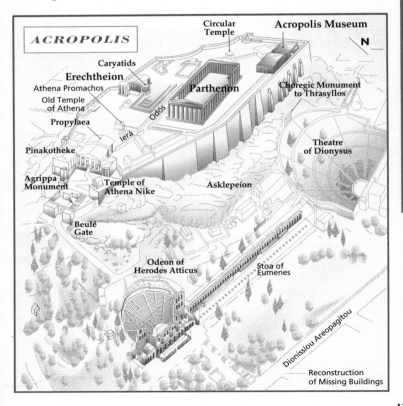

Athens

133

Phidias' secrets

Trying to attain visual perfection in the temple, Phidias strove to correct the optical illusions through a subtle use of lines. In choosing a peristyle with forty-six 10.43m-high columns (8 per façade, 17 for each side) he ensured the sanctuary a perfect balance between width and length. The shafts tapering upwards (1.90m in diameter at the base and 1.45m at the capitals) and their slightly inward curve, as well as the slight reinforcement of the corner columns and the imperceptible convexity of the horizontal elements, also contribute to the building's great harmony. Without these precautions the columns would indeed seem wider at the top than at the bottom, the corner columns would look less robust and the entablature would appear to be curved slightly inwards.

advantage: the figures are lying down, sitting, leaning or standing upright according to need. Besides the rare vestiges that remain, we know these works from the 200 drawings which the **Marquis de Nointel** had done in 1674.

In far better condition, the **frieze***** was composed of 92 metopes (slabs sculpted in relief) between each triglyph on a red background featuring mythological scenes. Lastly, the **architrave** supported golden shields offered by Alexander the Great.

One went **inside** (*access is forbidden, but it is visible through the colonnade*) through a 10m-high door cut out of the **eastern portico**. This gave onto the pronaos, a vestibule preceding the holy of holies (*naos*) containing the **chryselephantine statue of Athena**, a huge 12m-high sculpture in gold and ivory (over a wood and marble frame) rising all the way up to the ceiling. A two-storey colonnade on each side marked the limits of the central space, complemented by an ambulatory. Behind this, the Parthenon itself housed the **treasury** of the Delian League led by Athens; behind the building you can still see the four Ionic columns that supported the ceiling. The famous **frieze of the Panathenaea** (preserved in part in Paris and in London) depicting the sacred procession ran along the outside wall of the *naos*, under the peristyle, forming a superb band of sculpture nearly 160m long.

As you cross the esplanade towards the Erechtheion, take a look (*on the right*) at the foundations of two temples dedicated to Athena built in the 6C and 5C BC. The first is known as the **Hecatonpedon** ('the Temple of 100 Feet') and the second as the **Old Parthenon**.

The Erechtheion***

Walking along the northern façade of the Parthenon, the procession then reached the Erechtheion, another jewel of the Acropolis. Finished in 406 BC, this masterpiece of Ionic art successively housed a church, a palace, a harem and a powder magazine! Its restoration was begun in the 19C and completed in 1987.

Walk around the temple on the right in order to understand the way it was laid out and made more complex by the presence of several shrines inside, the largest of them dedicated respectively to **Athena**, to **Poseidon** and to **Erechtheos** and **Cecrops**, the two legendary kings of Athens.

In answer to the martial colonnade of the Parthenon, the famous porch of the korai or **Porch of the Caryatids***** responds with the grace and lightness of its six 2m-high statues of young women (*the originals are preserved in the Acropolis Museum*). The sensual bend in their knees and their nonchalant elegance are underscored by the parallel folds of their tunics evoking the fluting on the columns they replace. On the right, the six Ionic columns of the **eastern portico*** open onto the sanctuary containing the site's oldest **statue of Athena**, made of olive wood. The **western façade** was modified during the Roman era. An **olive tree** in the adjacent courtyard recalls the place where people came to worship the sacred tree of Athena (which explains why there is no roof).

This side of the Acropolis is where the <u>Mycenaean settlement</u> lay (1400-1125 BC), its rare vestiges of stone blocks scattered here and there around the Erechtheion. Continuing towards the eastern tip of the hill at its highest point, one discovers the remains of a **sanctuary dedicated to Zeus Polieus**. The Romans later built a **circular temple** next to it dedicated to Rome and Augustus, which can be picked out by its few standing columns and accompanying cypress trees.

The tip forms a slight promontory from which there is a **view★★** over the roofs of Pláka. By turning around you can see the back of the Parthenon *(watch out for the wind, which is sometimes very strong here)*. It is particularly impressive when Athens is glowing in the sunset.

The Acropolis Museum★★★

Cleverly hidden in a hollow, this richly endowed museum contains mainly sculptures and objects from the monuments and excavations on the site, in particular from its early buildings. On display in **Rooms 1 and 2** are **Archaic works★★** from the 7C and 6C BC, including fragments of **pediments★** in tufa which still show blue and red traces of their original colours. The Labours of Heracles, including his struggle with the Triton, are the subject of several sculptures. Of particular interest is the famous **Moscophoros★★★** or Calf Carrier *(Room 2)*, unquestionably one of the most graceful statues from the Archaic Period.

Room 3 boasts a stunning sculpture of a **bull★** being attacked by two lions, while **Room 4** has a prestigious **collection of korai★★**, as well as the **Rampin Horseman★**, another Archaic statue with a legendary smile.

Room 5 contains a **group of sculptures★** from the old Temple of Athena featuring a remarkable gigantomachia (the Battle between the Olympian Gods and the Giants). Not to be missed in **Room 6**: the fine votive relief of **Athena mourning★★** (or 'pensive'), as well as the **Fair Head★★** of a young man, the **Kritios Boy** and the beautiful **Euthydikos kore★★**.

Rooms 7 and 8 contain casts of **sculptures★★** from the Parthenon and the Temple of Athena Nike, as well as the **Caryatids★★★** from the Erechtheion – the real ones! – protected in glass cases. In the last room there is a **bust of Alexander the Great★**, a **statue of Procne★** by a student of Phidias, and a wonderful **head of a philosopher★**.

On leaving the museum walk along the southern edge of the hill for a **view★** over the Theatre of Dionysus and, further to the left, of the Temple of Zeus and the Stadium. The striking feature at the south-west tip of the temenos is the elegant **Temple of Athena Nike★** ('Victorious'). The building and surrounding area are closed for restoration, so you will have to contemplate its lovely Ionic façade completed in 410 BC from afar. It juts out like a watchtower in front of the Propylaea. From this rocky outcrop, from which you can see the coast, old **Aegeus** is said to have thrown himself into the sea that now bears his name. Indeed, he thought his son **Theseus** was dead when he saw a black sail – instead of a white one – hoisted on the mast of the ship bringing him home from Crete after having defeated the Minotaur. Since the temple is out of bounds, enjoy the **view★★** overlooking the amphitheatre of the **Odeon of Herodes Atticus★★** (Plan III, B4) *(only open during musical performances)*.

Around the Acropolis★★ (Plan III, C4)

The Theatre of Dionysus★ (Dioníssou Théatrou)

Access (hidden behind a fence): from Odós Dionissiou Areopagitou, 10m after the Makrigiáni bus stop at the top of the steps. 8am-6.30pm. Entrance fee. To conclude (or precede) your exploration of the Acropolis, you may want to see the oldest theatre from Antiquity. It was also the most prestigious, because this is where the masterpieces from the classical repertory – by **Aeschylus**, **Sophocles**, **Euripides** and **Aristophanes** – were all staged in the 5C BC.

Born in the Athens Agora, **tragedy** was originally staged in simple wooden theatres before being moved in the 6C BC to this well-chosen site. Indeed, the place already possessed a sanctuary dedicated to **Dionysus Eleutherios**, tutelary god of the dramatic arts, as the Dionysiac festivals included choruses, mime and dance. This basic set-up, probably a simple earthen embankment, was replaced by a real theatre with wooden tiers in the following century. While retaining the same structure and dimensions, the stone theatre dates from the time of **Lycurgus** (4C BC) and owes its current form to the Romans.

Only a few vestiges remain – from the wall and colonnades – of the vast **portico** that stood in front of the entrance to the theatre. Through their proportions, the tiers★ create a feeling of both space and intimacy. Moreover the perfect shape of the cavea, built against the rock face of the Acropolis, ensured ideal **acoustics**. It could accommodate nearly 17 000 spectators (compared to 12 000 in Epidaurus in the Peloponnese), each of whom brought his own cushion.

Built under the reign of Nero (1C), the sculptures on the frieze★ decorating the proskenion evoke the myth of Dionysus. Note the bearded Silenus, crouching in the position of Atlas, the only character whose head is intact. Grouped around the altar dedicated to Dionysus, the chorus stood in the middle of a **lozenge** formed by the marble paving. In the first row, slightly above the seats reserved for dignitaries, is the **seat** of the high priest of Dionysus. High on top of the tiers, two Corinthian columns mark the site of the **choregic monument to Thrasyllos** along with other honorific structures.

There is a splendid **view★** from on top of the tiers over the columns of the Temple of Olympian Zeus and the Stadium, below to the left. Closer by to the left of the amphitheatre lie the ruins of the **Odeon of Pericles**, mainly used for rehearsals and music competitions.

The sanctuary of Asklepios (Asklepeíon)

Adjacent to the theatre, the rather disorderly ruins of this sanctuary dedicated to **Asklepios** (the god of medicine) are not exactly inspiring; but the walk through the cypress trees has a certain charm to it. From the upper part of the theatre, follow the path along the huge wall of the **portico of Eumenes**. Built in the mid-2C by Eumenes II, King of Pergamon, this monumental stoa was 163m long on one floor. You then reach (*on your right*) the terrace with the ruins of the **Asklepeíon**, which included two sanctuaries from different eras. At the foot of the rock face stand the remains of the first **portico**, a 50m-long Doric gallery (4C BC) where patients slept as they waited to have a dream in which the god would reveal what form of therapy they should follow. Adjoining the gallery, a **tholos** (circular temple) housed the sacred spring where patients came to purify themselves. Excavations have also unearthed fragments of a **basilica** devoted to Saints Cosmas and Damian, two Christian doctors of Arab origin – a sign that, while replacing the old gods, the new religion preserved the sanctuary's medical vocation. Further on are the ruins of an **Ionic portico** (circa 420 BC).

Have a rest in the shady woods surrounding Filopápos Hill, or enjoy a gastronomic meal at the famed Dionysus restaurant at the foot of the hill – a real institution where you can taste the most refined dishes in Greek cuisine.

On the hill of the Muses★ (Mousseíon or Lófos Filopápou) (Plan II, B4)

A wide paved path leads through the trees to the foot of the Mousseíon, the hill dedicated to the muses. This piece of greenery in the heart of Athens is among the most pleasant sites in the city. After the pretty **Ágios Dimítrios Loumbardiáris** Chapel, a path (*on your right*) follows along the line of the **wall of Themistocles** (built around Athens in 460-457 BC) and winds through the pine trees to the summit past a series of former **troglodyte cave-dwellings**, one of which was held to be **Socrates' prison** according to a fanciful tradition. Crowned by the **Filopápos monument★★**

(114-116 AD), from which the hill derives its name, the summit affords a magnificent **view**★★ of the Acropolis, particularly at sunset. The monument, a giant stele, contained the remains of a prince of Syrian origin who became a Roman consul, as well as a citizen and benefactor of Athens. Its striking 10m-high **concave façade**★ preceded a funerary chamber containing the sarcophagus. The deceased is shown standing in a quadriga on the bas-relief.

Walking back down, take the last path on the left. It leads to the **Pnyx** (Pníka) (Plan II, B3), literally 'the place where people are squashed together', a natural amphitheatre where the **Assembly of the People** was held from the 6C to the 4C BC. During these democratic meetings, citizens discussed laws being proposed, and each man had the right to speak once. Attendance was so low by the 4C that the constabulary had to force people to go in order to reach the quorum of 5 000! On summer evenings the Acropolis **son et lumière** show is held here *(see page 163)*.

Pláka★★ (Plan III)
Allow a whole day

You will love Pláka from your first step inside this maze of colourful, sometimes quiet and sometimes hectic streets dotted with churches, busy squares and autumnal-coloured houses. This neighbourhood with a provincial feel blends many eras, from Antiquity to the Ottomans. Its many vestiges bring alive the story of Greece, transporting you to a village in the Cyclades or to Arcadia. In short, this is the best place in the city to go for a stroll.

To begin your explorations, start with the **Church of Sotíra Lykodímou**★ (E3)(*on the corner of Odós Filelínon and Odós Souri*), the largest medieval building in Athens (11C). Partly damaged during the War of Independence, this former abbey-church was acquired by Czar Nicholas I who offered to have it restored for the Russian community in Athens. It is decorated with **frescoes** by the German painter Thiersch. From Odós Filelínon head into the heart of Pláka on Kidathinéon, a pedestrian street. Tall cypress trees herald the **Church of Sotíra tou Kotáki** (D3) (*on your right*), also known as **Agía Sofía**. Built in the 11C-12C, it has lost its beautiful brick face, which is covered over with an awful roughcast added when it was restored in 1908. But the admirable dome has remained intact.

Just opposite it is the **Museum of Greek Folk Art**★★ (D3) (*10am-2pm; closed on Monday; entrance fee*) which contains a magnificent collection ranging from the mid-17C to the present. It features all of the country's traditions, including Balkan, Mediterranean and Oriental influences. The ground floor has a collection of **embroidery**★ often of Byzantine inspiration from the Dodecanese, Epirus, Thrace, Crete and Skíros. The mezzanine is devoted among other things to works in wood, metal and ceramics, as well as to the famous shadow theatre, **Karaghiózis** *(see page 73)*. In addition to a room devoted to temporary exhibitions, the 1st floor contains paintings by the naive painter **Theóphilos Hatzimichaíl** (1868-1934). In his works, this representative of popular culture brings together figures such as Alexander the Great and Kolokotrónis, a hero from the War of Independence. The 2nd floor has a display of **silver and gold objects**, and the upper floor features textiles (costumes, weaving) and stone sculptures.

Filomoússou Eterías★ (D3), a pleasantly shady square, is a Mecca for gastronomic tourists with its countless restaurants in neo-Classical buildings. At rush hour (ie 1pm and 8pm) a tout holding menus in several languages is sent out by each establishment in the hope of enticing passers-by to stop off at its several-metre-long territory; then it is the turn of his colleague from the neighbouring taverna...

Follow Odós Farmáki (*on the left*) to the apse of **Agía Ekateríni**★ (D3) (11C-12C), one of Athens' most beautiful Byzantine churches, whose interior has just been renovated. Its square, shaded by tall palm trees, is distinctly lower than the rest of the district; at its far end are some Roman remains sunk almost 2m below the present-day street level — proof of the dynamism of urban development in this part of the city.

Only a few metres away stands the **Lysicrates monument**★ (D3) (erected in 334 BC), the sole survivor among the choregic monuments that dotted the route connecting the Theatre of Dionysus and the Agora. Standing at the end of Odós Tripódon – a name evoking the bronze tripods offered to winners of the Dionysiac contests, which they then displayed all along the way – this structure was restored by the French School of Archaeology in Athens in 1845 and used to be known as the **Lantern of Demosthenes**. Above its Corinthian columns is a frieze in which Dionysus can be seen transforming pirates into dolphins, presumed to be the subject of the drama contest won by Lysicrates.

Enjoy lunch or a short break here and cool off in the delicious shade of the large tree.

Upper Pláka: Anafiótika★★ (Plan III, C3)

Lined with pretty ochre-coloured houses, the little street of **Odós Epimenídi**★ (D4) takes you into a part of Pláka far from the madding crowd that has remained intact and quiet *(when you reach Thrassílou, the continuation of Strátonos, turn right towards Anafiótika)*. On your left, olive trees stretch out to the foot of the Acropolis cliffs crowned with its powerful fortifications, while far off to the right is the silhouette of Mt Lycabettos. In 1834, a law forbade all construction around the Acropolis. Despite this, the inhabitants of the island of **Anáfi** (east of Santoríni), who had taken refuge in Athens at the beginning of the War of Independence, settled on the side of the sacred hill, giving Athens a genuine village with low-lying houses. Later growth in Pláka spread to this world apart without penetrating inside it.

Stroll through this maze of narrow alleys fragrant with the sweet scent of ripe figs. Turn left, then left again after a set of stairs, to climb up to the highest houses in the 'village', where there is a beautiful **view**★ of Athens, particularly at sundown.

Disappearing into its maze of lanes, where the only creatures you will run into are napping cats (or lost visitors!), you will eventually find your way back to Odós Pritaníou by the Church of **Ági Anárgiri Kolokinthí**★ (C3) (17C) perched just above the Psaras restaurant.

The Aérides Quarter★ (Plan III)

If you liked the Anafiótika quarter, then you ought to also enjoy **Odós Thólou**★ (C3) and **Odós Aretoússas**★ (C3) *(turn left onto Pritaníou)*. They delimit one of the most beautiful parts of Pláka, full of houses from the late 19C. However, they were badly damaged by the earthquake of 15 September 1999, and most of them are awaiting restoration.

At the beginning of Odós Thólou, first you will pass on your left the **Old University**★ (1833) or **Kléanthis House** (C3), recognisable by its rust-coloured rendering. Designed by the architect of the same name, it housed the first university of the young Greek government from 1837 to 1842.

The **Kanelópoulos Museum**★★ *(8.30am-3pm; closed on Monday; entrance fee)*, created to preserve the treasures bequeathed to the State in 1976 by collectors Pavlos and Alexandra Kanelópoulos, stands at the corner of Odós Aretoússa and Odós Panós in a superb neo-Classical house built in 1884. It contains all kinds of works of art and archaeology – Cycladic, Minoan and Mycenaean clay figurines, Coptic textiles, Byzantine and post-Byzantine icons and funerary masks from Faiyum, bronzes and jewellery – from the Hellenic peninsula and archipelago, Asia Minor and the Middle East. The choice of objects was intended by the collectors to show the continuity and evolution in Greek art in time and space.

Have a break at the **Neféli café** *(at the end of Odós Aretoússa)* or at one of the tables at the **Diskoúron café**, tucked away at the end of little Odós Mitróou. These establishments on the edge of the Agora afford a beautiful **view**★★ of Athens.

A few metres away *(via Odós Andokídou)* stands the **Tower of the Winds**★★ (C2), a strange octagonal building each side of which features an *aéride*, or winged figure, representing one of the eight winds that blow in Athens. Boreas, the cold north wind, is shown in the form of a bearded man (*facing Odós Eólou*), while flowers are blown from the cloak of gentle Zephyr on the western face. These **Aérides** gave their name to the district around the Roman Forum between Pláka and Monastiráki. Built to the east of the Roman Forum under the reign of Julius Caesar (1C BC), the tower served a double purpose: first it sported a weathervane indicating the direction of the wind, then it had a hydraulic clock hidden inside that was driven by the **Klepsidra spring** on the north slope of the Acropolis hill. Since then, the name clepsydra has designated this type of water clock device.

Music-lovers may want to pay a brief visit to the nearby little **Museum of Music**★ (C2) (*10am-2pm, Wednesday: 12pm-6pm; closed on Monday; free admission*). Housed in a building dating from 1842, it has close to 1 200 folk music instruments from the 18C to the present, collected by musicologist Fívos Anoyanákis. Headphones (*commentary in Greek and in English*) placed in front of each case explain the various types of Greek instruments, from the bouzoúki to the sandoúri, as well as the cymbals and spoons. The museum also has a bookshop and a pretty garden (where concerts are held).

The **Plátanos taverna**, one of the most pleasant in Pláka with its shady terrace, awaits you only a few steps away on Odós Diogénous.

The flattened dome and columned porch behind the Tower of the Winds is the **Fetiye Djami Mosque**★★ (C2) (15C), or Victory Mosque (referring to Mehmet the Conqueror's taking of Constantinople), more prosaically nicknamed Djami tou Staropazarou, the 'wheat market mosque', by locals.

It adjoins the **Roman Forum**★ (B2) (*8.30am-3pm; closed on Monday; entrance fee*), a wide quadrilateral where the city's commercial activity was concentrated, and which the Turks turned into a cereal market. It stretched all the way to the colossal **Gate of Athena Archegetis**★★ (*at the other end of the site, facing Odós Pikílis*), and was framed by a **portico** dating from the 1C BC, the remains of which are still visible. Odós Dexípou provides a fine view over **Hadrian's Library** (*not open to the public*), a vast complex built in 131-32 AD. A part of the wall is still standing (*on the right, in Odós Eólou*), which formed the actual library wing and reading rooms. To the left, at the other end of the site, the west wall has preserved a fine group of columns. Have a look at the **frescoes**★ across the street in the **Taxiárhes Church**★ (B2) ('of the Archangels'), a building from the 11C-12C that was completely rebuilt in 1852. Nearby are the **wicker merchants** whose cluttered stalls overflow with treasures: how about a pair of bulrush slippers or a sumptuous flowerpot-holder made in China?

Monastiráki★, the old Turkish bazaar (Plan III)

Walk down Odós Áeros, a traditional hangout for the last surviving hippies and others who feel nostalgic for those days. The whole range of seventies fashions – genuine hippie jewellery, embroidered purple tunics, military surplus accessories – stretches all the way to Platía Monastiráki a bit further up.

Dzistaráki Mosque★ (B2) (1759) contains a rich **ceramics collection**★ (*9am-2.30pm; closed on Tuesday; entrance fee except on Sunday*) from the Museum of Greek Folk Art. In addition to some beautiful decorative works by well-known ceramicists, a variety of early 20C pieces from Greek and Cypriot workshops are cleverly displayed so as to highlight the building's architecture, which is worth a visit in itself. Right next to it is Platía Monastiráki, the heart of the former Turkish quarter, which has unfortunately been encumbered with barriers while work is being done on the metro. On the right however you can see the fine **tower**★ of the **Church of Panagía Pandánassa**★ (C1). Nicknamed *Monastiráki*, the 'little monastery', it gave its name to the local bazaar which stretched all the way to the Roman Forum in Ottoman times. The **flea market**★★ (B1), a dense maze of alleyways, takes up all the space between Odós Adrianoú and Odós Ermoú. Formerly the domain of metalworkers,

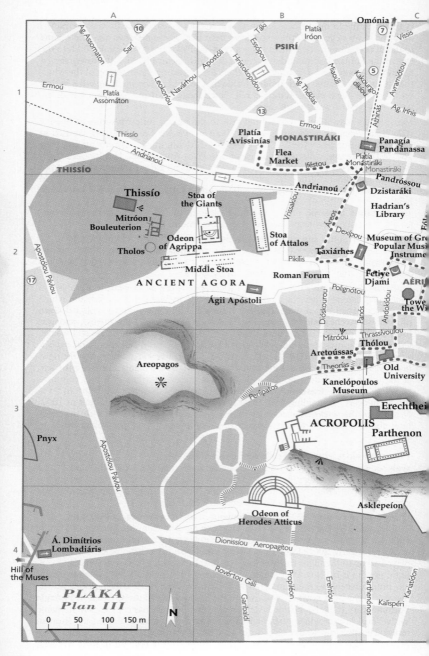

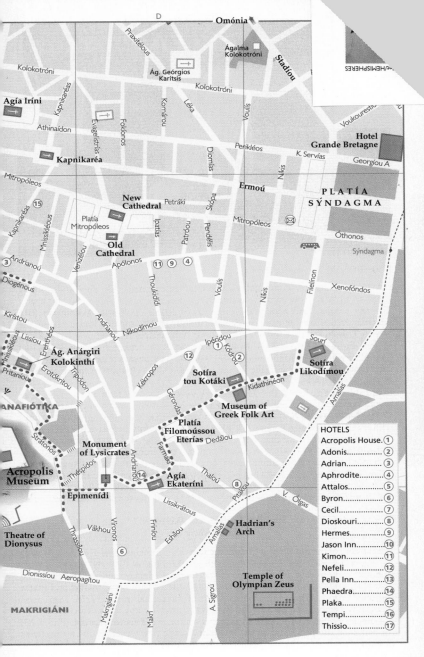

Praxitélous

Ágalma
Kolokotróni

Stadíou

Kolokotróni

Ág. Geórgios
Karítsis

Kolokotróni

Kapnikaréas

Agía Iríni

Komárou

Léka

Periklées

Voukourestíou

Athinaídon

Evangelistrías

Fokíonos

Diomías

Hotel
Grande Bretagne

K. Servías

Georgíou A

Kapnikaréa

Nikis

Mitropóleos

Ermoú

PLATÍA
SÝNDAGMA

New
Cathedral

Petráki

Ýpsros

Kapnikaréas

15

Mnisikléous

Platía
Mitropóleos

Ipatías

Mitropóleos

Óthonos

Venizélou

Old
Cathedral

Patróou

Pendélis

Syndagma

Andrianoú

3

Apólonos

11 9 4

Thoukidídi

Voulís

Nikis

Filelínon

Xenofóndos

Diogénous

Kirístou

Andrianoú

Nikodímou

Mnisikléous Lissíou

Ipérdou

1

Kódrou

Souri

Erehthéos

Ág. Anárgiri
Kolokinthí

Erotókrítou

Tripódon

Kékropos

12

Kódrou

2

Sotíra tou Kotáki

Sotíra
Likodímou

Pritaníou

ANAFIÓTIKA

Stratonos

Gérondas

Kidathinéon

Amalías

Museum of
Greek Folk Art

Platía
Filomoússou
Eterías

Dedálou

Monument
of Lysicrates

Thespídos

Farmáki

Thaloú

Acropolis
Museum

Andrianoú

14

Agía
Ekateríni

8

Epimenídi

Lissikrátous

V. Ólgas

Theatre of
Dionysus

Vákhou

Vironos

Frýnou

Eshílou

Amalías

Pittakou

Hadrian's
Arch

6

Dionissíou Aeropagítou

Thrassílou

MAKRIGIÁNI

Makrigiáni

Miari

A. Sígou

Temple of
Olympian Zeus

Monastiráki, the flea market district

Odós Iféstou has been converted into more tourist-oriented trade: shoe and clothing shops of all kinds now compete with antique dealers and souvenir shops for space. The real second-hand goods dealers are to be found on **Platía Avissinías**★ (B1), which is particularly animated on Sunday mornings. The surrounding streets all the way to **Thissío** station echo with the sounds of languages from all over Central and Eastern Europe. This is where to find that pair of binoculars from the Red Army (complete with star, hammer and sickle) that you have always dreamed of. Then you can enjoy a break at one of the terrace cafés on Odós Adrianoú set up at the edge of the railway tracks.

If you still haven't found 'the' gift you were looking for after taking this route, there is one radical solution left: go back to Platía Monastiráki and plunge into narrow **Odós Pandróssou**★ (C2). This market, so touristy that it is amusing, features shops with jewellery, clothing, ceramics, leather and the most kitschy souvenirs packed one next to the other. And if that isn't enough, walk around Hadrian's Library and take **Odós Adrianoú**★ (B2) which crosses the entire Pláka from Platía Monastiráki to Agía Ekateríni Church. This beautiful paved street is also lined with a host of tourist shops selling natural sponges, leather goods (although the classic sandals from the 1970s are increasingly giving way to big sports name brands), and piles of hideous T-shirts, not to mention reproductions of various objects and masterpieces from Antiquity.

In the heart of Athens★★
Allow a whole day

Use the cool of the morning to explore the two other principal sites of ancient Athens: the Agora and Keramikós Cemetery, both as charming as they are rich in history. Continue your voyage back in time at the **Central Market** and the old shopping district around Odós Athínas and Odós Eólou between the central market and **Platía Omónia** (Plan II, C2), which was the heart of the capital in the 1930s. Don't miss the nearby National Archaeological Museum, a must for any visitor to Greece.

For lunch or a refreshing break, head for the attractive **Thissío quarter** (Plan II, B3) (in particular the pedestrian street, Iraklídon), while in the evening the lively streets of **Psirí** (Plan II, B2) offer the perfect setting for a delicious dinner.

The Agora★★ (Plan III, A2-B2)

There are three ways to reach the Agora: at the end of Odós Polignótou (at the far end of the Roman Forum), at the bottom of Odós Adrianoú (in Monastiráki) and via Odós Apostólou Pávlou. 8am-3pm; closed on Monday. Entrance fee (the ticket is also valid for the museum). Allow 2hr.

Take time to walk around this city centre garden of stone, the heart of ancient Athens. It has been excavated since the 1930s by the **American School of Archaeology**, which is also responsible for replanting the area in order to beautify it and to evoke the ancient city's vegetation. At first glance, however, the place looks more like a chaotic maze of ruins; but the two **plans** – one at the Odós Adrianoú entrance and the other on the terrace in front of the façade of the Hephaisteion – give a good overall idea of the layout *(brochures are available at the ticket office)*.

The Agora was the focal point of life in the city, and the citizens of Athens spent a great deal of time here. Markets were held here, as well as certain religious festivals with their processions and theatrical or athletic contests. It was here, too, that citizens came to discuss public affairs and to listen to orators in the shade of the *stoas*, the long porticoes sheltering shops and administrative offices.

While the Agora was first laid out in the 6C BC, it did not take on its final form until the 2C BC. Bounded by various administrative buildings, temples and porticoes, it spread out over 2.5ha and was crossed diagonally by the **Panathenaic Way**. An open space was preserved in the centre, where, starting with Augustus, the Romans built temples to the glory of Rome as well as a monumental odeon.

Overlooking the ruins, the lofty façade of the **Theseion**★★★ (Thissío or Hephaisteion) *(100m from the entrance on Odós Apostólou Pávlou)* immediately catches your attention. Perched on a 65m-high mound, it is the best starting point for exploring the site and affords a striking **view**★ of the Acropolis. Dedicated to the worship of Athena and her brother **Hephaestus**, the god of smiths and metalworkers – of which there were many in the neighbouring area at the time *(now clustered around Odós Ermoú)* – this majestic Doric temple (449-444 BC) is one of the best preserved in the Greek world. While the **sculptures** on its two pediments have completely disappeared (there are a few fragments in the museum), it has kept the highly eroded decorative **motifs**★ from its metopes and outer frieze in Parian marble, evoking the adventures of Heracles and Theseus. Hence the old nickname Thissío (or Theseíon) given to the building and the nearby district. One rare feature was the **garden** that embellished the area around the sanctuary, scented with potted pomegranates, myrtle trees and vines. Another was the east portico, or pronaos, which has preserved its **coffered marble ceiling**★.

At the foot of the mound *(on the right)* stood the **tholos**, a circular building that housed the **Council of the Prytaneis**, a kind of executive branch of Athenian democracy, as well as the standard weights and measures. The **Council of Five Hundred**, the Assembly of Athens, was held in the nearby **bouleuterion**, while the **Metróon**, a temple to the Mother of the gods, was where state archives were kept. The statues in the centre of the esplanade indicate the site of the **Stoa of the Giants** that preceded the **Odeon of Agrippa**, a 1 000-seat performance hall. The rows of columns behind it give an idea of the size of the **Middle Stoa**. Don't miss the **frescoes**★ (the ones in the dome are from the 18C) in the **Church of Ágii Apóstoli**★ (the Holy Apostles) built in the late 10C and now fortunately rid of its 19C modifications.

Now imagine that you are a citizen of ancient Athens and stroll through the huge **Stoa of Attalos**★ (125-122 BC), a superb two-storey gallery that is 116m long by 20m wide. Offered to the city by Attalos III, King of Pergamon, it was reconstructed in 1956 by the American School of Archaeology to house the findings from its excavations, its archives and the researchers' workshops. The 'public antiquities' in the **museum**★ are open to the public. They include voting tokens, tools designed for picking court juries, weights and measures, etc, a striking testimony to the political, judicial and commercial life of the young Athenian democracy. In addition to these objects, there are all the artefacts discovered in the tombs and dwellings – a wide variety of **ceramics** – as well as sculptures that decorated the Agora. On the 1st floor there is also an interesting **model**★ of the Agora and the Acropolis.

Close by the Agora lies the old **Gázi district** (Plan II, A2), where the first stages of industrialisation in the capital took place between the late 19C and the early 20C. The area owes its name to the public gaslights installed there in 1877. It is now the site of the **Technópolis M Hantzidákis**, a cultural park where concerts and exhibitions are held. Artists' workshops, and a few trendy restaurants and bars show that this is one of the city's up-and-coming areas.

Keramikós Cemetery★ (Plan II, B2)

Odós Ermoú 148. Thissío metro station. 8am-3pm, 8.30am on Sundays and holidays; closed on Monday. Entrance fee (same ticket for the museum). Less frequented than the Acropolis and the area around it, the site of the largest and oldest necropolis in Attica invites you to take a voyage in the shade of its olive and cypress trees beyond the Styx, the river of Hades; it features a whole range of Greek funerary art waiting to be explored.

Located outside the ancient city, the **necropolis** takes its name from the clay (*kéramos*) used in making the funerary vases and objects that were placed near the deceased. Beginning in the 6C, and depending on the fortune – and vanity – of the deceased, tombs were adorned with steles, stone vases, statues and even small chapels, structures that reached the height of luxury during the Age of Pericles.

To the left of the entrance is a **museum** containing some of the objects discovered on the site, while the path in front of you leads to the **Street of the Tombs**★ (*on the left*), lined with plots belonging to rich Athenian families. On the right, a path leads to the **Sacred Gate** (5C BC), built as an extension of the Sacred Way connecting Eleusis and Athens.

Parallel to the Sacred Way, the **Academy Road** led to the **Dipylon**★, the main gate to Athens. This 'double gate' which had two towers – one facing the city and the other facing out – was part of the fortified wall around the city.

A stone's throw from Keramikós, you can plunge into the narrow streets of the **Psirí district**★ (Plan III, B1) a colourful, charming and unpretentious area where old – often dilapidated – houses and soulless recent buildings rub shoulders. There are lots of little cafés tucked away, but the area is at its best in the evening, when you can stroll around before ending up on the terrace of a *mezedopolío* for a tasty dinner (on Platía Iróon, or Odós Táki). In short, this is the ideal place to come after a day of sightseeing. Psirí has become quite a trendy place in recent years. It has a wealth of cafés, bars and restaurants, and not a week goes by without a new establishment opening its doors here. On Sundays, the exotic scent of the Far East permeates the atmosphere with the **Spice Market**, where the capital's Asian communities (Indians and Filipinos, among others) come to do their shopping.

The Central Market District★ (Plan II)

Take **Odós Eólou**★ (C1-2-3), a long, narrow pedestrian street lined with textile and inexpensive clothing shops that leads to the old Athens market. In the past, when the city was still of a reasonable size, this maze of winding streets was where its commercial heart beat most strongly. While it may not be as prosperous as in former times, the activity here is still frenetic.

In passing, have a look at the **Aiolou** café (a very good one) across from the white church of **Agía Iríni**; it has preserved its metal-framed **awnings** typical of the neighbourhood. In the same style of architecture – though on a much larger scale – the **central market**★ (Kendrikí Agorá) (C2) (*closed on Sunday*) is lively, noisy and colourful, as well as being a place of strong smells (not recommended immediately after breakfast). In the wee hours of the morning, night owls gather in the little restaurants in the area to have some *patsá*, or tripe soup, the supreme remedy for stomachs that have been ill-treated by strong drink.

At night the area is also a hangout for homeless people of all kinds. It's a place of contrasts; by day, poverty gives way to speculators – large and small – on Odós Sofokléous where the **Stock Exchange** (krimatistírio) stands with its pompous Doric colonnade.

Further on, the large **Platía Ethnikís Andístassis** (National Resistance Square) (C2) contains the **Athens City Hall** *(on the left)* and the fine neo-Classical buildings of the National Bank of Greece *(on the right)*. A number of examples of architecture from the beginning of the century are hidden among the modern buildings in the centre of Athens. Of particular note are the 1920 **frescoes*** on the building on the corner of Athinás and Likoúrgou.

Platía Omónia (C2) ('Concord' Square), a hectic, deafening place that is almost always congested – and devoid of all charm – is only a stone's throw away. It is hard to believe that during the Belle Époque, with its palm trees, groves, luxury hotels (now dilapidated) and chic cafés, it was as elegant as Platía Sýndagma. The intense traffic, the deterioration of neighbouring areas and a whole series of building works have reduced it to a mere place of passage where people take the metro. It also has an unsavoury night-time reputation.

But this is the way to the National Archaeological Museum *(it is only 600m from Platía Omónia via Leofóros 28 Oktomvríou)*. On your way, have a look at the **façade*** of the **Polytechnic School** (C1) (1862-76, enlarged in the 1920s and 1950s) the work of the talented and prolific Kaftantzóglou.

National Archaeological Museum*** (Plan II, C1)

Open daily 8am-7pm, including Sundays and holidays, Mondays: 12.30pm-7pm. Entrance fee. This is a must! Devoted to ancient art, from the Neolithic to the Roman Period, the Athens museum is one of the richest in the world, boasting innumerable masterpieces from the major Greek archaeological sites, with the exception of Delphi, Olympia, Crete and some Macedonian sites. Constructed between 1866 and 1889, the neo-Classical building was gradually enlarged according to need. Theoretically,

The central market in the heart of the modern Agora

R. Manin/HOA QUI

Athens

works are presented **in chronological order** and based on the materials used and private collections, but on top of the restoration and modernisation work on certain rooms, the earthquake in September 1999 completely disrupted this well-ordered plan. Thus, the 1st floor (ceramics, frescoes and ceramics from Santoríni) has been closed to visitors for an indeterminate period, and a significant part of the museum has been subjected to temporary arrangements which the official **catalogue** is hard put to keep up with. Apart from the recently remodelled rooms, the central part of the building has no air conditioning. With the heat and crowds in summer, be prepared for high temperatures; and given the large number of pieces displayed in each room, all it takes is two or three groups on a guided tour to spoil your pleasure. So don't hesitate to upset the chronology and look at objects randomly; or go when there are the fewest people – at opening and closing times. Finally, signs (not always very legible) and descriptive panels are in Greek and English.

■ Begin your trip through the past in **Room 5**, devoted to the **Neolithic Period**, containing **terracotta figurines** *(nos 5894 and 5937)* from Sesklo (Thessaly): a male idol with disproportionate genitals suggesting that it is a fertility god, and a female idol holding a child in her arms. Note the fine **vase** *(no 5922)* from Dimini (Thessaly), which already shows highly developed decoration.

■ **Room 6** has **Cycladic antiquities★★** (3000-2000 BC), vases and marvellous **marble idols**. There are four exceptional pieces: the **goddess** of Amorgós *(no 3978)*, the **Amorgós head** *(no 3909)* and the two **statuettes of musicians** *(nos 3910 and 3908)* with their harmonious lines.

■ **Room 4** contains the fabulous treasures from the **Mycenaean Period★★★** (1600-1100 BC) that have made the museum's reputation. Most of the pieces on display come from Mycenae, excavated from 1876 onwards by Schliemann and his successors. It also has some precious objects unearthed at other Mycenaean sites such as Tírintha, Árgos and Pílos. The central cases contain some magnificent **gold funerary objects**, including the famous **mask of Agamemnon★★★** *(no 624)* which Schliemann wrongly attributed to the 'king of kings', and which, perhaps due to its expressive power, is far superior to the others. Diadems, inlaid daggers, and engraved rings complete this incredible array, along with embossed metal goblets, a splendid **rhyton★** (drinking vessel) in the shape of a bull's head, a duck-shaped vessel made of rock crystal, and small ivory objects attesting to the link between the Mycenaean world and the Orient. Don't miss the **warrior vase** *(no 1426)*, the delicate **woman's head** in limestone *(no 4575)* and the frescoes, including the **Mycenaean woman★** *(no 11670)*, exhibiting a striking suggestion of perspective.

■ Return to the entrance hall to reach the rooms devoted to **Geometric and Archaic Art★★** (10C-6C BC). The major piece in **Room 7** *(next to the cloakroom)* is the monumental **geometric amphora★★** *(no 804)* from the mid-8C from a tomb in Keramikós Cemetery with a geometric pattern framing a funeral procession.

Room 8 features a **Dipylon Head★** *(no 3372)*, found near the gate of the same name; it belonged to the oldest known kouros, which was standing on the tomb. The huge **votive kouros** *(no 2720)* stood in front of the temple to Poseidon at Cape Soúnion.

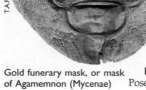
Gold funerary mask, or mask of Agamemnon (Mycenae)

T.A.P.

Attica

Room 9 contains the charming and graceful **kouros** and **kore** from the Cyclades and Attica. Of particular note is the **Phrasikleia kore** (no 4889) with its crown and dress decorated with flowers, as well as the **Winged Victory** (Nike) once placed as an acroterion on top of a temple (no 21).

In the centre of **Room 10** stands the very noble **Volomandra kouros★★** (no 1906), whose extremely fine face contrasts with the relatively rustic rendering of the body.

Go back to Room 8 to reach **Room 11**, where you must stop to look at the **funerary stele of Aristion★** (no 29), or 'the warrior of Marathon'. This sculpture of a warrior is by Aristokles, whose name can be seen on the base.

Room 12 contains the strange **funerary stele of a running hoplite** (no 1959), so-called because it represents a hoplite (soldier) who is running; then again, it could be a dancer...

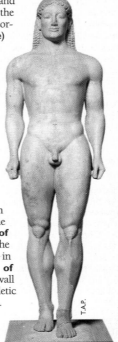

In **Room 13** is a superb **funerary kouros★** (no 3851) from Attica (530 BC). An inscription at the bottom says that the statue adorned the tomb of Kroisos. The **statue of Aristodikos** (no 3938), one of the last kouroi from the Archaic Period, shows the transition into classical art in which the body was freed from the stone. Two **bases of statues** (nos 3476 and 3477) discovered in Themistocles' wall are decorated with bas-reliefs showing youths doing athletic exercises, and an amusing fight between a dog and a cat. Among the votive and **funerary steles** in **Room 14**, don't miss the votive **relief** (no 739) in honour of a girl named Amphotto holding an apple, and the **Attic relief** (no 3344) of an Ephebe putting on a crown, illustrating the beginning of classical art.

Kouros: an early depiction of the body

■ **Classical Art★★** (5C-3C BC):

Room 15 contains two of the museum's masterpieces: the extraordinary **Artemision Poseidon★★** (no 15161) (c 460-450), a bronze statue salvaged in 1928 off the coast of Cape Artemision (at the northern end of Euboea). Standing in a superb pose, the god of the Sea wears a stern face above a powerful body, his right hand clasping what was once a trident. Another masterpiece is the wonderfully expressive **Eleusinian relief★★** (no 126) (c 440-430) with its solemn figures. Demeter (on the left), the goddess of fertility and patron of agriculture, is shown with her daughter Persephone giving an ear of corn to Triptolemos, son of the King of Eleusis, charged with teaching agriculture to mankind.

Outstanding among the many steles cluttering **Room 16** is the **great funerary lekythos** (no 4485), a narrow vase found in Platía Sýndagma. Hermes, in the centre, is taking a young woman to the Acherón, the river leading to the kingdom of the dead, while her family bids her farewell.

Of particular note in **Room 17**, devoted to **classical sculptures** and **votive reliefs**, is a **relief of Hermes★** (no 1738) with both sides sculpted, as well as one dedicated to **Dionysus** (no 1500).

In **Room 18**, **Hegeso's tombstone★★** (no 3624) shows a seated young girl studying a piece of jewellery taken from a case handed to her by her servant. This work of exceptionally elegant design, tinged with sorrow, is attributed to Kallimachos (c 410), one of Phidias' main students.

The following rooms have **classical sculptures**: statues from the 5C and 4C BC that are classical copies of the originals, including the famous (lost) chryselephantine **Athena** by Phidias that stood in the Parthenon.

Room 21 contains the remarkable **Jockey of Artemision**★ *(no 15177)*, a Hellenistic bronze from the 2C BC, which was salvaged from the waves – like the statue of Poseidon – off Cape Artemision. The artist has captured the galloping horse and spirited young rider with great realism.

Go past Rooms 34 and 35, which have various sculptures and votive reliefs, to **Room 36** featuring the **Karapánou collection**★ which includes figurines and small **bronze** objects from the 8C to the 3C BC. The most remarkable pieces are from the sanctuary of Zeus at Dodona (Epirus), in particular the delicate little bronze of **Zeus** *(no 16546)*, a horse *(no 16547)*, and a **statuette of a 'colonel'** *(no 16727)*.

Room 37 contains **objects** (8C-4C BC) from the islands, Thessaly and north-west Greece, Olympia, Crete and the Peloponnese; note the **Athena Promachos** from the Acropolis *(no 6447)*.

Go back to Room 21.

Rooms 22 to 24, devoted to art from the 4C BC, have a series of **sculptures** from the tholos at the Temple of Asklepios in Epidaurus *(Room 22)*, as well as **funerary monuments** *(Room 26)* and **votive reliefs** *(Rooms 25 and 27)*.

There are three pieces of note in **Room 28**: a **high-relief**★ *(no 4464)* of a spirited horse held by a black slave, which came from a funerary monument dating from the 2C BC that was found in Athens. The very lively and lifelike piece is a wonderful example of the transition between classical and Hellenistic art. The **Ephebe of Antikythera** *(no 13396)* is a bronze statue found in the sea off the island of Antikythera representing Paris giving the famous apple to Aphrodite. The **Head of Hygeia** *(no 3602)*, the daughter of Asklepios, attributed to Scopas, is striking for its introspective expression and gentle contours.

■ **Hellenistic Art**★★ (3C-2C BC):

The sculptures in **Room 29** include a fine **statue of a Gaul**★ *(no 247)*. **Room 30** features a colossal **statue of Poseidon**★★ (2C BC) which dominates the entire space. Don't miss the two bronze heads, which are highly individualised and expressive portraits: a **head of a philosopher** *(no 13400)* (3C BC) and a **man's head** *(no 14612)* (c 100 BC), as well as the **group with Aphrodite**, Eros and Pan *(no 3355, created c 100 BC)*.

■ Save up some energy for **Roman Art**★, illustrated by reliefs and statues produced in various Greek workshops in the 1C BC. In the centre of **Room 31** is the haughty **equestrian statue of Augustus** (fragment). The piece next to it is a group of funerary **portraits** from steles (2C-3C AD) discovered near the Tower of the Winds.

Rooms 32 and 33 contain Greek pieces from the Roman Period (2C-3C AD), including a lovely **sleeping maenad**★ *(no 261)* and numerous busts: the **philosopher Metrodorus** *(no 368)*, a **head** *(no 3085)* from a funerary monument, another **head of a woman** *(no 3087)*, and one of a **young man** *(no 420)*. Note the museum director's thoughtful touch in putting side by side **Antinoüs** *(no 417)* and the **Emperor Hadrian** *(no 249, see also no 3729)*, a reminder of the insatiable passion which the former inspired in the latter.

End your visit of the Roman section with the great **sarcophagus** *(no 1497)* from Attica and a **relief** representing a family portrait *(no 3239)*.

■ If your legs are still willing, finish your tour with an African escapade in the **Egyptian antiquities collection**★. With its 7 000 pieces (only some of which are on display), the **Dimitriou collection**★★ in **Rooms 40-41** covers the entire history of Ancient Egypt, from the pre-dynastic period to the Ptolemaic Era (5000-1C BC). Statues in wood, granite, clay, alabaster and bronze, as well as jars, vases, amphorae, knife fragments, votive reliefs, tablets covered in hieroglyphics, jewellery, masks and funerary statuettes illustrate the amazing consistency of Egyptian art throughout the centuries.

Attica

■ In the shadowy light of **Room 42** lies the sparkling **antique and Byzantine gold jewellery**★★ from the **Helene Stathátou collection**, from Macedonia and especially from Thessaly (*be careful not to brush against the cases, as the alarms go off at the slightest touch*).

For a welcome break in a cool (but not air conditioned) place, you have a choice between the museum café (Museum Garden) located at the entrance to **Aréos Park**★ (Plan II, D1) – one of Athens' biggest green spaces – and Green Park. Or you might feel like a complete change of scene altogether, and go to Platía Exarhíon or Odós Kalidromíou. At the foot of **Stréfi Hill**, west of Lycabettos, **Exárhia** (Plan II, C1) is a lively and colourful area where students, fringe groups and dissidents of all kinds hang out. The area has many tavernas featuring simple, tasty and inexpensive food, making it a good place for an evening meal.

Neo-Classical Athens★
Around Platía Sýndagma (Plan II, D3)

What could they do to rebuild Pericles' prestigious city? The people who shaped modern Athens for a whole century (1830-1930) were obsessed by this dream. No building was to be without its marble colonnade! And what better choice as an introduction and model for this new city than the two ancient monuments to **Hadrian**, the philhellenic Roman Emperor?

A great admirer of Athens and of Greek culture, Hadrian stayed in the capital on several occasions and embellished it with numerous buildings. The Athenians honoured their powerful benefactor by erecting a sort of triumphal arch to him in the Roman style in 131 AD, at the point where Athens and the Roman quarter met. Inscriptions engraved on the frieze of **Hadrian's Arch**★ (Plan III, D4) proclaim, on the Pláka side: 'This is the town of Athens, the ancient city of Theseus', while the opposite side says: 'This is the city of Hadrian, not of Theseus'. By putting the mythological hero and the Roman Emperor on the same level, the Athenians acknowledged their noble visitor... and played up to his vanity.

Temple of Olympian Zeus★★ (Plan III, E4)

Go around Hadrian's Arch to the left to reach the entrance to the site (on your right at the beginning of Leofóros Vasillíssis Ólgas). 8.30am-3pm; closed on Monday; entrance fee.

Paintings, drawings and stories all attest to the fact that no traveller ever passed through Athens without being moved by the fallen majesty of these powerful columns standing in the middle of a bare esplanade. More than the monuments on the Acropolis, which were remodelled by its various occupants and hardly recognisable, the Temple of Olympian Zeus was the ultimate ruin possessing the melancholy air so dear to European romantics. They were also moved by its colossal dimensions recalling an era of giants: with its **triple colonnade** of 104 Corinthian columns (in all), the building formed a 107.75m by 41.1m rectangle, making it one of the largest temples in the Greek world.

Pausanias thought that **Deucalion**, the mythical ancestor of the Greeks, was the originator of the sanctuary. On a more prosaic level, archaeologists estimate the oldest foundations to be from the era of the **Peisistratid tyranny** (546-510 BC). Abandoned with the rise of democracy, work was resumed in 174 BC thanks to the Seleucid King Antiochus IV and completed by Emperor Hadrian in 132 AD. The building's fate is uncertain, but there is no doubt that its huge quantities of marble were sent to the limekilns. When Cyriacus of Ancona visited Athens in 1436, there were only 21 columns left.

Near the entrance to the site, on the right, are the foundations of the **Baths of Hadrian**, whose actual baths have preserved their marble **mosaics**.

For a taste of the neo-Classical, go down Leofóros Vasillíssis Ólgas towards the **Olympic Stadium**★★ (Plan II, D4), built for the first **Modern Olympic Games** in April 1896. Abandoning the original wooden stadium (330 BC), General Herodes Atticus gave the city (in 144 AD) a building in Pentelic marble more in keeping with the prestige of the Panathenaic athletic contests. The present stadium is a faithful replica of that building. It can accommodate 70 000 spectators, who come to admire the athletes or to enjoy the beautiful **view**★ of the National Garden and the Acropolis.

Leave the traffic on Leofóros Vassiléos Konstandínou for the quiet park opposite. At the end of a lovely tree-lined path stands the neo-Classical façade of the **Zappeion (Zápio)** (Plan II, D3) (1874-88), a huge **exhibition hall** designed by talented architects T Hanser and F Boulanger. It was above all the dream of one man, K Zappas, a rich Greek from Alexandria. He put his entire – substantial – fortune into trying to rebuild Athens through what had been its greatest glory: architecture, art and athletics.

Walk around the building on the left, then enter the cool shade of the **National Garden**★ (Plan II, D3), an oasis in the heart of the city that is open from dawn to dusk.

Platía Sýndagma★ (Plan II, D3)

Leaving the garden via Leofóros Amalías, return to Platía Sýndagma, 'Constitution Square'. Swamped by the intense traffic that reigns all around it – most of Athens' buses and trolleybuses stop here – not to mention the countless bitterly fought-over taxis, it has lost its former charm from the days when it was lined with terrace cafés. However, the new green spaces and the fountain gushing forth in the centre by the brand new metro stop are very welcome additions. But with its banks and two huge fast-food restaurants, Sýndagma has turned into a mere place of passage, of feverish activity, which fills up and empties according to the rhythm of office hours.

At the foot of the old royal palace (1836-42), which became the **Parliament** (Voulí) in 1935, the *evzónes* wearing *foustanèlles* (pleated kilts that are the traditional Albanian costume which came into fashion with Otto) and *tsaroúchia* (pom-pom shoes) stand guard in front of the **Tomb of the Unknown Soldier**. The changing of the guard *(every hour)* is the occasion for a little **ceremony** – a kind of military dance – that has always been very popular with tourists.

The **Hotel Grande-Bretagne** (1843) on the right, undoubtedly the most prestigious in the city, probably has no memory of having housed the **French School of Archaeology** (now in Kolonáki) between 1856 and 1873.

A stroll down Odós Ermoú

Take Odós Voulís to **Odós Ermoú**, a long pedestrian shopping street that forms a breach through the city from the colonnade of the Voulí all the way to Keramikós Cemetery.

When you reach Evangelistrías, a street running off at right angles, have a look *(on the left)* at the two cathedrals. The work of architects and a monarch, the **New Cathedral (Mitrópolis)** (Plan III, D2) built in 1842-62, flattens Platía Mitropóleos with its graceless mass. More interesting is its tiny neighbour, the **Old Cathedral**★★, a lovely Byzantine chapel from the 12C dedicated to Panagía Gorgoepíkoos, the 'Virgin who answers (prayers) quickly'. Many elements dating from ancient and medieval times used in its construction can be seen in the outer walls.

Another treasure of Byzantine art, the **Church of Kapnikaréa**★★ (Plan III, C1) (11C-13C) stands in the middle of Odós Ermoú, a few metres away. Its fine brick façade is set off by friezes and two elegant little marble columns.

A maze of narrow streets lined with shops of all kinds takes you to **Platía Klafthmónos** (Plan II, C2) and its verdant esplanade. In the shade cast by the trees, the **Church of Ágii Theódori**★ seems to have been placed here by some spell. Rebuilt in the 11C on the foundations of a 9C sanctuary, it has some striking patterns of Arab origin on its outer walls.

The little Byzantine Church of Kapnikaréa squeezed between modern buildings

Between 1836 and 1842, the Greek sovereigns resided at **Vouros Palace** (1834) on Odós Paparigopoúlou, the present location of the **Museum of the City of Athens★** (Plan II, C2) (*9am-1.30pm; closed Tuesday and Thursday; entrance fee*), also called the Vouros-Eutaxia Museum. Paintings, drawings and engravings from the 17C-20C (*on the ground floor and 2nd floor*), as well as a large **model of Athens★** from 1842, recall the capital's urban history. On the 1st floor are Otto's and Amalia's furnished **salons**, which are livened up by a few historical pieces such as a copy of the **Treaty of London** in French signed by Talleyrand. The atmosphere is evocative of the bourgeois household of a small monarchy with fewer than one million subjects...

Head for **Panepistimíou★** (Plan II, C2) (officially called Eleftériou Venizélou, but no one uses that name). The University avenue has some of the finest of Greek neo-Classical buildings: from left to right, the **National Library** (1887-1902), the **University** (1839-64) and the **Academy** (1859-87). With its fine Ionic colonnade flanked by two high columns supporting statues of Athena and Apollo, the latter is perhaps the greatest of the three. These 'temples of culture' form a harmonious whole that is imposing without being too monumental. Financed by Greeks from the diaspora – the only ones capable of raising the kind of money needed for such projects – they were entrusted to two Danish architects living in Greece: the **Hansen brothers**, who left their mark on what is known as the neo-Hellenic style. Relax in the cool shade (rather rare in this part of Athens) of the terrace café hidden in a corner of the **Athens City Hall Cultural Centre** (Plan II, D2) (*take the pedestrian street, Odós Massalías*), whose ground floor houses the **Theatre Museum** (*Monday-Friday, 9am-2.30pm; free admission*) devoted to modern Greek theatre. If you are getting hungry, try some meze at Athinaïkon or Andréas' on Odós Themistokléous.

Kolonáki★ and the Museum District

*Leofóros Vassilíssis Sofías and its museums
are close to Platía Filikís Eterías (Kolonakíou).*

The preserve of intellectuals, politicians (the Prime Minister lives on Odós Anagnostópoulou), professional people, well-heeled foreigners, chic shops and cafés where people go to see and be seen, Kolonáki stretches out at the foot of Lycabettos, forming a regular grid of shady (and often congested) streets of which **Skoufá** and **Patriárhi Ioakím** are the backbone. It is also a district with a multitude of museums to be explored during the hottest time of day before going for a drink on top of the mountain.

Benáki Museum★★★ (Plan II, D3)

Access via Odós Neofýtou Doúka or via Leofóros Vassilíssis Sofías. 9am-5pm, Thursday 9am-midnight, Sunday 9am-3pm; closed Monday. Entrance fee). Like the Kanelópoulos, this museum is first and foremost the work of one man, **Adonis Benáki** (1873-1954), who had a passion for all forms of expression of Hellenism throughout the ages. Born into a wealthy family from the Greek diaspora in Alexandria, Egypt, Benáki created the museum in 1930 as a showcase for his collections. Enriched with numerous later donations, they occupy the family home, a magnificent neo-Classical residence from the early 20C. Long closed to the public, the museum has been completely remodelled and is now open again. Everything has been very thoughtfully laid out, from the presentation to the reception, the shop, the rooftop terrace café and documentation *(bring a sweater, however, as the air conditioning is a bit on the chilly side)*.

Presented in chronological order from prehistoric times to contemporary Greece, the many forms of expression of Greek identity gathered here – whether artistic or linked to everyday life – will take you on a fascinating voyage through the country's history. **Rooms 1 to 8** *(from prehistoric times to the 6C AD)* contain in particular an exceptional collection of **gold objects★** (3200-2800 BC) and **Hellenistic jewellery**, as well as a fine amphora in the geometric style and two portraits from Faiyum. **Rooms 9-12** *(Byzantine and post-Byzantine eras)* feature some delicate **rock-crystal pendants, illuminated manuscripts of the Gospels**, some very beautiful **icons★★**, in particular two early works by El Greco, and some sculpted wooden **iconostases**. On the 1st floor, **Rooms 13-24** *(the period of Ottoman and Venetian rule)* are the realm of precious fabrics, brocades and silks from Venice, a superb collection of **costumes★★** and jewellery from the 18C and 19C. They also contain **interior decorations★★** from various regions of Greece with wood panelling and furniture. Finally, the last two floors recall the War of Independence and some aspects of modern Greek history through paintings, weapons and various documents.

Museum of Cycladic Art★★ (Goulandrís Foundation) (Plan II, D3)

10am-4pm, Saturday 10am-3pm; closed Tuesday and Sunday. Entrance fee. Created in 1986, this remarkable museum is devoted to Aegean civilisation, in particular to the prehistoric Cyclades. The objects on display – over a thousand – cover a period ranging from 3000 BC to the 4C AD. Excellent explanatory texts with maps and sketches provide a better understanding of the collections and of Cycladic culture, its art and funerary customs.

Since 1991, the museum has been enlarged to include the **Stathátos Palace** *(the new wing is connected via a glass passageway)*, the elegant adjoining neo-Classical home which is now used for long-term exhibitions. For the time being, there is a fascinating exhibition entitled **'The city beneath the city'**, featuring 500 of the innumerable discoveries made while the metro was being built. A bronze head, marble sculptures, ceramics with black designs, and numerous lekythoi (narrow vases) with white bases are the finest pieces.

Back in the **main building**, white marble stairs – evoking the Aegean w[...] to the 1st floor and the famous **Cycladic idols★★★**. Whether large or small[...] than 10cm to 1.4m for the tallest), their simple forms and strikingly m[...] lines make these white marble figurines some of the most precious obje[...] historic art. While they have preserved some of their mystery, they are [...] have been connected to funerary worship (thus the folded arms) and lain down hor-izontally (perhaps near the deceased), which would explain their pointed feet.

The 2nd floor contains works of art and various utilitarian pieces dating from 2000 BC to the 4C AD. The most important pieces are the **bronzes**, red-figure **ceramics★★★** and **large amphorae★★★**. Note the touching little **doll** with movable joints (*no 197*) taken from a child's tomb. The 4th floor (the 3rd floor houses tem-porary exhibitions) has the highly varied, excellent **Charles and Rita Polítis collection★★** (ceramics, Byzantine lamps, statuettes, helmets, swords, etc). Of par-ticular note are the elegant **statuettes of women★** (*no 73-76*).

Byzantine Museum★★ (Plan II, E3)

8.30am-3pm; closed on Monday. Entrance fee. The museum is in a handsome neo-Renaissance house built in 1848 for the **Duchess of Piacenza**, an important figure in the philhellenic movement and in Athens society during the reign of Otto. While it is a very well-endowed collection, the presentation is unfortunately not of the same standard (it could use more space and better explanations). However, this may be remedied by the renovations currently being carried out.

Don't miss the two **reconstructions of churches★**: one of a **Christian basilica** from the 5C-7C (*Room 2*), with a **sculpture of the good shepherd★** (*on the right*), and another of the **dome★** of a Greek-cross church (*Room 4*). Take time to admire the **icons★★** in Room 7, some of which are exceptional. In particular the **Archangel Michael★★★** (14C), and the **Panagía Glikó Filoússa★** (literally 'the Virgin who kisses sweetly'), not to mention the **mosaic of the Visitation** (14C) (*on the right at the end of the room*). The next room has some pretty **frescoes** and small objects (jewellery, crosses, ceramics, rock-crystal glasses, metal utensils) from the early Byzantine era. The visit ends with various **silver and gold** objects and **clerical garments**.

If you have any time left...

Art lovers may want to visit the **National Gallery★** (Alexander Soútsos Museum) (Plan II, E3) (*across from the Hilton Hotel, Monday and Wednesday 9am-3pm and 6pm-9pm, Thursday, Friday, Saturday 9am-3pm, Sunday 10am-2pm; closed on Tuesday; entrance fee*) which has three paintings by **El Greco★★**, including the famous *Concert of the Angels*, as well as Cretan and post-Byzantine icons. It also contains the most representative trends in **neo-Hellenic painting**, in particular 18C works from the Ionian Islands and those by the main masters of the Munich school (**Gýsis**, **Lytrás**, **Iacovídes**, **Volanákis**, etc). A room (*on the 1st floor*) is devoted to the painter **K Parthénis** (1878-1967), who had a decisive influence on 20C Greek art. There are also ten frescoes by the naive painter **Theóphilos** and works by the sculptor **I Halepás** occupying two rooms and the garden.

On Mt Lycabettos★★ (Plan II, D2)

By the road or the funicular (at the corner of Odós Aristípou and Odós Ploutárchou); leaves every 10 min, every day from 8.45am-0.15am, Thursday 10.30am-0.15am. Why not end your exploration of Athens with the spectacular **panorama★★** over the capital and its environs from the top of Mt Lycabettos? Legend has it that Athena was carrying this huge 278m-high boulder to the Acropolis in order to lift up her temple and bring it closer to the heavens. But two black birds appeared in the sky, predicting bad news for her. Full of anger, the goddess dropped her boulder... and left it there. Ever since, the 'Hill of the Wolves' has stood right in the centre of the Athens basin which is bounded by far-off Pentelikon, Parnes and Hymettus. Completely deforested during

Athens

Mt Lycabettos: a rock rising out of concrete

the Ottoman era, Lycabettos got back its fragrant pine and cypress trees at the end of the 19C. Standing like a lighthouse above the **open-air amphitheatre** is the little **Church of Ágios Geórgos**, which provides shade for the restaurant terrace. This is the ideal place to come at the end of the day to watch the city being lit up by the rays of the setting sun, then sparkling with a thousand electric stars.

COMING AND GOING

See also (page 166), 'Making the most of Piraeus'.

By air – The new **Elefthérios Venizélos** Airport was opened in April 2001 in Spáta (27km south-east of the city centre). The Greek capital's other two airports have been permanently closed and all air traffic is now concentrated at Venizélos, including international, domestic and charter flights. This huge airport hopes to become one of the most modern new hubs in Europe. Its first task will be accommodating the millions of visitors arriving for the first Olympic Games of the 3rd millennium. Services available – all brand new – include car rentals, travel agencies, shops, left-luggage lockers, hotels, restaurants, banks, money changers, etc.

For information, call: ☎ (01) 36 98 300 / 35 31 000. You might also want to have a look at the airport's very clear Web site: www.athensairport-2001.gr It features timetables for all flights and contact information for all domestic and international airline companies that have flights to Athens.

Access: Shuttle bus service 24 hours a day to the centre of Athens and Piraeus. The Athens shuttle leaves from Platía Sýndagma ('Airport-Spáta' bus).

To get to the airport by car: from Sýndagma, take Leofóros Vassilíssis Sofías (alongside the Parliament) (see page 127 Plan II, D3-E3). This feeds into the new 6-lane expressway built for the airport. Travel times vary according to traffic of course, so allow extra time (45min).

If you take a taxi, make sure the meter is working properly (rate 1 during the day, rate 2 after midnight, on Sundays and holidays).

By train – Athens has 2 railway stations, used by Hellenic Railways (OSE), right next to each other: the first, **Peloponnese Station** (Plan II, B1), Leofóros Theódorou Deligiáni (get off at Deligiáni station, line 2) is for trains going to southern Greece; the second, **Lárissa Station** (Plan II, B1), Platía Laríssis (get off at Lárissa station, line 2), is for northern Greece.

By bus / metro – Piraeus-centre is served by blue and yellow **bus 040**; departs from Platía Sýndagma (Plan III, E2), at the beginning of Odós Filelínon. To get to the main harbour of Piraeus, take metro line 1.

The KTEL company's orange buses serve Attica, in particular the ports of Rafína and Lávrio and the Soúnion site. The terminal is located on Platía Egíptou, Odós Mavromáteon, in front of Áreos Park (Plan II, C1) (5min from Victoria station on line 1).

For the north and south, go to bus terminal A, 'KTEL Kifissoú', 100 Odós Kifissoú (Plan II, C2). It is served by bus 051; the stop is on the corner of Odós Zínonos and Odós Menándrou, near Omónia. Buses go to the Peloponnese, the Ionian Islands, and Thessaloníki.

For central Greece: terminal B, 'KTEL Liossíon', Odós Liossíon 260, served by bus 024, the stop for which is on Leofóros Amalías (Plan II, D3). Buses go to Delphi, Galaxídi, Tríkala (Metéora), Vólos (Pelion), etc.

FINDING YOUR WAY

An accurate and practical plan of the city is given away free at the information office, 4 Odós Amerikís. Other city plans, which vary in quality, are for sale at stands and in bookshops. The historical map of Athens published by the Ministry of Culture (€3) is by far the best, but its one-square-metre size makes it a bit unwieldy. It is available, along with others, at **Elefteroudákis** (Leofóros Panepistimíou 15), **Road Edition** (Odós Ipokrátous 39) and at the **National Archaeological Museum**. Don't be shy about asking your way (most people understand some English), as local people will be delighted to give you directions.

GETTING AROUND

By bus – **Blue buses** (centre and outskirts), **mini-buses** (centre) and **trolley-buses** (centre) run from 5am to 0.30am. Tickets ('isitíria') are valid for buses and trolleybuses (but only for one trip; around 35 cents) and are sold at stands near stops, at Sýndagma (there is a ticket machine by the 040 bus stop) and at

Omónia. Make sure you cancel your ticket when you get on the bus. Buses are crowded at rush hour (between 3pm and 5pm) and move slowly through the centre due to traffic jams. The map of Athens offered by the information office indicates the routes taken by the trolley-buses and 4 mini-bus lines.

By metro – Athens has 3 metro lines, open from 5am to 0.15am. The oldest line ('ilektrikó') runs between Piraeus and Kifissiá, via Thissío (Keramikós and the Agora), Monastiráki and Omónia (The National Museum is halfway between Omónia and Victoria, the next station). A ticket costs around 60 cents, or 75 cents if you plan to continue your trip on the other 2 brand new metro lines.

The 2 new lines, which cost around 75 cents, are linked by 3 connecting stations: **Omónia** connects lines 1 and 2; **Atikí** and **Sýndagma** connect lines 2 and 3. Opened in December 1999, this new network is not in full service yet, and some stations are still under construction. Some connections indicated on maps are not accessible yet, in particular Monastiráki station; which is only accessible via line 1 for the time being.

By taxi – Taxis are relatively inexpensive and numerous. Don't be surprised if your taxi lets on other customers during rush hour; this is an accepted custom. The driver must then deduct the cost of each passenger's trip (make sure he does). Besides the 60 cent pick-up charge (or more if you reserve a car by telephone, and a small extra charge for baggage), there are 2 rates: **rate 1** (during the day) and **rate 2** (at night, midnight-5am, on Sundays and holidays, or outside the city limits, double rate 1).

Finding a taxi on Platía Sýndagma, where the traffic is deafening, is a demanding sport that has at least two rules: go out to meet them, while avoiding the buses and trolleybuses, and clearly articulate your destination. If the taxi already has passengers, it will flash its headlights and slow down rather than coming to a complete stop. That's when you must state your destination out loud. A broad 'A' followed by your mouth closing around the sound $\Delta\rho$ ('drr') will signify 'aero-drómio', or airport, without fail.

Car rentals – Nearly all the companies, large and small, have offices on **Leofóros Sigroú** (at the beginning) (Plan II, C4). The lowest rates for renting a car run from €45 to €55 per day during peak season. Sliding rates are available depending on the length of rental. Small companies offer lower rates, but make sure you get the equivalent in terms of coverage for accidents and breakdowns.

Hertz, Leofóros Sigroú 12, ☎ (01) 922 01 02-04.

Budget, Leofóros Sigroú 8, ☎ (01) 921 47 71-73.

Athens Car, Odós Filelínon 10, ☎ (01) 323 37 83.

Autorent, Leofóros Sigroú 94 and Odós Vizándiou 11 (right angles to Sigroú), ☎ (01) 923 25 14 / 923 84 38.

Roadside Assistance – Contact **ELPA**, the Greek Automobile Touring Club, for any technical problems, ☎ 104.

Address book

Tourist information – **EOT, the Information Bureau of the Greek National Tourism Organisation**, Odós Amerikís 4 (near Sýndagma) (Plan II, D2), ☎ (01) 331 05 61 / 2 / 5. 9am-7pm, Saturday 10am-3pm; closed on Sunday. They can provide a great deal of information not only about Athens, but also regarding all means of transport in Greece (schedules and rates): to the islands, Attica, the Peloponnese and northern Greece. The hostesses are very friendly even though they are often over-burdened with work. Free brochures and three magazines in English containing a wealth of information on cultural life in the city during the summer (performances, concerts, films, etc) are also available.

Embassies / consulates –

United Kingdom, Odós Ploutárchou 1, 106 75 Athens, ☎ (01) 727 2600, Fax (01) 727 2720, info@athens. mail.fco.gov.uk

United States, Leofóros Vassilíssis Sofías 91, 101 60 Athens, ☎ (01) 721 2951.

Canada, Odós Ioánnou Gennadíou 4, 115 21 Athens, ☎ (01) 727 3400, Fax (01) 727 3480.

Australia, Odós Dimitríou Soútsou 37, ☎ (01) 645 0404, Fax (01) 646 6595, ausembgr@hol.gr

Cultural centres –
British Council, Platía Kolonáki 17.
The Hellenic American Union, Massalías 22.
The French Institute, Sína 29 / Massalías 1.

Travel agencies – There are many travel agencies in the area between Sýndagma, Filelínon and Pláka. Tickets and schedules for ferryboats to the islands are available, and you can book rooms there.

Airline companies – Olympic Airways, Odós Filelínon 15 (Plan III, E2), ☎ (01) 92 67 444 / 92 67 555 / 92 67 663. Arrivals-Departures, ☎ (01) 93 63 363. International flights, ☎ (01) 96 94 111.

British Airways, Leofóros Vouliagménis 130, ☎ (01) 89 06 666 / 96 01 444.

Air France, Leofóros Vouliagménis 18 (Plan II, C4), ☎ (01) 96 01 100 / 96 01 444, Airport, ☎ (01) 35 30 110.

Canadian Airlines, Leofóros Sigroú 7 (Plan II, C4), ☎ (01) 92 12 470.

Delta, Odós Óthonos 4 (Plan III, E2), ☎ (01) 33 11 660.

Swissair, Odós Óthonos 4 (Plan III, E2), ☎ (01) 33 70 520, Airport, ☎ (01) 35 30 152.

Banks / Currency exchange – There are cash dispensers all over Athens. All the major banks have branches at Sýndagma. Currency exchange bureaux are preferable to banks (closing time: 2pm), which take a higher commission and you might have to wait in line (especially at the National Bank). They are located in areas with many tourists such as Omónia, Monastiráki, Pláka, Sýndagma and the major avenues. **Eurocambio** (on the corner of Akadimías and Sína) offers the best rates with no commission.

Post offices – The **Sýndagma branch** (on the corner of Odós Mitropóleos) (Plan III, E2) is open 7am-8pm daily, Saturday 7.30am-2pm, Sunday 9am-1pm.

The **Omónia branch** (100 Odós Aiolou) has the same hours.

Internet – Athens is full of Internet cafés.
Gr Net, on the corner of 28 Oktomvríou and Irakliou, near the National Museum.
Sky Net Centers, Odós Apóllonos 10, in Pláka.
Bytes & Bites, Odós Akadimías 78 (on the corner of Odós E Benáki).

Media – Newspapers and magazines can be purchased at news-stands on Platía Sýndagma and Platía Kolonáki. *Athens News*, the English daily, is available free at the information office.

Emergencies – In the event of a problem (health concerns, theft, mugging, accidents, etc) call the **tourist police**, ☎ 171 or **police emergency service**, ☎ 100.
Emergency medical assistance, ☎ 166.

Bookshops – Compendium, Níkis 28.
Elefteroudákis, Leofóros Panepistimíou 15. The 1st floor has a large section with maps and tourist books (in Greek and English).
Road Edition, Odós Ipokrátous 39. This company, which publishes maps – the best – and guidebooks, has a small shop that is well-stocked with tourist literature.

Laundry – Launderettes are few and far between in Athens. Try a dry cleaner's ('stegnokatharístria'); some hotels provide this service.

WHERE TO STAY

Prices shown are for a double room at peak season including breakfast except where indicated to the contrary. Hotels will lower their rates for stays longer than 2 days. For those on a tight budget, the youth hostel is about the only place in Athens where you can stay for under €23; but it is usually taken by storm, and finding a bed there is a rare occurrence indeed. The best areas to stay in – combining a lively atmosphere, good facilities, and a practical location for getting to the major sites – are Pláka, Monastiráki and Eólou (very central and full of shops), Thissío and Exárhia (very lively in the evening, although a bit out of the way). Kolonáki is the most chic area.

• **Pláka** (Plan III)

Between €25 and €30

Phaedra, Odós Herefóndos 16, on the corner of Odós Lissicrátous, ☎ (01) 32 27 795 / 32 38 461 – 21rm. ✒ ⌧ Shared showers, supplement for breakfast. Across from beautiful Agía Ekateríni Church. What this little hotel lacks in comfort is made up for by its location in the heart of Pláka.

Dioskouri, Odós Pitakoú 6, ☎ (01) 32 48 165 – 20rm. ⌧ ⌧ An old building with a worn-out façade, run by an English-speaking couple. Youth hostel atmosphere, with a pretty inner courtyard full of flowers.

Between €30 and €45

Kimon, Odós Apóllonos 17, ☎ (01) 33 14 658 – 13rm. ⌧ ✒ ⌧ ⌧ The entrance isn't much to look at, but the rooms are decent and it has a pretty terrace with a view of the Acropolis.

Between €60 and €75

Adonis, Odós Kódrou 3, ☎ (01) 32 49 737 / 32 49 741, Fax (01) 32 31 602 – 27rm. ✒ ⌧ ▤ ⌧ ⌧ Extremely well-situated in the heart of Pláka, this handsome, comfortable hotel has all the amenities and very reasonable prices. Superb view of the Acropolis from its terrace, which has a little bar for a drink in the evening. Excellent value for money, and if you do without air conditioning they knock off €9.

Acropolis House, Odós Kódrou 6-8, ☎ (01) 32 22 344 / 32 26 241, Fax (01) 32 44 143 – 19rm. ▤ ⌧ ⌧ This charming hotel (with antique furniture and murals) has all the modern comforts in a pretty, neo-Classical house. The proprietors are very welcoming. You can save €15 by doing without air conditioning.

Aphrodite, Odós Apóllonos 21, ☎ (01) 32 34 357-9, Fax (01) 32 25 244 – 84rm. ✒ ⌧ ▤ ⌧ The decor in this modern hotel is a bit dreary (the terrace could really do with some sprucing up), but the rooms are better than the 1970s-style marble lobby. Still, this establishment in the Pláka is good value for money.

Ómiros, Odós Apóllonos 15, ☎ (01) 32 35 486-7, Fax (01) 32 28 059 – 37rm. ✒ ⌧ ▤ ⌧ ⌧ ⌧ This

modern hotel is not particularly attractive, but it is comfortable. The terrace is a pleasant place to have breakfast.

Nefeli, Odós Iperídou 16, ☎ (01) 322 80 44-5, Fax (01) 322 58 00 – 18rm. ✒ ⌧ ▤ ⌧ Very well-situated on a quiet street in Pláka across from a beautiful (and, unfortunately, highly damaged) neo-Classical home. This pleasant little hotel has recently installed air conditioning and has consequently raised its prices a bit too much.

Adrian, Odós Adrianoú 74, ☎ (01) 32 21 553 / 32 50 454, Fax (01) 32 50 461 – 22rm. ✒ ⌧ ▤ ⌧ ⌧ ⌧ In the heart of Pláka a few metres from the Tower of the Winds, this is another small hotel with impeccable comforts and a really beautiful shady terrace from which you can see the Erechtheion. The interior decoration is quite elegant. Ask for a room on the far side of the building.

Between €75 and €90

Austria, Odós Moussón 7 (Plan II), at the foot of Filopápos Hill, ☎ (01) 92 35 151-3, Fax (01) 92 47 350, austria@hol.gr – 37rm. ✒ ⌧ ▤ ⌧ ⌧ ⌧ A fine hotel located in one of the quietest areas in the city. Terrace and balconies with views of the Acropolis.

Lycabette, Odós Valarítou 6 (Plan II), ☎ (01) 36 33 514-7, Fax (01) 36 33 518 – 39rm. ✒ ⌧ ▤ ⌧ ✕ ⌧ ⌧ In a quiet pedestrian street nestled between Stadíou and Panepistimíou. This clean and comfortable establishment above the elegant Florian café has rooms with balconies. Good value for money.

Pláka, Odós Kapnikaréas 7, ☎ (01) 32 22 096-8, Fax (01) 32 22 412, rofos@ath.forthnet.gr – 67rm. ✒ ⌧ ▤ ⌧ ✕ ⌧ ⌧ Comfortable and attractively decorated rooms. The ones facing the Acropolis are naturally more in demand. If they are already taken, try to get the price lowered a bit. There is always the terrace for the view.

Byron, Odós Víronos 19, ☎ (01) 32 30 327 / 32 53 554, Fax (01) 32 20 276 – 22rm. ✒ ⌧ ▤ ⌧ ⌧ ⌧ This is one of the oldest buildings on the street, which says a lot. Fortunately, this hotel has recently been modernised so you will find all the comforts here, as well as a friendly welcome. From the terrace there is a view of the southern slope of the Acropolis and the roofs of Pláka.

Hermes, Odós Apóllonos 19, ☎ (01) 32 35 514, Fax (01) 32 32 073 – 45rm. ✆ ⚒ 📠 📺 ✕ 💳 It's a pity this modern hotel doesn't have a terrace. But its rooms are large and all have balconies, some the size of verandas. This comfortable hotel – with all the amenities and well-kept communal areas – also doubles as a travel agency.

• **Athinás, Eólou, Monastiráki** (Plan III)

Around €33

Témpi, Odós Eólou 29, ☎ (01) 32 13 175 / 32 42 940, Fax (01) 32 54 179, tempihotel@travelling.gr – 24rm. ✆ ⚒ ✕ Very well-situated on Eólou, a traffic-free street at the entrance to Pláka, near Agía Iríni Church, an area that is quiet in the evening and lively during the day. Modest, but with a warm welcome; and there's a laundry in the hotel. Breakfast not served.

Pella Inn, Odós Ermoú 104, ☎ (01) 32 50 598 / 32 12 229 – 21rm. ✆ ⚒ ✕ ⛲ Hidden behind the construction work on the metro, this is a small, backpacker-style hotel with an outdated and gaudy decor. Modest comforts and reasonably clean. Ask for a room on Odós Karaïskáki, as Ermoú is noisy in the evening. They also offer services such as money deposits and a travel agency.

Around €53

Attalós, Odós Athinás 29, ☎ (01) 32 12 801-3, Fax (01) 32 43 124, atthot@hol.gr – 80rm. ✆ ⚒ 📠 📺 💳 Lovely rooftop terrace. At the beginning of Athinás just next to Monastiráki (a noisy, but very lively, area). Clean and comfortable. View of the Acropolis from the balconies.

⚙**Cecil**, Odós Athinás 39, ☎ and Fax (01) 32 17 079 / 32 18 005 / 32 19 606 – 40rm. ✆ ⚒ 📠 ⛲ 💳 This hotel in a beautiful neo-Classical building was recently renovated. The rooms, which have wooden floors, are charming, some noisier than others (ask for one on the little corner street). Warm welcome.

• **Thissío** (Plan III)

Around €38

Erechtheion, Odós Flamarion 8 on the corner of Odós Agías Marínas (Plan II), ☎ (01) 34 59 606 / 34 59 626, Fax (01) 34 62 756 – 22rm. ✆ ⚒ 📠 📺 ⛲ A stone's throw from Agía Marína Church and the Observatory, on a very quiet street. Run by two very friendly ladies, this hotel has preserved its 1960s decor; but the rooms are clean and comfortable, and very quiet. It's a pity the terrace isn't really useable.

Thissío, Odós Apostólou Pávlou 25 on the corner of Odós Agías Marínas, ☎ (01) 34 67 634 / 34 67 655, Fax (01) 34 62 756 – 18rm. ✆ ⚒ 📠 ✕ ✕ ⛲ 💳 This building, a bit more modern than the previous one, is from the 1970s. The rooms are clean and comfortable, but the air conditioning is old and sometimes just as noisy as Odós Apostólou Pávlou. Pretty terrace. Good value for money.

Around €55

Jason Inn, Odós Assomáton 12, ☎ (01) 32 51 106, Fax (01) 32 43 132 – 57rm. ✆ ⚒ 📠 📺 ✕ 💳 Right near the Agora and across from Keramikós, this modern hotel has every possible comfort at affordable prices. While standard, the decor is not lacking in taste. Every room has its own balcony.

• **Omónia, Exárhia** (Plan II)

Omónia and the area around the two railway stations is the cheapest part of Athens, but it is noisy. The lively nightlife in Exárhia is a particular attraction.

Around €18

Youth Hostel Victor Hugo, Odós Victoros Hugo 16, ☎ (01) 52 34 170, Fax (01) 52 34 015 – 138rm (2-4 people). A fairly recent (1994) and well-kept youth hostel. Rooms are light and soundproofed, with or without bathroom. Safes and lock-up cupboards, left-luggage lockers, communal kitchen. Breakfast is not served, but the hostel is expanding to include more services. A very good place, but it is often full.

Around €27

Orion, Odós Dryádon 4 (the first steep little street on the left after the intersection of Odós Benáki and Odós

Kalidromíou), 25min from Pláka, ☎ (01) 38 27 362 / 38 20 191 / 38 27 116, Fax (01) 380 51 93 – 20rm. 🏌 🛬 🏠 While a bit out of the way, this establishment and the neighbouring Dryádes (see below) are worth mentioning. Built on a slope on the edge of little Strefi Park, they overlook the pleasant Exárhia district (cafés, bars and tavernas). Friendly welcome and 'glamorous' atmosphere (models of both sexes like to stay in both hotels). In both cases, avoid the rooms overlooking the neighbouring basketball court, which gets noisy in the evening. The Orion has one shower for 2 rooms. The rooms are clean and quiet, and some have lovely views.

Between €45 and €55
Dryádes, next to the previous hotel – 15rm. 🏌 🏮 🛬 🏠 The same address and management as the Orion, but more comfortable. Try to get one of the 3 rooms on the top floor, which have magnificent views.

Athinéa, Odós Vilará 9, 5min from Platía Omónia and 15min from Pláka, ☎ (01) 52 43 884-5 / 52 45 737 – 42rm. 🏌 🏮 📧 📺 ✗ 🏠 🆑 This modern hotel is clean and comfortable, and is located on a quiet pedestrian street lined with cafés near the large Church of Ágios Konstandínos. Excellent value for money.

• **Kolonáki** (Plan II)

Around €68
🏨 **Athenian Inn**, Háritos 22, 10min from Pláka, ☎ (01) 72 38 097 / 72 39 552 / 72 18 756, Fax (01) 72 42 268 – 28rm. 🏌 🏮 📧 🆑 In the heart of the chic Kolonáki district in a quiet street lined with shops, near the museums. The end of Odós Háritos is pedestrian (bars and an open-air cinema). This is a very comfortable little family hotel with well-designed decor (works by Greek painters) and a high standard of service. Laurence Durrell, the English writer who was a great connoisseur of Greece, is said to have stayed in this hotel whenever he was in Athens.

• **Koukáki** (Plan II)

Around €43
Tony's, Zaharísta 26, ☎ (01) 92 36 370 / 92 30 561 / 92 35 761 – 13rm. 🏌 🏮 🏠 Breakfast not served. The rooms are clean

and relatively comfortable, some with balconies.
🏨 **Marble House**, a cul-de-sac off Odós Zini, between Odós Dimitrakopoúlou and Odós Androútsou, ☎ (01) 92 34 058 / 92 26 461 – 8rm: 🏌 🏮 📧 🏠 🆑 6rm: 🏌 🏮 🛬 🏠 🆑 6rm: 🏌 🛬 🏠 🆑 Depending on the category: €45, €40 and €33. A recent building at the end of a quiet alley. A large bougainvillaea brightens up the marble façade, and the decor inside is simple but elegant. Pretty terrace. Extra charge for breakfast.

Around €53
🏨 **Art Gallery**, Odós Erehthíou 5, ☎ (01) 92 38 376 / 92 31 933, Fax (01) 92 33 025 – 21rm. 🏌 🏮 🛬 🏠 Very near Pláka, but in an area that has its own charm thanks to the cafés and restaurants on Platía Gargarettas. In a fine house from the late 19C that belongs to an artist whose paintings adorn the walls. Remodelled by architects, the hotel has a simple but elegant decor with wooden floors. Warm welcome, pretty terrace for breakfast or for a drink in the evening. Dry cleaning service.

Around €88
Hera, Odós Fálirou 9, ☎ (01) 92 36 682 / 92 35 618, Fax (01) 92 47 334, hhera@hol.gr – 49rm. 🏌 🏮 📧 📺 ✗ 🏠 🆑 In the Makrigiáni district near the Acropolis and Pláka, this modern hotel has a terrace with a view of the Acropolis, lounges, and a pleasant bar and patio, in addition to the usual comforts for this category. The reception is quite friendly for an establishment of this standing.

EATING OUT
Depending on your appetite, you can pick a restaurant ('estiatório') or taverna, which serve traditional Greek dishes, or an ouzo bar (or 'mezedopolío') if you feel like snacking on meze. To help you make your culinary choices, see the chapter on Greek cuisine, page 88. Tavernas not catering to tourists are usually closed for lunch.

• **Kolonáki area** (Plan II)
Under €12
Rozia, Odós Aristípou 44 (E2). Closed on Sunday. This taverna serves simple, delicious food in a cool garden at the foot of Lycabettos.

Rozalia, Odós Valtetsíou 58 (E2). Open for lunch. This taverna frequented by regulars serves simple and very inexpensive dishes in a little courtyard beneath a leafy arbour. Choose your food inside and try the house rosé which is quite decent.

Athinaïkón, Odós Themistokléous 2 (C2). Mezedopolío. Open for lunch. A pleasant air-conditioned room with traditional white marble tables. This is an ideal place to spend the hot early hours of the afternoon in a typically Athenian atmosphere.

Andréas kai Yiós, Odós Themistokléous 18 (C2) (in a cul-de-sac on the right). Mezedopolío. Open for lunch, closed on Sunday. It doesn't look like much, but they have delicious fish meze with ouzo or white wine to accompany them.

Dexaméni, Platía Dexaméni (D2). Ouzo bar. Open for lunch. People come here at all hours to have a chat while snacking on a salad and some meze, or to quench their thirst with a cool beer under the shade of the trees lining the street; the atmosphere feels a bit like being out in the country.

Around €23

47 Maritsa's, Odós Voukourestíou 47 (D2). Mezedopolío. Air-conditioned room and outdoor tables (very pleasant in the evening). Don't let the rather starchy look of the place put you off. The meze have an incomparable flavour. A simple plate of steamed courgettes with a dash of olive oil and a few drops of lemon juice can make a great dish, especially when it is accompanied by bits of grilled octopus.

• Gázi (Plan II)

Between €12 and €15

Mamacas, Odós Persefónis 41 (A2). Open for lunch. Venture into the Gázi district lined with old houses and enjoy some 'traditional nouvelle cuisine' there. In other words, Greek flavours with a touch of the exotic. This restaurant is located in a charming all-white little house with tables in the shade in front. Try the meatballs in cumin and tomato sauce.

Kallixorou, Odós Persefónis 31 (A2). This restaurant in a pretty pink-coloured house – with a decor that is both modern and rustic – offers a wide range of appetisers to get you started and some tasty dishes to complete your meal. Have dinner on the terrace in the evening.

• Pláka (Plan III)

Under €11

Plátanos, Odós Diogénous 4 (C2). Closed on Sunday, open for lunch. In the shade of a eucalyptus tree, a vine arbour and a plane tree, and a stone's throw from the Tower of the Winds. Plátanos taverna is an old Pláka classic. Try the tasty moussaká with a salad and a refreshing beer in this delightful setting.

Trípodon, Odós Tripódon 14 (D3). Ouzo bar. Open for lunch. The two ladies of the house serve a wide assortment of meze on large platters – from which you choose the dishes you want – under a delightful pergola shaded by vines.

Tó Kafenío, Odós Epiharmou (D3), just beyond the previous establishment. Closed for lunch. The tables are set out on both sides of a pretty little street in Pláka with a charming neighbourhood atmosphere. Some good, simple dishes including fried aubergines ('melidzánes'), tzatzíki, 'saganáki' (cooked slice of cheese), 'keftedákia' (meatballs), and salad.

Xinou, Odós Angélou Gérondas 4 (D3). Taverna. Another Pláka 'classic', because of its garden and its moussaká, its spaghetti and meatballs lightly flavoured with cinnamon and its nostalgic music (in the evening).

Glikis, Odós Angélou Gérondas 2 (D3). Ouzo bar. Open for lunch. Choose between the 'pikilía' (assortment) for one, two or three people, or twenty or so meze. Covered in vines, the pergola is probably one of the most attractive in Pláka.

Between €12 and €15

Tou Psará, Odós Erehthéos 16 and Odós Erotókritou 12 (C3). Open for lunch. Located on a little square where several streets cross, the oldest taverna in Pláka has a charming setting and delicious food (don't miss the meat with sauce). Take time to mull over the abundant menu. One of the best places in Pláka.

Kafé Avissinia, Platía Avissinías. Meze-dopolío (B1). For lunch. The inside is a bit like an old Parisian bistro. The owner brings out his tables as the antique dealers put away their wares. Excellent meze, and the rice pilaf with mussels won't disappoint you.

Under €20
Dionysos, Odós Rovértou Gáli 43 (B4). Restaurant. Terrace or air-conditioned room. Alongside its international menu (hence the tour buses parked all around), this restaurant has a solid reputation for Greek gastronomy. This is the place to taste some real 'dolmádes', light 'pítes' (flaky-pastry pies) and a deliciously oriental baklava.

● **Exárhia** (Plan II, D1)

Under €11
Lefká, Odós Mavromiháli 121. Closed on Sunday. A courtyard and a few huge wine casks make up the decor in this unpretentious taverna where the food is simple (salads, a few starters and grilled meats) and inexpensive.

Ama Lahi, Odós Kalidromíou 71 or Odós Methónis 66. Taverna. A neo-Classical house with a large, shady courtyard giving onto two streets. Try the 'moshári stamnáto', a tasty beef stew. This pleasantly cool place makes you want to linger, especially since the neighbouring bars are so inviting.

Bárba Iánnis, Odós E Benáki 94. Open for lunch. A taverna with tables set out on a pedestrian street in the heart of the Exárhia district. Try one of the cuts of meat with sauce and a good salad washed down with some retsína (on sale downstairs).

Between €12 and €15
Stréfis to Stéki tis Xánthis, Odós Irínis Athinéas 5, on the corner of Odós Poulherías. Closed on Sunday. A magnificent flower-decked terrace crowns this pretty neo-Classical house located at the foot of Stréfi Hill. An ideal place for a tête-à-tête, where taverna fare with a slightly more sophisticated touch is served.

● **Psirí**

Under €12
Platía Iróon, Platía Iróon 1 (Plan III, B1). Mezedopolío. In the heart of this old Athens neighbourhood where the evenings are lively. Tables on the square. For anyone who wants to learn about meze, the menu theoretically has 250 varieties! The service can be a bit slow, but it's worth it.

Náxos, Odós Christokopídou, next to the church (Plan III, B1). Mezedopolío. Open for lunch. Delicious grilled, fried or marinated fish meze. Psirí atmosphere, although a bit out of the way.

Telys, Odós Evripídou 86 (Plan II, B2). Closed on Sunday, open for lunch. Specialises in charcoal-grilled meats. Aside from a few salads and fries, the only fare is chops, rib steak, mutton, beef or pork fillet. A very inexpensive taverna.

● **Pagrati** (Plan II, D4)

Around €9
Karavitis, on the corner of Odós Arktinou and Odós Pafsanía, 5min from the stadium. This taverna – an institution – has 2 addresses: a winter one, and a summer one in a courtyard with a vine arbour, a very pleasant place to have something from the grill.

HAVING A DRINK

July and August are not the best months for exploring Athens' night-life, because the numerous cabarets, theatres, cinemas, and many bars are closed. Apart from air-conditioned places, which aren't very pleasant in the evening, the only establishments that remain open are those with an outside area.

Cafés, bars – There is a semblance of activity around the large and small terrace cafés on Odós Tsakálof and Platía Filikís Etairías in Kolonáki, but the neighbourhood is quite deserted between 1 and 20 August. The most lively spots are the big cafés on Odós Iraklídon (pedestrian) and Odós Nileos in Psirí and Thissío:

Clepsídra, a small, intimate terrace on the corner of Odós Thrassívoulou and Odós Clepsídras (Plan III, C3), offers a welcome halt after exploring the Aérides quarter.

Níkis, Odós Níkis (Plan III, E2), a small street at right angles to long Odós Ermoú. A little café for regulars with a few tables on the pavement, very near the

many shops on Ermoú, but still quiet. Ideal for a coffee break. It has good music (jazz, Cuban, etc), a wood decor, and is unpretentious and very pleasant.
Stavlos, Odós Iraklídon 10, Thissío (Plan II, B3), a bar-restaurant with an exhibition area in a very beautiful old home.
Tango, Odós Anargíron 21-23, in Psirí (Plan II, B2). Pleasant bar that is also a restaurant.
Dío epí Tría ('2x3'), Odós N Apostóli, in Pláka (Plan III, B1), at the beginning of Odós Adrianoú. This place by the railway tracks is very pleasant in the evening.
In Exárhia (Plan II, C1-D1), there is a pleasant atmosphere in the cafés on Platía Exarhíon and in the bars on Odós Kalidromíou, in particular at **Mílos** and across the street at **55**, as well as at **Kalidromíou** (on the corner of the street of the same name and Odós Zossimadon).

Open-air cinemas – Open-air cinemas are naturally made for watching films, but a sandwich and a beer or a soft drink are all part of the experience, as is the break in the middle of the film (your chance to get another beer, soft drink...). And it's also an opportunity to see an old classic or a film from last year. In Greece, films are sub-titled in Greek, but never dubbed. The sound is usually not as loud for the second showing, for the neighbours' sake; so don't sit too far from the speakers. The programme for the cinemas is listed in Athens News (in English).

🎞 **Dexaméni**, Platía Dexaméni, Kolonáki (Plan II, A4). With its 2 bars, this is undoubtedly one of the nicest places in Athens. The sound is quite loud, except when the security team of the Prime Minister, who lives next door, makes it known that he would like to get some rest.
Thissíon, Odós Apostólou Pávlou 7 (Plan III, A3). Chairs with cushions, a view of the Acropolis and many cafés nearby where you can discuss the films afterwards.
Ciné Paris, Platía Filomoússou Etairías. On a terrace in the heart of Pláka. Photos from old films on sale at the entrance.
🎞 **Cine Psirí**, Odós Sarí 40-44, Psirí (Plan II, B2). The best screening conditions in one of the oldest areas of Athens.

OTHER THINGS TO DO
Athens Festival Office, Odós Stadíou 4 (near Sýndagma) (Plan II, C2), in the Spyromilíou gallery, ☎ (01) 32 21 459. For information about performances at the Odeon of Herodes Atticus and Lycabettos, and about the Pnyx son et lumière show. Monday-Friday 9am-3pm, Saturday 9am-2pm.

Son et lumière – At the Pnyx site, every evening at 9pm. For information, contact the above-mentioned festival office. Shows in all languages.

Traditional dancing – Dóra Strátou Theatre, information available at: Odós Scholíou 8, in Pláka. Traditional Greek dance performances are held every night except Monday at 10.15pm on Filopápos Hill (main entrance on Platía Apoloníou in Koukáki). Additional performances at 8.15pm on Wednesday and Sunday.

SHOPPING GUIDE

Miscellaneous – For classic souvenirs, go to Pláka where they have copies of everything ever produced by Greek civilisation from the Age of Pericles to modern times – from plaster statuettes of Athena to komboloí (worry beads), not to mention natural sponges and the inescapable T-shirts. In the same vein, but much more chic, are the **reproductions of antiquities** from the capital's major museums. For the best deals, buy them straight from the workshop that supplies the museums... and sells them at better prices: **Arionas**, Odós G Drossini 19, Ilioúpoli, a 20min drive from the centre of Athens.

Second-hand / flea market – In the area around Odós Ermoú there are timeless shops where the standard items on sale, which haven't changed since 1880, now amount to second-hand goods. Hunt around at the flea market too, or in the shops in **Monastiráki**, where you might find a 'bríki', a little pot for making Greek coffee, a storm lantern, or a fine brass church censer.

Culinary specialities – In desperation you can also fall back on ouzo (the best brands are, among others, Barbayiánni, Plomario, Mini and Babatzim) and pistachios from Égina.

PIRAEUS
(PIREÁS)

Province of Central·Greece – Capital of the district of Attica – 10km from Athens
Regional map page 123 and page 125 – Michelin map 980 fold 30
Pop 182 671 (476 304 with bordering townships)

Not to be missed
The Archaeological Museum.
The sunset over Athens from Munychia Hill (Kastélla).

And remember...
Avoid walking around Piraeus in the middle of the day in summer
as the heat is scorching.

Polluted and scorching hot Piraeus is not exactly a resort destination. So you will probably only go there if your boat to the islands casts off early in the morning, or if you arrive late at night. If you have a few hours to kill there, seek out the hidden spots frequented by the locals far from the noise and heat.

Piraeus has three harbours, each with a different atmosphere: the **main harbour** (Mégas Límano) where ferries to the islands leave from, and which has a metro stop and is full of frenzied activity; the quieter **Zéa Marina** reserved for hydrofoils, and **Mikrolímano**, a small sailing harbour further away that is peaceful and charming in the daytime but which throbs to the beat of noisy discotheques at night.

The country's biggest harbour

Piraeus was built by Themistocles in the 5C BC to replace the port of **Fáliron** which was too exposed to the wind. The new harbour was linked to Athens by a long fortified boulevard called the "Long Walls". There is scarcely anything left of this port, which had several centuries of great prosperity before the Romans burnt and sacked it in 85 BC under Sulla's orders. That was probably when the museum's superb bronze statues were stored in the basement of a shop – where they were discovered by accident in 1959 – while waiting to be shipped to Rome.

Piraeus experienced a further setback in the 19C when Ermoúpoli, capital of the island of Síros, was chosen as the country's main port. At Otto of Bavaria's coronation in 1834, the town had no more than 50 inhabitants. But it came back into favour when Athens was made capital of the liberated nation and the Corinth Canal was opened in 1893.

Visiting the town

Morning is the best time to visit the two museums in Piraeus, which close between 2pm and 2.30pm. After lunch in Zéa Marina, rest during the afternoon heat and wait until later in the day to go for a walk. In the evening, try one of the cafés at Mikrolímano.

The Archaeological Museum★★

Odós Hariláou Trikoúpi 13. From the main harbour go along Aktí Miaoúlis – on your left when facing the sea. Turn left into Odós H Trikoúpi just before reaching the imposing Ágios Nikólaos Church. The museum is 150m further along (allow 20min to get there on foot from the metro). 8am-2.30pm; closed on Monday. Entrance fee.

The museum is housed in a modern building that is cool and quiet. At the entrance is a huge **sitting lion★** from a 4C BC funerary edifice discovered in the neighbouring Mosháto district. The museum has a fine series of **bas-reliefs** and the monumental remains of a **mausoleum★** from the 4C BC built in memory of a man and his son.

Attica

On the first floor there is a magnificent collection of **funerary steles** showing living and dying figures saying their last goodbyes. But the museum's gems are its **four bronze statues** (*see above*) which are thought to be from Delos. Two of them are of **Artemis** with her right hand stretched out, and the third is a remarkably well-preserved 2.35m-tall statue of **Athena** wearing a peplos and crested helmet from the 4C BC. The fourth statue, the famous **Apollo of Piraeus**, is the most important piece in the museum. This masterpiece, created in the late 6C BC in the severe style, is the oldest known Greek bronze.

From the first floor there is a view of the remains – the orchestra and first tiers – of the **Ancient theatre of Zéa**.

On leaving the museum, go along Odós H Trikoúpi to lively Zéa harbour, where there are places to eat. Continuing on the right, you reach the entrance to the harbour. The Maritime Museum is on the quayside.

The Maritime Museum*
Aktí Themistokléous. 9am-2pm; closed on Sunday, Monday, and in August. Entrance fee.
This new building, right on the Zéa Marina quay, was built around a section of the wall dating back to the time of Themistocles. The museum tells the story of the Greek navy from 8000 BC to the present through 2 000 objects with explanatory texts in Greek and English. Models, maps, uniforms, decorations, flags, paintings of naval battles and photographs illustrating the heyday of 20C Greek shipowners are mixed with bone objects sculpted by French sailors who were taken prisoner during the Napoleonic Wars. Of particular note are a **papyrus model of a boat** made in Corfu during Antiquity, and another of the **Averof**, the flagship of the Greek fleet until 1951. The boat itself, which has been turned into a museum, is anchored in Álimos harbour a few kilometres to the south.

Have a look around Zéa Marina and continue your walk along the seaside to Mikrolímano.

Mikrolímano and Kastélla

The well-named Mikrolímano ("little port") – a picturesque harbour full of yachts and colourful fishing boats – is the prettiest harbour in Piraeus. This is where to find the trendy bars and clubs whose tables spill over onto the pavement. If you're a walker, climb up **Kastélla Hill** above Mikrolímano (*a 30min walk in the direction of the "bowling center"*). It is a genuine village – far from the surrounding urban chaos – with working-class tavernas, single-storey houses, and chairs lined up along the pavement for long discussions in the evening. At the very top is a dead-end square with a large café (and a bowling alley) that has a huge terrace affording a fabulous **view** of the area: beneath you lies Mikrolímano; Piraeus is on your right, and Greater Athens stretches out endlessly in front of you – blanketed with the impenetrable *néfos*, the layer of smog hovering over the capital.

Piraeus

Making the most of Piraeus

As we said earlier, Piraeus *(Pireás)* (Plan I) is not exactly a resort destination. So you are only likely to stay there if you have an early boat or flight to catch. Piraeus has three harbours: the *main harbour*, right by the metro station, where ferries leave for the islands; *Zéa Marina* reserved for hydrofoils, and *Mikrolímano*, a small sailing harbour that is very lively in the evenings.

COMING AND GOING

By bus – *Coming from Athens*: from Sýndagma, take green bus *no* 40, which leaves every 15min, from 5am to midnight. Get off at Platía Grivas before the last stop (allow 30min, more at rush hour). From Omónia: take bus *no* 49, get off at Platía Themostokléous in Piraeus, on the left as you come out of the metro station.

Coming from the airport: an express bus runs 24 hours a day. Get off at the 'Harbour' stop (about 1hr).

To go to the airport: take the same bus from Platía Karaïskáki a few hundred metres on the left as you come out of the metro station. From the Piraeus metro station to Zéa Marina, take bus *no* 905 or trolleybus *no* 20.

By metro – Piraeus is the southern terminus for the Kifissiá-Piraeus line. Trains leave every 10min from 5am to midnight. Count on a 20min trip from Monastiráki, 25min from Omónia.

By train – Piraeus has 2 stations: **Peloponnese Station**, just to the right as you come out of the metro station, ☎ (01) 41 78 335, only serving cities on the peninsula; and the **station for northern Greece (Lárissa)**, across from the metro on the other side of the basin (go around the latter on the right), ☎ (01) 46 12 734.

By taxi – Ask the price of a trip before getting into a taxi (€15 on average to go to the centre of Athens). **To reserve by telephone, call** ☎ (01) 41 35 888 / 49 33 811 / 41 15 200.

GOING TO THE ISLANDS

Tickets can be bought at the same price in any agency at the harbour, where they will tell you the name of the boat and the quay.

Ferries – When taking a taxi to the main harbour in Piraeus (where the ferries leave from), tell the driver which island you are going to so that he can drop you off at the appropriate quay. When arriving by metro, the quays (or 'Gates') on your right are, successively, B, A, then H; on the left is quay G, just next to the metro, then quays D and E.

These are the main destinations and names of the corresponding quays: A and B for islands in the North Aegean (Chios, Lesbos, Ikaría, Sámos); E for the Dodecanese Islands; G and E for the Saronic Gulf; A for Crete; B for the Cyclades (Kíthnos, Sérifos, Sífnos, Kímolos, Mílos, Astipálea, Folégandros); G and D for Síros, Mýkonos, Íos, Tínos, Santoríni, Irárklia, Schinoússa, Koufoníssi, Amorgós, Donoússa; G for Páros and Náxos.

Hydrofoils – They leave from Zéa Marina, except for the ones to Égina (main harbour).

For information and schedules, contact the **Piraeus main harbour police**, ☎ (01) 42 26 000; for hydrofoils at **Zéa Marina**, ☎ (01) 45 25 315; and on the internet at: www.gtpnet.com

ADDRESS BOOK

Banks / Currency exchange – There are several banks facing the harbour: **National Bank** and **Eurobank** on the right as you come out of the metro, **Western Union** on the left.

Post office – ☎ (01) 41 71 584.

Police – Main harbour branch, ☎ (01) 42 26 000.

Medical service – Hospital, ☎ (01) 49 15 061.

WHERE TO STAY

Choose a hotel based on its proximity to your embarkation quay, or because they agree to drive you to the boat. Don't be taken in by the young people waving hotel brochures at you as you leave the metro. First ask them to show you on a map exactly how close the hotel is to your embarkation quay, and where the nearest bus stop is.

• **Piraeus Harbour**

€45

Eva, Odós Notará 2, ☎ (01) 41 70 110, Fax (01) 41 70 350. 🖋 📶 🍽 📺 The rooms in this new, pleasant hotel are small but comfortable and attractively decorated. The quietest ones are on the 6th floor. Its only drawback: there is no breakfast, and the closest café is three streets away.

Zacharátos, on the corner of Odós Notará and Odós Evangelistrías, ☎ (01) 41 78 830 – 59rm. 🖋 📶 🍽 🍴 📺 Just across from the Hotel Eva, this establishment is older but clean and comfortable.

Around €60

Anita-Argo, Odós Notará 23-25, ☎ (01) 41 21 795, Fax (01) 41 22 420 – 57rm. `⌁` `▤` `TV` Behind the metro station. As a last resort. They take you by minibus to the harbour and even to the airport.

Poseidónio, Odós Hariláou Trikoúpi 3, ☎ (01) 42 86 651, Fax (01) 42 99 220 – 54rm. `✎` `⌁` `▤` `TV` `CC` This recently renovated 10-storey building – a bit far from the harbour – has very comfortable rooms. There is no restaurant, but guests can have cooked meals delivered.

Noufara, Odós Iróon Polytehníou 45, ☎ (01) 41 15 541, Fax (01) 41 34 292 – 84rm. `✎` `⌁` `▤` `TV` `CC` As comfortable as the Poseidónio (same owner), this modern hotel has the advantage of being closer to the harbour.

Between €60 and €98

The Park, Odós Kolokotróni 103, ☎ (01) 45 24 611, Fax (01) 45 24 615 – 80rm. `✎` `⌁` `▤` `TV` `✕` `⌂` `CC` This comfortable hotel – popular with businessmen and less than a 10min walk from the harbour – is a good place to get away from the heat in Piraeus. The flower-decked terrace crowning the building is quite delightful for breakfast (continental or buffet). Nearly all the rooms have a balcony, and 24 of them also have saunas.

• **Zéa Marina (Passalimáni)**

Between €57 and €60

Lília, Odós Zéas 131, ☎ (01) 41 79 108, Fax (01) 41 14 311 – 20rm. `✎` `⌁` `▤` `TV` `CC` This small, quiet hotel is in a pretty little street overlooking Zéa Marina. Ask for a room overlooking the street (the others give onto a wall). Upon request, a free shuttle service will take you from the hotel to the harbour (in the morning) and from the harbour to the hotel (in the afternoon).

EATING OUT
The best establishments are only known to locals and are too far to reach on foot from the seafront. What is left along the harbour are fast-food joints and the usual greasy spoons. However, there are a few pleasant surprises in the adjoining streets, mostly in the area around the **municipal theatre**. To get there from the main harbour, turn left when facing the seafront and follow Aktí Posidónios. Go past the cathedral and continue down Leofóros Vassilíou Georgíou for 100m. Just behind the theatre is a charming square full of cafés and tavernas. Stay away from the tourist restaurants along Mikrolímano harbour, which are expensive and often dreadful.

• **Around Zéa Marina (Passalimáni)**

Between €7.50 and €9

To palió tis katsíkas, Odós Ipsilándou. This old taverna, which has been re-modelled, is directly opposite the Olympiakos shop – the kind of place where you choose your dinner in the kitchen and enjoy it while watching the news on TV.

Tá ennéa Adélphia ('the 9 brothers'), Odós Sotíros. From Zéa Marina, go up Odós Lambrákis as far as the first street on the right. The taverna is hidden behind the trees on a little square. This institution, a local favourite, has a wide variety of well-cooked traditional Greek dishes to choose from.

Around €23

🍲 **Pétrino**, on the corner of Odós Merarhías and Odós Ipsilándou, ☎ (01) 89 45 861. Local people are very fond of this restaurant. Its fanciful decor (stone walls covered with photographs of famous people, an overdone ceiling, artificial flowers, etc) is matched by its appealing menu. As for the service, it is fast and friendly.

HAVING A DRINK
If you are spending an evening in Piraeus, head for the centre of town around the municipal theatre, or for Zéa Marina (near the metro, bus *no* 905 or yellow trolleybus *no* 20). You could also take a taxi to delightful little **Mikrolímano harbour** where most of the town's trendy bars are located. There is a **bowling alley** at the top of Kastélla Hill.

Making the most of Piraeus

SOUTH OF ATHENS★
CAPE SOÚNION (AKROTÍRIO SOÚNIO)★★★

Province of Central Greece – District of Attica
Regional map page 123 – Michelin map 980 folds 30-31
A 155km tour starting from Athens – Allow 1 or 2 days

Not to be missed
Kessarianí Monastery.
The Temple of Poseidon at Soúnion, preferably at sunset.
The Sanctuary of Artemis at Vravróna (Brauron).

And remember...
Plan this excursion for a Saturday morning when the Vorrés Museum is open
(only at weekends) and before the Athenians have left the capital.
Avoid the beaches on the Apollo Coast, which are crowded with Athenians
(including late at night in summer).

Don't leave Athens without making the pilgrimage to Soúnion to watch the sunset over the ruins of the majestic Temple dedicated to Poseidon. Now is the time to explore this peaceful peninsula and salute its resistance – but for how much longer? – to the inexorable encroachment of the Athens suburbs. After the highly urbanised area around Ellinikó Airport – a dreary grid of offices and housing for the new middle class – there is a string of upmarket seaside resorts along the Apollo Coast almost to the tip of the peninsula. But at the end of the road are woods and countryside, less crowded beaches and a few secret spots looming up from the past: Antiquity in the ancient stones of Brauron, and the Middle Ages inside the serene walls of Moní Kessarianí.

The southern suburbs of Athens

By car, leave Athens via Odós Vassilíssis Sofías, which starts to the left of the Parliament. Once past the Hilton Hotel, take Odós Mesógion, and follow the signs for "Marathónas" and "Agía Paraskeví". Turn towards the airport to go to Moní Kessarianí (5km from the centre of Athens) or continue straight ahead for Peanía.
Moní Kessarianí can be reached by the no 223 and 224 buses (stops on Platía Kanigos, behind the National Museum, on Leofóros Akadémias, or on Leofóros Venizélou). The last stop is 30min on foot from the monastery. Taxis are also available. The surrounding woods are a pleasant place to have a picnic.

■ **Kessarianí Monastery**★★ – *8.30am-2.30pm; closed on Monday. Entrance fee.* Tucked away in a little valley covered with pine, plane and cypress trees in the shadow of Mt Hymettus, this little Byzantine monastery is one of the most attractive in the Athens area (and is very popular at weekends). Founded in the 10C, its nearly intact buildings enclose a **little garden**★ overrun with flowers and birds – a veritable Garden of Eden out of a medieval illumination. Hundred-year-old cypress trees keep a close watch over the **church** (katholikón), dedicated to the Presentation of the Virgin. Inside are some magnificent 16C and 17C **frescoes**★★ that replaced the original murals. Of particular note is the *Christ Pantocrator* covering the centre of the dome and the frescoes in the narthex by Peloponnese painter Ioánnis Ipatos. In addition to the finely drawn features and colours, they provide a moving account of the life of the monks in the 17C. The other side of the courtyard is lined with **monastery buildings**, including the refectory, bakery, mill and baths.
Continue this delightful walk into **Kessarianí Woods** (*from dawn to dusk*), destroyed during the Second World War and replanted in 1945 thanks to the efforts of a foundation. The main path leads all the way to the **top of Mt Hymettus** (1 026m), whose beehives were already famous in Antiquity.

Attica

From Moní Kessarianí (by car) go straight ahead past the monastery to get back to the main road, then take the road to Lávrio / Soúnion (12km).

■ **Peanía** – The only thing of interest in this dusty and soulless city founded by Demosthenes is the **Vorrés Museum**★ *(ask for directions from the centre of town; Saturday and Sunday only, 10am-2pm; entrance fee;* ☎ *(01) 66 42 520 / 66 44 771)*, a contemporary art foundation created by Ian Vorre, a local resident. It is housed in a huge estate divided into two distinct visiting areas. At the entrance is a modern **exhibition space**★ with hundreds of paintings and sculptures by Greek artists from the second half of the 20C. Behind it – surrounded by a magnificent **garden**★ – stands an elegantly furnished **traditional home**.

From Peanía, take the airport road and follow the coast south. From Athens, take Leofóros Amalías near the Parliament, go around the Temple of Olympian Zeus, then turn right into Odós Vouliagméni. Go past the airport (10km) and straight on to Soúnion (65km). If you don't have a car, take the A2 or A3 bus to Glifáda, then change to the 115 or the 116 which head south.

The Apollo Coast

Despite its name promising beauty, the Apollo Coast is rather disappointing with its string of crowded and over-developed beaches and a broad seafront avenue packed with cars. But after **Glifáda**, which is close to Athens *(14km)* and thus overpopulated and noisy due to the airport, the beaches become more and more pleasant the further you get from the capital. There are attractive beaches at **Vouliagméni**, a pleasant residential town well away from the noise of aircraft, as well as at **Voúla** and **Várkiza**, full of flowers and trees, all the way to the area around Soúnion with its quiet, sandy beaches at **Lagoníssi** and **Anávissos**.

■ **Cape Soúnion**★★★ (Akrotírio Soúnio) – *To go straight to Soúnion, either take the no 60 bus from Áreos Park near the National Museum (Plan II D1, page 127), which leaves every hour from 6.30am to 6pm; or take the bus from Platía Egíptou (same plan, C1), which leaves every 30min from 6.30am to 7.30pm. Car park and cafeteria at the site entrance.*

Twilight at Cape Soúnion

B. Kaufmann/MICHELIN

The only real jewel along the Apollo Coast belongs to Poseidon. Sunset over the temple dedicated to this sea god is one of Attica's major attractions; so do not expect to be alone while admiring it.

After the short walk up, the sight of the **Temple of Poseidon★★** (8am to dusk; entrance fee; allow 1hr) standing alone on its bare promontory is dramatic indeed. Like a lookout post at the southern tip of Attica, on what Homer called the "sacred rock", this grandiose site perched on the edge of a cliff 60m above the waves seems supremely indifferent to the ferryboats shuttling around the Aegean. The slender columns stand out like dazzlingly bright swords against the blue sky. Resisting the assault of time and weather, they mirror the greatness of the god whom they honoured.

Thus, even amid the crowds, you cannot escape the charm and evocative power of what was once called the "Cape of Columns". A landmark for sailors and a sentinel stationed at the entrance to the Saronic Gulf, the sanctuary was raised on a platform specially levelled for it, and protected by a (partly preserved) **defensive wall**. You walk past it – like a pilgrim in Ancient times – to reach the **propylaea** that led into the heart of the temenos (sacred area). Only a trace of its wide staircase remains – in the grooves from chariot wheels left in the central stone ramp. On the right, an imposing (levelled) **portico** housed pilgrims. It precedes the temple, standing majestically on its high **terrace** reached by a ramp. Built between 444 and 440 BC, at the same time as the Parthenon, it succeeded a previous temple to Athena destroyed during the second Persian War (ruins visible down and to the right from the road). Besides the cella walls, which were partially raised, 15 of the 34 **Doric columns** that surrounded it are still standing. As they are not curved – in order to better resist corrosion from the sea – they are more slender than traditional Doric columns and have 16 rather than 20 arrises. Likewise, the metopes dotting the frieze have no trace of any sculptures – too fragile here. Linger a moment at the **north pillar** of the cella. Like an avatar of modern times it is covered with graffiti, including some carved by Lord Byron in 1810.

Poseidon, a touchy god

After evicting Cronus, his three sons divided up the universe. Hades took the underworld, and Zeus became master of heaven and holder of the supreme title. As for Poseidon, he took possession of the waters and ruled the Earth's movements. Thus, the earthquakes that regularly rock Greece are ascribed to him, as well as the storms that the god unleashes as he howls and strikes the sea with his trident. Wild-tempered Poseidon – known for the irrepressible wrath that made Olympus itself quake – was feared above all by sailors, who always remembered to honour him. They paid tribute to him whenever they sailed around the tip of Soúnion, praying the god of the waves to grant them a smooth crossing. Even today, the long avenue leading to the seaside towns south of Piraeus has been dedicated to Poseidon by sailors.

The East Coast

From Soúnion, head northeast towards Lávrio

■ **Lávrio** – 9km from Soúnion. Lávrio, a former mining town with neo-Classical houses, is now filled with the desolate ruins of the establishments that once made it prosperous. Yet the **argentiferous lead mines** (close to 2 000 shafts!) discovered in 484 BC contributed to the power of Athens and Attica. Themistocles, the founder of Piraeus, used them to build 200 triremes that took part in the Greek victory over the Persians at Salamis, and they enabled the city to strike coins and finance Pericles' great works. Exploitation of the mines stopped in the 2C AD and was only started again in 1864 when new processes were developed for treating the ore. It continued until 1981 under the aegis of a French mining company. The only vestiges of this golden age are the **Museum of Mineralogy** (Odós Andrea

Kordela; Wednesday, Saturday and Sunday, variable times) and, in Thoriko *(1km north of the city at the end of the road)*, the remains of a **theatre** from the 5C or 4C BC – overrun with vegetation – that could hold 5 000 spectators.

■ From Lávrio take the road that goes across the **Mesógia** (Midland) covered with olive trees, woods and vineyards. In **Markópoulo**, where *Kourtákis* retsína is made, stop off at the **Daréma bakery** on the main square to taste the *moustokoúlora*, delicious cookies made with grape juice.

■ Then turn right towards **Pórto Ráfti**, a pretty harbour fringed with sandy beaches (which is not always the case on this coast).

From Pórto Ráfti, take the coast road to the seaside resort of Brauron (8km to the north). Drive through the town and head inland until you reach the archaeological site.

■ **Brauron★** (Vravróna) – *Even when the site is closed, the ruins are easily visible from the outside. Allow 90min including the museum.* According to Euripides (in *Iphigeneia in Tauris*), Agamemnon's daughter brought a sacred statue of Artemis with her when she came back to spend her last days in Brauron, thus introducing the cult of the goddess to Attica. But one day a she-bear – Artemis' totem animal – threatened her sister. A young man saved her by killing the bear, immediately provoking the wrath of the goddess. To make amends, Iphigeneia dedicated a sanctuary to her that was watched over by young priestesses called "Little She-Bears". A pilgrimage held there every four years was one of the most important in Attica in the 5C BC.

The ruins of the **Sanctuary of Artemis★** *(8.30am-2.30pm; closed Monday, Tuesday and Wednesday; entrance fee)* are scattered over a peaceful field surrounded by eucalyptus trees. To reach the site, walk down to the white **Ágios Geórgios Chapel** *(closed)* overlooking it. A path on the right runs past the foundations of a **sacred house**, behind which a crevice in the rock has been identified as the **Tomb of Iphigeneia**. Below it lie the foundations of the **temple** itself, around which the sanctuary was set up. Twelve of its columns have been re-erected – part of the **Stoa of the Bears** whose architraves the birds use to perch on. It was here that the girls did their "bear dance".

As you leave the sanctuary, take the by-road that runs alongside the site towards the **museum★** *(500m further on; 8.30am-2.30pm; closed on Monday; entrance fee)* at the edge of the field. Despite the rather dated style of the museum, there are a few pieces discovered in the sanctuary which are worth having a look at: the 9C-8C BC **vases** with geometric motifs, the collection of **bone flutes**, the **bas-reliefs** from the 5C to the 3C BC illustrating the goddess Artemis before a procession of pilgrims, and above all *(in Room 2)* the beautiful **statuettes★** of the "Little She-Bears" and other children. A **model** at the entrance provides a reconstruction of the site.

■ Fifteen kilometres to the north lies **Rafina** *(131km from Athens)*, the second-largest port after Piraeus for ships serving the Aegean Islands.

Little She-Bears
The young priestesses who worshipped Artemis of Brauron were called "little she-bears" in memory of the violent death of the goddess' she-bear. They were initiated into the cult at the age of seven, along with a number of boys. During the Brauronia celebration held every four years in the goddess' honour, they wore saffron-yellow robes and imitated a bear walking in an expiatory dance. Contrary to what was long believed, it seems that the girls only lived on the site during the celebrations.

Attica

COMING AND GOING

By bus – See map of Athens page 126-127. For **Glifáda**: bus A3 from Sýndagma, (blue) bus A2 and E2 Express from Leofóros Amalías (the stop is just across from the entrance to the National Gardens). Weekdays, every 20min from 8am-4.30pm.

For **Vouliagméni** and **Várkiza**: (blue) bus A3 goes through Sýndagma and ends in Glifáda. From there, transfer to the 114 or 115.

For **Voúla**: (blue) bus A2, the stop is at Sýndagma. For **Brauron**: (blue) bus A5, the stop is on Leofóros Academías. For **Moní Kessarianí**: (blue) bus 224, the stop is on Leofóros Vassilíssis Sofías.

For **Peanía**: (blue) bus A5 on Leofóros Academías, then transfer to the 307, 308 or 310. For **Soúnion**: the coastal buses (*paraliaká*) leave every hour (on the half hour) from the Mavromatéon bus terminal and stop on Odós Filelínon near Sýndagma 10min later (2hr trip).

WHERE TO STAY

Most hotels are located on the Apollo Coast, as the East Coast is reserved for seasonal rentals for Athenians. Since most of these establishments are pricey and campsites rare, use Athens as a base or treat yourself to one night in the Soúnion area.

• Glifáda

Between €45 and €55

Ilion, Odós Kondíli 4, ☎ (01) 894 60 11. ⚎ 𝓟 This pleasant – although rather antiquated – hotel in a quiet area in the heart of Glifáda is supposedly the least expensive in town. Breakfast (not included) and other meals can be taken in a pleasant taverna across the street.

Around €90

Sea View, Odós Xánthou 4, on the seafront 100m south of the former airport, ☎ (01) 894 76 81 – 74rm. ⚎ 𝓟 ▤ TV ✗ ⚲ ⚲ A modern 5-storey hotel right across from Astir beach with comfortable rooms and a nice pool. It's a shame that it's so close to the noisy avenue running along the seafront. The (high) rates include breakfast.

• Anávissos

Between €45 and €55

Calypso Beach, ☎ and Fax (0291) 601 70 to 74 – 70rm. ⚎ 𝓟 ✗ ⚲ 🏠 This pleasant establishment built almost on top of a grey pebble beach has rooms in a main building and in bungalows (with air conditioning). A warm welcome and peaceful environment on a wooded peninsula next to a calm bay.

€75

🛏 **Mávro Lithári**, ☎ (0291) 549 72 to 74, Fax (0291) 549 75 – 18 studios. ⚎ 𝓟 TV ✗ ⚲ ⚱ 🏠 A clean and modern complex – only recently opened – and one of the most pleasant on the coast. The huge studios are elegant (slate floors, blue fabrics, terraces), well furnished (beds, sofa beds, kitchenettes, etc) and can comfortably accommodate up to 5 people. There are 3 terraces overlooking the sea where you can dine, and the beach is only 150m away. Ask for a room with a view of the Saronic Gulf but far enough from the piano bar if you like going to bed early.

Around €90 with half-board

Xenia Helios, 49km from Athens, 15km from Soúnion, ☎ (0291) 370 24, Fax (0291) 369 98 – 104rm. ⚎ 𝓟 ▤ ✗ ⚲ 🏠 A fine pyramid-shaped establishment from the 1970s which is a hotel management school during the school year and is open to the public from 1 June to 25 September. The service is well attended to by the school's students and teachers, giving the place a friendly atmosphere. The comfortable rooms all have terraces and overlook the sea (2 adjoining beaches).

• Legrená

Between €30 and €38

Minos, a little way from the village, ☎ (0292) 513 21 to 23 – 72rm. ⚎ ✗ Although it is named after a fabulously wealthy king, the only luxury in this hotel is its clean and spacious rooms. The welcome and the electrical system, however, seem quite worn out. Breakfast not included. Open all year.

• **Soúnion**

Between €60 and €75

Cape Soúnion Beach, 3km from the temple, ☎ (0292)398 24 / 393 91, ☎ in Athens (01) 861 78 37, Fax (01) 861 64 73 – 26rm. 🍴 🖉 ✗ ⛱ 🏊 🍸 ♨ 🎏 The bungalows at this hotel are scattered over a wooded hill and all have a fantastic view of the temple across the way. The surrounding park is well maintained and the beach can be reached through a tunnel under the road. Pity about the lack of air conditioning and the rather faded decor. Rates include half-board.

Aegaeon, 1.5km west of the Temple of Poseidon, ☎ (0292) 392 00, ☎ and Fax (0292) 392 34 – 89rm. 🍴 🖉 📺 ✗ 🏊 This hotel located in a quiet spot on the seashore is the closest to the temple of Soúnion. The advantageous location is almost enough to make you forget the somewhat dated facilities and decor in the rooms. Breakfast not included. There are two tavernas at the nearby beach.

• **Vravróna**

Between €68 and €75

Mare Nostrum, on the seafront, ☎ (0294) 484 34, Fax (0294) 477 90 – 352rm. 🍴 🖉 🍽 ✗ ⛱ 🏊 ♨ 🎏 This recently renovated, enormous complex built in the 1980s is one of the few hotels on the east coast. It has all the best of what you would expect from this kind of establishment: games, activities, shops, etc, as well as a nearby thalassotherapy centre.

EATING OUT

The whole coast is lined with the usual array of pizzerias and fast-food joints, but the fishing harbours also have restaurants with very fresh grilled fish. Ask the price of the fish beforehand if there is no set menu, otherwise you may be in for an unpleasant surprise. Octopus *(octapódi)* and squid *(kalamári)* are the cheapest deals around.

HAVING A DRINK

Cafés, bars – Kastro, in Pórto Ráfti. This trendy bar on a hill catering to a chic clientele from Athens is housed in an extravagant concrete fortress complete with watch turrets, machicolations and "Knights of the Round Table" furniture! Lunch is served on Sundays. It isn't cheap, but there is a fabulous view of Pórto Ráfti and the coast. Daily from 4 June to the end of August; the rest of the year on Saturday from 4pm-1am and on Sunday from 12pm to 1am.

Vouliagméni Yachting Club, a chic establishment at the marina entrance.

Night-clubs – The Apollo Coast has an impressive array of bars and night-clubs which are particularly lively in summer when the Athenians migrate out here.

OTHER THINGS TO DO

Outdoor pursuits – In Loútsa, there are several **windsurfing** clubs and one **scuba-diving** club.

In Glifáda, **Bowling Blanos** is in the centre of town. There is a **go-cart** track in the Ágios Kosmás district on Leofóros Poseidón, which runs alongside the sea.

Sailing harbours – Alimos (Kalamakí), the largest one on the coast, ☎ (01) 98 80 003; **Flisvos** (P Faliro), ☎ (01) 98 822 18 / 98 874 22; **Vouliagméni**, ☎ (01) 896 00 12; **Lávrio** (Olympic Marines), ☎ (0292) 610 18.

Excursions – One-day excursions to Cape Soúnion are quite common from Athens. Enquire in one of the many travel agencies.

EUBOEA★★ (ÉVIA)
Province of Central Greece – District of Euboea
Regional map page 127 – Michelin map 980 folds 18-30-31
3 654km² – Pop approx 205 500

Not to be missed
The mountain road along the southern tip of the island.
The remains of ancient Erétria.
A siesta in the shade of the pine trees on the unspoilt beaches south of Límni.
And remember...
Driving is the most practical way to get around. But given the size of the island,
allow more time for the long distances and winding roads
where you must drive slowly.

There is nothing really unforgettable in Euboea, although it is the second largest Greek island after Crete. But the variety of landscapes, the magnificent views, peaceful villages and seaside resorts add up to an alluring getaway, which is all the easier as its coasts brush up against those of Attica – a stone's throw from Athens. Whereas the west coast across from the mainland is dotted with beaches backed by stretches of agricultural land, the east coast is wilder with steep contours. Cool mists from the thick forests cover the mountains in the central area. The richly wooded land in the north (pine, chestnut and olive trees) is in stark contrast to the bare, rocky landscapes at the island's remote southern tip.

Not quite an island
Euboea may be an island but it doesn't have the insular feeling that is a distinctive feature of the little islands off the coast. The sea is not always visible from the bends along the mountain ridge over 150km long, and the southern tip is closer to Athens than to the northern part of the island. You could easily think you were on the mainland, which Euboea used to be part of before Poseidon separated them with his trident (or more prosaically, before an earthquake). There is only one bridge linking it to Attica, which already spanned the **Evrípos Channel** in the 6C BC.
Tourist facilities are rather scanty and mainly aimed at Greek tourists, especially Athenians fleeing the oppressive heat in the capital in summer and **people taking the waters**.

The Great Crossing
A tour of about 625km by car. Allow at least 3 days.

■ **Halkída (Chalcis) –** The capital of the island, the starting point of your journey, lies just on the far side of the **metal bridge** connecting Euboea to the mainland (*a 45min drive from Athens*). With a population of over 50 000, this large, cosmopolitan and noisy town is the focal point for trade and industry on the island. Two or three hours is long enough to have a pleasant walk along its vast **quays★** facing the Evrípos Channel (there is frequently a market along the seafront).
Before strolling through town and exploring its vestiges from the past – it was an important city state allied with Athens in the 5C BC – stop by the **Archaeological Museum★** (*Odós Venizélou 13, 8.30am-1pm; closed on Monday; entrance fee*). It has some fine prehistoric, Hellenistic and Roman pieces which were discovered locally. Then have a walk in the **Kástro district★★** (*to the south-east, behind the old metal bridge; not to be confused with the ruins of the Turkish fortress standing across from it on the mainland*), the former stronghold of the Turkish community, which remained in Halkída until 1923 – almost a century after the last Ottoman garrison had left (in

1833). There is an antiquated feeling about its sleepy little streets with their **traditional houses** with overhanging upper floors, some of which are quite rundown. Recently settled by Muslims from Thrace, it has preserved its 15C **mosque**★ (closed) with an adjoining marble **fountain**★, as well as a large 13C Byzantine basilica, **Agía Paraskeví**★ (visits during services), decorated with fine **mosaics** and a **marble iconostasis**. Just across from it stands the elegant façade of the **Venetian Vazelis house**. The nearby **synagogue** (19C) on Varatásou is a reminder of the Jewish presence here going back over 2 500 years.

Head north out of Halkída; turn right at Néa Artáki.

■ **Stení**★★ – *31km from Halkída*. This is the first foray into the verdant mountains in the centre. After the city heat it feels good to stop off in this peaceful village up in the cool heights. The splashing and gurgling of its many **fountains** and springs can be heard throughout its little streets – from the *kafenía* to the sleepy old houses – and a stream winds through the village in the shade of tall plane trees.

■ *After Stení, the road lined with beehives climbs up to the pass 8km further along.* Pull over and enjoy the **view**★★ of the sea from both sides of the pass. With the right shoes you can start out here on a **hike**★★ up to the bare summit of **Mt Dhírfis**★★, the highest peak on the island (1 743m) (*enquire in the village of Stení; allow 2hr30min to hike up; take a sweater, some water and food*). After a walk in the shade of dense, varied vegetation that changes as you go higher, deciduous trees give way to pines, then to a jumble of bare rocks at the summit with a magnificent **panorama**★★ of the island and the sea.

After the climb, carry on along the road which descends the north-eastern slopes of Mt Dhírfis.

■ Just before reaching the village of Metóhi, turn left onto a pleasant, nearly deserted track (*for 17km*) that runs through planes, chestnuts, pines, ferns, fields and orchards. The little streams are easily fordable. Stretching out at the end of the path is beautiful **Hiliadoú beach** (*signposted*), a pleasant place to relax after a hike.

Back in Metóhi (about 24km after Stení), a good paved road takes you straight to the village of Kími (24km further on).

■ **Kími** – Situated on a rocky plateau 250m above the sea, the village of Kími overlooks its harbour and the pretty, sandy beach of **Paralía Kímis**★ nestling below it 4km away. Anyone interested in local traditions might like to make a brief stop at the **Folk Art Museum** (*10am-1pm / 5pm-7.30pm*) located between the village and the harbour (which has a collection of local costumes).

From Kími, continue south towards Káristos. The road, although very beautiful, is long (about 105km) and winding. After a while it opens onto a peaceful plain of scrubby pastureland dotted here and there with **Byzantine chapels**.

■ **Lépoura** – (*35km*) Lépoura is the gateway to the southern part of Euboea, an arid and desolate area with scattered villages that have an Albanian flavour. The road gets steeper, winding up and down the slopes of bare mountains. Dotting the rocky moon-like landscape are large white **wind turbines** – modern windmills – contrasting with the last Lombard and Venetian **lookout towers** still keeping watch over the sea.

Between **Stíra** (marble quarries) and **Káristos**, the **eagle road**★★ runs at nearly 800m along the mountain ridge. There are few birds of prey despite its name, but it affords spectacular **views**★★ of the **Petalión Gulf**. The wind is strong here as it slams into the abrupt slopes of **Mt Óhi**★ (1 398m), where the cipolin marble **quarries** have been worked since Antiquity.

■ **Káristos*** – Now the landscape becomes more welcoming, with a fertile plain dotted with vineyards and olive trees. It opens onto a large, sheltered bay with the bustling port of Káristos – the southernmost city on the island. This large seaside resort features some fine **neo-Classical architecture**. Káristos was planned by the Bavarian architect Bierbach for King Otto, who contemplated transferring the capital of the young Greek nation here. The **Bourzi****, the remains of a 14C **Venetian fortress** inlaid with ancient marble from the Temple of Apollo, stands at the eastern end of the quay. The waterfront is a pleasant place for a stroll – and it's possible to carry on to the extensive beaches stretching out on both sides of the city (such as **Psilí Ámmos** to the west, a lovely – although often windy – beach).

Those keen on art and history might also stop off at the modest **Archaeological Museum** *(across from the Bourzi, 8.30am-2.30pm; closed on Monday; entrance fee)*.

From Káristos, take a tour of the heights above the city *(3.1km)*, where the pretty town of **Míli*** is shaded by plane trees and oleanders.

From here a minor road leads almost to the foot of **Castel Rosso****, an impressive fortress perched on a rocky promontory, which owes its name to the red-coloured stone *(it can also be reached on foot from the town in 20min)*. It is worth a trip for the incomparable **view***** of the city, the bay, southern Euboea and the Cyclades.

It is also worth venturing down to the **southern tip of the island**** on the coast road. It is paved for 8km, then turns into a stony track, but you are rewarded with a number of remote coves and beaches. The southern tip of the island can also be explored by boat *(enquire at the harbour)*.

Take the same road out of Káristos that you came in on, and when you reach Lépoura (68km, stopping off at Néa Stíra for a quick swim) turn left towards Alivéri.

The landscape changes west of **Alivéri** *(9km)* and **Amárinthos** *(16km)*. The coast – lined with beaches where the sea is calm – has been spoiled by all the hotel complexes and vacation homes.

■ **Erétria**** – *9km.* With its 19C architecture, Erétria is more attractive than neighbouring Halkída. It has preserved many remains from its ancient past as a prosperous city renowned for its powerful merchant fleet, as well as for its **philosophy school** that was very influential until the city was destroyed by the Romans in 87 AD.

Have a walk inside the walls of the ancient **acropolis**** *(behind the museum in the northern part of the town)* overlooking the ruins of a palace, a temple, a gymnasium and a theatre with an underground passageway for the actors.

Don't miss the **Archaeological Museum**** *(8.30am-3pm; closed on Monday; entrance fee)* containing a wealth of objects from the prehistoric site of Xiroropolis, from the necropolis at Lefkandi (11C-9C BC) and from Ancient Erétria, including **tombs** from the Classical, Hellenistic and Roman Eras, **funerary vases**, fragments and a reconstructed pediment from the Temple of Apollo, etc. There are also funerary monuments, pottery and mosaics in the courtyard.

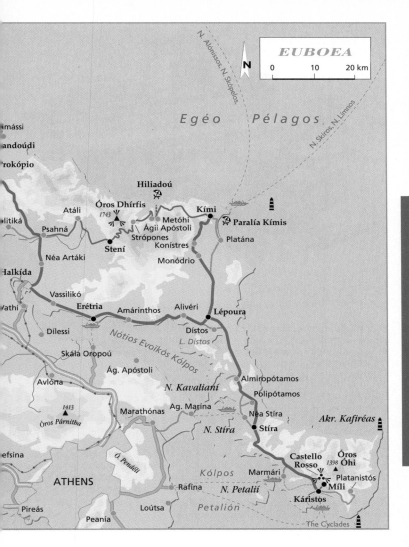

The **House of Mosaics****, an ancient villa 300m east of the museum (*free admission; ask the museum guard for the keys*) is a must to round off your visit. Built around 370 BC and destroyed a century later, it has nevertheless preserved a few reception rooms, where you can see some magnificent ornamental **pebble mosaics**** with mythological themes.

Return to Halkída, 22km to the west, and continue north towards Límni.

G. de Benoist/MICHELIN

Repairing nets at the harbour

Heading north*

After Halkída, the winding road climbs up through a superb pine forest. A river runs through a small valley with lush vegetation between **Prokópio** (*41km*) – known for its unsightly **Ágios Ioánnis Rossos Monastery** – and **Mandoúdi** (*8km further on*). A charming place to have a picnic or a siesta.

In Strofiliá (8km away), turn left towards Límni, 19km further on.

Límni** – The old houses in this pretty fishing village perched on a mountainside run all the way down to the sea. The modest, serene setting is favoured by artists as well as retired folk who converse endlessly in their favourite cafés.

From the village, the very pretty **coast road**** heads south. After the *To Ástro* restaurant (*see the "Eating out" section*) the paved road turns into a dirt track, which disappears into a thick pine forest covering the slopes of **Mt Kandíli** all the way to the sea. There are many beautiful places to go swimming tucked away in a totally untamed setting. Continuing straight ahead, you reach large **Glifá Beach**** – in fact several successive beaches – with its calm and clear waters. A a perfect place to relax.

Go back towards Límni and climb up to **Galatáki*** (*8km from Límni; signposted; theoretically open in the morning and late afternoon; free admission*), a peaceful and remote convent at the tip of a promontory overlooking the gulf. The nuns will lend women a dress, but they won't hesitate to turn away any men whose knees are showing! The **katholikón** has 16C frescoes.

Back in Límni, continue your journey by taking the cliff road leading to Loutrá Edipsoú (31km). There is a magnificent **view**** *over the sea from the entire stretch of road. Stop off for a swim along the way at the beach below the village of* **Roviés**.

■ **Loutrá Edipsoú**, a thermal spa, has been known since Ancient times for the therapeutic properties of its **sulphurous waters**. Finding food and lodging is easy because of the host of spa hotels, guesthouses and restaurants, but there is nothing else of interest in the town.

■ Beyond Loutrá Edipsoú the road soon runs along a wide, nearly deserted bay with a glorious, uncrowded sandy **beach★★**. At the other end of the bay is **Loutrá Giáltron** *(15km)*, a place known for its **hot springs** with sulphur steam (for drinking and bathing) flowing straight into the sea.

Return to Loutrá Edipsoú and turn left in a north-easterly direction.

The north-east coast

■ After going around a bend, just before reaching Oreí, there is a beautiful, inviting beach with a **watchtower** perched on a little island where you can have a swim. The quay in the picturesque fishing town of **Oreí** *(16km from Loutrá Edipsoú)* extends into a beach. The little cafés lined up next to each other are wonderful places to contemplate the **sunset** over the mainland across the way.

■ The northern tip of Euboea is less developed and less accessible. The main road runs almost straight to the unprotected beaches on the east coast, which are not always very clean. Rather than going to the beach at Pefkí, for instance, go to the much more attractive one at **Elliniká★** *(about 25km after Istiéa)*, a busy town with many markets.

■ Before reaching Strofiliá, where you join the road back to Halkída, have one last stop in the quiet village of **Agía Ána★** *(57km from Istiéa)*, where the old women still wear traditional costumes.

Making the most of Euboea

COMING AND GOING

By boat – Ferries leave for Erétria from the little port of **Skála Oropoú** every 30min between 6am and 11pm and return every 30min between 5am and 10pm in summer. Other ferries run from the mainland to ports on the west coast of the island: from Glífa to Agiókambos, from Arkítsa to Loutrá Edipsoú, from Agía Marína to Néa Stíra, and from Rafína to Marmári and Káristos.

By **hydrofoil** (Flying Dolphins): from Rafína (east of Athens) to Káristos, Marmári, N Stíra, Alivéri, etc. The terminal in Halkída is north-east of the channel, on the mainland side. Boats leave from Káristos for the islands of Ándros, Tínos and Mýkonos on a regular basis.

By bus – From Athens (terminal B) there are buses every 30min for Halkída between 7.45am and 9pm (1hr40min). For Kími: 4 or 5 buses a day. For Loutrá Edipsoú: 3 buses a day.

To find the stop in **Halkída**, walk 400m up Odós Kotsou from the bridge. It is 50m to the right. For Kími from Erétria: 9 buses a day (2hr30min). For Káristos via Erétria: 3 buses a day (3hr30min). For Límni: 4 buses a day (2hr30min).

By air – From Athens: 3 flights a day. Other flights from Thessaloníki and Lesbos.

By train – Trains leave every hour from Athens (Laríssis Station) for Halkída. The station in Halkída is on the mainland side of the channel, south of the fortress.

GETTING AROUND

By boat – In summer, numerous daily hydrofoils (Flying Dolphins) run between Halkída and Loutrá Edipsoú via Límni (1hr).

By bus – Buses run on the main road from Halkída to the island's main urban centres: Káristos in the south-east, Límni and Loutrá Edipsoú in the north-west, and Kími in the east.

By car – This is the most practical option. Given the considerable distances and the often very strong winds on mountain ridges, avoid two-wheel vehicles except for off-road motorcycles. The easiest way is to rent a car in Athens (about an hour's trip) or in the centre of Halkída (around the waterfront).

ADDRESS BOOK (HALKÍDA)

Besides Halkída, only the two large resorts of Káristos and Loutrá Edipsoú offer a whole range of services. Límni has banks, a post office and an OTE office.

Tourist information – *Negroponte Agency (EOT)*, Angeligovioú 22, ☎ (0221) 282 90 / 761 33.

In Káristos, the **SET-Kosmos agencies** are on the western side of the central esplanade, and at the western end of the quayside, ☎ (0224) 26 200 / 25 700, Fax (0224) 29 011.

Tourist police – ☎ (0221) 83 333.

Harbourmaster's office – ☎ (0221) 28 888.

Banks / Currency exchange – Around Odós Eleftheríou and near the quayside.

Post office / Telephone – *Main post office*, Odós Karamourtzoúni. *OTE*, Odós Venizélou, near the museum.

Medical service – *Hospital*, ☎ (0221) 21 901.

WHERE TO STAY

Under €27

Halkída is not a very pleasant place to stay. Try Loutrá Edipsoú, which is less noisy and has many spa establishments. The best plan is to stop off in one of the following villages or towns:

• Stení

The two hotels overlooking the village have fine views of the little valley. An ideal place to enjoy the cool air and restful setting.

Dirfys, up to the left of the road, ☎ (0228) 51 217 / 51 370 – 18rm. ⌐| ✕ ☞ A rather nonchalant welcome. Rooms are spacious but a bit rustic. Pleasant outdoor terrace for breakfast.

⌂ **Hotel Stení**, next to the Dirfys, ☎ (0228) 51 221 – 35rm. ⌐| TV ✕ ⌐ ☞ The rooms in this hotel are very comfortable, well kept, quiet and spacious, with pretty wood panelling and a beautiful view of the valley.

• Kími Beach (Paralía Kímis)

There are several rooms for rent in the hilltop village of Kími.

Between €27 and €38

Corali Hotel, 300m south of the harbour, 150m up and to the right,

☎ (0222) 22 212 / 22 002, Fax (0222) 23 353 – 25rm. ⌐| ℰ ▤ TV Very quiet, spacious and comfortable.

Beis Hotel, on the seafront, to the north, ☎ (0222) 22 870, Fax (0222) 22 604 – 40rm. ⌐| ℰ ▤ TV ✕ ☞ This modern hotel lacks charm but provides comfortable rooms with a view of the sea. It is next to the embarkation quay, which is practical for anyone taking the ferry, although rather noisy.

• Káristos

Between €27 and €38

Hotel Galaxy, at the western end of the quayside, ☎ (0224) 22 600 / 22 603 – 60rm. ⌐| ℰ ▤ TV ☞ CC This establishment has a large capacity, but the decor is outdated. The rooms are decent, with views over the quayside or street.

Around €45

⌂ **Karystion Hotel**, Kriezótou 3 (at the far eastern end of the quay, after the "Bourzi"), ☎ (0224) 22 391 / 22 191, Fax (0224) 22 727 – 39rm. ⌐| ℰ ▤ TV ⌐ ☞ CC A modern, tastefully furnished and very comfortable hotel with highly professional service. Ask for a room facing west so that you can enjoy the sunset from your terrace. The sumptuous breakfast – with the freshest ingredients – is served on the garden terrace.

• Amárinthos

Although Amárinthos is not a particularly pleasant town, it is a practical place from which to visit Erétria, 9km away.

Around €27

Hotel Apartments Iliathídes, on the main road north of town next to the Shell fuel station, ☎ (0229) 37 605 / 37 215 – 16rm. ⌐| ℰ ▤ TV ☞ CC This establishment offers good value for money. In addition to spacious and comfortable flats with kitchens, it has views of the harbour and a friendly owner.

Over €38

Hotel Artemis, ☎ (0229) 36 168 / 38 632, Fax (0229) 38 655 – 22rm. ⌐| ℰ ▤ TV ⌐ ⌐ ☞ CC This upmarket hotel is located on the waterfront. Rooms have balconies, are comfortable and well equipped, but rather expensive.

• Erétria

Campsite (around €23)

Milos campsite, as you leave Erétria (towards Halkída), ☎ (0229) 60 420 / 60 421, Fax (0229) 60 360 – 60 pitches. 🏕 ⚒ [CC] Located on the waterfront. Bar and shop. Very clean.

• Límni

Around €27

Plaza Hotel, at the harbour under the arcades, ☎ (0227) 31 235 – 8rm. A modest hotel (showers off the corridor) in a traditional home run by some friendly elderly ladies. Charming, but rather expensive given the level of comfort.

🍴 **Límni Hotel**, south of the quayside, ☎ (0227) 31 316 / 31 748 – 27rm. 🏕 🏊 This hotel is comfortable, inexpensive, and away from the hustle and bustle of the harbour. 20 rooms with sea views. Breakfast not included.

To Ástro (Ioannou Brothers' Taverna), see restaurant of the same name below.

• Roviés

Campsite (around €12)

Camping Rovies, as you come from Límni heading towards Loutrá Edipsoú, go past the village of Roviés; the campsite is on the left, ☎ (0227) 71 120 / 71 123. About a hundred shaded spaces next to a pleasant beach.

EATING OUT

Because most of the visitors who come here are Greek, most restaurants only provide menus in Greek.

• Halkída

Between €9 and €15

There are dozens of restaurants on the seafront that are quite expensive and of mediocre quality. None are really worth mentioning.

• Steni

Under €9

Sakafliás, on the main square in the old part of the village (to the right of the road as you go up). 🍽 This little taverna has no menu and they do not speak English, but hand gestures work quite well to explain what you want. The tasty regional dishes are copious and inexpensive.

Around €9

Kissos, on the left side of the road, ☎ (0228) 51 226 / 51 227. 🍽 This large restaurant with several terraces has a wide range of dishes at reasonable prices.

• Kími

Around €9

Several decent seafront tavernas.

• Káristos

There are many quite good tavernas along the seafront, where you can have a pleasant stroll in the evening.

🍴 **Cavo d'oro**, Párodos Sahtoúri (an alleyway at right angles to the quayside after the esplanade). 🍽 A traditional taverna where the culinary delights are shown in the window. It's a good thing, because the menu is only in Greek. There is no fish, but the dishes with sauce are delicious and copious.

🍴 **Ta Kalámia**, further west, at the beginning of the beach. 🍽 A nice taverna on the water, far from the tourists. It has no English menu, but its traditional dishes – which you can have a look at in the kitchen – are inexpensive and tasty.

• Límni

Around €9

🍴 **O Plátanos**, under the only plane tree on the quayside. 🍽 This establishment with its very pleasant shaded terrace is well known and appreciated by the locals. Specialities include grilled and fried fish, grilled meat and other dishes. Family-run and efficient. Only open at weekends during the low season.

O Sténios, on the quayside right next to O Platanos. 🍽 A pleasant and inexpensive ouzo bar.

Between €9 and €15

🍴 **To Ástro (Ioánnou Brothers' Taverna)**, 3.5km south of Límni on the coast road in a tiny hamlet on the water, ☎ (0227) 31 487 / 32 426. 🍽 This is the place for a romantic dinner. Meals are served on a large terrace in a charming setting. The food is traditional, but quite varied and of high quality. This establishment also has 10 modest rooms 200m away overlooking the sea (enquire at the restaurant).

FROM ATTICA TO BOEOTIA (VIOTÍA)★★
EXCURSIONS NORTH OF ATHENS
Province of Central Greece – Districts of Attica and Boeotia
Regional map page 123 – Michelin map 980 folds 29-30-31

Not to be missed
The Ancient Temple of Nemesis in Ramnoús.
The Byzantine monasteries of Dafní and Óssios Loukás.

And remember...
Plan on driving since the public transport network in Boeotia
(north-west of Athens towards Delphi) is not well developed.
Don't try to find lodging along the way, as accommodation is limited.

Mainly frequented by Greek tourists for its beaches, mountains and pure air, northern Attica is little known by foreigners. This is probably because they are pressed for time and imagine the area north of Athens as one big noisy and dusty suburb not worth investigating. Yet, just past the suburbs there is a bucolic region where charming little valleys full of olive trees alternate with mountain forests. It is ideal for a day's excursion from Athens before taking the road north or towards the Peloponnese.

In fact, the finest places in Attica are hidden in Boeotia on the shores of the Gulf of Corinth. Barely out of Athens, Dafní Monastery heralds another side of Greece, a serene and verdant region you will enjoy exploring (or returning to) after the hustle and bustle of the capital.

Northern Attica★
North-east of Athens
A 170km tour. Allow one day. Sites close around 2.30pm, so do your sightseeing in the morning and spend a night in the heart of Mt Parnes.

Leave Athens via Leofóros Vassilíssis Sofías, which runs left of the Parliament (Platía Sýndagma, Plan II page 126-127), then go straight on towards Rafína).

■ **Rafína** *(25km from Athens)*, the first stop on your tour, is built on a human scale despite being the port from which ferries and hydrofoils leave for the Aegean. Tavernas and fish stalls crowd the quays, and the beach turns out to be quite pleasant if you have a few hours to kill while waiting for your boat. But the most attractive beaches lined with pine trees lie to the north between **Máti**, a seaside resort favoured by Athenians, and **Néa Mákri**.

■ **Marathon** (Marathónas) – *20km from Rafína. 8am-2.30pm; closed on Monday. Entrance fee. Museum visit included in price of ticket.* Marathon would be nothing more than a dreary plain if its name weren't synonymous with one of the most famous battles in Antiquity. All that remains of that event is a **tumulus** with the ashes of the 192 Greek soldiers who died and were cremated at the site of the battle. Enclosed within a public garden, the burial mound forms a 10m-high knoll with a circumference of 180m. Its weed-covered slopes once had steles with the names of the dead on them.

History buffs might want to visit the **museum**, reached via country lanes *(5km from the site, near the town of Marathon; 8am-2.30pm; closed on Monday; entrance fee).* Near another burial mound with the ashes of the Plataean soldiers, the museum houses findings from the Marathon plain – which in fact have nothing to do with the famous battle. The oldest pieces are of Neolithic **pottery** (4000-2700 BC). The most recent pieces, objects from the 2C with Egyptian features, come from the Marathon estate of Herodes Atticus, a rich Roman dignitary *(see page 292).*

As you enter Marathon, turn right towards Ramnoús. The site is 10km to the east.

■ **Ramnoús**** − *8am-5.30pm weekdays; closed on Monday; 8am-5pm on Sunday. Entrance fee.* The ruins of the peaceful and quiet **Temple of Nemesis**, goddess of retribution, are scattered on top of a knoll caressed by a gentle wind that rustles through the pines. The first temple was built a third of the way up a long Sacred Way that still climbs the hill. From the present entrance to the site, it continued to the shore to the site of the fortress of Rhamnonte (Ramnoús), which controlled the straits of Evrípos. As excavations are underway all over the site, only the first section of the Sacred Way can be visited in addition to the sanctuary.

Heroes and a herald

On 10 August in the year 490 BC, a 20 000-25 000-man Persian army landed on the shores of Attica. The opposing Greek army had only 10 000 men, including 1 000 Plataeans. To compensate for this numerical inferiority, the Greek General Miltiádes sent a handful of soldiers into the middle of the battlefield to draw in the enemy, while positioning the main body of his troops on the flanks. As planned, the Persians rushed in and were caught in the middle. 6 000 of them were killed, whereas the Greeks lost only 192 men. To spread news of their victory as fast as possible in Athens, they sent a messenger named Pheidippides who ran the 42.195km to the capital without stopping. When he got there, he barely had time to say "Enikísame!" ("we won!") before dying of exhaustion. In memory of his heroic act, the famous marathon race was created in 1896 covering exactly the same distance run by Pheidippides.

With the attendant's dog in tow − delighted to come along − walk down the **Sacred Way** dotted with **funerary monuments**, including the ruins of the **Tomb of Menestides** and his descendants (*on the right*), the biggest mausoleum on the Sacred Way with sides measuring 7.50m (4C BC).

On top of the mound − made into a terrace to accommodate the Temple of Nemesis − are the remains of **two temples**. Several sections of the walls discovered by archaeologists indicate the location of the oldest − and smallest − temple built in the 6C BC to house sacred objects. The more recent, larger temple (435 BC), which has preserved a few of its remarkably white **Doric columns**, contained a statue of the goddess made by a student of Phidias. The head of this noble work of art is in the British Museum in London.

Go back towards the motorway. After crossing "Marathon Lake", a reservoir for Athens created in a beautiful mountain landscape, take the motorway towards Halkída-Thebes (Thíva). Exit at Malakása and follow the signs for Skála Oropoú / Amfiaraío.

■ **The Amphiaraion of Oropós*** (Amfiaraío) − *33km from Marathon. 8.30am-2.30pm; closed on Monday. Entrance fee.* Nestling in a pine forest covering a hillside, the ancient sanctuary of Oropós is situated in a highly romantic setting. This "healing centre" owes its name to Amphiaraios, a local hero famous for the healing powers he derived from the sacred spring of Oropós.

After making your way through the blocks of stone scattered around a **temple**, you pass the foundations of an **altar** where each patient had to sacrifice a ram. Then a long row of truncated **Doric columns** marks the spot of an **incubating portico**. Patients would spend the night there on a **bench** wrapped in the bloody skin of the ram they had sacrificed; in the morning the priests delivered their tailor-made prescription.

Just above the portico are the ruins of the tiers of an impressive **theatre***, whose **stage** has been well preserved, together with five **marble seats** reserved for notables.

Head back towards Athens on the motorway, and exit at Varimbómbi.

■ Before returning to the hustle and bustle of the capital, make one last foray into the countryside and wander down the little mountain roads on the wooded slopes of **Mt Parnes*** (Óros Párnitha). You will discover a deep and delightfully scented **forest**

Ramnoús

only 40km from Athens, where pines are mixed with other Mediterranean species such as Judas trees and kermes oaks. This little world teeming with fresh springs must be crossed slowly so as not to crush the hundred-year-old **tortoises** calmly walking across the road here and there! Then you are brought crashing back to civilisation on the **summit** of Mt Parnes, where there is a luxury hotel with a casino. But the climb up *(by the road or the cable-car)* is worth the trip for the magnificent **view★★** of the surrounding massif. *Cable-car:* ☏ *(01) 24 69 111; goes up every 10min from 8am to 4am the next morning; inexpensive tickets for daytime (8am-6pm) and night-time (6pm-4am).*

Excursions around Boeotia★★
From Dafní to Delphi
A 200km tour starting from Athens. Allow a day.
Lodging in Delphi (see page 196, and the "Making the most of" section page 189).

Rather than leaving Athens via the main road to make a straight dash to Delphi, take the little roads that cross the grassy Boeotian countryside and forget about the highway with its heat and traffic. Take time to explore the heart of eternal Greece with its ancient citadels and Byzantine monasteries. This is a Greece of hillsides and mellow valleys dotted with olive trees, whose branches rustle in the wind to tell of past battles and the religious fervour which is still very much alive.

10km west of Athens. Leave the capital by the main road (Leofóros Athinón) in the direction of Corinth. After 10km, take the interchange that brings you back towards Athens. Dafní is 3km further on.

■ **Dafní Monastery★★** — *8.30am-3pm; closed on Monday. Entrance fee. Allow 1hr. Car park.* Caught in a stranglehold between the overcrowded highway and the dusty suburbs of Athens, Dafní Monastery is not very inviting at first glance. But once past the threshold, you are instantly transported to the Middle Ages in a thriving, peaceful haven still protected by part of the laurel woods *(dafné* in Greek) which gave the place its name. Dedicated to the Dormition of the Virgin, this majestic Byzantine ensemble was built in several stages during the Middle Ages with the stone from an ancient temple to Apollo along the Sacred Way connecting Athens to the Sanctuary at Eleusis. You enter the monastery through a beautiful **Cistercian cloister★★** built by disciples of St Bernard during the Frankish occupation. Its light arcades line a **paved courtyard** off which lie the monks' cells (16C), with two **medieval sarcophagi** in front of them. Steps flanked by two cypress trees lead to a domed **Byzantine church★★★**. It was built in the 11C, and several **chapels** were added in the 13C where the monks could say mass simultaneously. The marble ornament that ran along the base of the walls has disappeared, but the upper sections have preserved most of their **mosaics with a gold background★★★**. The roughness of the walls offsets the light and delicate figures all the more, displaying a rarely equalled fineness of design and harmony of colours. Among the most beautiful panels is the severe **Christ Pantocrator (Christ in Majesty)★★** on the dome holding the Bible. Also of note are some remarkable episodes from the New Testament, in particular the panels near the entrance portraying the **Last Supper★**, the **Washing of the Feet★** and a wonderful **Betrayal by Judas★★**.

A **Gothic exonarthex** was added to the southern end of the church *(on the right as you leave)*, whereas the **refectory** (in ruins) was built against the north side.

Continue on towards Corinth.

The ancient fortress of Egósthena, keeper of the olive trees

B. Kaufmann/MICHELIN

■ Those keen on archaeology might make a brief stop at **Eleusis** (Elefsína) to contemplate the meagre remains of the great **Sanctuary of Demeter**, surrounded by the modern city and refineries *(8am-2.30pm; closed on Monday; entrance fee)*. During Antiquity this very important place of worship drew vast numbers of pilgrims who came from all over the Greek world to attend the initiatory rites at Eleusis. The famous **Mysteries** celebrates the return to Earth six months out of the year of Demeter's daughter Persephone who was abducted by Hades, the god of the Underworld.

Leave Eleusis and the Corinth road and take the Magoúla-Thebes road.

At last you can leave the oppressive heat of Athens behind and enter a serene landscape of hills covered with olive trees where the only sound is the cicadas chirping and the wind whispering sweetly through the foliage. Two fortresses positioned high up on both sides of the road linking Athens and Thebes have stood there since the beginning of time, as if watching over it. Built in the 4C BC in a beautiful setting, they are both remarkably well preserved.

Leaving Vília on your left, enter the hamlet of Kaza on your right; a dirt road leads up to the first fortress.

■ The first one you come to is **Eleutherae Fortress** (Eleftherés) *(26km from Eleusis; free admission; allow 30min)*. The fortress is positioned at the edge of a rocky mound surrounded by gullies, its high, white-stone wall full of doors and posterns standing out against the sky. At regular intervals, the wall, which one can go around on a **walkway**, is reinforced by powerful **square towers**.

Cross the road towards Vília and Pórto Germenó.

■ **Aegosthena Fortress*** (Egósthena) — even better preserved, having been restored by the Franks in the 13C — stands guard on the other side of the highway overlooking the Gulf of Corinth *(allow 30min)*. Leave your car next to a field of olive trees and climb up to a pretty white chapel hidden among the trees. Soon you reach an impressive, 180m-long **stone wall** with doors that have heavy **lintels** (still standing), **posterns** and **towers** over 10m high. From the walls, you have a superb **panorama*** of the Gulf of Corinth and the peaceful surrounding countryside.

■ From the fortress, go down to the edge of the gulf between the Aleppo pines and olive trees. The road stops at **Pórto Germenó***, a charming harbour nestled in a quiet cove covered with vegetation. It is an ideal place to stop for lunch in one of the

The Óssios Loukás Monastery under the Boeotian skies

fish tavernas dotting the waterfront. In summer and at weekends, however, crowds of Athenians come for the surrounding **beaches** overlooked by the village's white houses clambering up the slopes of Mt Cithaeron.

Go back to the highway.

■ **Thebes** (Thíva) – After crossing the great fertile plains of Bóeotia, you soon reach legendary Thebes. But there are few **architectural remains** – scattered throughout the city – to remind you of the brilliant and tragic past of Oedipus (*see page 51*). The

Athens' "wall"
Focusing on Antiquity's masterpieces, we often forget that it was an age of fratricidal wars among the Greek city states, in particular between Athens and Sparta. Those conflicts left their marks, such as the series of fortresses which Athens had built around it – after its defeat by Sparta in 404 BC – in an attempt to limit its formidable enemy's expansionist aims. Three of the fortresses are still visible: Ramnoús, across from Euboea, Eleutherae on the Thebes road, and Egósthena on the Gulf of Corinth that was designed to stop any invasions coming from the sea.

museum★ (*8.30am-3pm; closed on Monday; entrance fee*) opened in 1962, features a remarkable series of objects from Boeotia including a very noble 6C BC **kouros**★ (*to the right of the entrance*), some black stone funerary steles from the 5C BC and, in the last room, several **painted sarcophagi**★ from the Mycenaean Era portraying mourners and funerary rites.

Get back on the road to Delphi. After Livadiá, take the first road on the left.

■ **Óssios Loukás**★★★ – *22km from Thebes, 40km from Delphi and 150km from Athens. 8am-2pm / 4pm-7pm from May to mid-September; 8am-5pm the rest of the year. Entrance fee. Wear appropriate clothing. Allow 90min.*
Built on the edge of a majestic natural amphitheatre bounded by gently sloping mountains, Óssios Loukás and its setting are equally impressive. This is one of the most beautiful Byzantine monasteries in Greece both for the originality of its architecture – its octagonal plan was adopted in late Byzantine architecture – and for the extraordinary wealth of mosaics on a gold background, frescoes, icons and polychrome marble paving. Such treasures naturally draw crowds of visitors, despite the monastery's rather remote location far from the main highways. The size of the car park in front of the entrance is self-explanatory...
Óssios Loukás was built in the 11C on a site where a small oratory had been erected 150 years earlier by a local hermit, **Luke of Stiri**. You enter the monastery through a door put in just beneath a 19C **clock tower**. On the right near the ticket office is the **old refectory**★, turned into a **museum** housing some architectural elements and a collection of religious objects.
An imposing **building**★ on the left side of the **courtyard** contains the monks' **cells**; slightly to the right stands the **katholikón**★★★, a magnificent edifice topped by a red-tiled dome. Its finely made brick-and-stone walls are set off by white marble friezes. Dedicated to St Luke, it was built above a crypt containing the remains of the holy man and against the older church dedicated to the Virgin.
Entering the church through the **narthex**, one finds a profusion of mosaics on a gold background, including scenes from the **Passion of Christ**★★ and, crowning the door, a hieratic **Christ holding the Gospel**★★.
Past the narthex, the eye is drawn up to the dome with its grand **Christ Pantocrator**, a 17C fresco that replaced a mosaic destroyed during an earthquake. All around it is a flurry of frescoes, sculpted capitals, icons and an amazing wealth of coloured marble paving offset by more magnificent mosaics on a gold background. Of particular note are the peaceful **Virgin and Child**★★★ adorning the apse and, on the squinch arch in the south-west corner, a remarkable **Baptism of Christ**★★★ where the Jordan's waters swirl like strips of lace.

Mosaics on a gold background at Óssios Loukás: a jewel of Byzantine art

To the left of the choir, a passageway containing the **relics of St Luke** leads to the **Church of the Virgin Mary**** (10C), which has a feeling of great nobility due to its more austere architectural style.

Turn left out of the main church and take the passageway leading to the **crypt*****. The ceiling in this underground chapel – dug out in the 10C to hold the first **Tomb of St Luke** – has some wonderful, recently restored 11C **frescoes*****. Next to episodes from the life and passion of Jesus are portraits of numerous saints, surrounded by predominantly red, black and white geometrical patterns. Of particular note is a Last Supper (in the dark unfortunately) and to the right of that, a **Deposition** and a moving **Entombment**.

Turn left again as you leave the crypt and enter the monastery's **second courtyard** framed by various utilitarian monastic buildings *(in ruins)*. There is a fine **view**** of the Phocis Valley below.

Attica

B. Kaufmann/MICHELIN

Making the most of northern Attica

COMING AND GOING

By bus – Buses for **Rafína** leave from the Mavromatéon bus station in Athens. Numerous departures from 5.30am to 10.30pm (1hr).

To get to **Mt Parnes**, take the metro to Kifissiá, then the 503 or 537 buses (every 20min) which stop at Varimbómbi.

Or get the (free) private bus from the casino at Zápio (Plan II D3, page 127). Leaves at 5.15pm, 9pm and 11.30pm; returns to Athens at 10.15pm, 1.45am and 4am (1hr).

GETTING AROUND

By train – The Athens-Halkída railway line runs across Mt Parnes, terminating about fifteen stations further on. For information, call: ☎ (01) 513 16 01.

WHERE TO STAY

The north-east coast of Attica is studded with little resort hotels, usually full of Greek families, and hotel complexes for groups. There are also a few campsites near the seaside. The very well-situated (luxury) hotel at Mt Parnes is another unusual feature of note.

• **Mt Parnes (Aharnés)**
Between €76 and €122
Mount Parnes, in Aharnés, on top of Mt Parnes, ☎ (01) 246 91 11, Fax (01) 246 07 68 – 64rm and 10 suites. ⚓ ♨ ⚓ This establishment perched up on top of the mountain – away from the scorching heat of Athens – exudes the splendour of yesteryear. The spacious rooms have marble bathrooms and spectacular views of the entire mountain range. But the pool is a bit worn around the edges, and roulette and black-jack fans still haunt the gigantic passageways.

OTHER THINGS TO DO

Outdoor pursuits – IOBOP Riding Club, at the foot of Mt Parnes in Varimbómbi, next to the road ☎ (01) 816 95 64 or 620 42 21.

Karavi, near Agía Marína, ☎ (0294) 55 950 (on the web at www.karavi.gr) is a gigantic games and sports club (volleyball, water-skiing, surfing, etc) which attracts many young Athenians. It has its own restaurant, bars, sound system and a well-guarded car park. A clientele of 18-30-year-olds.

Excursions – Mt Parnes is a well-known site for excursions and hiking. For refuge addresses, enquire at the **Federation of Greek Mountain-Climbing Clubs**, Odós Karageorgi Servias 7, 10563 Athens, ☎ (01) 323 45 55.

Activities for children – Makri, a small amusement park (with merry-go-rounds).

Making the most of Boeotia

COMING AND GOING

By bus – For **Dafní** and **Eleusis**, take the blue A16 bus. The Athens stop is at Platía Eleftherías (see Plan II B2 page 126). Leaves every 30min (20min). Get off at the "Psychiatricó" stop (the monastery is opposite a psychiatric hospital).

For **Óssios Loukás**, take the blue 024 bus. Leaves between 5.50am and 8.30pm from Leofóros Amalías, Platía Sýndagma and Leofóros Panepistimíou (2hr). Returns between 6am and 8pm weekdays, 6pm on Sunday. Enquire about where the bus drops you, usually in the village of Dístomo 9km from the site. From there, negotiate a round-trip taxi fare. For **Thebes** (Thíva), there are numerous departures between 6.30am and 9pm (90min). Bus stops at Leofóros Amalías, Platía Sýndagma and Leofóros Panepistimíou.

OTHER THINGS TO DO

Festivals – Dafní, mid-July to mid-September: wine festival (tickets for the site come with free Greek wine tastings and folk performances). **Óssios Loukás**: monastery festivals on 5 February and 3 May.

DELPHI★★★
(DELFÍ)
Province of Central Greece – District of Phocis
Regional map page 122 – Michelin map 980 fold 41
Alt 573m – Pop 2 426

Not to be missed
The stadium and the theatre, also for the view.
The museum, which has a large collection.

And remember...
Bring a sweater as it can get cool at the end of the day, even in summer.

The tiered white ruins of the Sacred Precinct – clinging to a steep mountainside – are scattered among pine, olive and cypress trees. The Sanctuary overlooks the Pleistos Valley, a narrow grey-green carpet of velvet snaking towards the sea. Above it stand the **Phaedriades Cliffs**, impressive 300m-high ramparts of red sandstone, and outlined against the sky – when not totally covered in mist – is the blue ridge of Mt Kirfis. Delphi is striking both for its rich remains and for the beauty of its setting. But it is on the UNESCO World Heritage list and is one of the most frequently visited sites in all of Greece. Whatever the season, you will not be alone; and you may have to elbow your way through the crowds in order to see certain monuments and some of the museum's treasures. Instead of vainly trying to ignore the crowds, think of yourself as one of the pilgrims who used to come here by the thousands to pay tribute to the god of the Arts and Beauty. Indeed, in its heyday, Delphi was one of the most popular sanctuaries in the Ancient World, and the reputation of its oracle drew in visitors from everywhere.

The centre of the world
Delphi was considered to be the hub of the universe. There was already a sanctuary to Gaea – the Earth, source of all life – on the slopes of Parnassus in the 2nd millennium BC. The site's theatricality – with its caves, chasms, faults and dizzying rock faces – inspired the Ancients who interpreted the rumblings from its depths and its babbling brooks as divine speech. An oracle was born and was guarded by the serpent Python, who gave the site its original name – Putho.

So it was only natural that Zeus, king of the gods and master of the world, should make it the centre of his kingdom – the *omphalós*, or umbilicus. In the end it was his son, Apollo, who was given the honour of being worshipped there. But the first thing Apollo did upon arriving was to shoot all the arrows in his quiver at Python on the pretext that he was bothering his mother (Leto). To celebrate his victory, the young god even claimed the title of Pythian Apollo, the oracle-maker, founded the **Pythian Games** (*Pythia*), and rechristened the site Delphi, in honour of the legendary dolphin who led him there.

Laurel Love
Apollo the seducer fell in love with beautiful Daphne. But the nymph refused his advances and asked for help from her father, who turned her into a superb laurel tree just as Apollo was about to catch her. In Ovid's words, Apollo then said: "Since you refuse to be my wife, at least you will be my tree. My hair, my cithara and my quiver will ever be adorned with you, Oh laurel tree [...]. And at the entrance to Augustus' dwelling, it is again you – most faithful guardian – who will stand before the door." Thus the laurel – "daphne" in Greek – became Apollo's totem tree.

The **Pythian Games** started out as a musical contest but soon took on greater importance, particularly after 582 BC when the Athenians linked worship of Dionysus and Athena to them. From that point on, they became a huge artistic and athletic event comparable to the one in Olympia. The oracle prospered a great deal from the taxes charged to those consulting the **Pythia**.

Despite wars, earthquakes and pillaging (by Sulla and Nero among others), the Sacred Precinct continued to function until the reign of Hadrian (2C AD). But the advent of Christianity sounded the death knell for the Delphic oracle. **Julian the Apostate** (331-63), the last pagan emperor, received this final oracle from the Pythian priestess, which sounds like an epitaph: "Go and tell

The Pythia, Apollo's int
The Pythian priestess, Apo
was chosen from among
drinking water from t'
near the temple (said to en
with the gift of prophecy) the youn
went into a cell (the "adyton") and sa
a tripod above the Python's cave, out of
which sprang vapours from burning laurels.
To help induce a trance, she also chewed
laurel leaves. Her enigmatic cries and gestures were interpreted by attendant priests
who transmitted the divine messages to the
pilgrims waiting patiently at the entrance of
the temple.

the king that the fine building is on the ground, Apollo no longer has a hut or prophetic laurel tree, the spring has dried up and the water that once spoke is silent." The sanctuary closed its doors permanently to pilgrims in 381, before Byzantine emperor **Constantine the Great** took its remaining treasures. In 1892, Delphi came back to life thanks to the efforts of a prestigious team from the **French School of Archaeology in Athens**, which is still carrying out excavation work on the site.

7.30am-7pm. Entrance fee. Allow nearly a whole day to do everything, including visiting the museum and contemplating the landscape. The site starts east of the village and comprises two areas: the Sacred Precinct and the Marmaria, which can be seen from the road below before reaching the car park. It's best to arrive early in the morning in order to avoid the crowds. Wear sturdy shoes as you will climb up a mountain path. Brochures with a reconstruction of the site as it was in Ancient times are on sale at the entrance. There is a place to get drinking water between the theatre and the stadium, as well as two toilets (one at the entrance to the site and another one by the stadium).

The Sacred Precinct★★
Access on the right of the road, up an easy path

Like pilgrims in Ancient times, visitors first go through the **agora**, a little rectangular square preceding the temenos, the sacred area of the sanctuary. Shops selling ex-votos to be offered to Apollo line the **portico** built into the hillside here *(to the right)*.

From treasure to treasure
After going through one of the nine doors to the temenos, you start up the Sacred Way, a fine avenue paved with marble that winds from terrace to terrace all the way to the top. First, the Sacred Way goes by the **ex-voto area** dotted with columns, steles, statues and **treasuries**, or small buildings resembling temples erected by the Greek city states to house their offerings. With time and the increasing number of such structures, the place began to look like an open-air museum *(most of their decorations are now in the museum)*.

The cylindrical stone stele on the left as you round the first bend is a replica of the **omphalos** on which the temple of Apollo was built. The temple – standing a bit further up – is next to the **Treasury of the Athenians★**, a small Doric "temple" in white marble which Athens had built with spoils taken from the Medians at the famous **Battle of Marathon** (490 BC). The retaining wall of the terrace has a **dedicatory inscription★**, while the walls – also covered with inscriptions – are embellished with laurel wreaths, the symbol of Apollo.

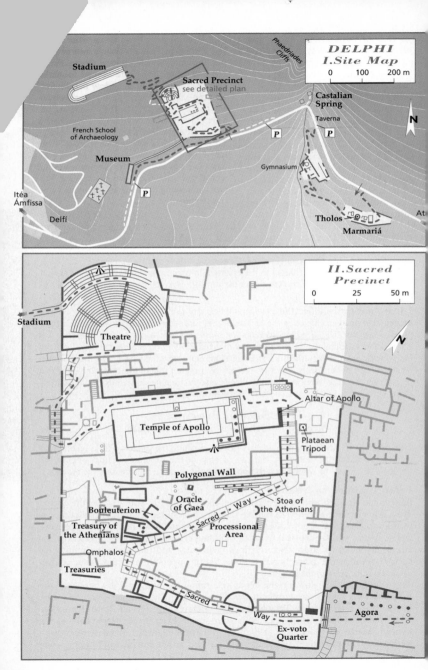

DELPHI
I. Site Map
0   100   200 m

Stadium

Sacred Precinct
see detailed plan

Phaedriades Cliffs

Castalian Spring

Taverna

N

French School of Archaeology

Museum

P

P

Itéa Ámfissa

Delfí

Gymnasium

P

Tholos

Marmariá

At

II. Sacred Precinct
0   25   50 m

N

Stadium

Theatre

Altar of Apollo

Temple of Apollo

Plataean Tripod

Polygonal Wall

Oracle of Gaea

Bouleuterion

Treasury of the Athenians

Stoa of the Athenians

Sacred Way

Processional Area

Omphalos

Treasuries

Sacred Way

Agora

Ex-voto Quarter

Next to the treasury stood the **bouleuterion**, the administrative headquarters of Delphi, of which only the base remains. A curious pile of rocks overlooking it is where the original **oracle** dedicated to Gaea was jealously guarded by Python before he was slain by Apollo.

Towards the Temple of Apollo

The Sacred Way leads to the Temple of Apollo, built on a wide terrace affording a splendid view of the mountains. An impressive (6C) **polygonal wall**★★ made of huge blocks – covered with **inscriptions** from the Hellenistic and Roman Eras – stretches out for 83m. Archaeologists have recorded 800 registered deeds of slaves who were emancipated. Standing in front of the wall are three slender columns, the modest remains of the (5C BC) **Stoa of the Athenians** – another votive monument containing naval trophies taken from the Persians. Across from the portico on the other side of the Sacred Way lies the area where **processions** formed to go to the temple. During the preparations, priests would relax on the elegant marble **exedra**★ surrounding the square.

From here, a staircase on the side of the terrace leads up to a square in front of the temple. On the right is the circular base of the **Plataean Tripod**, all that remains of the column commemorating the Battle of Plataea. The column was made of three intertwined serpents whose heads – at the top – supported a large basin with a flame in it. Emperor Constantine took it back to Constantinople to decorate his hippodrome (it is still standing there, although badly defaced).

On the right in front of the entrance to the temple is the imposing **Altar of Apollo** (or **Altar of the Chiotes**), built in the 5C BC by the inhabitants of the island of Chios (Híos). Just behind it stand the tall columns of the **Temple of Apollo**★, built in the 4C on the ruins of a temple that was two centuries older and had been destroyed by an earthquake. The **cella** contained altars and statues, whereas the **adyton** – the secret lair of the oracle – was the preserve of the Pythian priestess, who sat on her tripod there near the omphalos. You are now standing at the centre of the universe...

The temple – 60.30m by 23.80m – was framed by 12m-high Doric columns made of tufa covered with stucco. Six of them were put back in place, but only one is complete, making it very hard to imagine the scale of the building. However, you will never tire of the magnificent **panorama**★★★ of the valley and of the Kirfis' peaks.

An even more beautiful view awaits you a bit higher up, from the top of the tiers of the superb stone **theatre**★★ fanning out on the hillside, which was remodelled by the Romans in the 2C. It had a capacity of no less than 5 000 spectators, who came to attend recitals given in honour of Apollo and Dionysus. The first row was reserved for priests. Take the time to sit down and contemplate the landscape here. Behind you, the high wall of the Phaedriades Cliffs seems almost within reach. With a bit of luck you might see an eagle – a messenger of Zeus – soaring on the rising air currents. Legend has it that the 6C BC fable-writer **Aesop** was thrown from the top for mocking the priests of Apollo.

After so much culture, how about a little sports activity? It's time for a race in the **stadium**★. From the *diázoma* (the corridor overlooking the theatre), a path leads up to the sanctuary's highest terrace where athletic activities were held. A **monumental gate** (the remains of an abutment) built by Herodes Atticus (*see page 292*) in the 2C AD stood at the entrance. A 178m-long **track**★ stretches

Apollo's Officials

The religious domain of Delphi included the whole Pleistos Valley all the way to the coast. The administration of this huge territory was entrusted to the Amphictyonic League, a kind of Greek "United Nations" of 12 city states, each of which had two representatives. The sanctuary was run by two high priests, an administrator, a treasurer, five priests (of which Plutarch was one) and several acolyte priests who assisted the Pythian priestess.

through a resin-scented pine forest and is surrounded by tiers, some of which are carved directly out of the north rock face of the hill. Six thousand five hundred spectators were lined up on either side of the grandstand, which can be made out in the centre. The starting and finishing lines – made of marble slabs – are intact.

The Museum**

Coming back down from the stadium, the museum is on your right – a characterless modern building, which is fortunately hidden among the trees. It houses a superb collection of pieces discovered during the excavations. Of particular note is the **Agrenon** at the top of the stairs – a conical block of marble covered with sculpted lattice-work. This is the Hellenistic equivalent of the **omphalos** that stood in the crypt of the Temple of Apollo.

Cross the **Hall of Shields** and enter the **Hall of the Siphnian Treasury** on the right. It contains sculptures from the Archaic Period (6C BC), such as the stunning **Winged Sphinx***** that stood on top of the column of the Naxians. The room takes its name from the remarkable **frieze*** decorating the walls of the Siphnian Treasury, which still has polychrome traces on it. The scenes depict the Trojan War (with fine horses) and a gigantomachia (battle between the gods and the giants).

The **Hall of the Kouroi** has some striking colossal statues of **ephebes**** from the 6C BC. Next comes the **Hall of the Bull** containing various objects for worship discovered in two pits under the Sacred Way. At the time, it was common practice to throw out ex-votos and other objects that had become too old or outmoded – a real gold mine for archaeologists! One of the finest pieces is a wooden **bull**** covered with silver plate on copper bands (6C BC). Don't miss the two **statuettes*** – an ivory one of a god taming a wild animal, and one in repoussé gold – as well as a delicate bronze **incense burner*** held by a young girl (5C BC).

The next room contains the sculpted decor from the **Athenian Treasury****, with exquisite metopes illustrating the legends of Heracles and Theseus. The charming **"dancers"**** is a magnificent group of three bacchantes (priestesses of Dionysus) crowning a marble Corinthian capital. It adorned the **acanthus column** – a gift from the Athenians – that stood on the square in front of the Temple of Apollo.

In the corner is a fine statue of the **athlete Agías***, a marble replica of a bronze by Lysippus of one of the great pancratium (wrestling) champions at the Olympic and Delphic Games.

But the museum's prize piece is without a doubt the **Charioteer***** (478 BC), an extraordinary bronze statue that is one of the masterpieces of late Archaic art. Discovered in 1896 near the theatre, it is a life-size figure (1.80m) of a charioteer who won the quadriga race at the Olympic Games in 474-473 BC. It was given to the Sacred Precinct by Polyzalos, the tyrant of Gela (Sicily). The four horses whose reins the charioteer still holds are no longer there; nor is the statue of Polyzalos, who was probably standing to the right of the charioteer. The stunningly beautiful head – with a victory band around it – is remarkably well preserved, particularly the eyes with their white enamel in contrast to the bronze. The exquisite features, hair and folds of the clothing are flawlessly realistic.

It could almost cause you to miss the white **libation cup****, another masterpiece exhibited nearby. It shows a seated Apollo wearing a laurel wreath and playing his kithara while making a libation under the watchful gaze of a raven, his totem bird. The visit ends with the fine **statue of Antinous*** (2C AD), a favourite of the Emperor Hadrian who was deified after death. On the way out, have a look at the **paleo-Christian mosaics** discovered near the town.

The Charioteer of Delphi

Marmariá★

Below the road. Same ticket and hours as the Sacred Precinct. Allow 30min.

Examples of circular temples *(tholos)* are rare. And the one in Marmariá, dedicated to the mother goddess Gaea, is located in a beautiful setting. Before going to the Sacred Precinct, pilgrims used to come here to salute the goddess and Athena. Today there are few remains of the sanctuary of the two goddesses because its stones were used as a quarry (hence the nickname of this part of the site meaning "marble"). Nevertheless, archaeologists did manage to find enough elements to reconstruct the entire base of the tholos★ (4C BC) and to set three of its columns back upright.
Nearby, among the piles of stone blocks, is a little rectangle drawn on the ground. This is all that remains of the entirely demolished **Temple of Athena**. The upper terrace has more remains, from the Roman Period. A gymnasium, a palaestra and baths completed the sanctuary, whose stones are now scattered among the olive trees.

Don't leave Delphi without seeing the **Castalian Spring★** hidden in the hollow of a roughly hewn cleft in the Phaedriades Cliffs. Water from this spring has irrigated the surrounding olive trees since ancient times. Pilgrims came here to perform their ritual ablutions. The fountain's name comes from a nymph who is supposed to have drowned here while trying to escape Apollo's advances. A few traces of the ancient layout subsist, including several **basins**, one of which is carved right out of the base of the rock wall.

Making the most of Delphi

COMING AND GOING

By bus – Be careful, as times vary from one year to the next. So it is a good idea to enquire before leaving, or get to the bus station early.
From Athens, 6 buses a day (3hr) at 7.30am, 10.30am, 1pm, 3.30pm, 5.30pm and 8pm. Four of them go on to Itéa and Galaxídi. Departures from Odós Liossíon 260 north-west of Athens (see plan page 126). For information, call ☎ (01) 83 17 096.
5 buses a day for Athens, at 5.30am (7am on Sundays and holidays), 9am (except on Sundays and holidays), 11am, 1.30pm, 4pm and 6pm.
From Thessaloníki, 1 bus a day at 3pm (5hr). Change at Ámfissa at weekends (30min). Buses leave from Odós Monastiríou 51 (see plan page 422), ☎ (0315) 25 876.
From Patras, the bus boards a ferry-boat, then takes you to Delphi (3hr). Departures at 10.30am and 5.45pm from Odós Óthonos 47 and Amalías, ☎ (0616) 21 200. Otherwise you can go to **Itéa** then take another bus (7 buses a day for Delphi).
From Náfpaktos (where the ferryboat also stops), 6 departures a day between

5.45am and 7pm. For information, call ☎ (0634) 27 241.
By boat – For maritime connections to the Peloponnese via Itéa and Náfpaktos, see "Making the most of Patras", page 300.

ADDRESS BOOK

Tourist information – The EOT in Delphi has two entrances: Odós Apóllonos 11 and Odós Pávlou & Frideríkis 12 (at the top of a flight of steps), ☎ (0265) 82 900. 8am-2.30pm; closed on Sundays and holidays. This is one of the best tourist information offices in Greece, and the director is very helpful. Free maps of the town are available.

Banks / Currency exchange – There are several banks with cash dispensers in Delphi on Odós Pávlou & Frideríkis. Money can also be changed at the OTE.

Post office / Telephone – The Delphi post office is to the right of the tourist information office on Odós Pávlou & Frideríkis. **OTE**, Odós Pávlou & Frideríkis, 7.30am-3pm, Monday to Friday.

Tourist police – In Delphi, on Odós Sikelianoú 3, not far from the church,

☎ (0265) 82 220. **Police**, ☎ (0265) 82 222. In Aráhova, ☎ (0267) 31 333.

Taxis – In Delphi, ☎ (0265) 82 000. In Aráhova, ☎ (0267) 31 566. In Galaxídi, ☎ (0265) 41 272 / 41 243.

Medical service – In **Delphi**, there is a dispensary practically opposite the bus stop on Odós Pávlou & Frideríkis, ☎ (0265) 82 307. Pharmacy, ☎ (0265) 82 700. In **Aráhova**, dispensary, ☎ (0267) 31 300; pharmacy, ☎ (0267) 31793. Dispensary in **Galaxídi**, ☎ (0265) 91 255.

WHERE TO STAY

The town of Delphi, built on a mountainside, has one road zigzagging through it from top to bottom that changes its name halfway along. The hotels, clinging to the hillside, often have two entrances – one up above and one below, with the upper floors offering a magnificent panorama of the valley. When they are packed (in summer), you can take refuge in **Aráhova** 13km to the east – a real mountain village with pretty stone houses. The atmosphere there is more welcoming than in Delphi, and the hotels are noticeably cheaper.

• **Delphi**

Campsites (around €12)

The Apóllo, 1.5km from Delphi on the Itéa road, ☎ (0265) 82 762. ⌇ This is the closest campsite to Delphi and is a pleasant place due to its large pool and its view of the gulf. Beware of crowds in summer and some rather noisy pitches near the road.

The Delphí, 3km from Delphi on the Hrissó road, ☎ (0265) 82 363. ⌇ ✖ Without a doubt the most pleasant of the three campsites in the area with its shady terraces, its little pool and the view from its taverna.

Between €30 and €38

Thólos, Odós Apóllonos 31, ☎ and Fax (0265) 82 268. ⌇ ℰ This hotel (converted youth hostel) is practically opposite the church and has small but clean rooms. Breakfast is served on the terrace of the establishment next door (breathtaking view).

Between €38 and €45

Pan, Odós Pávlou & Frideríkis, between the bus station and the post office, ☎ (0265) 82 294 / 82 328, Fax (0265) 82 320 – 25rm. ⌇ ℰ TV A traditional establishment with modest but attractive rooms run by a charming elderly lady. If the hotel is full, they will send you to the nearby **Hotel Pythia** (50rm) which is of a similar standard and has a restaurant.

Between €55 and €75

Iníohos, in the centre of town, ☎ (0265) 82 710 – 40rm. ⌇ ℰ ▤ TV ✖ Renovated in 1998, this reasonable hotel has clean and stylish rooms, all with balconies.

Between €82.50 and €128

King Iníohos, above the village, ☎ (0265) 82 151 to 3, Fax (0265) 82 644 – 116rm. ⌇ ℰ ▤ TV ✖ 🏋 A handsome and superbly situated mountain hotel with a view of the Gulf of Corinth on one side and the slopes of Mt Parnassus on the other. Some of its very comfortable suites (especially in winter) have fireplaces. The restaurant has a good, varied menu.

Delphi Xénia, on the slopes of Mt Parnassus, ☎ (0265) 82 151 – 82rm. ⌇ ℰ ▤ TV ✖ ⛱ ✾ 🏋 This luxury establishment in natural surroundings has a panoramic view of the entire valley. The rooms are more conventional than at the King Iníohos, but the pool looks out over the Gulf of Corinth and there is a fitness club.

• **Aráhova**

The village of Aráhova, halfway between the Gulf of Corinth and the ski slopes, has many hotels, which are more expensive in winter than in summer (due to winter sports).

Between €30 and €45

Nóstos, in the centre of town, ☎ (0267) 31 385, mobile 093 53 13 72, Fax (0267) 31 765. ⌇ ℰ An old house turned into a hotel, run with great care by an elderly gentleman. He has a minibus to take guests sightseeing in the area. Excellent value for money (breakfast included).

Between €38 and €60

Filoxénia, at the end of a little alleyway, slightly out-of-the-way, ☎ (0267)

31 046, Fax (0267) 31 215 – 11rm and 3 studios with kitchenettes. 📶 𝒫 TV A friendly, traditional hotel. The rooms have balconies looking out over the olive trees below. In winter, ask for one of the (more spacious) rooms with a fireplace. Open all year.

Xénia, ☎ (0267) 31 230, Fax (0267) 32 175 – 42rm. 📶 𝒫 ▤ TV 🚗 Spacious rooms with large bathrooms off corridors as anonymous as the reception.

Between €60 and €75
Anemoliá, ☎ (0267) 31 640, Fax (0267) 31 642 – 55rm and 8 suites. 📶 𝒫 ▤ TV ✕ ⬛ 🚗 CC This hotel built in the 1970s has an attractive interior design all in wood, and its warmly decorated rooms are furnished with local rugs. The covered pool, open all year, also has a fitness club.

• **Galaxídi**
This charming fishing harbour 18km south-west of Delphi is a great place for a stopover. But the Athenians are very fond of coming here, and it is taken by storm at weekends and during holidays. Reservations a must.

Between €60 and €75
Argó, 100m from the sea on a street at right angles to the harbour, ☎ (0265) 41 996 / 42 100, Fax (0265) 41 878 – 16rm. 📶 𝒫 ▤ TV This recent, all-white building houses a comfortable and clean hotel with marble floors. Rooms are small but pleasant. Home-made jams and cakes at breakfast. Open year round.
🏠 **Galaxá**, Odós Eleftherías & Kénnedy, 100m from the sea, ☎ (0265) 41620 / 41625, ☎ in Athens (01) 77 97 665 / 65 22 092, 18rm. 📶 𝒫 ▤ TV ✕ 🚗 This small, all-white hotel in a former captain's home is our favourite. Everything is serene here, from the smiling owner to the family atmosphere and immaculately white – almost monastic – rooms. The hotel will take you on a boat ride in their caique and on day excursions to Delphi. Breakfast included. Open year round.

Between €38 and €60
Lykoreía, outside Itéa on the Delphi road, ☎ (0267) 31 180 – 20rm. 📶 𝒫 TV ✕ CC All the rooms in this comfortable and discreet little hotel have a pleasant terrace overlooking the valley.

Breakfast not included unless you stay for a week. Closed in July and August.

EATING OUT
Don't expect anything exceptional from the pizzerias and tavernas for tourists which are all over Delphi. If possible, choose one of the friendly tavernas in Aráhova which are known for their copious meals and inventive cooking.

• **Aráhova**
Around €7
I Géfira ("the bridge"), just after the bridge on the valley side. A traditional mountain taverna serving copious local dishes in a village atmosphere. At teatime they serve Middle Eastern cakes and yoghurt with honey. Good value for money.
Neón, enjoy an excellent assortment of meze in a decor of white stone and varnished wood.

Around €11
Flox, Athenians are very fond of this fashionable establishment where the cooking – like the music – ranges from Greek to international (fine assortment of kebabs and salads with Parmesan cheese).

HAVING A DRINK
Cafés, bars

• **Delphi**
Café (it has no name), at the bottom of the site, on the road that leads down to the tholos. Breathtaking view of the valley. Naturally, the iced coffee is expensive (€2!).

• **Aráhova**
For a peaceful evening, try one of the café-bars on the main street. If you're into loud music, head for one of the very lively night-clubs, **Show-Me** and **Banana-Moon**.

OTHER THINGS TO DO
Feasts & festivals – The inhabitants of Delphi have an **Easter** parade for which they dress in traditional costumes and serve mutton kebabs up and down the street. 23 April is the Aráhova village festival, which lasts 3 days and ends with a feast.

Arts and crafts – Carpets, cushions and curtains made of woven cotton. In Delphi, **Níkos Giannópoulos** in the upper part of the town has a good selection. In Aráhova, they are sold in the various shops lining the main street.

Antiques – In Delphi, **Demétrios Fekás'** beautiful shop at Odós Apóllonos 56 has a superb choice of traditional everyday objects (pottery, old signs, fabrics, etc) but the prices are high.

Local delicacies – Besides the olive oil and wildflower honey, try the **staphylopsomiá** (raisin biscuits) and in Aráhova taste the **formaéla**, the cheese with which (toasted) "saganáki" is made. These can be bought in grocery stores in Aráhova, such as **Ioánnis Sýros'** splendid shop in the centre of the village.

Making the most of Náfpaktos

102km west of Delphi. If you are going on to the Peloponnese, spend a night at Náfpaktos, a quiet town with a pleasant beach and an imposing Venetian citadel.

COMING AND GOING

By bus – Buses leave every 3hr for Itéa and Delphi. But check on timetables when you get there just to be sure (the bus station is in the centre of town).

By boat – **Ferries** run every day (approximately every 30min) between Andírio, 10km west of Náfpaktos, and Río (on the far side of the gulf, 7km from Patras). Timetables vary according to the season, so enquire at the harbour police or at one of the tourist agencies in town.

ADDRESS BOOK

Tourist agencies – **Adractas**, ☏ (0634) 22 285 / 22 286, **Zambaras**, ☏ (0634) 22 290, **Lepando**, ☏ (0634) 23 391. For information about boats, buses and lodging.

Harbour police – ☏ (0634) 27 909.

Taxis – ☏ (0634) 25 111 / 27 678.

Medical service – **Medical centre**, ☏ (0634) 23 690 to 94.

WHERE TO STAY

In addition to hotels, many people rent out rooms in their homes which are a bit cheaper.

Between €23 and €30
Hotel Amaryllis, on the seafront, ☏ (0634) 27 237 – 28rm. 🕯 ▤ ✕ This charming little hotel is quite modest, but it is also clean, pleasant and near the harbour. Warm reception.

Between €38 and €45
Hotel Lépando Beach, Odós Grímbovo, ☏ (0634) 27 798 – 93rm. 🕯 ▤ ℰ TV ⚑ CC A large hotel with a standard level of comfort and a garden between it and the sea.

Between €33 and €51
Hotel Akti, east of town, facing the sea, ☏ (0634) 28 464, Fax (0634) 24 171 – 113rm including 4 luxury suites. 🕯 ▤ ℰ TV ⚑ CC This remodelled establishment has a very contemporary look and all modern comforts. All of the rooms have a balcony overlooking the sea.

EATING OUT

Around €11
Taverna Spittikó, a small, traditional taverna on the beach that is popular with the locals. Good menu.

Taverna Ilіópoulos, in Monastiráki, about 12km from Náfpaktos in the direction of Delphi (past the town church, take the steps leading down to the beach). Pleasant local dishes and fresh fish.

The Gulf of Messinía

THE PELOPONNESE

The Peloponnese became an island in 1893 when the Corinth Canal was built. But in reality the isthmus linking it to the mainland was never wide enough for it to consider itself anything other than a land apart.

Protruding from the south of the country and separating the Ionian Sea from the Aegean, the Peloponnese stretches out like a hand as though to catch hold of Crete. In the east is the green Argolis, sticking out like a thumb. Then come three fingers: the rocky Monemvassiá point, the wild Máni Peninsula, and lastly, in the west, the softer contours of Messinía.

The four headlands have jagged coastlines, reflecting the dramatic relief of the peninsula. But between the chains of mountains are fertile plains with Mediterranean vegetation where olives, vines, cereals and fruit trees compose peaceful pastoral scenes evoking ancient Arcadia.

Such topography favoured the emergence of powerful city states – including the redoubtable Sparta – that continuously asserted their individuality by engaging in fratricidal warfare. But today their ruins offer visitors a heritage that is as rich as it is beautiful. Of all the regions in Greece, the Argolid is probably the one with the highest concentration of archaeological sites per square metre. But travelling from shore to shore and plain to plain, you will find that the Peloponnese has many other surprises, among them Nestor's Mycenaean Palace, the temple at Bassae deep in the mountains, and the ramparts of ancient Messene. And the history of the peninsula does not stop with antique times, as is borne out by the evocative remains of an eventful Middle Ages and a flamboyant Byzantine Renaissance. Testifying to this are Monemvassiá, crowned in glory, Mistra, with its slumbering magnificence, and along the coast, dozens of Frankish, Venetian and Ottoman citadels placed like crowns on hilltops to protect the ever coveted land.

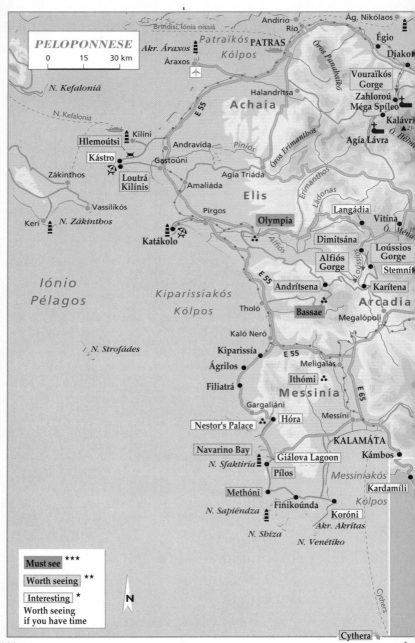

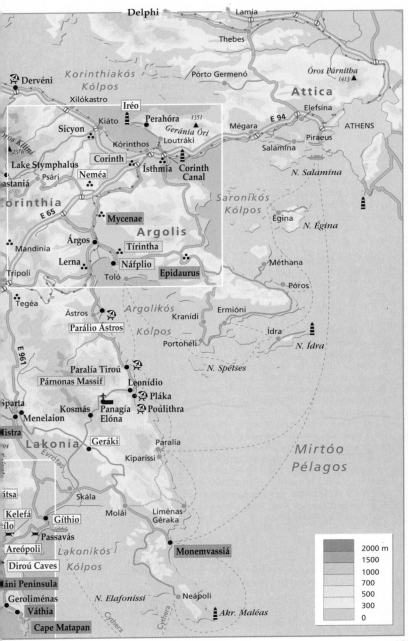

A TOUR OF CORINTHÍA ★

Province of the Peloponnese – District of Corinthía – Regional map page 202
Michelin map 980 fold 29 – Tour of one or two days

Not to be missed
The Corinth Canal.
The Heraíon at Perahóra (Iréo).
The site of Neméa.

And remember...
Begin the tour in Corinth but choose somewhere to stay in places round about
(see page 207).

Eighty kilometres of motorway separate Athens from the immense Peloponnese
Peninsula – or rather island, as all that connect it to the mainland are two bridges
across a dead straight canal. The bridges lead to Corinthía, a vast region lying between
two bays, stretching from the Saronic Gulf to the Gulf of Corinth, dominated in the
middle by the **Kilíni Massif** (2 376m). Before visiting ancient Corinth, take a day or
two to explore the surrounding area. Starting from the modern town, you can cross
from shore to shore, enjoying delightfully bucolic landscapes and a view of the canal
itself.

The Corinth Canal★★

Looking as though it was gouged out by some giant instrument forged in the smithy
of Hephaestus, the canal is as straight as a die, with smooth vertical sides. The two
white walls are 80m high and barely 25m apart. The canal is 8m deep and so narrow that boats – liners and coasters only – pulled by a tug, are always touching the
sides. The best **view**★★ of the
canal is from the two bridges
(both one-way) that span it. If
you are put off by the bars,
kiosks and souvenir shops that
line the **Ísthmia bridge** (north-
east, on the Athens-Peloponnese
road) go to the **Posidonía
bridge** (further south, on the edge
of the Gulf of Corinth), which is a
little more removed from the
tourist bustle. When a boat ap-
proaches, the **wooden roadway**
in the centre of the bridge sinks
into the water to let it pass – a
slow, silent spectacle (about
20min) stoically contemplated by
drivers.

A 2 500-year-old project
In Antiquity, the triremes transporting goods from
Piraeus to Italy had to go round the Peloponnese.
In addition to the time wasted by the detour, the
voyage was a dangerous one because of the countless rocky headlands on the coast of the peninsula. In the 6C or 7C BC, the diolkós a paved
portage-road, was built across the isthmus, thus
allowing ships to be transported on trolleys along
the 6.5km that separated the two gulfs. But it was
the Romans who had the idea of building a canal.
However, after Nero had symbolically inaugurated the digging with a golden shovel, the work
was interrupted due to a lack of sufficiently robust tools to pierce the rock (limestone and marl).
It was only taken up again seventeen centuries
later, on 1 May 1882, and lasted eleven years.

From shore...

*From Corinth, drive along the north coast to the Posidonía bridge, cross the canal and
continue to the Heraíon at Perahóra, 25km north-west. Allow 2 to 3hr, including a swim
and an ouzo at sunset. Don't forget your swimsuit.*

■ Beyond **Loutráki**, a large resort without any charm but renowned for its spa, the
road disappears into a huge forest, unfortunately damaged here and there by fire.
Once past **Perahóra** (*take the first road left when you enter the town*), you come to the

romantic shores of **Lake Vouliagménis***. This is linked to the sea by a narrow channel and has several shady tavernas (**beach** at the north-west end).

■ 3km further on, the road ends at the **Perahóra Heraíon*** (Iréo), a delightful ancient site shaded by pines. This sanctuary dedicated to Hera, a haven of peace and serenity, rises in tiers above a small cove. While the foundations of the **temple** are hardly spectacular, you can, however, clearly make out a large Hellenistic **cistern** without a roof in the middle of the lower terrace and, on the right, the remains of the **harbour**, drowned in crystal-clear water in which you can swim.

...to shore

■ **Ísthmia** – *Coming from Corinth, take the last road on the right before the canal. The ruins of Ísthmia (8km) are outside the village of Vrísi. Allow 2hr, more if you go to the beach at Loutrá Elénis.* More than an intense archaeological experience, a trip to Ísthmia is an excuse to explore the north-east of the Peloponnese. Of the sanctuary founded in the 7C BC and dedicated to Poseidon, there are but modest remains: the low walls of the **temple** – which, nonetheless, was the largest in the Peloponnese along with Olympia – several tiers of the **theatre**, and the **starting line** of a very large **stadium**. More interesting are the **mosaics*** that covered the floor of a **Roman bath**, featuring Tritons and Nereids. Nothing else recalls the glorious **Isthmian Games**, which together with those organised at Olympia, Delphi and Neméa (*see below*) made up the four great pan-Hellenic events.

At the entrance to the site on the left, the **museum*** (*8am-3pm; closed Monday; free*) displays the objects found at Ísthmia and Cenchreae, particularly panels of **painted glass mosaics**. These are very rare and probably came from Egypt.

■ On leaving Ísthmia, take the coast road past **Cenchreae**, the eastern port for ancient Corinth (*see page 208*). Beneath the water you can see the **foundations of the south jetty**. The road continues south to the large pebble beach at **Loutrá Elénis**, dominated by green hills, and to the sandy beach at **Almirí**.

West of Corinth

■ **Sicyon** (Sikióna) – *From Corinth, follow the coast westwards. After 5km you go past Léheo (ancient Lechaeum, the main port of ancient Corinth). 22km further on, leave the main road at Kiáto, and take the road in the direction of Traganá. The ruins are 6km further on, outside Vassilikó; 8.30am-3pm; closed Monday. Free. Allow 1hr.* In comparison with the ruins of Corinth, there's nothing spectacular about those of the Hellenistic city of Sicyon. But they make for a delightful excursion if you like solitude and Mediterranean vegetation buzzing with the hum of cicadas. The town was built on a plateau in the year 300 to take the place of an older city on the site of present-day Kiáto. A **museum** at the entrance to the site has been installed in the **Roman baths**, which are in fairly good condition. There you can see finds from Sicyon and Stymphalus, including **architectural items** from different periods and **Hellenistic statues**.

As you leave, take the road that climbs up the neighbouring hill, which is topped by the remains of the acropolis. Two hundred metres further on are the ruins of the **gymnasium** extending over two terraces. It has kept two lovely **nymphaea** (monumental fountains), one of which still has its walls and the columns with their architrave on the façade.

Back on the road, 200m further on the left at the foot of the acropolis, you will see the well-preserved terraces of the **theatre**. The **arched passageways** on its sides once linking the upper terraces to the acropolis can still be seen.

At the gates of Arcadia⋆

The Nemean Lion

Two of the Twelve Labours of Heracles (Hercules) took place in Corinthía: at Stymphalus (see following box), and at Neméa, where the demigod killed a supposedly invulnerable lion that devoured shepherds and flocks of sheep. The monster lived in a cave with two entrances. With his club, Heracles forced the lion into its den and blocked one of the entrances. He then leapt upon the beast and choked it with his bare hands. Afterwards he used its skin as a coat and its head as a helmet. To thank Heracles for avenging the death of one of his sons killed by the lion, the shepherd Molorchus offered Zeus the Saviour his finest ram. It is on the very site of this sacrifice that Heracles founded the Nemean Games, in honour of his father, the god Zeus.

If you only have 2hr, give priority to a tour of Neméa, 35km from Corinth along the Corinth-Trípoli motorway. Note that the site is only open in the morning. A trip into the lonely mountains of Corinthía (150km there and back from Corinth) will take a day, including lunch at Psári, or at Láfka or Kastaniá located beyond Lake Stymphalus.

■ **Neméa**⋆ – *8am-2.30pm; closed Monday. The ticket includes a tour of the site and entry into the museum.* Though Neméa is slightly off the classic tour for archaeology lovers, it is worth a visit not only for its beautiful setting in a peaceful valley ridged with vines but also for the site itself, which is maintained as a public garden. From the mid-4C BC onwards, the **Nemean Games**, one of the four major Panhellenic festivals were held here every two years. Admittedly, the remains of the sports facilities (*currently being excavated*) are not particularly inspiring. However, note, to the left of the entrance, the remains of the **baths** and just beside them those of the **lodgings** for the athletes and visitors. Further on are three **Doric columns** of a **temple** built in the 4C BC to the glory of Zeus, standing as though mirrored by the cypress trees round about.

A **museum** at the entrance to the site houses the objects discovered here, which include architectural fragments, bronzes, pottery, as well as **models** of the site at different times. An exhibition provides interesting information on the games held in the stadium in Antiquity, the rules governing them, the diverse disciplines, etc.

As you leave the museum, turn left to return to the main road, and then left again.

A hundred metres further on (*on the right, but poorly signposted*), hidden among bay trees, pines and cypresses is the **stadium**⋆ (*same times as the main site; entrance fee*), the most evocative part of Neméa. A short distance beyond the ticket office, on the right, the bases of about ten columns mark the site of a building that was used by athletes and officials. A well-cleared **tunnel** connects it directly with the stadium (the **graffiti** on the walls date from those times). The **track**, stretching out for 100m from the **starting line**, which is intact, lies between the grass embankments formerly covered in tiered wooden terraces where the spectators would sit.

Cross the village of Neméa and continue straight ahead for about 30km.

■ The beautiful **road**⋆ disappears into the wild scenery of the lonely mountains of Corinthía. The terrain it crosses varies from fertile valleys planted with vines – which since Antiquity have produced a red wine called **Nemean wine** or "blood of Heracles" – to austere mountains where you will see not a soul.

The Stymphalian Birds

The other mission that Heracles had in Corinthía was to kill the birds of prey that haunted the lake of Stymphalus. They had multiplied to such an extent that they ravaged the entire region, devouring everything in their path, fruit, crops and animals, even going as far as humans (according to some traditions). Heracles used bronze rattles to frighten them out of the forest. As they flew up from the foliage he shot them with arrows.

It is in this unreal setting between Arcadia and the Argolid that **Lake Stymphalus** (Stimfalía) lies. The immense reed-covered marsh is home to thousands of birds, as well as to sheep. These graze with their legs in the water under the dreamy gaze of young Albanian shepherds listening to their personal stereos.

■ The tour ends at the end of a winding road at **Kastaniá**, a charming mountain village lost among the firs and chestnuts at a height of 920m. The **traditional houses** still have their wooden balconies.

For a different route back to Corinth, make your way to the Gulf of Corinth via Krionéri and Sicyon (see above). But, in addition to the fact that the Sicyon site closes at 3pm, the landscape is less enchanting and the coast road very crowded.

Making the most of Corinthía

GETTING AROUND

By bus – See *"Making the most of Corinth"*, page 213.

WHERE TO STAY

• **Loutráki**

Between €55 and €75
Agelídis Palace, Odós G Lékka 19, on the main thoroughfare heading north out of town, ☎ (0744) 26 695 / 26 696, Fax (0744) 63 164 – 43rm. ⌂ 🖳 🖉 TV ✗ 🐾 CC A luxury hotel dating from the 1920s with huge and comfortable rooms. For those who like stucco, gilding and chandeliers (in the dining room). The only hotel in town that really stands out. The rooms overlooking the sea have balconies.

• **Ísthmia**

Campsite (around €12)
Ísthmia Beach campsite, ☎ (0741) 37 447 or 37 131 (in winter), Fax (0741) 37 710. A huge, well-equipped campsite covering an area of 2.5 hectares, giving onto a long sandy beach. The pitches are separated by bushes. There are water-sports facilities, and rooms, tents, caravans and vehicles for hire.

Between €60 and €120 (half-board for 2 people)
Kalamáki Beach, ☎ (0741) 37 331-4 – 76rm. ⌂ 🖳 🖉 TV ✗ 🛋 🐾 🍽 🕭 CC A large, very new international hotel beside the sea with an extensive garden. All the rooms are spacious and have terraces. Many activities and a wide range of water sports (windsurfing school).

EATING OUT, HAVING A DRINK

• **Lake Vouliagménis**
The shores of the lake are dotted with pleasant little tavernas right beside the water.

• **Neméa**
Two café-tavernas stand facing each other in the middle of the village. The one on the left as you come from the site is also a grocery store (provisions for picnics). Closed during siesta time.

• **Posidonía**
To the left of the bridge across the Corinth Canal, on the west side, is the **Diolkós** café-taverna, which has the best view of the canal and the shipping traffic. To the right, the **Posidónio** bar is right beside the water and is an ideal spot at sunset.

OTHER THINGS TO DO

Excursions – Short boat trips are organised between Corinth and Lake Vouliagménis. Hydrofoils from Ísthmia serve the islands in the Saronic Gulf.

Open-air cinema – In **Loutráki**, on the main avenue, Leofóros Venizélou, between the thermal baths and the Agelídis Palace Hotel.

Newspapers – In Loutráki, **International Press** bookshop on the main avenue, at Leofóros Venizélou 26.

SHOPPING GUIDE

Local delicacies – Try the **Nemean wine** or "blood of Heracles", produced for 2 500 years. It is dark red, full-bodied and spicy.

ANCIENT CORINTH★★

(ARHÉA KÓRINTHOS)

Province of the Peloponnese – District of Corinthía
Regional map page 202 – Michelin map 980 fold 29

Not to be missed
The Fountain of Peirene.
The view from the top of Acrocorinth.

And remember...
Rather than staying in Corinth itself, which has little charm, opt for the village near
the site of ancient Corinth, or one of the resorts in the region
(see below "Making the most of Corinth", and the previous chapter).

Once past the new town of Corinth, the road lined with oleanders crosses a landscape that seems to have remained unchanged since Antiquity. Over plain and valley, fields of cereals ripple in the sun, alternating with olive groves, vineyards and pasture for sheep. The picture is one of complete harmony – you could almost be in the gardens of Arcadia! The atmosphere recalls Homer's descriptions of Greece, or French paintings from the 18C. Rising out of this bucolic setting are the ruined walls of ancient Corinth, inviting you to continue your journey beyond Athens into the heart of Hellenic Antiquity.

The gateway to the Peloponnese

The ancient city of Kórinthos was established as the capital of Corinthía (*see previous chapter*) on the edge of the isthmus that separates the Saronic Gulf from the Gulf of Corinth. It had been inhabited since Neolithic times and very soon became the richest and busiest commercial city in Ancient Greece. This was thanks not only to the countless springs that made the region fertile, and to the pottery and bronzeware that was highly sought after throughout the Mediterranean between 650 and 550 BC, but also to the city's exceptional position. Ancient Corinth dominated the whole of the northern Peloponnese, and whoever transported goods from the East to the West necessarily passed through. The city reached its height between 630 and 590 BC, when the majestic Temple of Apollo was built, reflecting its immense prosperity.

Such commercial power was bound to be coveted by the **Romans**, who took Corinth in 146 BC, massacring and looting shamelessly, sparing neither the temple nor the other buildings. However, a hundred years after the sacking, Julius Caesar set up a colony for veterans there. The buildings that were still standing were repaired and converted, and the city gradually recovered its splendour – with a population of 300 000 in the 1C AD – to become the **capital of Roman Greece**, a status it retained for three centuries.

Although the city was little affected by the barbarian invasions, the earthquakes that

Business and pleasure

Already at the time of the early Greeks, Corinth was known for its unbounded luxury and licentiousness, to which the austere philosopher Diogenes took an opposing stance by deciding to live in a barrel. In addition to the many courtesans in the city, the priestesses in the Temple of Aphrodite engaged in sacred prostitution, and the dancers and musicians at banquets were known for their loose morals. When the city fell to the Romans, becoming a cosmopolitan town with Romans, freed Greeks and Jewish merchants, it regained its opulence and dissolute ways, which attracted crowds of visitors, traders, sailors and travellers of every kind. This earned it castigation by St Paul, who rebuked the inhabitants for their evil ways when he wrote his Epistle to the Corinthians in the middle of the 1C.

struck in the 6C were to toll the knell of its second golden age. Through the centuries that followed, Corinth was reduced to a modest market town, renowned from the 14C onwards for its **currants**. Only the fortified acropolis, Acrocorinth, was to keep a certain strategic importance, while the ancient city disappeared gradually beneath Ottoman constructions, which spared little other than the Temple of Apollo.

A new capital
It is traditionally believed that the person who invented the Corinthian column was the sculptor Callimachus, who was born in Corinth in the 5C BC. The idea came to him when he saw a wickerwork basket which had been placed on top of an acanthus plant, whose leaves had subsequently grown up around it.

Modern Corinth

Paradoxically, it was another earthquake, in 1858, that brought ancient Corinth to light. The new town was entirely ruined and rebuilt on the coast to the north, near the canal, thus making room for American archaeologists who, beginning in 1896, gradually uncovered the ancient ruins.

The new town, a district centre with a population of 23 000, was built to a strict grid pattern without any charm. There is little to retain the traveller, and so you will probably only use it as a starting point for a tour of Corinthía. The only attraction is the **Historical and Folk Museum** (*at the bottom of Odós Ermoú, opposite the marina, 8am-1pm; closed Monday; entrance fee*), that displays clothes, jewellery, old embroideries and traditional tools.

In the heart of the ancient city★★

On leaving Corinth, take the motorway towards Trípoli. After 6km, follow the signs to Arhéa Kórinthos, which is 1km further on.

Leaving aside the souvenir shops that crowd the centre, the **village** close to ancient Corinth is fairly authentic, contrasting with the impersonal tourist resorts you find around most large archaeological sites. The tour starting from here is in two parts: the ancient city, which is mainly Roman, and the climb to Acrocorinth, the citadel that dominates it.

Go through the village. The site is a few hundred metres away as you go up towards Acrocorinth Hill. 8am-7pm from July to October. Entrance fee (including the museum). Allow 2hr.

Even though the ruins suggest that ancient Corinth was a very large town, it is not easy to appreciate all the economic and strategic power that it wielded. The city spread out within concentric walls that started from Acrocorinth and formed a wide circle around it. From there it continued as a kind of corridor for several kilometres on either side of the Lechaeum Way. This led to the western port, while a second road linked the city to the eastern port at Cenchreae, south of Ísthmia (*see page 205*). Near the car park before you reach the entrance you will see on the left a ruined **theatre**. This was built in the 5C BC before being remodelled by the Romans to hold nautical events. Further up (*towards the entrance*), in the shade of cypress trees are the remains of a **Roman odeon** (1C AD). Most of the rows of terraced seats were carved out of the hillside.

Beyond the ticket office, the path leads to the right, past three Corinthian columns. These still hold up part of the architrave of the **Temple of Octavia**, dedicated to the sister of Emperor Augustus.

Keep the museum for the end of the tour and go into the city past the low ruined walls of countless **shops** – testifying to Corinth's major commercial role – which stood in rows facing the **agora**.

On the left, a path leads round the ruins of a **sanctuary to Hera** to the impressive rock of the **Glauce Fountain**, whose four **cisterns** were hewn out of the rock and supplied with water by an aqueduct from Lake Stymphalus.

On the other side of the path, on the right, rises the ochre-coloured **Temple of Apollo**★ (550 BC), one of the oldest in Greece. Its seven monolithic Doric columns made of tufa – and on which part of the entablature rests – are all that remain of the building's original 38 columns. The temple stands on high ground affording a fine **view**★ of Acrocorinth to the south and the shimmering Gulf of Corinth to the north. Below, looking towards the sea, you can make out the **north market** shops, whose side and back walls can still be seen.

The Roman agora★

Turn away from the temple to discover the huge open space of the Roman agora, which dates back to the 1C. It was built on two terraces, measuring almost 200mx100m. The first terrace or **lower forum** was demarcated (at your feet) by an impressive row of **fifteen shops** that are in fairly good condition. The largest, in the middle, has even kept its **vaulted roof**.

At the end of the row on the left, steps lead down to the underground spring of a **sacred fountain**, which was reserved for priests. One of them would hide here, passing himself off as Apollo, and answer the questions put by worshippers.

On the right (*not far from the museum*) were several **small temples** whose foundations can still be made out. At the back stands another **row of shops**, interrupted in the middle by the **orators' platform** (Bema), where St Paul had discussions with the Jews of Corinth.

Behind this lies the **upper forum**, marked by an immense **portico** (stoa). You can see the bases of a **double colonnade**, where the administrative buildings stood. On the right was the council building or **bouleuterion**, recognisable by its oval foundations and the stone benches up against the wall.

The fortified hill of Acrocorinth

The fourth side of the agora is taken up by the **Julian Basilica**, a long building that served as a law court. Just in front of it you can see the **starting lines** for the races that were organised during votive festivals.

Turning back and going left, you reach the **propylaea** that opened onto the Lechaeum Way. They are flanked on the left by a second **Roman basilica**, whose façade was once adorned with four large **statues of captives** (two are in the museum).

On the right stands the superb **Fountain of Peirene****. Its name derives from the tragedy of one of the

Glauce, or love's burns

In his quest for the Golden Fleece, Jason, the leader of the Argonauts, was helped by the beautiful enchantress Medea and fell in love with her. When his adventure ended, he married her and they settled in Corinth. But Jason's gratitude and love only lasted for a while, and he ended up by repudiating his wife to marry Glauce, the daughter of King Creon. Thirsting for revenge, the enchantress gave her rival a poisoned tunic. When Glauce put it on, she was burned so badly that she threw herself into the water to try to soothe the pain. It is to her that the fountain is dedicated.

daughters of the river god Asopus, who bore Poseidon two sons, Lechaeum and Cenchreae (also the names of the two ports of Corinth). When one of them was accidentally killed by Artemis, the inconsolable mother shed so many tears that she was turned into a spring, whose water, which has been highly reputed since earliest Antiquity, still flows today and supplies the modern village. The fountain was built in the 6C BC and remodelled by the Romans in the 2C. It consists of a paved **court** with a rectangular **basin** in the middle where the water flows. This is framed by three semicircular drawing basins that form the **nymphaeum**. At the back, six **arches**

precede a row of basins and reservoirs. As you cannot go inside, lean forward into the structure and when your eyes are accustomed to the half-light you will be able to make out the **balustrades** decorated with small Ionic columns, and traces of **polychrome painting** on the walls.

Now walk down the **Lechaeum Way**, which has kept its paving and many of the shops and monuments that lined it. On the right are the well-preserved **public latrines** and the **baths**.

Retrace your steps to end the tour at the **Archaeological Museum** that contains the finds from the site. Room 1, to the right of the entrance, displays **Corinthian ceramics** dating from the Geometric to the Classical Era, as well as a 6C BC **sphinx**. Room 2 contains the **statues** of the family of Augustus that adorned the Julian Basilica. Lastly, on the patio you will find various architectural fragments from the town buildings, particularly the theatre.

Acrocorinth★★

The track to the acropolis (3km) leads off just to the right of the entrance to ancient Corinth, and then forks left. On foot, it is a tough 90min walk uphill, often in the blazing sun. Instead, take a taxi, which will drop you off and then come back to collect you (phone booth in the taverna-café, at the foot of the car park). The best time to visit is at dusk or in the morning before the heat haze sets in. Bring good walking shoes. Allow 2hr. Open until 7pm. Free access.

Although from Corinth, Acrocorinth looks like nothing more than a steep rocky hill (576m), don't deprive yourself of the pleasure of wandering through the majestic ruins of what in ancient times was the bastion of Corinth and, in the Middle Ages, the largest citadel in Greece. Once there, you will appreciate the sheer size of the place. The many remains from successive eras merge in with the rocks. In the silence barely disturbed by the whistling of the wind, you will have an exceptional **view★★** of the Gulf of Corinth and the northern Peloponnese.

A much coveted citadel

Whereas Roman Corinth with its emphasis on trade declined in the 6C AD, the military fortress of Acrocorinth outlasted it by almost eleven centuries. Ideally placed on a hill from where it could keep watch and give warning of enemy attacks, it also benefited from springs that supplied enough water to survive a siege. Needless to say all these assets made it a strategic prize of the highest importance. Consequently, in spite of powerful ramparts, it passed from hand to hand, notably falling to the **Franks**, who managed to take it after a five-year siege. In the end, it came under Turkish rule from the 15C onwards, with a Venetian interlude between 1687 and 1715.

Tour of the site

A paved ramp leads from the car park up to the fortress, where in a single glance you can take in some of the 2.5km of **ramparts★** that surrounded the town. You have a spectacular panorama of the three lines of defence and the three well-preserved **monumental gates★★**, which were built over the remains of the ancient ramparts at different times in history. The first one, dating from the 14C, was built by the Turks, and the second, of the same age, by the Franks, before being remodelled by the Venetians. The third, flanked by two massive towers, dates back to the Byzantine Era.

Once through the third gate, you enter the fortress itself, an immense plateau covering an area of 24ha, where, strewn among the rocks are the ruins of numerous buildings. By following the path past a renovated **chapel** on the left, you come to a fairly well-preserved **mosque**, then, further up on the right, to an enormous **cistern★** whose roof, which forms a kind of platform, is flanked by a truncated **minaret**.

From here, a steep stony path overgrown with bushes leads to a junction. If you have the energy and suitable shoes, you can continue the climb: the left-hand path leads to the insignificant remains of the **Temple of Aphrodite**, stronghold of the famous sacred prostitutes whose behaviour provoked the indignation of St Paul. The middle path leads to the **upper Fountain of Peirene**, which is reached via steps.

Making the most of Corinth

COMING AND GOING

By bus – The terminal is on the corner of Odós Ermoú and Odós Koliátsou, ☎ (0741) 24 481. Buses to Athens (about thirty a day), Loutráki, Ísthmia and Neméa. To see the canal, get off at Isthmós.
Buses to the Peloponnese: station on the corner of Odós Ethníkis Antístasis and Odós Arátou, ☎ (0741) 24 403. Connections with Mycenae, Árgos and Náfplio. To get to ancient Corinth (travelling time 20min), take a bus from the main square, near Odós Koliátsou (1 bus an hour).

By train – The station, ☎ (0741) 22 523, is in Odós Demokratías. 14 trains a day to and from Athens via Ísthmia (travelling time 2hr), 8 to Patras (2hr30min to 3hr30min depending on the train), 2 to Náfplio (75min), 4 to Árgos (1hr), Trípoli (2hr) and Kalamáta (5hr). Left luggage.

By taxi – There is a taxi rank in the main square, ☎ (0741) 22 361 or 24 844.

ADDRESS BOOK

Police – Odós Ermoú, opposite the main square.

Tourist police – Upstairs, above the police station, ☎ (0741) 23 282.

Medical service – **Hospital**, Leofóros Athinón 53, on the way out of town on the Athens road, ☎ (0741) 25 711 / 12.

WHERE TO STAY

Avoid Corinth, as its hotels lack charm. Instead, try the village at ancient Corinth or the small resorts along the east coast (see page 207). In summer, when demand is much greater than supply, book as soon as possible.

• **Ancient Corinth**
Around €23
Tássos, on the right beyond the post office, ☎ (0741) 31 225 / 31 183 – 10rm. ⌂ 🚿 ✗ 🆑 Accommodation above a taverna. Modest rooms with balconies or shared terraces. Avoid the ones giving onto the street (noisy). Open all year.

Around €33
Marínos, in the first road on the right beyond the Tássos taverna, ☎ (0741) 31 209 / 31 180 – 25rm. ⌂ Some of the rooms have no bathroom. Otherwise, this large house among the pines is very comfortable and welcoming to families. The quietest rooms are in a wing behind the main house. No room service, but breakfast is included.

EATING OUT

• **Ancient Corinth**
Between €6 and €7.50
Tássos, a taverna where every detail helps create a typically Greek atmosphere: *souvláki* being grilled, good-humoured personnel, Greek music, and backfiring mopeds scraping past your table.

€12
🍽 **Marínos**, the restaurant at the guesthouse with the same name (not to be confused with the Marinos taverna in the town centre). An excellent taverna with tables laid out beneath the trees. Generous set menu (wine included).

MYCENAE★★★
(MIKÍNES)
Province of the Peloponnese – District of Argolis
Regional map page 202 – Michelin map 980 fold 29
38km from Corinth, 10km north of Árgos and 90km from Athens

Not to be missed
The Lion Gate.
The circle of royal tombs on the acropolis.
Clytemnestra's tomb and the Treasury of Atreus.

And remember...
Wear good walking shoes (the rocks are slippery), and cover up from the sun.
Bring a torch to see the tombs and the cistern.

The rocky sun-scorched hilltop on which the powerful citadel of Mycenae was built in 1600 BC looks over a bucolic landscape, in what at the time, according to Homer, was the most remote part of the fertile Argolis. And yet this peaceful setting was the scene of one of the bloodiest Greek tragedies – that of the royal house of Atreus, whose soul still seems to haunt the site. So many murders committed in such a restricted space makes Mycenae the dramatic stage of an open-air theatre where, for want of unity of time, there was certainly that of place. You will only make sense of the ruins, from the ancient city to the tombs of its rulers, if you recall the different episodes in this cruel story. And so, as the stone walls come to life, so do the mythical characters that lived within them.

From Corinth, take the main road through the Argolid and turn off at Fíhti. Go through the modern village of Mycenae with its many tavernas, and continue for another 2km to the ancient site.

Mycenae, the city "rich in gold"
According to myth, Mycenae was founded by **Perseus**, the son of Zeus and Danae. The walls of its acropolis (citadel) were built by the **Cyclopes**, the one-eyed giants with superhuman strength. History, as usual, is a little more prosaic, showing how, in the year 2000 BC (beginning of the Bronze Age) the first inhabitants, the **Achaeans**, arrived. They reigned for centuries over a large part of mainland Greece, firmly establishing their way of life. During the reign of **Agamemnon** in the 13C BC, Mycenae became the main city in the Achaean world, holding sway over all the surrounding domains. It was deeply influenced by the Minoan civilisation of Crete, and such was its prosperity that Homer described the city as *polýchrysos*, "rich in gold".

Schliemann, a self-taught genius
Nothing predisposed the German grocer's assistant Heinrich Schliemann (1822-90) to become the father of modern archaeology and one of the greatest discoverers of the Greek world. Nothing, apart from a consuming passion for Antiquity – the Iliad had always been his bedside book – and European languages, including Russian, and Arabic, which he taught himself. By the age of 45 he had become a wealthy banker, heading the Imperial Bank in St Petersburg, and decided to devote his fortune and his time to looking for the sites described by Homer, which contemporary scholars believed to be the stuff of legend. In 1871, his discovery of Troy at the entrance to the Dardanelles proved that Homer's accounts were based on real fact. His discovery of the royal tombs at Mycenae in 1874 confirmed the existence of a civilisation that was thought to be mythical but could now be dated back to the time of Amenophis III thanks to the objects laid in the tombs beside the dead.

Mycenae, the first circle of tombs

Nobody knows exactly what ruined the Mycenaean palaces around 1200 BC. It may have been earthquakes, or peasant revolts against the all-powerful lords, or the **Dorians** who swept through from the north, devastating everything in their path. Whatever the case, the destruction of the palaces tolled the knell of the Mycenaean civilisation. After that disaster, it took the Greeks several centuries to rebuild a social and administrative structure that was as organised as the one that had originated here.

The blood of the House of Atreus, a family tragedy (Homer.)

Of all the ancient dramas, the most tragic was indisputably the one that befell the house of **Atreus**, the family who reigned over Mycenae in the 13C BC. In customary fashion, the tragedy took place in several acts.

Act I. **Atreus**, first king of Mycenae and father of the royal line, decides to punish his twin brother, the adulterous Thyestes, by killing three of his sons, cutting them up into pieces and serving them to their unfortunate father at a banquet. In his suffering, Thyestes has Atreus killed and becomes king in his place. All this barbarity, however, incites the wrath of the gods. They put an eternal curse on Atreus' children.

Act II. The two sons of Atreus are now brought into play: **Agamemnon**, who drives his uncle Thyestes from the throne, and **Menelaus**, whose wife **Helen** is carried off by **Paris**, the son of Priam, king of Troy. To get back his unfaithful wife, Menelaus declares war on Troy, where the lovers have taken refuge, and asks neighbouring kings to join him. Agamemnon leads the expedition.

A feudal society

During the high period of the Mycenaean civilisation, the Argolid was divided into several small kingdoms. Each was ruled by an all-powerful king who held within his hands political power, the organisation of military operations and the spoils of war. He was surrounded by various lords who lived in grand style in their palaces, subjecting craftsmen and farmers to a life of drudgery. This very organised society recorded its needs in terms of men, weapons and animals, engraving them on tablets with the help of a stylet.

215

I. The gods, who are maintaining the curse on the house of Atreus, refuse to vide a favourable wind which will allow the Greek fleet to make for Troy unless gamemnon sacrifices his youngest daughter **Iphigenia**. Giving in to blackmail, Agamemnon carries out the sacrifice, to the utter despair of his wife **Clytemnestra** and her two other children, **Orestes** and **Electra**.

Act IV. Alone in Mycenae, which she has been ruling for the ten years of the war, Clytemnestra takes a lover, **Aegisthus**, and plots her revenge with him. When her husband Agamemnon returns, she and her lover murder him within the palace walls.

Act V. To avenge the death of their father, Orestes and Electra kill their mother and her lover. It is after this murder that the wise goddess Athena decides to put an end to the curse by acquitting Orestes and his sister.

The acropolis★★★

8am-7pm; closed on public holidays. Entrance fee includes a tour of the Treasury of Atreus. Come early to avoid the tourist buses and the worst of the sun that beats down on the treeless hillside. Allow a good two hours, beginning with the acropolis and then continuing with Clytemnestra's tomb and the Treasury of Atreus, not far from the car park.

When you are in the city, try if you can to forget the crowds and imagine Mycenae the way it was from the 16C BC to the 12C BC, one of the oldest citadels in history. Crowning the hill are the impressive **Cyclopean walls**★★, an assemblage of enormous blocks of stone jointed with admirable precision, in places up to 8m thick. A narrow lane flanked by two bastions leads to the famous **Lion Gate**★★★ (the animals are probably lionesses), cut into the walls in the 13C BC. The gateway is made of four massive blocks of stone, including a monolithic relieving triangle above the lintel, carved with two headless lions standing on either side of a column. You are left speechless before the sheer power of the structure, both so simple and yet so forceful. The feature is unusual for a civilisation that made little use of monumental sculpture, and is moreover the only decorative element in the austere ensemble.

Once through the gate you enter the citadel (acropolis) along the path that led to the royal palace. A few dozen metres further on, you come to the **royal circle**★★ on the right, the first Mycenaean necropolis discovered by Schliemann. Demarcated by **orthostates**, upright stone slabs, this wide circular area (26.50m in diameter) contained **six tombs** *(off-limits)* in which were buried, in foetal position, 19 royals –

The splendours of Mycenae

Apart from its talent for power, Mycenaean society was also outstanding for its arts, particularly its work with precious metals, of which many examples were found in the citadel tombs. Among them were gold-encrusted bronze swords, ivory sculptures, seals set with precious stones, vases made of chased gold or silver, and death masks made of gold leaf. The mask that Schliemann mistakenly thought to belong to Agamemnon is now one of the showpieces in the Archaeological Museum in Athens. The polychrome frescoes that covered all the palace walls could be compared with the masterpieces in the Minoan city of Knossós. Their colour and refinement contrasted strikingly with the deliberate austerity and might of the complex's outer walls.

kings and members of their families. Around the remains were piles of jewels, gold-encrusted swords and other sumptuous offerings intended to accompany the dead person into the world beyond. A **gold death mask** covered every face, moulded over the skin.

The ruins lining the paved way *(slippery)* that leads to the top of the acropolis are more difficult to identify. However, you will easily make out the **Royal Palace**★ set on a wide built-up terrace dominating the Argolis Plain. This marks the site of the largest palace **courtyard**, which was originally reached on the right by a **grand staircase** that has kept 18 of its steps. At the back was the **megaron**, the main chamber in the complex (*see lexicon page 45*), where the king had his throne. There was a **round hearth** in the centre surrounded by four columns that supported the roof and whose bases are extant. The palace was laid out on terraces and consisted of several floors, but only the foundations of the first level can still be seen today. It is traditionally believed that it was in these apartments that Queen Clytemnestra and her lover Aegisthus murdered Agamemnon on his return from Troy.

Mycenaean funerary architecture

Several types of grave have been found at Mycenae. Those in the two royal circles are rectangular pit graves, dug into the ground and marked by funerary steles. The most spectacular are the domed graves, of which the finest example is the Treasury of Atreus. Hidden under a mound of earth, they form high circular chambers in the shape of a beehive, reached via a long open-air corridor. The tombs of ordinary citizens were square, carved out of the rock and then covered with a stone slab.

If the heat is not too much for you, keep climbing to the upper part of the citadel, not so much for the remains of the **Temple of Athena** (*on the left as you leave the palace*), nor for the scattered ruins of the craftsmen's workshops, but for the fine **view★** over the valley (*from the postern, right at the end on the right*). At the very end on the left, an **underground staircase** leads down to a **secret cistern**. This was fed by a neighbouring spring and was intended to supply the town with water in case of siege. Only go down if you have good shoes and an electric torch... and if you are energetic enough to face the 99 steep steps back up again.

Retrace your steps and leave the acropolis through the Lion Gate. Walk about a hundred metres down the hill to a series of tombs on the left.

Mycenae

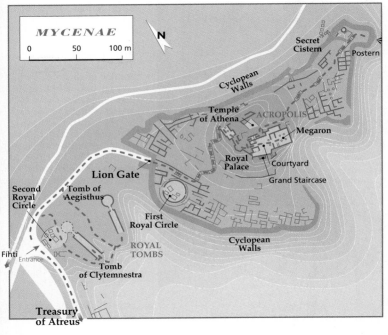

MYCENAE

0   50   100 m

N

Secret Cistern

Postern

Cyclopean Walls

Temple of Athena

ACROPOLIS

Megaron

Royal Palace

Courtyard

Grand Staircase

Lion Gate

Second Royal Circle

Tomb of Aegisthus

First Royal Circle

ROYAL TOMBS

Cyclopean Walls

Fíhti

Entrance

Tomb of Clytemnestra

Treasury of Atreus

The royal tombs***

Nine graves have been excavated outside the citadel enclosure, below the walls. The earth tumuli each contain a round chamber topped by a dome (tholos). Not all are in the same state of preservation, so don't spend much time at the **Tomb of Aegisthus** *(the first on the left)*, where the dome has caved in, but go on to the neighbouring one, the 14C BC **Tomb of Clytemnestra****. You reach it via a 35m-long **corridor***, hollowed out of the tumulus and consolidated by walls made of large blocks of conglomerate rock. Above the lintel over the **door***, made of carved marble, is a relieving triangle, in this case hollowed out, which took the weight of the roofing off the lintel, spreading it directly onto the abutments. The inside of the tomb has been carefully restored and forms a vast round chamber, with perfect walls, where the pure lines of the **dome**** rise to a height of 12.95m.

Once out into the sunlight, continue left to a **second circle of royal tombs**. Older and less spectacular than the circle in the acropolis, this nonetheless contained 24 royal tombs and 14 pit graves, filled with precious offerings, as well as 10 small sepulchres carved out of the rock, for people of lower rank.

Return to the car park and drive to the Treasury of Atreus, 500m further down the road, on the right.

The **Treasury of Atreus*****, the name given to the grandest of the domed tombs found at Mycenae, the only one with two chambers, is also preceded by a 36m-long **corridor***. Schliemann thought it belonged to Agamemnon... mistakenly, because it was built more than a century before the Trojan War, in the 14C BC. But the sheer size and perfection of the work undeniably make you think that it was built for the mortal remains of a great king, perhaps Atreus himself.

Once through the door with its amazing 9m-long monolithic lintel** – weighing some 120t – you are first of all struck by the very welcome cool temperature inside. Once your eyes are accustomed to the dark in the round chamber (14.50m in diameter), note the outstanding arrangement of the **33 rows of stones**, skilfully corbelled with perfect curves, right up to the top of the dome, which reaches a height of 13.20m. The royal sepulchre with its accompanying weapons and provisions stood in the middle of the chamber, just beneath the keystone. On the right, a second, smaller chamber contained an ossuary (which may be seen by torchlight).

Mycenae, the enormous monolith of the Lion Gate

B. Kaufmann/MICHELIN

COMING AND GOING

By bus – There's a bus every hour from Corinth that will drop you off at **Fíhti**, 3km from the site. From Náfplio, 3 buses a day to Mycenae (travelling time 1hr). From Árgos, 6 buses a day (30min).

By train – Mycenae station is 2km from the centre of the village. 5 trains a day to Athens (travelling time 3hr30min), 2 trains to Náfplio, 3 to Árgos, Trípoli and Kalamáta.

By taxi – Dimítrios Mavroyánnis, ☎ 094 366223 (mobile).

WHERE TO STAY

Although Mycenae village has no special charm, there are several hotels should you wish to spend the night here.

Campsite (around €12)

Atreus campsite, at the entrance to Mycenae village, 2.5km before you reach the site, ☎ (0751) 76 221 (in winter: 76 735), Fax (0751) 76 760. This welcoming, family-run campsite has 44 shady pitches, clean, simple facilities, a cafeteria, a small shop (no gas cylinders) and a swimming pool. Avoid the noisy pitches beside the road.

€30

Belle Hélène, in the middle of the village, on the right as you come from Mycenae, ☎ (0751) 76 225 / 76 434, Fax (0751) 76 179 – 8rm. ✕ ⚏ If you

don't mind bathrooms at the end of the corridor. An old hotel built in 1862, with rooms whose furniture and photos date from the same period. Honour to whom honour is due: room *no* 3, formerly occupied by the archaeologist Schliemann, is the only one with a basin! On the ground floor, a rather unsightly restaurant has been built onto the old façade of the building. Open from the beginning of March to the end of November.

Around €75

Petite Planète, between the village and the archaeological site, ☎ (0751) 76 240, Fax (0751) 76 610 – 56rm. ⚏ ⚏ ⚏ ✕ ⚏ ⚏ A recent hotel with pleasant, comfortable rooms with terraces. The swimming pool is particularly welcome. There is a magnificent view of the Argolid from the restaurant.

EATING OUT

There are tavernas all along the main street. The one beside the Belle Hélène hotel is one of the few with air conditioning.

Around €7.50

Kafé-bar Éllinas, in the main street, on the left as you come down from Mycenae. A few tables in a vine arbour create a pleasant setting. An unpretentious taverna serving pizzas, omelettes and the day's specials at reasonable prices.

IN THE ARGOLID★★
ÁRGOS AND TÍRINTHA★★
Province of the Peloponnese – District of Argolis
Regional map page 202 – Michelin map 980 fold 29

Not to be missed
The Greek theatre and the Roman baths in Árgos.
The acropolis and its Cyclopean walls in Tírintha.
The Byzantine church of Agía Triáda.

And remember...
Tour the archaeological sites in the morning, as they mostly close at 3pm.
Bring your swimsuit: you are always within easy reach of the coast.

It is hard to find anything attractive to say about Árgos, the economic capital of the Argolid, a stifling modern town with dusty streets jammed with cars. You can begin, however, by dreaming about the treasures in the basements, buried beneath dismal buildings, as the town has been inhabited constantly since prehistoric times and is considered to be the oldest city in Greece, founded by one of Zeus' many descendants. But the only remnant from the past still standing is a fortified castle perched atop a bare hill, its high walls keeping watch over the town. To see the impressive Greek theatre at the foot of which the Romans built equally large baths, you have to go into the heart of the unsightly suburbs. Most visitors neglect the baths, so you will find them almost deserted and can take the time to wander around.

Leaving Árgos to its hectic pace, you can then drive along a peaceful road through huge citrus plantations with neat rows of trees. Rising above the greenery, the ruins of Tírintha stand out against the sky. The power and wealth of the citadel were on a par with those of its contemporary, Mycenae. The fortress is a thrilling example of 13C BC military architecture, and its Cyclopean ramparts with their extraordinary width continue to impress visitors thirty-four centuries after they were built.

■ Árgos
3 to 4hr are enough to tour the town and the ancient ruins.

When you come from Mycenae, the main road runs directly into the town and leads to the main square, Platía Agíou Pétrou, on which stand the banks, cafés and the museum. Begin your tour at the museum to get an immediate idea of the city's past, before heading off in search of its remains.

From Neolithic to modern times
After Mycenae and Tírintha had fallen into the hands of the **Dorians** (*see page 215*), the newcomers established themselves in Árgos, giving the town its first golden age. In the 7C BC its opulence was such that Sparta became jealous, and after the ensuing war, which Sparta won, the latter replaced Árgos as the region's political and economic capital. Árgos however, continued its influence thanks to its bronze and pottery, and more especially, in the 6C BC, to the fame of its school of sculpture, in which **Ageladas** and **Polyclitus** distinguished themselves. When the Romans arrived, Árgos was greatly embellished, growing very rapidly and seeing most of its buildings remodelled in the Roman style. The Visigoths, however, who ravaged the town in 395, brought in a period of disturbance during which the town changed hands several times between Turks and Venetians. It was freed when the Lárissa citadel was taken in 1829, after the first Greek National Assembly had held sittings in the town (1821).

The **museum**★ is housed in a modern building hidden behind a hedge (*from Platía Agíou Pétrou, take Odós Vassilíssis Ólgas which runs alongside the Café Retro Pizzeria; 8.30am-3pm; closed Monday; entrance fee*). The only sight in the town centre, the museum contains the finds excavated at Árgos and in the environs by the French School of Archaeology. You are welcomed by a large **jar**★ from the Geometric Era, covered in painted motifs arranged in a patchwork pattern. The showpieces in the first room, immense **funerary vases**★★ from the second millennium BC stand beside an amazingly well-preserved **breastplate** and **helmet** made of bronze dating from the 8C BC (the time of the Trojan War). Displays on the first floor include copies of **Roman sculptures** and delicate 4C **mosaics**.

When you leave the museum, turn right and make your way to Lárissa Hill, outside the town on the Trípoli road.

In search of ancient Árgos

8.30am-3pm. Free. From the ticket office, follow the wide lane that runs alongside the Roman baths on the left, and which leads directly to the theatre. Built in the 4C BC on a hill near Lárissa, the **Árgos theatre**★★ was one of the largest in Greece. One is struck by its sheer size – its light-coloured terraces (well restored) spread out like a huge fan on the steep hillside. The tiers were either built up or hewn out of the rock (in the centre). The theatre could accommodate no less than 20 000 spectators, 5 000 more than its prestigious rival Epidaurus. Later the Romans converted the **orchestra** into a pool to hold nautical events. The back of the stage still has part of its **brick wall** (once covered in marble), pierced with alcoves in which statues once stood.

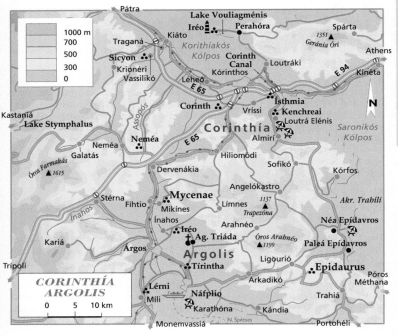

Turning away from the theatre, make your way (right) to the **Roman baths*** below. Many of the walls of this vast complex built in the 2C are intact, some still reaching a height of 10m. You enter from the hill through a large **apsidal chamber** that probably served as a reception room. From here you can walk from room to room, to the hot baths, which you will easily locate when you see the chequerboard of heating stacks, the small flat-brick columns that made up the under-floor heating system **(hypocaust)**.

The other remains of the site are less evocative. All the same, take the lane between the baths and the theatre to the **odeon**, a small 1C edifice that was probably remodelled in the 3C. It has kept some of its tiered seating carved out of stone, its side corridors paved with **mosaics**, and the back of the stage (stripped of its marble covering). Beyond, you come to the ruins of the **Sanctuary of Aphrodite**, of which only part of the foundations has been excavated.

Lastly, the **agora** – or at least what remains of it – stretches out on the other side of the road. In spite of being encumbered by modern constructions, the excavations have uncovered portions of the public buildings that surrounded it, as well as traces of the starting line of a **stadium** from the Classical Era. All in all, when you consider how important the living heart of the city was in Antiquity, there's not much left today.

■ **Lárissa Citadel*** – *From Platía Agíou Pétrou, head towards Mycenae, taking the road (signposted) up to the castle (5km). If you are on foot, you can climb the hill from the ancient theatre (allow for a fairly tiring walk of between 45min and 1hr). Free.* Crowning a sun-scorched hill, Lárissa's monumental **kástro** has lost none of its grandeur in spite of the ravages of time. It was built in the 10C by the Byzantines with material from an ancient acropolis, and then altered several times by the Venetians and the Turks. If you lack the energy to go round the two **defensive walls**★★, which protect a small ruined **church**, at least enjoy the **panoramic view*** of Árgos, and beyond to the kástro in Náfplio, whose outline can be seen on the horizon.

Leave Árgos on the Mycenae road and fork right towards Límnes. At Ínahos follow the signs to Néo Iréo, then to "Ancient Iréo".

■ **The Argive Heraíon** (Iréo) – *9km north-east of Árgos. 8am-2.30pm; closed Monday. Free.* Archaeology enthusiasts will make the effort to tour this sanctuary dedicated to Hera, the tutelary goddess of the Argolid. The place is mainly worthwhile for its beautiful **site**★★, a vast solitary plain carpeted with orange and olive groves. Built during Mycenaean times and still active under the Romans, the sanctuary was one of the largest in Antiquity, laid out over three **terraces**. The second and third terraces bear the foundations of two Doric temples. Armed with the *Iliad*, you may find the place where the Greek chiefs swore an oath of allegiance to Agamemnon before setting out for the Trojan War.

■ Tírintha★★

8km south-east of Árgos, 4km north-west of Náfplio. There's a bus between the two towns every half-hour. 8am-7pm. Entrance fee. Allow 45min.

The hillock on which Tírintha stands had been inhabited since prehistoric times but its definitive adaptation as an acropolis dates from 1200 BC. Sumptuously appointed and powerfully defended, Tírintha was nonetheless vulnerable to earthquakes, which damaged it on several occasions. But, in the same way as for Mycenae (*see page 214*), we do not know whether it was a new earthquake that abruptly caused its downfall soon after the building had been completed, or the short-lived occupation by the **Dorians**. Whatever the case, once they were inside the stronghold, the Dorians destroyed the palace, building in its place a temple dedicated to Hera, which restored a degree of influence to Tírintha. But the war with the **Argives**, who laid Tírintha waste, tolled the knell of the city, and it was abandoned for good in the 5C BC. Since then only flocks of sheep have haunted its ruins.

Tour of the site

You only have to look at the countryside to understand the strategic position of the citadel, and the need for such a powerfully fortified castle. Built on a slight rise (18m), Tírintha was in fact more exposed to enemy attacks than if it had been perched on a rocky spur. Hence the need for sufficiently thick and ingeniously designed ramparts to discourage any intrusion. Behind its formidable walls, the city was laid out in two distinct areas: an upper terrace reserved for the luxurious palace, and a lower terrace for diverse workshops, living quarters and shops.

A **ramp** broad enough to let wagons pass leads into the citadel. Once through the **first gateway** cut into the **ramparts****, you come to a sort of **security chamber**, formerly surrounded by high walls, where intruders who had managed to get through the first gate were trapped and came under attack by archers. You leave

The work of the Cyclopes

Impressed by the massive size of the ramparts at Tírintha, the ancient Greeks thought that the Cyclopes – the giants with just one eye in the middle of their foreheads – had built them. In fact, we still do not know how simple men could lift such heavy blocks of stone, some of them weighing more than 13t. It is also difficult to explain how they assembled them to form such a mighty wall, 8 to 10m thick, perched on a bluff. But we do know that the work took a very long time, beginning in 1400 BC and continuing for almost two centuries.

The brick and stone walls of the Byzantine church of Agía Triáda

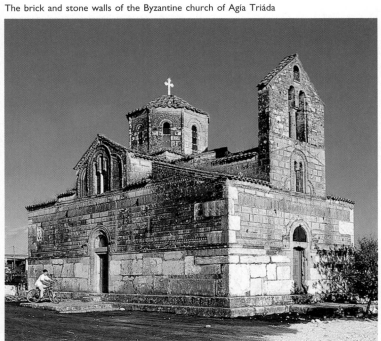

the security chamber through another **monumental gateway** – note on the ground the **holes for the hinges** of its door – which opens onto the **lower terrace**, a huge rectangular esplanade. At the end, as you go down to the left, you reach the **east casemates★★**, an amazing series of galleries built into the thickness of the ramparts, which served as shelter in wartime and storerooms in peace. Note the **vaults**, made of skilfully arranged flat stones.

Back on the terrace, go through the **propylaea** (*left*), recognisable by the bluish stone threshold, and enter the outer **palace** courtyard. A staircase on the left leads to the **south casemates★**, similar to those in the eastern ramparts, while on the right you have the palace's **inner courtyard**. This has kept its wide cement flooring as well as part of the altar that once stood here (*right*). The rooms of the palace proper, the **megaron**, surrounded another courtyard that was once roofed and whose walls were adorned with frescoes. A **circular hearth** occupied the centre, and the **royal throne** stood on the right.

Once through the megaron, turn left to the western walls where you will see the remains of a **tower**. Inside there is a narrow stone **staircase★★** cut into the thickness of the ramparts. The 80 well-preserved steps lead down to the outside of the citadel, coming out just at the foot of a postern gate. Here too, any attacker (or someone trying to escape) stood no chance of dodging the arrows of the archers. When you reach the bottom, walk to the right alongside the ramparts to see the vaulted **cisterns**. These were intended to collect drinking water from two springs, and were connected to the citadel by underground passages.

On leaving the citadel, take the Árgos road north-east and then, 5km further on fork towards Agía Triáda.

■ **Agía Triáda** – If you have the time, it is worth making a detour to the village of Agía Triáda. As you enter the village, you will see a delightful 12C **Byzantine church★★** dedicated to the Assumption of the Virgin, and surrounded by a cemetery. The interior, which has preserved the remains of **frescoes**, is being restored after a fire and is often closed. If you cannot enter, at least take the time to walk around the church to admire its beautiful **walls★**, which are made of a mixture of ancient stones and bricks arranged in geometric patterns.

Venetian streets
in the Peloponnese

COMING AND GOING

By bus – You can buy tickets at the *bus station* on Platía Agíou Pétrou, ☏ (0751) 67 324 / 66 300 / 23 570. Note that buses leave from two different stations depending on the destination. *For the Argolid and Athens*, go to Odós Kapodistríou (which begins at Platía Agíou Pétrou): buses every 30min to Náfplio (travelling time 30min), every hour to Athens (2hr), six buses a day to Mycenae (25min), and two buses to Neméa (1hr).
For Arcadia and Lakonía, the station is in Odós Phéidonos, which leads into Odós Vassilíssis Ólgas (the street with the museum). Nine buses a day to Trípoli (travelling time 75min), eight to Sparta via Trípoli (2hr30min), and one to Leonídio (3hr).

By train – The *railway station* is 500m south-east of Platía Agíou Pétrou. Seven trains a day to Athens (travelling time 3hr – one hour longer than by bus!) via Mycenae (10min) and Corinth (1hr). Four to Trípoli (1hr) and Kalamáta (almost 4hr).

ADDRESS BOOK

Banks / Currency exchange – Most of the banks are on Platía Agíou Pétrou (cash dispensers).

Main post office – In Odós Kapodistríou that leads to Platía Agíou Pétrou, ☏ (0751) 67 366.

Telephone – *OTE*, in Odós Nikitará, which heads off from Platía Agíou Pétrou, beside the National Bank, ☏ (0751) 67 599.

Police – ☏ (0751) 67 222. There is no tourist police office.

Medical service – The *hospital* is on the way out of Árgos, on the Mycenae road, ☏ (0751) 24 455.

Taxis – Taxi rank on Platía Agíou Pétrou.

Market – A large and lively market is held on a square near the museum on Wednesday and Saturday mornings.

WHERE TO STAY, EATING OUT

There's nothing to keep you at Árgos, whose rather charmless hotels are grouped around Platía Agíou Pétrou. It is much pleasanter (and simpler) to stay in Náfplio (see page 229).

You shouldn't expect much of the food in Árgos either. Avoid the noisy, expensive main square and look for a taverna in the country.

NÁFPLIO★★
(NAUPLIA)
Province of the Peloponnese – Capital of the district of Argolis
60km south of Corinth, 80km north of Trípoli, 12km south of Árgos
Regional map page 202 – Michelin map 980 fold 29 – Pop 11 900

Not to be missed
The Archaeological Museum and Palamedes Fort.
A walk through the old town.

And remember...
Náfplio is an ideal base for touring the Argolid.
For swimming, the beach at Karathóna is less crowded than the one at Toló.

Adorned with marble and stucco, and washed by the blue waters of the Gulf of Argolis, Náfplio is indisputably one of the most attractive towns in Greece. It has carefully maintained all the traces of its past. All its invaders left their imprint, and Náfplio has seen in turn medieval houses tightly packed along narrow alleyways,

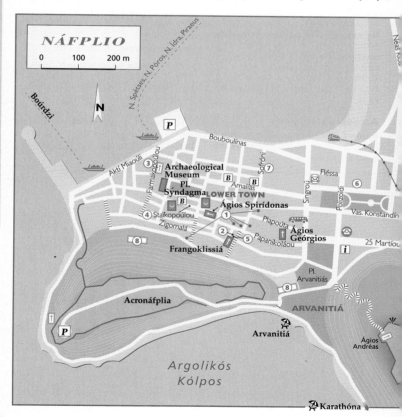

elegant 17C and 18C Venetian mansions, neo-Classical houses with fine balconies, mosques converted into churches and churches converted into mosques. The townscape as a whole could have looked ill assorted. It is in fact surprisingly homogeneous, as though each occupant had made it a point of honour to cover the roofs with the same red tiles, roughcast the walls with the same pastel colours and pave the streets and squares with the same marble. In sum, Náfplio is one of those charming places that it is easy to feel at home in. It invites visitors to sample all the typical holiday enjoyments: shopping in the old town's fashionable boutiques, swimming at a neighbouring beach, and when the sun goes down having an ouzo in the shade of a palm tree at one of the cafés looking out to sea.

A town with three forts

Although for a long time Náfplio served as a military and commercial port for its neighbour Árgos, it has preserved few remains dating from Antiquity. Among them are several Mycenaean tombs, and the walls of an acropolis which the Byzantines used to build the town's first fort, Acronáfplia, which was later reinforced by the Franks and then by the Venetians. In the 15C, having defeated the Turks, the Venetians added the fort on Boúrdzi islet, which stands guard over the entrance to the harbour. Two centuries later, they built the imposing Palamedes Fort on the highest hill in the town – a defensive structure designed to dissuade even the most enterprising invader. However, it didn't prevent the Turks from taking the town in 1715. Later, at the beginning of the War of Independence, the Greek fleet blockaded the harbour. On 30 November 1822 it ousted the Ottoman troops from Palamedes Fort, thus giving the country one of its early victories. It followed naturally, therefore, that after a short time on Égina, the government of the new Republic should establish itself in Náfplio, in 1828. As capital of Greece until 1834, the town enjoyed unprecedented prosperity; it was restored and rebuilt, giving it the appearance which it has kept up to the present.

The lower town★★

Leave your car in the harbour car park and wander on foot through the narrow streets. You will only need your car again to drive up to Palamedes Fort, then down to the beach at Karathóna, 3km away (you can also get there by taxi) or up to Acronáfplia to see the sunset. Even though a tour of the different sights and the Archaeological Museum barely takes more than 2hr, allow a day to thoroughly enjoy everything.

As you leave the car park, you will notice **Boúrdzi islet and its Venetian fort★** *(closed for renovation)* rising out of the sea just beyond the harbour. The fort later became the residence of the public executioner of Náfplio before being converted into a smart hotel.

You enter the town along Odós Farmakopoúlou *(to the right of the former Hotel Grande-Bretagne)*. The street passes behind the

Árgos

Ammonís

kos

Árgous

Kléous

Bouboulínas

PRÓNIA

Jíras Merarhías

Kíprou

Asklipioú

Toló

25 Martíou

Palamedes Fort

lamedes Fort

P

HOTELS

Acronafplia	①
Byron	②
King Otto	③
Leto	④
Marianna	⑤
Nausimedon	⑥
Omorphi Poli	⑦
Xenia	⑧

Náfplio, sunset over Boúrdzi islet

Church of the Panagía, and opens onto the elegant **Platía Sýndagma***, favoured by pedestrians and outdoor cafés. A certain nobility emanates from the high façades of the patrician houses, matched by the two former **mosques** (the one at the end is now a cinema, and the other housed the first Greek Parliament).

Beneath the airy arches of the Venetian arsenal *(right)*, you enter the fascinating **Archaeological Museum**** *(8.30am-3pm; closed Monday and public holidays, entrance fee)*. The first floor, devoted to prehistory, has some outstanding displays, including a 15C BC **Mycenaean cuirass**** – the oldest known to date – surmounted by a boar's-tusk **helmet****. There are also **fragments of frescoes**** from the palaces at Mycenae and Tírintha, which will give you a good idea of the former polychrome decoration at the sites. In a display case to the left of the entrance, you can see an amazing series of 13C BC **female votive statues**** found at Mycenae.

On the floor above, as well as more recent ceramics, there are notably a **bronze helmet***, some **ritual masks*** and two small 7C BC terracotta **shields** from Tírintha.

From church to church

On leaving Platía Sýndagma, you can pepper your walk with short stops at some of the town's many churches, each of which in its own way recounts an episode of Náfplio's history. The **Church of Ágios Spirídonas** witnessed the assassination of Ioánnis Kapodístrias, the first president of Greece, after a political conspiracy in 1831. The 16C **Church of Ágios Geórgios** – the Cathedral – contains the throne of the first king of Greece, the young Otto of Bavaria. The **Catholic Church of Frangoklissiá** *(on the climb up to Acronáfplia)* is a former mosque, as is suggested by the ruins of a **minaret** that once stood beside the entrance. It was converted into a church by Otto, a Catholic, and contains a **commemorative plaque**, a memorial to the Philhellenes who fell in the Greek War of Independence.

Acronáfplia

By car, go up Acronáfplia Hill on the road alongside Leofóros Singroú, between the old and modern parts of the town, heading towards the beach at Arvanitiá. On foot, take the lift up to one of the two Xenia hotels (the one in the west), Odós Zigomalá, at the end of Odós Farmakopoúlou. 8am-6.45pm, Sunday 5.45pm. Free. Allow 30min.

The promontory with its bird's-eye **views*** over the town, the Gulf of Argolis and the surrounding countryside, will appeal to romantics and photographers alike. The Acronáfplia Citadel consists of four bastions corresponding to four successive periods

G. de Benoist/MICHELIN

in history. The first two were built by the Venetians: the **Castel Toro** in 1450, alas occupied by one of the Xenia hotels, and the **Grimani Bastion** in 1706. Further along is the **Frankish section**, and at the end of the promontory, the **Byzantine section**, laid out over the remains of ancient fortifications. When the Venetians built Palamedes Fort, they connected the two citadels by a **covered stairway**, which was sheltered from enemy fire, hewn out of the rock and closed by several gateways. As you go down, you can stop at **Arvanitiá beach**.

Palamedes Fort★★

There are two possible access routes. The first, on foot, is up the stairway mentioned above, which leads off from near the tourist office. Remember, however, that there are 857 rather steep steps to climb, so take a deep breath and a bottle of water (no refreshments at the fort). The second is by car (3km). Head towards Toló and then fork right up to the top of the hill. 8am-6.45pm. Entrance fee. Allow between 45min and 1hr.

Perched on an imposing rock (216m), the fort that bears the name of Náfplio's symbolic hero dominates the entire town. Built by the Venetians in the early 18C, it is one of the most impressive in Greece despite its single circle of walls. Originally there were **seven forts**, designed to be self-sufficient in the case of attack, and connected by a network of secret corridors. You enter through the **Andréas bastion** also known as the **Venetians' bastion★**, whose parade ground has a thoroughly Italian elegance that softens the military aspect of the place. Near **St Andrew's Chapel** is the cell in which Kolokotrónis, one of the heroes of the revolution, was imprisoned after a political conspiracy. Above all, you should take the **parapet walk★** around the fort, which affords magnificent **views★** of the town and the fortified walls of Acronáfplia.

Then, if you feel like a swim or lunch beside the sea, follow the road to the right on leaving the fort for 4km, which will bring you to the pleasant **Karathóna beach**

Making the most of Náfplio

COMING AND GOING

By boat – Several weekly boat connections between Piraeus (Zéa Marina) and Náfplio, via Póros, Hydra, Ermióni, Spétses and Portohéli (crossing 4hr). At Portohéli you can take another boat to Monemvassiá via Tirós, Leonídio, Kiparíssi and Gérakas (Liménas Géraka). Every morning in summer there's a hydrofoil to Spétses and Hydra. Enquire at the **Yannópoulos Agency**, Platía Sýndagma, ☎ (0752) 22 393.

By train – 2 trains a day to Athens via Árgos, Corinth and Piraeus (travelling time 3hr). Tickets are sold in an old railway carriage at Náfplio station and at the **Staïkós Agency**, Aktí Bouboulínas 50, on the right as you leave the station.

By bus – Terminal on Leofóros Singroú. Buses leave every hour for **Athens** (travelling time 3hr) and for the resort at **Toló**, south-east of the town (between 7am and 8.30pm). 6 buses a day to the theatre at **Epidaurus** (special bus at 7.30pm on Friday and Saturday for performances), 4 to **Mycenae**. 4 buses to **Trípoli**. 1 bus every 30min to **Árgos** and **Tírintha**.

GETTING AROUND

Since the old town is not very big, you can easily get around on foot.

Making the most of Náfplio

By taxi – Taxi rank opposite the bus station, ☎ (0752) 24 120.

By car – Plenty of hire companies, particularly in Aktí Bouboulínas on the waterfront, between the railway station and the car park.

ADDRESS BOOK

Tourist information – Leofóros 25 Martíou, ☎ (0752) 24 444. Open daily, 9am-1pm / 4pm-8pm. Well stocked with street maps and various brochures. Changes money.

Banks / Currency exchange – Several banks in Odós Amalías and Platía Sýndagma have cash dispensers.

Post office / Telephone – On the corner of Leofóros Singroú and Odós Fléssa. **OTE**, Leofóros 25 Martíou, almost opposite the tourist office.

Police – Odós Fotomará 16, ☎ (0752) 28 131. As you leave the old town along Leofóros 25 Martíou, the police station is halfway between the tourist office and the stairway up to Palamedes Fort.

Tourist police – Same address as the police, ☎ (0752) 27 776.

Medical service – *Hospital*, Leofóros Asklipioú, ☎ (0752) 27 309. Leave the old town along Leofóros 25 Martíou. At the first fork, bear left into Odós Kíprou, which then becomes Leofóros Asklipioú. The hospital is on the right, in the fifth block of buildings.

Laundry – *Astrafteró*, self-service, Odós Papanikoláou 22, ☎ (0752) 21 783. 9am-1.30pm / 5.30pm-8pm; closed Sunday.

WHERE TO STAY

As the tourist flagship of the Argolid, Náfplio has very good hotel facilities. It is worth bearing in mind that the charming hotels in restored mansions in the heart of the old town are hardly more expensive than the more ordinary places. The town is packed in summer, so you should book ahead. For budget accommodation, the tourist office provides a list of the many campsites along the coast.

• **Old Town**

Between €15 and €60

🏨 *Acronafplia*, Odós Ágios Spirídonas 6, ☎ (0752) 24 481, mobile 094 59 36 80. Five old mansions dotted about the old town, including one in Odós Ágios Spirídonas. You have a choice between a room without a private bathroom (€15-€27) or an apartment for 4 people with a bathroom, kitchenette, air conditioning and television (€45-€60). Some of the best value for money in town.

Between €38 and €55

Omorphi Poli, Odós Sofróni 5, harbour end of the street, ☎ (0752) 21 565 – 7rm, including 2 suites. 🍴 🖉 📺 ✕ 🆑 This small, inventively decorated hotel recreates the atmosphere of a traditional Greek house, in which each room has its own style. A *kafenío* on the ground floor serves a good selection of meze. Good value for money.

🏨 *King Otto*, Odós Farmakopoúlou 4, ☎ and Fax (0752) 27 595 – 11rm. 🍴 🖉 📺 Ideally located between the waterfront and the old town. A friendly hotel in a tastefully refurbished neo-Classical house. An amazing wooden staircase leads up to the small though comfortable rooms. You have breakfast (copious) in a delightful walled garden. Probably the best hotel in Náfplio.

Between €60 and €68

🏨 *Nausimedon*, Odós Merarhías 9, between the post office and the old railway station, ☎ (0752) 25 060, Fax (0752) 26 913 – 13rm, including a suite. 🍴 🖉 📺 🆑 This old, magnificently restored mansion has high-ceilinged rooms with an old-fashioned, homely atmosphere.

• **Acronáfplia**

Between €24 and €38

Leto, Odós Zigomalá 28, ☎ (0752) 28 093 – 12rm. 🍴 🆑 A modest, unpretentious place enabling you to stay in Náfplio reasonably cheaply. Ask for one of the rooms with a view on the upper floors. About €3 extra for breakfast.

Between €38 and €55

Marianna, Odós Potamianoú 9, ☎ (0752) 24 256 / 26 730, mobile 095 30 1691, Fax (0752) 21 783 – 8rm. 🍴 🖉 ✕ 📺 🏠 🆑 All the rooms in this bright clean house give onto the town and the harbour. To avoid the tiring climb on foot, get a taxi to drop you off in front of the Xenia hotel (west).

Between €45 and €75

Byron, Odós Plátonos 2, ☎ (0752) 22 351, Fax (0752) 26 338, byronhotel@otenet.gr – 7rm. 🛏 ♫ 🗙 CC Recognisable by its elegant ochre façade and coloured windows, this charming, tall hotel is one of the local showpieces. Unfortunately, the beds are hard and the place tends to overbook and charge extra for air conditioning, TV, etc.

Between €97.50 and €113

Xenia, the main entrance is in Odós Letó where a lift goes up to the reception, ☎ (0752) 28 581, Fax (0752) 28 987 – 50rm, plus 54 in bungalows. 🛏 ♫ 🗐 TV 🗙 🚿 🛎 CC The hotel consists of two large buildings that irremediably disfigure Acronáfplia Hill and are typical of 1970s architecture. The rooms have not changed since then, and although they are very spacious the decor is rather outdated. Nonetheless, the place is comfortable and the swimming pool on its flower-filled terrace has a clear view of the town and Boúrdzi islet.

EATING OUT

You can eat well in Náfplio, as long as you avoid the expensive places with their touts on the seafront and Platía Sýndagma, as well as most of the rather tourist-oriented tavernas in Odós Staïkopoúlou.

Between €4.50 and €7.50

To Sokáki, between Platía Sýndagma and the King Otto Hotel. Excellent full breakfasts, giant pancakes, and if you are still hungry, enormous mixed ice creams.

Between €7.50 and €11

🍴 **O Noúlis**, Odós Moutsourídou 22, an alley parallel to Leofóros Singroú, near the Astrafteró laundry. A traditional taverna away from the crowds and popular with local people. The tray with ten different types of meze is a meal in itself: meatballs with herbs, *tirópita*, anchovies in vinegar, grilled octopus, etc.

Omorphi Poli, Odós Sofróni 5, harbour end of the street. The young people who run the place make excellent meze and traditional dishes that attract a crowd every evening.

HAVING A DRINK

Cafés, bars – Most of the bars and cafés are either on the seafront, where the palm trees make an ideal spot for watching the sun set over Boúrdzi islet, or on the beautiful Platía Sýndagma.

🍴 **Stathmós**, a good place if you feel nostalgic about old trains. The bar is in the old Náfplio railway station, beside the disused tracks. It is cool, pleasant and original.

Igloo, Odós Anastasíou, between Platía Sýndagma and the King Otto hotel, serves the best ice cream in town. Open late.

Night-clubs – Most of the night-clubs and discos are in **Midéa**, 5km north of Náfplio, a dismal seafront suburb.

Liquid, a disco with rather tasteless neo-Moorish decor.

Pérama, live Greek music every Friday, Saturday and Sunday evening.

OTHER THINGS TO DO

Outdoor pursuits – **Water-sports School**, on the beach at Karathóna, south of Palamedes Fort, ☎ and Fax (0752) 27 301. From mid-April to mid-September.

Excursions – Day trips by boat to the Saronic Gulf Islands and Monemvassiá (see page 238). Caique trips out to sea from the harbour. The tourist office sometimes sells tickets for the Epidaurus festival.

Newspapers – Odós Farmakopoúlou, in the shop called **Mycanaes Popular Art**, and in the **Odyssey** bookshop on Platía Sýndagma.

Local festival – In June a festival of classical music is held in town.

SHOPPING GUIDE

Yánnis Kókkoris' shop, Odós Staïkopoúlou, ☎ (0752) 21 143. A workshop where craftsmen still make traditional figures out of paper and cloth for Karaghiózis, the Greek shadow theatre.

Market – On Saturday, on Leofóros 25 Martíou (near the tourist office).

EPIDAURUS ★★★
(EPÍDAVROS)
Province of the Peloponnese – District of Argolis
Regional map page 202 – Michelin map 980 fold 30
68km south of Corinth – 30km from Náfplio

Not to be missed
The theatre, if possible during one of the festival performances.
And remember...
Try to get to the site early before the crowds arrive.

On leaving Náfplio, the road soon winds through sparsely populated countryside among gently rounded hills and green plains. The heart of the Argolid is a peaceful bucolic land, echoing to the sound of cicadas and dotted with Mycenaean ruins: here a tholos, there a bridge, and further on the eroded walls of a long-forgotten acropolis. Beyond Ligourió the road suddenly widens, ending up in an enormous car park congested with buses. Here you are at the gates of one of the most famous sanctuaries dedicated to Asklepios the god of healing, where worshippers and the sick from the four corners of Greece once gathered... as do hordes of tourists today. Of all the buildings that once formed the vast complex – for healing both body and mind – only the theatre remains intact. But what a theatre! A masterpiece that the ancients themselves considered perfect.

Once through Ligourió, turn right at the sign for Ancient Epidaurus (not to be confused with the villages of Néa Epídavros and Paleá Epídavros, recently renamed Arhéa Epídavros).

Tour of the site
8am-7pm from Tuesday to Sunday, 12noon-7pm Monday, 5pm in winter.
Entrance fee. The ticket to the site includes the museum. Allow 2 to 3hr.

The theatre★★★
You should keep your first sense of amazement for the theatre, which appears, dazzling, at the end of a lane through the trees. It is extraordinarily well preserved and has regained all its lustre through careful restoration. Backed up against the northwest slope of **Mt Kynortión**, facing the **sacred valley of Asklepios**, it spreads out like a superb white marble conch set among the pines. Built in the 4C BC by the architect **Polyclitus the Younger** (descendant of the 5C BC sculptor), the Epidaurus theatre is one of the most complete in the ancient world, its perfection unequalled. You reach it through the **stage★** (orchestra), a perfect circle 20m in diameter, at the centre of which traces of an **altar** to Dionysus, the god of drama, can still be seen. This was where the ancient chorus officiated, while the actors performed slightly further back, on the platform of the **proskenion**, which they reached through the two high gateways on the sides, the **paradoi★**.

A godly doctor
Asklepios (Aesculapius to the Romans) was born of the union between the god Apollo and the mortal Coronis. These unworthy parents abandoned him as soon as he was born but he survived thanks to the centaur Chiron, who fed him goat's milk and taught him surgery and the art of healing with plants. The young Asklepios soon became an outstanding doctor, renowned throughout the land for being able to heal all ills and even resuscitate the dead. Unfortunately, this power, hitherto reserved for the gods, earned him a thunderbolt from Zeus, who was unwilling to share his prerogatives with humans. Asklepios was buried at Epidaurus, which was already devoted to medicine – as is borne out by an ancient sanctuary dedicated to Apollo (also a god of healing). From then on, the site became a seat of the cult of Asklepios (6C BC).

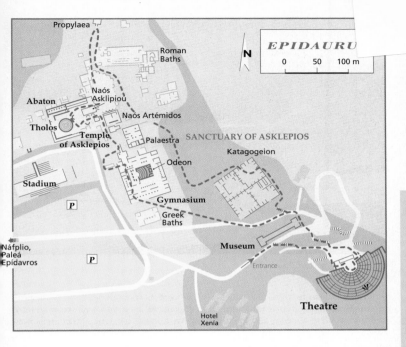

The dazzling **cavea****, punctuated by stairways, was built at two different times. The lower part could accommodate 6 210 spectators, with the first row reserved for leading citizens, who had stone **armchairs** with headboards and armrests. Two centuries later, 21 extra rows were added, thus bringing the seating capacity up to 12 300. This could have had an adverse affect on the top rows perched 22.5m above the level of the orchestra. But this was not so: no matter where you are in the theatre, you will hear sounds from the stage with the same clarity. If there are two of you, try for yourselves: strike a match or recite a poem *mezza vocce*, and your companion seated in the very top row will hear everything. On the condition, of course, that you are alone, as more often than not hundreds of tourists amazed at the exceptional acoustics of the place are all doing the same thing, in all languages and in all tones of voice.

The museum

Same times as the site and included in the site ticket. The modest Epidaurus Museum, set between the theatre and the ruins of the sanctuary, evokes

Revival of the theatre

The Epidaurus theatre held performances over a period of 800 years, from the time it was built to the 5C AD, when Christians condemned it to silence and oblivion. In the 19C, however, there was some restoration, when the olive trees that had invaded the seats were removed. But it wasn't until the 1950s that it recovered its original function, with the staging of ancient plays and mythology-inspired operas. Maria Callas was among those who gave phenomenal performances here. Since then, every summer, texts by Aeschylus, Sophocles, Euripides and Aristophanes come to life in the age-old decor under the starry sky. Don't miss the chance to attend one of these evenings to drink in the language of the ancient poets (if you can, buy the text in English beforehand, as no simultaneous translation is provided).

Epidaurus, the perfect theatre

the life of the doctors and the patients at the centre. You can see bronze **surgical instruments** dating from Roman times *(in a display case at the entrance)*, **steles** bearing inscriptions on treatments, and **ex-votos** engraved on marble. One of them tells how Asklepios healed a man suffering from an abscess on his neck and cancer of the ear.

The Sanctuary of Asklepios

To the right of the museum, up a few steps. When compared with the theatre, the remains of the sanctuary, a grid pattern of low walls and neatly arranged blocks of stone, are disappointing. And yet the sanctuary buildings were once the most important part of the complex. As if to complicate matters, you enter on the opposite side from the old official entrance, which means you have to cross an area of secondary importance. On the ground on the right you can see the square shape of an inn **(katagogeion)** where pilgrims were lodged. Then the remains of the **Greek baths** appear, followed by a huge **gymnasium** whose courtyard was occupied by an **odeon** in Roman times.

The **sanctuary** itself, currently being restored, was surrounded by a **wall** guarded by a vast number of sacred snakes – the symbol of the doctor's caduceus. The most remarkable feature is the **tholos*** *(left)*, once a huge circular building whose ruins mark out a maze-like design on the ground. It was in fact a cleverly arranged network of **concentric corridors** linked together by passages, with the centre probably serving as a place of sacrifice in honour of Asklepios.

Beyond the tholos, several columns which are currently being re-erected mark the site of the **abaton**, or sacred dormitory. After having undergone various rituals such as fasting, taking a purifying bath and sacrificing animals, the sick would come here to sleep. As they slept, Asklepios would appear to them, indicating through coded messages the method to follow in order to regain health. When the patients woke up, doctor-priests would interpret the god's words and issue an ad hoc prescription. To the right of the tholos are the foundations of what was once the **Temple of Asklepios**. Lastly, don't leave without seeing the **stadium***, hidden behind an embankment where several **tiered seats** are still intact. Music and gymnastics competitions are held here every four years.

Short trip to the sea

As the coast is only fifteen kilometres from Epidaurus, you can easily go there for a swim. Return to Ligourió then take the road right that winds through bay trees and orange groves. Leave the village of **Néa Epídavros**, with its rather ordinary black sand beach, and head right towards the neighbouring **Arhéa Epídavros** (or Paleá Epídavros), a delightful resort nestling in a bay surrounded by woods. In addition to its many **beaches**, the village has a small ancient **theatre**, which was excavated in 1971, but is unfortunately surrounded by houses. Performances are given here in summer.

Making the most of Epidaurus

COMING AND GOING

By bus – 6 buses a day from Náfplio (travelling time 1hr). Special buses at 7.30pm on Friday and Saturday for performances in the theatre. 2 buses from **Athens**, 4 from Arhéa Epídavros. Travel agents in **Athens**, Corinth, Náfplio and the Saronic Gulf Islands also organise day trips.

By taxi – Bookings: ☎ (0753) 23 322.

By boat – In summer, two hydrofoil connections a day between Piraeus (Zéa Marina) and Arhéa (Paleá) Epídavros. Tickets from the **Ceres Agency** in the harbour, ☎ (0753) 42 010.

USEFUL INFORMATION

You will find various services at the entrance to the site: a police station, a post office that changes money, a card-operated phone booth, and WC.

WHERE TO STAY

As the Epidaurus area is some distance from the major holiday centres, it has a limited choice of hotels. If you want to stay here, it is essential to book, particularly during the festival. Otherwise, go to one of the neighbouring resorts, such as Arhéa (Paleá) Epídavros, Néa Epídavros or Náfplio.

• Epidaurus
Between €97.50 and €113
Xenia, ☎ (0753) 22 003, Fax (0753) 22 219 – 48rm. ⚏ ℐ 🍽 TV ✕ CC The most comfortable (though expensive) hotel in the area. Its unobtrusive layout consists of stone-built bungalows dotted among the pines, blending in well with the site.

• Ligourió
Between €23 and €38
Asclipioú, main street, ☎ and Fax (0753) 22 251 – 8rm. A large house dating from the 1950s, with decor and facilities that have not changed since. Not a very cheerful place, in spite of the friendliness of the owner.

Alkión, at the junction of the main road and the road to the theatre, ☎ (0753) 22 002, Fax (0753) 22 552 – 11rm. ⚏ ℐ ⚱ ✕ CC A charmless place on the side of the road. But it is close to the sanctuary and does have a restaurant.

Ávato, less than 1km from the entrance to the site, ☎ (0753) 22 178 / 22 059, Fax (0753) 23 059 – 16rm. ⚏ ℐ This simple hotel is the most acceptable in Ligourió, in spite of the rather dour owners. In summer, the place is packed with festival performers, who rehearse on the main lawn. Some rooms have fans.

EATING OUT

If you want to eat before the performance, bring a picnic (the snacks at the cafeteria are very expensive) or go to the nearby **Xenia** (see "Where to stay", closing time 9pm). Otherwise, try one of the many tavernas in Ligourió, open before and after the performance.

EPIDAURUS FESTIVAL

In July and August, on Friday and Saturday at 9pm. Given the huge popularity of the festival, it is advisable to book tickets in advance. They can be bought on the spot 3hr before the performance begins, ☎ (0753) 22 026, or in Náfplio, at the tourist office in Leofóros 25 Martíou, ☎ (0752) 24 444, and also in Athens at the **Athens Festival Box Office**, Odós Stadíou 4, ☎ (01) 322 14 59 / 331 24 00.

THE ARCADIAN COAST★
FROM NÁFPLIO TO MONEMVASSIÁ
Province of the Peloponnese – District of Argolis
Regional map page 202 – Michelin map 980 folds 29-41 – 200km itinerary

Not to be missed
The Byzantine fortress and the churches in Geráki.
And remember...
With an early start, you can do the trip in a day.

Rather than heading for the south-east of the Peloponnese along the main Trípoli-Gíthio road, take the coast road. Admittedly longer, it nonetheless goes through more varied scenery. The trip starts out rather monotonously along rocky shores and dizzy bends, but here and there you will come across peaceful coves with crystal-clear water. Once past Leonídio, you enter another world, dominated by the Párnonas Massif, where the cool sweet-smelling slopes are home to long-horned goats. When you come out of the mountains and into Geráki you have reached the border, leaving Arcadia for Lakonía.

On the slopes of Mt Párnonas

■ 14km beyond Náfplio, you come to the village of **Míli**, formerly surrounded by marshes. A track to the left leads to a small archaeological site, whose name is associated with the Labours of Heracles and the Hydra, the terrible swamp creature. However, **Lerna** (Lérni) (*8.30am-3pm, 2.30pm in winter; entrance fee; allow 15min*) will only be of interest to archaeology enthusiasts. Not much remains between the ruined walls of the oldest known town in the Argolid (c 2200 BC).

■ Nor does the road to **Ástros** (*22km from Lérni*) leave a permanent impression, apart from the fact that it leads to **Parálio Ástros★**, the most extensive sandy beach on the coast. Beyond, however, the landscape becomes more attractive. Leaving the sea below, the road winds up into the olive carpeted foothills of the Párnonas Massif, above wide bays given over to fish farming. Indenting the coastline are small coves such as **Paralía Tiroú**, its shore covered in pebbles.

■ **Leonídio** – *86km from Náfplio*. The only real town on the Arcadian Coast, Leonídio with its small neighbouring ports makes for a good stopping point halfway through the trip (*it is also time to fill up with fuel as there are no service stations between Leonídio and Geráki*). The highway runs through Leonídio, forming a bottleneck (traffic jams are unavoidable), and so the place has lost its charm. But if you take the time, you will come across some fine **neo-Classical houses**, albeit dilapidated, which once earned Leonídio a reputation for elegance.

Instead, make the most of the attractive little harbour at **Pláka** (*4km down the coast*) with its pebble beach lined with old tavernas. You could also try **Poúlithra** further south.

The marsh Hydra
The Hydra of Lerna, a hideous snake whose nine heads grew again as soon as they were cut off, was probably just as real as the other monsters that Heracles had to overcome (see page 50). The myth, however, could be a symbol for a very real phenomenon: the ancients' permanent struggle against the coastal marshes constantly flooded by the poorly diked seawater.

The landscape changes when you leave Leonídio and head inland. The sun-scorched rocks on the coast are replaced by the cool and fragrant pine-covered slopes of the **Párnonas Massif★★**

The superb road that winds above the **Badron Gorge★** affords spectacular **panoramas★★**. After 17km you come round a bend to see the white **Convent of Panagía Elóna** (*free, suitable clothing required*) clinging to the rock like a bird of prey.

■ **Geráki*** — Set on an outlying spur of the Párnonas Massif, the village peacefully contemplates the Lakonía Plain stretching out below. Several **Byzantine churches*** from Geráki's medieval past deserve a visit. Most are in the southern part of the village and are often closed. However, take the time to walk around the outsides to see the beautiful **walls** that combine brick and stone.

Other churches, which are usually open, are on the slopes of a hill where a **Frankish city*** was founded in the 13C (*3km south of Geráki, along a road on the left, 8.30am-3pm; closed Monday; free; allow 45min*). As you climb to the top of the hill, which is dominated by the ghostly outline of the former **kástro**, go into each of the churches along the way. Nearly all have preserved lovely fragments of medieval **frescoes**. The last, the **Church of Ágios Geórgios*** (the least deteriorated), is perched right at the top, within the fortress walls. In addition to its 13C **frescoes**, note on the left, a large funerary recess bearing the **heraldic emblems** of the Franks. On leaving, go round the **parapet walk** that looks over the surrounding countryside, affording a wonderful **view****.

Making the most of the Arcadian Coast

COMING AND GOING

By boat – In summer, several hydrofoils serve the east coast of the Peloponnese, from Zéa Marina in Piraeus down to Monemvassiá. They are either direct (travelling time 2hr30min), or stop at Hydra (Ídra), Spétses, Portohéli, Toló, Tirós (Paralía Tiroú), Pláka (the port for Leonídio), Kiparíssi and Gérakas (4hr15min). Another boat leaves from Náfplio on Thursday morning.

By bus – From **Leonídio**, three buses a day go to **Athens** via Árgos and Corinth (travelling time 5hr). Two buses to Trípoli, two also to Geráki and Monemvassiá. The station is on the road going down to Pláka.

GETTING AROUND

Either by boat (see above) or by bus.

By bus – Buses from **Leonídio** regularly go to the ports of **Pláka** and **Poúlithra**, as well as to the village of **Kosmás** (in the mountains, a short distance beyond Panagía Elóna).

ADDRESS BOOK (LEONÍDIO)

Banks and the post office are on the square, Platía 25 Martíou.

Police – ☎ (0757) 22 222.

Medical service – **Dispensary**, ☎ (0757) 22 950.

WHERE TO STAY

Every village or slightly developed beach has at least one hotel, a campsite beside the water, or rooms in guesthouses.

● **Paralía Tiroú**

Campsite (around €12)

Repodina campsite, in Ágios Andréas, 4km south of Ástros, ☎ (0755) 31 282. ✗ ☜ Terraces for tents have been laid out between the road and the private beach. Recent bathroom facilities, a self-service restaurant and a grocery store.

Around €30

Apollo, beside the sea, south of the village, ☎ (0755) 41 393 – 23rm. ☜ ▤ ☜ A clean, well-run, relatively recent hotel. Kitchen facilities available. The most pleasant rooms are the ones overlooking the sea (with large balconies).

● **Leonídio**

Around €23

Alexákis (To Neon), in Odós Agías Ekaterínis, at right angles to the main street, ☎ (0757) 22 383 – 23rm. ☜ As a back-up. This fairly comfortable hotel is in a good position in the town centre. Open all year round.

● **Kosmás (Vitína)**

Around €23

☜ **To Balkóni tis Kynourías**, on the main square in the village of Vitína, near Kosmás, halfway between Leonídio and Geráki, ☎ (0757) 22 821 / 22 532 or in Athens (01) 67 11 386 – 10rm. Perched at a height of 1 150m hidden among pine, cedar and chestnut trees, this hundred-year-old house has been converted into a family guesthouse. The level of comfort is modest but the atmosphere friendly. Open from April to November.

MONEMVASSIÁ ★★★

Province of the Peloponnese – District of Lakonía
Regional map page 202 – Michelin map 980 fold 42
350km from Athens, 97km from Sparta, 67km from Gíthio – Pop 768

Not to be missed
A walk through the lower town.
St Sophia's Church.
And remember...
As the cobblestones in the alleyways are slippery, even in dry weather, sneakers are
more suitable than sandals.

After crossing Arcadia in the heat and dust, the sea is a welcome sight indeed. The
road that leads into Lakonía stops at the entrance to the modest town of **Géfira**. As
a backdrop, an unusual rock peninsula looms imposingly on the horizon. The visitor

is naturally curious to see what happens on the other side, on the slope facing the sea. And there, behind the huge stone escarpment is a jewel of a medieval city. One of the most beautiful in Europe, it is intact, and could have come straight out of a Byzantine fresco. Invisible from the coast behind its steep rock face, Monemvassiá seems to stand at the end of the world, an impression that is reinforced by a rough sea and the strong, ever-present wind. The positive result of this isolation – dictated by safety requirements many years ago – is that the town has been spared the torments of modernity. No concrete here, nor any recent constructions, all of which are reserved for Géfira (Néa Monemvassiá), the modern suburb. You won't find any haphazard renovation here either, or any cars for that matter. Only donkeys may pass through the silent narrow alleys.

A city with "only one entrance"

Nestling at the foot of a steep cliff 300m high, Monemvassiá is protected by a causeway to the west, and rises in successive terraces facing the water. Originally the "rock" – as it is still known today – was linked to the mainland by a tongue of land that formed a single ("moni") access ("emvassía"). When this was destroyed by an

B. Kaufmann/MICHELIN

Monemvassiá

earthquake in 375, the Byzantines took advantage of the disaster to build a town – behind the rock but facing the sea – with defences considered to be a model of their kind. In spite of this, Monemvassiá fell into the hands of **Guillaume II de Villehardouin** (1249), and then, through ransom, into those of the emperor of Byzantium (1263-1460), before being taken over by the Pope for four years, and then by the **Venetians** and lastly the Turks, in 1715. It was coveted for its strategic position in the south of the Peloponnese and for the commercial role it played between the East and the West. These two major assets enabled the inhabitants to amass huge fortunes, as is borne out by the town's many palaces, towers and churches.

A second life for Monemvassiá

In the early 1970s, Monemvassiá – then in ruins and practically emptied of its population – was dying from a general lack of interest, when a handful of Athenian sophisticates chose it as a place for holidays. The renovation of the first houses attracted craftsmen and enough other visitors to justify the reopening of several cafés, followed by one or two hotels. In less than ten years, the forgotten town had become one of the upmarket destinations for the country's intellectual and artistic elite. Today the houses bought by rich Greeks and foreigners are considered to be the most expensive in Greece along with those on Mýkonos. Renovation, and in some cases almost total reconstruction, is firmly controlled by the archaeology department and has to be carried out in strict accordance with the style of the original houses. This means that electricity cables, meters and air-conditioning systems have to be completely camouflaged.

Tour of the town
Allow a good half-day

The Lower Town*** (Kástro)

Leave your car in the car park at the bridge on the road into town. Come early in summer, as there is an acute shortage of spaces. Otherwise, take the bus (ticket) that runs between Géfira and Kástro every 15min. Allow 2hr to give yourself enough time to stroll through the town.

You enter Kástro through the main gateway in the walls. There were once five entrances. Once through the **chicane**, designed to slow down the approach of attackers, you come to the **main street**, which is named after the poet Yánnis Rítsos (1909-90), who was born in the town. Many of his poems were put to music by Míkis Theodorákis, and part of his family still lives in Monemvassiá. In spite of the town's many souvenir shops, the picturesquely irregular paving, stone walls and arched doorways are enough to plunge you into an enchanting medieval atmosphere.

A little further on, you can escape from the crowd by heading down to the right to the peaceful **main square**, on which stands the 13C **Church of Chrístos Elkomenós**. It has an elegant 17C **Venetian portal** adorned with two peacocks, and inside, several **icons**. Opposite, a former **mosque*** dating from the 16C houses the town's modest **archaeological**

Malmsey

Monemvassiá owes its international fame to its wine, which it produced for centuries, first on the island, to the north of the town, and then, when demand outstripped supply, on other land round about. Malmsey (from "Napoli di Malvasia", the name the Venetians gave the town) was a sweet white wine with a fairly high alcohol content, particularly prized by European courts. Tradition has it that it was in a butt of Malmsey that the treacherous George, Duke of Clarence, was drowned in 1478 while a prisoner in the Tower of London. Although it is no longer made as such, varieties of the vine can be found in several Mediterranean regions, both islands and mainland.

collection *(8am-7pm, Monday 12noon-7pm; free)*. It is worth having a look, not so much for the objects that evoke daily life in the old days (pipes, crockery, etc) as for the architecture of the building, now well restored.

Next, head towards the sea along the alleyway to the right of the church. Stone stairways and vaulted passages lead you through some delightful, silent quarters. Here and there are buildings that bear the mark of the various people who ruled the town. You see crenellated walls, Byzantine churches with a touch of Venetian grace, and noble Greek houses set off by **Ottoman loggias** where the women could see out without being seen. Below the city, the **ramparts** run all the way to the **Portello** district, where a stairway descends to the waterside (concrete quayside).

Back on the square with the church of Chrístos Elkomenós, cross the main street to begin your climb to the upper town. Stop on the way at the 18C church of **Panagía Mirtidiótissa**, whose parvis once served as a parade ground. If the church is closed (which is often the case), try peering through the keyhole in the portal. In the half-light you will be able to make out the richly carved **lintels★** on the old iconostasis.

The Upper Town★★ (Citadel)

A path to the left of the church of Panagía Mirtidiótissa zigzags up to the citadel, perched on top of the rock. You need a lot of energy (the slope is steep) and some water. Allow 15min for the climb and a good hour to walk around.

If you can, it is worth making an excursion to the upper town, which is at its most pleasant in the cool of the morning or in the late afternoon. Standing on top of the rock, which forms a huge plateau, the citadel dominates the sea, affording staggering **views★★★**, an enchanting sight at sunset. A **portal** cut into the ramparts guards the entrance. Inside the walls, you at first see only a windswept field of ruins covered in wild grass. Remains emerge here and there, including those of a 17C **hammam**, as well as a number of **old cisterns** surrounded by bushes. Then, at the end of a steep lane, the **Church of St Sophia★** appears, a delightful building restored in the 1950s. Once beyond the **Venetian loggia** which forms the façade, you are struck by the peace and the refreshing coolness of the place. Note the impressive **brick dome★**, the fragments of 13C **frescoes** and the finely carved **marble capitals**.

Lastly, take the time to walk around the plateau among the melancholy ruins. A vertiginous **panorama★★★** opens out over the gulf and the lower city with its red and pink roofs.

Monemvassiá

Making the most of Monemvassiá

COMING AND GOING

By boat – Hydrofoil: several connections a day with Piraeus (Zéa Marina). Travelling time: 2hr30min if direct, 4hr15min with stops at Gérakas, Kiparíssi, Leonídio, Paralía Tiroú, Spétses, Hydra and Póros. Tickets on sale at the **Angelakos Agency**, at the entrance to the bridge, ☎ (0732) 61 219.

Daily connections also with Náfplio and Cythera. Boats are more convenient than buses (which first go to Molái where you have to change to go on to Náfplio).

By ferry: 3 connections a week with **Athens** (travelling time 4hr30min).

By bus – 3 buses a day to **Athens** (6hr), via Molái, Sparta, Trípoli and Corinth. Bus station in front of the post office in Géfira. 1 bus a day in summer to **Githio**. Tickets on sale at the **Malvasia Agency**, opposite the bus station, ☎ (0732) 61 752 / 61 432, Fax (0732) 61 432.

By taxi – ☎ (0732) 61 274.

By rental vehicle – Fuel station near the bridge. You can hire cars and two-wheelers at the **Malvasia Agency**, opposite the bus station, ☎ (0732) 61 752 / 61 432, Fax (0732) 61 432.

ADDRESS BOOK (GÉFIRA)

Banks / Currency exchange – You can change money either at the post office or, just on the left, at the **Ethnikí Bank** (cash dispenser).

Main post office – On the main street, facing the Malvasia Agency, ☎ (0732) 61 231. Changes money.

Police – Near the post office, ☎ (0732) 61 210.

WHERE TO STAY

The two areas to stay in Monemvassiá are Géfira, the modern suburb, and Kástro, where you will find some charming hotels. Check out the rates for the latter (not all are exorbitant) and book ahead in summer and at weekends. In Géfira choose a room that looks onto a quiet street and has air conditioning, so you can sleep in the cool away from the noise and the mosquitoes. Avoid the unfriendly Filoxénia hotel.

Campsite (around €13.50)
Paradise Capsis campsite, 4km south of Monemvassiá, ☎ (0732) 61 123, Fax (0732) 61 680, Paradise@mail.otenet.gr ✗ ☼ A bit far from everything, but quiet (except near the cafeteria with its booming sound system). A large, pleasant place with trees and two beaches (one with sand). Mini-market and a restaurant, which serves vegetarian dishes. To get to Kástro, you can take the bus (2 a day), a taxi-boat or hire one of the campsite's mountain bikes. In the height of summer when hotel accommodation is scarce, the campsite also hires out tents and caravans.

• Géfira (Néa Monemvassiá)

Between €23 and €38
Villa Doúka, 3km north of the town, ☎ (0732) 61 181, Fax (0732) 61 751. In Athens, ☎ (01) 97 61 044, Fax (01) 97 05 197 – 8 studios and 12 apartments for 4 to 7 people. ⌖ ℘ ⚘ ☼ ☼ 🍴 ✗ [CC] A modern place whose apartments give onto a huge garden bursting with bougainvillaea and bay trees. All sorts of activities, including ping-pong and basketball. Ideal for families with cars (no transport into town).

🛏 **Beléssis**, to the right of the main road, 50m before entering Géfira, ☎ and Fax (0732) 61 217 – 10rm and 5 apartments. ⌖ [TV] Kitchenettes. As the rooms in the old traditional house are near the road, you may prefer the more recent rooms set back a little off a quiet, flower-filled patio. Friendly welcome.

Between €43 and €54
🛏 **Villa Diamantí**, in the Topalti district, just before Géfira, ☎ (0732) 61 196 / 61 534 – 9rm in the hotel (on the left of the road) and 12 bungalows on the right. ⌖ ⚘ [TV] ☼ Decent rooms in the hotel. The attractive bungalows, dotted about on a hillside, are new, well-equipped and have terraces. Very friendly welcome.

• Kástro

Between €33 and €38
🛏 **Malvasia**, reception in the main street, ☎ (0732) 61 323 / 61 113, Fax (0732) 61 722 – 28rm. ⌖ ℘ ▦ [TV]

The Peloponnese

[CC] Three old mansions dotted about the town have magnificent rooms with traditional decor (exposed beams, stone fireplaces, carpets, woven cushions, etc), tempting you to stay a few days in Monemvassiá. At the foot of one of the houses (Ritsou) there's a beach with a cement swimming platform.

Between €30 and €60
Byzantinó, in the centre of Kástro, ☎ (0732) 61 254 / 61 351, Fax (0732) 61 992 – 22rm. ⌁ ▤ [CC] In the same way as the place above, the charming rooms are dotted about in old mansions, some with a view of the sea. Very up-market, but marred by an unfriendly welcome.

Between €55 and €60
🛏**Kellia**, right at the bottom of Kástro, on the square where the Church of Panagía Chrissafítissa stands, ☎ (0732) 61 520, Fax (0732) 61 767 – 12rm. ⌁ ♪ 🔆 🍴 🛏 Far away from everything except the sea, which you can hear lapping below. A long building with attractively decorated rooms. A good place if you want peace and quiet. In summer, however, it can be hot in spite of the fans.

Between €60 and €105
Lazareto, on the causeway linking Kástro to the mainland, ☎ (0732) 61 990, Fax (0732) 61 994 / 61 331. ⌁ ♪ ▤ [TV] ✕ 🛏 [CC] This large house, built in the style of Kástro's noble mansions, opened in 1987 and is one of the smartest hotels in the area. Each room has its own decor and looks out onto a peaceful flower garden. Breakfast is not included in the price.

EATING OUT

The most pleasant, elegant and expensive restaurants are of course in Kástro. But you can also find friendly tavernas in Géfira where prices are more reasonable.

• **Kástro**
Around €11
🛏**Matoúla**, below the main street. The tables are set out in the shade of a large fig tree facing the sea. In a pleasant atmosphere you are served excellent dishes such as *saganáki*, cheese cooked in an earthenware dish, and delicious *arnáki*, lamb with lemon sauce.

To Kanóni, to the right of the main street. The restaurant terrace looks out over the dome of the museum. Serves a good plate of *pikilía* (appetisers). Slightly more expensive than the place above.

• **Géfira**
Around €4
Fótis, at the beginning of the road along the seafront. An unpretentious eatery with a canvas awning for shade, where you can have inexpensive *píta* or *souvláki*.

Limanáki, to the right of the road, just before the bridge. A traditional taverna where you choose your dishes in the kitchen, as in the good old days. The tables are set out in an arbour.

HAVING A DRINK

• **Géfira**
Traditional cake shop (no name) below the Minoa hotel, on the main street. Almond shortbread biscuits, doughnuts, etc, to eat in or take away.
Rock Café, opposite the Minoa hotel, in the middle of the village. Very loud music.

OTHER THINGS TO DO

Beaches – You can swim off the pontoon at **Portello** below the ramparts in Monemvassiá, as well as at the sandy **Pori Beach** in Géfira, or off the cement platforms to the right of the causeway, a short distance before the entrance to Kástro.

Feasts & festivals – For 5 days around 23 July the town celebrates its liberation from the Turks. Traditional singing and dancing in front of the church of Panagía Chrissafítissa.

Making the most of Monemvassiá

THE MÁNI PENINSULA★★★

Province of the Peloponnese – District of Lakonía
Regional map page 202 – Michelin map 980 fold 41
Tour of 240km from Gíthio to Kalamáta along the coast (at least 2 to 3 days)

Not to be missed
A walk through the streets of Gíthio and Areópoli.
The south of the peninsula, especially Váthia and Cape Matapan.
The coast road between Areópoli and Kalamáta.
And remember...
As there is little in the way of public transport, hire a car or a two-wheeler
(from Gíthio).

Isolated from the rest of the Peloponnese by the natural barrier of **Mt Taíyetos** (Óros Taígetos), the high, jagged Máni Peninsula is a land apart. It is a harsh, windswept region where the sun beats down on the stony ground and the inhabitants are known for their ungovernable passion. For many years, family clans engaged in ruthless feuds, as is borne out by the hundreds of fortified towers that spike the landscape. Now that arms have been laid down and the descendants have emigrated, the towers have been converted into hotels and second homes. But in places the smell of gunpowder and spilt blood still seems to hang in the air. As a counterpoint to these martial buildings, dozens of Byzantine chapels are a reminder of the intense religious life that also reigned here. On the walls of some of them are strikingly beautiful frescoes preaching a message of mercy and forgiveness. It is hard to work out whether this is pure paradox or was intended to serve as an antidote. Be that as it may, you will not remain indifferent to this strange land where war and peace are so intimately mixed.

The southernmost point of the Peloponnese

Squeezed between the Gulf of Messinía and the Gulf of Lakonía, the Máni Peninsula is a narrow stretch of rock about sixty kilometres long and barely fifteen wide. It forms the southern tip of the Taíyetos range that begins near Kalamáta and ends at **Cape Matapan** (Akrotírio Ténaro), the southernmost point of the Peloponnese. Little Máni has two faces: north of Ítilo the **Messinían Máni** or Outer Máni that clings to the green foothills of Mt Taíyetos, and in the south the desolate hills of the **Lakonían Máni** or Inner Máni, the most spectacular part.

Maniots: furious characters

Down through the centuries, the isolated peninsula served as a refuge for all the country's outcasts. Not least the **Spartans**, who were disappointed by the decline of their city. These proud, touchy soldiers defended their freedom so ardently that they were nicknamed the Maniots, from the Greek adjective *maniódis* (furious). A character trait that they wished to assert, even in the choice of name for their regional capital **Areópoli**, a direct reference to Ares, the god of war. Preceded by their flattering reputation for belligerence, the Maniots managed to maintain a de facto autonomy from the succession of occupying forces, Franks, Byzantines, Slavs, Albanians, Venetians and Turks. And when they rose up against the latter in 1769 and 1821, they gave the War of Independence one of its most valorous leaders, **Petrobéy Mavromichális**. Turned in on itself, the peninsula saw barely any intermarriage with other peoples. Furthermore, it remained isolated from the great movements in history for many years (the region was pagan until the 9C) and after Greece had become independent, had a lot of trouble adapting to the national laws.

Lakonían Máni★★★
The south of the peninsula
Allow 2 days

■ **Gíthio★ –** Gíthio, the Máni Peninsula's eastern port, nestles in the curve of the Gulf of Lakonía, its waterfront lined with attractive façades with coloured shutters. When you arrive from the east you can make a detour to see the **theatre**, the only noteworthy remains of Sparta's ancient port (*on entering the town take the first road on the right, which is signposted, then the second right and the first left. The theatre adjoins some barracks; free*). A dozen rows of **tiered seats** have been excavated, some of which still have their stone backs.

Go through the town, dotted with **Ottoman houses** with **wooden balconies**, and you soon come out onto the jetty, a very lively place in summer with its fish tavernas. Attractive **neo-Classical houses** rise in tiers on a hillside covered with olive trees. They look out over the sea and the green outline of the **islet of Kranaï★**, now linked to the mainland. It is believed to have been the place where the lovers Paris and Helen spent their first night together before embarking for Cythera and then Troy. Walk through the pines to the tower that has been converted into a **museum** on the history of the Máni Peninsula (*9.30am-9pm; entrance fee*). The first floor has an interesting exhibition on the architecture of the fortified towers in the area. If you feel like a swim, there are **beaches** south of the town. **Mavrovoúni** is outside the village of the same name (*3km*). **Vathí Bay** (*10km*) is very popular, and **Skoutário★** (*20km*) has three small beaches of fine sand that are still havens of peace.

From Gíthio, you can take the road inland to Sparta and Mistra (*see page 265 and 268*). It's a lot less attractive than the Kalamáta road, but shorter (*43km*).

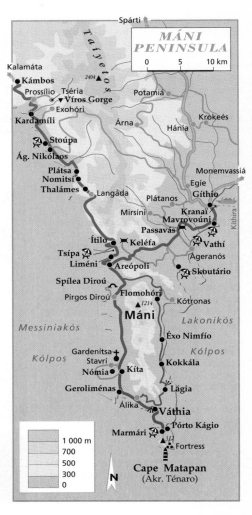

MÁNI PENINSULA

0   5   10 km

Spárti

Taÿyetos

Kalamáta
Kámbos
Prossílio   Tséria
▼ Víros Gorge
Exohóri
Kardamíli

Potamiá

Krokeés
Árna   Hánia

Stoúpa
Ág. Nikólaos

Plátsa
Nomitsí
Thalámes   Langáda
Mirsíni
Plátanos

Monemvassiá
Egié
Gíthio
Kranaï
Mavrovoúni
Passavás
Ítilo   Keléfa
Tsípa
Liméni   Areópoli
Vathí
Ageranós
Skoutário

Spílea Diroú
Pírgos Diroú   Flomohóri
▲1214
Mání   Kótronas
Lakonikós

Messiniakós

Éxo Nimfío

Kólpos
Gardenítsa
Stavrí
Nómia   Kíta
Geroliménas
Álika

Kólpos
Kokkála

Lágia

Váthia
Pórto Kágio
Marmári
▲31?
Fortress

1 000 m
700
500
300
0

N

Cape Matapan
(Akr. Ténaro)

The Máni Peninsula

Towers, watch out

A law unto itself, the Máni Peninsula was organised into clans led by invincible chiefs. In the 15C, each clan asserted its power by building fortified towers 15m to 25m high. These square or rectangular buildings had very few windows and consisted of three or four floors with just one room each, connected by simple ladders, without any stairs. In the case of surprise attack, all the people had to do was take refuge on one of the floors, pull up the ladder and fire on the intruders. For centuries, people set about killing one another, with feuds going on between villages, families, or friends. They would fight over a patch of land, or because of an unappeased lust for power or simply because someone smiled at their neighbour's daughter. In the late 19C, the Máni Peninsula still had 800 of these towers, mainly concentrated in the south.

■ The **road★** that runs inland from Vathí to Areópoli crosses a splendid landscape of green hills dotted with old villages. It goes past the foot of **Passavás Castle** *(not visible from the road)*, built in the 13C by the Governor of Morea, the Frenchman Jean de Neuilly. If you do not feel like climbing the grassy path up to it *(15min)*, you can opt for another castle, **Keléfa★**, with an easier approach *(5km before Areópoli a small signposted road leads off to the right and passes through a village, after which there is a practicable track to the castle)*. Partly ruined, this impressive 17C Ottoman fortress stands in complete isolation dominating **Ítilo Bay** (Ormos Limeníou).

■ **Areópoli★** – *27km from Githio.* The peaceful capital of the Máni Peninsula stretches out at the foot of a bare mountain not far from the Gulf of Messinía. The town is the gateway to the Inner Máni, a good base from which to explore the surrounding area for a day or two. Cross the modern square where the buses pull in, and lose yourself in the streets of the well-restored **old town** which wind past towers and old **stone houses** with red-tiled roofs. Once past Platía Darkákou with its traditional shops, you come to the square where the Maniots proclaimed the beginning of the War of Independence on 17 March 1821. Recognisable by its tall, detached bell-tower, the **Taxiárhes Church** *(often closed)* is adorned on its outside walls with **carved marble plaques** featuring the signs of the Zodiac.

The southern tip★★★

Head south from Areópoli towards the southern shores of the Inner Máni. 73km tour. Allow one day, including a swim.

■ Your first stop is at the **Diroú Caves★** (Spílea Diroú) *(8km; 9am-4pm from June to September, 8am-2.15pm from October to May; entrance fee)*. Piled into a boat, you glide along an underground river, head down to avoid the stalactites. Here you see the "pink apartments" with their walls covered in a kind of pink crystal sponge, there the "red apartments" with crimson concretions.

■ At **Pírgos Diroú** you enter the most picturesque part of the Máni Peninsula where hamlets and villages punctuate a rugged landscape of rocky scrubland, olive trees and prickly pears. On either side of the road, the

The Peloponnese

towers of **Nómia** and **Kíta** stand facing each other, like two warriors on the qui vive. Their story is a good example of the damage caused in the past by local aggression. For thirty years in the 19C, these two villages were at each other's throats because a young man had held a pretty neighbour too close while dancing.

■ Four kilometres further south, the small fishing port of **Geroliménas** lies tucked into a bay dominated by cliffs. Beyond, the already arid countryside almost turns into a desert.

The vendetta, a Maniot export?
If the chief of a clan had not managed to avenge his honour during his lifetime, it fell to his descendants to take on the fatal "gdhikiomós" or settling of the blood feud. It is believed that when some Maniots left the Máni Peninsula and settled in Corsica under the protection of the Republic of Genoa in the 17C, they imported this tradition of vengeance, which became known there as the "vendetta".

■ The atmosphere becomes increasingly strange, permeated by a deep silence, when **Váthia★★★** rises up on the horizon, its many towers standing out atop a solitary spur in a scene of dramatic austerity. The soul of the Máni Peninsula seems to be concentrated in this village in the middle of nowhere. About ten years ago, the tower houses began to come alive again, partly restored and rehabilitated as hotels by the national tourism organisation (EOT). Unfortunately everything is now closed, as the latest owners have neglected the place, and the streets are once again home to stray dogs.

■ For refreshment, go on to **Marmári★**, driving alongside the jagged rocks lining **Marmári Bay★★**. The resort has a lovely **sandy beach★★**.

Váthia, a forgotten village in the Máni Peninsula

J. Malburet/MICHELIN

■ You could also go to **Pórto Kágio** (Quail Port) on the east coast. Surrounded by bare mountains, this stopover for migratory birds has retained almost nothing of the **Máni Fortress** built in the 13C by Guillaume de Villehardouin. Ramblers, however, can start out from here on a superb walk to **Cape Matapan**★★★ (Akrotírio Ténaro), a spectacular windswept promontory which served for many years as a base for pirates of all kinds, chiefly Maniots.

■ From here, make your way back north along the coast through the villages of **Lágia**★, **Kokkála**★ and **Éxo Nimfío**★★, with its impressive towers clinging to the hillside. The houses in **Flomohóri**★ are believed to be the tallest in the Máni Peninsula.

Return to Areópoli along the road that crosses the peninsula.

Messinían Máni★★
From Areópoli to Kalamáta
80km from Areópoli to Kalamáta. Allow half a day, or a whole day including a walk into the Víros Gorge.

The road leaves the harsh landscape of the southern part of the peninsula to pass through some of the most attractive, varied countryside in the Peloponnese. It winds between the bare foothills of Mt Taíyetos and the green shores of the Gulf of Messinía with its inviting blue water (in summer the resorts are hugely popular). The setting becomes increasingly rustic. Maniot towers give way to Byzantine chapels that line the road, often leaving their doors open to visitors.

■ Driving along the west coast you soon come to the small fishing port of **Liméni**, hugging the curve of a superb rocky inlet. You may like to stop at one of the tavernas right beside the water, but if you want to swim, you will have to continue to the beach at **Tsípa**.

■ Five kilometres north of Areópoli, **Ítilo**★, the former capital of the region, is the gateway to Messinían Máni. Formerly protected by **Keléfa Castle** (*see above*), the old village stretches out peacefully at the foot of the fortress. A plaque on the main square – a dead end – recalls in Greek and French that in the 17C the town was the departure point for Maniots leaving for Corsica, and that the town is twinned with Cargèse in Corsica.

■ Moving on up towards Kalamáta, you reach **Thalámes**. Rather than wasting your time at the private museum of Folk Art and Traditions, of minor interest, keep going to the **Church of the Metamórfosis**★ (*as you leave the village*), which has fine capitals carved with animals.

Towers of war, domes of peace
As though to offset the warlike image created by the fortified towers, the Maniot countryside is dotted with Byzantine churches and chapels, the oldest dating back to the 11C. All have the same plan: a dome resting on a Greek cross. The walls, beneath the stone-tiled roofs, are built of alternating stone, brick and delicate fragments of ancient or paleo-Christian marble. The interiors are just as worthwhile (don't hesitate to go in if they're open. If not, ask the nearest neighbour for the key). You will see extraordinarily fine frescoes, albeit damaged by the ravages of time and human negligence.

■ One kilometre further on, at **Nomitsí**, the **Church of Anárgiri** still has some lovely frescoes. Richer still, the neighbouring village of **Plátsa**★ boasts several **Byzantine churches**, whose beautiful frescoes are very moving.

■ The coast further north becomes much more tourist-oriented. Beyond the attractive port of **Ágios Nikólaos** the gleaming resort of **Stoúpa** stretches along the finest **beach**★ in the region, and is obviously very popular.

■ Then you come to the green coastal village of **Kardamíli***, dominated by a **medieval wall** that has kept its tower, and by the delicately carved pointed belfry of the **Church of Ágios Spirídonas**.

■ Beyond Kardamíli the road enters ever-denser woodland and then runs through the sombre **Víros Gorge*** (*if you want to do this excursion on foot, leave your car near the Church of Ágios Spirídonas and take a taxi to the village of Tséria 10km north-east. Bring good walking shoes and a picnic, allow half a day*). The steep-sided canyon disappears into the Vassilikis forest to the east and comes out at the sea north of Kardamíli. You go down along a magnificent paved track before slowly climbing up to Exohóri, between the monasteries clinging to the heights. Then you return to the Church of Ágios Spirídonas.

■ Finally, if you still have the strength, don't miss the **Church of Ágii Theódori*** at **Kámbos**, recognisable by its portal carved with palm leaves. Inside, the rather damaged frescoes show martyrs with extraordinarily serene expressions on their faces. On the ceiling is a Christ in Majesty surrounded by signs of the Zodiac.

Beyond, you reach the border of the western Máni, ending the tour at Kalamáta.

COMING AND GOING

By boat – In summer from Gíthio, 2 daily connections (3 on Saturday) with the port of Agía Pelagía on Cythera, on the *Maria Piá* ferry (2hr30min crossing). For Crete (Kastéli), two weekly connections (times change every year so you should enquire).

By air – The nearest airport is at **Kalamáta** (see page 262).

By bus – From **Athens**, 3 buses a day to Areópoli via Piraeus, Corinth, Trípoli, Sparta and Gíthio (travelling time 6hr). In Areópoli, the bus station is on the main square, in front of the Europa Grill café, ☎ (0735) 51 229.

GETTING AROUND

By bus – From **Gíthio**, six buses a day to Sparta, between 7.30am and 7pm. Four to Areópoli, between 6am and 7pm, two to Kalamáta via Sparta, and one to Monemvassía.
From **Areópoli**, four buses a day to Gíthio, from 8am to 6pm. Two to Geroliménas. Three to Kalamáta (change at Ítilo). Three to Sparta.

By rental vehicle – Car rental in Gíthio, at **Mákis**. Motorcycles for hire

on the jetty, not far from the islet of Kranaï, ☎ (0733) 25 111, mobile 09 77 57 37 64. Service stations in Gíthio, Areópoli and Pírgos Diroú.

ADDRESS BOOK

Tourist information – In Gíthio, Odós Vassilíou Georgíou 20, ☎ (0733) 24 484.

Banks / Currency exchange – In Areópoli, **National Bank**. The cash dispenser is in the street leading into the town when you come from Gíthio.

Main post office – In **Areópoli**, beside the bank, opposite the Mani hotel, ☎ (0733) 51 230. No currency exchange. In **Gíthio**, in Odós Ermoú, which opens onto the seafront.

Police – In **Areópoli**, ☎ (0733) 51 209.

Medical service – **Areópoli medical centre**, ☎ (0733) 51 215 / 51 259.

WHERE TO STAY

For several years, the number of small hotels and rooms to let has been growing, increasing the peninsula's accommodation possibilities. On the other hand, don't count on hotels formerly run by the EOT, as they have either been closed until further notice (in **Váthia**), or are poorly run by private owners (Kapetános Tower in Areópoli). And don't expect to find campsites in the middle of the peninsula, most are on the north-west coast or south of Gíthio in Vathí Bay.

• **Gíthio**

You will find a large concentration of hotels and rooms to let along the seafront, from the town itself all the way to the Vathí Peninsula. You are spoilt for choice.

Between €38 and €55
Aktaion, Odós Vassilíou Pávlou 30, ☎ (0733) 23 500 / 1, Fax (0733) 22 294 – 20rm and 2 suites. ⌁ ℰ 🖳 📺 cc On the avenue that runs beside the sea. A large building with several storeys. Pleasant rooms, all with balconies overlooking the harbour. Comfortable bathrooms. Open all year.
Gythion, Odós Vassilíou Pávlou 33, ☎ (0733) 23 452, Fax (0733) 23 523 – 7rm. ⌁ ℰ 🖳 📺 A small hotel in a 19C house with a more attractive façade than its neighbour. The rooms, which have no special charm, all give onto the sea and onto some lively cafés (a little noisy in the evening).

• **Vathí**

Campsites (around €11)
Gíthion Bay, 3km west of Gíthio on the sandy beach at Mavrovoúni, ☎ (0733) 22 522, Fax (0733) 23 523. Very popular with German campers. A large, well-organised site, shaded by hundreds of fruit trees. A good place for families (children's games and a variety of sports equipment). Open all year.
Mégas Aléxandros, 10km south of Gíthio, ☎ (0733) 93 160. A decent campsite in a eucalyptus forest beside a superb sandy beach. Unfortunately, too few bathrooms to cope with all the guests in the height of summer. Open from May to October.

• **Areópoli**

Between €38 and €45
Pierros Bozagregos, on a square, just behind the Taxiárhes Church, ☎ (0733) 51 354 / 51 403 – 7rm. ⌁ In a peaceful part of town. A tower with huge,

plain but clean rooms on the first floor. Breakfast is served on the attractively restored ground floor.
Ta Sfentónia, just opposite the Pierros Bozagregos, ☎ (0735) 33 570 – 5rm, 2 studios and 1 apartment for 5 people. ⌁ ✕ 📺 This guesthouse in a real Maniot tower will delight all who love the vivacity of Greek families... and colourful decor. Amid a jumble of cuddly toys and plaster dogs are various war souvenirs belonging to the grandfather, a resistance fighter.

• **Marmári**

Between €30 and €38
The Castle, ☎ (0733) 52 111 – 8rm. ⌁ ✕ 🐾 🏠 Overlooking a beautiful sandy beach. The more attractive of the two places in this small resort in the south-west of the peninsula. The modest but charming rooms have frescoes on the walls. Decent restaurant. Magnificent view over the sea at sunset.

Between €24 and €45
Marmari, at the top of the village, ☎ (0733) 51 680 / 1, in Athens (01) 99 14 597 – 5rm. ⌁ 🏠 This rather basic hotel has three rooms with 3 beds and a kitchenette, and two rooms with 2 beds. The lady owner is a little hard of hearing.

• **Stavrí**

Between €45 and €60
🏨 **Tsitsiris Castle**, ☎ (0733) 56 297, Fax (0733) 56 297. In Athens, ☎ (01) 68 58 960 / 61, Fax (01) 68 58 962 – 20rm. ⌁ 🖳 ✕ cc In a tiny village lost in the middle of nowhere. In the late 1980s, five brothers made this superb hotel out of several towers. The rooms are all different and give onto cobbled patios adorned with large earthenware jars. The very courteous owners collect guests who don't have their own transport at the bus stop 2km below. Open from April to the end of October and around Christmas.

• **Liméni**

The whole coast is dotted with hotels and rooms to let, so you will always find somewhere to stay.

Between €38 and €63
Liméni Village, 4km north of Areópoli, ☎ (0733) 51 111 / 112, Fax (0733)

51 182 – 35rm. 🛏️ 📋 🅿️ 📺 ✕ ⚓ 🏛️
CC 18 towers clinging to the steep slope that drops down to the azure sea have been converted into rooms to form an ensemble that is as comfortable as it is elegant. Rooms and suites have fridges. Breakfast included. Open all year.

EATING OUT

• Gíthio
Around €9
To Nissí, as you come onto the islet of Kranaï, surrounded by pines. One of the best places in Gíthio: high-quality cooking (good salads and fresh grilled fish), and espresso... which could almost be Italian.

• Areópoli
Around €7.50
🏛️ **O Bárba Pétros**, in the main street,☎ (0733) 51 205. The best place in town offers a bucolic setting in a little flower-filled courtyard, together with well-prepared traditional Greek dishes. The local white wine is served chilled, with a smile from the very welcoming owners.

• Stavrí
Around €9
Tsitsiris Castle, the restaurant of the hotel with the same name. Generous – although rather expensive – portions served in a peaceful and attractive white courtyard.

• Geroliménas
Around €6
Theodorákis, at the end of the harbour. This taverna doesn't look very appealing but serves fresh grilled fish and good traditional Greek dishes (octopus in vinegar, moussaká, different meats in sauce, etc). Warm welcome and mainly Greek clientele.

• Ítilo
Around €6
Pétrini Goniá, on the main square in the old village. A café-taverna with tables set out under trees. A peaceful place to try decent Greek dishes at very reasonable prices.

HAVING A DRINK

• Pírgos Diroú
La Cueva Café-Club, a large place beside the road. Gaudy decor with a mock tower adorned with a mock fountain. Depending on the time of day, you can eat, drink or dance here (English and American music). Open from 11am to 5am.

OTHER THINGS TO DO

Local festivals – In Gíthio the **Marathoníssia Festival** with plays and concerts takes place from 15 July to 15 August.

SHOPPING GUIDE

Antiques – In **Gíthio** you will find a good antique shop (tools, jars, lamps, engravings, etc) on the seafront near the Aktaion hotel. In **Areópoli**, on Platía Darkákou, venture into the bazaar run by the Mitsákos, a friendly elderly couple who will let you dig around in their incredible collection of bric-a-brac. At the back of the shop, you will find traditional Greek sheets sold by the metre, hard to come by these days.

CYTHERA★★
(KÍTHIRA)

Ionian Islands – District of Attica – Michelin map 980 folds 41-42
284km² – Pop 3 000 – Allow 3 days

Not to be missed
Hóra (Kíthira), Kapsáli, Milopótamos, Agía Sofía and Paleohóra.
The Monastery of Ágios Theódoros. Potamós.

And remember...
As there is little public transport and the taxis are heavily booked, either bring your
own vehicle to the island or hire one on the spot.

"Island of feasting hearts and secret joys!
Like a fragrance, the voluptuary ghost
Of Aphrodite floats above your shores,
Inflaming minds with languor and with love."

Baudelaire, *A Voyage to Cythera* (extract), *The Flowers of Evil*.

Made famous by the painting by Antoine Watteau, *Pilgrimage to Cythera*, the island
of love where Aphrodite landed has been sung by many a poet. However, it is not
the traces of a mythological past or the ancient remains (very few) that you will
be seeking on this windswept island, but the authentic Greek atmosphere and the
pleasing architecture that harmoniously combines the whiteness of the Cyclades
with Venetian features. Before the new airport begins to disgorge hordes of tourists,
make the most of the island landscapes, which range from verdant plains to wild
ravines. Enjoy too the lovely towns: Kíthira, the capital, Kapsáli, a resort that comes
vividly to life in the evening, and, in the north, Potamós, the commercial heart of
Cythera.

Two sides to the island

The most southerly of the Ionian Islands has two different faces. The south consists
of wild gorges full of myrtles, and the north, with more springs, is covered in heath
with a scattering of pinewoods. This geographical division once corresponded to a
political one, as the Venetians established a border at **Dókana** (Customs) in the middle of the island where travellers had to pay a tax. This separation, still alive in people's
minds, means that the inhabitants in the south refer to themselves as coming from
"inside", in other words from the Venetian area dominated by the citadel at Kíthira, as
opposed to those from the north who come from "outside".

Aphrodite's isle

Cythera, the mythical land of love, was visited by two of legend's most beautiful women, Helen and the goddess Aphrodite. Born from the foam ("aphrós" in Greek) produced in the sea by the severed genitals of Uranus (cut off by his son Cronus), the goddess made for Cythera aboard a shell, poised on it like a pearl. Blown on her way by Zephyrus, she landed at Cythera where Eros and the satyrs rushed to meet her. She only escaped them by hiding in a myrtle bush, a plant that then became her emblem. A sanctuary, of which nothing remains, was dedicated to her at Paleókastro. It was called the palace of Menelaus, in memory of the time Helen and her Trojan lover Paris stayed on the island, a visit that in no way pleased the goddess, who was jealous of Helen's beauty.

Strategic stakes

Because of its position south of the Peloponnese, isolating it from the other Ionian Islands, Cythera has been fought over throughout the ages. Athens and Sparta went to war over it, then Antony

The Peloponnese

and Augustus, and in the 13C, pirates from Monemvassiá. Nor should we forget the Venetians: having taken it after a hard-fought struggle, the troops of the Venetian Republic exercised their domination here until the arrival of the French in 1797. The latter, exalted by the ideas of the French Revolution, inspired the inhabitants with a desire for democracy that had been repressed for too long... which ended up with the nobles being massacred by the peasants in the citadel at Kíthira. During the War of Independence in 1821 Cythera

Greek kangaroos

In winter, Cythera is emptied of its living strength. The only people who stay behind are the elderly, kept going by the money sent by their children who have emigrated to the United States or to Australia. Today more than 60 000 people born on the island now live in Australia, earning Cythera the nickname "Kangaroo Island", and Australia that of "Big Cythera"! As a sign of gratitude the inhabitants have built a monument to their émigrés in the village of Frátsia.

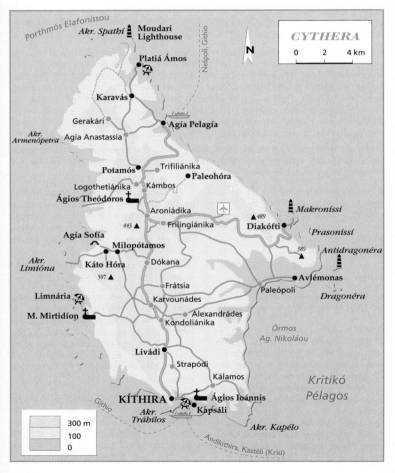

served as a refuge to two Greek patriots, **Kolokotrónis** and the future father of the nation, **Venizélos**. After having been occupied by the Russians and the British, who began its modernisation, the island became part of Greece in 1864.

Kíthira and the south★★

■ **Kíthira**★★★ (Hóra) – *The narrow streets fill quickly in summer, so park at the entrance to the town. Allow 2hr.* As you go into the capital of Cythera, you are dazzled by the immaculate whiteness of the walls, set off wonderfully by architectural detailing of Venetian origin. The main street leads to a rocky spur where the Venetian Republic built a **citadel**★ in the early 16C. From its ramparts is a superb **view**★★ of the twin bay of Kapsáli. Diverse buildings inside *(closed)* include **four Byzantine churches** and an old seigneurial mansion. There are also several cannons.

At the foot of the citadel, an alleyway leads off to the right to the **Mésa Voúrgo district** whose **Byzantine churches** contain frescoes from the 15C and the 18C. Outside the town, on the right, you can visit the little **Archaeological Museum** *(9.45am-3pm from Tuesday to Saturday, 9.30am-2.30pm on Sunday and public holidays; entrance fee)* which displays Minoan and Mycenaean objects found on the island.

■ **Kapsáli**★ – *2.5km below. No bus service, so take a taxi or hitch-hike.* With its two curved bays separated by a small rocky promontory, Kapsáli has become Cythera's fashionable beach, very lively in the evening, and the place where the yachts come alongside. A small pebbly harbour flanks the **main beach** (on the left), where fishing boats moor. On the right is a small sheltered beach, reached by a wooden pontoon. Above Kapsáli, a road, unfortunately closed on account of landslides, leads to the **Ágios Ioánnis Monastery** where, according to legend, St John the Apostle began writing the *Apocalypse*, which he finished on Pátmos.

Follow the main road northwards, taking minor roads off it to various sites in the south. On leaving Livádi, a former place of residence for the British, take the first road left and continue straight ahead for 15km.

■ **Moní Mirtidíon** – *Free. Suitable clothing available for visitors, near the portal. Allow 1hr.* At the bottom of a green **valley**★ invaded by myrtles and pines, stands a monastery dedicated to the Panagía Mirtidiótissa, the Virgin of the Myrtles. Whereas the 19C architecture is of little interest, the charming, well-kept garden is enjoyable and the church contains a lovely **icon**★ of a Black Virgin. A practicable track goes down from the monastery to the small **beach at Limnária** *(2km away)*.

Go back the way you came for 3.5km, and take the first road left to Milopótamos, the starting point for a lovely walk, a round trip of 7km (allow 2 to 3hr on foot in all).

■ Without being very spectacular, the drowsy village of **Milopótamos**★ is not without a certain charm with its **neo-Classical houses** adorned with elegant balconies, its taverna shaded by plane trees, and its fountain. You can have a break at the only café in the place and then set off to stroll through the abandoned streets of the neighbouring citadel, Káto Hóra *(1km away)*.

An icon in the myrtles
One 24 September in the 12C, a shepherd found an icon of the Virgin Mary in some myrtles and took it home. But, strangely, the holy icon returned twice to where it had been discovered. So the shepherd decided to build a chapel for it on the spot. From that moment on, the icon began to show powers of healing, quickly attracting a large number of pilgrims. It was not until the mid-19C that the present church was built for it.

■ **Káto Hóra Citadel**★★ – Without making a detour to see the **Kataráktis Neráïda** waterfall, spoiled by litter, continue to the magnificent Venetian fortress built in 1565. Crowning a rocky spur between two ravines, it appears like a figurehead on the prow of a ship advancing over a sea of trees. Go through the portal at the entrance, adorned with the **lion of St Mark** and you will discover a whole town with its streets and houses now exposed to the winds. Time seems to have stopped just a short while ago, freezing the place as it was the day it was abandoned. Only the **Byzantine chapels** (*closed*) have been restored.

■ On leaving, take the road and then a dirt track to the **Cave of Agía Sofía**★ two kilometres further on (*3pm-8pm from Monday to Friday, 11am-5pm at weekends; entrance fee. Bring non-slip shoes*). The cave, where St Sophia is believed to have stayed, is 50m above the sea. The small chapel at the entrance is dedicated to the saint and has a moving 12C (or perhaps 14C) **iconostasis**★. Beyond, you plunge into a maze of narrow passages and chambers with **stalactites** and **stalagmites**.

Back on the main road, head off to explore the east of the island, not so much for its bare rocky landscapes as for its sandy **beaches**★, among Cythera's finest. You have a choice between two roads, one south, and the other north. The road in the south ends at the charming port of **Avlémonas**★ (*10km beyond Frátsia*), where old stone houses surround a small recently restored **Venetian fortress**. The road in the north, which runs past the airport, stops at the new port of **Diakófti** (*25km beyond Aroniádika*), which has a superb **sandy beach**★★.

In the streets
of Hóra, Cythera

G. de Benoist/MICHELIN

Cythera

The north★★

By car, allow one day (about 50km) from Kíthira, including time for a swim.

■ **Paleohóra**★★ — *Take the main road, go past Aroniádika and then bear right onto the dirt track (currently being improved) that leads to Paleohóra 4km further on. On foot, allow 1hr, preferably in the cool of the morning or the evening.* The track crosses an austere rocky landscape and then opens onto a spectacular **mountain cirque**★★. The peak in the middle, surrounded by precipices, was once home to the old Byzantine capital of Cythera. There, the inhabitants, who came from Monemvassiá and founded the place in the 12C, thought they would be safe from pirates. Indeed, with their **70 churches** (*some have been restored but are closed to the public*), they lived in peace until 1537, when the troops of **Barbarossa** managed to climb the walls of the city, thus heralding its tragic end. The pirates burnt the houses and reduced the inhabitants to slavery, driving the rest of the population to commit group suicide, as is borne out by the discovery of bones at the bottom of the rocks. Today, windswept and overgrown, the remains of the city, like all towns that have met the same fate, exude an atmosphere of deep sadness... which shouldn't mean that you lose all sense of prudence (*take heed of the danger signs at the foot of unstable walls*).

Retrace your steps, turn right onto the main road, and less than 1km further on, bear left to the Monastery of Ágios Theódoros nearby.

■ **The Monastery of Ágios Theódoros**★★ — Barely have you gone through the entrance when the quiet of the place and the whiteness of the walls, stark against the dark green of the pines, plunge you into an atmosphere of light and silence. You enter a square courtyard. On the left are the monastery buildings, at the back a cultural centre dating from the time of the British, and on the right, a **church**★ dedicated in the 12C or 13C to the monk Ágios Theódoros, protector of Cythera. The whitewashed **façade**★ with its pure lines — note especially the beautiful **marble lintel** at the entrance — is set off by delicate yellow bands and various carved motifs. Inside, have a look at the painted wood **iconostasis**, which stands near the ruined wall of an early sanctuary built in the 4C in honour of St Sergios and St Vackos (Bacchus).

■ **Potamós**★ — Far from the tourist bustle in the south, the island's largest village (*less than 2km north of the monastery*) has plenty of authentic atmosphere. It is a cheerful place, especially on Sunday when the local **market** is held. The delightfully shaded main square is a picturesque spot for a drink before having a wander around the streets, where you will see **neo-Classical houses** with graceful wrought-iron balconies. Potamós is also the starting point for pleasant **excursions**, on foot or by car, into Cythera's green north.

■ Without being of any great interest, **Agía Pelagía**, a port of call for ferries, nonetheless has some sandy beaches where you can while away the time before catching a boat to the mainland.

■ **Karavás**★ — 5km further north, in the heart of the greener part of the island. You should not miss this steep little village with its stream, considered to be one of the best preserved and most atmospheric places on Cythera. From here, walkers can set off on the mountain road that links the village to **Amos beach** (*2km away*) and then bear left onto a footpath. This leads 5km northwards (*allow a good hour*) to the **Moudari lighthouse** built by the British, where there is a fine **view**★ of the sea and, in the distance, the coast of the mainland.

Making the most of Cythera

COMING AND GOING

By boat – Cythera has two ports. The first, **Agía Pelagía** serves the ferries from **Neápoli** (Monday and Tuesday: 8am, 11am, 5pm. Wednesday and Thursday: 8am, 12noon, 5pm. Friday, Saturday and Sunday: 8am, 11am, 2pm, 5pm). To **Neápoli**: Monday, Tuesday, 9.30am, 12.30pm and 6.30pm. Wednesday, 9.15am, 3.30pm, 6.30pm. Thursday, Friday, Saturday and Sunday: 9.15am, 3pm, 6.30pm (50min crossing). Enquiries, harbour police in Neápoli, ☎ (0734) 22 660 / 23 004, or harbour police in Agía Pelagía, ☎ (0736) 34 371 / 34 372. Some ferries go to **Gíthio** on the east coast of the Máni Peninsula (2hr30min crossing). The second port, modern **Diakófti** , is reserved for Flying Dolphins to Piraeus (4 to 5hr crossing depending on the number of stops – Monemvassiá, Kiparissía, Géraka, Portohéli, Spétses, Hydra and Zéa Marina in Piraeus). Also serves **Crete**, ☎ (0736) 33 490. 4hr30min crossing.

For other enquiries, try **Porphyra Travel** in Livádi, ☎ (0736) 31 888 / 9 or the **Megalokonomou Agency** at the harbour in Agía Pelagía, ☎ (0736) 34 490 / 33 890. It is advisable to book ahead of time for your car.

By air – **Olympic Airways**, on Cythera: ☎ (0736) 33 362 / 33 292, or (01) 96 66 666. Athens-Cythera: in summer, 3 connections a day during the week, 1 on Sunday. Cythera's airport is 15km north-east of Kíthira (with taxi rank). The airport is being extended and should now be handling much increased traffic.

By bus – Several connections by road from Athens: George Drakakis, ☎ (0736) 31 160 or 09 32 41 52 66, Níkos Karydis, ☎ (0736) 31 049 or 09 44 44 14 82.

GETTING AROUND

By bus – Just one bus a day serves the main villages on the island early in the morning.

By taxi – ☎ (0736) 31 160 / 31 860, mobile 0932 415266 / 0944 746246.

By rental vehicle – In summer, you should book in advance. The best agency is **Panayotis**, which hires out two-wheelers and cars (as well as canoes and pedalos), ☎ in Kapsáli: (0736) 31 600 / 31 789, Fax (0736) 31 789, in Hóra (Kíthira): ☎ (0736) 31 004, in Agía Pelagía: ☎ (0736) 33 194, in Tsikalariá: (0736) 31 551, in Diakófti: 0944 263757.

Motorcycles at **Easy Rider**, ☎ (0736) 33 486 and **Níkos**, in Kapsáli, ☎ (0736) 31 190.

Service stations in Potamós, Logothetiánika and Kondoliánika.

By boat – Limited facilities in **Kapsáli** harbour. A man comes round selling fresh water once a day. Harbour police next to the **Ambassy** café, ☎ (0736) 31 222.

ADDRESS BOOK

Tourist information – For want of an official tourist office, Cythera has several information places, such as the one at **Agía Pelagía**, on the left when you leave the landing-stage, ☎ (0736) 33 815, which provides boat timetables and hotel addresses, and will call a taxi.

Banks / Currency exchange – In Hóra (Kíthira) on the main square, two banks change money and have cash dispensers. In Potamós the **National Bank** on the main square cashes travellers' cheques, and takes credit cards. Currency exchange also at Agía Pelagía at the **Megalokonómou Agency** on the jetty.

Main post office – In Hóra, on the main square. In Kapsáli, in a caravan behind the harbour. In Potamós, near the main square.

Telephone – **OTE**, in Hóra, on the main square. In Potamós, above the main square.

Internet – The island has a Web site in English, German and Greek: www.kythira.com

Police – In Kíthira, ☎ (0736) 31 206.

Medical service – In Kíthira, **dispensary** on the right as you enter the town, open in the morning from Monday to Friday, ☎ (0736) 31 243. **Dr Tserpenákis**, mobile ☎ 09 44 87 78 62. **Hospital**, ☎ (0736) 33 325. **Dentist** in Livádi, ☎ (0736) 31 536, or 09 44 24 95 51.

WHERE TO STAY

Each village has hotels and rooms to let and sometimes charming self-catering places. In August it is essential to book.

• Hóra (Kíthira)
Around €38
Castello, at the foot of the citadel, to the left of an antiques shop, ☎ and Fax (0736) 31 069 / 31 869 – 6rm and 3 studios. ⚒ ✈ ♞ cc In a modern house surrounding a garden. Simple, clean rooms with fridges. Good value for money.
Between €38 and €68
🦞**Margarita**, in an alley leading off the main street to the right, ☎ (0736) 31 711, Fax (0736) 31 325 – 12rm. ⚒ 🍽 ♞ TV cc A charming hotel in a very well-renovated 19C house in the heart of the capital. Breakfast is served on one of the two peaceful terraces looking out over the countryside.

• Kapsáli
Campsite (around €12)
Kapsáli campsite, ☎ (0736) 31 580. The only campsite on the island. Looks out over Kapsáli from a forest of pines and eucalyptus that gets very hot in summer. An attractive site but the sanitary facilities are notoriously inadequate. No fixed reception times.
Between €99 and €120
Raikos, on a hill overlooking Kapsáli Bay, ☎ (0736) 31 629 / 766, Fax (0736) 31 801 – 24rm. ⚒ 🍽 ♞ ⚓ 🏊 cc A fine group of modern white-washed buildings. Bright rooms with small terraces with views. Pleasant swimming pool but no restaurant. Booking essential.

• Pitsinádes
Some of the hundred-year-old houses in this attractively restored hamlet have

been converted into charming self-catering guesthouses.
Between €55 and €75
Pitsinádes, ☎ (0736) 33 877 or in Piraeus (01) 41 73 702 – 6rm. ⚒ A lady owner runs this 170-year-old house which has beautiful vaulted rooms with built-in furnishings, opening onto a shared patio. Two rooms have kitchenettes. Breakfast and cleaning included. Open from April to October.
🦞**Ta Sfentónia**, ☎ (0736) 33 570, annie@ath.forthnet.gr – 5 studios. ⚒ The spacious, naturally cool studios with kitchenettes are in two magnificently restored 16C and 17C houses decorated with old tools and implements. The private terraces look out onto the peaceful countryside as far as the eye can see, and the hostess, Anna, is very welcoming. A little expensive, however (no room service).

• Aroniádika
Between €23 and €38
Rouga, ☎ (0736) 33 596 – 4rm. ⚒ cc In the heart of an old village currently being restored. Rooms in an old private house belonging to a Greek-British couple. A decent standard of comfort (kitchenettes) at a reasonable price. Open all year.
Kamáres, ☎ (0736) 33 420 or (01) 41 32 512 – 5rm. ⚒ ♞ 🍽 Completely renovated recently. Rooms with kitchenettes. The architecture of the hundred-year-old house has been respected, as has the traditional masonry for the furnishings. Wide view of the surrounding countryside from the shared terrace. Open all year.

EATING OUT

• Hóra
Between €15 and €23
Zorba's Taverna is far from being the best or the friendliest taverna in Hóra, but it is the only one in the town centre. **Crêperie Marketo**, on the main street, is tucked away in a small garden 20m beyond Zorba's, and has a better atmosphere. Good pancakes with different fillings.

- **Kapsáli**

Between €15 and €23

🐌 **Hydragogío**, far from the noise of the bars, and with a good view of the harbour. The best taverna in Kapsáli. Tables in arbours thick with vines. The young owners create cheerful, inventive dishes, with tasty honey doughnuts to finish off the meal. Come before 8.30pm to get a table.

- **Logothetiánika**

Between €15 and €23

María Yorgopoúlou, this grocery store-cum-taverna has a limited menu but you are served in true Greek tradition by the indefatigable Maria or a member of her family.

Taverna-ouzo bar (no name), opposite the church, in a private house with a garden. The dishes are served in generous portions (lamb chops, aubergine fritters, etc) washed down with a local rosé. On some evenings there are rembétiko concerts.

- **Potamós**

Between €12 and €18

Panaretos, an open-air restaurant in the main square where you can try local dishes, including *loukánika* (island sausages) and excellent oriental pastries.

- **Diakófti**

Under €15

Zephiros, opposite the Flying Dolphins harbour, right on the beach, looking out to sea. A pleasant hut serving unpretentious Greek fare and good grilled fish.

HAVING A DRINK

- **Potamós**

Ouzerí Roúla, sheltered by large pines in the main square, this is the best place to enjoy ouzo and grilled octopus with the locals.

Kafenío Alexandros, in the street heading downhill left of the bank. A kafenío worthy of the film director Angelópoulos, with its dark wooden tables and bar, its collection of old clocks and its távli players hidden in the half-light.

- **Kapsáli**

Barbarossa, a friendly night-club on the jetty with rock and Greek music. Good atmosphere.

OTHER THINGS TO DO

Outdoor pursuits – In Kapsáli, **Panayótis**, ☎ (0736) 31 600, hires out canoes and pedalos, and gives water-skiing instruction.

Beaches – The beaches suitable for families are at **Kapsáli** (main beach) and around **Agía Pelagía**. The fine red sandy beach at **Firí Ámos** (at the end of an impracticable track) is popular with nudists. Other possibilities are the beaches at **Límni** and **Diakófti** on the east coast, and those on the west, which are hard to reach but washed by a warm sea.

Boat trips – In Kapsáli, the **Alexandros**, ☎ (0736) 31 991, serves the isolated beaches on the south coast.

Feasts & festivals – On 12 May, the Monastery of Ágios Theódoros celebrates the saint's feast day. In early August, there are two festivals celebrated with singing, dancing and a Greek dinner: the wine festival at **Mitáta**, and the Portokália (orange tree) festival at **Karavás**. 15 August: **Potamós** festival. 20 September: feast of **Agía Pelagía**. 24 September: **Moní Mirtidíon** celebrates the saint's feast day.

SHOPPING GUIDE

Market – Every Sunday morning in **Potamós**, farmers sell their produce in the main square, and the shops set out their goods on the pavement.

Local delicacies – Thyme honey, jams, medicinal herbs and olives at **Stávros** in Hóra, below the museum, and in Potamós at **Mariánthi Kassimátis**, on the left as you come into town.

Other – Attractive hand-decorated ceramics on sale at **Galerie Roússos** in Hóra, and in the workshop at **Káto Livádi** on the Livádi-Kálamos road.

KALAMÁTA
ITHÓMI★★

Province of the Peloponnese – Kalamáta, capital of Messinía
Regional map page 202 – Michelin map 980 fold 40
78km from Areópoli, 70km from Sparta and 52km from Pílos – Pop 42 000

Not to be missed
A trip to the archaeological site at Ithómi, especially a tour of its walls.

And remember...
Tour Ithómi at the end of the day when the site is bathed in golden light.
Bring water, as the sun beats down hard on the ruins.

Kalamáta, capital of fertile Messinía and main port for the south of the Peloponnese, is probably not the perfect place for a holiday. But its airport and choice position between the Máni Peninsula, Pílos and Sparta mean that you necessarily go through it at some stage, and it is an ideal starting point for excursions to the south. It is from here, also, that you will leave to explore the underrated archaeological site at Ithómi, ancient Messene. Neglected by most tourist itineraries, this ancient city will not fail to impress you as you stand alone, or almost, within its mighty walls. Currently being excavated, the site rings with the clicking of archaeologists' tools and the chirping of cicadas. It has not yet revealed all its riches, but once the buildings have been restored, Ithómi will definitely be one of the greatest archaeological sites in Greece.

Short tour of Kalamáta
Allow 2hr

Kalamáta has three distinct districts: the seafront, the residential quarter with its strict grid plan, and the old town with its more confusing layout. Exploration of the town generally begins at the **seafront**, which has all the attributes of a resort: hotels, cafés and a clean **beach★** with good facilities, not forgetting the usual *kamáki* (skirt chasers!). The only real attraction, however, are the **old trains** exhibited in a small public garden behind the tourist police office.

To get from the beach to the old town, either take Odós Akríta, which is at right angles to the commercial port, or Odós Néodontos, just beyond the marina, which runs alongside the railway.

Go straight through the **residential quarter** in the town centre, which was rebuilt after the 1986 earthquake that killed 20 people and left 12 000 homeless. The **old town** stretching between the railway station and the Frankish citadel is the liveliest part of Kalamáta. It feels like an oriental city, with its network of hot noisy streets packed with small shops and cars. Here and there you can still see **neo-Classical houses**, currently being renovated.

A flight of steps up the hill leads to the former **Frankish citadel**, built by Geoffroi I de Villehardouin in the early 13C. All that remain are the **keep** and an **outer wall** that affords a good **view★** of the town and the Gulf of Messinía. At the entrance, an open-air theatre holds the annual International Dance Festival. In the north, there is a small **Byzantine church** dedicated to the Virgin of Kalomata ("with an approving eye"), to whom the town may owe its name.

Back down the hill, you come to the **Ipapándi Cathedral**, flanked on the right by the **Monastery of St Constantine and St Helen**, where the nuns still weave and embroider silk. On the left is the **Benáki Museum** (*Tuesday-Friday 8am-2.30pm, Saturday and Sunday 8.30am-3pm; closed Monday; entrance fee*) where archaeological remains and souvenirs from the War of Independence are displayed.

Ithómi, ancient Messene★★

22.5km from Kalamáta. Leave Kalamáta, heading north of the railway station towards the airport. After going through modern Messíni, head for Mavromáti. The site of Ithómi (signposted Ancient Messene) is outside the village, on the left. Take the stony track (practicable) that goes down to the remains. Free. Allow 2hr30min. The small museum to the left of the entrance is currently closed.

The town built by Epaminondas

In 371 BC at the end of the Battle of Leuctra, the Theban general **Epaminondas** gave orders that Ithómi should be built, following the example of the cities of Megalopolis, Mantineia and Árgos, in an effort to put a stop to Spartan expansionism. The Messenians in exile were thus invited to settle in the new city, which became the capital of the independent state of Messinía. Protected by 9km of formidable fortifications, the town prospered until the arrival of the Visigoths in the early 4C. The very precise description made by the Greek geographer **Pausanias**, who visited the city in the 2C, indicates that it was an important political and artistic centre. Excavations on the site, which began in 1895 but were interrupted several times, are continuing, and each year new discoveries are made.

Tour of the site

The remains of what was once the largest town in ancient Messinía are either still being excavated or have been restored, and cover a huge slope dotted with olive and fruit trees. You begin your exploration with some of the **arches** of a **theatre**, which can be seen on the right. Further on, on the left, a **water channel** snakes along to a round basin with a **fountain**. Just beside it are the foundations of a **temple** built in honour of the Greek gods and of Epaminondas.

One hundred metres below is the **agora**★, dating from Hellenistic times. It forms a wide rectangular esplanade, surrounded by a portico with a double colonnade. The latter's access **stairway** and about twenty **columns** have been restored. In the middle once stood a **temple dedicated to Asklepios** – the god of healing and a member of the family of the kings of Messene – of which there remain the foundations, and the base of a very large **altar** *(left)*. Go clockwise round the esplanade: on the left side, behind the altar *(to the east)* are the restored tiered seats of the **theatre**★★ (ekklesiasterion), set around an **orchestra**★★ with polychrome marble paving. Apart from being used for plays and ritual ceremonies, the theatre also served as a meeting room when the neighbouring **synedrion** proved too small. The latter has kept its stone **bench**, which runs all the way along the inner walls.

Below the agora, and leaning against its retaining wall, are the remains of a small **heroon**, where the deceased of one of the town's noble families once lay. You then see the more impressive **paved chambers** of the **baths**. On the third side of the esplanade there was once a small **temple dedicated to Artemis**.

With the sound of cicadas or mechanical excavators echoing in your ears, go down to the southern end of the site (under excavation) to the **gymnasium** and the **stadium**★, where part of the tiered seating has been unearthed. Some of the white marble **columns** of the double colonnade on the north side have been re-erected. To the east and west, simple Doric porticoes closed off the edifice at the end of the **track**, which also marks the southern limit of the town.

Return to where you began and take the road on the left.

Tour of the ramparts★★

The huge **walls**★★ that once protected the city are a fine sight, in their day a model for military architecture. Now hidden by vegetation, now rising above the olive trees and cypresses, the outsize 3m-thick stone wall snakes 9km down the mountainside, faithfully following every contour. There are several **towers**★, some round, others square, which accommodated the garrisons. Between the towers stand **monumental**

gateways. One in particular, the **Arcadia Gate****, 2km from Mavrománti, is well worth a look. It is probably the best preserved on the site and has **two entrances** separated by a vast **circular courtyard**. Note the art and precision – right down to the last millimetre – with which the masons cut and fitted the thousands of stones that made up the work.

To end the tour, you can either go down into the valley by following the walls, or retrace your steps to **Mavrománti**. Built in the shape of an amphitheatre among the olive trees and vines on the slopes of Mt Ithómi, this peaceful isolated village stands around a **fountain** with cool pure water.

COMING AND GOING

By boat – Kalamáta port is currently only used for freight. To go to Cythera, take a boat from Gíthio or Neápoli.

By air – *Kalamáta airport*, 8km north-west of the town, is mainly used by charters, ☎ (0721) 69 009, and has only 3 weekly connections with Athens. There's a bus every 30min to Kalamáta. Taxi rank.

Olympic Airways, ☎ (0721) 22 376, opposite the railway station in town. Monday-Friday, 8am-3.30pm.

By bus – The bus station is at the end of Odós Artémidos, west of the kástro. 12 daily connections with Athens, about ten buses to Pílos and Methóni, 3 to Areópoli and Gíthio, 2 to Patras, 2 to ancient Messene (except Sunday) and 2 to Mistra and Sparta. 3 weekly connections with Thessaloníki.

By train – The railway station is in the west of town, halfway between the fortress and the waterfront, ☎ (0721) 23 904. *Ticket office*: 7am-9am / 10.30am-11.15pm. Five trains a day to Trípoli, Árgos, Corinth, Athens and Piraeus, and three to Patras.

GETTING AROUND

By bus – Good bus network in the town itself. Stops on the waterfront (buses every 20min) and a shuttle between Kalamáta and Messíni via the airport (every 30min). ☎ (0721) 22 851.

By taxi – *Radio Taxi*, ☎ (0721) 26 565.

By rental vehicle – Several rental companies at the airport, around the seafront and at the marina, west of the commercial port. Among them, *Alamo Rent a Car*, ☎ (0721) 94 030 / 96 262.

By boat – *Kalamáta's yachting harbour* is 176 nautical miles from Piraeus and can accommodate 255 boats. Modern and well equipped (electricity, water, fuel, boat repairs, shower, WC, telephone, laundry, etc), it is the only one in the region, until the one at Pílos opens in a few years' time. *Harbour*, ☎ (0721) 22 059 / 21 959 / 21 054. *Harbourmaster's Office*, ☎ (0721) 22 218.

ADDRESS BOOK

Tourist information – Two offices: one at the marina (Monday-Friday, 7am-2.30pm), the other at the airport (closed on Sunday).

Tourist police – Aktí Miaoúli 30, at the intersection of the harbour and the marina, in a yellow building opposite a department store, ☎ (0721) 86 868.

Banks / Currency exchange – Plenty of banks in the area around the railway station (Platía Vassilíou Georgíou) and on the waterfront. *National Bank*, on the corner of Leofóros Navarínou and Odós Akríta.

Post office / Telephone – Two offices: one in Odós Iatropoúlou near the railway station, and the other near the tourist police at the harbour. *OTE*, on Platía Vassilíou Georgíou.

Police – ☎ (0721) 22 622.

Medical service – *Hospital*, behind the railway station, west of the railway line as you go towards Messíni ☎ (0721) 85 203 / 94 500 / 25 555.

WHERE TO STAY

Most of the mid- to top-of-the-range hotels are along the seafront. More modest places are near the railway station.

The Peloponnese

- **Railway station district**
Around €23
George, on the corner of Odós Dagre and Odós Frantzí, just beside the station, ☎ (0721) 27 225 / 29 127 – 7rm. 🛏 ✆ This small, clean, nicely laid-out hotel (but with no fans) fills up quickly in summer and at weekends. The young owners speak English. You have breakfast in a neighbouring café.
Byzantio, Odós Stathmoú 13, ☎ (0721) 83 251 – 86rm. 🛏 ✆ Near the place above. A modern, simple but comfortable hotel that charges reasonable rates.

- **Seafront**
Between €44 and €55
Elite, on the jetty, on the corner of Odós Vérga and Leofóros Navarínou, ☎ (0721) 22 434 – 57rm and 87 bungalows for 2 to 5 people. 🛏 🖥 ✆ 📺 ✕ ⛱ 🏊 ✖ CC This pleasant new hotel is surrounded by trees. All the bright, clean comfortable rooms have balconies looking onto the beach. You are given a courteous welcome in English. Good value for money.
Between €55 and €75
Filoxénia, at the beginning of Leofóros Navarínou when you arrive from the south, ☎ (0721) 23 166 to 8, Fax (0721) 23 343 – 210rm. 🛏 ✆ 🖥 📺 ✕ ⛱ ✖ 🏛 CC A large, modern and comfortable international hotel complex with restaurants both inside and out, a swimming pool, games for children, and a piano-bar with deep armchairs.

- **Old town**
Between €84.50 and €105
Rex, Odós Aristoménous 26, ☎ (0721) 27 492 / 21 227 – 42rm and 2 suites. 🛏 ✆ 🖥 📺 ✕ CC The illustrious Panhellinion hotel was destroyed by the earthquake in 1986, and reopened in 1999, 100 years after it was first built. It is back with its sumptuous old-fashioned decor, turn-of-the-century verandas and luxurious (and expensive) standard of comfort.

EATING OUT
Most of the modest tavernas and little fish restaurants may be found either around the marina, beyond the commercial port, or on Platía Vassilíou Georgíou, a sort of "rambla" west of the station that is fairly lively in the evening.

- **Seafront**
A small bar (no name) on Leofóros Navarínou, opposite the National Bank, prepares inexpensive *píta* and *souvláki*. Ideal for picnics and snacks for less than €4.
Around €7.50
I Psaropoúla, Leofóros Navarínou 14, a taverna right beside the water where the tables look onto a small fishing port. Excellent Greek dishes: grilled fish and *kokorétsi* (assorted offal kebabs, including goat), and quick, cheerful service.

- **Marina district**
Around €8
🍴**O Háris**, Odós Salamínos 17, with a private house and garden atmosphere. The very welcoming owner serves you the delicious dishes cooked by his wife. Try the *bakaliáro me skordaliá* (cod with garlic), washed down with a pleasant rosé.

HAVING A DRINK
Ice-cream parlour – Igloo, on Leofóros Navarínou, opposite the National Bank. One of the best ice-cream makers in town.

Cafés, bars – Roi Mat, in the middle of the seafront opposite the I Psaropoúla restaurant. A café with pool tables, pinball machines and video games.

Night-clubs – Mostly east of the waterfront near the campsites.

OTHER THINGS TO DO
Outdoor pursuits – Two **amusement parks** for children on Leofóros Navarínou, beside the sea, including one opposite Pharaoe Palace.

Market – Between the station and the citadel. Open every morning. One of the town sights, with its abundant offerings and feverish activity.

Local festivals – End of June to mid-July: **International Dance Festival**.

SHOPPING GUIDE
Arts and crafts – Household linen made of cotton or silk. Woven, embroidered or dyed by the nuns at the Monastery of St Constantine and St Helen, at the foot of the fortress, to the right of Ipapándi Cathedral.

Local delicacies – The famous **black Kalamáta olives**, as well as oranges, dried figs and *pastélli* (sesame cakes).

SPARTA
(SPÁRTI)
Province of the Peloponnese – Capital of the district of Lakonía
Regional map page 202 – Michelin map 980 folds 29-41
43km from Gíthio – 60km from Kalamáta (airport) – Pop 11 900

Not to be missed
The Museum.

Sparta, the ancient rival of Athens, had a curious fate. Quick to take offence, austere and bellicose, it had so little in the way of luxury and comfort and virtually no monuments or adornment that it has left nothing to posterity to evoke its past. Nothing, apart from a very few ruins and the memory of a particularly anti-democratic civilisation that put the peninsula to fire and the sword throughout the Peloponnesian War. Ironically, modern Sparta is an extremely peaceful provincial capital. It was designed to a grid plan by the engineers of King Otto in the mid-19C. Without much character, but close to Mistra and halfway between Trípoli and Gíthio, Sparta can serve as a convenient base for your excursions into Lakonía.

Order and inequality
In Mycenaean times, the city of Sparta was home to **Menelaus** and his beautiful wife **Helen** (an almost incongruous female figure in this world of men). It later exercised its forceful influence in the Peloponnese, and then throughout Greece, from the 9C to the 4C BC. The city's constitution, drawn up by the legislator **Lycurgus** in about 900 BC, provided for an oligarchy ruled by two kings, who were also military leaders, assisted by a council of 28 elders and 5 *ephors* who had executive power.

Spartan society was divided into three classes. First were the **hómoioi** or **equals** (at the very least, "more equal" than the others) who devoted themselves to warfare and governmental functions, all the while living off the land which they did not cultivate themselves. Then came the **períoikoi**, whose name means "dwellers from round about" (the state of Sparta), in other words, traders, craftsmen and farmers, free men who nonetheless had to pay tax. Lastly, at the bottom of the scale were the **Helots**, the most numerous but the people with the fewest civic rights. Reduced to slavery, they led a life of drudgery in an atmosphere of terror skilfully maintained by the dominant class.

An iron education
Life for members of the class of equals was extremely regimented. They were forbidden to work and mainly lived in barracks where they ate the famous black **broth**, pork stewed in the animal's blood with vinegar and salt. At the age of 7, the boys were chosen to be future warriors depending on their physical ability. Rather than becoming a burden on society, unfit or disabled children were thrown into a ravine from the top of a ridge 500m from today's village of Trípi in the Taíyetos Massif.

Laconic Lakonians
Not only were the Spartans of Lakonía strictly against any decorative flourishes or any superfluousness in their architectural style but they also despised the art of oratory as practised by the Athenians. So the citizens were asked to express themselves effectively and economically, leaving out all affectation or useless detail. This terseness of speech is at the origin of our word "laconic".

Able-bodied boys were drafted into youth troops in institutions without any comfort, where they underwent physical training and learnt the art of stealing (without getting caught). On reaching adulthood, they were taken to the Sanctuary of Artemis Orthia for a series of initiation tests or **krypteia**, during which they were flogged, sometimes to death. They were then abandoned without resources in the countryside where they proved their courage and virility by killing any Helots who tarried out of doors after dark. The girls also were given to strenuous exercise and, after reaching puberty, their role was to become the mothers of future warriors.

Tour of the town
Allow 2hr

This provincial town which King Otto wished to make capital of Greece is laid out around the main avenue, Leofóros Konstandínou Paleológou, a large thoroughfare planted with palm trees.

Museum★
In a public garden at the junction of Odós Likoúrgou and Leofóros K Paleológou. 8am-2pm; closed Monday. Entrance fee. Allow 30min. The oldest provincial museum in Greece is housed in a neo-Classical building and displays some interesting ancient works dating from the Archaic Era to Roman times. The first room, on the right, contains a series of 3C BC **mosaics★** that decorated the city's rich Hellenistic and Roman houses, including a **head of Medusa★** and, above the door, the portraits of six **Nereids**. The following room contains architectural elements from the Archaic Era (6C BC). The showpiece of the third room is the 5C BC **bust of a Spartan**, executed in the so-called "severe" style and thought to be King Leonidas of Sparta.

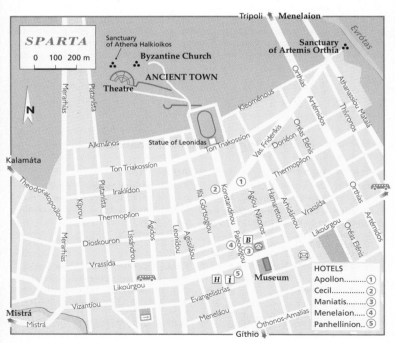

HOTELS
Apollon..........①
Cecil..............②
Maniatis.........③
Menelaion.....④
Panhellinion..⑤

other side of the entrance hall you can see an unusual collection of terracotta **ive masks***, used during the sacred dances performed in the Sanctuary of Artemis Orthia. There is also a **terracotta model of a Roman galley**, dating from the late 1C AD. Go up to the mezzanine to see a collection of 16C-13C BC objects from **Mycenaean tombs**, including pottery, jewellery and weapons.

Remains of the ancient town

Drive from the centre of town along Leofóros K Paleológou in the direction of Trípoli. When you reach the statue of Leonidas turn left and follow the signs. Leave your car at the foot of the hill. Free. Allow 30min. As Sparta was never fortified, when it began to decline it was particularly vulnerable to ruin and looting. What is left of the ancient city therefore consists mostly of the remains of the acropolis, dotted about a hill covered in olive trees. After walking past the ruins of a 10C **Byzantine church**, recognisable by its brick and stone walls, you follow the outline of an ancient **rampart** uphill. On the left, hewn out of the hillside opposite Mt Taÿgetos, the **theatre** now only comprises several dismantled rows of **tiered seats**, since the stones were used to build Mistra. Lastly, a few metres further on, you will see the foundations of a **sanctuary dedicated to Athena Halkioikos**.

Archaeology and history enthusiasts may like to continue to the **Sanctuary of Artemis Orthia** (Limenaíon), the site where the ritual endurance tests of young Spartans took place. All that remain are several **seats from Roman times** *(return to the statue of Leonidas, bear left into Odós Frideríkis, and then immediately right at the beginning of the main road to Trípoli).*

Similarly, the **Menelaion** *(4km east of Sparta. Take the Trípoli road, then the one on the right for Geráki. Next, bear right into a cement road, which ends up as a stony track. Allow 1hr there and back),* a monument built by the Spartans in honour of Menelaus and his wife Helen, will only interest history enthusiasts. Already austere when first erected, it is barely more evocative today with just a few blocks of grey stone on top of a solitary rise. The site is mainly worthwhile for the bird's-eye **view*** over the vast wooded plain of Sparta, blocked on the horizon by the tall outline of Mt Taÿgetos.

Making the most of Sparta

COMING AND GOING

By air – The nearest airport is 60km away at Kalamáta (see page 262).

By bus – 8 buses a day to Athens via Trípoli, 6 to Molái, 5 to Gíthio, 3 to Areópoli, 3 to Monemvassiá, and 2 to Kalamáta. The bus station is at the end of Odós Likoúrgou. ***Lakonía KTEL company***, ☎ (0731) 26 441 / 22 857.

GETTING AROUND

By taxi – Taxi rank on Leofóros K Paleológou, at the Menelaion hotel, ☎ (0731) 24 100 / 26 666 / 26 667.

ADDRESS BOOK

Tourist information – To find it, go to the main square, bear left round the former town hall (now a café) and climb the steps to the first floor. You will be given a charming welcome (in English) and a plan of the town. ☎ (0731) 24 852.

Banks / Currency exchange – Most of the banks are on Leofóros K Paleológou. The ***National Bank*** opposite the Menelaion hotel changes money and has a cash dispenser.

Police – ☎ (0731) 26 229 / 26 252.

Tourist police – ☎ (0731) 20 492.
Medical service – Hospital, ☎ (0731) 28 671 / 29 100 to 9.

WHERE TO STAY

Nearly all the hotels are on or around Leofóros K Paleológou.

Under €30

Panhellinion, Leofóros K Paleológou 65, ☎ (0731) 28 031 – 8rm. Probably the most spartan place in town: no private bathrooms, few fans, no dining room (breakfast is in the café opposite), and a rather vague attempt at sweeping. But it is central and relatively inexpensive.

Between €30 and €45

Cecil, Leofóros K Paleológou 125, ☎ (0731) 24 980, Fax (0731) 81 318 – 23rm. 📶 ♂ TV A little out of the town centre. A modest though clean and friendly place in a pre-war building. You can have breakfast (not included) at the nearby café.

Apollon, Odós Thermopílon 84, ☎ (0731) 22 491, Fax (071) 23 936. 📶 📧 ♂ TV ✕ cc An impersonal, rather faded hotel whose rooms with balconies give onto a quiet street.

Between €55 and €60

Maniatis, Leofóros K Paleológou 72-76, ☎ (0731) 22 665, Fax (0731) 29 994 – 80rm. 📶 📧 ♂ TV ✕ cc In a good central position. A pleasant place, in spite of the small rooms and bathrooms. The decor, which has been completely renovated, is pleasant and adds a bright touch. All the rooms have balconies and radios (background music).

Menelaion, Leofóros K Paleológou 91, ☎ (0731) 22 161, Fax (0731) 26 332 – 48rm. 📶 📧 ♂ TV ✕ ⅃ cc A hotel in a very good position, with spacious rooms and bathrooms, double glazing, and above all a swimming pool open from 7am to 7pm. However, the place could do with a little freshening up.

EATING OUT

Around €8

Elysé, Leofóros K Paleológou 113, to the right of the Menelaion hotel. A small candy-pink restaurant where they serve traditional dishes as well as some more unusual ones, such as "petit cochon aux aubergines" (in French on the menu) washed down with a pleasant local rosé.

Around €11.50

Maniatis, Leofóros K Paleológou 72-76, the restaurant in the hotel of the same name. Fairly pleasant with its neo-Spartan decor and cool airconditioning. Although there is a limited choice of desserts (4 dishes), the typically Greek menu also includes several French specialities. Closed on Sunday.

Menelaion, Leofóros K Paleológou 91. The restaurant, one of Sparta's elegant venues, is on a fairly cool patio beside the pool in the hotel of the same name. The menu offers a mixture of Greek and French dishes, including quiche Lorraine, pancakes and mushrooms with cream.

HAVING A DRINK

Cafés, bars – The best place for a quiet drink is the main square, which is lined with outdoor cafés. If you want something a little more hip, try the **Ministry Music Hall** (on Leofóros K Paleológou, opposite the Menelaion hotel).

Night-clubs – There are several discos in the suburbs of Sparta, especially on the Mistra road.

OTHER THINGS TO DO

Walking – The Taíyetos Massif is a wonderful area for walking and has a number of well-marked paths. Information and addresses for refuges provided by the **Sparta Climbing Club**, Odós Górtsoglou 97, ☎ (0731) 22 574.

Excursions – Various tours of the region are organised by local travel agents, such as **Skouros**, beside the Apollon hotel.

Feasts & festivals – 26 November: feast day of Ágios Níkonos, the town's patron saint.

SHOPPING GUIDE

Local delicacies – Black olives and juicy **oranges**, practically all year round.

MISTRA ★★★
(MISTRÁS)
Province of the Peloponnese – District of Lakonía
Regional map page 202 – Michelin map 980 fold 41
5km from Sparta – Accommodation in Sparta or Mistra

Not to be missed
The Church of St Sophia in the Upper Town, and the whole of the Lower Town.
And if you have any strength left, the De Villehardouin Castle.

And remember...
Leave for Mistra early in the morning to tour the place before it gets too hot.
Bring good walking shoes, a hat and water.
If you go to Mistra from Kalamáta by car,
fill up before crossing the Taíyetos Massif.

A steep hill standing out dramatically against the Taíyetos Massif is the setting for one of the most spellbinding places in Greece: Mistra, the former Byzantine capital of Morea, now listed as a UNESCO World Heritage site. Mistra's influence was such that, even in ruins, its palaces, churches, monasteries and seigneurial dwellings still testify to its magnificence. Though it may now be a ghost town, it still stands guard over Sparta and the Evrótas Plain, and is not as dead as some writers have made it out to be. At the very most it is slumbering in the shade of the cypress trees. Exquisite frescoes shimmer on the walls of its churches, and wild orchids flower symbolically among the stones in the spring.

The Mitrópoli of Ágios Dimítrios, Mistra

R. Mazza/ON LOCATION

From Franks to Byzantines

The first edifice of the future city was the castle built in 1249 by **Guillaume de Villehardouin**, Prince of Morea, who came from Champagne in France. Perched on its rock at a height of 621m facing the Evrótas Valley, it occupied an ideal position to protect Lakonía from incursions by the **Slav** peoples living on Mt Taíyetos. However, this Frankish domination lasted only ten years. Taken prisoner in Macedonia by the Byzantine emperor **Michael VIII Paleologus**, then reigning in Nicaea, Guillaume only recovered his freedom three years later by relinquishing his castle at Mistra and the fortresses at Monemvassiá and Maina. And so when he returned to Lakonía, he saw the future town being built without ever being able to recapture his castle. Mistra then became the seat of the Byzantine governor of the province. In the 14C, the town was made **capital of Morea**, which covered almost the whole of the Peloponnese and was reserved for the "despots", the younger sons or brothers of the Cantacuzenus and Paleologus emperors. It was there that the last Byzantine emperor, **Constantine Paleologus** was crowned before dying at the hands of the Turks during the siege of Constantinople (1449).

Livelier Christian art

The churches built in Mistra under the impetus of the despots had a traditional Byzantine plan (cruciform with domes) but showed great Western influence, with Italian belltowers, extended naves, and arcaded porches in the Cistercian style. Partly neglecting marble and mosaics that were a little too hieratic, the artists focused keenly on expressive, colourful frescoes. These showed a desire for realism and lively figures, with a vast number of picturesque details taken from everyday life.

Splendour...

Under the leadership of the despots, Mistra quickly became the main centre for the revival of Hellenic politics and culture. The inhabitants grew rich on the lucrative **silk** industry, and palaces, churches and mansions were built on the hill. Mistra exercised an unprecedented intellectual influence over the whole region. Renowned artists, scholars and philosophers, some of whom had studied in Italy, flocked to the town. Among them were **Manuel Chrisolorás**, who had taught Neo-Platonic philosophy in Florence in 1397, and the humanist **Plethon** (1360-1452), who called himself the Renaissance Plato. A Greek philosopher and humanist, Geórgios Gemistós introduced Greek letters to Renaissance Italy. A great admirer of Plato, he showed little modesty in calling himself Plethon, which in Greek means a man gifted with every talent, knowing everything about everything. During the lively discussions between Byzantines and Italians on the impossible union of the Roman Catholic and Orthodox Churches, he visited Florence in 1439 and founded an Academy of Neo-Platonism. There he advocated revolutionary ideas, including social reform through limiting the

Mistra

rights of the land-owning classes (the aristocracy and the Church), the renewal of moral values, and the reinforcement of Christian dogma with the theories professed by Plato.

... and decline

In 1460, Mistra was surrendered to the Ottomans by Demetrius Paleologus, Emperor Constantine's brother. The churches were converted into mosques and the Despots' Palace became the residence of the Pasha. In the 17C, the town was still flourishing thanks to the silk industry, which the Ottomans encouraged, and the inhabitants numbered 42 000. Despite a short Venetian interlude (1687-1715), the town remained Ottoman until the country's independence. Its first ordeals occurred in 1770 when Russian troops under **Count Orloff** put it to fire and the sword, brutally massacring the population. The Turks took their revenge with a ten-year period of violent acts and killings. Nonetheless, when Chateaubriand visited Mistra in 1806, the town was still thriving with 8 000 inhabitants. The deathblow was given by the Egyptian troops of **Ibrahim Pasha** during the War of Independence. Afterwards, the city was completely abandoned by King Otto, and its status as regional capital was given up in favour of Sparta in 1834.

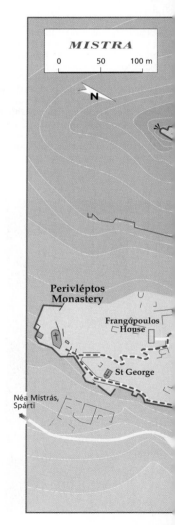

Head west out of Sparta in the direction of Mistra. There are two entrances to the site, one at the bottom of the hill (beside the Xenía restaurant), and the other at the top. As the terrain is steep, it is advisable to begin the tour at the top, starting with the castle and then continuing down the hill. Drive directly up to the top entrance (car park), and at the end of the tour take a taxi back up the road (card-operated phone at the site exit), or hitchhike.

The bus from Sparta drops you off and collects you from the bottom (see "Making the most of Mistra"). So to get to the top, you have to either take a taxi or get a lift.

Mistra hill is divided into three sections: the castle (kástro), which dominates the whole site, and the two walled districts of the city below, the Upper and Lower Town, connected by Monemvassiá Gate. 8am-7pm (in theory). Entrance fee. Allow a good half day, including 1hr there and back to see the castle. Bring suitable clothing to enter the churches.

The Kástro and Upper Town★

Castle★ (kástro)

You either get there directly by bus, or walk along a steep winding track that leads off to the right of the entrance to the Upper Town. The climb is quite tough, so allow a good quarter of an hour. The castle was built by the De Villehardouins and then altered by the Byzantines and the Turks. It has spectacular **double walls★** that you can walk along. Heading left alongside the first rampart, you come to a **vaulted gateway**, flanked by a **stout tower**, which marks the entrance. Inside is the second rampart, which protected the seigneurial mansion. This is where Guillaume II de Villehardouin and his wife Anna Comnenus held court in grand style surrounded by their Frankish knights. The place is in ruins and is mainly worthwhile for the impressive **views★★** over the sheer ravines facing Mt Taíyetos and over the red roofs of the town facing the plain.

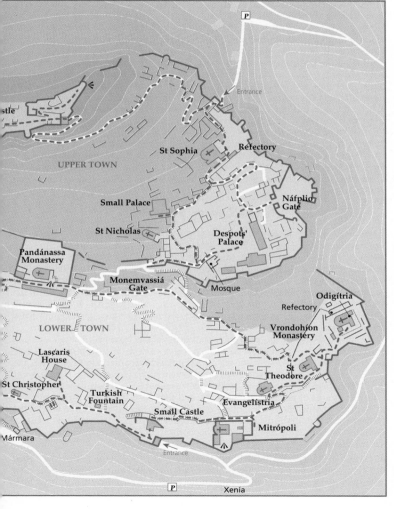

The Upper Town★★

Access along a paved path that goes down as far as the Despots' Palace, surrounded by seigneurial mansions. The first edifice you reach is the **Church of St Sophia★**, standing just beyond an arch. It was built in the mid-14C by Manuel Cantacuzenus, the first Despot of Mistra, and was so called as a tribute to the great basilica in Constantinople with the same name. Inside its detached bell-tower, of which only two levels remain, is a spiral staircase suggesting that the tower was used as a minaret under the Turks. Inside the church are well-restored walls and, on the floor, the remains of polychrome marble **paving**. In the soft light filtering through the windows in the dome you can see portions of **frescoes★** including a peaceful Christ in Majesty *(in the apse)* and, in the chapel on the right, the Nativity of the Virgin. Just to the left of the entrance is the imposing façade of a **monastery refectory**, a long building with windows and niches.

When you come to the first fork, head right to the **Small Palace** (Palatáki), Mistra's oldest and largest seigneurial mansion *(in ruins)*. Standing out just below is the **Church of St Nicholas**, the town's only post-Byzantine church.

Closing off the Upper Town, the **Despots' Palace★** (Despotikó Anáktoro) *(currently being restored; closed)* occupies two sides of an immense **esplanade** once used for public meetings and celebrations. This is where you can imagine the philosopher Plethon having discussions with his followers. The oldest part is on the right, probably built in the time of Guillaume de Villehardouin. The **pointed windows** and the stone **balcony** are reminiscent of Western architecture. The other buildings were erected under successive despots between the 14C and 15C.

By going left round the palace, you come to the **Náfplio Gate**, formerly the main entrance to the Upper Town. Further down, you reach the **Monemvassiá Gate★**, the only access between the upper and lower parts of the town. It is protected by a massive **square tower** pierced with loopholes, and once had a heavy iron portcullis.

The Lower Town★★

Pandánassa Monastery★★

The narrow cobbled alleyway from the Monemvassiá Gate leads directly to one of the most outstanding buildings in Mistra, the Pandánassa Monastery. This is the only building still inhabited, by nuns, who will welcome you into a lovely flower-filled courtyard cooled by a fountain. After being offered some Turkish delight, you will be asked to put on suitable clothing for the tour. The monastery was founded in the 15C by John Frangópoulos, the chief Paleologian minister of Mistra. It has been well restored and the buildings form a harmonious synthesis of all the architectural styles used in Mistra.

Climb the steps up to the **church★★** dedicated to the Pandánassa Virgin (Queen of the Universe). The façade is flanked by a superb French-inspired Gothic **porch-belfry★** with trefoil oculi, set off by pinnacles (corner towers). Inside, the church has a basilical plan which becomes cruciform at the upper level to support the domes. Take the time to look at the **wall frescoes★★**. These form one of the most complete groups of paintings in the town, and they have the most marked sense of realism, as is borne out by the expressiveness of the people depicted, the flow of the garments and the use of the complex architectural setting. Don't miss the beautiful *Ascension*, beneath the dome behind the iconostasis, or *Christ's entry into Jerusalem* in the left transept.

By leaving the monastery through the door at the back, you come to the paved path that continues down the hill. It goes past **Frangópoulos House**, which has kept its majestic 15C façade set off by a long **stone balcony★** onto which open two high windows.

Perivléptos Monastery★★★

A short distance below Frangópoulos House, you come to the restrained **arched gateway** of the Perivléptos Monastery. On it is a **monogram** of the motto *"Perivleptos"* ("seen from every side") flanked by two lions. Of the former monastery there remain the **refectory**, on the ground floor of a **high tower**, and the **church★★**, flanked by two funerary chapels. The church was built in the 13C with a Greek-cross plan and a detached bell-tower. When it was altered in the 14C, it was decorated with exceptionally beautiful **frescoes★★★** illustrating the New Testament and the Life of the Virgin. Picturesque, inventively detailed and wonderfully coloured, these are indisputably the finest in Mistra. In the dome is a Christ Pantocrator (in Majesty), surrounded by the Virgin Mary and the Apostles. Dotted about on either side are twelve scenes from the Life of Christ, particularly a wonderful *Nativity* (where Mary is resting on a rock), a *Baptism of Jesus* and an *Entry into Jerusalem* enlivened with children playing. Note, in the *Resurrection of Lazarus*, the moving expression of the man's friends in mourning, and the two weeping angels in the *Descent from the Cross*. Above the entrance door is a magnificent composition of the *Dormition of the Virgin*, in which Christ is shown standing behind the tomb, holding his mother's soul represented by a baby. In the left apse are two processions of angels from the *Holy Liturgy*, another of Mistra's masterpieces. The lively movements, graceful garments and exquisite colours are unequalled.

Outside, as you continue downhill, note the stone and brick facing on the nearby **funerary chapels★** built by the local nobility. The first chapel is dedicated to **St George**, and the second, further on, to **St Christopher**.

Just above the second chapel, you will see the façade of the **Lascaris House**. Although quite badly damaged, it is a fine example of a 14C Byzantine mansion. The vaulted ground floor probably served as stables, above which were two floors of living quarters.

Mistra

Byzantine masterpieces: frescoes in Pandánassa Monastery

R. Meazza/ON LOCATION

Back on the main path, you soon come to a shady esplanade with a **Turkish fountain**. Then you reach an **arched passageway** over which a house was built. Go past the **small castle**, which marked the former entrance to the town (*near the present access to the site*), and turn right.

Mitrópoli★★ (Ágios Dimítrios Cathedral)

Founded by the metropolitan bishop Eugenius in the late 13C, the Mitrópoli is the oldest church in Mistra. You reach it through a courtyard off which a **monumental stairway** leads down to the church square. In the 15C, the original basilica with a nave and two aisles had a floor added with a **gynaeceum**, a gallery for women (*closed for restoration*). When the five domes were built, most of the early paintings in the transept were seriously damaged but the multicoloured marble **paving★** was saved. The best-preserved **frescoes★★** are in the north aisle on the courtyard side, where you can see eleven scenes of the **torture of St Demetrius★** (14C). But the most characteristic work, in the opposite aisle, is the grandiose composition covering the vault and illustrating the theme of the **Hetoimasía**, (Preparation). It shows an empty throne surmounted by the Byzantine cross and surrounded by angels with ecstatic expressions on their faces. The image symbolises the expectation of the Second Coming of Christ for the Last Judgement. All the neighbouring frescoes also evoke the Last Judgement, including those of two beautiful angels holding the records of Good and Evil.

Outside, the church square extends left into a second courtyard, dating from the 18C, where there is a superb **view★** over the plain. A **Roman sarcophagus** there was once used as a basin for the Mármara Fountain. To the left, a wooden staircase leads to a small **museum** (*same times as the site; closed on Monday*) containing diverse objects found at Mistra: icons, fresco fragments, pottery remains dating from the Middle Ages, and in a display case, the hair and dress of a woman whose tomb has been exhumed.

On leaving the Cathedral, you pass by the church of the Evangelistria (well-restored but closed).

Vrondohíon Monastery★★

The last call on your tour is the Vrondohíon Monastery, which served as a sort of cultural centre where the philosopher Plethon taught. Within its walls are two great churches. The first, dedicated to **St Theodore★** (Ágii Theódori) (late 13C) is mainly noteworthy for its **great dome★**, the highest in Mistra. It is supported by eight pillars and rests on a 16-sided drum. This majestic structure encouraged worshippers to look upwards, where they would see an immense **Christ Pantocrator★**. The walls were once adorned with **polychrome marble** (fragments).

The **Church of Odigítria★★** (Afendikó), is twenty years younger. It is dedicated to the Virgin "who shows the way", and is characteristic of Mistra's architectural style: a basilical plan with a nave and two aisles separated by rows of three columns, surmounted by an upper level which has a cruciform plan and is topped by domes. Like its neighbour, the church had polychrome marble (no longer visible) on the walls framing portraits of prelate saints: Gregory of Nyssa, Basil, John Chrysostom, etc. But it is also decorated with magnificent 14C **wall paintings★★** by different schools. In the narthex are the Miracles performed by Jesus (Healing of the Blind Man, the Samaritan at the Well, the Marriage at Cana, etc), masterpieces whose detail, freshness and harmony of colour suggest the influence of Duccio or Giotto. At the far end of the narthex, on the left, a funerary chapel contains the **Tomb of Pachomius**, the founder of the monastery, and the **Tomb of Theodore II Paleologus**, shown on the wall as despot (*left*) and as the monk he became at the end of his life (*right*). Higher up on the same side is a very well preserved **Procession of Martyrs★★**, one of the jewels of the church. In a second chapel, at the other end of the narthex, are the Greek texts of **chrysobulls**, imperial decrees granting rights and privileges to the monastery.

A narrow stairway leads from the chapel to the floor with the **gynaeceum**, also decorated with brilliantly coloured paintings, among them the *Resurrection* and the *Flight into Egypt*. On the side walls are full-length paintings of **70 apostles**.

Outside, several buildings (most in ruins) form part of the monastery precinct, including the **refectory**, a long narrow building behind the bell-tower.

To leave the site, retrace your steps to the small castle.

Making the most of Mistra

COMING AND GOING

See also *"Making the most of Sparta"*, page 266.

By bus – Runs every hour between Sparta and Mistra. Buses leave from the corner of Odós Likoúrgou and Odós Leonídou, terminus near the Xenía restaurant. Be warned: not all the buses go up to the restaurant. Enquire when you board and get your ticket.

By taxi – Radio-taxi, ☎ (0731) 83 450.

ADDRESS BOOK

Police – ☎ (0731) 83 315.

Medical service – *Mistra medical centre*, ☎ (0731) 51 215 / 51 259.

WHERE TO STAY

The new village of Mistra has few possibilities for accommodation, so it is best to stay in Sparta.

Campsites (around €12)

Castle View, outside the village on the Sparta road, ☎ (0731) 83 303. ✗ ⚊ A shady, clean, well-equipped site with a swimming pool and a good taverna. The Sparta bus stops just at the entrance.

Palaiológo, on the Sparta road, halfway between the two towns, ☎ (0731) 25 256. ✗ ⚊ A large field shaded by orange trees and open all year. A welcome swimming pool in summer. Minibus shuttle service to Sparta (2km).

Between €45 and €68

Hotel Byzántion, in the middle of the village, ☎ (0731) 83 309, Fax (0731) 20 019 – 26rm. ⌁ ▤ ♂ ⎘ 🅲🅲 This pleasant, recently renovated hotel is clean and comfortable (spacious rooms and bathrooms, most with a view over ancient Mistra hill).

EATING OUT

Mistra has restaurants of all categories, ranging from elegant tavernas to modest fast-food places.

• Mistra

Around €7.50

O Palaiológos, ☎ (0731) 83 373, in the middle of the village, with a terrace set among the fruit trees. With its friendly atmosphere and traditional Greek dishes, it's a favourite with families from Sparta.

Around €12

Xenía, above the village, ☎ (0731) 20 500. Surrounded by greenery and dominating the whole of the Sparta plain. A good restaurant serving excellent traditional Greek dishes, washed down with a pleasant carafe of rosé. Very popular with local polite society, it is literally taken by storm at weekends. Arrive before 8.30pm to get a table on the terrace.

• Trípi

A little mountain village surrounded by chestnut trees in the Taíyetos Massif, 9km west of Mistra. On very hot evenings, the local inhabitants get together in the airy tavernas.

OTHER THINGS TO DO

Local festivals – For 3 days at the end of May, the **Paleológia** festivities are held in honour of the ancient city, with religious ceremonies, *son et lumière* shows, etc. During the village festival from 26 to 31 August, there is a market as well as concerts of traditional music.

Cake shop, in the middle of the village, where you can try tasty "Byzantine" pastries.

THE METHÓNI PENINSULA★

FROM KALAMÁTA TO KIPARISSÍA ALONG THE COAST

Province of the Peloponnese – District of Messinía – Regional map page 202
Michelin map 980 folds 28-40 – 170km tour – Allow 2 days
Accommodation in Pílos or in one of the peninsula's many hotels

Not to be missed
A trip aboard a caique in Navarino Bay.
Methóni Fortress and Nestor's Palace.

And remember...
To appreciate the wildlife of the Giálova Lagoon, get there in the early morning
and bring a pair of binoculars.

Although somewhat off the beaten track and overshadowed by lofty Mistra and the Máni citadels – the Methóni Peninsula is nevertheless full of charm and character. The landscapes are mellower and less rugged here, inviting travellers to spend a few days relaxing. When not swimming at one of the peninsula's long sandy beaches watched over by a Venetian fortress, you can also catch a glimpse of history: Homeric Greece at the Palace of Nestor, who was one of the heroes of the Trojan War; and the Battle of Navarino Bay that set Pílos harbour ablaze in the 19C.

Southern landscape

Wedding Gift

According to legend, it was a young bride who caused Messinía to be settled. When **Messene**, daughter of a prince of Árgos, married Polykaon, son of the King of Lelegia, she persuaded her warrior husband to invade the peninsula and settle there. It was quite a gift, because the region later described by Euripides as "bearing fine fruit" turned out to be full of springs and watercourses.

The inhabitants of the peninsula, who had become Achaeans in 1500 BC, fought in the Trojan War under one of their most famous princes, **Nestor**, King of Pílos. Thereafter its history resembles that of many regions of Greece; it became a Roman province in 146 BC, then a Frankish domain in the Middle Ages before being taken over alternately by the Venetians and the Turks. On 20 October 1827, **Navarino Bay** (now Pílos) was the site of one of the greatest naval battles of the War of Independence – a decisive event in Greece's liberation.

The east coast of the peninsula★

The peninsula can be reached either by the highway directly connecting Kalamáta and Pílos or by the far prettier coast road running along the Gulf of Messinía (our choice).

■ **Koróni★** – *50km from Kalamáta. Allow 2hr on foot.* This charming, peaceful city perched on a rocky promontory overlooking the sea was an important maritime centre in the Middle Ages. Little lanes and stairways lined with trim **medieval houses** with coloured shutters lead up to the **old town** *(follow the signs for the "Hotel Panorama").* After a pause on the graceful **arcaded square★** – a reminder of the Venetian and

B. Kaufmann/MICHELIN

A highly coveted place

The peninsula where Methóni Fortress stands – the ideal place for watching over the entrance to the Ionian Sea – was already the site of an ancient city and a medieval town. On their way back from the Crusades, the Venetians built a powerful fortress here that also contained dwellings. Its defences were so strong that it took 100 000 men, 500 cannons and a month of bombarding for Ottoman General Beyazit to capture it in 1500. The citadel remained in the hands of the Turks for nearly three centuries except for a second Venetian occupation from 1686 to 1715. It was attacked by Greek Admiral Miaoúlis in 1824 and was finally seized in 1828 by General Maison.

Genoese presence here – you reach the imposing **Gothic door** of the **citadel**★. Inland, a vast wooded plateau still has a few **churches** and a **Byzantine monastery**.

Continuing all the way down you reach **Zanga beach**★ (*20min on foot from the centre of town*), below the **gardens of Panagía Eleistra Church**.

■ You might prefer the beach in the village of **Finikoúnda** (*25km to the west*), which is equally attractive in its setting of hills covered with vineyards and crops grown under glass.

■ **Methóni**★★ – *38km from Koróni and 13km from Finikoúnda. Allow 2hr including a swim.* This southernmost town on the west coast of the Peloponnese is quite a pleasant place with its old houses and wrought-iron balconies. Full of flowers and well-equipped for tourism, Methóni is mainly known for its magnificent **sandy beach**★ and its **Venetian citadel**★★, one of the best preserved in the entire Mediterranean (*cross town to the promontory where it stands and leave your vehicle in the car park; 8am-8pm weekdays, 9am-8pm on Sunday; free entrance; allow 1hr*).

After crossing the majestic **stone bridge**★ built in 1828 by the French, you enter a paved street on the left surrounded by high walls. Here there are **three gateways**, creating a medieval atmosphere not unlike the streets of Rhodes, but without the crowds. They lead inside the fortress, a vast esplanade where weeds and caper bushes run wild. The **granite column** used to be topped by a lion of St Mark. Follow the eastern ramparts (*on the left*) lined with the ruins of several buildings: a **Turkish bath**, some **cisterns**, a **powder magazine** and a **Roman Catholic cathedral**. An octagonal Turkish tower (16C), the **Boúrtzi Tower**★★, rises from the sea at the southern tip of the citadel at the end of another **stone bridge** battered by the waves. Climb up to its sentry walk to see the superb **panorama**★★ that takes in the fort, the bay and the islands of **Sapiéntza** and **Schíza** emerging from the blue waters of the Ionian Sea. Walk back to your starting point on the western side.

Drive 12km north along the west coast to Pílos.

The graceful arches of Sotíros Church shaded by cypress trees (Pílos)

G. de Rénoise/MICHELIN

■ **Pílos**★★ (Navarino) — *Allow a morning of walking (1 entire day including an excursion in the bay).* Sheltered on the west by the rocky wall of Sfaktiría Island, the Bay of Pílos is one of the finest and most secure in the whole Mediterranean. The city itself, spreading out like an amphitheatre facing the sea, was founded by French expeditionary forces in 1829.

Take time to wander down the steep little streets and stairs leading to **Platía Tríon Navárhon (Three Admirals Square)**★ with its peaceful cafés shaded by gigantic plane trees. In the centre stands a monument dedicated to the victors of the Battle of Navarino Bay.

The exposed little **harbour**, which has a marina, is overlooked by fine old houses including the birthplace of **Kostís Tsiklitíras**, a high-jump and long-jump champion at the London Olympics of 1908 and again at Stockholm in 1912.

Have a look inside the **Archaeological Museum** (*Odós Filelínon, which starts at Platía Tríon Navárhon next to the Agricultural Bank; 8.30am-3pm; closed on Monday; entrance fee*). The few display cases contain objects ranging from prehistoric times (stone tools, at the entrance) to the Hellenistic Period (three fine, well-preserved **coloured-glass vases**).

On your way out of town on the Methóni road, be sure to climb up to the **citadel**★ (Neókastro) ("new castle") built by the Turks in 1573 and restored by the French not long after the Battle of Navarino Bay (*Tuesday-Sunday, 8.30am-3pm; entrance fee; allow 1hr*). Its

Navarino, an improvised battle

Far from being decided by staff headquarters, the naval battle preceding Greece's independence was in fact the result of what English King George IV called a "terrible misunderstanding". The 26 English, French and Russian ships that had taken up position around Pílos Bay on that 20 October 1827 were only meant to intimidate the Turko-Egyptian fleet anchored there, not to attack them. But the Turks didn't get the message. At first sight of the Allied ships they fired a few cannonballs, triggering a response... and the subsequent battle. Despite their superior fire power (2 400 cannons and backup from the artillery at Neókastro), the Turks were surrounded on all sides and lost 82 ships and 6 000 men (compared to 174 on the Allied side).

powerful **ramparts**, reinforced on the southern side by impressive **towers**★, form a defensive wall 1 566m long, enclosing an area offering a superb **panorama**★★ over the bay. It is crowned by a **hexagonal fort**, or **"redoubt"**, forming an inner bastion. Chirping crickets have replaced the roar of cannon, but the atmosphere inside these high walls still evokes the various episodes in the citadel's history. A **museum** to the left of the entrance contains souvenirs from the War of Independence. **Sotíros Church**, further along on the right, is a former mosque converted by the Franks.

■ **Tour of Navarino Bay**★★ — *See also "Making the most of Pílos".* If you have time, treat yourself to a delightful tour of Navarino Bay by caique (*4-5hr*), with several short stops. On **Sfaktiría Island**, closed off on the bay side by magnificent **cliffs**★★, there are funerary monuments dedicated to Greek and foreign heroes who died in the War of Independence. On the northern side of the island, the well-preserved walls of a **medieval fortress** are still standing on top of a high rock (*allow 30min to climb up*). An underground passageway connects it to a cave known as **Nestor's Cave**, a natural cavity adorned with stalactites where the King of Pílos is supposed to have sheltered his cattle. There is a funerary monument in memory of 540 French sailors who died in the battle of Navarino Bay on the **small island of Pílos** at the foot of the citadel in the southern part of the island.

Go through the village of Giálova 8km north of Pílos, then turn left towards "Golden Beach". Follow the beach between two rows of eucalyptus trees until you reach a dirt road (suitable for cars, but very narrow in places). Drive slowly.

The Methóni Peninsula

■ The dirt road disappears into **Giálova lagoon★**, a vast stretch of still waters where over **250 species of birds** live, together with **chameleons** and **logger-head sea turtles** (harder to see). The best time to explore the area is early in the morning when this beautiful aquatic landscape can be seen in the soft light of dawn, bathed in a deep silence that is only broken by the birds frolicking in the reeds. For a swim, head for **Golden beach★**, a lovely beach with fine sand (*taverna, parasols, etc*).

Beyond Giálova go through the village of Korifássi and follow the signs for Nestor's Palace.

■ **Nestor's Palace★** – *20km from Pílos, 48km from Kiparissía. The bus from Pílos to Kiparissía stops near the palace and the museum in Hóra. 8.30am-3pm; closed on Monday. Entrance fee. Allow 1hr.* The three buildings composing the palace of this hero of the Trojan War, which stand on a hilltop amid a sea of olive trees, are sheltered now-adays by a metal canopy that mars the landscape a bit. But the site is worth the trip. With its 1m-high walls and remains of stairs, this group of royal buildings is one of the best-preserved Mycenaean palaces. Nestor's Palace – built at the same time as the ones in Mycenae and Tírintha (13C BC) – was also destroyed in the 12C BC (*see page 19*). Unlike them it has no ramparts, which gives it a particularly peaceful feeling.

Nestor, the wise hero

Nestor, King of Pílos, was described by Homer as a wise man, one of the few who tried to bring peace to the Greek camp during the Trojan War. He lived to a ripe old age and took part in several legendary expeditions: the Argonauts' voyage to bring back the Golden Fleece (see page 50), the battle against the Centaurs in which he fought on the side of Theseus and the Lap-iths, and the Trojan War. On returning home from that war, he welcomed inside his palace the young Telemachus who was searching for his father, Odysseus.

The official rooms, or **main palace**, are reached through a **propylaea** with a **guardroom** on the right and an **archival room** on the left where 1 250 terracotta tablets inscribed in "Linear B" were discovered, facilitating the de-ciphering of Ancient Greek writing (*see page 19*). Beyond the courtyard is a once richly decorated **megaron**, or throne room, with an open hearth and holes for the four columns that sup-ported the ceiling. A long **corridor** on the right gives onto various waiting rooms and storerooms, the outlines of which are clearly delineated by what is left of the walls, as well as the first eight steps of a staircase that led up to the first floor. Behind the guardroom, where there was another staircase, are the **queen's quarters**, which also had an open hearth and a **bathroom** (*on the right*) that still contains a bathtub.

To the left of the main palace past a paved courtyard are the remains of an **older palace**. On the other side are the **outbuildings**, **storerooms** for oil and wine, and administrative offices, along with a little **sanctuary**.

One hundred metres past the car park are numerous **beehive tombs** (tholos) adjoining the palace that look like the ones at Mycenae (*see page 218*).

Take the road to Kiparissía and stop off at Hóra, 4km to the north. The museum is at the top of the village.

■ The **Hóra Archaeological Museum★** (*8.30am-3pm; closed on Monday; entrance fee; allow 30min*) contains finds from the site of Nestor's Palace and the nearby beehive tombs – 4 000 items from various eras. The first room mainly has **gold cups★** and other pieces of **gold jewellery** discovered in a tholos. The second room has mag-nificent **frescoes★** from the palace, as well as a fine collection of **vases** and **votive pottery**. In the last room stands a huge **pithos** (earthenware jar) nearly 2m tall and **two chimneys** also from the palace. Don't miss the display case with a pair of per-fectly balanced **scales**.

- Continuing through the vineyards and olive groves towards Kiparissía, the road runs through the villages of **Filiatrá**, with its miniature Eiffel Tower, and **Ágrilos**, whose main attraction has nothing to do with Classical – or even neo-Classical – architecture: the **Castle of the Fairytales** (*only the outside can be visited*), a strange, unclassifiable construction built by local folk artist Konstantínos Broumídis (1805-80). Its spiky red roofs, many-coloured coats of arms and giant sculptures look out sadly over the rocky coast.

- Halfway between Methóni and Pírgos (Olympia), the seaside resort of **Kiparissía** is a useful place to stay – particularly as it has the region's only **railway station**, with daily connections to Athens. It also has a fine **sandy beach** and a **Frankish castle** (*free entrance; best seen at sunset*). Good for a one-night stay, but not for a longer holiday.

Making the most of the Methóni Peninsula

COMING AND GOING

By air – The closest airport is 52km away, in Kalamáta (see page 262).

By bus – 6 buses run daily between Pílos and Kalamáta, going around the peninsula. The **Pílos bus station** is located on the main square under the arcades, ☎ (0723) 22 230.

There are 2 buses a day to Athens from **Pílos**.

By train – The region's only railway station is in **Kiparissía**. 10 trains a day run between Pírgos (Olympia), Patras, Diakoftó, Corinth and Athens (about 10hr).

GETTING AROUND

By taxi – In **Pílos**, ☎ (0723) 22 555. In **Methóni**, ☎ (0723) 31 333.

ADDRESS BOOK

Tourist information – Although there is no official tourist information office, the villages all have travel agencies that can arrange accommodation and transport.

In Koróni, **Pelasgi Agency**, ☎ (0723) 22 717, on a pedestrian street below the fortress. In Pílos, **M-Travel**, Odós Filelínon 11, ☎ (0723) 22 696, Fax (0723) 22 676, eleonas@otenet.gr

Banks / Currency exchange – In **Koróni**, the Agricultural Bank is on a pretty square in the old town. In **Pílos**, the National Bank on the main square has a cash dispenser. In **Kiparissía**, the Agricultural Bank is on the main square (Platía Dimárhou) in the centre of town. Cash dispenser.

Post office – In **Pílos**: from the main square follow signs for the "Hotel Arvaniti", then for the post office. In **Kiparissía**: on the main square (Platía Dimárhou) in the centre of town.

Telephone – In **Pílos**, there is card-operated phone by the "O Aetós" café near the pier. The OTE is on the same street as the post office.

Police – In **Koróni**, ☎ (0725) 22 422. In **Pílos**, ☎ (0723) 22316. In **Methóni**, ☎ (0723) 31 203.

Medical service – Doctor on call in **Koróni**, ☎ (0725) 73 218. **Pílos Hospital**, ☎ (0723) 22 315. There is a pharmacy under the arcades on the main square. Another doctor on call in **Methóni**, ☎ (0723) 31 456.

WHERE TO STAY

The peninsula is quite popular and has numerous hotels, campsites and rooms for rent, particularly in tourist centres such as Pílos, Methóni and Koróni.

• Koróni

Campsite (around €12)
Koróni campsite, north of town near a bus stop, ☎ and Fax (0725) 22 119. ⚓ 📺 ✗ ⚒ 🅿 🐾 A nice campsite – with a pool shaded by a palm tree – that also rents out bungalows with kitchens and TVs.

Around €38
Inn on the beach, 3km south-west of town, ☎ (0725) 22 401 – 93rm. ⚓ 🅿 ✗ 🐾 A nice hotel that is slightly out-of-the-way, usually full of groups (reservations recommended). Animals allowed. Open all year.

• Methóni

Between €30 and €45
Áris, in the centre of town on a quiet little square 150m from the sea, ☎ (0723) 31 125 – 28rm. ⚓ All the rooms in this modest but comfortable family-run hotel have balconies. When you call to book, ask for one with a view.

Between €40 and €57
Kástello, not far from the citadel, 50m from the sea, ☎ and Fax (0723) 31 300 – 24rm. ⚓ A recent hotel (1990) with a garden. Rooms are modest but comfortable, some with balconies. Animals allowed. Open all year.

• Pílos

Between €43 and €54
Hotel Karalís, Odós Kalamáta 26, ☎ (0723) 22960, Fax (0723) 22970 – 35rm. ⚓ 📺 🅿 📺 🆑 A charming hotel – like a family home – in an old house on the coast road leading down to the centre of town. The small but comfortable rooms have balconies and a 1930s-style decor. Hearty breakfast.

Between €58 and €66
🦞**Karalís Beach Hotel**, between the fortress and the beach, ☎ (0723) 23 021 / 22, Fax (0723) 22 970 – 14rm. ⚓ 📺 🅿 📺 🆑 This is definitely the best hotel in town, and it is very well situated, nestling in a pine forest at the very end of a road below the fortress 20m from the sea (little beach with a landing-stage). The comfortable rooms have large bathrooms, and those overlooking the sea have balconies. The little terrace bar is an inviting place to have a drink to the sound of lapping waves and soft music.

• Giálova

Campsite (around €12)
Navarino Beach Camping, at the entrance to the village. The tents are set up to the right of the road as you arrive from Pílos. The reception and restaurant are by the beach. Modest facilities, a mini-market and a few games for children.

Between €24 and €51
Zoé, along the beach, ☎ (0723) 22 025, Fax (0723) 22 026 – 35rm or apartments with kitchens. ⚓ ✗ 🐾 🆑 A row of banana and tamarisk trees separates the beach from this modest but friendly hotel. The restaurant tables set up under the trees are as Greek as they come. Reservations recommended. If the hotel is full, they will find a room for you in the "annex" on the way out of the village, a clean and new building but in a less pleasant setting.

Between €36 and €60
Villa Marías (Eleónas Cottage), on the way out of the village on the Korifássi road, at the end of a practicable (and signposted) road; the property is managed by the M Travel agency, ☎ (0723) 22 696, Fax (0723) 22 676 – 14 bungalows and 2 apartments. ⚓ 🏠 🆑 A series of smart, well-equipped modern houses scattered over a hillside covered with fruit trees 800m from the sea. Quiet, peaceful and a little out-of-the-way (personal transport is the most practical solution here).

• Kiparissía

Campsite (around €12)
🦞**Kyparisía**, a really pretty spot at the end of the village by the seaside,

☎ (0761) 23 491, Fax (0761) 24 519. Buildings in the local style. Warm welcome. Games for children. Note that places are hard to come by in August.

Between €27 and €38
Iónion, just across from the railway station, ☎ (0761) 22 511, Fax (0761) 22 512. ⚄ 🍽 🖊 🆃🆅 🆑🆑 Clean but anonymous rooms whose only advantage is in being opposite the station in case of an unexpected stopover.

Kiparissía Beach, 10m from the shore at the southern end of town, ☎ (0761) 24 492 to 94, Fax (0761) 24 495 – 26rm. ⚄ 🍽 🖊 🆃🆅 ⚒ 🐾 🆑🆑 A recent hotel which is rather soulless despite its swimming pool bordered by banana and palm trees. There is a fridge for keeping drinks cool.

EATING OUT

• Koróni

€5.50
Symposium, on the main street, ☎ (0725) 22 385. The most popular place in town, run by a very friendly Greek-American. Excellent grilled food and fresh fish of the day. There are a few rooms for rent above the taverna.

• Methóni

Between €9 and €12
Eléni, the best establishment here, is located on a peaceful square by the beach at the end of town. Nice "gígantes" (giant beans), aubergine salad and an appealing menu with various meat dishes.

• Pílos

Bars and restaurants are cheaper at the harbour than in the centre of town. But on windy days you can barely stand up there.

Around €7.50
O Grigóris, on a little triangular square to the right of and above the main square when facing the sea. A garden-taverna with several flower-decked terraces where they serve good Greek food to the sound of local music.

Around €11
1930, on the same square as O Grigóris, but protected from passers-by with a row of flowerpots. Traditional Greek menu with a few international dishes (melon-prosciutto, avocado with shrimp, etc).

HAVING A DRINK

Cafés, bars – Life in **Pílos** is centred around the cafés and tavernas squeezed under the plane trees on Platía Tríon Navárhon.

Night-clubs – There are several trendy night-clubs, such as **Zoglo** and the **Koynta Club**, on the road between Pílos and Methóni.

OTHER THINGS TO DO

Outdoor pursuits – Fishing in summer on the islands of **Sapiéntza** and **Schíza** off the coast of Methóni. For information, contact one of the tourist agencies in town.

Excursions – Caique tours in Pílos Bay (4-5hr). Information available at the harbourside stand or in the café on the corner of the harbour and Platía Tríon Navárhon. Rates vary according to the number of passengers.

Market – On Saturday mornings in **Kiparissía**.

Feasts & festivals – On 20 October in Pílos they celebrate the **Navarinia**, commemorating the Battle of Navarino Bay.

IN THE MOUNTAINS OF ELIS (ILÍA)★★
THE TEMPLE OF BASSAE★★★
Province of the Peloponnese – District of Elis
Regional map page 202 – Michelin map 980 fold 28

Not to be missed
The temple of Bassae.
The hilltop villages of Andrítsena, Karítena, Stemnítsa and Dimitsána.

And remember...
A car is a must for getting around this rather isolated region.
Hikers will want to set out early in the morning to explore Loússios Gorge.

Whether you are coming down the road along the Gulf of Kiparissía or from Olympia, you will want to visit the green mountains of Elis rising up between Trípoli and the Ionian Sea. The region has preserved a rare, rustic charm and authenticity far from the most popular archaeological sites in the Peloponnese. This part of Arcadia may not have the bucolic atmosphere attributed to it by painters and poets but many aspects of traditional life have retained their vigour in the stone and timber villages clinging to their steep mountain slopes. This area also contains one of the best-preserved monuments from the Ancient World, the Temple of Bassae, nestling in a remote and majestic mountain spot.

The Temple of Bassae★★★ (Vassés)
31km from the coast. From Taxiárhes or Tholó on the coast, head for Figália.
8am-7pm. Entrance fee. Allow 30min.

Emerging from a forest of plane and pine trees, the road winds steeply upwards through rocks and bushes where herds of goats gather. The Temple of Bassae suddenly appears out of nowhere in the middle of a plateau hemmed in by high peaks. The setting is breathtaking and unforgettable. First of all because you don't expect to find a temple here; but also because the gigantic tent temporarily protecting it creates an intimate atmosphere between you and the temple, making its beauty all the more captivating.

According to Pausanias, who visited it in the 2C AD, the temple was built in the middle of the 5C BC by **Ictinus**, one of the architects of the Parthenon. It is said to have been commissioned by the inhabitants of the ancient village of Figália, halfway between the site and the Ionian Sea, to thank Apollo Epicurius for saving them from the plague that raged during one of the Peloponnesian Wars.

Neglected, then resurrected
The Temple of Apollo Epicurius was neglected for centuries before being rediscovered in 1765 by Joachim Bocher, a French architect working for the Venetians. The study was undertaken 50 years later. The edifice, built in local limestone, was severely damaged by alternating summer heat waves and winter frosts, as well as by violent storms and earthquakes. Although it is one of the best-preserved Greek temples, it was about to collapse when restoration began in 1975. Since then an ambitious renovation programme has been undertaken under the sponsorship of the European Union. It has now been propped up like an invalid and will be protected by the marquee from further assaults until around 2010.

Under the marquee
Beneath their vast canopy, the temple's pale **colonnades**★★ are breathtaking. Some rather unusual characteristics distinguish the building from traditional Classical architecture: its unusual length (15 columns on the sides and 6 on the façade, instead of the traditional 13 for 6); a Doric style mixed with Ionic

The Peloponnese

and Corinthian features that was quite unusual at the time; a north-south rather than an east-west orientation; an opening on the east side designed to light up the statue of Apollo; and, finally, Ionic columns in the cella where the statue stood that were connected with buttresses to the wall. A **frieze** (now in the British Museum) running along the upper part of the room depicted the battle of the Greeks and the Amazons, as well as that of the Lapiths (from Thessaly) and the Centaurs.

Explore the surrounding ruins of Archaic and Classical buildings, then walk up to the guard's house for an **overall view*** of the site.

In the mountain villages**

From the Temple of Bassae, the winding **road**** to Dimitsána goes through some beautiful mountain villages. In winter, the snow blanketing the mountains and stone-roofed houses provides a stark contrast with the dark wooden loggias and overhangs.

■ **Andrítsena****, the first village, stretches along a main street lined with old **shops with painted woodwork** where you can still find things like metal oil lamps and handcrafted bells. A huge plane tree stands in the picturesque square in front of the town hall – a genuine agora where the old people and farmers congregate at the Friday morning market. A house just below it has been turned into an **Ethnographic Museum** (*for the key, enquire at the taverna next door*) cluttered with furniture, tools and old-fashioned clothing. Hidden above the little cobblestone alleyways are houses and ancient tavernas where you can enjoy the timeless taste of traditional Greek coffee.

■ Past Andrítsena, the road snakes along until you reach the little village of **Karítena**** (*29km*) whose houses are built in terraces on narrow alleyways, climbing up between a 13C **Frankish castle** (in ruins) and the dizzying **Alfiós Gorge****. An **old bridge*** built by the Franks in the 13C still spans the river at the bottom of the gorge on the road to Megalópoli. Restored in 1439, it retains four original arches topped by a tiny **chapel** accessible via a stone staircase.

A landscape in Elis: the Frankish castle at Karítena

G. Simeone/DIAF

Forty-day construction sites

In Elis, a region known for its builders, legend has it that in the 19C most of the churches in Langádia were built in 40 days – and not a day more. Véli Pasha, son of the Pasha of Ioánnina, who ruled the area, issued a decree limiting the construction time of all Orthodox buildings to a few weeks, probably in an attempt to keep their numbers down. The Church of the Archangel on the main square, built in 1808, is one of them. You can recognise it from the bas-relief on one of the outside walls – a simple and moving Christ on the cross.

■ **Stemnítsa*** *(10km further north)* an important metalworking centre in the Middle Ages, has a stylish look due to its large, well-preserved stone houses from those prosperous times. Not far from the centre, the **Basilica of Trión Ierarhón**, covered with frescoes, is one of the most interesting of the 18 medieval churches in town.

Stemnítsa is also the starting point for some great hiking in **Loússios Gorge**** *(beware of snakes)*, in a wild setting of rocky ground and scrubland *(go through the village in the direction of Moní Prodrómou and take the first path on the left leading down to the valley; maps of the gorge can be bought at the newsstand on the main square)*. A beautiful 2hr walk takes you to **Ioánnis Prodrómou Monastery**, whose monks paint icons. The hike continues on to **ancient Gortys** *(2hr30min)*, a city from the 4C BC deep in a valley, where the remains of a **sanctuary dedicated to Asklepios** lie next to a small 11C **church**. From there, you can either retrace your steps (but the path is very steep) or go to Dimitsána *(allow 5-6hr more, or another day's walk)*.

■ **Dimitsána**** is only 12km away by road. This large mountain town – spread out over two hills facing one another – had its golden age in the 18C when gunpowder was manufactured here in a number of factories. From those prosperous days Dimitsána has preserved and renovated its patrician houses, solid-looking two-storey buildings with wrought-iron balconies. Take the time to explore the pretty cobble-stone alleyways and admire the red roofs that create a sea of pantiles below.

A few kilometres below the village is the **Open-Air Water Power Museum** *(10am-2pm / 5pm-7pm; closed on Tuesday; entrance fee)*, a quite well-designed museum showing the various ways in which the energy from mountain streams was used in watermills, tannery mills, etc.

■ The road divides north of Dimitsána. To the east it leads to **Vitína** *(15km)*, a town in the plains without much character but with the best hotel on this tour *(see the "Where to stay" section)*. The road to Olympia to the west takes you through **Langádia*** *(11km)*, a large town devoted to traditional crafts where you can buy a carved wooden cane or spindle, as well as coloured wool rugs, embroidered table-cloths, etc.

Making the most of the mountains of Elis

COMING AND GOING

By bus – KTEL buses connect Athens to Trípoli (2hr15min) and Megalópoli, where you can hire a car. For information in Athens, ☎ (01) 51 32 834. Two buses a day run between Andrítsena and Olympia, and two a week (Monday and Friday at 8.45am) go from Olympia to Dimitsána.

By train – Regular service between Athens and Trípoli, ☎ in Athens (01) 51 31 601.

ADDRESS BOOK

In Dimitsána

Banks / Currency exchange – There is only one bank, the National Bank on the **main street**. Currency exchange is inside and the cash dispenser is outside.

Telephone – OTE, on the main street next to the National Bank. There are several card-operated phone booths around town.

Medical services – Dispensary at the northern end of the village.

In Andrítsena

Medical service – Dispensary, ☎ (0626) 22 222 / 31 401.

Police – ☎ (0626) 22 209.

WHERE TO STAY

The few hotels built in the 1970s dotting the Andrítsena road are rather dreary and fusty. If you're planning to stay 2 or 3 days, choose a hotel in Stemnítsa or Vitína where the accommodation is better.

• Andrítsena

€38

Theoxénia, at the entrance to the village, ☎ (0626) 22 219 – 45rm. ⚑ ✗ This large hotel, whose heyday was in the 1970s, has quite outdated facilities (no airconditioning, which is a must in summer). Its only advantage is being the closest hotel to the Temple of Bassae. Open from March to September.

• Stemnítsa

Under €30

Trikoloneíon, in the middle of the village, ☎ (0795) 91 297, Fax (0795) 81 483 – 20rm. ⚑ ✗ With its drystone walls and wooden balconies, this large house – a typical example of Arcadian architecture – fits well into the landscape. The modest rooms are heated in winter during the skiing season. In summer maps of Loússios Gorge are provided. (Hearty) breakfast included.

• Dimitsána

€48

Dimitsána, in the village, ☎ (0795) 31 518 – 24rm. ⚑ ℰ As this is the only hotel in the village, it gets credit for simply existing. Otherwise – except for the large private balconies overlooking the valley – everything is old and expensive.

• Vitína

Between €48 and €60

⌂ Menalon Art Hotel, on a quiet square not far from the centre of town, ☎ (0795) 22 217 / 22 200 – 50rm. ⚑ ℰ TV This relatively recent establishment (1992) is by far the best hotel in the entire region, as well as the most friendly. It also has the most interesting decor, which is understandable since the owner has an art gallery.

EATING OUT

All of the mountain villages have at least one taverna where you can try traditional Greek dishes made with local produce. Try the "loukániko", a delicious mountain sausage.

• Vitína

€9

Ta Aïdónia, on the street leading down from the main square, to the right of the souvenir shop. The best restaurant in town. Enjoy goat ("katzíki") cooked in oregano and lightly resinated white wine while sitting in the shady garden.

HAVING A DRINK

• Andrítsena

Tsigoúri Taverna, halfway up the stairs leading to the main square. An old-fashioned taverna with blackened "bríki" (coffee pots), oilcloths and a friendly proprietress, who keeps the keys to the Ethnographic Museum.

OTHER THINGS TO DO

Outdoor pursuits – In season, skiing and other winter sports are the main attraction. Hiking enthusiasts will also appreciate the many mountain trails in the area.

SHOPPING GUIDE

Arts and crafts – In Stemnítsa and Vitína: carved wooden boxes, canes and toys. In Langádia, **carpets** and old **embroidery**, and carved wooden canes.

Local delicacies – Mintzíthra, a fresh soft white cheese, as well as mountain honey and pasta from Dimitsána.

OLYMPIA ★★★
(OLIMBÍA)
Province of the Peloponnese – District of Elis
Regional map page 202 – Michelin map 980 fold 28
324km from Athens – 113km from Patras – 193km from Sparta

Not to be missed
The museum, especially the pediment room.
And remember...
Start your visit early, saving the museum for later in the day when it gets hot.
Bring along a bottle of water (sold in the car park).

Without a doubt, the birthplace of the Olympic games holds a special place in the history of Greek sanctuaries, and in history in general. It is the only one of all the great sites created by mankind whose initial activity is still going on over 2 700 years later – and with such success! Such glory might have made the site a bit full of itself. But Olympia – far from the mountainous grandeur of Delphi or the unashamed wealth of Delos out in the Aegean Sea – exudes only peace. Its pine-shaded ruins – disorderly only in appearance – spread out at the foot of tranquil **Mt Kronion** (hill of Cronus), a green hill barely 125m high. It's as if all that remained of the many struggles that have taken place here was the feeling of duty accomplished by the athletes. The thrill of those athletic events and exploits may no longer run through the stadium, which has been thoroughly cleaned out; but what remains is still impressive; and the museum – where nearly everything found on the site is displayed – is one of the finest in the country.

The sacred forest of Heracles
Olympia is situated in a fertile valley with two rivers running through it, the **Alfiós (Alpheus)** – which Heracles diverted in order to clean the stables of Augeas – and its tributary, the **Kládios (Cladeus)**. In Ancient times there was a forest of olive, oak and pine trees here around which Heracles built a fence to create a sacred grove, or **altis**. This is where two legendary victors were first honoured – Zeus, who had dislodged his father Cronus from Olympus (*see page 47*), and King Pelops, who had won the Peloponnesian throne after a hard-fought struggle.

In those days, Elis was ruled by King Oenomaus whose daughter, Hippodamia, was of marrying age. After learning from an oracle that his future son-in-law would kill him in order to take the throne, the king challenged Hippodamia's suitors to chariot races in which the losers were put to death. Naturally the races were fixed and always ended with a victory for Oenomaus, whose team of horses – given to him by Ares – was invincible. Enter Pelops, son of Tantalus and future father of Atreus (*see page 215*). Through trickery he got Oenomaus' charioteer to damage one of the wheels on the royal chariot, causing it to crash. Pelops the victor took over the kingdom, married Hippodamia and killed the king, if only to make the oracle come true.

Twelve centuries of games
These two victories were commemorated from the 8C BC onwards through athletic games that took place every four years between June and September during the full moon. For twelve centuries, from 776 BC to 393 AD, Olympia brought all the Greek cities together – friends and enemies – under the same ideal. Even the most remote colonies sent their athletes there from the 5C BC. When the dates for the Games were announced by heralds all across the country, everyone set aside arms and discord out of respect for the **sacred truce**.

The Games were highly religious and were first held in front of the Temple of Zeus. As the number of athletes and spectators increased, more appropriate facilities were built. It was a unifying celebration that drew in large crowds estimated at 150 000 and even 200 000 people. The events themselves were held during five days. The rest of the month was devoted to the athletes, who trained under the watchful eye of the judges, to religious and political festivities (diplomacy was in full swing, and numerous conflicts between cities were settled during the Games), and to various commercial and cultural events such as concerts, conferences, exhibitions, etc.

It was four centuries – in the late 4C BC – before the sanctuary took on its permanent configuration. The Romans, who arrived two centuries later, added more luxury but also heralded its decline by gradually doing away with the event's political and religious substance. Then Theodosius banned pagan worship, and the last Olympic Games were held in 393. The Temple of Zeus was destroyed, the statue of the god was sent to Constantinople where it disappeared in a fire, and the site ended up as ruins beneath the dwellings of a Byzantine town.

The Athletes

Numerous religious processions accompanied by offerings to Zeus and Pelops preceded the events. Before competing, the athletes went to the bouleuterion (*see below*) where they swore on the altar of Zeus to respect and obey the Olympic rules. Then, naked and rubbed down with olive oil, they gave themselves over to their sport. **Horse** and **chariot races** were held in the hippodrome; the stadium opened at dawn for **foot races**, races for armed soldiers (*hoplitodromia*), **wrestling**, **boxing** and **pancratium** (a combination of wrestling and boxing) contests, and finally the **pentathlon**, involving discus, javelin, running, jumping and wrestling events.

At the end of each event, the victor was given a palm. On the last day of the Games, he and all the other winners were crowned with a **kallistéphanos** ("beautiful crown"), a wreath of olive branches cut from the sacred olive tree with a golden billhook. At the banquet held in their honour, poets such as **Pindar** sang their praises and sculptors immortalised them in stone. Their native cities had ex-votos or treasuries erected in Olympia to acknowledge the gods; and when the victors came home, they were treated as demigods.

Coubertin and the revival of the Olympic Games

Credit for reviving the Olympic Games 1 503 years after they died out goes to the Frenchman Pierre Frédy, Baron de Coubertin (1863-1937). Convinced that sports were the best way of learning about freedom and group responsibility, he put all his energy into resurrecting this noble institution. He wrote articles, founded associations, launched petitions and subscriptions, sparing no effort, and organised the "Congress to re-establish the Olympic Games" at the Sorbonne on 25 November 1892, which convinced those who were still undecided. The first modern Olympic Games were inaugurated four years later on 5 April 1896 to a cheering crowd of 60 000 spectators in the **Olympic Stadium in Athens** rebuilt with funds provided by Greek philanthropist **Geórges Avérof**. From then on, the Games were held every four years except during times of war, as the truce observed in Antiquity unfortunately no longer exists. They were such a success, even generating economic development, that they gave rise to the **Winter Olympics** in Chamonix in 1924. Appropriately, the first Olympic Games in the 3rd millennium will take place in Athens in 2004. As for Pierre de Coubertin, his heart is buried near the stadium at Olympia in a mausoleum built by the Greeks after he died.

Olympia

Visiting the site
8am-7pm; 8.30am-3pm Saturday, Sunday and holidays. Allow 3hr.

The site is reached by going up the main street that runs through the modern town. Lined with (noisy) hotels, fast-food joints and souvenir shops, it won't entice you to slow down for a look. But those interested in the story of the modern Olympic Games may nevertheless want to make a brief stop at the **Olympic Games Museum**, created by the International Olympic Committee (*at the end of the street that is at right angles to the Ilis Hotel; 8am-3.30pm weekdays, 9am-4.30pm Sundays and holidays; entrance fee; allow 20min*). It features display cases with medals and mascots, as well as photographs of legendary athletes and various important events such as the first female Olympic medallist, British tennis player Charlotte Cooper, receiving a gold medal in 1900.

The rediscovery of Olympia
Buried under 3-4m of debris that had accumulated over the centuries, Olympia only resurfaced in 1723 when Dom Montfaucon, a Parisian Benedictine, urged the Archbishop of Corfu to take an interest in it. In 1766, Englishman Richard Chandler identified the site. But it was the French under the direction of Abel Blouet who unearthed the first fragments in 1829: three metopes and some mosaics from the Temple of Zeus, which they immediately sent to the Louvre. Upset by this "pillaging", the Greeks stopped the excavations, entrusting them later on to German archaeologists, who were responsible for nearly the entire restoration of the sanctuary in two phases, from 1875 to 1881 and from 1936 to 1941.

The archaeological site has three main areas: in the middle is the **sanctuary**, a wide quadrilateral bounded by a wall with **annex** buildings all around it – a kind of "Olympic village" – for athletic training and for welcoming priests, delegations and important guests (ordinary pilgrims camped outside). Finally, the eastern tip of the site contains the actual **athletic facilities** such as the stadium and the hippodrome.

The Annex Quarter
The path first runs along the **outer wall of the sanctuary** (*on the left*) and one of the **porticoes** framing the **Gymnasium** (*on the right*), a vast 120m-wide by 220m-long courtyard where athletes trained in disciplines requiring a lot of space such as javelin and discus throwing, foot races, etc.

The **Palaestra**★ next to it, a peristylar courtyard with 66m-long sides and a **double colonnade**, was reserved for wrestlers, boxers and jumpers.

Beyond them on the right are the remains of a Roman villa and a Byzantine church. Just behind that is the **Workshop of Phidias**★, identified by the numerous tools found there. It was built so that the famous sculptor could create the statue of Zeus that was to decorate the temple.

A few metres away stand the Doric columns of the **Leonidaion**, a huge hostel built in the 4C BC by Leonidas of Náxos where important guests and foreign officials stayed.

Back on the main path, look for three steps leading to a door flanked by **two columns** which marks the beginning of the **Processional Way** created by the Romans, which is dotted with remains of **ex-votos** (bases) and various levelled buildings. Further along on the right is the **Bouleuterion**, the council chamber for the management of the sanctuary. It is composed of two wings closed off by apses whose outline can be seen on the ground. A square room also housed the **Altar of Oaths** where athletes swore an oath before competing. The **South Gate** behind the bouleuterion closed off the site.

Turning your back to the bouleuterion, enter the sanctuary.

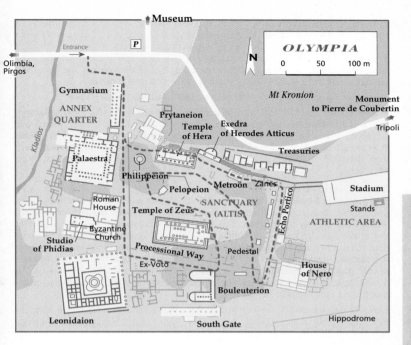

The Sanctuary (Altis)

According to legend, this square with 220m sides containing the temples, altars and other monuments dedicated to worship was designed by Heracles himself.

The **Temple of Zeus**★, built in the centre on a wide terrace that is reached by a **ramp**, was meant to impress the pilgrims and had to be the biggest and most luxurious monument. Even lying chaotically on the ground (since the earthquake that destroyed the building in the 6C), its gigantic columns, sliced into pieces like so many sausages, are enormously impressive. There were six **Doric columns** along the façade of the temple and 13 on each side. The equally impressive decor was composed of a colossal statue of Zeus standing in the cella, and the wonderful bas-reliefs and sculptures – metopes and pediments – enhancing the outside (all on display in the museum).

Phidias' Wonder

Given the proportions of the chryselephantine (made of gold and ivory) statue designed for the Temple of Zeus, Phidias must have made it on site. This considerable task took him no less than ten years to complete – between 430 and 420 BC. The naked parts of the body were sculpted in wood and covered with ivory, whereas gold leaf was laid over the hair, beard and accessories. The god was seated on a throne of ebony and bronze embellished with gold, ivory and precious gems, holding a sceptre with an eagle on it in his left hand and a small chryselephantine Victory ("Níke") in his right hand. The statue, one of the Seven Wonders of the Ancient World, was 13.5m tall and almost touched the ceiling of the temple. When Pausanias discovered it in the 2C, there was a small basin of water at its feet for humidifying the atmosphere and protecting the visible ivory and invisible wood. The statue was taken to Constantinople, where it perished in a fire in 475.

Scattered stonework near the temple indicates the location of the **Pelopeion**, a temple to Pelops near which a sacred olive tree grew. It adjoins the **Temple of Hera**★ (Heraíon), older (600 BC) than her spouse's temple. Its **tufa columns**★ with their more pronounced fluting are a fine example of the evolution of the Doric style. The interior contained a number of statues, including one of the goddess and Praxiteles' famous statue of Hermes, one of the gems in the Olympia museum.

Retrace your steps and leave the Altis via the right (east) side, heading south.

Hurry past the insignificant ruins of the **House of Nero** without looking for any traces of the **hippodrome** (609m by 320m) that stretched out nearby and was destroyed when the Alfiós flooded. Then walk up along the ruins of the **Echo Portico**, a long gallery with colonnades built in the 4C BC to separate the sanctuary from the athletic facilities. The name comes from the seven echoes produced by its acoustics.

The Athletic Area

Don't miss the **Stadium**★, built in the 3C BC, all that is left of the area devoted to the contests. It is reached through the only remaining **vaulted corridor** (kryptè), which leads directly to the track. This fine bed of sand measures exactly 192.27m, the length fixed by Heracles equalling 600 times the length of his foot (a bit more than 32cm, meaning the demigod wore size 16 shoes!). The **finishing line** – near the entrance – and the **starting line** are still visible, but scarcely anything remains of the marble **grandstand** where important figures sat *(on the right)*. The 45 000 spectators which the stadium could hold sat on wooden stands on grassy mounds on either side of the track.

Leave the stadium and go straight ahead on the path along the north side of the Altis.

Excavated into the side of Mt Kronion, the **Terrace of the Treasuries**★ at the top of a wide flight of stairs is lined with ruins of a dozen "treasuries", the small buildings commissioned by city states and Greek colonies to house their offerings to the gods. The pedestals along the bottom of the terrace supported the **Zanes**, statues of Zeus financed with fines imposed on cheaters by referees of the Games.

Go past the ruins on the left of the **Metroön**, a temple built in the 4C BC in honour of Cybele, mother of the gods, and continue to the end of the terrace of the treasuries. A wide, well-preserved stone semicircle marks the site of the **Exedra of Herodes Atticus**★. Built in 160, it was named after the rich Roman patron from Athens who commissioned it along with Athens' first marble stadium and the odeon at the foot of the Acropolis. More than a mere marble bench, it was a luxurious nymphaeum (monumental fountain) into which flowed spring water that fed the entire sanctuary via an aqueduct and a network of pipes. **Niches** embellishing the two superimposed **basins** contained statues of the imperial family and of Herodes Atticus.

On the left as you leave the sanctuary is the circular base of the **Philippeion** (4C BC), a tholos devoted to the cult of the dynasty of Philip II of Macedon. Then, on the right, stands the **Prytaneion**, the administrators' headquarters where official banquets were held. This is where the **sacred flame** burned continually.

The Museum★★★

Tuesday-Sunday: 8am-7pm, Monday: 12pm-7pm. Entrance fee. Allow at least 90min, more if you lose track of time while contemplating the pediments at the Temple of Zeus or the Hermes by Praxiteles. This modern and well-designed museum hidden among the trees *(behind the car park)* contains objects discovered on the site which are presented in chronological order. Take time to look over the **two models**★ of the site in the vestibule, which are very instructive. On the left is **Room 1**, devoted to objects from the Prehistoric and Geometric Periods. Next to a delicate little **bronze horse**★ from the 9C-8C BC is a striking **helmet with wild-boar tusks**★ from 3500 BC.

The very long **Room 2** contains bronze objects from the Geometric and Archaic Periods: **armour★**, including beaten-metal helmets in very good condition, **oriental-style statues** from the 7C BC, and **beaten bronze sheets** depicting mythological scenes. One of them *(display case 8)* shows a moving farewell scene between a warrior going off to battle and his wife carrying their child on her shoulders. The graceful **head of Hera★** on the wall was found in the Temple of Hera.

Room 3, devoted to works from the 6C BC, contains a reconstruction of the **pediment of the treasury of Megara** whose theme is the battle between Zeus and the Giants.

The Archaic and Classical masterpieces begin in **Room 4**: on the left is a superb terracotta composition (470 BC) with polychrome traces showing **Zeus abducting Ganymede★★★**. A display case on the right has various objects from the **studio of Phidias**, including tools, terracotta moulds used to make the statue of Zeus and a small vase with an inscription "I belong to Phidias" that helped in identifying the sculptor's workshop.

A large alcove on the left is devoted entirely to the **Winged Victory by Paeonius★★**, a striking 2.11m-tall sculpture in Parian marble. The slender *Nike* wearing a short robe has come down from Olympus to announce the victory of the Messenians and the Naupactians over Sparta. The sculptor has captured the moment when her foot is gracefully touching down (actually on an eagle).

The Pediment Room★★★ occupying the central area of the museum is the most spectacular. It contains sculptures in high-relief that decorated the **Temple of Zeus**, including **metopes★★** featuring the Twelve Labours of Heracles, and pediments that are masterpieces in the severe style. The **west pediment★★★** on the left-hand wall shows the marriage of Deidamia (daughter of the king of the Lapiths) and Peirithous, in which the Lapiths drive back the drunken Centaurs – representing the brute force of

Hermes by Praxiteles, the height of realism (Olympia Archaeological Museum)

Olympia

B. Kaufmann/MICHELIN

293

nature – who are trying to abduct the women and their young folk. Apollo appears still and serene as he gives advice to the men in the midst of the violent, chaotic fray.

The **east pediment★★★** just across from it portrays the preparations for a chariot race between Pelops and Oenomaus. In contrast to the west pediment, in which all is sound and fury, the protagonists here have a reflective attitude as they concentrate before the fight: Zeus is in the centre, young Pelops is on his right, and on his left is Oenomaus wearing a cloak and accompanied by Hippodamia with her arms crossed. Even the horses are posing.

Back in Room 4, a door on the right leads to **Room 5** which has several sculptures from the Classical Period, then to **Room 6** containing the magnificent **Hermes by Praxiteles★★★**. Sculpted in Parian marble in the 4C BC, Hermes is wearing winged sandals and holding a newborn baby, Dionysus, the son of Zeus and Semele, whom the messenger of the gods is taking off to the Nymphs to protect him from jealous Hera. In a rather unlikely gesture for a child of that age, Dionysus is trying to grasp a bunch of grapes – soon to be his favourite fruit – that Hermes was probably holding out to him. Note the progress – between this work from the late Classical Period and the pediments from the Temple of Zeus that were sculpted a century earlier – in the quest for realism.

Rooms 7 and 8, the last ones, are devoted to the Hellenistic Period. Of particular note are the **Roman statue of Antinous★**, Emperor Hadrian's favourite, and the accessories relating to the Olympic Games.

Pierre de Coubertin Monument

Pass the archaeological site going east. A track 1.5km down the road, behind a well-trimmed hedge on the left, leads to the **Mausoleum** built in 1938 which holds the heart of Pierre de Coubertin. Just next to it is the **altar of the Olympian flame** with the five intertwined circles symbolising the union of the five continents.

Making the most of Olympia

COMING AND GOING

By bus – Pírgos-Olympia: 15 buses a day on weekdays, 9 on Sunday (40min trip). Olympia-Trípoli: 3 buses a day, 2 on weekends (3hr30min). Olympia-Andrítsena: 1 bus a day except on Sunday. Olympia-Dimitsána: 2 a week (Monday and Friday at 8.45am). The bus stop is opposite the tourist office on the main street.

By train – The Olympia railway station is closed, so you have to get off in *Pírgos* (18km away), then take a bus or taxi. There are 5 trains a day from Athens to Pírgos.

GETTING AROUND

By bus – There are 10 buses a day connecting Pírgos to Patras (2hr), Itéa (4hr30min) and Athens (6hr). Daily buses to Kalamáta (2hr).

By taxi – ☎ (0624) 22 555 / 22 788.

ADDRESS BOOK

Tourist information – In a little building in the middle of the main street, ☎ (0624) 23 100 / 23 173, Fax (0624) 23 125.

Banks / Currency exchange – Several banks on the main street have cash dispensers and currency exchange. However, the rate at the tourist information office is sometimes better.

Post office – On the street to the left of the tourist information office, ☎ (0624) 22 599.

Police – Behind the post office, ☎ (0624) 22 100.

Medical service – There is a *hospital* on the street to the right of the Olympic Games Museum (signposted), ☎ (0624) 22 252. There is a *medical practice* in front of the Hercule hotel where English is spoken, ☎ (0624) 22 197. *Pharmacy*, ☎ (0624) 23 306 / 22 000.

WHERE TO STAY

The hotels in Olympia are rather disappointing and may discourage visitors even for one night as they are often worn around the edges – and sometimes dirty. For the hotels listed below, which have been thoroughly tested, reservations are recommended during the high season.

Campsite (around €12)
Diana campsite, behind the Olympic Games Museum, ☎ (0624) 22 314 / 22 425. Laid out on terraces (which fill up fast in summer), this welcoming and attractive campsite is only 200m from the centre of town and 800m from the archaeological site. Good washing facilities and a small pool shaded by trees. Open from March to October.

Between €23 and €30
Poseidón, on a quiet, slightly out-of-the-way street above Odós Kondíli, ☎ (0624) 22 567 – 10rm. ✖ cc A modest, but clean and quiet establishment. Communal showers. Some rooms have fans. The young owner is very friendly. Breakfast included. Meals are served in the shade of the taverna next door.

Around €30
Krónio, Odós Kondíli (the main street), ☎ (0624) 22 188 – 24rm. ☐ ✐ ✖ cc This hotel is one of the best in town regarding value for money and is open all year. Adequate comfort, rooms with balconies, and bathrooms with bathtubs. Copious breakfast (not included in the price of the room).

Around €45
Ilis, in the middle of Odós Kondíli, not far from the Olympic Games Museum, ☎ (0624) 22 547 – 60rm. ☐ ☐ cc This uninspiring "modern" building has ordinary rooms with a rather worn

decor. But the welcome is friendly and you can use the pool at the Antonios hotel, 200m up the hill.

Between €75 and €105
Antonios, above town, ☎ (0624) 22 348 – 65rm. ☐ ☐ ✐ ✖ ☐ cc A large, modern establishment surrounded by pine trees... near the cemetery. Could that be why the welcome is so icy? The rooms are very comfortable, however, and the pool is pleasant, especially in summer.

Europa, on the hill overlooking Olympia, ☎ (0624) 22 650, Fax (0624) 22 166 – 80rm including 2 suites. ☐ ☐ ✐ ☐ ✖ ✗ cc The best establishment in town (and also the most expensive) is situated in the middle of a huge wooded park a few kilometres from the archaeological site. It has everything to make guests happy, from marble bathrooms, a taverna under the trees and a pool to facilities for the handicapped. Open all year.

EATING OUT

One does not eat well in Olympia. The main street is one long succession of pizzerias and fast-food joints; and the restaurants in adjacent streets boasting "Greek cooking" overcharge.

• **Mirakas**
If you have a car, go to Mirakas (take the first road on the left after the archaeological site all the way to this village, nestling in the hills a few kilometres from the centre of Olympia). Go straight past the "Drosiá" restaurant, which is quite unpleasant, and stop 100m further on.

Around €7.50
Bacchus, this village taverna with a pleasant decor serves local food that is inventive and enjoyable. Try the aubergine fritters, sausage ("loukániko") or kebabs cooked just right. The first pitcher of wine is on the house, in honour of the taverna's name.

OTHER THINGS TO DO

Local festivals – *Theatre and music festival* in Olympia's new theatre on the edge of town. For information, contact the tourist office.

THE NORTHERN COAST
OF THE PELOPONNESE
FROM OLYMPIA TO CORINTH

Province of the Peloponnese – Districts of Elis, Achaia and Corinthía
Regional map page 202 – Michelin map 980 folds 28-29
340km tour – Allow 2-3 days

Not to be missed
The Frankish castle at Hlemoútsi.
A trip through the Vouraïkós Gorge on the little train from Kalávrita.
And remember...
Try to avoid staying in Patras, a noisy city with constant traffic jams.

The northern coast of the Peloponnese is not much more than a succession of seaside villages with sandy or pebble beaches stretching along the Gulf of Corinth. The inland areas with olive groves and vineyards rippling across the foothills are not lacking in charm. But the two overcrowded main roads linking Patras and Athens have created a kind of barrier between the two areas. It would be a pity, however, not to stop off at the Frankish castle of Hlemoútsi, the largest on the peninsula, or to travel through the spectacular Vouraïkós Gorge on the little rack railway that has wound through it for over a century.

Katákolo, a little port with all the flavour of the Mediterranean

Bouquet/DIAF

From Olympia to Patras

130km. Head for Pírgos out of Olympia.

It's only a quarter of an hour from Olympia to **Pírgos**, a dreary modern town that has nothing to keep you, and in fifteen more minutes you can wade into the Ionian Sea.

■ The first beach is at **Katákolo**, a colourful port that is a pleasant place to stop for lunch. It's a shame that cars are allowed on its sands.

■ A better plan is to go straight across the long agricultural plain opening out in front of you, then exit at **Gastoúni** and go on to the coastal village of **Loutrá Kilínis** *(43km from Pírgos)*. **Golden Beach★★**, a magnificent and well-named beach with fine sand, stretches out for kilometres under the shade of a thick pine forest. Empty buildings hidden here and there among the trees are a reminder that the site was a spa at the time of the colonels' junta and collapsed along with them. During the high season, the beach attracts large crowds of Greek and Scandinavian holidaymakers.

The village of Kástro is 7km inland from Loutrá Kilínis. A bus shuttles between the two villages several times a day.

■ **The castle of Hlemoútsi★★** – *8am-8pm on weekdays, 8am-2.30pm on Sundays and holidays; closed on Mondays. Free admission. Make your visit in the early morning before the haze sets in.* The houses in the town of **Kástro★**, perched high up on a hillside overlooking the sea, are squeezed together in the shade of an impressive Frankish citadel. Its recently restored sandy-coloured walls stand out against the sky like a majestic crown. Hlemoútsi is the best preserved, as well as the largest, fortress in the Peloponnese. Built in around 1220 by **Geoffroi I de Villehardouin**, the "Château de Clairmont" was handed down over the centuries until it was finally abandoned... then restored.

You enter through a **monumental gate★** made by the Turks in the 13C. The **first wall★** delimits a huge "lower courtyard" with outbuildings. Only a few chimneys are left, as well as some razed walls including those of a **mosque**, just to the right as you enter. The **second wall★★** of the fortress, which protected the knights' quarters, has an **arched portico★** of striking proportions. It gives onto a two-storey **chapel** on the left, while on the right a 70m-long **vaulted passageway★★** runs alongside the ramparts. Crossing the inner, hexagonal

Beware of traffic jams!

courtyard you reach the **seigneurial abode**★ whose large vaulted rooms have preserved their elegant windows and some stone fireplaces. Before leaving, climb up to the outside terraces for a wide **view**★★ of the Ionian Islands (from left to right: Zacynthus, Cephalonia, Ithaca, recognisable by its two steep hills, and Leucas).

■ **Patras** (Pátra) – *113km from Olympia.* The third largest city in Greece – after Athens and Thessaloníki – is a roadway junction and a major port with all the crowds, noise, heat and pollution that one hopes to avoid on holidays. If you have to spend a few hours there while waiting to catch a boat, head for the **kástro** at the end of town where it is cooler and greener. Otherwise, you can sit under the shade of the palm trees on the big square, **Platía Tríon Symmáhon**, which has plenty of open-air cafés *(between the harbour and the railway station)*. All the services you need are to be found here: banks, hotels, post office, etc.

From Patras to Athens

210km tour. As you leave Patras, avoid the main road which gets congested with trucks. Although it is narrower, take the two-lane toll road that turns into a motorway at Égio. It runs alongside a series of little seaside towns.

■ **Égio** – Among the modest seaside resorts dotting the northern coast, Égio boasts an **Archaeological Museum** housed in a covered market from the neo-Classical Period. It contains various objects found in the region, the oldest of which is an 800-year-old painted **fruit dish**★. The most recent piece is a fine **statue of Zeus Aigiochos** in the Classical style although made in the 1C BC.

■ **Diakoftó** – Between beaches and fields of olive trees, the road soon reaches the peaceful town of Diakoftó, overflowing with lemon and orange trees. Although this charming setting has no particularly noteworthy sights, it is a pleasant place to stop off. The village is best known as the starting point for the famous Vouraïkós Gorge.

■ **Vouraïkós Gorge**★★ – *It is easier to reach the Monastery of Méga Spíleo and Kastriá Cave by car (allow 75min one way, and between a half and a whole day in all, depending on your programme). But the most spectacular route is the one taken by the little rack railway. Its station adjoins the main Diakoftó railway station. 4 trains a day go up to Zahloroú and Kalávrita, with additional trains in summer. Get there 15min before departure time in order to have a seat, preferably just behind the driver (for the breathtaking panoramas). Buy return tickets in advance and check the return schedule. If you are only visiting the Monastery of Méga Spíleo, buy a ticket to Zahloroú. The first section is the most striking in any case. If you get to Kalávrita and are stuck because of an awkward return schedule, you can visit Kastriá Cave (by taxi) or go back down to your starting point (also by taxi). The station is on the town's main square.*

A hundred years after its inauguration in 1896, the little narrow gauge **rack railway**, or **"odondotó"**, is back in service and has become one of the (rare) attractions in this part of the Peloponnese. It makes the 22km run between Diakoftó and Kalávrita in 65min, crossing the dizzying Vouraïkós Gorge in the process, a real adventure. It runs at the pace of a "choo-choo" train from another age, going from green meadows scented with pine, oleander and wild oregano to steep slopes where the rack attachment really proves its worth. On the way it trundles along over narrow bridges, spans bottomless cliffs and disappears into Lilliputian tunnels dug out of the mountainside. After 40 intense minutes, the train makes a short stop *(10min)* at **Zahloroú** station. If you are charmed by the place, it is possible to spend the night *(hotel near the station)*. Then the voyage continues on to **Méga Spíleo Monastery**★ *(closed 1pm-3pm; allow 2hr of walking and 1hr of sightseeing; bring a good pair of shoes for the road and decent clothes for the monastery; beware of snakes on the stony path)* clinging to the smooth, vertical rock face, as if suspended above the abyss. Destroyed several times (the last time was in 1943) then rebuilt, Megá Spíleo looks from the outside like a strange combination of disparate elements added one after the other. The first thing you see inside is the **cave**, from which the monastery took its name *(spíleo)*, where a miraculous 8C icon of the Virgin was found. The upper floors house a small **museum** (illuminated manuscripts, icons, embroidered fabrics, liturgical objects) overlooked by the cool and peaceful 17C **church**. It contains 17C **frescoes**★★, as well as the famous **icon** attributed to St Luke the evangelist.

The last stop on this railway journey is **Kalávrita**, a peaceful mountain town that turns into a base camp for skiers in winter. The **church clock** in the centre of town still reads 2.34pm, a reminder of the hour when German soldiers shot Kalávrita's 1 436 male inhabitants on 13 December 1943 before setting fire to the town. The names of the martyrs, the oldest of whom was 80 and the youngest barely 12, are engraved in stone on the **memorial** built on a hill.

A taxi from the main square will take you 6km south-west of town to the **Monastery of Agía Lávra** *(10am-1pm / 4pm-5pm)*, an imposing building of sandy-coloured stone founded in 961. Few elements remain from that time, but the place – one of Greece's most venerated sites – is regarded as the starting point of the War of Independence, which was launched in 1821 to the cry of "Freedom or death".

■ But you would probably rather visit **Kastriá Cave**★ *(16.5km to the south-east; theoretically from 9am-6pm, but opening times vary according to the season, ☎ (0692) 31 633 / 31 262; bring non-slip shoes)*. This 2km-long labyrinth has a series of **thirteen underground lakes** on three levels. It is reached via a manmade tunnel leading to the second storey; then you cross footbridges and pontoons that take you down stunning corridors, anterooms and galleries whose walls sculpted with coloured stalactites are reflected in the supernatural-looking blue-green water.

■ The sandy beach at **Dervéni** is a good place to make one last stop before heading back to Attica, unless you prefer to wander inland around Sicyon *(see page 205, exit at Kiáto)* or ancient Corinth *(see page 208)*.

COMING AND GOING

By boat – From the port of **Kilíni**, ☎ (0623) 922 11, there are daily ferries for the Ionian Islands: Zacynthus (90min), Cephalonia (2hr to the port of Póros, 3hr30min to Argostóli).

From **Patras**: daily domestic links with Ágios Nikólaos 30km west of Itéa (1hr) and to the Ionian Islands. International links with Italy: 4-5 boats to Ancona, Bari and Brindisi. The Superfast Company's ferries are the quickest (7pm; 2.30pm for Bari). T Philópoulos and K Parthenópoulos Agency, Óthonos & Amalías 12 in Patras, ☎ (061) 62 25 00, Fax (061) 62 35 74.

Timetables and reservations can be obtained at the following Web site: www.gtpnet.com

From **Río** (7km north of Patras), ferries every 15min for **Andírio** (about 10km from Náfpaktos on the mainland; 30min trip). Buses leave from the Patras bus station every 15min for the port of Río. In 2004, the ferries will be replaced by a 2 300m-long suspension bridge between Río and Andírio.

From **Égio** (Aíghion) there are 8 ferries a day (from 7.30am to 8pm, return from 8.30am to 10pm) for Ágios Nikólaos, 35km from Delphi on the mainland (1hr trip).

By air – **Áraxos** airport, 30km west of Patras, handles charters during the season and military activities year round. There is a taxi rank in front of the airport (bring some cash, as there are no cash dispensers).

By bus – In **Patras**, the bus terminal is at the harbour near Gate 6, ☎ (061) 62 38 86. There are 32 departures daily for Athens, including 10 which are direct (4hr trip); 15 departures for Pírgos on weekdays, and 9 on Sunday (40min; connections to Olympia). 2 for Kalamáta. About fifteen for Río (with connections to Delphi) and Égio. 2 for Trípoli (with connections to Sparta).

By train – **Patras**: the railway station (with left-luggage facilities) is centrally located in the harbour area. 8 trains a day for Athens (6hr trip) and 8 for Pírgos (2hr) including 7 for Kiparissía. 4 trains daily for Kalamáta.

GETTING AROUND

By taxi – In Kilíni, ☎ (0623) 95 278. They speak Greek... and German.

By rental vehicle – In Kilíni, two-wheeled vehicles can be rented at **Voúltsos**, ☎ (mobile) 09 37 01 33 06. Car rental in Patras at **Delta**, Odós Amalías 44, 500m to the right of the landing-stage.

ADDRESS BOOK (PATRAS)

Tourist information – The tourist information office at Gate 6 at the embarkation harbour provides lists of hotels in the Peloponnese, but doesn't call them for you. Fortunately, the tourist office directly opposite is more obliging.

Medical service – **Red Cross** emergency centre, ☎ (061) 27 386.

Left-luggage – At Gate 6 at the harbour and at the railway station.

WHERE TO STAY

There is no shortage of rooms to rent in this popular coastal area. Avoid arriving without reservations during the Patras carnival and around 15 August when places are fully booked.

• Arkoúdi-Loutrá Kilínis

A little seaside resort adjoining Loutrá Kilínis that is peaceful, although quite popular with groups.

Between €33 and €38

Arcoudi, slightly out-of-the-way near a wooded area, ☎ (0623) 96 480, Fax (0623) 96 494, www.travelgreece. com – 47rm. ⊓ ▤ ℘ ▣ ✕ ⚊ ⌂ This recent hotel 300m from the beach is pleasant and comfortable. The pool also has a children's pool and playing area, and there are electronic games and a billiard table inside. One hitch: air conditioning and individual fridges cost extra, jacking up the price quite a bit.

• Kástro

€45

⌨ **Catherine Lepida**, in the centre of town on the left as you go up, ☎ (0623) 95 224 / 95 380, in winter, ☎ (0623) 95 444 – 5 studios. ⊓ ⊼ ℘ ▣ Catherine's large studios, renovated in 1998, are quiet, cheerful and well equipped (fully equipped kitchens and screens on the windows to keep out mosquitoes). The owner is very welcoming.

Between €45 and €55

Paradise, beside a minor road between Kástro and Kilíni, ☎ (0623) 95 209 / 95 450, Fax (0623) 95 451 – 40rm. ⁋ 🗐 ✐ ✗ ⌿ ✹ CC This pleasant, modern establishment has a garden with trees as well as a large swimming pool and a playground for children. Water-skiing and parascending are also possible at the neighbouring club. The only drawback is that it is a bit far from everything, so a vehicle is essential.

● **Patras**

The highest concentration of hotels is around Platía Tríon Symmáhon between Odós Agíou Andréou running along its northern side and Odós Agíou Nikoláou at right angles to it.

Between €40 and €45

Galaxy, Odós Agíou Nikoláou 9, ☎ (061) 27 52 81 – 55rm. ⁋ 🗐 ✐ TV CC This fusty hotel should only be used as a last resort. However, the bathrooms do have real bathtubs.

€45

Méditerranée, Odós Agíou Nikoláou 18, ☎ (061) 27 96 02 / 27 96 24, Fax (061) 22 33 27 – 95rm. ⁋ ✐ TV CC Practically opposite the preceding hotel. This establishment with several storeys is a bit noisy and has no character, but is clean and centrally located. Ask for a room with air conditioning (extra charge). (Buffet) breakfast not included. Open all year.

● **Diakoftó**

Between €38 and €45

Chris-Paul, in the centre of the village, ☎ (0691) 41 715 / 41 855, Fax (0691) 42 128 – 25rm. ⁋ ✐ 🗐 TV ⌿ 🕱 This comfortable hotel 80m from the station (with a swimming pool) is a good place to stop for the night. Our only regret was the somewhat impersonal welcome and the fact that the hot water was shut off at 8.30am.

EATING OUT

● **Kástro**

Around €10

🍽 **Castello**, right next to Catherine Lepida's rooms, has a shady terrace and good-quality cuisine that contrasts sharply with the usual cheap restaurants. Some of their welcome culinary attractions include beef in filo pastry, grilled meats that melt in your mouth, and homemade taramosaláta, all washed down with a rather pleasant, slightly smoky white wine.

● **Patras**

It will come as no surprise that the establishments closest to the harbour (and therefore the most accessible when you are passing through) are also the worst and most expensive. Go across town to the foot of the kástro – quite a way – to find a more pleasant place.

HAVING A DRINK

Cafés, bars

● **Kalávrita**

Air-music Club, a few kilometres from the entrance to Kalávrita, is a bar/night-club inside a real Olympic Airways Boeing 737 that seems to have landed here by some miracle! There is also a play area for children.

OTHER THINGS TO DO

English-language newspapers – In **Patras**: Book's Corner, Odós Agíou Nikoláou 32 and at stands along the harbour.

Local festivals – In **Hlemoútsi**, a theatre, dance and music festival is held in the castle in July and August. For information, contact Catherine Lepida.

The "Karnavali" in **Patras** – from mid-January to Ash Wednesday – is one of Greece's most famous carnivals. There is a gigantic parade on the last Sunday of the festival.

SHOPPING GUIDE

Arts and crafts – In Kástro, a shop called **Camara** (in the street going down to the left from the centre) sells attractive pottery.

The hilltop village of Dílofo: the Zagória region

THESSALY
AND EPIRUS

Together, Thessaly and Epirus form a region which stretches from the Aegean to the Ionian coasts, sharing between them a colourful landscape of mountains and forests, deep valleys and vast plains, where timeless Greece alternates with the harsh Balkan countryside. Their strategic position on the routes between Macedonia and southern Greece, between Rome and Byzantium, and, finally, between the West and the East, has brought them into many conflicts over the centuries. And it is the relics of this tormented past which have generated an extraordinary heritage. This includes the theatre of **Dodona**, the ancient city of **Nikópoli**, the Byzantine churches of **Ioánnina**, as well as the myriad mountain villages, cut off from the world, where the way of life has not changed for centuries, its rhythm marked by the seasonal movement of livestock.

Epirus has long been preserved from external influences by its mountainous terrain, and also by the **Pindus Chain**, with the spectacular **Víkos Gorge** which cuts through it. The mountains rise to 2 687m and form the border with Thessaly. Vast forests of beech trees and conifers still provide shelter for bears, lynx and wolves. Further south, the sun beats down on the plains of **Árta** and **Préveza**, the domain of orange trees, rice fields and early fruit and vegetable crops. In the very heart of Greece, encircled by the highest mountains in the land, which include Pindus to the west and **Mt Olympus** to the north, Thessaly consists of a fertile agricultural basin, where wheat, barley, maize, sugar-beet, fodder-crops and cotton are cultivated. But the main point of interest here lies in the **Metéora**, strange rock formations sculpted by erosion. Continuing towards Epirus, the road goes through the **Katára Pass**, the highest in Greece (1 705m). Situated at the opposite end of the province is the **Pelion Peninsula**, a region of magnificent mountains and forests, where apple and olive trees are grown, and where there are remarkable villages of stone houses.

From the Molossi to the Romans

Ruled by aristocratic clans for several centuries, Thessaly was invaded in the 4C BC by the tyrants of Pherae, Thebes, and then by Philip II of Macedon.

As for Epirus, the first great kingdom there was that of the **Molossi** (4C BC), founded by the **Aeacidae** who claimed to be descended from Achilles. Soon to come under Macedonian rule, the kingdom had its period of glory, during the reign of **Pyrrhus** (297-272 BC). However, weakened by palace squabbles and rioting in the streets, the kingdom disappeared with the Aeacidae, around 232 BC.

Unhappily trapped in a position between the principal powers of the period, Rome and Macedonia, Epirus tried in vain to preserve its neutrality. During the Third Macedonian War (171-168 BC), the region was used as a battlefield by the warring factions. The Roman victory at **Pydna** opened the way for a period of pillaging, destruction and reprisal killings unrivalled in Greece. Having become a Roman province in 146 BC, at the same time as Thessaly, Epirus suffered further tribulations during the following century. After Dodona was destroyed by **Mithradates VI**, king of Pontus, it was subjected to, in turn, Caesar's campaign against Pompey, Antony's campaign against Cassius and Brutus, and finally that of Octavian. To celebrate his victory over Antony at **Actium** (31 BC), Octavian (later known as Augustus) set about building the city of Nikópoli which enjoyed great prestige.

The Byzantine Era

In the early Byzantine Era (4C), the region continued to be heavily influenced by the heritage of Antiquity, but the spread of **Christianity** and the construction of numerous basilicas brought drastic changes to both the artistic and social background. The 6C, however, saw the dawn of a "Dark Age": Slavs, Arabs, Bulgars, Venetians and Normans ruled in succession, until the Vlachs established themselves in the Pindus in the 11C.

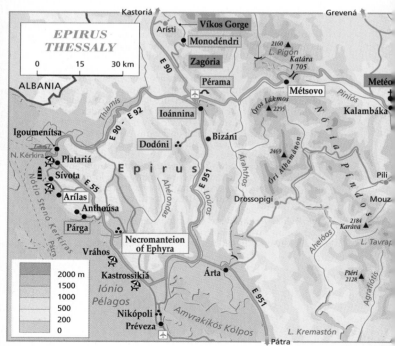

A new era began with the fall of Constantinople to the **Crusaders** (1204). **Michael Angelus Ducas** succeeded in creating an independent state, which would become the **Despotate of Epirus**, while all other Greek territories, including Thessaly, came under Latin control (except for the Empire of Nicaea in Asia Minor). **Theodore Ducas**, who succeeded him, took possession of Thessaly and Macedonia, and even went so far as to stake a claim to the Byzantine legacy. The rivalry between the two Greek nations continued until 1265, after the restoration of the Byzantine Empire. Under threat from all sides, the dynasty of Epirus ended with the assassination of the despot Thomas, in 1318. Epirus and Thessaly, occupied in turn by the Byzantines, the **Serbs** and the **Albanians**, then experienced one of the darkest periods of their history. To conquer the Albanians, the Serbs made the mistake of appealing to the Turks for help.

Epirus the rebellious

Conquered by the Ottomans in 1430, Epirus was never to be completely free of conflict. Throughout the entire period, its mountains were used as a hideout by bands of patriotic bandits who enjoyed great popularity and played a major role during the insurrection against the Turks in 1821. At the same time, the *pashalik* **Ali Pasha** *(see page 324)* also defied the Sublime Porte, before meeting his tragic end.

Although the region of Fthiótida became part of Greece in 1831, the rest of Thessaly would have to wait until 1881. As for Epirus, its turn would come in 1913, with the exception of its northernmost territory, which became part of Albania. The Orthodox minority which lives there was at the root of an upsurge of tension between the two countries in the early 1990s.

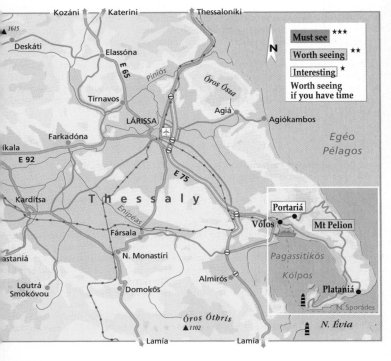

PELION ★★
VÓLOS

Province of Thessaly – District of Magnissía – Regional map page 304
Michelin map 980 folds 17-18 – Tour of around 200km (2 days)
In the hills, the climate is cool and damp

Not to be missed
The Archaeological Museum in Vólos.
The villages of Pelion and its coastal resorts.

And remember...
Avoid visiting Pelion at weekends, when the demand for accommodation
is overwhelming.
Drive carefully on the narrow, winding roads.

To the south of Vólos, the Pelion Peninsula has a wild landscape of forests and mountains, emphasised by the flat, blue expanse of the Aegean Sea. In contrast to the ski
resorts and mountain villages with their beautiful traditional houses, the coastline is
dotted with holiday resorts complete with sun-drenched beaches. In short, this is a
region with many attractions, the privileged holiday haunt of the inhabitants of Vólos
and of those tourists who come to explore the north of the country.

A centre for Greek renaissance
Inhabited since early times, the peninsula suffered numerous invasions before finally
experiencing a period of relative peace under Byzantine rule in the 13C. The threat
of piracy, however, meant that the villages were mainly built high up in the hills.
Paradoxically, it was under the Ottomans, who settled in Vólos and in the coastal
villages, that Pelion had its golden age (18C), thanks to the booming silk industry
that originated here. Enjoying the advantages of its autonomous status, the region
became a centre for the Hellenic renaissance, with the creation of many schools
financed by the local gentry. After Pelion became part of Greece in 1881, Vólos
came to dominate all the economic activity of the peninsula, which was disadvantaged by its remoteness. The conflicts of the Second World War merely exacerbated
its decline.

Tour of Vólos
Allow half a day

Set in the vast **Bay of Pagassitikós**, Vólos (pop 77 000) occupies the site of ancient
Iolkos, where several cities were built. Often hit by earthquakes – the most recent
was in 1955 – it was rebuilt on each occasion, and today looks much like any other
modern town, devoid of all the charm that the passing of time brings with it. The
third largest port in Greece, it has become an established centre for exports to Europe
(cotton, tobacco, olives, oil, wine, fruit) and to the Middle East (industrial goods).
In short, the town has few attractions for the traveller, apart from the **Archaeological
Museum**★★ *(follow the quays south to Odós Athanassáki; open 8.30am-3pm; closed
Monday; entrance fee)* which houses a magnificent collection of funereal steles. Leading
off the entrance hall, where there is a very poignant sarcophagus of a 6-year-old child,
there is a room displaying the superb **steles of Demetrias**★★, decorated with very
vivid frescoes (3C BC). The room devoted to the **Neolithic Period** (habitat, stone
and terracotta figurines, pottery, tools) is equally interesting. The museum also has
a remarkable collection of gold **jewellery** (necklaces, pendants, rings, gold-leaf
crowns), and also **amphorae**, **Mycenaean vases** (2nd millennium BC), **terracotta
pieces**, and Greek and Roman **pottery**.

Exploring Mt Pelion★★ (Óros Pílio)
Tour takes 2 days by car, starting out from Vólos.
See also "Making the most of Mt Pelion".

A narrow rocky ridge hemmed in between the Gulf of Pagassitikós and the Aegean Sea, the Pelion range sweeps southwards into the Magnissía Peninsula, shaped like a long hook which ends in a curl in the vast Gulf of Pagassitikós. Rising to 1 551m, Pelion boasts stunning scenery, its flora alternating between Mediterranean (olive trees) and mountainous (orchards and woods of walnut, beech, oak, fig, chestnut and pine trees, and ferns). The setting is further enhanced by the villages, dotted in the depths of the valleys, which so strongly characterise the region: traditional stone-roofed houses with projecting upper storeys still predominate here, and each village has its big *platia*, sheltered by both an enormous plane tree and a venerable church with its bell-tower.

A land of legends

Tradition holds that during the gigantomachia – the combat which took place between the gods and the Giants, the offspring of Heaven and Earth – the giants defied Olympus by trying to stack Pelion on top of Óssa (the mountains further north). It is also said that the famous centaur, Chiron, lived in the heart of Mt Pelion. This wise and knowledgeable centaur instructed Achilles, one of the heroes of the Trojan War, as well as the healing god, Asklepios, and Jason, whose epic tale is also closely linked to Pelion: it was here that he built the ship in which, together with his fifty Argonauts, he sailed to the Black Sea to bring back the famous Golden Fleece (see page 50)...

■ **Anakassiá** – *5km west of Vólos.* Housed in an elegant building in the heart of the village that was home to the Kondós family (1830) is the **Theóphilos Museum** *(8am-3pm; closed Monday)*. On display is an unusual series of allegorical **frescoes***** depicting the War of Independence, painted by the naive artist Theóphilos (1872-1934).

The road continues to climb, with superb views down over the Bay of Vólos.

■ **Portariá*** – *8km.* Tucked away at an altitude of 600m, Portariá delivers the customary ration of traditional houses, plane trees, tavernas, shops... and churches, including the **Chapel of Panagía**, inside which there are some lovely **frescoes** (16C), and the **Church of Ágios Nikólaos**, with its curious portico set on squat, short, sturdy columns.

■ **Makrinítsa**** – *3km from Portariá on a road to the left. Leave your car at the entrance to the village.* Lined with shops selling herbs and crystallized fruits, a long and narrow street leads to the delightful village **square****, the silence disturbed only by the sound of the fountains and the wind in the plane trees. The **church** (18C) contains an **iconostasis** flanked by beautiful icons. You should also take a stroll through the village to admire the palace-sized **houses**, some adorned with ceramic friezes. From here, continue up into the hills where the **Church of Panagía** (18C) is perched: look out for its pretty bell-tower. It contains some Roman and Byzantine inscriptions. Even more striking is the magnificent **view***, which stretches as far as the sea.

Beyond Portariá, the road becomes very winding, and with the constant distraction of the **vertiginous panorama****, drivers may find it difficult to concentrate (this is the time, however, for extreme caution!). From the **mountain pass of Hánia**, at an altitude of 1 200m *(12km from Portariá)*, you can either continue to the winter-sports resort of **Agriólefkes** *(2km from the pass)*, or turn left in the direction of Zagorá, on the eastern face of Mt Pelion.

■ **Zagorá** – *18km from Agriólefkes.* Tucked away in the midst of a thick cover of forest, Pelion's largest village (pop 3 000) is less attractive than its neighbours. It was, however, an important centre for the Hellenic cultural renaissance which took place during the Ottoman Era, as well as the centre for the textile industry. Today, the surrounding orchards are the main source of income. Among the various churches, it is worth having a look at **Agía Kiriakí**, near the post office, and **Agíos Geórgios** *(beyond the Horeftó crossroads)*, with its entrance **porch-cum-tower**. Inside there is a pulpit and a richly carved wooden **iconostasis***.

From the village, a road leads down to the resort of **Horeftó** *(8km)*, flanked by a **beach★** which stretches as far as the eye can see.

Go back the way you came, passing through Zagorá. When you come to a crossroads in the open countryside (15km), turn left and continue for 12km.

■ **Kissós★** – Surrounded by woodland, the village has a timeless quality about it which you can savour in the pretty little squares shaded by plane trees as you admire the breathtaking **view★★** over the Aegean Sea. Like all the villages in the area, Kissós is inhabited by rugged mountain folk, who nevertheless are known for their welcoming ways. Do not leave without visiting the great **Church of Agía Marína★** (18C). Crowned by five cupolas, its nave and aisles are decorated with frescoes and contain an **iconostasis★** which is a masterpiece.

■ You return to a more Mediterranean atmosphere in the resort of **Ágios Ioánnis** *(6km from Kissós)*, which has a huge **beach**. *After a stop for a swim, rejoin the main road to Mouréssi.*

■ **Tsangaráda★** – *9km from Ágios Ioánnis.* An enchanting village, its houses are dotted along the many paths through the woods which fill the air with an intoxicating freshness. But, as typical of the area and as lovely as the houses and churches are, the star attraction here is undoubtedly the truly colossal **plane tree★** in the main square. Purported to be a thousand years old, its foliage has a spread of nearly 15m!

The village of Makrinítsa in the peaceful Pelion Mountains

Pelion

G. de Benoist/MICHELIN

You could stop off here or carry on to **Milopótamos★** *(8km)*, which clings to the cliff-side, overlooking bays fringed with **beaches★** reached by steps.

Continue along the main road, and 20km further on, turn left at the major road junction.

■ **Miliés★** – *22km from Tsangaráda*. A charming village crisscrossed by flagstone alley-ways which constantly echo to the refreshing trickle of an ancient fountain, Miliés is another good place for a stopover; and make sure you don't leave without sampling a *tyrópsomo* (cheese tart), the local speciality. As well as its charming atmosphere, the village is mainly famous for having been a centre of Hellenic renaissance under the Ottomans.

If you are interested in history (albeit its darker moments) you could visit the small **Folk Museum** *(10am-2pm; closed Monday)*, which has a collection of photos depicting the tragic massacre perpetrated here by the Nazis in 1943, as well as some of the 1955 earthquake. It also houses an exhibition of craftwork and paintings by local artists. Above all, do not miss the **library★** *(9am-2pm; closed Sunday)*, with its incredible collection of 3 000 ancient books inherited from the famous Miliés school (18C). A beautiful example of the local architecture, the **Church of the Taxiárhes★** (17C) houses a glorious gilded wood **iconostasis★**, and some vivid **frescoes**. Lastly, take a look at the old **disused railway station**, below the village *(20min walk)*.

■ Continuing along the small road past Miliés, you come to the charming little town of **Vizítsa★** *(2km)*, its mass of **traditional houses★** worthy of a cinema set. Another attraction is the **panorama★★**.

On the west coast
Returning to the road junction (4km), take the road to the right which winds down to the west coast, which you then drive along to the south.

Platanídia, **Maláki**, **Káto Gadzéa**, **Kalá Nerá**... the further you go down the west coast from Vólos the more charming the resorts. The mountains also begin to give way to a softer Mediterranean landscape.

■ You could stop for a while in **Áfissos** *(14km from Miliés)*, an attractive and lively resort, its quayside lined with café and restaurant terraces. If you need to cool off, head for the small, shady square, and the stream that runs through it. And if you fancy a swim, there are three **beaches** nearby.

■ A small, quiet port with several hotels and restaurants, **Hórto** *(15km)* also boasts two **beaches** in the vicinity. But if it is not lively enough for you, you would do better to head for the resort of **Milína** *(3km from Hórto)*, with the same beautiful **view★** over the bay.

■ From Milína, you can set off for the westernmost point of the peninsula *(30km)*, or head for **Platániá** *(17km)* on the south coast. While the town takes on the appearance of a pleasant little seaside resort during the summer months, it devotes the rest of the year to its fishing activities.

Making the most of Vólos

COMING AND GOING

By train – The *station* is situated to the west of Platía Ríga Feréou, on Odós Papadiamandí. There are seven direct services to Athens, between 5.35am and 9.08pm (7hr), and two express trains, at 6.25am and 7.06pm (5hr). To Thessaloníki, eight trains daily, between 5.35am and 9.08pm (4hr). There are also frequent services (daily) to Lárissa.

By bus – The **terminal** is in Odós Grigoríou Lambráki: to Lárissa, services depart approximately every hour, from
6am to 9pm (1hr); to Kalambáka, 4 services, from 6am to 9pm (3hr); to Thessaloníki, 6 services, from 6.15am to
8.30pm (3hr); to Athens, 9 services,
from 7.30am to 10pm (5hr). Note that
services are much less frequent from
October to May.

By ferry – The landing-stage is in Odós
Argonaftón, at the bottom of Odós Elefthériou Venizélou. From July to September, three to five sailings daily to
Skiáthos (3hr30min); Skópelos
(4hr30min); to Alónissos, one sailing
daily, except Wednesday (5hr30min).

By hydrofoil – In summer, frequent
services to Skiáthos (1hr15min), Skópelos (2hr) and Alónissos (2hr30min).

GETTING AROUND

By rental vehicle – **Avis**, Odós Argonaftón 41, ☎ (0421) 20 849,
Fax (0421) 32 360. **Europcar**, Odós Iásonos 83, ☎ (0421) 24 381, Fax (0421)
24 192. Also hires out motorcycles.
Hertz, airport, ☎ (0421) 22 544.
Theofanídis Hellas, Odós Iásonos 137,
☎ (0421) 32 360 / 36 238.

ADDRESS BOOK

Tourist information – **EOT**, Platía
Ríga Feréou, ☎ (0421) 23 500,
Fax (0421) 24 750. In summer, Monday-Friday 7am-2.30pm / 6pm-8.30pm,
weekends 9am-12.30pm / 6pm-
8.30pm; in winter, 7am-2.30pm; closed
at weekends. Information on the Pelion
region.

Tourist police – Odós 28 Oktomvríou
179, ☎ (0421) 72 421.

Banks / Currency exchange –
National Bank of Greece, seafront.
Open Monday-Thursday 8am-2pm, Fri-
day 8am-1.30pm. Cash dispenser.

Post office – Odós Pávlou Melá 45, entrance is easily missed. Poste restante.

Telephone – Local code: 0421. **OTE**,
Odós Eleftheríou Venizélou 22.

Internet – Odós Topáli 14, near Hotel
Selecta. (Open Monday-Saturday, 9am-
1am, Sunday 4pm-1am).

Travel agencies – **Les Hirondelles**,
Odós Koumoundoúrou 19, ☎ (0421)
32 171, Fax (0421) 35 030. This agency
offers a range of sporting activities (hiking, mountain biking, horse-riding,
diving, kayaks) and also hires out cars.

Taxis – ☎ (0421) 52 222.

WHERE TO STAY

Under €23

Hotel Iolkos, Odós Dimitriádos 37,
near the tourist information office,
☎ (0421) 23 416 – 15rm. ⛖ TV
Slightly run down but good value for
money.

Between €23 and €45

Iasonas, Odós Pávlou Melá 1, ☎ (0421)
26 075, Fax (0421) 26 975 – 40rm. ⌑
♪ TV Very acceptable accommodation
in comfortable, well-kept rooms. Only
the white tiles and pink and green walls
are of rather dubious taste...

Admitos, Odós A Diákou 5, ☎ (0421)
21 117, Fax (0421) 21 119 – 33rm. ⌑
▤ ♪ TV A quiet hotel, very close to
Odós Dimitriádos, with simple but spotlessly clean rooms, with balcony. English spoken. Prices are considerably
higher in summer.

Electra, Odós Topáli 24, ☎ (0421)
32 671, Fax (0421) 31 224 – 38rm. ⌑
▤ ♪ TV CC The rooms are small and
lack character, but are impeccably clean
and comfortable. The hotel is in a pleasant little shopping street in the town
centre.

Over €60

Aegli Pallas, Odós Argonaftón 24-26,
☎ (0421) 24 471, Fax (0421) 33 006 –
75rm. ⌑ ▤ ♪ TV CC This old hotel
with its neo-Classical architecture has
been recently renovated. Pleasant rooms
with fitted carpets and views over the
port. Breakfast is included.

EATING OUT, HAVING A DRINK

There are plenty of seafood restaurants
along the quayside. The cafés are mostly
located at the eastern end of Odós Dimitriádos, on the seafront.

Making the most of Mt Pelion

COMING AND GOING

By bus – Most of the Pelion mountain villages can be reached from Vólos (see above).

By train – At weekends, the train which travels between Vólos and Miliés leaves at 11am (1hr) and returns at 4pm.

ADDRESS BOOK

Telephone – Local codes: Makrinítsa, Hánia (0428), Tsangaráda, Milopótamos (0426), Áfissos and Plataniá (0423).

WHERE TO STAY

There are rooms to let – sometimes in magnificent buildings – in nearly all of the villages, but make sure you book ahead in winter and at Easter (prices are considerably higher). On the coast, however, most hotels close in the winter, and summer is the high season.

• Makrinítsa

Under €38

Domátia Makrópoulo, near the church, in the hills above the village, ☎ (0428) 99 016, Fax (0428) 99 073 – 8rm. ⁊ A small, very quiet guesthouse with simple but spotlessly clean rooms. Reasonable prices and a friendly welcome. The terrace has views down over the whole village.

Between €45 and €60

Archontikó Roútsou, ☎ (0428) 994 30, Fax (0428) 99 114 – 9rm. ⁊ This guesthouse lacks the charm of some of the more traditional houses, but is pleasant all the same. The owners, who are very friendly, also have other rooms to let.

Archontikó Xiradákis, in the main street, follow the signs, ☎ (0428) 99 250 – 12rm. ⁊ In a very striking building which is around two hundred years old, with a terrace, this guesthouse enjoys a splendid view. The rooms have a monastic feel but are not without charm. Breakfast is included.

Archontikó Repaná, main street, ☎ (0428) 99 548 – 7rm. ⁊ ℐ TV This enchanting 19C house, which also has a magnificent view, has pretty rooms furnished with antiques. You can have breakfast (extra) in the garden.

Over €75

Archontikó Karamarlí, main street, on the left, ☎ (0428) 99 570, Fax (0428) 99 779 – 9rm. ⁊ ℐ TV The rooms in this amazing 17C house were decorated and furnished by the owner, a stage designer by profession... but this is reflected in the prices. Have your breakfast (included) on the panoramic terrace.

• Kissós

Under €30

Sofoklís Garoufaliás, left of the church, ☎ (0426) 31 214 – 8rm. ⁊ ✗ Simple and comfortable rooms. Warm welcome and excellent family cooking. Breakfast is included.

• Tsangaráda

Under €60

Parádisos Pension, main street, on the right-hand side, ☎ (0426) 49 209, Fax (0426) 49 551 – 40rm. ⁊ ℐ TV ✗ CC A comfortable, welcoming hotel run by the Rigákis brothers. Ask for one of the rooms facing the road, noisier, but worth it for the view.

Xenia, follow the signs from the village, ☎ (0426) 49 205, Fax (0426) 49 496 – 46rm. ⁊ ℐ TV A comfortable establishment, due to be renovated in the near future (a pool is planned). Ask for an upstairs room, with balcony and sea view. The restaurant is only open in winter (breakfast is included).

• Vizítsa

Under €38

Domátia Georgáras, as you enter the village, ☎ (0423) 86 359 – 5rm. ⁊ ℐ TV ✗ This new hotel, traditional in style but lacking in charm, has comfortable, well-kept rooms.

Over €75

Blanas Mansion, from the car park, take the alley off to the right, ☎ (0423) 86 359 – 4 rm. ⁊ ⚵ ℐ TV CC A magnificent old house, with wood panelling and stone flags. Full of atmosphere and extremely comfortable (sauna). Panoramic lounge on the first floor.

- **Áfissos**

Under €30

Domátia Réna, at the end of the quayside, ☎ (0423) 33 297, Fax (0423) 33 439 – 10rm. ⚲ A pleasant guesthouse facing the sea with comfortable, spacious studio-apartments (although a bit noisy) with kitchens. Good value for money.

Over €55

Maïstráli, at the end of the village, near Abovos beach, ☎ (0423) 33 472, Fax (0423) 33 149 – 5rm. ⚲ 🗏 🐾 [TV] ✗ 🌿 [CC] Comfortable, well-kept rooms, balconies with sea view, at a reasonable price. The professional and friendly staff speak English.

Katia Hotel, behind the main square, ☎ (0423) 33 297, Fax (0423) 33 023 – 22rm. ⚲ 🗏 🐾 [TV] [CC] This small luxurious hotel has extremely comfortable – though somewhat small – rooms. Rather lethargic reception.

- **Plataniá**

Under €30

Domátia Nikólaos Papastamatíou, at the harbour, ☎ (0423) 71 535 – 5rm. Monastic-style rooms and welcome, but comfortable enough for the price.

Hotel Drosseró Akrogiáli, at the harbour, ☎ (0423) 71 210 – 30rm. ⚲ 🐾 ✗ A long building several storeys high, with comfortable rooms but no sea view. The friendly owner, who speaks only Greek, also runs the Kastri campsite on the road into the village.

EATING OUT

- **Makrinítsa**

Psystariá, main street, left-hand side. 🍴 Roast meats, chicken, *spet-*

sofáy (sausages)... all the local delicacies are served here. Furthermore, the service is quick and friendly. Try to get a table on the terrace – the view is superb.

Panthéon, village square, ☎ (0428) 99 143. 🍴 Another place to try *spetsofáy* and bean soup.

- **Miliés**

To Panórama, opposite the museum. 🍴 Its specialities are chicken, pork in wine, spinach tart. You can choose between the terrace and the upstairs dining room, with fine views.

Kira Marías, church square. 🍴 The cooking is simple (cheese tarts, salads), served in the shade of a plane tree.

- **Vizítsa**

Mpalkonáki, 🍴 Delicious local delicacies served in the shade of a plane tree.

- **Áfissos**

I Psátha, at the end of the quayside, ☎ (0423) 33 587. 🍴 An excellent restaurant for Greek cuisine and seafood, very friendly. The chef is French.

Café Óasis, near the square, on the seafront. 🍴 An ideal place for breakfast or a drink in the evening. Also has bicycles for hire.

- **Plataniá**

Nikólaos Papastamatíou, 🍴 Greek cuisine and fish from the morning's catch.

OTHER THINGS TO DO

Excursions – There are caiques to the peninsula's more isolated beaches. Book at **Les Hirondelles** agency in Ágios Ioánnis, ☎ (0426) 31 181, Fax (0426) 31 180. See also in Vólos.

MÉTÉORA ★★★

Province of Thessaly – District of Tríkala
20km from Tríkala and 125km from Ioánnina
Regional map page 304 – Michelin map 980 fold 16

Not to be missed
The cathedral in Kalambáka.
The hilltop monasteries.

And remember...
Visit Megálo Metéoro and Varlaám in the morning and the other monasteries
in the afternoon.
Avoid the busiest periods, at Easter and Christmas.
Wear respectable clothing (no bare legs or shoulders)
and take comfortable shoes and a hat.

On the edge of the Pindus mountain chain, where it meets the plain of Thessaly, an extraordinary forest of rocks rears up, with smooth, vertiginous walls, like sugarloaves on a bed of greenery. These curious promontories have been used since the 11C as celestial perches for the monasteries which are aptly named Metéora: "suspended in the air". Indeed, such a unique location (listed as a UNESCO World Heritage site) could only serve as an inspiration to men who, since the dawn of time, have heaped legends upon it... and it has even been used – albeit in a rather less orthodox context – as a setting for the adventures of James Bond. Although often confused with Mt Athos, another dazzling example of monastic architecture *(see page 444)*, the comparison stops there. This is because the Metéora have ceased to be a pilgrimage shrine: instead, hordes of tourists flock here each year, and it is a near miracle that the place has lost nothing of its magical atmosphere which remains just as intense.

Nearer to God

The first monks settled in the Metéora in 11C, inspired by the example of **St Simeon Stylites**, the Syrian ascetic (5C), who for 36 years remained perched on a column (*stylos* in Greek) 25m above the ground. They first settled in caves which lent themselves to asceticism and mystical contemplation, and came down to Doúpiani every Sunday to celebrate a communal Mass. During the 14C, however, there was a shake-up in proceedings, instigated by St Athanasius, who came from Mt Athos and laid down rules governing the lives of the anchorites. Soon the Metéora were bristling with monasteries, built in precarious conditions up above the abyss. The Orthodox Serbians, who dominated the region at the time, proved to be devout and generous protectors, and from the 15C, there were no fewer than 24 monasteries, decorated by the greatest artists of the time, including **Theophanes of Crete**.

Paradoxically, the Ottoman invasion in no way hindered the development of the monasteries and they were even the beneficiaries, in the 16C, of the generosity of Süleyman the Magnificent. This was not to last: a long period of decline ensued, brought about by the levying of taxes and disputes between the communities about the management of the huge landed estates. Integration with Greece in 1881 did nothing to check this decline, and the monks' domains were confiscated in the 1920s. In 1949, however, in the aftermath of the civil war, some of the monasteries were providing shelter for refugees, and even for some tourists! Then, thanks to Bishop **Dionysus**, monasticism underwent a revival, and there are now 5 monasteries still in operation, as well as one convent.

The Metéora, a taste for the high life (Agía Triáda)

...te has no fewer than sixty of ...rocky towers – some more than ... – sculpted and polished by the va... erosion into gigantic pebbles. They ...fact blocks of sandstone that are much ...der than the limestone of the Pindus ...hain, which was gradually worn away by the River Piniós and its tributaries, eventually leaving a maze of narrow gorges at their feet. As water streamed down through the rocks, the gorges became furrowed with gullies. With the passage of time, the sandstone base was broken up into rocky outcrops, exposed and scrubbed clean by erosion to create this amazing landscape of natural pillars which tower up over the plain.

But the removable ladders and the system of hoists, which were once the usual way up for the monks or their provisions, have been abandoned in favour of roads and steps, thereby opening up the Metéora to tourism. The revenues generated by these 'heaven-sent' visitors are considerable and are supplemented by grants from the European Union for the restoration of the monasteries. In short, monastic life is now a little less austere: it is not unusual to see monks with mobile telephones or driving cars, and most monasteries now have bookshops and souvenir shops.

At the foot of the Metéora

Kalambáka

Tucked away at the foot of the Metéora, this large, bustling village serves as the main base for the millions of tourists who come to visit the area every year. Look out for the majestic rocks: omnipresent, they appear at the corner of every street. The village stretches out along Odós Trikálon, the long principal thoroughfare that runs through **Platía R Feréou** (the main square), then the **town hall square**, where most of the bars, restaurants, hotels and souvenir shops are to be found.

As a prelude to exploring the suspended monasteries, pay a visit to the **cathedral★** (Mitrópoli), high in the upper part of the village (*in the continuation of Odós Vlachavá; 8am-1pm / 4pm-8pm; variable opening times*). Probably built in the 12C, the church contains a magnificent marble **ambo★★** – the only one in Greece – set with pieces recycled from the Early-Christian Period. Pavement **mosaics** from an earlier shrine have been discovered and, in the gloom pierced by the occasional ray of light, you can make out the mural **frescoes** from the 13C, 14C and 16C, which are sadly very discoloured.

Odós Trikálon then continues on to the neighbouring village of **Kastráki** (*2km*) on the other side of the first massif. This is the best place to stay, as it is quieter and nearer to the monasteries.

Between heaven and earth

Beyond Kastráki, the road climbs up towards the monasteries. Allow 1 day. Please note that you are not allowed to take flash photographs of the frescoes.

As well as the six large monasteries, the Metéora site also conceals a number of abandoned sanctuaries – some of which are undergoing restoration – a good excuse for a beautiful walk; but be careful not to get lost! Perched on the heights, some are virtually inaccessible, unless you follow the example of the highly-skilled mountaineers, for whom climbing up the steep vertical rock-face holds no fears. The great majority of tourists prefer to get there in comfortable air-conditioned coaches, and when visiting the main monasteries, the aim of the game is to time your visit in the interval between the arrivals of two coach-loads...

■ **Ágios Nikólaos Anapáfsas★★** – *Open every day, 9am-5.45pm. Entrance fee.*
Crowning a slender peak, of which it almost seems to be part, is the monastery dedicated to St Nicholas, which probably dates from the 15C, if not the 14C or even the 13C. At the top of the steps is the **refectory**, used as a reception room, and then

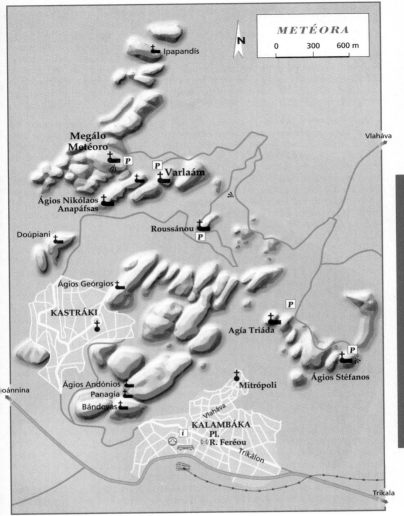

the **katholikón** (16C), the very narrow church topped with a windowless dome, the top floor of which houses the monks' cells. In contrast, the narthex seems more spacious and luminous. In the absence of a courtyard, it was actually used as a study room. Linger to look at the **frescoes★★**, masterpieces of expression, the work of the great artist Theophanes of Crete (16C). In particular, note the very appealing Virgin and Child, the Dormition of St Ephraim the Syrian, and the large composition representing the Last Judgement. Finally, at the far end of the promontory, there is a superb **panorama★★** over the Metéora, stretching as far as the eye can see.

■ **Roussánou**★ (Agía Barbára) – *Open every day, 9am-6pm. Entrance fee.* Another hilltop domain, the monastery of St Barbara occupies an unassailable position at the summit of a rocky outcrop with vertiginous walls. Luckily for visitors, the ancient system of mobile ladders has been replaced by steep steps leading to two **stone bridges** which are suspended above the drop, adding to the beauty of the setting. Probably constructed in the 14C, the monastery was renovated in the 16C, and the domed **katholikón** has some beautiful **frescoes** (1561). But you should also climb to the top of the nearby hill to enjoy the **view**★★ back down over the monastery, its noble silhouette highlighted against the backdrop of the majestic Pindus Chain.

■ **Varlaám**★★★ – *Open every day except Friday, 9am-1pm / 3.20pm-6pm. Entrance fee.* Larger than the previous ones, this monastery owes its name to the first ascetic who settled on the summit of this 373m peak in 1350. Erected by the Aparas brothers, noblemen from Ioánnina (16C), the sanctuary flourished rapidly. Having been bombed during the Second World War, it underwent restoration and is once more home to a monastic community. A ramp hewn out of the rock means it can be reached without difficulty. According to legend, it took 22 years to gather together the materials to construct the **katholikón**★ (1544) and only 20 days to actually build it. All nooks and crannies, it has inside a pretty wooden **iconostasis**★, some furniture inlaid with mother-of-pearl and ivory, and also some **frescoes**★★ by Frango Catellano (1548), one of the masters of post-Byzantine art. The ones in the narthex (1566), where the tombs of the Aparas brothers lie, depict the Last Judgement and the Life of John the Baptist. In the **Chapel of the Three Hierarchs**, on the site of the original oratory, the Dormition of St John Chrysostom and the Dormition of St Ephraim the Syrian (17C) illustrate the influence of both the Cretan school and western style. The visit continues with the treasures of the **refectory**★, where you can see some gold-embroidered **liturgical vestments**, some icons, a **Gospel**★★★ (960) which once belonged to Emperor Constantine Porphyrogenitus and some carved wooden **crosses**. Lastly, past the **storeroom** with an enormous **barrel** which can hold 12 000 litres, the tour comes to an end at the **Vrizoni Tower**, which has retained its **windlass**.

■ **Great Meteoron**★★★ (Megálo Metéoro) – *Open every day except Tuesday, 9am-1pm / 3.20pm-6pm. Entrance fee.* Perched atop an impressive 400m-high rock, the Great Meteoron, or Monastery of the Transfiguration, was founded by St Athanasius in 1356. His successor and disciple, St Ioasáf, the heir to the Serbian Despotate of Epirus, spent 40 years of his life here and endowed it with some sumptuous works of art. Although damaged by bombing during the war, it still remains one of the most important monasteries in Greece. As you climb up the steps, you pass in front of the **cave** where Athanasius lived as a hermit. Then you come to the **Vrizoni Tower**, which was used to winch up provisions, and from where there is a superb **panorama**★★, which takes in the Varlaám Monastery.

At the centre of the complex stands the **katholikón**, its cruciform plan emphasised by lateral conches. It is crowned with a high dome, decorated with the figure of Christ against a gold background. The **frescoes**★★, a splendid example of post-Byzantine art, were the work of Theophanes of Crete or his pupils (16C). Beyond the exonarthex, with its walls adorned with plates, you enter the narthex, where Athanasius and Ioasáf lie, at the foot of frescoes depicting various martyrs. Separated from the nave by an **iconostasis** with some remarkable **icons**★★, the sanctuary – the only original part of the church (1388) – contains some frescoes depicting various saints in suits of armour.

The monastery has three other churches, but even more impressive is the **refectory**★, with its domed ceiling and colonnade. Note the **icons**, ancient **manuscripts**, crockery and chandeliers set on enormous wooden tables. Next to it is the **kitchen** where the utensils are covered in a layer of fine dust, as if suddenly abandoned. You

Fresco of the Dormition of the Virgin, in the Varlaám Monastery

should also visit the **storeroom**, where jars, barrels and an assortment of tools are kept, as well as the **ossuary** where skulls have been carefully arranged on shelves, and the **Folk Museum**.

■ **Agía Triáda**★★ (Holy Trinity) – *Open every day except Thursday, 9am-12.30pm / 3pm-5pm. Entrance fee.* Just as spectacular is the site of the monastery of the Holy Trinity (14C or 15C), atop an enormous pillar of rock. From the road, a path leads to steps cut into the rock. Your efforts will be generously rewarded by the **view**★★ down over Kalambáka and the other monasteries. Legend has it that it took 70 years to hoist all the building materials up to the top! The monastery has retained its winching system intact, near the **Chapel of St John the Baptist** which was hewn out of the rock. A quaint little domed building, the **katholikón**★★ (15C) houses a number of magnificent **frescoes**★ as well as an iconostasis covered with some beautiful portable **icons**★. The fabulous treasure that it held has sadly disappeared, pillaged by the Germans during the Second World War.

■ **Ágios Stéfanos**★★ (St Stephen) – *Open every day except Monday, 9am-1pm / 3.20pm-6pm. Entrance fee.* Like a fortified castle, this monastery stands on a rock separated from the mountain by a ravine spanned by a **stone bridge**. Built on the site of a 12C hermitage, its prosperity dates from the 14C, when the Byzantine Emperor Andronicus Paleologus heaped riches upon it in thanks for the welcome he received there. Elevated to the status of patriarchate in 1545, it occupied an important position in the hierarchy of the Metéora, but was also pillaged by the Germans during the war. Since 1961, it has housed a convent where the nuns maintain the traditions of icon painting and music.

Repainted after the war, the **frescoes** of the **Church of St Haralámbos** (18C) have replaced those destroyed during a German bombing raid, although without the patina of time they are rather bright; but the sumptuous wooden **iconostasis**★ is original, as is the **reliquary** which contains the venerated skull of the saint. The **Chapel of Ágios Stéfanos** (15C) at the other end of the courtyard is not usually included in the visit, but you can console yourself with the **refectory**, where you can see some splendid **icons**★★ (16C-19C), a 6C **manuscript**★★, a **letter from the Patriarch of Constantinople**★★★ (16C), as well as some incense burners and priests' vestments. Last of all, at the end of the plateau allow yourself time to relish the magnificent **view**★★★ over Kalambáka and the Piniós plain.

Making the most of the Metéora

COMING AND GOING

By train – Four trains a day link Kalambáka with Athens (5-6hr). *Kalambáka station*, ☎ (0432) 22 451.

By bus – The terminal is down from the taxi rank. Frequent services to Tríkala (30min), from 6.15am to 9.15pm (from 7am on Sunday). From there, you can get a train or a bus to Athens or Thessaloníki. To Métsovo (1hr30min) and Ioánnina (3hr), departures at 8.45am and 3.20pm, and to Vólos (3hr), at 7am, 11am, 2.30pm and 6.30pm.

GETTING AROUND

By bus – From Kalambáka, there is a bus service (summer only) to the main monasteries of the Metéora: Megálo Metéoro, Ágios Nikólaos, Varlaám and Roussánou. Monday-Friday: 9am, 10am, 1.20pm; weekends: 8.20am, 9.45am, 1.20pm. Also frequent services to Kastráki (from 6.30am to 9.30pm).

By taxi – The taxi rank is in the town hall square, ☎ (0432) 22 310, 22 822.

By rental motorcycle and bicycle – *Papadzimópoulos*, on the Kastráki road.

ADDRESS BOOK (KALAMBÁKA)

Tourist information – Town hall square. Open every day, 8am-10pm from May to October; opening times vary during the rest of the year. The friendly and efficient staff can supply all kinds of information on transport, accommodation and the monasteries.

Tourist police – Odós Hadzipétrou 10, ☎ (0432) 22 109.

Banks / Currency exchange – *National Bank of Greece*, Platía R Feréou. Monday-Thursday, 8am-2pm, Friday, 8am-1pm. Currency exchange and cash dispenser.

Moneda, Odós Sidirodrómou 1, near Platía R Feréou. Exchange bureau open 24hr a day.

Post office – *Main post office*, Odós Trikálon. Monday-Friday, 7.30am-2pm.

Telephone – Local code: 0432. *OTE*, Odós Ioannínon. Monday-Friday, 7.30am-10pm, Saturday, 7.20am-3pm.

Internet – *Hollywood Cafe*, Odós Trikálon, on the right-hand side before Platía R Feréou. A trendy bar, with a giant screen and a few computers.

Cocktail Cafe, on the corner of Odós Deligiári and Odós Dimoúla. From 8am until late at night.

WHERE TO STAY

The hotels are reasonably priced, although slightly more expensive in summer.

• Kalambáka

Campsite (around €12)

Kalambáka campsite, take the street to the right as you come into town, ☎ (0432) 22 309 – 40 pitches. ✗ ⊿ On the side of a hill, this is a pleasant campsite, shaded by trees.

Under €30

Hotel Meteora, Odós Ploútarchou 13, from the town hall square, take the Kastráki road, turning immediately right into the street that goes up, ☎ (0432) 22 367 – 10rm. ◢⃠ A small, simple establishment with quiet rooms that are spotlessly clean. Friendly staff who speak English.

Hotel Aeolic Star, Odós A Diákou 4, up from the town hall square, ☎ (0432) 22 325 – 16rm. ◢⃠ Decorated with dried flowers, this stylish hotel has simple but well-appointed rooms. Some have a television and balcony.

Over €45

Hotel Helvetia, Odós P Dimitríou 45, on the way out of town, towards Kastráki, ☎ (0432) 23 041, Fax (0432) 25 241 – 18rm. ◢⃠ ✗ 🅣 A rather gloomy hotel, but comfortable enough. The prices seem rather high, so don't hesitate to negotiate.

Hotel Edelweiss, Odós E Venizélou 3, in the town centre, ☎ (0432) 23 966, Fax (0432) 24 733 – 48rm. ◢⃠ 🍽 ✗ 🅣 ✗ ⊿ 🆑 A three-storey building with clean, but rather uninspiring rooms. Caters mainly for groups. The swimming pool, however, with its view of the Metéora, is amazing. Prices are high, so negotiate.

• **Kastráki**

Vráchos-Kastráki campsite, on the way into the village, opposite Hotel France, ☎ (0432) 22 293, Fax (0432) 23 134 – 300 pitches. ✕ ⵜ Open all year round, this campsite has everything you need: mini-market, kitchens and barbecues, washing machines, and a children's play area. The owners extend a warm welcome and can supply lots of information on the Metéora. Moreover, the bus stops right in front.

Under €30

Domátia Patavális, opposite the fork in the road leading to Domátia Tsikéli, ☎ (0432) 22 801 – 7rm. ⵜ Small, impersonal rooms, but comfortable enough. The terrace with a view is very pleasant, but the lady owner does not speak English.

Vasilikí & Gregóry Ziógas, above the village, ☎ (0432) 24 037 – 10rm. ⵜ A friendly welcome, and the rooms, although modest, are clean and comfortable, with a view over the Metéora. More like a hotel than a guesthouse.

Domátia Tsikéli, on the way out of Kalambáka, take the street which goes off diagonally to the left, ☎ (0432) 22 438, Fax (0432) 77 872 – 18rm. ⵜ ℱ 📺 A pleasant place, warm welcome, breakfast served in a room complete with hearth which opens onto the garden. Some rooms have an unrivalled view of the Metéora.

Hotel France, on the way into the village, opposite the campsite, ☎ (0432) 24 186, Fax (0432) 75 186 – 26rm. ⵜ ℱ A hotel run by a very friendly Franco-Greek couple. The owner will be pleased to point out walks for you to go on, and might even act as a guide if he is available. The rooms cannot be faulted, and some have a view over the Metéora.

Dupani House, above the village, turn left and continue for 150m, ☎ and Fax (0432) 75 326 – 11rm. ⵜ 🍽 ℱ 💳 A very friendly welcome awaits at this quiet, secluded hotel, which enjoys the most beautiful view over its surroundings. Breakfast on the terrace in the sun.

Over €45

Hotel Kastráki, ☎ (0432) 75 336, Fax (0432) 75 335 – 27rm. ⵜ 🍽 ℱ 📺 ✕ On the bend as you head out of the village towards the Metéora. A modern,

very comfortable hotel. Some rooms have a view of the Metéora. Breakfast is included.

• **Kalambáka**

Under €15

Panellínion, Platía Dimarheíou. 🍴 One of three restaurants on this square. Good for a drink or good, plain Greek food.

• **Kastráki**

Under €15

Kosmikí Taverna, in the main street, near the church. 🍴 A beautiful terrace with a view over the Metéora, serving hearty meals. It is a pity that the staff are so unfriendly.

Bakaliarákia Taverna, near the church. 🍴 No surprises here, just delicious home cooking (salads, seafood), served with a modest local wine. On nights when there is no football on, there is Greek music in the restaurant. The cheapest in the area.

Philoxénia Taverna, above the village, past the church. 🍴 A pleasant place, which serves souvláki and spit-roast chicken.

Walking – Alpine Club, Platía Dimoúla. **Sideris**, Odós Patríou Dimitríou. A specialist shop selling walking equipment.

Festivals – Traditional folk dances are held in Kalambáka and Kastráki on Easter Sunday. In May, in Tríkala, dances and sports competitions are held **(Hatzipetriá)**.

Markets – On Thursday evenings and Friday mornings, the villagers from the surrounding area come to Kalambáka to sell their produce (olives, tomatoes, lettuces, grapes).

Antiques – Korákis Bros, Platía R Feréou. An Ali Baba's cave with assorted objects made from wood (tools, various utensils) and copper (lamps, trays), icons and jewellery.

Newspapers – Maria, Platía R Feréou. Newspapers and maps of the area.

MÉTSOVO★

Province of Epirus – District of Ioánnina – 56km from Ioánnina
Regional map page 304 – Michelin map 980 fold 16
Pop 4 000 – Alt 1 160m – Climate cool

Not to be missed
The Tosítsa house, converted into a museum.
A walk in the surrounding area.

With its sturdy, stone houses with their wooden upper storeys, Métsovo has something of Switzerland about it. But there is no room for doubt: you are well and truly in the heart of Epirus, a far cry from the sunny beaches of the Aegean coast. The old women in their long skirts, embroidered aprons and dark headscarves, the villagers getting around on mules... the town throws up some traditional clichés from times gone by, now charmingly outmoded. You come here to fill your lungs with the mountain air, all the more exhilarating and perfumed in this part of Greece, and to explore the mountains in all their majesty. Or to indulge your passion for winter sports.

Tour of the town
Allow one day

Leaving the Metéora, you cross the **Katára Pass** (1 705m), which marks the border between Thessaly and Epirus. The superb **view★★** stretches as far as Métsovo, seemingly clinging to the sides of a huge mountain range that curves round in a circle. It is easy to find your way around the town, which stretches the length of a sloping main street that comes out onto the **main square**. In an unchanging ritual, the old folk of Métsovo gather here after their siesta to sit and chat on the benches in the shade of the ancient trees. Right next to the square, the **Church of Agía Paraskeví** contains an ornate **iconostasis** (18C) with a profusion of carved motifs.
But the main charm of the place lies in the maze of little alleyways lined with attractive **stone houses★★** with projecting upper floors and stone roofs. Well worth a visit is the **Tosítsa House★★** *(from the main street, go up the steps near the Shell petrol pump; open every day except Thursday, 9am-1.30pm / 4pm-6pm; 30min guided tour; entrance fee)*, a sturdy building erected by Baron Michael Tosítsa in the 19C and now transformed into a Museum of Folk Art. The rooms with their tapestries, wood panelling and carved ceilings, evoke magnificently the splendour of this illustrious family, one of

The Vlachs – proud shepherds
Situated at the crossing point between the Aegean and the Ionian coasts, Métsovo has, since Antiquity, enjoyed great autonomy from the central powers, first the Byzantines and then the Ottomans. In return, the inhabitants of the region, who were descended from the Vlach shepherds, would guide travellers across the mountain passes of the Pindus Chain. A major crafts centre, Métsovo also became a trading centre for gold, silver and textiles, and the French established a trading post here in 1719. In the 19C, a number of successful families, including the Avérofs and the Tosítsas, who had made their fortunes from Egyptian cotton, generously contributed to the prosperity of the town.

whose members was the Minister of Foreign Affairs under Konstantínos Karamanlís. The museum houses a fine collection of jewellery, costumes and examples of **local craftwork**.
Art lovers might also be interested in the **Avérof Gallery** *(from the main square, take the street to the left of the National Bank; open every day except Thursday, 10am-4.30pm, 7pm from July to September; entrance fee)*. Founded by Evángelos Avérof-Tosítsa, it presents an interesting panorama of 19C and 20C **Greek painting**.

Thessaly and Epirus

The surrounding countryside offers plenty of opportunities for keen walkers. One path leads to the **Monastery of Ágios Nikólaos**, tucked away in the trees near a spring (*30min away, starting from the Hotel Athens*). With its rough stone walls, the building looks more like a sheepfold. Probably constructed in the 14C, it was rebuilt in about 1700 and decorated with post-Byzantine **frescoes**.

Making the most of Métsovo

COMING AND GOING

By bus – The bus stop is in the main square. To Ioánnina, 4 services daily (90min). To Tríkala, near the Metéora, 2 or 3 services daily (2hr30min).

ADDRESS BOOK

Greek Alpine Club – *Piktos Club*, next to Hotel Egnatia, ☎ (0656) 41 207. Monday-Friday, 7.30am-3pm. The club supplies excellent maps of the paths in the region and can arrange for a guide.

Banks / Currency exchange – National Bank of Greece, main square. Monday-Friday, 8am-2pm. Cash dispenser.

Post office – In the main street, just before the main square. Monday-Friday, 7.30am-2pm.

Telephone – *OTE*, main square. Monday-Friday, 7.30am-3pm.

WHERE TO STAY

Under €30
Hotel Athens, from the main square, take the street which goes down beside the bank, ☎ (0656) 41 332 – 9rm. ⚐ ✕ A large building with rustic-style rooms, but good value for money. Friendly reception and English is spoken. Try the breakfast: honey-flavoured yoghurt with rose petals...

Domátia Tsanaká, 100m from the main square, past the police station, ☎ (0656) 41 202, Fax (0656) 41 124 – 10rm. ⚐ TV A clean and comfortable establishment, with shared or private kitchens.

Filoxénia Hotel, near the Avérof Gallery, ☎ (0656) 41 725 – 16rm. ⚐ TV The building has been recently decorated in traditional style. The rooms are uninspiring but comfortable (some have a balcony with a superb view).

Hotel Egnatia, main street, before the main square, ☎ (0656) 41 263, Fax (0656) 41 485 – 35rm. ⚐ ℰ TV CC Clean, comfortable rooms. The owner, a member of the Alpine Club, can supply information and advice on walks in the

area, and offers minibus tours. Prices drop considerably in the low season.

Hotel Galaxías, near the bus stop, ☎ (0656) 41 202, Fax (0656) 41 124 – 10rm. ⚐ ℰ TV ✕ CC Very professional staff, English spoken. The rooms are comfortable and decorated with wood panelling and traditional fabrics. Prices significantly lower in the low season.

Between €30 and €60
Hotel Olympic, take the street which goes up from the main square, then follow the signs, ☎ (0656) 41 337, Fax (0656) 41 837 – 20rm. ⚐ ℰ TV CC Comfortable rooms with wood panelling and carpets, an oasis of calm and an unbeatable view over the valley. Little garden. Breakfast is included.

Hotel Apollon, near the main square, ☎ (0656) 41 844, Fax (0656) 42 110 – 43rm. ⚐ ℰ TV CC Car park. An enormous, three-storey hotel. Attractive rooms with carpets and wood panelling (some have a balcony). Prices drop considerably in the low season.

EATING OUT, HAVING A DRINK

Between €9 and €13
Athens, in the hotel of the same name. ⚐ You eat on the terrace or in the (rustic-style) dining room. The food is hearty, fresh and inexpensive.

Galaxías, near the hotel of the same name. Prices are slightly higher than the previous entry, but the fish and pasta are excellent. Also ideal for breakfast.

Cafés – *Café Pétrino*, on the left as you come into the main square. A small, unpretentious café frequented by backgammon players. Superb view.

SHOPPING GUIDE

Arts and crafts – In the main square and main street, there are many shops selling articles crafted from wood and geometrically-patterned woollen fabrics.

IOÁNNINA ★★

ANCIENT DODONA (DODÓNI) ★★

Capital of the province of Epirus and of the district of Ioánnina
100km from Igoumenítsa – Regional map page 304 – Michelin map 980 fold 15
Alt 520m – Pop 57 000 – Mild climate

Not to be missed
The kástro in Ioánnina and the island of Nissí Ioanínon in the lake.
Pérama Cave.
The ancient theatre of Dodona.

And remember...
Take a light woollen garment when you visit Pérama Cave.
If you are in a group, take a taxi to Dodona.

As soon as you leave the sunny climes of the Ionian coastline, another Greece, wild and unknown, reveals itself. Tucked away in the hollow of a vast ring of mountains, on the verdant banks of a lake, Ioánnina enjoys a luxuriant setting. The capital of Epirus, it is also a modern, vibrant city, which takes pride in its double role as university town and commercial centre. But there is also another side to Ioánnina, with a softer, almost Oriental feel, that lies hidden in its narrow streets, along the lakeside promenade, and within the walls of the citadel. This quiet atmosphere of ancient charm is also reflected in the romantic monasteries on Nissí Ioanínon, an island set upon the lake like a frail barque. Ioánnina itself has plenty to make visitors want to stay, and there are numerous treasures tucked away in the surrounding countryside, such as Pérama Cave, the Dodona oracle and the villages of Zagória. It is impossible to leave without a twinge of regret...

Despots and tyrants

Founded under Justinian (6C), for centuries Ioánnina remained largely unaffected by great historical events. But history caught up with it when the Norman **Bohemond**, pursued by Alexius Comnenus, took refuge in the town, surrounding it with ramparts (1082). After the occupation of Constantinople by the Latins (1204), the Greek Michael Angelus Ducas founded the **Despotate of Epirus**, of which Árta became the capital. He set about embellishing Ioánnina, the second city of the state, and had the first monasteries built on the island of Nissí Ioanínon. In the early 14C, the Byzantine Empire recaptured the city but granted it a certain degree of autonomy and the status of religious metropolis.

There was a new twist at the end of the 14C, when the city fell into the hands of the **Serbian tyrant, Preljubovic**, who made the town the capital of his despotate. To counter the threat from Albania, he made an appeal for help to the newcomers on the Balkan scene: the **Turks**. In 1430, Ioánnina gave itself up to them without a fight, thus preserving itself from pillaging and conserving its privileges. The 16C brought great prosperity to the region, both in economic and artistic terms. However, in 1611, the **rebellion of Bishop Dionysus** provoked a violent reaction from the Turks, who abolished the privileges accorded to the city and threw the Christians out of the citadel. Despite everything, Ioánnina has retained its commercial dynamism. In the 17C, many churches were built, its schools achieved great renown, and, in the following century, it became established as one of the centres of Greek Enlightenment. A shadow would fall across the scene, however: declared *pashalik* of Epirus in 1788, the ruthless **Ali Pasha** conducted a merciless campaign against the Souliot rebels. Anxious to quell his ambitions, the Sublime Porte then sent an army of 50 000 men to besiege the town that Ali Pasha had fortified. He took refuge on the island of Nissí Ioanínon, and was finally assassinated in 1822. However, the nationalists would have to wait

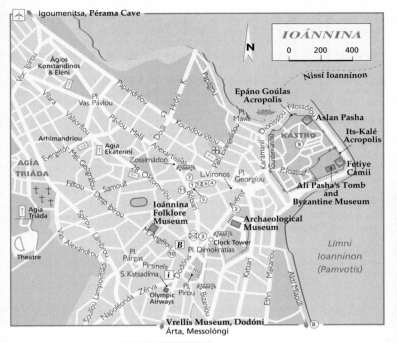

Igoumenítsa, Pérama Cave

IOÁNNINA
N   0   200   400

Nissí Ioannínon

Ágios Konstandínos & Eléni

Epáno Goúlas Acropolis

Aslan Pasha

Its-Kalé Acropolis

KÁSTRO (9)

Fetiye Camii

Ali Pasha's Tomb and Byzantine Museum

AGÍA TRIÁDA

Agía Ekateríni

Zossimádon

Agía Triáda

Ioánnina Folklore Museum

Archaeological Museum

Límni Ioannínon (Pamvotís)

Theatre

Clock Tower
Pl. Dimokratías

Vrellís Museum, Dodóni
Árta, Messolóngi

Olympic Airways

Ioánnina

HOTELS

Agapi	①	Hermes	⑦
Astoria	②	Hôtel du Lac	⑧
Bretania	③	Kastro	⑨
Dioni	④	Olympic	⑩
Egnatia	⑤	Palladion	⑪
El Greco	⑥	Paris	⑫

until 1913 to see the arrival of **Greek** troops. The **Second World War** was to strike a final historical blow with German bombing raids and the deportation of the Jewish community, which had existed there since the 14C.

Tour of the town
Allow 2 days including Nissí Ioannínon

Disheartened by the tangled maze of narrow streets, drivers are quick to abandon their cars and wander through the town on foot, setting off along Odós Avérof, the main street, which leads from the modern part to the lower town and citadel.

The Archaeological Museum★
In the city park, Odós Avérof. Open every day, 8.30am-3pm; entrance fee. Among the objects displayed in **Room A**, which is devoted to Dodona, Vitsa and the Necromanteion of Ephyra, there is a 200 000-year-old **carved stone**, which is said to be the oldest tool ever found in Greece. You can also see an enormous terracotta jar, two beautiful bronze jugs, some jewellery and a helmet from the 5C BC, as well as some superb **bronze statuettes**★. But the star exhibits of the museum are the **tablets from the oracle of Dodona**★★, depicting the questions that the pilgrims asked Zeus. Often very moving ("Am I my father's son?"), they also sometimes reveal more prosaic concerns ("Timoxanos asks Zeus whether he should enter into earthly trade with the profits of his silver mine; the response is positive, he should remain in the town and do the deal").

In **Room B**, devoted to Classical and Roman sculpture, you can see a **Roman sarcophagus** decorated with a bas-relief (2C BC), as well as a marble lion by Michalítsi (4C BC). **Room C**, of equal interest, contains various funereal objects, as well as another Roman sarcophagus adorned with bas-reliefs. The last room has a display of works by various 18C-19C Greek artists.

If you are interested in the local traditions, visit the **Ioánnina Folklore Museum** (*Odós M Angélou, 8am-3pm; closed Sunday and Monday*), which houses a fine collection of the **furniture**, **jewellery** and **traditional costumes** of Epirus (19C-20C).

The kástro**

Since the 11C, Ioánnina has dwelt under the watchful eye of the kástro built up high on the peninsula which looks down over the lake, to the north-east of the town. Beyond the thick defensive wall built by Ali Pasha (early 19C) which combines elements from the Byzantine Period, you will be struck by the quietness that reigns inside these walls, in the paved alleyways lined with **Ottoman houses**. At the end of Odós Ioustinianoú stands the **synagogue**, the only vestige of the Jewish community. The main attractions of this tour are the two acropolises of the citadel.

The Its-Kalé Acropolis* – *Go back up Odós P Ioasáf.* Beyond the **monumental gate**, is the former **guardroom** and the **kitchens**, an attractive stone-roofed building which has been converted into a cafeteria. From there, you come out onto the esplanade, where the **Fetiye Camii** mosque stands *(closed to the public)*, like a big white cube pinned to the earth, flanked by a minaret. Constructed in 1611 using the walls of a 13C church, it was rebuilt by Ali Pasha in 1795. Just in front of it, surmounted by a beautiful piece of wrought-iron work, stands the **tomb** containing the decapitated corpse of Ali Pasha.

To the right of the mosque, the **Byzantine Museum** *(open Monday 12.30pm-7pm, Tuesday-Saturday 8am-7pm; entrance fee; keep your ticket to visit the annex)* occupies an elegant building constructed on the site of Ali Pasha's seraglio. It covers a period from the Early-Christian Era right up to the 19C, and contains various **funereal objects**, **sculptures**, **icons** and pottery unearthed in the Epirus region.

Ioánnina: a city, an island and a lake in the heart of Epirus

B. Kaufmann/MICHELIN

Do not leave without visiting the **annex to the museum*** (*also located on the esplanade*), which houses a remarkable collection of silver **crosses**, **crockery** and **jewellery**. The **tower** (1082) that you can see at the back is the only vestige of the kástro built by the Normans.

Leave the Its-Kalé Acropolis and return to the north of the citadel.

The Epáno Goúlas Acropolis – Formerly the domain of the Byzantine palaces, this second acropolis is now dominated by the slim silhouette of the minaret of the **Aslan Pasha Mosque*** (1618), built after the destruction of the Church of St John. A gallery runs around the old prayer room, now transformed into the **Municipal Museum** (*8.30am-3pm; closed Monday*). The Greek, Turkish and Jewish communities that lived together in Ioánnina until the 20C, are represented here by way of a very interesting collection of **traditional costumes**, **women's jewellery**, **weapons** and **silverware** (the town has long been famed for its silverware). From the terrace, there is a wonderful **view*** over the lake and the mountains.

Before you leave the citadel, take another look at the **old powder magazine**, in a cave reached by the steps near a **medieval tower**. Several gateways lead to the pleasant **lakeside promenade**, a popular place for courting couples.

The island of Ioánnina** (Nissí Ioannínon)
The landing-stage for boats to the island is to the north, Platía Mavíli. A paradise for frogs and eels – the town's local delicacies – **Lake Pamvotís** surrounds a little haven of greenery and tranquillity, seemingly cut off from time. As well as its monasteries, which are masterpieces of post-Byzantine art, the island is home to a fishing village with enchanting **stone-roofed houses***.

From the landing-stage, go through the village until you come to the 16C **Monastery of Pandeleímonas** (*open every day, 8am-11pm in summer, 9am-8pm in winter*), where Ali Pasha was assassinated. In his memory, a pretty cottage has been converted into a **museum** (carpets, engravings, etc.).

Further on is the **Monastery of St John the Baptist** (Ágios Ioánnis Pródromos) with its 16C church (the **frescoes** are being restored), and a **cave** containing a hermitage. Lovers of Byzantine art should not miss the **Filanthropiní Monastery*** (Spanós), which stands atop a hillock on the other side of the village. Built in the 13C and modified in the 16C, it contains a superb – although rather sinister – cycle of **frescoes**** (16C), depicting the persecution of the Christians and the boundless creativity of their persecutors, whose methods included decapitation, beating, castration, skinning alive, drowning, burning, dismembering...

100m further on, the enchanting **Monastery of Ágios Nikólaos Dílios*** (Stratigópoulos) (early 14C) enjoys a striking **view*** of Ioánnina. As well as a beautiful wooden **iconostasis**, the church contains some 16C **frescoes** with a more uplifting subject matter: a complete cycle on the life of the Virgin Mary, the only one from this period in the whole of Epirus.

Around Ioánnina
Situated 6km north of Ioánnina, the **Pérama Cave**** (*open every day, 8am-6.30pm; entrance fee; 45min*

A legendary oracle
As reported by Herodotus, tradition has it that two doves which set off from Thebes in Egypt were at the origin of the oracle. One flew to Libya, where it founded the Sanctuary of Zeus Ammon, and the other crossed the Mediterranean to get to Dodona. Perched on an oak tree, the bird announced to the inhabitants, with a human voice, that Zeus lived in the tree. The oracle, which manifested itself through the rustling of the leaves, was thereafter interpreted by seers who slept on site and never washed their feet, to keep in contact with the earth! The sanctuary appears in various legends and classical texts, notably in the story of the Golden Fleece when Jason puts a branch of the sacred oak in the stern of his ship to warn him of danger, and in the Odyssey when Odysseus consults the oracle to find the way to Ithaca.

guided tour) was a fortuitous discovery during the Second World War for the villagers who were looking for somewhere to shelter from the bombing. An 850m-long path leads to this strange forest of multicoloured, curiously shaped limestone concretions. From the exit at the top of the hill, you can enjoy one of the most beautiful **panoramas**★★ that there is of Ioánnina.

The work of the sculptor Pávlos Vrellís, the **Vrellís Wax Museum** in **Bizáni** *(13km away on the road to the south; open every day, 9.30am-5pm in summer, 10am-4pm in winter)* presents a somewhat biased version of the history of the national struggle (18C-20C), where the pale, unshaven, Greek patriot is constantly depicted as a victim of the boundless cruelty of the occupying Turkish forces. The scene of the decapitation of Ali Pasha is particularly realistic.

Dodona (Dodóni)★★
21km south of Ioánnina. Monday-Friday 8am-7pm, Saturday and Sunday 8.30am-3pm. Free admission on Sunday. Allow 1hr. See "Excursion to Dodona", page 331.

In a magnificent mountain setting dominated to the south-west by the **Tómaros Mountains** (1 974 and 1 816m), Dodona occupies an idyllic site, its serene and majestic location evoking its ancient sacred history.

The oldest oracle of Ancient Greece
The oracle of Dodona originated from a religious cult brought here by ancient Epirotes (3rd millennium BC), long before the arrival of the Greeks in the 16C BC who replaced this cult by the worship of Zeus. Rituals to its Great Goddess of abundance and fertility also continued to be practised, but she became known as **Dione**. At the end of the 5C BC, the sanctuary passed into the hands of the Molossi, before being pillaged, despite its highly sacred status, by the Aetolians (219 BC), then by the Romans (168 BC). The oracle was finally silenced forever when Theodosius decreed the closure of all pagan shrines. After this, the site seems to have been deserted following raids by Slavs. Excavations carried out in several stages from 1875 onwards have also unearthed ruins of various basilicas dating from the 5C-6C.

The official buildings
Remarkably well preserved, the **theatre**★★★ of Dodona was one of the largest in Ancient Greece, capable of holding 17 000 people! Although supported by the slope of a hill, the weight of the stones and the size of the construction meant that the builders had to raise the upper section of the tiered seating and add two strong lateral **supporting walls**. In front of the **stage**, which had two storeys, was a **portico** built on thirteen columns, the remains of which can still be seen. Built in the 3C BC, under Pyrrhus, the theatre was the venue for the famous **Naia Festival** which was held every four years. But times change, and Greek poetry gave way to the roars of lions and the screams of gladiators during the Roman Era. It was at this time that the first **tiers** were taken out and the spectators were separated from the arena by a wall and a drainage ditch.

From the top of the steps, the superb **view**★★, encompasses the whole of the site. Behind you, at the top of the hill, stood the **acropolis**, of which only part of the **defensive wall** remains (4C BC).

At the base of the theatre, you can make out the eastern end of the **stadium** (late 3C BC), where athletic competitions would take place during the Naia Festival. In the early 2C, these games were just as famous as those of Olympus and Corinth. The path then passes between the remains of the **bouleuterion** *(on the left)*, the council building, and the **prytaneion** (late 3C BC), the seat of the magistrates *(currently being excavated)*. The former, constructed on the side of a hill in a semi-circle, has retained a large section of its Doric colonnade, but virtually nothing remains of the tiered seating provided for the council members. Nevertheless, some fragments of bronze **statues** of Epirote generals (3C-2C BC) have been found.

The group of sanctuaries

Beyond the small **Temple to Aphrodite** and the temple to **Themis**, of which virtually nothing remains, you will eventually come to the **Sanctuary of Zeus Naios** (Hierá Oikiá), which was the site of the oracle. Originally (8C BC), the oracle was consulted in the open air beneath a sacred oak tree surrounded by cauldrons. The first building (4C BC) was followed by a succession of various temples and, after the Aetolian raid in 219 BC, the Epirotes and Macedonians built a larger monumental temple, with a large tetrastyle vestibule (with 4 rows of columns) and an Ionic propylaeum leading up to it. What you see today are the ruins of the latter construction – burnt by the Romans in the 2C – around an **oak tree** planted by archaeologists.

The visit ends with the ruins of the two **Temples of Dione** (4C and 3C BC) and of the **Temple of Heracles**, partly covered by the remains of a **basilica** with three aisles (5C-6C).

Making the most of Ioánnina

COMING AND GOING

By air – To get to the airport (5km), take the bus (*nos* 1, 7 or 13) Odós Avérof, near the clock tower. In summer, two flights daily to Athens and one to Thessaloníki.

By bus – The *bus station in Odós Zosimadon* in summer (reduced service in winter) operates services to: Athens, ☎ (0651) 26 286, 9 services daily (7hr30min); Thessaloníki, ☎ (0651) 27 442, 5 services daily (7hr). To Igoumenítsa, ☎ (0651) 26 211, 9 services daily (2hr30min). To Párga, one service daily (3hr); Métsovo, 4 services daily during the week and 2 daily at weekends; Tríkala, two services daily (3hr30min); Kónitsa, 11 services daily (2hr).

In summer, the *bus station in Odós Bizaníou*, ☎ (0651) 25 014, operates services to: Párga, one service daily (3hr); Préveza, 10 services daily (2hr); Árta, 10 services daily (2hr30min). To Pérama Cave and Dodona, see under "Other things to do".

GETTING AROUND

As the town is very compact, you will have no difficulty getting around on foot.

By taxi – Taxis can be found near the clock tower, ☎ (0651) 46 777 / 78 / 79.

ADDRESS BOOK

Tourist information – **EOT**, Odós Napoléonda Zervá 2, ☎ (0651) 25 086. Monday-Friday, 7.30am-2.30pm / 5.30pm-8.30pm, Saturday, 9am-1pm; in winter, only open in the morning.

Tourist police – Odós 28 Oktomvríou, opposite the post office, ☎ (0651) 25 673. Monday-Friday, 8am-10pm, weekends, 8am-9pm. Here you can obtain information regarding the opening times of the sites and transport services, as well as a map of the town.

Greek Alpine Club – **EOS**, Odós Despotátou Ipírou 2, ☎ (0651) 22 138. Monday-Friday, 7pm-9pm. A useful address for those who wish to go trekking in the region. See also under "Other things to do".

Banks / Currency exchange – You can change money in the large hotels, or use the many cash dispensers in the town centre.

National Bank of Greece, Odós M Angélou, near the Hotel Olympic. Monday-Thursday, 8am-2pm, Friday, 8am-1.30pm. Cash dispenser.

Post office – Odós 28 Oktomvríou; Odós Geórgiou Papandréou.

Telephone – Local code: 0651. **OTE**, Odós 28 Oktomvríou. Monday-Friday, 7am-10pm.

Internet – *Internet Café*, Odós Napoléonda Zervá 4-6 (7am-10pm; closed at weekends).

Kurdistó Portocáli, Odós Pirsinéla 5 (10am-1am). A slightly sinister basement games room, but offering good connections.

Car rental – **Hertz**, Odós Dodónis 105, ☎ (0651) 48 990.

Avis, Odós Dodónis 96, ☎ (0651) 46 333, Fax (0651) 46 188.

Airline – **Olympic Airways**, Odós Kadsadíma 7, ☎ (0651) 23 120 / 26 518.

WHERE TO STAY

If you want to stay with a local family, enquire at the tourist information office.

Under €30

Agapi, Odós Tsirigóti 6, ☎ (0651) 25 041 – 7rm. Very good value for money. Rooms are rather gloomy and basic, with shared bathroom.

Hotel Hermes, Odós Sína 2, ☎ (0651) 75 992 – 33rm. The rooms here have a cell-like atmosphere and are not that clean, but the price cannot be beaten. Don't hesitate to negotiate.

Hotel Paris, Odós Tsirigóti 6, near the main bus station, ☎ (0651) 25 041 – 15rm. Basic rooms which are not that clean, and not all have bathrooms. Will do at a pinch, but not good value for money.

Between €30 and €60

Hotel Egnatia, on the corner of Odós Daglí and Odós Aravadinoú, ☎ (0651) 25 667, Fax (0651) 75 060 – 52rm. ⌖ 𝒫 TV CC This friendly and comfortable hotel offers the best value for money in this category (prices are fixed all year). Underground car park nearby.

Dioni, Odós Tsirigóti 10, ☎ (0651) 27 864, Fax (0651) 29 950 – 53rm. ⌖ ▤ 𝒫 TV A modern hotel in the centre of town, with clean and comfortable rooms, although somewhat small and relatively expensive. Prices are fixed all year, but breakfast is extra. Underground car park nearby.

Hotel El Greco, Odós Tsirigóti 8, ☎ (0651) 30 726, Fax (0651) 30 728 – 36rm. ⌖ 𝒫 TV In the same category as the Dioni, slightly more comfortable. Good value for money (prices fixed all year), but breakfast is not served here.

Astoria, Odós Paraskevopoúlou 2, on the corner of Odós Avérof, ☎ (0651) 20 755, Fax (0651) 78 410 – 16rm. ⌖ ▤ 𝒫 Recently renovated, the Astoria has carpeted rooms, which cannot be faulted. Extra charge for breakfast. Staff speak English.

Hotel Olympic, Odós J Melanídis 2, ☎ (0651) 22 233, Fax (0651) 22 041 – 54rm. ⌖ ▤ 𝒫 TV In a good location, with very professional staff who speak English. Charming rooms, but small and expensive (extra charge for breakfast). Car park.

Hotel Bretania, Platía Kentrikí 11A, ☎ (0651) 29 396, Fax (0651) 33 589 – 23rm. ⌖ ▤ 𝒫 TV Clean and spacious rooms, but you might be put off by the rather unfriendly welcome.

Palladion, Odós Nóti Bótsari 1, ☎ (0651) 25 856, Fax (0651) 74 034 – 130rm. ⌖ ▤ 𝒫 TV ✕ CC Newly renovated, this town centre hotel is comfortable, with very professional staff (English spoken). Superb view of the lake from the upper floors. Prices negotiable in low season. Car park and satellite.

Over €60

🛏 **Hotel Kastro**, Odós Paleológou, ☎ (0651) 22 866 – 7rm. ⌖ 𝒫 TV CC In an old house in the kástro, this charming new hotel is superbly situated and very quiet. Rooms are comfortable and clean. Breakfast is included.

Hôtel du Lac, Odós Aktí Miaoúli, 1km south of the town centre, facing the lake, ☎ (0651) 59 100, Fax (0651) 59 200 – 129rm. ⌖ ▤ 𝒫 TV ✕ ⌇ CC A new luxury hotel with a marble interior and efficient staff. Thick carpets, mini-bars and satellite... the rooms are extremely comfortable. Breakfast included.

EATING OUT

In addition to those on Platía Georgíou, Odós Papágou has plenty of restaurants with terraces overlooking the lake. They stay open all day, and the food is respectable, but nothing special. To enjoy the trout or eel (the local delicacy) in a more peaceful setting, however, the tavernas on the island cannot be bettered.

- **Ioánnina**

Under €15

To Koumanio, Platía Georgíou, ☎ (0651) 38 044. ⌕ Smaller and less expensive than the neighbouring Manteio. Simple Greek fare (grills, spitroasts), but good quality. The service is quick, too.

To Mánteio Psistariá, Platía Georgíou. Same category and same fare on offer, but a bit livelier than the previous entry.

Restaurant Límni, Odós Papágou. ⌕ The last restaurant but one in this row, serving a delicious "bekrí mezzé" (beef in tomato sauce).

Itaki, Odós Papágou 20A, ☎ (0651) 73 012. 🍴 Often packed out, this restaurant is popular with the locals, which is always a good sign. But be prepared to wait, service is slow.

Over €15

Es Aei, Odós Koundouriótou 50, ☎ (0651) 34 571. In an old mansion tastefully decorated with antiques, this restaurant has a reputation for refined, creative cooking (try the "Es Aei", a tasty assortment of cheeses and kebabs). The subdued lighting and the background salsa music create a very pleasant atmosphere.

• **The island of Nissí Ioannínon**

Gripos, to the right of the landing-stage. 🍴 The grilled trout is excellent, but the fate of the crocodile confined to an aquarium near the toilets might be a cause for concern.

Propodes, near the Ali Pasha Museum. 🍴 A pleasant lakeside restaurant, with eel, crayfish and frog on the menu.

HAVING A DRINK

Bars – Platía Mavíli has a vast selection of bars with terraces overlooking the lake.

Fílistro, Odós Andréou Paleológou 20, in the citadel. A good place for a cup of tea, coffee or chocolate, or for a drink in the evening.

Bar Ev Ioannious, a very lively bar in a courtyard set back from Odós Karamanlí, near the citadel. In the evenings, the place is packed out with trendy youngsters.

OTHER THINGS TO DO

Boats to Nissí Ioannínon – Boats to the island leave every 30min from Platía Mavíli until 11pm in summer and 10pm in winter (10min crossing).

Excursion to Pérama – To visit Pérama Cave, catch the *no* 8 bus near the clock tower (departs every 20min, 15min trip).

Excursion to Dodona – Getting to Dodona by bus is a bit more of a challenge. Go by taxi if you are in a group (approximately €13 for the journey and €2 to wait for one hour). Buses depart from Odós Bizaníou (Monday, Tuesday, Wednesday, Friday and Saturday at 6.30am and 4.30pm, and Sunday at 6pm), but the return schedules do not allow for a lengthy visit. If you want to spend some time here, catch the **Zotikó** bus (Monday, Wednesday and Friday at 5.30am and 2pm) and get off at the top of the road which goes to Dodona, then continue on foot (2.5km).

Walking – *Robinson Expeditions*, ☎ (0651) 74 989, Fax (0651) 27 071. This agency specialises in the Zagória valley, and can organise every kind of activity (treks on foot or by mountain bike, climbing, paragliding, canyoning).

Festivals – In July and August, Dodona is the setting for the **Ta Epirótika** drama festival (information from the EOT). Also worth a visit is the **Zítsa wine festival** at the end of August (village 24km to the north-west).

SHOPPING GUIDE

Markets, shopping streets – There is a market in Odós Papafilou every morning except on Sunday. Odós Lórdou Víronos, a pedestrian street, is absolutely jam-packed with shops.

Antiques – *Ioánnis Kariofílis*, Odós Paleológou, in the citadel, ☎ (0651) 22 327. A vast selection of antique jewellery.

Bookshops – *Dodóni*, Odós M Angélou 27. A wide range of books in Greek and English.

Papazótou Zíkos, Odós P Ioassáf, just through the entrance to the citadel. Superb maps and old books at exorbitant prices, but worth a look.

THE ZAGÓRIA REGION★★★

Province of Epirus – District of Ioánnina
40km from Ioánnina and Kónitsa – Regional map page 304
Michelin map 980 fold 15 – Cool climate

Not to be missed
Víkos Gorge.
The villages of Monodéndri, Megálo Pápingo and Mikró Pápingo.
And remember...
The walk through the gorge is not very difficult,
but you need to be reasonably fit for trekking in the mountains.
The region is best explored with your own means of transport.

A classless society?

Traditionally, there has never been much distinction between the social classes in Zagória; but three groups could be distinguished: those who occupied a recognised position and had the right to possess goods (merchants, scholars, priests, etc); the Arvanites and Souliots, assimilated into the community, who set about protecting the villages, even taking to banditry; and finally, the gypsies, who owned no land and made a modest living as blacksmiths, musicians or upholsterers. The economy was based on wood, rearing stock, and agriculture as well as on money sent back to the area by Zagoriots who had emigrated from the 12C onwards. With the Industrial Revolution at the end of the 19C, the region went into an inexorable decline and the villages have hardly changed in appearance since then. Their buildings are packed tightly together, with a single centre, the "mesochóri", where the public buildings (school, church, café) are grouped. Around this, the houses are divided up into neighbourhoods ("mahallás") traversed by a network of paths and mule tracks ("kalderímia").

Scattered over the slopes of the Tímfi Massif, the 46 villages of the Zagória region melt into the background, their grey stonework and wooden balconies blending in with the spectacular landscape of mountains embellished with forests, gorges and torrents. In perfect harmony with this inviolate nature, the inhabitants of the region maintain their timeless way of life, its rhythm dictated by the seasonal movement of their livestock. But it is under threat, and some villages, such as Pápingo, Monodéndri and Tsepélovo, have only managed to survive by opening their doors to tourism. In addition to the spectacular grandeur of their location, they all hold plenty of attractions for the visitor, with traditional houses, churches adorned with frescoes, old stone bridges which span the rushing streams; this is a land of ages past which cries out to be explored.

The country "beyond the mountains"

Zagória owes its name to a term of Slavonic origin meaning "beyond the mountains". Covered in winter by a majestic mantle of snow, this hilly region is dotted with mountain peaks which range from 420m to 2 456m, including the **Tímfi Massif**, part of the northern Pindus Chain. A protected area, it is the site of the **Víkos-Aóos National Park** which covers most of the region. Crossed by the Aóos and the Voïdomátis, a trout stream which flows through the valleys of the Víkos Gorge, the region provides an exceptional habitat of maple, oak, willow, chestnut, cedar and thorn trees where deer, boar, wild goats and also a small number of **bears**, **wolves** and **wildcats** roam.

Inhabited since prehistoric times, the Zagória benefited from a high degree of autonomy during the Ottoman Era. The region thus became a refuge for patriots until November 1940 when it was the scene of violent fighting between the Greek and Italian armies.

From village to village

From Ioánnina, take the Kónitsa road north.
Allow a minimum of one day for the excursion.

When you reach Metamórfosi *(20km from Ioánnina)*, turn right and continue on to the **Noutsou bridge***(15km)*, a fine example of such constructions, built in 1750. Then, just before Kípi, the strange silhouette of the **Plakída bridge**★★ (1814) comes into sight at the bottom of a gorge, with its triple hump-back outline, slender and redundant (the road no longer goes this way), spanning the stream.

■ Perched on the southern flank of the Massif, **Tsepélovo** attracts fewer tourists than the nearby Víkos Gorge. However, this large village with its stone houses boasts a magnificent **panorama*** and there are some beautiful **walks** to be had in the surrounding mountains. Beyond Tsepélovo and Skamnéli, the road goes through a dark forest of conifers, through which you get occasional glimpses of the stark outline of the majestically beautiful **Tímfi Mountains***.

The Víkos Gorge★★★ (Farángi-Víkou)
As though hewn out by a giant, a deep (1 000m) vertiginous fault cuts into the side of the mountain, forming a bed for the Voïdomátis stream.
With the benefit of the best **panorama**★★ in the region, the village of **Monodéndri**★★ will be the starting point for your trek. But meanwhile, allow yourself a short stroll through its streets lined with flower-decked stone walls, followed by a *tirópita* (cheese flaky pastry), the local delicacy.
From the **Church of Ágios Minás**, walk to the **Monastery of Agía Paraskeví** (15C), a fascinating, small stronghold built of grey stone perched up over the gully on a rocky spur.

If you have your own transport, you can complete your excursion by taking the track *(7km)* which leads to **Oxía**, a rocky formation which overhangs the gorge, providing a breathtaking **viewpoint**★★★.

Senior citizens conversing

G. Guérard

The Zagória Region

Not far from the monastery, a path leads down to the bottom of the **gorge***** *(45min)* into an extraordinary mineral landscape with vertiginous walls. This route takes you all the way back to Víkos *(5hr walk)*, at the northern end, in the ever-present, almost oppressive, shadow of the cliffs.

Next is the village of **Víkos**, which is blessed with a pretty **church**, but most of all with its spectacular **panorama**** over the gorge and the Tímfi Mountains, a magnificent blue-tinged ridge which glows red at sunset. You can also enjoy this spectacle from the road to Arísti *(44km)*.

Then go back through Arísti to get to **Megálo Pápingo***** *(15km)*, a fairytale village which has managed to preserve its gentle way of life, far away from the modern world. Take time to savour the wild beauty of the **site**** as well as the charming **traditional architecture**** of its churches and houses, not to mention the respectful, yet warm reception that awaits you.

■ Positioned at the foot of a cliff, the village of **Mikró Pápingo***** *(2km)* also has a very pretty **church** with a side gallery, a local feature. Stroll through the alleyways where the paving stones echo with the hooves of horses, mules, goats or sheep... The plump bunches of grapes which you see hanging down from trellises are used to make a delicious wine. Something to fortify yourself with in preparation for one of the many tempting **walks** in the surrounding countryside!

Making the most of Zagória

COMING AND GOING

By bus – In Ioánnina, the **Odós Zosimádon bus station** operates a service to Zagória: Monodéndri (Monday, Wednesday and Friday at 5.30am and 4.30pm), Pápingo (Monday, Wednesday and Friday at 5am and 3pm, and Sunday at 9.30am), Tsepélovo (Monday, Wednesday and Friday at 5.30am and 3.15pm).

GETTING AROUND

By taxi – If you miss the last bus from Víkos, you will have to call a taxi from Kónitsa, ☎ (0655) 31 240, or from Ioánnina, ☎ (0651) 46 777 / 78 / 79.

By rental car – See Ioánnina.

ADDRESS BOOK

Tourist information – The **EOT** and **EOS** offices in Ioánnina supply a very useful map.

Telephone – Local code: 0653.

WHERE TO STAY

You will find a good selection of hotels and guesthouses in attractive buildings. However, it is advisable to book (the prices given rise in winter and at Easter). Most of the hotels have a restaurant where the famous "tirópita" is on the menu. However, breakfast is not usually included.

• **Tsepélovo**

Under €23

Pension Gouris, from the main square, go back up the narrow street and turn right at the sign, ☎ (0653) 81 214 – 8rm. ♨ A small, friendly and comfortable establishment run by a charming lady. Very reasonable prices.

Domátia Erasmía Deligiánni, up from the main square, ☎ (0653) 81 232 – 3rm. ♨ A small guesthouse in a traditional building run by a charming elderly couple who will give you the warmest welcome (but who only speak Greek). Use of kitchen allowed.

Between €30 and €45

Pension Fánis, above the village, ☎ (0653) 81 271 – 7rm. ▨ A superb old residence, rustic but comfortable, with a warm welcome. The owner organises treks, as well as horse and bicycle rides. You can eat here.

Over €45

Hotel Dracolímni, at the entrance to the village, ☎ (0653) 81 312, Fax (0653) 81 311 – 31rm. ▨ ✎ TV CC ✗ The biggest hotel in the village, with excellent facilities, mainly caters for groups (so goodbye to hospitality and tranquillity...). Breakfast is included.

• **Monodéndri**

Under €30

To Kalderíni, ☎ (0653) 71 510 – 5rm. ▨ This new hotel, in traditional style, has spacious, well-kept rooms. Breakfast is included, but be warned, the prices are doubled in high season.

Monodéndri Katerína, ☎ (0653) 71 300 – 7rm. ✗ A magnificent 17C building, an excellent restaurant and a warm reception; in short, the ideal place. The old building is more atmospheric, but the bathroom is outside.

Hotel Ladia, ☎ (0653) 71 483 – 10rm. ▨ A recent hotel, built in local style. The rooms are comfortable, but prices rise considerably in winter.

• **Vítsa**

Under €38

Selíni, ☎ (0653) 71 350 – 7rm. ▨ ✎ TV ✗ CC Before Vítsa, take the path on the right, which leads to this isolated little hotel with its superb view. Extremely comfortable and clean.

Beloi, ☎ (0653) 71 571 – 9rm. ▨ ✎ TV ✗ A recent hotel on the way into Vítsa, rather disadvantaged by its roadside location. But the rooms are comfortable, with fireplaces.

• **Víkos**

Under €38

Sotírios Karpoúzis, main square, ☎ (0653) 41 176 – 11rm. ▨ ✗ This rustic establishment, with its stone walls and fireplaces, is a haven of peace after the walk through the gorge. But the prices are a little steep.

• **Megálo Pápingo and Mikró Pápingo**

Under €38

Xenónas tou Koúli, Megálo Pápingo, ☎ (0653) 41 138 – 7rm. ▨ ✗ A traditional, comfortable and sturdy house with a pleasant welcome.

Xenónas Kalliópi, Megálo Pápingo, above the village, ☎ (0653) 41 081 – 8rm. ▨ ✗ This small hotel is quaint and welcoming and has various types of room at different prices. In the evenings, you can sample the produce of the vegetable garden on the restaurant terrace.

Dias, Mikró Pápingo, ☎ (0653) 41 257 – 12rm. ✗ Full of character, with an attractive shaded terrace. The spacious and comfortable rooms in the old building, with an unbeatable view, are more charming. But the newer ones have bathrooms.

EATING OUT

• **Monodéndri**

I Píta Tis Kikítsas, main square, ☎ (0653) 71 340. 🍴 An excellent place to sample "tirópita" (minimum 3 people), in the shade of a plane tree.

• **Megálo Pápingo**

Níkos Tsoumánis, ☎ (0653) 41 984. 🍴 Right at the heart of the village, this restaurant has a flower-decked terrace with a view of the mountains. Savoury tarts are the house speciality.

OTHER THINGS TO DO

Walking – Enquire at the hotels or try **Robinson Travel** (see "Making the most of Ioánnina", page 329).

THE IONIAN COAST★
PÁRGA
Province of Epirus – District of Préveza
From Igoumenítsa to Préveza, approximately 120km – Michelin map 980 fold 15
Regional map page 304 – Mediterranean climate

Not to be missed
A stroll through the streets of Párga.
A visit to the Necromanteion of Ephyra and Nikópoli.

And remember...
If you are travelling from Italy, book your place on the ferry to Igoumenítsa
well in advance.

As a contrast to the rugged mountainous landscape of the hinterland, the Ionian coast offers a softer version of Epirus, dedicated to the sun and the pleasures of the beach. Vertiginous cliffs which drop straight down to the sea, little coves lapped by turquoise waters, fishing ports tucked away in wonderful natural harbours... the western coastline is every bit as attractive as the islands of the Aegean. And despite the tourist influx, you can always manage to find a small resort with a friendly welcome and a beach away from the crowds.

Greece's window onto Italy, the region has for centuries nurtured an intimate relationship with Venice, which is evident in Préveza and Párga. But its history goes back to well before the Middle Ages: as you will discover at the Necromanteion of Ephyra, the site of a famous oracle dedicated to the gods of the Underworld which gives a thrilling insight into the mystical world of the ancient Greeks.

Párga, on the blue waters
of the Ionian Sea

Along the coastline
*50km itinerary from Igoumenítsa to Párga
along the coast,
then 67km from Párga to Préveza.*

■ The principal port for ferries between Greece and Italy and for the Ionian Islands, **Igoumenítsa** has no special attractions, but its large number of hotels, restaurants and travel agencies make it a handy place for a stopover.

South of Igoumenítsa, you can go directly to Párga (51km) or take the longer way there – our option – following the coastline and its string of resorts.

■ The first stop on your tour, **Plataria** *(12km)* stretches the length of the **beach** which curves around a large bay. The road then climbs up a steep mountainside overhanging the sea, from where there is a magnificent **panorama★** which extends as far as Corfu.

■ Next en route is **Sívota** (*10km from Plataria, along the coast road*), a quiet resort with a small marina sheltered by two **islets**. If you fancy a swim, there are several **beaches** in the vicinity.

■ Further on, you come to **Arílas★** (*12km*), its houses scattered over the undulating hills. Down below is an enchanting cove, lapped by blue waters. Also in the vicinity is a **marina** and a number of secluded **beaches** tucked away along the coastline.

The road then takes you through a wonderful **landscape★★** of hills carpeted with olive groves, looking down over coves fringed with **beaches**. Then, a short distance before Párga, look out for the great **Citadel of Anthoúsa** (*12.5km*), perched high up in the hills.

■ Párga★★
Allow one day

Párga occupies a unique site, straddling two little bays enclosed by a rocky islet creating the illusion of a lake. Despite the sudden invasion of mass tourism, this old fishing village has managed to retain its charm. Sheltering under the protection of a Venetian fort, a maze of narrow streets tumbles down the hillside to the harbour, the centre of Párga (from where cars have been banned); the neighbouring bay, which is much quieter, has a pleasant beach.

Between the Sublime and the Serenissima
Continuously occupied since the Mycenaean Era, Párga became a great object of desire in the Middle Ages as an advanced post of the Christian world against the Turks. When the Crusaders took Constantinople, the town came under the control

B. Kaufmann/MICHELIN

of the **Normans**, who kept it until 1400. To regain its freedom, the town appealed to the **Venetians**, with whom a treaty was signed in 1401. The presence of the Serenissima was to last for 400 years, ensuring Párga's prosperity and liberty, in spite of assaults by the Sublime Porte, which destroyed it on several occasions during the 16C. After the Treaty of Passarowitz (1718), many Greeks from the region took refuge here, while a new threat arrived in the form of **Ali Pasha**, who would not rest until he had conquered it. Handed over to France by the Treaty of Campo Formio (1797), the town then passed into the hands of the British in 1816, but they disposed of it to the Turks in 1819, provoking an exodus of the population. Párga became part of the Greek nation on 22 March 1913.

A witness to this turbulent history, the citadel (1572) crowns a rocky peninsula, encircled by cypress and pine trees. There is a superb **view★** over the town from the summit, and you can even make out the chapels and French fort on the **Island of Panagía**.

You might also want to explore the surrounding area which has many beaches, including the one at **Váltos** *(on the far side of the citadel, on foot or by caique)*, which is quite large. Even more enticing is the beach at **Lichnós★**, an enchanting ribbon of sand *(3km south of Párga; tavernas, hotels)* which flanks a bay overlooked by cliffs and hills covered with olive and cypress trees.

South of Párga, the road follows the coastline and leads to a succession of sandy crescent-shaped beaches which are almost deserted.

In Messopótamo (20km from Párga), turn left before the stream and continue for 2km.

■ **The Necromanteion of Ephyra★** (Nekromandío Efíras) – *Open every day 8am-7pm. Entrance fee.* Here you are at the entrance to the Underworld! On a small hill, with cypress trees to set the tone (the funereal tree par excellence), overlooking the confluence of the **Acherón** – "the river of woe" – and the **Cocytus** – the "river of lamentation", flowing with the tears of the dead left unburied – stood one of the most famous oracles of Ancient Greece, dedicated to Hades and Persephone. There, the living could make contact with the souls of the dead...

Protected by a defensive wall of which only the base remains, the first impression of the Necromanteion is of a vast complex with thick stone walls. Various passageways led to the heart of the sanctuary, which had several rooms as well as a **vaulted crypt**, where the priests would pronounce the oracles amidst the sulphurous vapours. Concealed there was a powerful mechanism allowing strange figures to be hoisted up, supposedly evoking the spirits of the dead. In order to prepare them for this trial, the pilgrims were shut away for several days, in rooms nearby. Immersed in darkness and silence, they would consume nothing but hallucinogenic substances. And then slowly they were brought nearer to the **sacred labyrinth**, where they would finally go through the three gates to the Underworld.

The gateway to the Underworld

After following a turbulent course through wild gorges, the Acherón flows across the Fanári Plain, where, in Antiquity, the marshy Lake Acheroussía was located. Reputed to be the gateway to the Underworld, this mysterious and inaccessible lagoon had to be crossed by the souls of the deceased to reach the infernal realm of Hades and his wife Persephone. The dead who had not been buried in accordance with the customary rituals were condemned to wander eternally through its forests of reeds. The others, after they had paid the obligatory fee of one obol to the guardian Charon, took their place aboard his boat to reach the bowels of the earth, guarded by Cerberus, the dog with several heads. Only two living beings managed to enter the realm of the dead: Heracles, who completed one of his Twelve Labours there, and Orpheus, whose lyre enabled him to snatch the nymph Eurydice from the claws of the infernal gods... before he lost her again because he looked at her before they had left the Underworld.

Oranges galore

A primitive sanctuary was already in existence here in the Mycenaean Period, but the site was at its peak of glory in the 3C-2C BC – the ruins that can be seen date from this time – before it was completely destroyed by the Romans. Items discovered here are on display in the Museum in Ioánnina *(see page 325)*.

Leave Hades' lair behind you and follow the coast road, dotted with a succession of long **beaches★★**. Can you resist an impromptu stop on the sands at **Vráhos** or **Kastrossikiá**?

■ **Préveza** – *56km south of the fork off to Párga. Allow one day.* Positioned at the head of the vast Bay of Árta, Préveza is both a yachting marina and the departure point for ferries to Áktio and the island of Leucas. The small seaside town has little of interest, but there is enough going on to make it a pleasant place to stay, particularly if interspersed with jaunts to the beaches nearby or to the site of Nikópoli.

Late to make an appearance in historical records (15C), Préveza passed into Venetian hands at the end of the 16C, where it would remain for three centuries, apart from a few Ottoman interludes. In 1797, the town was awarded to France by the Treaty of Campo Formio, but in the following year, Ali Pasha managed to take possession of it. It remained Turkish until 1912. Three main streets run from north to south through Préveza. **Odós Irínis**, along which you travel as you arrive from Árta, **Odós Ethnikís Antístasis**, the main commercial thoroughfare (largely

The day that decided the fate of Rome
On 2 September in the year 31 BC, the entrance to the Bay of Árta was the scene of one of the most famous naval battles in history, the Battle of Actium. The stroke of genius of Octavian and his general Agrippa, who had established their headquarters near Nikópoli, was to refuse to engage combat where Antony's fleet was expecting it, first to the north-west of Préveza, then in the bay, near the marshy mouth of the Loúros. Agrippa profited from this by capturing the island of Leucas, thus cutting Antony off from the rear of his fleet, and leading him out onto the high sea, where his light and nimble boats performed marvellously. Defeated, Antony and his companion Cleopatra were forced to abandon their fleet and flee to Alexandria, leaving the way clear for Caesar's adopted son, who then took the title of Augustus and established the Empire.

pedestrianised), and lastly **Odós Venizélou**, along the seafront, where you will probably spend most of your time. It springs to life in the mornings, when the fishermen come back into port, and again in the evenings when the whole town converges on the café terraces.

At the northern end of the quayside, opposite the marina, the **Venetian citadel**, restored by Ali Pasha, affords a beautiful panorama over the bay.

Drive north on the road to Ioánnina and Árta.

■ **Nikópoli** – *8km from Préveza. Entrance fee. The site is very extensive, so allow 90min, starting with the museum.* Founded in 30 BC by Octavian after the battle of Actium, Nikópoli, the "town of victory" (*"níke"* in Greek), is said to have been visited by St Paul in 64 AD. Indeed, it rapidly became an active centre for Christianity and was the birthplace of Pope St Eleutherius (2C). Destroyed in the 6C by the Vandals and Goths, the town was rebuilt by Justinian and entered a new golden age before being razed once more by the Bulgars in the 11C. In 1798, French and Souliot troops were massacred there (*see page 332*) by Ali Pasha's army.

At first, the road runs alongside a strong **Byzantine defensive wall**★ (6C) flanked by **towers**. Then, on the bend, a path leads behind the ramparts to the ruins of the **Basilica of Doumetios** (A) (around 575), which still has a few sections of **mosaic floor** (*generally covered with sand*).

On display in the **museum** (*Monday-Friday 8am-7pm, weekends 8am-2.30pm*) are a few Hellenistic and Roman pieces: a funereal lion (3C BC), a marble tomb, a **statue of Minerva** (4C BC), another with a sumptuous drape, as well as a delicate **glass urn**. The star exhibit is without doubt the **marble base**★ of a statue of a Roman Emperor, decorated with a remarkable bas-relief.

Continue your exploration of the site with what was the marvel of Nikópoli, in all its exquisite splendour, the ancient cathedral, or **Basilica of Alkison** (B) (*300m away, on the other side of the road leading to the theatre*), constructed in the 5C-6C. Unfortunately, nothing remains of its five aisles, apart from its **mosaics**.

One and a half kilometres further on, in the hills above the Árta road, stands the **Theatre of Augustus**★ in a beautiful fan-shape of stone and brick. In use until the end of the 3C, it has been restored and you can now walk up the steps, interspersed with thistles, a perfect playground for the colonies of lizards and crickets. From the top, the **panorama**★ extends over the whole of the site, as far as the sea.

On the other side of the road, the ruins of a portal mark the entrance to the **stadium**, the route of the tracks still discernible against the embankment.

Finally, if you have time, follow the little road to the top of the hill, to the ruins of the **monument** erected by Augustus, marking the place from which he directed the battle of Actium (*currently being excavated*).

COMING AND GOING

By ferry – In July and Aukgust, it can prove difficult to find space for a car on a ferry. It is therefore better to book well in advance. Get your ticket from the ferry company rather than from a travel agency, and always make a booking.

To Corfu, sailings approximately every hour, from 5am-10pm (90min).

To Italy, most ferries stop off at Corfu. Check-in 2hr before departure. There are 6-8 sailings daily to Brindisi (11hr) and 2 to Bari (13hr). There are also services to Ancona, Otranto, Venice and Trieste.

By bus – To Ioánnina, 9 services daily (2hr); to Thessaloníki, one daily (8hr); to Párga, 5 daily (1hr); to Préveza, 2 daily (2hr30min); to Athens, 3 daily (8hr).

ADDRESS BOOK

Tourist information – At the old port, ☎ (0665) 22 227. 7am-2.30pm.

Telephone – Local code: 0665.

Travel agencies – *Sívota Travel*, ☎ (0665) 93 439, Fax (0665) 93 355. Reservations for air and ferry travel, hotels, car rental.

WHERE TO STAY

The summer prices (quoted here) are 25-50% higher than in winter.

Under €30

Hotel Akropolis, near the Minoan agency, ☎ (0665) 28 346 – 32rm. Basic accommodation for travellers who are easily pleased. Not very well maintained and staff don't speak English.

Over €45

Hotel Aktaion, Agíon Apostólon 17, opposite the quay for boats to Corfu, ☎ (0665) 22 707, Fax (0684) 22 330 – 18rm. ⚐ 🗐 🅿 📺 🆑 A well-run, very comfortable, but rather pricey establishment. The friendly staff speak English.

Hotel Oscar, Agíon Apostólon 149, opposite the new port, ☎ (0665) 22 675, Fax (0684) 23 557 – 30rm. ⚐ 🗐 🅿 📺 Smart, comfortable rooms, but somewhat uninspiring. Good value for money, however. Staff speak English.

COMING AND GOING

By bus – The **bus station** is in Odós Alexándrou Bága, behind the church, ☎ (0684) 31 218. To Igoumenítsa, 4 services daily (1hr); to Préveza, 5 daily (2hr); to Ioánnina, one daily in summer (3hr); to Athens, 3 services daily (7hr).

GETTING AROUND

By rental vehicle – *Avis*, Odós Spírou Livadá 2, ☎ and Fax (0684) 32 732.

Hertz, Odós Anexartisías 37-39, ☎ (0684) 31 833.

ITS, see "Travel agencies" below. Car and motorcycle rental.

ADDRESS BOOK

Tourist information – No address; just a telephone number: ☎ (0684) 32 107.

Port authorities – On the quayside, to the right of the landing-stage, ☎ (0684) 31 227.

Tourist police – Odós Alexándrou Bága, near the bus station, ☎ (0684) 31 222.

Banks / Currency exchange – *National Bank of Greece*, Odós Spírou Livadá. Cash dispenser.

Post office – Odós Alexándrou Bága, near the bus station.

Telephone – Local code: 0684. **OTE**, Odós Spírou Livadá, on the corner of Odós Alexándrou Bága, opposite the church.

Airlines – **Olympic Airways**, ☎ (0684) 28 343.

Travel agencies – **ITS**, on the quayside, Odós A Afthanasíou and Odós Anexartisías, ☎ (0684) 31 833 / 31 910, Fax (0684) 31 834. Tours to Dodona, Ioánnina, Víkos Gorge and Corfu.

WHERE TO STAY

Summer prices are given here and are 50-100% higher than prices charged in the low season.

Under €45

Hotel San Nectarios, Odós Spírou Livadá, on the way into town, ☎ (0684) 31 150, Fax (0684) 32 150 – 20rm. ⌐⎤ ⏁ ♪ 📺 A two-storey hotel (no lift) with simple, respectable rooms. Good value for money.

Villa Vergos, at the beginning of the street at the far end of Krionéri beach, ☎ (0684) 31 617– 13rm. ⌐⎤ Rooms with balcony or terrace (ask for one of the brighter ones upstairs). Closed October-May.

Hotel Paradise, Odós Spírou Livadá, in the direction of Váltos, near the church, ☎ (0684) 31 229, Fax (0684) 31 266 – 15rm. ⌐⎤ ♪ 📺 ⌐⌐ An attractive two-storey hotel (no lift) with pleasant rooms with balconies. Prices are significantly lower in winter.

🐌**Achilleas Hotel**, at the beginning of the street at the end of Krionéri beach, ☎ (0684) 31 600, Fax (0684) 31 879 – 23rm. ⌐⎤ 🗐 ♪ 📺 ⏁ ⌐⌐ The comfortable and well-kept rooms are set around an interior courtyard. The hotel has direct access onto Paleó Krionéri Bay and has a very pleasant bar at the top of the promontory.

Between €45 and €60

Parga Palace Hotel, Krionéri beach, ☎ (0684) 32 330 – 18rm. ⌐⎤ ♪ ✗ ⏁ In a great location opposite the beach, the rooms here are spacious and comfortable. Buffet-style breakfast.

Villa Koralli, Krionéri beach, ☎ (0684) 31 069, Fax (0684) 32 469 – 15rm. ⌐⎤ 🗐 / ⏁ ♪ 📺 A large white building, with facilities more suited to a

hotel than a guesthouse. It is friendly and very well run. In short, good value for money. Breakfast is served on a terrace opposite the beach.

Hotel Acropol, Platía Agíon Apostólon 4, signposted from the church square, ☎ (0684) 31 239 – 8rm. ⌐⎤ 🗐 📺 ✗ The oldest hotel in town, according to the owner, with renovation and extension work planned.

EATING OUT

Under €15

Zorba, on the quayside, to the right of the landing-stage. ⟰ A seafood restaurant.

Rudi's, in the same location. ⟰ More sophisticated and refined.

H Altana, near the Castello. ⟰ Greek cuisine served on a beautiful terrace looking down over the alleyways.

Over €15

Castello, in the Hotel Acropol (see above). ⟰ A very popular restaurant, often full, serving Greek, Italian and French cuisine. Good wine list. Booking recommended (same telephone as hotel).

HAVING A DRINK

Bars – Among the many bars on the quayside, you could try the **Caravel** (look out for the salmon-coloured façade), an ideal place for breakfast or a drink on the terrace.

OTHER THINGS TO DO

Excursions – As well as small boats which go to the **beaches** of Sarakinikó (departure 11am, return 5pm) and Lichnós (departure every hour, 10am-2pm and return every hour, 2pm-6pm), there are boat trips to **Paxós** and **Antípaxos** (departure 9.30am, return 5.15pm). You also have the option of a 1hr boat trip to **Aphrodite's cave**.

The travel agencies also offer a bus trip to the **Necromanteion of Ephyra**, 45min away.

SHOPPING GUIDE

Bookshop – You will find books and **newspapers** in the small bookshop to the right of the landing-stage, near the customs.

COMING AND GOING

By air – The *airport* is at Áktio, on the other side of the strait, and can be reached by ferry (departures every 30min), ☎ (0682) 22 355. There are three or four flights to Athens weekly.

By bus – The *bus station* is in Odós Irínis, on the corner of Odós Bizániou. To Párga, 5 services daily (2hr), to Igoumenítsa, 2 services daily (2hr30min), to Ioánnina, 10 services daily (2hr), to Árta, 5 services daily (1hr), to Athens, 4 services daily (6hr), to Thessaloníki, 1 service daily (8hr).

ADDRESS BOOK

Tourist information – *EOT*, Odós Venizélou, halfway along the quayside, near the post office.

Banks / Currency exchange – *Alphabank*, Odós E Antístasis, behind the post office. Cash dispenser.
National Bank of Greece, on the corner of the quayside and Odós Theofaniou, near the post office.

Post office – Odós Venizélou, halfway along the quayside.

Telephone – Local code: 0682. *OTE*, on the corner of Odós Irínis and Odós Kariotáki.

Internet – *Cafeteria Ascot*, Odós Balkou. Open every day, 9am-2am.

Travel agencies – *Leópoulos Travel*, Odós Venizélou, near the Avra hotel, ☎ (0682) 24 473, Fax (0682) 25 671. Reservations for ferries and air travel, car rental.

WHERE TO STAY

The summer rates shown here are 20-30% higher than in the low season.
Campsite (around €12)
Kalamítsi, 4km from Préveza, on the Párga road, ☎ (0682) 22 192, Fax (0682) 28 660 – 116 pitches. ⚑ ✗ ⤢ ⚘ A very friendly and well-run campsite with plenty of shade, near Nikópoli. Pitches for caravans and even a few rooms to let. Open all year.

Under €45
Préveza City, Odós L Irínis 61, ☎ (0682) 27 370, Fax (0682) 23 872 – 51rm. ⚑ ℘ TV ✗ CC The marble foyer and the restaurant with its post-modern furnishings are just an illusion, because upstairs the true nature of the hotel is revealed, with its faded carpets and wallpaper. A pity, because the rooms are comfortable.
Minos, Odós 28 Oktomvríou 11, ☎ (0682) 28 424 – 23rm. ⚑ ℘ TV Simple, clean, recently-renovated rooms with little balconies. Good value for money, although the staff can be rather brusque.
Between €45 and €60
Avra, Odós E Venizélou 19, ☎ (0682) 21 230, Fax (0682) 26 454 – 28rm. ⚑ ▤ ℘ TV ✗ A comfortable hotel in a white three-storey building, just opposite the landing-stage for ferries to Áktio. Beautiful view over the bay of Árta.
Dioni, Platía T Papageorgíou, ☎ (0682) 27 381, Fax (0682) 27 384 – 37rm. ⚑ ▤ ℘ TV CC A short distance from the quayside in a quiet alleyway in the pedestrian shopping district. The rooms are a bit down-at-heel, but bright and comfortable.

EATING OUT, HAVING A DRINK

🍴 **Ambrosios**, Odós Grigoríou, at right angles to the quayside. ⌂ This popular taverna, one of the oldest in Préveza, serves good plain food. Try the fish in white wine, under the shade of the trellis: a moment of pure harmony.
Peponís Gregóri, Odós Niklaba 1. ⌂ In a shady alleyway at right angles to the quayside, a small restaurant serving fish, soups and salads at reasonable prices.
Cafe-pizza Profil, Odós E Venizélou 12. ⌂ A good choice for a hearty breakfast. You can also have a drink or a snack here.

ÁRTA

Province of Epirus – District of Árta – 77km from Ioánnina
Regional map page 304 – Michelin map 980 fold 15
Pop 19 000

Not to be missed
Panagía Parigorítissa.
The Vlachérna Monastery.

Nestling in a bend of the River Árahthos in the southern foothills of Epirus, Árta does not attract many tourists, being more of a convenient stopping point on the route from Préveza to Ioánnina. However, this quiet town with its modern architecture harbours a few jewels of Byzantine art, especially the superb Church of Panagía Parigorítissa.

The two ages of Árta

Founded by Corinth in the 8C BC as a bridgehead in northern Greece, ancient *Ambracia* passed into Macedonian hands four centuries later. It had its period of glory under King **Pyrrhus** in the 3C BC, before being pillaged by the Romans in 189 BC and then abandoned by its inhabitants when Nikópoli was founded a century later. The town was not brought back to life until the 13C-14C, when the **despots of Epirus** decided to make it their capital, adorning it with sumptuous churches. But Árta was captured by the **Turks** in 1449, and held by them until 1881.

A Byzantine walk
Allow 2hr for visit

Odós Skoufá, partly pedestrianised, is the liveliest street in the **old town**. The local young people, couples out on a jaunt and families all stroll peacefully here, or linger on the terraces of the cafés in **Platía Ethnikís Antístasis**.

Famed throughout the Balkans, the majestic 17C **bridge*** with its four arches and humpback silhouette, spans the Árahthos on the edge of the town. According to legend, as recounted by the poet Níkos Kazantzákis, the architect used his wife's corpse to reinforce the foundations!

Right next to it, you might like to visit the small **Folk Museum** *(9am-1.30pm; closed Monday)*, before having a drink in one of the nearby **cafés**.

Definitely worth a visit is the town's main attraction, the **Church of Panagía Parigorítissa****, dedicated to the Virgin Comforter *(8am-2.30pm; closed Monday; entrance fee)*. From the outside, it seems massive and resembles a huge cube crowned with a dome and turrets, its surface decorated with a delicate pattern of brick and stone. Built in 1290, the church reveals a mixture of architectural styles, inspired by the sanctuaries of Constantinople, but original in more ways than one: at its base, it is arranged on an octagonal plan, while the higher storeys take the form of a cross. Take some time to observe the astonishing **elevation of the cupola****, with its triple levels of cantilevered pilasters. Note also the **mosaic**** in the dome, depicting Christ surrounded by the prophets: a pure masterpiece, executed in the best workshops in Constantinople. Today, the brick walls seem almost bare, but you can still make out a few **frescoes***, especially in the apse (16C). The church also contains some remarkable 18C **icons**, particularly those of the Virgin and of Christ, in the iconostasis.

To the right of the church, the old canteen houses an **Archaeological Museum** *(same opening times as the church)* where various Roman pieces are on display: **bronze statuettes** and moulds, **marble statues**, numerous **terracotta** objects, as well as some amazing **puppets** from children's tombs. The long building *(currently being excavated)* enclosing the courtyard behind the church once housed the monks' **cells**.

Go back up Odós Pírrou Vassilís and turn into Odós Plastíra.

Much smaller, but no less charming, the **Church of Agía Theodóra*** *(open every day, 7am-1pm / 5pm-8pm)* is equally worth a detour. Built in the 11C-12C, it has an elegant brick exterior. Its basilica with three aisles, covered with a wooden frame-work, was once part of a convent. It was enlarged and decorated at the end of the 13C, when Theodora, the wife of the despot Michael II, went into retreat there. Inside, take time to examine the very ornate Corinthian **capitals***, taken from Early-Christian buildings, as well as the carved marble **sarcophagus*** of Theodora. The newly constructed **iconostasis** incorporates a few 11C fragments.

Go along Odós Kiprou in the direction of the citadel.

With its indented and undulating friezes, the enamelled ceramic tiles contrasting with the red of its bricks, and the thousand arabesques dancing on its walls, the 14C **Church of Ágios Vassílios*** looks quite wonderful. The interior is just as inspiring, with its **paintings** which brighten up the apse (17C or 18C) and the two unusual plaques in varnished terracotta, set into the adjacent wall (15C), depicting the Crucifixion and the Three Hierarchs.

Before you go back to the town centre, have a look at the fortifications of the **citadel** (13C) which are only a stone's throw away.

The Vlachérna Monastery**

Go along the Préveza road and turn right at the first major crossroads, then follow the road which goes off to the right, 3km further on. Continue for about 3km as far as the village of Vlachérna. The monastery is closed during siesta time. Ask for the key at the kiosk on the square.

Atop a hill to the north of the Árahthos, the Vlachérna Monastery is an exciting tes-timony to Epirote architecture. The original sanctuary, founded in around 900, was incorporated in the 13C into a basilica with three aisles crowned by a dome. The elegant marble **bas-reliefs*** are pieces recycled from the Roman, Early-Christian and Medieval Eras, and include a superb 13C **Archangel Michael****. As well as the **tomb** of the despot Michael II, the church contains some splendid 13C **frescoes***, particu-larly in the narthex, but unfortunately badly damaged. Also of interest is the floor, decorated with a beautiful **opus sectile** (marble mosaic).

Making the most of Árta

COMING AND GOING

By bus – The main **bus station** is to the east of town, outside the ramparts. Ten or so services daily to Ioánnina (90min) and 5 to Préveza (1hr). Connections to Athens (5hr), and Thessaloníki (7hr30min).

ADDRESS BOOK

Bank – *National Bank of Greece*, near the Cronos Hotel. Cash dispenser.

Post office – Odós Amvrakías.

Telephone – Local code: 0681. *OTE*, Platía Ethnikís Antístasis.

WHERE TO STAY, EATING OUT

The summer prices shown here are about 25% higher than those charged during the rest of the year. You will find restaurants and snack-bars on Platía Kilkís, Platía Ethnikís Antístasis and Platía 24 Iouníou.

Under €45

Amvrakia, Odós Priovódou 13, ☎ (0681) 28 311, Fax (0681) 31 544 – 60rm. ♒ ⸁cc⸂ Simple but comfortable and very clean rooms with balconies. Some have a bathroom, television and air conditioning.

Cronos Hotel, Kilkís, ☎ (0681) 22 211, Fax (0681) 73 795 – 55rm. ⸁⸂ ♒ ⸁TV⸂ ⸁cc⸂ In the same category as the Amvrakia, this hotel has more comfort-able rooms that are only slightly more expensive. The only credit card accepted is MasterCard.

SHOPPING GUIDE

Market – A vegetable market is held in the morning on the corner of Odós Pír-rou Vassilís and Odós Manoláki.

Corfu, the Venetian bell-tower of Ágios Spirídonas

THE IONIAN ISLANDS

The brilliant blue waters of the Ionian Sea are home to a long chain of islands. Lying off the coast of Epirus and stretching down to the tip of the Peloponnese, the Ionian archipelago is made up of seven islands (hence its Greek name, **Heptánese**). Set apart from the others, Cythera *(see page 252)* is situated off the little known and wild Máni Peninsula. With its drier climate and softer contours, the island of *Kíthira* differs from the others, its villages of white houses more reminiscent of the Cyclades than the nearby shores of Italy.

For a long time, Italy, and in particular, the Venetian Republic were to base themselves on these islands, strategically poised between two coastlines.

Beneath their red-tiled roofs the houses have pale yellow façades. With the windows outlined in white, and despite the numerous earthquakes that have shaken the archipelago – the one in 1953 spared only Corfu – the bell-towers of the churches, a tribute to the Campanile of St Mark's in Venice, still stretch proudly skywards. Across the countryside, they tower above the villages, as straight as a die, cutting into the sky with their perfectly aligned bells. The green hills of Corfu, Leucas and Cephalonia are again reminiscent of Italy, with their clumps of cypresses and stretches of olive trees, vines or sweet-smelling lemon trees. And when night falls, the terraces of the cafés come alive and the aromas of Italy mingle with the sweetness of the air, already laden with the perfume of *espresso coffee* and the occasional *gelato al limone...*

But the Ionian Islands are proud of their Greek origins and the fact that they belong to the land of Homer. Was Ithaca not home to Odysseus? And while the Ionian School of painting which flourished here in the 19C to some extent perpetuated the art of the Renaissance, its main achievement was to give a new boost to the Byzantine tradition, and establish a firmer foothold for everything it represented to the young Greek nation.

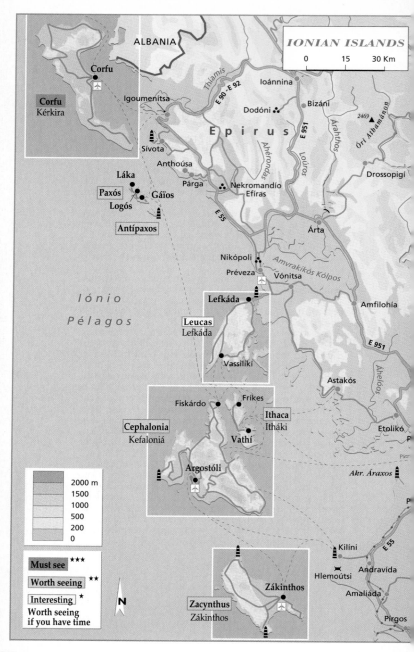

IONIAN ISLANDS

0   15   30 Km

ALBANIA

Corfu

Corfu
Kérkira

Igoumenítsa

Thíamis

Ioánnina

Dodóni

Bizáni

E 90 - E 92

E p i r u s

E 951

Órt Athamánon
2469

Arahthos

Sívota

Anthoúsa

Párga

Nekromandío
Efíras

Loúros

Aherondas

Drossopigí

Láka

Paxós

Gáïos

Logós

Antípaxos

E 55

Árta

Amvrakikós Kólpos

Nikópoli

Préveza

Vónitsa

Amfilohía

Iónio

Pélagos

Lefkáda

Leucas
Lefkáda

Vassilikí

E 951

Ahelóos

Astakós

Fiskárdo

Fríkes

Ithaca
Itháki

Cephalonia
Kefaloniá

Vathí

Etolikó

Argostóli

Akr. Áraxos

Pátr

Kilíni

E 55

Andravída

Hlemoútsi

Zákinthos

Amaliáda

Zacynthus
Zákinthos

Pirgos

2000 m
1500
1000
500
200
0

Must see ★★★

Worth seeing ★★

Interesting ★
Worth seeing
if you have time

N

348

CORFU★★★
(KÉRKIRA)

Ionian Islands – Capital of the district of Corfu –
Regional map opposite – Michelin map 980 fold 14 – Map of
Pop 107 000 – Mediterranean climate – Allow

Not to be missed
The old town of Corfu.
The rocky beaches of the west coast.
The spectacular views from Pélekas, Paleokastrítsa and Mt Pandokrátor.

And remember...
Make time for a stroll along the deserted inland roads.
Buy a map for exploring the more remote areas.
Almost all the museums are closed on Mondays.

Spared by the terrible earthquake of 1953, the jewel of the Ionian Islands conjures up all the charm of the many cultures and civilisations which succeeded each other here: with the passing of the centuries, the harmonious mosaic of its Greek and Byzantine heritage was followed by the dominion of the lion of St Mark, symbol of the Venetian Republic, and the calming influence of the British Protectorate. But there is no doubt that Corfu remains predominantly Greek, and that the soul of the Homeric heroes beats in its breast. Could this be the fertile *Scheria* of the poet, the country of the Phaeacians and their king Alcinous, a prominent figure in the Odyssey? No-one knows. But everywhere, in its white-washed monasteries, beneath its ancient olive trees, in its charming villages, you will feel the heartbeat of Greece (as sung by another poet, the Corfiote **Lorenzo Mavilis**).

At one time Corfu was attached to the Albanian coast, today only a narrow channel barely 3km wide separates it from the mainland. Its east coast, dotted with anchorages and peaceful bays, is more serene than the west coast, which is buffeted by winds and indented with rocky creeks. In the centre of the island, there is yet another kind of landscape, with gentle contours, a succession of green hills culminating in **Mt Pandokrátor** (917m). The vegetation is lush and was described by Homer: myrtle and broom, orange and lemon trees, and, of course, the ubiquitous olive tree. Undoubtedly the face of the island has changed a great deal since Antiquity – the tourist business is almost a century old here – but almost 70 % of Corfiotes still earn a living from farming. And it is up to you to leave the beaten track and discover the authentic charm of the most beautiful of the Ionian Islands.

A Corinthian colony

Corfu did not make its entrance in history until 734 BC, when the **Corinthians** established a colony at Paleópolis, south of the present capital. The island, then known as **Corcyra**, developed rapidly and by the 5C it had the second-largest Greek fleet after Athens. However, conflict and war led to a rapid decline, until the Peloponnesian War (431 BC) which left the island drained of its resources. Now weakened, it passed through many hands, before being annexed by Rome in 229 BC.

In exchange for the use of its harbours, **Rome** granted Corcyra a large degree of autonomy. As a result the island regained some of its prosperity, and undertook a prestigious building programme. After the reign of Diocletian (284-305 AD), who tried in vain to repress the evangelisation begun by **Jason** and **Sosipater**, the disciples of Paul, the island was soon annexed to the Eastern Empire and followed the fate of Byzantium from 395 until 1267. The Church of Corfu then became one of the twelve great Orthodox archbishoprics of Greece.

Corfu

349

...der constant attack by the barbarians, Goths and Vandals, the capital ...transferred to a site that was better protected, the two promontories of ...were to give the island its new name: *Ton Koryphón*, the city with "two ...its". The effort was wasted: Corfu and its citadel were again invaded by the ...rmans, the Venetians and pirates... before falling in 1267 into the hands of the **...evins of Naples**. Upon the death of Charles II of Naples, the island agreed to come under the protection of its powerful neighbour, Venice, which purchased Corfu in 1386... for 30 000 gold ducats.

Under the banner of the Serenissima

Now out of reach of the Ottoman Empire, Corfu was placed under the slightly lighter yoke of the Serenissima (the Venetian Republic), which granted the islanders a certain amount of autonomy and the nobles their privileges. The Venetians also encouraged trade and the cultivation of olives. But the weight of labour and taxes led to many peasant **revolts**, the devastating effects of which, combined with the **plague** and **attacks by the Turks** (1537 and 1716), were to decimate the population. The haemorrhage was not to cease until the arrival of the Cretans, who themselves were fleeing the Turks: they brought a new dynamism to the island, together with the talent of their painters, including **Emmanuél Tzanès** (1610-90).

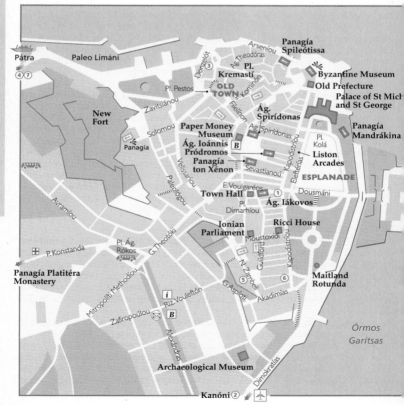

Modern Corfu

After a long period of decline which began in the 18C, the Venetian Republic was toppled by **Napoleon Bonaparte**, who, while he was at it, took possession of the Ionian Islands. After that, Corfu followed the fate of its sister islands, coming successively under French, Turkish, Russian and then British domination. The 19C was to be a period of intensive cultural development for the island, with the creation of the **Ionian Academy**, which was to produce scholars and poets, including the famous **Solomós**, author of the national anthem (*see sidebar page 401*). When the Ionian Islands were annexed by Greece (1864), Corfu, which had had to dismantle its fortifications, was proclaimed a neutral area, along with Paxós. This did not prevent the French and the Serbs from installing themselves on the island during the 1914-18 War, nor the Italians in 1923, nor, finally, between 1943 and 1945, the Germans, who bombarded the capital on two occasions. At the end of the war, peace was finally restored to Corfu... until the island was invaded by tourists, who flock here each year from all over the world.

Corfu Town★★★

Allow a whole day if you wish to spend time strolling through the streets.

**KÉRKIRA
(Corfu Town)**

0   100   200 m

N

Iráki

Old Fort

Ágios
Geórgios

HOTELS
Arcadion....................①
Archontico................②
Astron........................③
Atlantis......................④
Bella Venezia............⑤
Cavalieri....................⑥
Ionion........................⑦

The old town of Corfu stretches from the Spianada (the esplanade to the east) to the New Fort (to the west) and is built on a complex plan: at first the streets are laid out in an orderly way at right angles to **Kapodistríou**, the main thoroughfare of the town, but gradually become more winding as they approach the old harbour, which reveals a complex maze of *kantounia*, those little streets where it is so easy to get lost. Further out from the centre, to the south-west, the streets broaden out again, and are dotted with flowering bougainvillaea, quince trees and vine-laden trellises shading doorways. In the avenues planted with acacia trees, where the Corfiotes attempt to escape the heat, the foliage vibrates to the sound of crickets – until evening, when the town resonates to the deafening sound of aircraft. A cosmopolitan town, Corfu is a blend of tranquillity and restlessness, with any number of surprises awaiting those who take the time to explore it thoroughly, going wherever their fancy takes them. But, if you wish to avoid the main flow of tourists, follow our itinerary...

The Esplanade★ (Spianada)

Planted with trees by the French at the beginning of the 19C, the Spianada, the old fortified square built by the Venetians in front of the citadel, is now the heart of the town. This is where all the Corfiotes meet, where they like to be seen, perhaps nibbling a *kalambóki* (grilled corn on the cob) before strolling up and down the terraces lined with cafés once night has fallen.

There are various monuments decorating the area, including the **Maitland Rotunda**, erected in honour of a British High Commissioner. Another British legacy is the **cricket pitch** (!), which is still used on certain Sundays during the summer. Surrounding the Esplanade are the elegant arcades of the **Liston**★, built between 1807 and 1814 by the French, homesick for the Rue de Rivoli in Paris, under the supervision of the father of Ferdinand de Lesseps, who was to build the Suez Canal.

The Old Fort★★ (Paleó Froúrio)

8am-7pm in summer, 8am-3pm in winter; shop: 8.30am-3.30pm; closed at weekends. Free access to the fortress except for exhibitions, when there is an entrance fee. Allow 40min. Go in the morning: in the evening, the sun overhead interferes with the view over the town. It is also possible to visit the fort out of hours: the "Old Fortress Café" is set within its walls and stays open until late at night.

Originally built on the nearby island of Kanóni, the ancient town of Corfu was moved in the 6C to protect it from the incursions of the Goths. The Byzantine town lies in this citadel (or **Old Fort**) perched on its rock. In the 15C, the Venetians reinforced it with walls, encircling the **land fort** and the **sea fort**. They also dug a deep **moat** at the foot of the rock, giving the fortress the appearance of a little island in its own right. Between the two Turkish sieges (1537-71), the citadel was used strictly for military purposes. When it became too cramped, its last inhabitants moved out and founded the current town just outside the citadel.

From the Spianada, the Venetian moat is spanned by a bridge. Just beyond the bridge, in the building on the right, do not miss the **bas-reliefs** and the **Byzantine mosaics**★ (5C-6C) featuring animal motifs. Military strategy enthusiasts will also find the explanations about the Byzantine fortresses of Angelókastro and Gardíki very interesting.

After crossing a dry moat, you emerge onto the parade ground, surrounded by beautiful **Venetian reliefs** sheltered by arches. Beyond is the upper terrace, where there is an imposing **square clock tower**. From here, you can walk around the fort and discover, on the right, the austere façade of the **Church of Ágios Geórgios** (1840), a rather dull Doric building, while, on the left, British military buildings mingle with Venetian powder magazines and warehouses. To reach the top of the fort, take the passage to the right of the clock tower, then the steep cobbled pathway, alongside the British barracks. This leads to the land fort and its **lighthouse** (1822), where there is a fine **view**★★ over the town and out to sea. You might then want to head for the little pebble **beach** with its crystal-clear water on the right of the fort.

In the heart of the town

From the Spianada, take Odós Euvgeníou Voulgaréos, at the southern corner of the Liston arcades, opposite the entrance to the Old Fort. The first street on the right runs alongside the **town hall**★★ with its Renaissance façade and elegant arched windows decorated with medallions. Built between 1663 and 1691, at one time the building was a meeting place for the nobility on the island, hence its name, *Loggia Nobilei*. In the evening, head for the open-air cafés in the **Town Hall Square**, which is always buzzing with activity. On the left-hand side stands the **Church of Ágios Iákovos (St James)** (1553) and the former Roman Catholic Bishop's Palace (17C), which now houses the Bank of Greece.

Behind the town hall, on the right, take Odós Guildford – named after a British nobleman of philhellenic tendencies – famous for its restaurants with pleasant terraces.

In Odós Moustoxídi, on the right, at the end of the pedestrian precinct, stands **Ricci House**★, a fine patrician residence with seven arches decorated with grotesque figures. From its balcony, the Venetian *Proveditore* used to watch the horse races which took place in Strata Larga, then the main street of the town. A few metres further on, the Doric columns of the old **Ionian Parliament** (1855) come into view, where, in 1863, the vote was taken to restore the Ionian Islands to Greece.

Under the arcades of the Liston, Corfu

Retrace your steps and take the road on the left of a pink house, which will lead you back to Town Hall Square. This time take the road to the left of the town hall, Odós M Theotóki (beware: there are no fewer than four streets in Corfu with this name!).

After reaching a small square with a **well**, continue to Odós N Theotóki, at the corner of which stands the red and yellow bell-tower of **Panagía ton Xénon** (Virgin of the Foreigners). This basilica, which has a nave and two side aisles, and a **painted ceiling** by Nikólaos Koútouzis (18C), belonged to Epirotes who fled to Corfu during the Turkish occupation. They left many **votive offerings**.

On the other side of the street, cast a glance at the small church of **Ágios Ioánnis Pródromos*** (St John the Baptist), a sombre basilica with a single nave, flanked by an exonarthex (16C). All its charm lies in the moving simplicity of its pink façade. Note the marble **iconostasis*** and various **icons** painted by George Chryssóloras. In the vestibule preceding the nave, you should also go and see the rather extraordinary "museum", a strange collection of icons, crosses, candelabras, etc.

On the other side of the square, on the left, the Ionian Bank houses the banknote collection of the **Paper Money Museum** *(9am-2pm; closed Sundays; no charge)*, the only one of its kind in Greece. Aspiring forgers can become expert in the skills of paper-making and engraving techniques.

On the far left-hand side of the square, a gateway opens onto the town's most emblematic monument, the **Church of Ágios Spirídonas****. Built in 1589, it is dedicated to the patron saint of Corfu, who was originally from Cyprus, where he was a bishop in the 4C. Until recently, one out of every two boys baptised on the island bore his name. The mummified body was transferred to Corfu during the Fall of Constantinople (1453), and, since 1590, has rested in the crypt *(to the right of the sanctuary)*, protected by a 19C **silver coffin** which is the object of pious veneration after mass. A great procession on August 11 commemorates the day in 1716, when, according to the legend, Spirídon appeared to the Corfiotes, brandishing a torch which caused the Turks, who were besieging the town, to flee. There is a surprising contrast between the sobriety of its façade and bell-tower – the tallest on the island – and the exuberance of the interior decoration. Look up at the beautiful **ceiling★**, a 19C copy of some Baroque paintings by Panayiótis Doxarás (1727), the originals having been destroyed by damp. Note also the four **icons** in the narthex, works by the Corfiote artist... Spirídon Sperantzás, the **votive offerings**, and the two silver 18C **candelabras**.

Leave the church by the opposite door, step into Odós Ágios Spirídonas and turn left. The first street on the right winds along between stalls selling wooden knick-knacks of dubious origin. Turn left before the steps into Odós Filelínon, paved in beige-coloured flagstones. It leads to Platía Pestos with its restaurants on the terraces; then take the little street immediately on the right, then the second street on the left (Odós Kominón).

Around Platía Kremastí★★

An arch linking two ancient buildings, and a few steps lead to this charming little square, which plunges you straight into the atmosphere of 17C Venice. Surrounded by old houses with green shutters, and overlooked by the faded pink façade of the **Church of Panagía Kremastí** (16C), it has a richly decorated **well** (1699). The church, which owes its name to an icon of the Virgin Mary that hangs *(kremastí)* on the wall rather than being propped up on a support, as is more usual, only displays its treasures in the morning *(9am-1pm):* they include a stone **iconostasis** and some large **icons** by Spirídon Sperantzás.

Retrace your steps to Platía Pestos, and take the second little street on the left. The street emerges in front of a large white and yellow church, **Panagía Spileótissa★** (1577), the metropolitan church of Corfu. Behind its imposing Renaissance façade, the vast basilica has a nave and two side aisles. It houses the **relics** of St Theodora, which were formerly kept in Constantinople, and a **Byzantine iconostasis★★**. There are also some superb **icons★** of the Cretan and Ionian schools (16C-18C), the earliest being *Panagía tis Dimossianás*, painted in Ioánnina in the 14C.

Kapodístrias, a precursor of modern Europe
An emblematic figure in the tormented history of the island in the early 19C – Corfu changed hands six times between 1797 and 1816 – Count Giovanni Antonio Capo d'Istria (1776-1831) appears to have been very "European" long before the term existed. Judge for yourself: he studied Latin in Venice, science in Padua, he was a doctor in Corfu, Secretary of State of the Ionian Islands under Russo-Turkish domination (1803), a diplomat in Bucharest, and eventually became the Russian Minister of Foreign Affairs (1816-22). Over the years, he fought for Greek independence, and tried to persuade the great powers of the need to unify Europe. As President of the newly formed Greek Republic (1827-31), he devoted his efforts to developing a health service and educational establishments, thus laying the foundations of the new nation. But his authoritarianism and his reputation as a Russian agent made him unpopular. He was assassinated in Náfplio in 1831, and lies buried in the Monastery of Platitéra.

Walk down the long flight of steps leading to the old harbour, then take the first street on the right, and turn immediately right again. Dotted with fairground roundabouts, this square with its patchy lawns is a favourite haunt of the Corfiotes.

Turn right into Odós Donzelót, then into Odós Arseníou, which follows the seafront. Halfway along Odós Arseníou, on the right, a sign points to a little street that climbs up towards the Byzantine Museum.

Built in the 15C and now magnificently restored, the **Church of Panagía Antivouniotissa**★ houses the **Byzantine Museum**★ *(8.30am-3pm; 8am-2.30pm in winter; closed Mondays; entrance fee)*, which has one of the finest collections of icons dating from the 16C and 17C. In addition to the important works by Michael Damaskinós and Emmanuél Tzanès, who painted the superb **Noli me tangere**★★, do not miss the cruelly realistic **Stoning of St Stephen** (17C), nor the curious **Trinity** dating from the 16C in which the Father and the Son cover the world with their joined hands. Further on, look out for the original **Lamentation** (16C), framed by a sort of palanquin, and other works depicting the life of St John the Baptist. In the church itself there are still several fragments of the original **frescoes**, and an elaborate gold-painted wooden **ceiling**★★. Finally – a rare privilege – you can see the holy of holies, where the priest officiates, usually hidden behind a curtain. Notice the **Descent into Hell** (16C), in which Christ separates the blessed and the damned.

Go back down to Odós Arseníou and continue along the seafront to your right.

As you come round a bend, on the coast road, suddenly the massive silhouette of the **old prefecture of Corfu** (19C) appears, which is characteristic of the style implemented under the British Protectorate. It was built on the site of the birthplace of Ioánnis Kapodístrias, founder of the Greek state.

Devote some time to the **Palace of St Michael and St George**★ (or Royal Palace) *(8.30am-3pm; closed Mondays; no charge until the museum reopens; allow 25min)*. Designed by the British architect George Whitmore (1819-29), this neo-Classical building used to be the British High Commissioner's Residence. It owes its name to the Order of St Michael and St George, which rewarded services rendered to the British Crown in the Mediterranean. Later it was the seat of the Ionian Senate, before becoming the summer residence of the Greek royal family in 1864. Behind the Doric portico running along the façade, off the broad **vestibule** decorated with friezes depicting the Odyssey lies a labyrinth of rooms where portraits of the Presidents of the Ionian Senate and of George IV of England look down at the palace's rare visitors. Upstairs, the **throne room** and the **banqueting hall** evoke the former glory of the place. In the now silent **ballroom**, your steps will echo under the gilt caissoned dome. The **Asiatic Museum** situated within the palace walls houses the collections of two diplomats *(8am-3pm, 8.30am-3pm in winter; closed Mondays; entrance fee; allow 30min)*.

As you come out, to the right of the royal palace, do not miss the Lilliputian church of **Panagía Mandrákina**★★ (1700), with its disconcertingly bright red bell. On the right-hand side, a staircase leads down to the yacht harbour, situated in the outer moat of the old fort (citadel). Stop awhile in the nearby **garden** with its lovely terrace where you can sip an iced coffee while watching the sea.

And if you have time...

You can complete your exploration of the town by walking to the **New Fort**★ *(9am-10pm; entrance fee; allow 35min)*, erected by the Venetians between 1576 and 1588 to defend the north-western suburbs of the town against Turkish raids. To reach it, head along Odós Solomou, then climb a cobbled staircase that passes the **Church of the Panagía** with its pretty Italian bell-towers. The main attraction of the church is its **view**★ over the town, from the citadel to the Church of Ágios Spirídonas, and right across to the Albanian coast. After passing through several fortified gates, bastions and vaulted passages, you reach the **parade ground**, where music festivals are held in the summer. The barracks now house a café *(10am-4pm)* and an art gallery. A staircase and an ancient ladder lead to the top of the bastion, where the Greek flag flies defiantly next to a huge cross laden with electric bulbs.

Archaeology enthusiasts should head for the **Archaeological Museum**★ *(8.30am-3pm, 9am-2.30pm in winter; closed Mondays; entrance fee; allow 40min)*, which houses a remarkable collection of antiquities, dating from the Palaeolithic to the Roman Era: there are fragments of pottery, statues, funerary urns, bronzes and coins, etc. The most interesting exhibit is the **pediment of the Temple of Artemis★★**, known as the **Gorgon pediment**, discovered on the nearby island of Kanóni. This impressive relief, 17m wide, is one of the oldest examples of Greek sculpture (6C BC).

In the room on the north side of the museum is part of another **pediment** found at Figaréto (500 BC). It depicts Dionysus and a beautiful naked young man, sitting at table at a banquet. Note also the **Lion of Menecrates**, a 7C BC Corinthian sculpture from the necropolis of Garítsas, a bronze depicting a "comast" – a happy companion – (570 BC) and the small **kouros** head (530 BC) found at Mon Repos (*see below*). In the south room, also have a look at the strange lead plates on which the usurers of Paleópolis used to record pawn debts.

West of the town (*Odós Polihroníou Konstandá*), you can also visit the **Panagía Platitéra Monastery**, where Ioánnis Kapodístrias and the Corfiote historian Moustoxýdis are buried. The present buildings, reconstructed in the 19C, are of no particular interest, but you can see some splendid post-Byzantine **icons★★**.

The Kanóni Peninsula★★

The blue buses (line no 2; tickets from the office in Platía Theotóki) go to Kanóni. They leave from Odós Alexándras, 50m beyond the post office. If you go by car, drive along Garítsa Bay to the south of Corfu, following signs for Kanóni. Allow half a day.

South of the town of Corfu lies the Kanóni Peninsula, which owes its name to a cannon battery built and subsequently abandoned by Napoleon's troops. It was here that the first town of Corcyra was built, with its two harbours (Garítsas and Halikiópoulos), prior to being moved to the Citadel in the 5C BC. The residential area was situated on the west side of the peninsula while the sanctuaries were situated to the east. As you walk around, look out for remains of the original settlement. They appear here and there, on the corners of blocks of houses or in the setting of a quiet park.

■ A useful landmark as you leave the coast road is the **Douglas obelisk**, erected in honour of Ward Douglas, British High Commissioner from 1835 to 1841. The street to the right of the obelisk leads to the only surviving relic of the ancient necropolis, the **Tomb of Menecrates** (6C BC) who was consul of Corcyra (*no charge*). According to a tradition open to dispute, a lion, which can be seen in the Archaeological Museum, used to stand on the top of this round tumulus covered with stones.

■ A little further on, a road on the left leads to the **Church of St Jason and St Sosipater★** (*8.30am-2pm; no charge*), dedicated to the disciples of the Apostle Paul who evangelised the island in 48 AD. Built using old materials, this Byzantine jewel dating from the 13C is particularly charming because of the way stones and bricks have been employed alternately in its walls (the bell-tower is a Venetian addition). Unfortunately, the restoration work now in progress inside the building shows signs of carelessness: there are splashes of plaster on the frescoes, stuccoes have been damaged by scaffolding... Hopefully the damage will not prove to be permanent.

Go back to the road on which you arrived and follow signs for "Paleópolis" (signpost on the right).

■ Also worth a look are the ruins of the great **Basilica of Agía Kérkira**, at **Paleópolis** (*8.30am-2pm; no charge*). Of the original nave and four side aisles, only one remains, to which there is access when excavations are in progress. Again built of re-used ancient material, this Byzantine church dating from the 5C stood on the site of the agora of Corcyra. Despite the fact that it was destroyed by German bombing in 1943 you can still see some of its delicate **mosaics**, which are quite well-preserved.

■ To the right of the church, Odós Dörpfeld leads to the **Monastery of Ágii Theódori** and the Temple of Artemis. Only the west pediment, known as the Gorgon pediment (*on display at the Archaeological Museum*), the **monumental altar** (25m long) and some of the foundations testify to the size of this Doric temple, built in 590-580 BC.

■ Opposite Paleópolis is the archaeological park of **Mon Repos** (*8am-7pm; no charge*), which watches over the ruins of the ancient city. The elegant neo-Classical villa in the centre of the park used to be the summer residence of the British High Commissioners, and subsequently belonged to the Greek royal family (Prince Philip, the Duke of Edinburgh, was born here in 1921).
Take the road opposite the villa. It leads under foliage to the ruins of two temples (*turn left after the white church*): first, 50m further on, stands the **Temple of Hera** (7C BC), the most important temple of the ancient city, destroyed by Agrippa in the 1C BC. Three hundred metres further on, lower down, behind the pines fringing the coast, the beautiful ruins of the **Temple of Kardaki★** (6C BC) lie in perfect solitude. This building, 25m long, is the best preserved of the temples on the island. Amid the chaos of its Doric columns you may find votive offerings dedicated to Apollo or a statue of Cybele.

■ **Vlahérna Monastery★** (Moní Vlahérna) — *Reached by a flight of steps leading up left of the café. 8am-11pm. No charge.* Although this delightful little monastery, built on a tiny island, is the subject of some of the most beautiful picture postcards in Corfu, you will have to photograph it from close by in order not to reveal its surroundings which have changed a great deal since the 18C. Now the airport runway is a stone's throw away, generating a continuous stream of aircraft which almost clip its bell-tower every few minutes and create a deafening noise. It's a great pity, because the scene is really beautiful, the brilliant white church★ seeming to float on the calm waters of the lagoon. Go there at sunrise (in the evening, the sun sets to one side of

Corfu

A monastery on the water:
Vlahérna (Corfu)

G. de Benoist/MICHELIN

the monastery and the view is not so good). From the monastery, a caique (€1.5 *return ticket; a 3min ride*) will take you to the tiny nearby island of **Pondikoníssi**, which owes its name to the fact that it is shaped like a "mouse". Here, sheltered from the chaos of modern life behind its curtain of cypress trees stands the pretty **Pandokrátor Church** (*8am-11pm*), erected in the 11C.

The north of Corfu★★

Head north out of Corfu Town, following signs for Gouviá.
Allow most of the day, especially if you want to climb Mt Pandokrátor.

Apart from climbing Mt Pandokrátor, the main attraction in the north of the island is the series of **beaches** which have given it its reputation. To the north and west of Corfu Town, the coast is largely dominated by tourism, and the area has few attractions unless you stay in one of the hotel complexes at Dassiá (Club Med) or Ípsos (on the east coast). This is also where most of the campsites on the island are to be found (*between Ípsos and Pirgí*).

■ **Paleokastrítsa Bay★★** – *1 km beyond Gouviá, on the left*. The road leading to Paleokastrítsa, on the west coast, follows the shape of the huge bay: the stands of laurel trees and the last olive trees struggling to conceal the tavernas full of tourists or the constant flow of coaches. What was undoubtedly one of the most scenic parts of the island now attracts whole charter flights of visitors who for the most part have forsaken contemplation for sheer pleasure. However, the landscape is still superb: six sandy bays are lapped by a translucent sea which splashes against cliffs dotted with caves and highlighted by the green of the pines and the olive trees.

This delightful scenery is the setting of **Panagía Theotókos Monastery★** (18C) with its brilliant white walls (*7am-1pm / 3pm-8pm; open daily from 1 April to 31 October; long skirts are provided for female visitors*). Founded in 1228, the monastery was rebuilt in the 18C and 19C and the buildings themselves are of no particular interest. But you will fall under the spell of its **vaulted courtyard**, its terraces full of flowers, and the magnificent **view★★** across the bay. Offshore stands **Kolóvri Rock**, which is supposed to be the vessel used by Odysseus, turned into stone by Poseidon. Take a look at the **church** (1722), which houses a museum with a collection of Byzantine icons, liturgical objects and vestments.

Diving enthusiasts can give vent to their passion while others may like to climb up to the village of **Lákones★**, which has the most beautiful **view★** of the site.

Go back to the road from Corfu, then, at a hairpin bend 2km further on, turn left. After Lákones, continue along the same road to Makrádes.

■ There is a walk starting from **Makrádes**, a village famous for its red wine. From here, follow the road (*on the left, towards Kríni*) which climbs up to the ruins of **Sant'Angelo Castle★** (Angelókastro), a Byzantine fortress built in the 13C by the despot of Epirus to defend the island against pirate raids. The **view★★** from the top makes the effort worthwhile. The less adventurous can admire the castle from afar by driving along the road which winds along the upland plateaux.

Continue along the main road which passes through the villages of Priniílas and Ágios Geórgios. Then follow signs for "Ágios Geórgios Beach".

■ Nestling deep in a majestic bay surrounded by rocks, the sandy beach of **Ágios Geórgios★** (5km long) is one of the finest places on the west coast for a swim; what's more, it's fairly quiet, even in the high season.

Continue along the same road as far as the campsite, then after 500m, turn left (sign for "Arílas"). Then at the next crossroads, turn right.

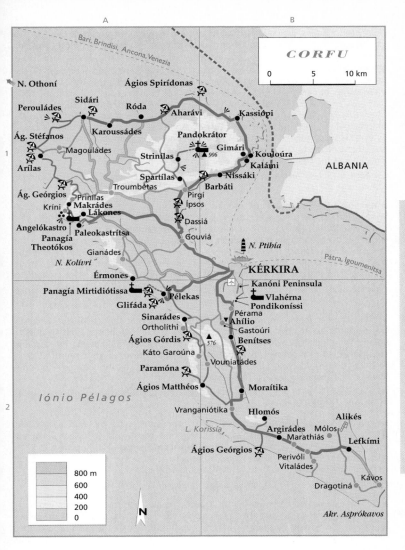

0   5   10 km

Bari, Brindisi, Ancona, Venezia

N. Othoní

Ágios Spirídonas

Perouládes   Sidári   Róda

Aharávi   Kassiópi

Ág. Stéfanos   Karoussádes

Magouládes   Pandokrátor

Arílas   Strinílas   Gimári

ALBANIA

Koulóura

Ág. Geórgios   Spartílas   Kalámi

Prinílas   Troumbétas   Níssáki

Kríni   Makrádes   Pirgí   Barbáti

Lákones   Ípsos

Angelókastro   Dassiá

Panagía   Paleokastrítsa

Theotókos   Gouviá

Gianádes

N. Kolívri   N. Ptihía

Érmones   KÉRKIRA

Pátra, Igoumenítsa

Panagía Mirtidiótissa   Kanóni Peninsula

Pélekas   Vlahérna

Glifáda   Pondikoníssi

Sinarádes   Pérama

Ortholíthi   Ahílio

Ágios Górdis   Gastoúri

Benítses

Káto Garoúna   576

Paramóna   Vouniatádes

Ágios Matthéos   Moraítika

Iónio Pélagos

Vranganiótika   Hlomós   Alikés

L. Korissía   Argirádes   Mólos

Marathiás   Lefkími

Ágios Geórgios   Perivóli

Vitaládes   Kávos

Dragotiná

Akr. Asprókavos

800 m
600
400
200
0

N

■ The village of **Arílas** also has two pleasant sandy but windy beaches: **Arílas beach**, situated next to a strange cluster of rocks sprouting out of the sea, and **Ágios Stéfanos** (*2km to the north*), surrounded by wooded hills. Beyond, the road to Sidári passes through some sleepy **villages**, dozing in the shade of the palms and olive trees.

■ **The Bay of Sidári** – There is a change of atmosphere when you arrive in Sidári, which has not escaped the ravages of the hotel industry. It's a pity, because the bay, with its numerous coves, is truly beautiful. The sea has patiently sculpted narrow channels, including the famous **channel of love** (*from the village, follow the signs "To great beach"*): legend has it that anyone swimming across the bay will meet their true love.

Ágios Ioánnis, the large beach east of Sidári, has little to recommend it, and all the hotels there are booked up year after year by British agencies. Instead, opt for **Perouládes beach***, which is less crowded (*3km; in Sidári take the road that follows the beach, on the left, then take the two following turnings. In the village, follow signs for "Sunset Beach" then "Restaurant Panorama"*). When the sea is rough, the wild magnificence of the grey and ochre **cliffs** that overlook the narrow strip of sand (*accessed by steps*) is spectacular. Take in the fine **view*** out to the Diapondia Islands. **Othoní**, the largest of them, is supposed to be the island where Calypso kept Odysseus in her clutches for eight years.

Go back to Sidári, and take the road left of the BP fuel station, following signs for Karoussádes (3km).

■ **Karoussádes*** is one of the prettiest villages in the north of the island: whitewashed houses, narrow streets, nothing has changed there for ages. From here you can reach **Róda** (*4km*), where archaeologists have excavated a temple dating from the 5C BC, certain fragments of which are on display at the Archaeological Museum in Corfu Town. Rather than go to its very busy beach, opt for **Aharávi beach**, the place where young Corfiotes meet (*1.5km to the east*). A multitude of tavernas line the long strip of sand and pebbles, but it can be difficult to find a place to stay.

Continue along the same road for 4km, to Ágios Spirídonas, where you turn left following the sign to "Taverna Lagoon".

■ **The beach of Ágios Spirídonas*** is still unspoilt. There are fine **views*** across to the nearby Albanian coast and the sea is glorious, the reflections constantly changing colour, from light green to lagoon blue. The ochre-coloured chapel on the beach is complemented by a pointed rock sprouting out of the waves. Even if you don't wish to swim, you could always linger over a fresh fish kebab on the terrace of the only taverna, and dangle your feet in the water.

Head back to the main road, then turn left in the direction of Kassiópi (well signposted). There are splendid **views**** out to sea from the coast road.

■ Dominated by the scanty remains of an Angevin **fortress**, the harbour at **Kassiópi**, which is now geared to mass tourism (diving, boat trips), probably does not merit a stopover. However, do have a look at the **Church of Panagía Kassiopítissa** (1590), where there is a fine icon of the Virgin by Poulakis. Caiques set sail from the harbour to the nearby islands of Othoní, Erikoússa and Mathráki.

Continue along the main road, in the direction of Kouloúra (well signposted).

■ Cut by valleys, and carpeted by pines and cypresses, the road crosses a promontory which undoubtedly has the finest sea **views**** on the island. Soon the white houses of the port of **Kouloúra*** appear, nestling in a rocky bay. An enchanting setting, where the tinkling of the rigging of the fishing boats mingles with the sound of the bells from the old church. The same peaceful calm must once have pervaded the nearby port of **Kalámi**, where the English writer **Lawrence Durrell** wrote *Prospero's Cell*, but now the place has become very popular.

■ The road runs along beside numerous bays, passing picturesque ports and villages: **Gimári** and its old houses, with their caves covered with vines, **Nissáki** (*take the left fork to the pretty beach of Agni Bay*), then **Barbáti*** and its white pebble beach, creating a strip of light between the dark green of the bare hills and the crystalline blue of the sea. Don't be put off by the rather uninspiring road and abandoned buildings: the beach at the end of it is lovely.

2km beyond Barbáti, in the village of Pirgí, take the right fork in the direction of Spartílas. 3km further on, turn right, and follow – carefully – the signs to the Pandokrátor Monastery. Allow 90min for the round trip.

If you have time, make a small detour to visit Mt Pandokrátor. The winding road leading up to it has wonderful **views★★** over terraces of olive trees, drystone walls and the blue bay of Gouviá.

■ In the village of **Spartílas★** *(5km higher up)* the white houses stand out from the dark hillside, among fig trees and broom. In the narrow streets, you may come across old ladies wearing elegant white shawls or bent double under the weight of a heavy bundle of firewood.

■ Further on, at a bend in the dry high plateau, the village of **Strinílas★**, another haven of peace, comes into view. In the main square, there are several tavernas with tables set in the shade of an age-old elm, where flocks of birds chatter among the foliage.

■ **Pandokrátor Monastery★** – *6km from Strinílas. 7am-12.30pm / 2.30pm-8pm. Open from April 1 to October 31. Long skirts are provided at the gate for female visitors. Small snack-bar. The concrete road leads to the top but because of the very steep slope, we recommend that you park as soon as possible and continue on foot.* Perched on the summit of the highest point of the island (906m), the Pandokrátor Monastery has exceptional **views★★**. This is the main purpose of the ascent: the site itself would be superb had the national television company not installed its gigantic masts, which dwarf the monastery buildings and the church. Founded in 1347, the monastery was rebuilt in the 17C. Its **katholikón** houses an 18C **iconostasis**, some post-Byzantine icons and some superb **frescoes★** covering the vault above the nave. Do not miss the **silver icon★** with the painted face *(on the right)*, which is stunningly beautiful. The surrounding countryside is equally striking: there are moon-like desert plateaux on one side, the sea and the Albanian lakes on the other. And if you are in Corfu between 1 and 7 August, you will be able to see the annual votive festival.

Retrace your steps to the coast road, turn right, and return to Corfu Town.

The south of Corfu★

Head south out of Corfu Town, following the coast road that goes in the direction of the airport, and follow signs for Lefkími. Allow a whole day; try to arrive at Pélekas at sunset. Keep an eye on your petrol tank as it can be difficult to find fuel on Sundays.

Once out of the town, there are several good **viewpoints★** on the winding road following the coast. Much less busy than the north, the south of the island has some pleasant surprises in store for travellers willing to take their time. Be careful however: apart from the road to Kávos via Moraítika, the others are all very winding and often turn into stony tracks.

Take the Benítses road as far as the village of Gastoúri, leaving the coast road that goes through Pérama, which has many large tourist complexes.

■ **The Achilleion★** (Ahílio) – *13 km from Corfu. Blue bus (no 10) departs from near Platía San Rocco. 8.30am-3.30pm. Entrance fee. Allow about 1hr. Try to get there early, before the crowds of tourists arrive.* Let's admit it: the Achilleion is one of the sites that has been ruined by mass tourism. After an hour of trying to catch a glimpse of some rather pretentious paintings through the crowds, even the most romantic visitors, their minds full of nostalgic films in glorious technicolour, will be cursing Sissi. The Empress **Elizabeth of Austria** went to great lengths to decorate this luxurious neo-Classical villa built in the Pompeiian style between 1889 and 1891 by two Italian architects. She named the villa after her favourite classical hero, Achilles, who, she wrote, "represents the Greek soul, the beauty of the earth". After the trials of her tumultuous life, she often came here in search of peace and quiet, to study Greek and the poems of Homer.

Sissi, a tragic destiny

One of the most beautiful princesses of her time, Elizabeth of Austria (1837-98) suffered from the same debilitating neurosis as several members of her family (notably her cousin, Ludwig II of Bavaria). This exacerbated the trials she suffered during her life, from the death of her daughter, Sophie, to that of her sister, who was burned alive in a terrible fire at the charity bazaar in Paris...not to mention the suicide of her son Rudolf at Mayerling in 1889. Separated from her husband, the Emperor Franz Joseph, she carried her unhappiness with her across Europe, spending most of her time at the castle of Gödöllö, near Budapest, and at the Achilleion in Corfu. A spirit enamoured of beauty and freedom, in Corfu she tried desperately to ease her troubled mind, far away from the intrigues of the Habsburg court. She was assassinated in Geneva in 1898 by an Italian anarchist.

Only the rooms on the ground floor are open to the public. They lead off either side of a monumental **entrance hall**, its ceiling covered in frescoes by the Italian painter Galopi, *The Four Seasons and the Hours*. You can also admire the famous **portrait of Sissi** by Winterhalter. To the left of the staircase, inspired by the one at the Paris Opera, the blue walls of the empress' **dining room** are dotted with stucco cherubs. The right-hand side of the villa incorporates the **chapel** and two rooms full of **souvenirs** of Elizabeth (photographs, letters, bibles) and of Kaiser Wilhelm II of Germany who took over the Achilleion in 1907. A French military hospital during the First World War, and the headquarters of Italian and then German forces during the Second World War, the Achilleion was then abandoned until 1962, when it became the municipal casino of Corfu until 1992. James Bond fans will remember the scenes from *For Your Eyes Only* which were filmed here. Go for a walk in the **gardens**, dotted with numerous statues. There is a superb **view★★** over the countryside and the lagoon. From the patio terrace, where Greek-style statues abound, you can see a huge, rather ostentatious fresco by Franz Matsch through a bay window.

Go back to the coast road heading for Benítses.

■ Two kilometres beyond **Kaiser's Bridge**, a ruined bridge which mysteriously disappears into the sea, lies the fishing town of **Benítses** with its gaily painted fishing boats and lemon trees. Having been invaded by the hotel industry, this village has lost much of its charm, rather like **Moraítika** *(7km to the south)*, where the beaches are swarming with people in summer. Wait till you reach the west coast for a swim.

1km beyond Moraítika, the main road turns right and crosses the village of Vranganiótika. 3km further on, there is a sign for Hlomós.

■ Thirty kilometres away from the chaos of the capital, the old village of **Hlomós** has retained all its former charm. Olive trees provide shade on either side of the road leading to it. Clinging to the hillside, its **houses** look out over a somewhat barren landscape, crisscrossed with drystone walls and arid plots of land.

After this detour, return to the main road and turn left in the direction of Argirádes.

■ If you fancy a break before continuing south, make a detour to the sandy beach of **Ágios Geórgios** *(after 1km, fork right)*, which is very popular, but long enough to dilute the crowds of swimmers: it stretches as far as **Lake Korissía**, further north. The sand has solidified into compact **dunes**, which look like rocks.

■ Continue in the direction of **Argirádes**, a village where time has stood still. Here smiling grandmothers in black headscarves pass the time by watching the tourists trying to negotiate the narrow streets, which are not really suitable for vehicles. Note the **traditional houses**, with architectural features from the Venetian period.

Stay on the main road which passes through the villages of Marathiás and Perivóli. 500m after Perivóli, the road curves left (do not take the right-hand fork to Vitaládes, unless you fancy a spot of peaceful sunbathing on its beach ringed with cliffs).

■ With 5 000 habitants, **Lefkími** (5km) is the largest town in the south of the island. Surrounded by vineyards and olive trees, it is built on the banks of a river and is dotted with tavernas. Every evening fishing boats make their way up the river.

■ Make a detour to visit the **salt marshes of Alikés** (sign on the left for "Alikés-Mólos"): the road ends at ruined buildings and the small rusty trucks that were once used for mining. On the ground, the short salt-burnt grass forms a whitish carpet that crunches underfoot. The actual marshes begin beyond the white chapel, and stretch as far as Cape Lefkími. Here you have to swim a long way before you get out of your depth.

Head north again without wasting any time at Kávos: head back towards Corfu Town, passing through Argirádes again. 9km further on, you pass through the village of Vranganiótika: turn left at the BP station towards Pélekas and Ágios Matthéos.

■ Beyond **Ágios Matthéos**, a pretty town built in the shape of an amphitheatre (tavernas), a road on the left leads down towards **Paramóna beach**, popular with local people. Continue along the main road through the delightful scenery of olive trees where battalions of cypresses keep watch.

3km beyond the village of Vouniatádes, turn left (sign for "Káto Garoúna") then, 500m further on, turn right (sign for "Ágios Górdis").

■ Surrounded by jagged rocks, the sandy **Ágios Górdis beach*** stretches for 5km. Although popular it is still pleasant. Like a tooth planted in the sea, **Ortholíthi** is reminiscent of a miniature Old Man of Hoy. Unfortunately, a rather lurid pink hotel has marred the harmony of the setting, a discordant note that jars with the pure blue of the waves, the green of the hills and the changing ochre hues of the cliffs.

Go past the abominable pink façade and continue straight on for 3km.

■ With its houses painted in pastel shades and its timeless *kafenío*, **Sinarádes**** is one of Corfu's most picturesque villages. Do not miss the enchanting **Folklore Museum*** (9.30am-2pm; closed Sundays; entrance fee; accessed by a little street on the left of the pink church, in the centre of the village; follow signs for "Folklore Museum"), situated in an old house which alone is worth a visit. You will see a reconstruction of the inside of a Corfiote house, traditional costumes and various objects associated with everyday life.

Turn left towards Pélekas, then, 50m further on, left again (sign for "Pélekas 5km"). After 3km, turn left at the "Yaliskari Palace Hotel" sign, then continue along the (good) track for 50m to the left of the hotel.

■ The track plunges down towards the long **beach of Pélekas****, an unspoilt bay circled by rocks and an ideal place for an afternoon swim.

Two kilometres further on is the village of **Pélekas***, famous for its magnificent sunsets. In front of the church, take the small road on the right and drive up to the top of the hill. From here there is a breathtaking **view***** in every direction, over the whole of the island. You get an idea of the width of the island when you see the two coastlines on either side. At the very top stands the **"Kaiser's Throne"**, a rock where Wilhelm II once watched the sunset.

Continue along the same road, then further on, turn left towards Glifáda. From here, you can reach Mirtidiótissa by driving north up a stony track on the left. Park in the small car park and continue on foot (10min).

■ Although **Glifáda** is one of the most popular beaches with Greek holidaymakers (green bus service from Corfu), **Mirtidiótissa beach*** is better. It might be more difficult to reach but is much more unspoilt: set in a superb creek and overlooked by

Corfu

verdant hills, this little beach of fine sand is one of the prettiest you could hope to find on the island. After all, we can assume that the artists who come here and set up their easels to paint the white **chapel**, the opal-green waves and the beach dotted with rocks know a good thing when they see it. The **Monastery of Panagía Mirtidiótissa**, set back in the hills behind, was named after an icon of the Virgin which was found among the myrtle bushes.

Turn left again onto the tarred road, then, 100m further on, turn right (sign for "Corfu"). At the next crossroads, turn left and continue to Érmones.

■ According to legend, this is the place where Odysseus, having been rejected by the waves, met Nausicaa, although **Érmones beach** is not very attractive with its rough sand and pebbles. Except for scuba divers and windsurfers, who will find this is the **perfect place** to practise their sports *(see the "Other things to do" section below)*.

— Making the most of Corfu —

COMING AND GOING

See also page 300 "Making the most of the northern coast of the Peloponnese".

By boat – Daily hydrofoil services to Paxós; departures at 3pm from the new harbour. 3 ferries a day run between Corfu and Igoumenítsa (coaches then connect to Athens, a 9hr bus ride), and a daily ferry runs between Patras and Corfu. Several ferries make the crossing from Italy: from Venice (4 times a week), Ancona and Brindisi (daily), and from Bari (3 times a week).

By air – Several flights daily between Athens and Corfu (50min), as well as direct charter flights from the main European airports. The airport is 3km outside the town, ☎ (0661) 30 180. Taxis and buses provide a service into the city centre. If you take a taxi, the fare into the town centre should be approximately €6.

GETTING AROUND

By bus – There are two kinds of bus: green and blue. The green buses leave from Odós Avramíou near the New Fort, ☎ (0661) 39 985. The blue buses leave from Platía San Rocco, ☎ (0661) 31 595. Ask at the tourist office for the timetables. Connections several times a day to: Paleokastrítsa, Róda, Aharávi, Ágios Stéfanos, Sidári, Kávos, and Glifáda.
The blue buses provide daily services to Kanóni, the Achilleion, Benítses, Ágios Ioánnis and Pélekas.

By taxi – The main taxi ranks are at the old harbour and on the Esplanade. A taxi for an hour costs about €21, a car with a driver €30 for a day (plus fuel). *Radio-taxis*, ☎ (0661) 33 811.

By horse-drawn carriage – Below the Old Fort. The route is fixed, but fares are negotiable: estimate €21 – €24.

By rental vehicle – The main rental companies have offices at the airport and an agency opposite the new port. The list of hire companies is available at the tourist office. A driving licence is required, even to hire a motorcycle. To hire a car for a day costs about €38, with unlimited mileage. *Budget*, at the airport, ☎ (0661) 28 208; *EuroHire*, at the new port, ☎ (0661) 22 062; *Suncars*, Leofóros Alexándras 40, ☎ (0661) 31 565.

ADDRESS BOOK

Tourist information – EOT, Odós Rizopastón Vouleftón, the road leading uphill opposite the post office, ☎ (0661) 37 520. Go up to the first floor. 8.30am-2.30pm; closed at weekends. There is also a branch of the tourist office at the ferry terminal (new port). The **tourist police**, in Odós Samartzí, near Platía San Rocco, ☎ (0661) 30 265, will also be able to help you. Daily 8.30am-8pm.

Banks – There are plenty of banks in the town, especially in the avenue leading to the main post office. Watch the time as they all close at 2pm. To receive money by express (Western Union): **Ergo Bank**, Odós Alexándras 31. 8am-2pm; closed Sunday and Monday.

Currency exchange – Acropol, Odós N Theotóki 37. There is another one on the Esplanade, just in front of the Arcadion hotel. Most of the banks also change money.

Post office / Telephone – Odós Alexándras 26, ☎ (0661) 39 604. Stamps and phone cards. Possible to change postal cheques and travellers' cheques (American Express). 7.30am-8pm, 7.30am-2pm on Saturday; closed Sunday. There are plenty of card phones in town. Phone cards can be purchased at newsagents and at the post office.

Internet – Cafe Net On Line, Odós Kapodistríou 28, next to the Esplanade; cafe_online1@yahoo.com Reasonable rates. Daily, 10am (6pm on Sunday)-2am.

Foreign newspapers – There are several newsagents on the Esplanade, in Odós Kapodistríou, and at Odós Alexándras 34 (near the post office).

Airlines – Olympic Airways, Odós Polilá, ☎ (0661) 38 694. Opening hours: 8am-3.45pm, 7am-2pm on Saturday. Airport office, ☎ (0661) 30 180, from 7am to 8pm.

Medical service – Hospital, Odós Ioulías Andreádi, near Platía San Rocco. ☎ (0661) 45 811.

WHERE TO STAY

• **Corfu Town**

Most of the hotels are near the Esplanade and around the harbours. For a long stay, head for the quieter seaside resorts.

€30

Hotel Ionion, Xen Stratigoú 46, ☎ (0661) 39 915 – 140rm. ⌖ ℘ CC Opposite the ferry terminal, an old-fashioned hotel with 1950s-type linoleum and wood decor. Simple rooms with clean bathrooms. One of the cheapest in town. Warm welcome.

Between €40 and €50

Hotel Archontico, M Athanassíou 61, Garítsa, ☎ (0661) 37 222, Fax (0661) 38 294 – 20rm. ⌖ ℘ TV This has the rather unusual charm of family-run hotels of yesteryear, in Garítsa Bay, a

10min walk from the town centre. Family welcome. Mini-bar.

Hotel Arcadion, Odós Kapodistríou 44, ☎ (0661) 37 670, Fax (0661) 45 087, arcadion@otenet.gr – 55rm. ⌖ ℘ ✗ CC Ideally situated, opposite the Esplanade and two minutes away from the old town, but quite noisy in the evening. Rooms painted sky blue, most have balconies, TV room, lift.

Around €70

Hotel Atlantis, Odós Xen Stratigoú 48, ☎ (0661) 35 560, Fax (0661) 46 480, atlanker@mail.otenet.gr – 55rm. ⌖ ▤ ℘ TV ✗ A fairly modern hotel, comfortable. Lacks character but right in front of the new port. Most rooms have a balcony overlooking the harbour.

Hotel Astron, Odós Donzelót 15, ☎ (0661) 39 505 / 39 986. ⌖ ℘ A hall decorated in pompous 19C style, with mythological paintings. The hotel has very "British-colonial" charm. The rooms, with balcony, overlook the harbour and the New Fort. Quite expensive for what it is.

⌂ **Hotel Bella Venezia**, Odós N Zambélli 4, ☎ (0661) 46 500, Fax (0661) 20 708, belvenht@hol.gr – 32rm. ⌖ ▤ ℘ TV CC A charming hotel with refined Italianate decoration in a beautiful 19C residence with a pleasant green terrace.

Over €90

Hotel Cavalieri, Odós Kapodistríou 4, ☎ (0661) 39 041, Fax (0661) 39 283 – 50rm. ⌖ ▤ ℘ TV CC The most luxurious establishment in the heart of the old town (category A), housed in an unusual 17C hotel with beautiful Anglo-Venetian decor (chintz, Venetian mirrors, etc). Splendid view over the sea and panoramic bar.

• **Pélekas** (A2)

€70

⌂ **Levant Hotel**, ☎ (0661) 94 230, Fax (0661) 94 115 – 25rm. ⌖ ▤ ℘ TV ✗ CC A charming hotel set in a beautifully finished neo-Classical villa. Warm welcome, good restaurant, romantic, cool rooms, with a magnificent view. The beaches of Glifáda and Mirtidiótissa are 3km away, there is horse-riding and a golf course 4 km away... In other words, a wonderful place to stay! Rooms with 4 beds for families.

Making the most of Corfu

- **Lákones** (A1)

€55

🏨 **Hotel Golden Fox**, ☎ (0663) 41 381 – 10 apartments. 📶 🅿 ✕ 🏊 **cc** This white-painted hotel dominating Paleokastrítsa has comfortable apartments, each with their own kitchenette and balcony (superb view). You are advised to book. Two restaurants, including the only vegetarian restaurant on the island.

- **Barbáti** (B1)

€50

Nautilus Hotel, ☎ (0661) 93 620, Fax (0661) 93 870 – 64rm. 📶 🅿 🏊 In the upper part of Barbáti, a very simple family hotel in a white-painted building complete with beams, with quiet rooms which mostly face the sea. The beach is 5min walk away.

- **Dafníla** (B1)

€65

🏨 **Hotel Neféli**, ☎ (0661) 91 033, Fax (0661) 90 290 – 45rm. 📶 🅿 ✕ 🏊 8km outside Corfu, a charming hotel set deep among olive trees. Spacious rooms with balcony overlooking the sea or the hills. The beach is 400m away. Good value for money.

- **Érmones** (A1)

€50

Érmones Golf Hotel, ☎ (0661) 94 236, Fax (0661) 94 605 – 41rm. 📶 🅿 📺 ✕ 🏊 ⚓ Two buildings, attractively decorated, frame a very pleasant swimming pool. Large rooms with balconies and sea views, just above Érmones beach.

- **Glifáda** (A2)

€90 (for 3 to 4 people)

Menigos Resort, ☎ (0661) 94 933 – 60 apartments. 📶 🅿 🏊 ⚓ Large bungalows built on terraces above the beach, some with a small garden. They are all different, furnished and well-equipped (kitchenette), and have a balcony with a sea view. Two types: category A for 3 to 4 people (35m²), and category B for 5 to 6 (from 60m² to 80m²). Small swimming pool, supermarket, snack bar, and tennis courts available at the large hotel nearby.

- **Aharávi** (A1)

€100

Beis Beach Hotel, ☎ (0661) 63 913, Fax (0661) 63 991 – 135rm. 📶 🅿 ✕ 🏊

⚓ 💧 **cc** A huge modern complex beside the beach, mainly frequented by Germans. Large square white rooms with a balcony. You will find all the facilities normally found in a hotel of this type: a shop, water sports, excursions, and evening entertainment. Half-board compulsory. It also has about 40 apartments to rent.

- **Paramóna** (A2)

€55

Paramonas Hotel, ☎ (0661) 76 595, Fax (0661) 75 686 – 22rm. 📶 🅿 ✕ Above the beach, a simple, clean hotel with cool white-painted rooms with marble floors. Large terraces overlooking the sea. The hotel restaurant is located in the **Sun Set hotel**, slightly lower down (the rooms, which have somewhat spartan comforts, are very cheap here: around €19 for a double). Closed from 30 October until 1 May.

- **Mirtidiótissa** (A2)

€25

Myrtiotissa Hotel, there is no telephone here yet! – 12rm. 📶 ✕ Comforts are basic but the beach is so beautiful... Family welcome and the rooms are clean. Vehicle access difficult. Closed from 30 October until 1 May.

- **Ágios Geórgios** (A1)

Campsite (around €10)

Ágios Geórgios campsite, 1km on the right beyond the beach, ☎ (0663) 51 194, Fax (0663) 51 759 – 300 pitches. ✕ A modest campsite (one of the few on the west coast), set deep among the olive trees, 600m from the beach. Bar, taverna, washing machine, small supermarket. Wooden bungalows with WC.

EATING OUT

- **Corfu Town**

There is no shortage of tavernas or "gíros", the most touristy ones being on Odós Kapodistríou, behind the Liston and on Town Hall Square. You will find venues that are more popular with the locals in the old port district. The following places have been chosen for their authenticity or charming setting.

Around €10

Taverna Nínos, Odós Sebastianoú 46 (corner of Odós M Theotóki), ☎ (0661)

46 175. Closed Sunday at lunchtime. ☎ Terrace in a small street parallel to Odós Kapodistríou. A restaurant famed since 1920 for its simple, fresh food and generous portions. The place is frequented by local people and comes alive in the evening to the strains of a singer who is a local star.

🍽 **Taverna Papyris**, Odós AG Theodóras 25, ☎ (0661) 30 228. Closed Saturday. ☎ A pleasant taverna in a square behind the Byzantine Museum. They serve real, freshly cooked, tasty Corfiote cuisine. The menu is in Greek, so you will have to rely on the owner's suggestions or go and inspect the various options in the kitchen!

Around €20

La Cucina, Odós Guildford 15, ☎ (0661) 45 029. ☎ Only open in the evening. Very good, freshly prepared, delightfully presented Italian cooking. You are advised to book: the terrace, which is pleasant in the evening, is quite small. The room inside has AC.

Restaurant Faliráki, corner of Odós Kapodistríou and Odós Arseníou, ☎ (0661) 30 392. ☎ ⅭⅭ Below the quay that runs from the royal palace to the old harbour, this municipal restaurant has a splendid view of the Old Fort from its terrace. Greek specialities, tasty fish dishes, spaghetti with crayfish, and delicious desserts (try the "kataífi" with walnuts, coated with chocolate).

🍽 **The Venetian Well**, Platía Kremastí, ☎ (0661) 44 761. Closed Sunday. ☎ The most beautiful open-air place to eat in Corfu, on a small square full of flowers, surrounded by Venetian houses. The cuisine is as refined as the setting, a happy combination of Italian and Greek gastronomy. Delicious swordfish kebabs with walnut caviar (book).

• **Lákones** (A1)

€10

Taverna O Boúlis, ☎ (0663) 41 929. Daily from April to October. ☎ A very simple taverna, far away from the greasy chip shops of Paleokastrítsa. Freshly prepared dishes with generous helpings, served inside or outside on the terrace: tzatzíki, keftédes (rissoles), saganáki (cheese covered in breadcrumbs, fried), delicious chicken and perfectly barbecued meats.

• **Ágios Spirídonas** (B2)

€10

Taverna Lagoon, ☎ (0663) 98 333. ☎ A large terrace by the beach, where you can get excellent fresh-fish kebabs and a selection of grilled fish. Courteous welcome and a magnificent view across to the nearby Albanian coast.

• **Kouloúra** (B1)

€13

Taverna Kouloúra, ☎ (0663) 91 253. ☎ Closed from the end of October until the beginning of April. Lovely terrace overlooking the peaceful harbour. Delicious fish specialities. Warm welcome.

HAVING A DRINK

Bars – You can watch the "passeggiata", the evening walk of the Corfiotes, from the huge bars located near the royal palace (the **Magnet** and the **Cofineta**), which stay open until about 2am.

Hotel Cavalieri, Odós Kapodistríou 4, south of the Esplanade on the way to Garítsa Bay. The panoramic 6th floor terrace has a splendid view over the Old Fort and the sea, especially at dusk. Open from 6pm. Dress code (no shorts).

Cafe Net On Line, see the "Internet" section above.

Night-clubs – All the most fashionable techno-music clubs are located to the north of the town, in the suburb of Mandoúki, beyond the new port. Some are worth a glance for their highly coloured papier-maché decor, especially the extravagant **Apocalypsi**.

OTHER THINGS TO DO

Concerts – Every year, from July to October, the town council organises a series of concerts (classical or traditional music) in the historic centre of Corfu (in Town Hall Square, at Ágios Spirídonas and at the New Fort), at 8pm on Tuesday evenings. Information available from the tourist office

There is also a **Guitar Festival** in the summer, with concerts at the New and Old Forts. ☎ (0661) 46 363.

Scuba diving – **Odissey Divers** ("Scuba Diving" sign), on the coast at Érmones, ☎ and Fax (0661) 94 053. Around €33 per person.

PAXÓS ★★

Ionian Islands – District of Corfu – Regional map page 348
Michelin map 980 fold 14 – 25km² (Antípaxos 3km²)
Pop 2 300 – Allow 2 days

Not to be missed
A boat trip around the island, including the cave of Ipapándi.
The harbour at Logós.
The sandy beaches of Antípaxos (on Paxós, there are just pebbles).
And remember...
Take your swimsuit if you go on a boat trip around the island.
Beware, the boats tend to leave earlier than the advertised time.
Avoid drinking the tap water, it's rather salty.

Although the etymological origin of Paxós is open to debate, the most attractive version is that it derives from the Latin *pax*: peace. In fact, no other term could better describe the serene atmosphere that pervades the island, which is further enhanced by the warm hospitality of its inhabitants. Still rather off the beaten track, Paxós has opted for a rather elitist form of tourism, refusing to have an airport, or any hotel complexes and night-clubs. It lends itself to visitors who want to relax; they will relish the peace and quiet of its three harbours and the tranquillity of its white-pebble beaches (particularly in the east). Even the landscape has a softness about it – Mt Ágios Isávros being no more than 250m high – except in the west, where the rocky coastline has been sculpted into cliffs, concealing caves which will delight diving enthusiasts. There is also the same beautiful white limestone that is one of the charming features of the old houses in the villages, the ruined windmills and the dry-stone walls which you see all over the island. And in this land, the olive tree reigns supreme. First planted by the Venetians, today it is often cultivated using organic farming methods and provides a decent income for the Paxiots.

Island of exile
Originally settled by Epirotes and by the Phoenicians, Paxós later came under Angevin domination like neighbouring Corfu, before closely following the destiny of the other Ionian Islands, until union with Greece in 1864. On several occasions, it served as a land of exile: in 1819, it gave shelter to the inhabitants of Párga who were fleeing the Turks, bringing with them their icons and traditions. Greek nationalists found exile here during the 1821 uprising, as did the elected nationalists of the Ionian parliament, and in 1922 refugees from Asia Minor arrived after the collapse of the Greek forces.

From Gáïos to Láka
9km tour. As the distances are very short, you could also opt for one of the many footpaths which crisscross the hills.

Gáïos★ – It has to be said that in summer, the capital of the island (with a population of 5 000) is no longer Greek but Italian: all the shopkeepers and restaurant owners will talk to you in Italian. With the yachts in the background and its carefree atmosphere, Gáïos is also reminiscent of St Tropez. Look out for the beautiful **Venetian houses**, which survived the 1953 earthquake; the most elegant being the old **Governor's house★** (18C), north of the harbour, which can be recognised by its roof crowned with three small arches. The scene that awaits you on arrival in the harbour on the boat from Corfu is enchanting: dotted with sailing boats, the sea is a translucent greenish-blue, edged by the rocky coastline, while the town itself, protected by two tiny islands, is hidden from view until the very last moment. On one side is **Ágios**

The Ionian Islands

Nikólaos, a nature reserve planted with pines, with the ruins of a 15C **fortress**. *(Visits can be arranged by the town hall, ☎ (0662) 32 100)*; on the other side is a low-lying island crowned with a small monastery, **Moní Panagía**, built on a rock and with a blue dome and white walls *(reached by boat; only open on August 15, for the festival of the Assumption; otherwise, ask for the key at the museum in Chryssantos)*.

In the harbour, do not miss the delightful bric-a-brac **museum** housed in the old school of Gáios *(7.30am-1.30pm / 7pm-12midnight; closed in winter)*. Founded in 1996 by a group of enterprising youngsters, it includes a host of objects – ranging from worked flints dating from the Palaeolithic Period to wireless sets from grandpa's time, pottery and costumes, to photos – which evoke a delightful picture of life on the island. There are reconstructions of a traditional kitchen and bedroom, and the guide will be only too pleased to tell you the story of each of the treasures in the museum.

At the southern end of the harbour stands the **statue** – painted a peculiar green colour – of the Paxiot sailor **Giórgios Anemoïánis**, hero of the War of Independence of 1821, who was hanged by the Turks at the age of 23 after he was caught attempting to set fire to the Turkish vessels moored at Náfpaktos.

■ Before commencing your tour of the north of the island, make time for a short outing to the south of Gáios. Off the road that follows the coastline are several rocky bays where you can swim in peace *(beware of sea urchins)*. The road then comes to the small port of **Spútzo**. The more energetic might like to set off on foot in search of the ruins of two Christian basilicas: **Agía Marína** *(visible on the right just in front of the harbour)* and **Ágios Stéfanos**, the apse of which opens onto a field.

From Spútzo, there is a stony track overlooking the **little island of Mongónissi** which is fringed by a delightful **beach** *(it is possible to cross the narrow channel by boat)*.

Return to Gáios. In the town centre, take the only road heading north and inland for 1.5km, then turn right and keep straight on for 3km.

■ From the village of **Magaziá**, a road on the left leads to the **Church of Ágii Apóstoloi** *(1.5km)*, perched on the edge of the **white cliffs of Eremítis**. From up here, the **view★** is superb, especially at sunset.

After Magaziá, continue north for 2km until the sign for "Ipapándi" on the left. If you decide not to take this route, Láka is 2km further on.

■ The hamlet of **Grámatikéika** has the distinction of having the only church in the Ionian Islands with two domes: a pretty Baroque bell-tower with a red roof stands next to it. The **church of Ipapándi** was built in 1601 by a number of wealthy families who lived in the vicinity. Tradition has it that there is an underground tunnel linking the church to the cave of Ipapándi, on the west coast.

■ **Láka★** – Hidden deep in a little bay reached by a narrow channel, Láka is situated far away from the cosmopolitan chaos of Gáios. In the harbour, there are no yachts, only small trawling boats belonging to the local fishermen, moored in a line opposite the tavernas. If diving is not your thing, you can visit the tiny **aquarium** *(10am-2pm / 7pm-10.30pm; only open in July and August; entrance fee)* where an elderly gentleman will proudly show you the fish, shellfish and crustaceans which inhabit the local coasts: they include groupers, scorpion fish and octopus.

Return to the Gáios road. After 2km, turn left, then immediately right (sign).

Refuge for divine lovers

Having taken refuge in a cave in order to escape marriage to Poseidon, the beautiful Amphitrite was then removed by a dolphin who left her on the island of Corfu. Poseidon then set about detaching the southern tip of the island with his trident, thereby forming Paxós. Found by the inhabitants of the island, the trident became the symbol of Paxós (but don't look for it in the local museums).

Paxós

- Overlooked by a white limestone hillock, the tiny harbour of **Logós**★★ *(3km)* attracts large numbers of pleasure seekers. Virtually deserted during the day, the harbour and its few tavernas come alive in the evening with the arrival of the sailing boats, while silence pervades the nearby ruins of the **olive oil factory**, a testimonial to the prosperous times when the green gold from Paxós was exported as far afield as Russia. Five hundred metres on either side of Logós, you will also find some lovely **beaches**: **Glifáda** to the north, and especially **Levrehió**★, to the south.

- To return to Gáios, leave Logós by the road leading out of the harbour and head south. The road passes a succession of pretty pebble beaches: **Kipiádi beach**★ *(left fork, then follow the footpath)* or the small **beaches of Kakí Lagáda** and **Kloní Vouli** which are easy to reach by taking the new road on the ridge (wonderful sea views).

Boat trip around the island★★

Three morning departures at 10am, 11am and 12noon. The trip lasts about 2hr, at which point the boat drops you off at Antípaxos for a swim; returns 5.30pm or 6.30pm; go down to the harbour and ask the boatmen for information. Estimate €9.

Initially the boat follows the low-lying, rocky east coast, which is dotted with beaches as far as Logós. After Orkos which is dominated by an elegant villa belonging to the owner of the Campari company, the coastline becomes more rugged, culminating in the long inlet forming the port of Láka. After passing the only lighthouse on the island, the boat then enters various magnificent creeks which are overlooked by tall **white cliffs**, a typical feature of the west coast. Eroded by the waves, some of the rocks have taken on peculiar animal-like shapes and are pitted with countless cavities. The most beautiful one is the **cave of Ipapándi**★★, a veritable limestone cathedral which is 70m long. Further south lie the white **cliffs of Erimítis**★, the sun's rays highlighting the powdery, streaked appearance of the rock formations. Next on the itinerary is the large **Bay of Ahái**★, where there is a cave hidden behind **three arches**★ carved out by the lapping of the waves. Finally, 200m to the south, the pointed rock of **Ortholithos** protrudes from the waves, marking the entrance to a vast cave where the boat turns round before continuing its journey.

Antípaxos★★

2km south of Paxós. Boat leaves from Gáios. See "Making the most of Paxós".

Do not leave without exploring this little island which is just as beautiful as neighbouring Paxós. Covered with vines and market gardens, Antípaxos is the garden of the Paxiots. You will also find some magnificent **sandy beaches** – which make a pleasant change from the pebbly beaches of Paxós – lapped by emerald-green water. If you fancy something to eat, there are two tavernas at **Vríka**, where most of the boats stop, before a last swim at **Voutoúmi** or **Agrapidiá**.

——— Making the most of Paxós ———

COMING AND GOING

By boat – From Corfu Town, a hydrofoil of the **Petrakis Line** runs a daily service to Gáios in 55min (tickets and departure times available at the new port). Another hydrofoil provides daily links between Igoumenítsa and Gáios in 40min. There is a daily ferry (passengers and vehicles) from Corfu to Paxós via Igoumenítsa (3hr crossing). A boat, the **Vicky**, runs a shuttle service between Gáios and Párga (80min crossing; buses then connect Párga to Préveza). There are also ferry and bus links between Gáios and Athens, 3 times a week. Since the schedules are very variable, consult a travel agency or the **harbour police**, ☎ (0662) 32 259.

GETTING AROUND

By bus – 6 or 7 connections a day between the 3 main villages: Gáïos (**bus station** at the top of the village, behind the main square), Láka and Logós. Timetable available from **Bouas Tours**, in Gáïos.

By taxi – ☎ (0662) 32 220.

By boat – Numerous boats provide a service to the beaches on Antípaxos (15min). Check the times for coming back.

By rental vehicle – Apply to the travel agencies in Gáïos and Láka. These agencies also hire motorboats and small sailing dinghies. You will find scooters and motorcycles at **Julia's Bike** in Logós, ☎ (0662) 31 330, and at **Moto Christos**, in Láka, ☎ (0662) 31 050.

ADDRESS BOOK

Tourist information – No tourist office on the island, but you can **Bouas Tours** in Gáïos, ☎ (0662) 32 401 (9am-1pm / 4pm-9pm), **Routsis Holidays** in Láka, ☎ (0662) 31 807 (8.30am-2.30pm / 5.30pm-10pm), and **Paxós Sun**, in Logós, ☎ (0662) 31 341.

Banks / Currency exchange – Visa cash dispenser at the **Commercial Bank of Greece**, on the main square in Gáïos. The travel agencies in Gáïos and Láka will change money.

Medical service – **Health centre** at Bogdanátika (2km west of Gáïos), ☎ (0662) 31 466.

WHERE TO STAY

Paxós has a grand total of two (luxury) hotels, both just outside Gáïos. On the other hand, you will find plenty of rooms to let in Gáïos, Logós and Láka, but they are in great demand in summer (estimate €23 for 2 people). For apartments, apply to the travel agencies. Note that everywhere in Paxós closes out of season (from October to April).

• Gáïos

Over €75 (half-board for 2)
Hotel Paxós Beach, ☎ (0662) 32 211 – 42rm. ⚓️📧 ✍ ✗ 🍴 🏊 1km outside Gáïos, a very peaceful place to stay. Stone bungalows set among pines and olive trees on land leading to a private beach. Bright rooms, painted in white and blue, with rattan furniture. Spotless bathrooms. Open from May to October. Warm welcome.

Over €75 (without half-board)
Hotel Paxós Club, ☎ (0662) 32 450, Fax (0662) 32 097 – 23 apartments. ⚓️ 📧 ✍ 📺 ✗ 🛏 💳 Jacuzzi, bar, money-changing facilities. In the hills 1km outside Gáïos, this fine modern hotel is based on the style of traditional local houses. Beautiful rooms and apartments, from studios to 4-rooms, all light and airy, with balcony, kitchenette and mini-bar. Breakfast included. Courtesy shuttle service to Gáïos and the beaches.

EATING OUT

There are numerous tavernas in Gáïos, Láka and Logós.

• Gáïos

Around €13
Taverna Annéta, 🍴 One of the best places to eat in the harbour, offering simple, freshly prepared dishes. Very warm welcome.

Restaurant Volcano, 🍴 On the main square in Gáïos, this family-run restaurant serves good, traditional cooking based on fresh fish and prawns.

• Logós

€12
🍷**Taverna Basílis**, 🍴 💳 In a pretty yellow house with stone floors, just in front of the old olive oil factory. Terrace by the water, where they serve fresh fish, lobster and mussels (a must), with excellent salads or tasty aubergine caviar.

HAVING A DRINK

Bar – **Roxi Bar**, in Logós, at the end of the jetty (10am-2am). Lively evenings.

OTHER THINGS TO DO

Pony-trekking – Horse-riding and pony-trekking in Láka (€18 an hour). Call Sandra at the "Harbour Lights Bar", ☎ (0662) 31 412 or on her mobile ☎ 09 322 7092.

Scuba diving – **Paxós Óasi Club** is open to experts and beginners alike, while **Dive & Fun**, in Láka, ☎ (0662) 30 004, only welcomes qualified divers. Full equipment provided in both cases.

Concerts – In September, the **Classical Music Festival** (started in 1985) attracts young musicians and artistes of international renown to Paxós (information from The Paxós Cultural Association at the harbour in Gáïos).

LEUCAS★
(LEFKÁDA)

Ionian Islands – Capital of the district of Lefkáda
Regional map page 348 – Michelin map 980 fold 14
305km² – Pop 24 000 – Allow 3 days

Not to be missed
The beach at Pórto Katsíki.
The village of Ágios Nikítas.
A boat trip around the islands in the Bay of Nidrí.

And remember...
Take your time and drive carefully:
the mountain roads are tiring and some of the routes cover long distances.
Watch the fuel gauge: there are only two filling stations,
both in the south of the island (in Nidrí and Vassilikí)

Leucas, "the white island", owes its name to the high white cliffs on the west coast. Here and there they make way for the magnificent sandy beaches for which the island is renowned. But basically Leucas is a mountainous land (mountains comprise 70 % of the terrain), with some high peaks (Mt Stavrotás is 1 158m high). Here wild torrents race down the gorges in the spring. It is a wild, impoverished island, where valleys and fertile plains are a rare phenomenon. The towns of Nidrí, Vassilikí and Lefkáda, the capital, have taken them over, and everywhere crops are cultivated on narrow terraces on the hillsides, supported by drystone walls. The lentils of yesteryear, which for a long time brought fame to the village of Englouví, have given way to the vine and the olive tree, while the inhabitants of the coast earn a living from fishing. But the new face of fortune is tourism, which has grown rapidly in the last twenty years – and not without spoiling some of the coastline. Fortunately, the minute you dive inland to the hills, there is any number of old villages to explore, the houses built like tiny fortresses to protect the population from the incursions of the pirates who once haunted its coasts. Time spent exploring these villages along with an excursion to a couple of beaches and maybe a boat trip will be the highlights of your stay here.

The captive sentinel
Separated from the mainland by a narrow channel, dug, according to Strabo, by the Corinthians in 650 BC, Leucas' strategic position has long been a cause for concern to its neighbours: enemies and then allies of the **Acarnanians** (the small kingdom situated on the promontory opposite Leucas), the island's inhabitants came successively under Roman, Frankish, Turkish (1479-1684), and then Venetian (1684-1797) dominion. Leucas changed hands five times between 1797 and 1810! The greed of its conquerors and constant harassment from pirates along the coast, along with the island's meagre natural resources suggest that Leucas was destined to suffer a difficult fate. It was also hit several times by devastating earthquakes, the most violent of which struck in 1769 and 1948.

Leucas... or Ithaca?
A disciple of the archaeologist Schliemann – who established that at least a part of the "Odyssey" was based on historical fact – Wilhelm Dörpfeld had a theory that Leucas was Odysseus' homeland. Relying on Homer's – albeit highly imprecise – description, he was to spend his whole life trying to solve the mystery. These days, although excavations have revealed significant evidence pointing to the existence of a Mycenaean principality (notably near Nidrí), it is the modern island of Ithaca that is regarded by experts as the site of Laertes' ancient kingdom.

But there was some respite: after the British Protectorate and union with Greece in 1864, it went through a period of relative prosperity only to see this end in 1900, when its vineyards were decimated by a parasite. Then followed a massive exodus to the United States. It wasn't until the late 1970s that tourism gave Leucas a new lease of life, attracting villagers from the mountains down to the sea.

Lefkáda Town*
Allow 1 day

Hugged by the sea on one side and the lagoon on the other, Lefkáda has the old-fashioned charm of a provincial town. The time to explore it is at nightfall, when the façades of its coloured houses soften in the glow of the street-lamps, and the crowds – which disappear during the afternoon – suddenly return, bringing the streets and the harbour back to life. In the calm of the adjacent streets, where people chat quietly on the doorsteps of the houses, are a number of curious old shops: a dusty bazaar with myriad hidden treasures, people selling icons and candlesticks, tiny cafés, some of which look as if they haven't changed for years, and a shop selling coffins, its wares piled up to the ceiling!

There are three main areas of activity: to the east, along the harbour, where the yachts are moored and the traffic roars past; to the west, on the side of the lagoon, where the young people of the island congregate in the numerous cafés; and finally the pedestrian precinct dividing the town into two, where the hotels, tavernas and shops are concentrated.

The island of poets
In the second half of the 19C, Leucas was the setting for a blossoming of literature without precedent in Greece. Brought about by the nationalist movement and the search for a Greek identity, its key protagonists were the great poets Aristotélis Valaorítis (1824-79) and, in particular, Ángelos Sikelianós (1884-1951), who revived the festival of Delphi, adopting a modern, optimistic and light-hearted vision of ancient civilisation. This literary legacy is still very much alive on the island, something borne out by the number of amateur theatrical associations and especially the Festival of Art and Literature which, for 37 years, has brought together poets, playwrights and musicians (see "Making the most of Leucas").

One kilometre before the entrance to the town, built on a narrow island, the **Santa Maura Fort** (Agía Mávra) controls access to the mainland. Erected at the beginning of the 14C by Giovanni Orsini to protect the island from attacks by pirates, it was altered by the Venetians in the early 18C. At that time it incorporated the whole town which was contained within its walls until the following century. Destroyed in 1888 by the explosion of a powder magazine, the interior is of no particular interest.

Odós Dörpfeld, which starts opposite the causeway, emerges in **Platía Ágios Spirídonas**, in the very centre of the town. Local brass bands come regularly to play to the packed terraces of the bars. On the north side of the square, the **Church of Ágios Spirídonas** (17C) has an elegant, richly decorated Venetian façade. Inside, you will find a fine wooden **iconostasis** by **Groppas**, a sculptor from the island of Zacynthus.

On the north-west side of the square, an interesting **Ethnographical Museum*** (*10am-2pm / 6pm-10pm; no charge*) contains photographs, costumes, embroidery and objects from daily life. Some of the rooms in this old house have been reconstructed with interiors typical of Leucas.

Just beyond it, have a look at the small **Phonograph Museum** (*signposted from Odós Dörpfeld; open in the evening*), which pays homage to some of Leucas' more well-known musicians, through photographs, instruments and phonographs.

One hundred metres further on, to the left, Odós Zabélion leads to two churches, **Ágios Nikólaos**, and **Ágios Dimítrios** (1688), which were also inspired by the Italian Baroque style. The three 18C icons housed in the latter, depicting the Life of Christ, are supposed to be the oldest on the island.

Leucas

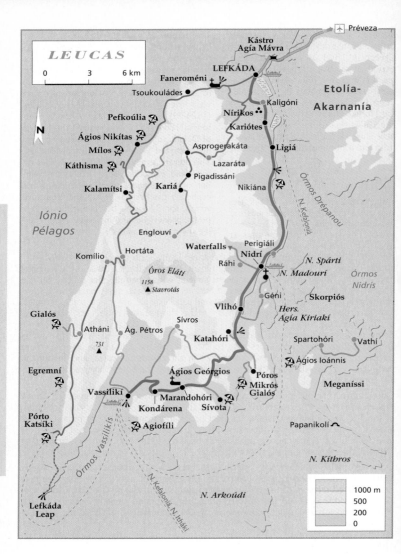

Return to the pedestrian precinct; it gradually widens, winding along between fruit and vegetable stalls, bookshops and cafés, to the **Church of Ágios Minás★** (1707) which contains an impressive gilt Baroque **iconostasis★**. Look out for the paintings by Konstantínos Kontarínis, a harmonious blend of the Greek Orthodox tradition and the Venetian influence.

Finally, do not miss the brand new **Cultural Centre**, where the **Archaeological Museum★** is located *(500m along the lagoon after the bridge, 8am-2.30pm / 9am-1.30pm Saturday and Sunday; no charge)*. Terracotta objects, statuettes, Archaic stone windmills, Hellenistic funerary steles, all sorts of artefacts, presented according to particular themes (the house, meals, the cult of the dead, etc) retrace the life of the island, from prehistoric times to Antiquity. There is also one room devoted to the discoveries made in the early 20C by the archaeologist **Wilhelm Dörpfeld**.

A short excursion inland*

26km tour. 1km from Lefkáda, take the right-hand fork, then the left fork 1km further on. Go through Lazaráta (after about 7km) then, at Asprogerakáta (1km), turn left again towards Kariá, situated 3km fur-

Anti-seismic architecture
Like a number of the churches in Leucas, Ágios Minás has a curious metal top to its bell-tower. This type of structure, which is lighter, more supple and less dangerous than stone in the event of an earthquake, began to appear after the quake of 1948. Similarly, the brightly painted houses of Leucas have stone bases with façades of wood or flat or corrugated sheet metal which give the town (and the rest of the island) a rather strange colonial atmosphere.

ther on. Before setting off to explore the island's coastline, why not make a short excursion inland to see the charming village of **Kariá***. Nestling in the mountains, it seems to have escaped the passing of time. High up on the barren plateaux, the **road**** leading to the village passes through some spectacular scenery. Around the main square of the village, the traditional houses, with their roofs of fluted tiles, have been built on a hillside covered with olive and cypress trees, overlooked by the old windmills, now in ruins. Kariá is the most important village of the hinterland and is famous for its embroidery and weaving, which you can admire in the small **museum** (*open daily in summer*) or buy in shops on the main street.

The west of Leucas: the unspoilt beaches*
Leave the town heading south-west, following signs for Ágios Nikítas.
Allow 1 day.

The most beautiful beaches on the island are located on the west coast. With access sometimes difficult and the sea being rougher than on the east coast (*be careful when swimming*) they have, until relatively recently, been spared the greed of entrepreneurs. Even though roads are now being built, the scenery is still unspoilt. But it won't last forever...

■ Three kilometres beyond the suburbs, the road winds uphill with fine views of Leucas. A right fork leads to the **Monastery of Faneroméni**, an important pilgrimage centre founded in the 17C. Rebuilt in the 19C after two fires, the buildings themselves are not very interesting, but you must stop to look at the **view****, which stretches all the way along the north coast.

■ Shortly after the sleepy village of **Tsoukouládes**, the road plunges downhill again towards the sea, and the pines are gradually replaced by olive trees. Below, you can see the huge **beach of Pefkoúlia**, lapped by a pale-blue sea (*reached by a small road on the right*).

■ **Ágios Nikítas**** – *12km from Lefkáda*. The atmosphere changes as you reach the coast. Despite the increasing influx of tourism, this old fishing village has remained largely unchanged and the centre of the village is a conservation area. On the hill overlooking the harbour, the **houses*** have pretty painted wooden balconies. Before heading for one of the tavernas on the harbour, enjoy a leisurely stroll along the paved street leading down to it. And if you fancy a swim, just beyond the rocky promontory facing the left-hand side of the harbour, there are two beautiful **sandy beaches: Mílos and Káthisma**.

A road winds uphill from the beach to the main road. After 2km, a right fork leads to Kalamítsi, further south, along a very wiggly road.

Leap of Love

Lefkáda Leap is associated with the "katapontismós" (jump into the sea), a sinister practice performed in around 1200 BC, which consisted in throwing victims off the cliff as a sacrifice. In classical times, innocent victims were replaced by criminals who were offered a kind of divine judgement, escaping with their lives if they survived. This place is also associated with the cult of Apollo. A (ruined) temple dedicated to the god once stood on the site of the present lighthouse. The god of purification, Apollo inspired a later adaptation of the "katapontismós": that of curing lovesickness. In her poems, the poetess Sappho gave rise to a legend according to which she herself jumped off the cliff to cure herself of her unhappy love for the handsome Phaon... and killed herself. Hence the name of the cliff, "Kávos tis Kirás": the Cape of the Lady.

■ **Kalamítsi** *(9km from Káthisma)* is tucked away on the slopes of Mt Ráhi, a refuge carefully chosen by the first inhabitants to make themselves invisible to the pirates roving along the coast. Famous for its fabrics, the little town slumbers below a few ruined **windmills**.

3km beyond Kalamítsi the road widens out. 1km beyond the village of Hortáta turn right off the main road towards Pórto Katsíki.

■ From the next village, **Atháni**, you are within striking distance of the lovely **beaches of Gialós and Egremní** which are usually quiet. Not very easy to get to *(quite a steep road leading to each, then a footpath; allow 10min on foot)*, but solitude has its price.

The **beach of Pórto Katsíki**★★, which is more accessible *(43km from Lefkáda)* is famous throughout the archipelago *(vehicle access as far as a rather unprepossessing car park, then, on the left, about 100 steps lead down to the beach)*. It's well worth the detour: the contrast between the stretch of fine sand and the steep cliffs towering above, bearing down on the translucent waves, makes for a stunning picture. Obviously, with the constant stream of tourists on boat trips from all over the island, *(Ágios Nikítas, Vassilikí and also Nidrí, on the east coast)*, you will not be alone.

From Pórto Katsíki, retrace your steps and, after 1.5km, turn right.

■ A rough track leads to the edge of a white rock face where there is a sheer drop of 70m down to the sea. Feared by sailors in Antiquity, this rocky promontory known as the **Lefkáda Leap**★ (Doukáto or Kávos tis Kirás) has a magnificent **view**★★ of the islands of Cephalonia and Ithaca. Especially at sunset, it is a moment to be savoured. The view of the cliff from the sea is also impressive – an option that will also save you the tiring drive *(take one of the boats leaving from Vassilikí)*.

On the east coast

Leave Lefkáda and head south-east, following the harbour in the direction of Nidrí.
Allow 1 day.

Greener than the west side of the island, the landscape in the east of Leucas is also softer, with long sandy beaches that are easily accessible from the road. The ideal place to develop an infrastructure for large-scale tourism...which has considerably spoilt this part of the coast.

■ Two kilometres from Lefkáda, on the outskirts of the village of **Kaligóni**, stand the modest ruins of **Nírikos**, the ancient capital of the island until the Byzantine Period: there are some sections of cyclopean walls and a few columns, while the remains of a small theatre lie scattered among the fields and the olive trees.

■ Further on, you come to **Kariótes** *(4km south of Lefkáda)* and the last **salt marshes** of Leucas. For a long time, these constituted one of the island's main sources of wealth. They used to stretch as far as Lefkáda, the southern part of which is built over ancient salt mines.

■ The road then passes through the little fishing port of **Ligiá**, with its brightly painted trawlers, after which it follows the coast. There are fine **views*** across to the mainland which is so close that the calm stretch of sea in between seems more like a lake.

■ **Nidrí** – After **Nikiána** *(9km)* and its long sandy beach *(numerous hotels below the road)*, the road passes through **Perigiáli**. It is then only a short distance to the extensive **Bay of Nidrí*** dotted with little green islands floating like water lilies on the deep blue sea. An ideal setting for windsurfers and scuba-diving enthusiasts. Unfortunately, there is nothing very exciting about the town: overrun with tourists from all over the world (in summer), it is nothing but a motley collection of travel agencies, tavernas and souvenir shops.

For this reason, more than anything else, Nidrí is the starting point for numerous **boat trips*** to the neighbouring islands *(information at the harbour)*. Most notably to **Skorpiós**, owned by the shipping tycoon **Aristotle Onássis**, with the white chapel where he married Jacqueline Kennedy in 1968. It is not possible to visit the island, but boats stop here for a brief swim.

Leucas

Green and blue: the huge Bay of Nidrí

B. Kaufmann/MICHELIN

Another private property, the **island of Madourí** is the site of the Italian-style villa of the poet Aristotélis Valaorítis (1824-79), famous for his poems calling for resistance to Turkish oppression.

■ You might want to spend more time on **Meganíssi**, the south-west coast of which has high cliffs indented with bays – (there is a beautiful beach at **Ágios Ioánnis**, where many of the boats stop for a swim). There are also marine caves here and there, the most interesting of which is **Papanikolí Cave**, whose white walls are reflected in the turquoise water. Its name comes from a Greek submarine which hid there in 1941, thwarting the plans of the German forces of occupation.

■ Three kilometres beyond Nidrí, two **waterfalls** provide a refreshing end to a walk, and are a particularly welcome sight in the afternoon (*from the town centre, follow signs for "Ráchi", then "Waterfalls"; when you reach the small car park, set off on the footpath opposite, a 15min walk*). First the path follows a tiny canal, then winds along in the shade following a limestone gorge dotted with stunted bushes. Acting as a sort of gateway, a **rock arch** stands in front of the falls, which appear one after the other. The second one is worth the short climb. Its water pours into a natural pool where you can swim (you will not be alone...).

Continuing south

Having been spared the onslaught of tourism more than the east of the island, there are some very pleasant beaches in the south of the island. These include **Póros** and **Sívota**, both nestling deep in narrow bays. Another must is a stroll around the harbour in the fishing port of Vassilikí which, despite its success as a tourist destination, has retained much of its charm.

■ Beyond Nidrí, there is a steep drop down from the road to the calm waters of the **Bay of Vlihó**, which is well protected by the long Agía Kiriakí Peninsula. Next to the small chapel is the tomb of the German archaeologist **Wilhelm Dörpfeld**.
At the far end of the bay lies **Vlihó** (*3km beyond Nidrí*), a delightful fishing port where the trawlers are still built using a technique that is famous all over the island.

■ Three kilometres beyond **Vlihó**, a concrete road (*on the right*) leads up to the village of **Katahóri**, where there are superb **views**** over the whole **Bay of Vlihó**.
Go back down to the main road and continue right towards Póros, 1km further on.

■ Another peaceful village, **Póros*** (*27km from Lefkáda*) turns its back on the sea, its pretty houses built on the hillside covered with olive trees. The ruins of a 4C BC **watchtower** can be seen on the top of the hill.
As you enter the village, a road on the right leads to **Mikrós Gialós** (*signs for "Póros Beach"*), a pleasant beach of white pebbles lined with tavernas that have been little touched by tourism (*rooms to let and campsite*). Offshore is the island of Arkoúdi.
Return to the main road, and turn left. 8km further on, turn left again at a hairpin bend (sign for "Sívota Bay").

■ **Sívota** offers the luxury of a long narrow bay resembling a Norwegian fjord. Lapped by waters that are especially calm and warm, it is a favourite anchorage for many yachts, even out of season. In the tavernas around the harbour, they serve delicious grilled fish, which you can select personally from a tank using a net. There's a small beach to the north of the bay.
Return to the main road, and turn left towards Vassilikí.

The road threads its way among the grey, bare mountains of the south of the island, passing through two charming villages: **Marandohóri**, near which stands the church of the old **Monastery of Ágios Geórgios** (*on the right*), with frescoes dating from the 16C (badly damaged), and **Kondárena**.

■ **Vassilikí** – *40km from Lefkáda*. The second largest tourist resort after Nidrí, Vassilikí stands on the edge of a vast bay which is a paradise for windsurfers and sailing enthusiasts. There is a school here, with all the necessary equipment and, more importantly, the wind, which blows from the sea in the morning (Force 2 to 3), and broadside (Force 5) in the afternoon, provides ideal conditions, even for the more experienced. But although the harbour has retained much of its charm, overlooked by eucalyptus and olive trees, the chaotic construction of modern buildings has largely disfigured the place (although there are fine **views★** of Cephalonia and Ithaca). Still very popular are the boat trips to these two islands, as well as the islands of Skorpiós and Meganíssi *(daily; information at the harbour; estimate €15 to visit several islands; boats leave at 10am, returning at 7pm)*.

There is a regular boat service *(all day; €3)* to the superb **beach of Agiofili★★** (10min), a tiny jewel of white pebbles hidden between steep cliffs. The sea is crystal-clear, an unbelievable "swimming-pool" blue. There are also boats serving the **beaches of Egremní** and **Pórto Katsíki**, on the west coast.

Making the most of Leucas

COMING AND GOING

By car – Now that a pontoon bridge (built in 1987) connects Leucas to the mainland, road access to the island is simple.

By bus – Regular services between Athens and Lefkáda: 4 buses a day, in both directions. For Préveza and Áktio airport: 4 or 5 buses a day.

By air – From Athens, 1 flight a day to Préveza (then bus or taxi).

By boat – From Lefkáda, daily connections to Fiskárdo (Cephalonia) and Fríkes (Ithaca). From Vassilikí, 1 ferry daily to Fríkes and Písso Aetós (Ithaca), Sámi and Fiskárdo (Cephalonia). It is also possible to reach Nidrí (south of Lefkáda) by ferry (1 daily departure). The timetables often change, so ask at the harbour.

GETTING AROUND

By bus – From the bus station, opposite the harbour, services depart to most places on the island, twice daily to the villages, and about every 2hr to the tourist resorts (Nidrí, Ágios Ioánnis, Vassilikí). Ask for a timetable at the bus station. The buses are fairly antiquated and noisy. Be patient at the ticket offices!

By taxi – In Lefkáda, in front of the pontoon bridge, ☎ (0645) 24 600 or 22 215, and in Nidrí, at the harbour, ☎ (0645) 92 202.

By rental vehicle – Most companies have cars for hire as well as scooters. *Budget* in Lefkáda, ☎ (0645) 25 274.

Europcar in Ágios Nikítas, ☎ (0645) 97 249 and Nidrí, ☎ (0645) 92 712. *Christos Alex* in Vassilikí, ☎ (0645) 31 580. *Avis* in Nidrí, ☎ (0645) 92 136.

ADDRESS BOOK

Tourist information – There is no tourist office on the island, and the tourist police in Lefkáda, in the main street, on the right, ☎ (0645) 26 450, do not have much in the way of information. You can always try the travel agencies: *Europlan* in Lefkáda, opposite the harbour, ☎ (0645) 25 398; *Borsalino Travel* in Nidrí, ☎ (0645) 92 528; and *Samba Tours* in Vassilikí, ☎ (0645) 31 520.

Banks / Currency exchange – There are several Visa cash dispensers in the main streets of Lefkáda and Nidrí. All the travel agencies on the island change money and some change travellers' cheques, notably *All Seasons Holidays* in Nidrí, ☎ (0645) 93 275.

Medical service – *Lefkáda Hospital*, ☎ (0645) 25 371, *health centre* in Vassilikí, ☎ (0645) 31 065. *Doctor* in Nidrí, ☎ (0645) 92 710.

WHERE TO STAY

• **Lefkáda**

Between €15 and €38

Hotel Byzántio, ☎ (0645) 21 315 – 15rm. At the beginning of the main street, a small old-fashioned family hotel: surly welcome and swallows flying through reception... Blue bedrooms with basic facilities (communal WC and showers), and lopsided ceilings. Small snack-bar on the ground floor. The cheapest place in town.

Between €38 and €60

Hotel Nírikos, ☎ (0645) 24 132, Fax (0645) 23 756 – 39rm. ⌨ ⤴ ℘ TV ✗ CC A large white hotel opposite the bridge leading across to the mainland. Simple rooms with views of the harbour or overlooking a little square. Rather shabby carpets, but clean bathrooms. Warm welcome.

⌖**Hotel Santa Maura**, near Platía Ágios Spirídonas, ☎ (0645) 21 308, Fax (0645) 26 253 – 18rm. ⌨ ▤ ℘ TV CC Situated in the heart of the town, but not too noisy, this newly refurbished charming hotel is housed in an old yellow-ochre building complete with green shutters, typical of Leucas. Lovely cool rooms painted in pastel shades, some with a view over the garden. Breakfast is served under an attractive pergola. Courteous welcome from the owner. In short, very comfortable and reasonably priced (reductions after the third day).

Over €60

Hotel Lefkás, ☎ (0645) 23 916, Fax (0645) 24 579 – 93rm. ⌨ ▤ ℘ TV ✗ CC As you enter Lefkáda, opposite the bridge. A large, rather grandiose hotel built in the 1970s (huge hall). White rooms with cream carpets, mini-bar, balconies with a view over the harbour. Quite expensive for what it is, but the hotels in Lefkáda get very busy in high season...

• **Nidrí**

Between €38 and €60

Hotel Áthos, ☎ (0645) 92 384, Fax (0645) 92 180 – 43rm. ⌨ ▤ ℘ ✗ ⌕ CC A white hotel at the end of the harbour, 500m from the beach. Cool rooms with balconies, housed in several different buildings. Jacuzzi. Evening entertainment, and boat trips can be arranged to the islands of Skorpiós and Meiganíssi... Family atmosphere.

• **Vassilikí**

Between €38 and €60

Hotel Lefkatás, ☎ (0645) 31 801, Fax (0645) 31 804 – 33rm. ⌨ ℘ CC In the centre of the village, this white, functional hotel with a marble entrance

hall is one of the most popular meeting places in Vassilikí for windsurfers. The white and blue rooms are spacious, have a balcony and most have AC. The hotel also has a few apartments to let.

Hotel Vassilikí Bay, ☎ (0645) 31 077, Fax (0645) 23 567 – 24rm. ⌨ ℘ CC The newest hotel in Vassilikí, in the heart of the town, 30m from the beach. Open from May to October. Very quiet, spacious white rooms, each with a balcony. Friendly welcome, and they will also help to arrange boat trips to the beaches at Pórto Katsíki and Agiofíli.

• **Ágios Nikítas**

In addition to the campsite, ☎ (0645) 97 301, and a few rooms to let in private houses, there are two good hotels, above the harbour:

Between €38 and €60

Hotel Neféli, ☎ (0645) 97 400, Fax (0645) 97 402 – 16rm. ⌨ ℘ A charming white hotel with green shutters, perched in the hills above the village, 100m from the beach. White, airy rooms (some have sea views), spotless bathrooms, mini-bar. Terrace overlooking a small garden, and numerous tavernas within easy reach. The owners, a charming couple, will give you a very friendly welcome. They also have four studios with kitchenette to rent.

Over €60

⌖**Hotel Odyssey**, ☎ (0645) 97 351, Fax (0645) 97 421 – 40rm. ⌨ ℘ ✗ ⌕ CC This rather elegant establishment, built in the local style and painted yellow, with three floors of terraces, is tucked among trees and flowers. Light and airy rooms with balcony (most have airconditioning), there is a gym, and the beach is 100m away. Pleasant rooftop restaurant with a superb view out to sea.

• **Póros**

Under €15

Poros Beach campsite, ☎ (0645) 95 452, Fax (0645) 95 152. ✗ ⌕ ⌖ Well located in the shade of olive trees, this campsite is just above the beach at Mikrós Gialós. Supermarket, small swimming pool and bar. They also have about 20 bungalows to let with bathrooms and kitchenette. Very busy in the high season.

• **Lefkáda**

The town tends to be fairly dead at lunchtime and many restaurants open only in the evening. Most of the decent tavernas and "gíros" are located on the main street and stay open until fairly late at night. You will also find – somewhat unexpectedly perhaps – numerous pancake houses. The tavernas down at the harbour have terraces right next to the road – not very attractive.

€11

Light House Tavern, Odós Philarmoníkí 14, ☎ (0645) 25 117. In a street at right angles to the main street, opposite the Church of Ágios Nikólaos. 5pm-1am, from April to October. 🍴 **CC** For more than 20 years, Mr Ventouras and his wife have been serving excellent food – grilled dishes, fresh fish and simple, freshly prepared starters. There are tables under a pretty ivy-covered arbour, a stone's throw away from the open-air theatre.

Taverna Romantica, Odós Mitropóleos 11, ☎ (0645) 22 235. From the main street, take the second street on the right after the Bank of Greece. 8.30am-1am. 🍴 Do not let yourself be put off by the huge pink and blue art-deco dining room: there is a pleasant airy terrace at the back. Frequented by Greeks, this taverna with its family atmosphere serves good local cuisine (fish, "pastítsio" and "maridópita", a sort of pizza with fried fish), and local musicians often come along to liven up the evening.

€12

Voglia di Pizza, Odós Ángelou Sikelianoú, ☎ (0645) 26 461. 7am-12midnight; closed in November. 🍴 If you fancy a pizza, this restaurant situated next to the lagoon, 50m from the new Cultural Centre, is ideal. From the dining room you can watch the *pizzaiolo* in action in front of his white oven, making excellent pizzas with a thin, crunchy base. They also serve pasta and other Italian specialities. It has a large terrace next to the water and is quieter than the tavernas in the main street.

• **Ágios Nikítas**

€11

Taverna Leftéris, in the main street, on the right just before you reach the sea. ☎ (0645) 97 495. Open between 9am

and 2am, from May to October. 🍴 **CC** The cooking is excellent and the dishes are freshly prepared, served on a large airy terrace. Specialities included fish, spaghetti with prawns, and delicious cakes. Friendly, courteous welcome.

• **Vassilikí**

€11

Taverna Stéllios, ☎ (0645) 31 581 – 10am-2am, from May to October. 🍴 Attractive shady terrace by the water, the ideal place to try some grilled fish.

• **Nidrí**

€9

Restaurant Iónion, ☎ (0645) 93 094 – 12.30pm-2am. 🍴 At the end of the harbour, on the right facing the sea. Good local cuisine accompanied by dry local wines, attentive service, a lovely pergola terrace decorated with a giant flowering purple lily. Quieter than the tavernas in the centre.

HAVING A DRINK

Bars – They are all located in Odós Angelou Sikelianou, next to the lagoon, and they come alive at dusk. The **Diverso Cafe** is one of the most fashionable.

Concerts – During the last two weeks of August, this is the setting for the **International Folk-dancing Festival**, with performances every evening at 9.30pm at the Cultural Centre (follow the lagoon for 500m beyond the bridge). From June to August: **Festival of Music, Arts and Literature**, with theatrical performances and concerts (classical, jazz, modern guitar, etc) held at Santa Maura Fort and the open-air theatre (look for the "Garden Theatre" sign on the main street).

Information from the Cultural Centre.

OTHER THINGS TO DO

Sailing – Sailing equipment and supplies, **Theódoros Koutchavtís**, in the main street of Lefkáda, on the right coming from the bridge, behind the stone fountain, ☎ (0645) 25 361.

Scuba diving – In Nidrí, **Lucky Scuba Divers**, Chrísanthos Politópoulos, mobile ☎ 093 681803.

Horse-riding – In Vassilikí, **Hippocampos**, ☎ (0645) 31 607.

Making the most of Leucas

CEPHALONIA★★
(KEFALONIÁ)
Ionian Islands – District of Cephalonia – 737km² – Regional map page 348
Michelin map 980 fold 27 – Allow 4 days – Pop 29 400

Not to be missed
A swim off the beach at Mirtós.
Fiskárdo, and especially the little harbour and the magnificent setting of Ássos.
Climbing Mt Énos.

And remember...
If your budget permits, rent a car; the coastline is difficult to negotiate and
this is the best way to get around without wasting any time.

The largest of the Ionian Islands has an extremely rugged landscape that has been
sculpted into various peninsulas, rocky capes, creeks, crescents of sand and deep
bays, watched over by Mt Énos, the highest peak in the Ionian Islands, its impressive black summit towering 1 628m above sea level. Austere and arid in the uplands,
which the long-haired goats have made their home, the island also has more serene,
even luxuriant, areas. In the south, for example, the cypresses vie with olive trees,
fruit trees and vines, the same vines that produce the tasty *Robola* wine. But, of course,
this is precisely what is so charming about Cephalonia: the varied landscape, where
remnants of the past – here a cracked bell-tower protruding from the pines, there a
forlorn gate opening onto the scrub – strike a romantic pose.

A committed people
Although a number of Mycenaean tombs have been discovered on the island,
Cephalonia lingered in the shadows throughout Antiquity. In the 11C, it was captured by the Normans of Sicily, before falling into the hands of the Frankish
Principality of Morea when it was part of one of the "great fiefs", the **Earldom of
Cephalonia**, which also took in Zacynthus and Ithaca. The island then came under
the protection of important Italian nobles, first the **Orsini** family (1155-1356) then
the **Tocchi** family, until 1478. The Turks only stayed for 20 years, put to flight by
the Venetians, under whom the island was to experience its golden age. Assisted by
Spanish troops, under **Gonzalo Fernández de Córdoba**, known as "El Gran
Capitán", the Serenissima held onto Cephalonia until 1797. From 1808, the British
established themselves on the island, a period of great civil works directed by **Sir
Charles Napier**. A very patriotic people, the Cephalonians participated passionately
in the War of Independence, and were praised by Lord Byron, who led the island
to rejoin Greece in 1864. Cephalonia is also the birthplace of scholars and politicians, such as **Ioánnis Metaxás** (1871-1941), the man who rejected the Italian
ultimatum on 28 October 1940 (now a national holiday).

Argostóli
Pop 10 000. Allow half a day.

Devastated by the terrible earthquake of 1953, the capital of the island is bereft of
any vestiges of the elegant city founded by the Venetians in 1757. However, the new
Argostóli is full of trees and flowers, the promenade along the seafront, planted with
palm trees, is delightful; its buildings, painted in pastel shades, are of modest proportions. But the town's charm no longer lies in its architecture; Argostóli's main
attraction is its unpretentious, peaceful atmosphere.
The town stands on the narrow **Koútavos Lagoon**, offering excellent moorings to
boats – mainly small ferries and pleasure craft. Spanning the lagoon just above the
level of the water, like a stone snake, **Bosset's Bridge★** (or English Bridge) connects

its two banks. Six hundred and fifty metres in length, it was built in 1810 by Major de Bosset. He was Swiss but worked for the British.

Running parallel to the seafront, **Odós Lithóstrotos** is the town's main commercial thoroughfare, a bustling, lively pedestrian precinct. Look out for the **Church of Ágios Spirídon***, one of the few remaining vestiges of the past. Uninspiring from the outside, it conceals a superb gilt wooden **iconostasis****.

Continuing north, the street emerges in a square where the small **Archaeological Museum** *(daily; closed Monday, 8.30am-3pm; entrance fee; allow 30min)* is located. Recently refurbished, it contains finds from excavations on the island, mainly from the Mycenaean sites of Metaxáta and Mazarakáta *(see below)*: pottery, jewellery and bronze weapons, also a **bronze head** dating from the 3C BC found at Sámi.

You might want to spend more time at the **Corgialenios Museum*** *(not far away, up Odós Rókou Vergóti, which runs at right angles to the seafront; 8.30am-1.30pm / 5pm-8pm; closed Sunday; entrance fee; allow 30min)*, named after the benefactor who set out

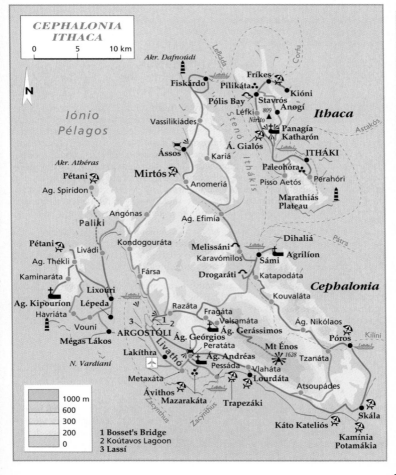

to recreate the daily life of the islanders from the 19C until 1953: there are pictures of old Argostóli, costumes, reconstructions of interiors of local houses and craft workshops, as well as some remarkable features from a church that is no longer standing. The museum also has a **library** with numerous historical texts about Cephalonia.

In the evening, head for **Platía Valiánou**∗ which is usually bursting with life (unless you prefer the peaceful but more touristy atmosphere of the quays). This large rectangular square is the heart of the town, its palm trees shading the terrace cafés and restaurants around the perimeter, where young people congregate to listen to music, drink iced coffee and chat late into the night.

North of Argostóli, the peninsula closing off the lagoon is dotted with small pebble beaches shaded by pine trees, and **katavóthres** (small chasms) around its tip (fine **view**∗ over the Bay of Argostóli and Lixoúri). The viewpoint has nothing of interest except the phenomenon itself: the sea rushing into the crevices, disappearing underground, only to re-emerge on the other side of the island, 30km away, in the underground lake of Melissáni (*see below*). The hydraulic power generated here was once used to drive **paddle wheels**, one example of which is still standing. From the tip of the peninsula, the road continues along the west shore to **Lássi**, the seaside resort of Argostóli, a large, crowded and rather characterless resort.

The Paliki Peninsula∗
Allow 1 day. Numerous shuttles daily.
(see "Making the most of Cephalonia").

Isolated on the other side of the blue Bay of Argostóli, the Paliki Peninsula looks a bit like a thumb (the rest of the island being the hand). Regarded as the garden of Cephalonia, the landscape here is greener, its hills carpeted with fruit trees, vines and olive trees. The ferry stops at **Lixoúri**, the second-largest town in Cephalonia (pop 6 000), almost opposite its large **central square** (*on the right*), a huge modern esplanade surrounded by restaurants and shops. Not very exciting, but the lively atmosphere in the nearby streets, full of small shops – spice shops, bakeries and fruit and vegetable shops – has a certain charm. The perfect chance to buy something for a picnic on the **beach of Pétani**∗∗, tucked away in a little bay dominated by two high white cliffs (*about 11km north-west, along a very steep, wiggly road*).

■ Following the coast south (*at the village of Kaminaráta, turn right*), at one point the **road** overlooks the small, squat **Monastery of Ágios Kipouríon**∗ (*after about 12km*). Painted white, it is perched on the edge of a precipice, the picturesque setting enhanced by vines and olive trees stretching down to the sea.

■ Fringed with beautiful beaches, the south of the peninsula will appeal to anyone in the mood for lounging around and having a swim. Choose between the long crescent of sand at **Mégas Lákos**∗ (*turn right at Vouni*) or the small sheltered creek of **Lépeda**∗ (*on the side of the bay; 4km south of Lixoúri*), a delightful place to watch the sunset (taverna set back from beach).

An expedition into the hills∗∗
Leave Argostóli by Bosset's Bridge and keep heading straight on, up the road that climbs into the mountains, following signs for Sámi.
Allow an afternoon.

On the far side of the bridge, the road immediately starts its ascent, winding up the side of hills bristling with cypress trees. Every so often there is a magnificent **view**∗∗ over the Koútavos Lagoon and the Bay of Argostóli. Then the road drops down, revealing a huge inland plateau dotted with a few villages.

After Razáta, turn right after 4km in the direction of Fragáta and Valsamáta.

■ A road shaded by tall trees leads to the secluded **Monastery of Ágios Gerássimos*** (11km from Argostóli; 8am-3.30pm), with an impressive **porch and bell-tower***. Inside the church, of which none of the original features remain (note the beautiful icons, however), the locals come to worship the relics of the patron saint of the island, which are kept in an enormous **silver casket***.

Also worth a visit is the **modern church**** nearby, an imposing red-brick construction, built in the traditional Byzantine architectural tradition. The interior is being lavishly decorated with **frescoes****, beautifully executed by a young artist who is taking his time to complete the task. An enormous **chandelier**** hangs in the crossing in front of a large white marble iconostasis. In addition to the beauty of the place – the view from the gallery is wonderful – you will also appreciate how cool it is.

Return to the main road and continue for 5km. Then turn right along a road which climbs slowly up the mountainside, for 3km.

■ Keen walkers will be pleased to know that you can climb **Mt Énos****, the highest peak in Cephalonia. Offering spectacular views, the mountain rises up from a thick forest – now protected – of native firs (*allow 2hr of easy walking, round trip*). Early on the road passes an **observatory**, recognisable by its huge dishes (4km), and then continues as far as the gate of the **nature reserve**, where the road then becomes a rough track (8km, allow 35min at a leisurely pace). Leave your car at the bend opposite the transmission masts and set off on foot along the path on the left which heads south (300m) following the ridge of the massif. At the next sign on the right, a well-marked footpath (yellow and green) winds up through the fir trees to the summit through the chaos of rocks. At this point the landscape changes completely and the cairn marking the summit appears in front of you, at the top of a steep rocky slope. There is only one sign of life up here: brown and black goats move up and down the steep slopes, with the agility of acrobats. As for the **view*****, which stretches right across the south of the island, you are unlikely to hang around admiring it since the wasps that live up here tend to hasten your descent.

The South*

About 70km. Allow 2 days, including time for swimming.
Leave Argostóli heading south, in the direction of Peratáta / Skála.

The Livathó Plain*
Short tour of about 35km. Follow the road skirting the lagoon and keep straight on for 5km. Once you have passed the end of the lagoon, hidden by the forest, the road continues through the green plain of Livathó, dotted with cypresses and centuries-old olive trees. The numerous villages form a veritable labyrinth and are well worth a visit. As if to compensate for the lack of attractive buildings – which were all destroyed in the 1953 earthquake – they rival each other in a profusion of flowers, with purple splashes of bougainvillaea brightening the streets, gardens and façades. This is the main attraction of Livathó, along with its fine views, which, every so often, open up across the plain sloping gently down to the sea.

■ At first sight, the **Fortress of Ágios Geórgios**** looks like an advance guard, a crown of greyish stone on the summit of a rocky knoll 320m high (*at the junction situated at the bottom of the hill, take the road that climbs up to it on the left*). Six hundred metres long, its defensive walls are pierced by a single, very well-preserved **arched gateway***, complete with its drawbridge and heavy iron grille. Three bastions defend this *kástro*, built in the 13C and altered by the Venetians, which housed the capital of the island until 1757 with a population of up to 15 000. Devastated by the earthquake of 1636, it was then abandoned in favour of Argostóli. Since restoration work is in progress, the doors may be closed (*usual hours: 8am-7pm, 3pm on Sunday; closed*

Monday), but try to get in if there is anyone working there. The interior contains the beautiful scattered ruins of the original buildings – a church, houses, etc – and the **view**★★ from the rampart walk and the north bastion stretches as far as Zacynthus.

Returning to the crossroads at the bottom of the hill, this time take the road on the right towards Peratáta (follow the signs for the Ionis hotel). Just after the hotel, before the village of Peratáta, take the small road on the right towards Metaxáta, then turn left.

■ Perched on a smaller rise not far away, is the **Monastery of Ágios Andréas**★ (Moní Milapidíon) *(9am-1.30pm / 5pm-8pm)*. It has a remarkable little 17C church, which has survived the earthquakes and been converted into a museum. Its lovely stone walls still bear fragments of **frescoes**★★, some of which come from the nearby church of Milapidía, no longer extant. There is also a magnificent 17C wooden **iconostasis**★★, various liturgical objects and some **icons**★★ painted on wood and metal. From the monastery, there is a wonderful **view**★ of the Fortress of Ágios Geórgios opposite.

Back on the Metaxáta road, turn left in the direction of Pessáda.

■ A short track to the right of the road leads *(after 100m)* to the **Mycenaean necropolis of Mazarakáta** *(there is a sort of ticket office, but access to the site appears to be free)*. Archaeology enthusiasts will jump at the chance to explore the interior of the many tombs dug out of the rock here. There are about 100 of them, packed close together and reached via narrow corridors.

Go back along the track to the Metaxáta road, and turn right towards the village of Lakíthra.

■ Situated on the flattish ridge of a small chain of hills, the main square in **Lakíthra**, dominated by the church, has a spectacular **viewpoint**★★. From here, you can see the whole plain of Livathó and its white villages, an expanse of green bristling with cypress trees against which the intense blue of the sea provides a fitting backdrop.

■ If you fancy a swim, head for the **beach of Ávithos**★ *(back in Metaxáta, turn right and continue beyond Kourkoumeláta)*, a beautiful curve of white sand, perfectly oriented so as to benefit from the sun all day *(taverna, showers)*.

Along the south coast★
About 35km. Head back to the main road to Skála, below the Fortress of Ágios Geórgios, and turn right towards Peratáta. At the village of Vlaháta, a road on the right descends towards the village of Lourdáta and the sea.

■ Immersed in vegetation, the main attraction of **Lourdáta** is the fact that it is cool, something the crickets seem to appreciate as much as the visitors. In the shade of a gigantic plane tree is a spring, and into the little square are crammed a tourist office, a grocer's, a taverna and even a junk shop.
From here, the road winds down towards the large **beach of Trapezáki**★ *(2km)*, divided into two parts by a small rocky promontory *(showers, loungers, pedalos and canoes for hire)*.
Right next to it is the **beach of Lourdáta**, another large expanse of sand and pebbles. Although less wild than its neighbour, it is peaceful here.

■ Running along a ridge between the sea and the mountains, the **road**★★ becomes increasingly picturesque towards Skála. It is not far to the **beach of Káto Kateliós**★. Sand dunes separate the beach from a marshy plain, from which rise electricity pylons and a number of uninspiring hotels. Further on, around the wide bay of Káto Kateliós there are several lovely beaches: **Kamínia** then **Potamákia** *(reached by a small road which turns into a track)*, attractive crescents of sand surrounded by vegetation.

■ Situated on the southern tip of the island, the pleasant seaside resort of **Skála** has a superb **beach**★★ fringed by a thick pine wood. Whilst it might be tempting to stay until the next day, the place has become the exclusive domain of British holiday-makers and it is very difficult to find any accommodation, most places being booked up from one year to the next. However, do have a look at the little **Roman villa** dating from the 3C AD which has been discovered just outside the town (*signposted*), and which has some fine mosaics (*8am-2pm; entrance fee*).

■ You stand a better chance of finding accommodation at **Póros**, a small seaside resort in a less attractive setting, although it can get very busy in the high season. Tucked away behind the rocks is the rather pretty harbour (ferries). Or continue to Sámi.

The North★★

110km tour. Allow 2 days.

■ **Sámi** – *30km from Póros.* The third-largest town in Cephalonia, the bustling town of Sámi stretches the length of an enormous sheltered bay, looking out towards the more austere coastline of Ithaca. While the terraces of the restaurants are situated on the seafront, the newer hotels are gradually making inroads into the hills above it, which has meant that the bustling old town centre has retained its charm. To the east, sealing off the bay of Sámi, lies the rocky promontory of **Dihaliá★★**. Carpeted in forest, this wild cape is the site of the ruins of ancient **Antisamos**, and the little **Monastery of Agrilíon★**, dominated by a majestic medieval tower. On the other side of the cape, lower down, the road passes a pretty, deserted **beach**.

While you are in Sámi you should pay a visit to **Melissáni Cave★** (*sign for "Melissáni Lake"; 3km to the north-west via the road to Agía Efimía, just outside Karavómilos along a road leading off to the left*). A flight of steps leads down into a gully and then to the edge of an underground lake, lit by a large hole where the roof has collapsed. You can take a boat (*20min*) to appreciate the intense blue of the water (especially at noon), the echo and the light, which combine to give the place a unique atmosphere. On either side of the cave, in two parts, underground tunnels connect with the *katavóthres* of Argostóli.

Another interesting phenomenon, the **Drogaráti Cave★** (*2km south-west of Sámi, on the Argostóli road, then take the road on the right for 2km*) was discovered four centuries ago and was opened to the public in 1963. Buried 60m below the ground

Fiskárdo: a little port from days gone by

G. de Benoist/MICHELIN

(steps), a single huge cave (1 000m²) is covered by a dome sculpted with a veritable forest of stalactites. The stalagmites have been removed to create a huge circular area which is used for concerts of classical music in the high season.

Leave Sámi and head for Agía Efimía (7km). To get to Fiskárdo from here, be sure to take the right road: at the end of the harbour, at the Mirtós sign turn left, then immediately right into the little road leading uphill; this emerges on the Fiskárdo road, which runs above the village parallel to the road to Mirtós.

■ A tiny port nestling in the crook of a deep inlet, **Fiskárdo**★★ *(38km from Sámi)* is the only village on the island to have been spared by the 1953 earthquake. Much of its old-fashioned charm emanates from the row of brightly coloured houses which overlook the harbour. The oldest of them, (now a bar), to the right of the steps leading up towards the church, dates from the 17C. Fiskárdo was named after Robert Guiscard, one of the Norman kings of Sicily, who died here in 1085. It is rumoured that he was buried at the **ruined church** with two Norman towers that stands on the far side of the inlet. Nowadays with the village attracting large numbers of visitors the place has lost some of its charming authenticity, and the number of quite expensive restaurants, fashionable bars and souvenir shops continues to multiply.

■ You may prefer **Ássos**★★, situated a little further along the west coast *(22km from Fiskárdo)*. As the road leading to it gradually gains height, it reveals wonderful **views**★★★ over the sea and the mountains with flocks of goats. The village soon appears below the road, at the beginning of a small peninsula crowned by a Venetian fortress (16C). Although less touristy and more subdued than Fiskárdo, Ássos also boasts an incredibly beautiful **setting**★★★. Nestling among sweet-smelling pines and laurels, its few houses skirt the edge of a blue lagoon, basking in splendid isolation. On Platía Paris – which was rebuilt exactly as it was by the city of Paris in 1953 – are a number of tavernas where you can linger over a drink, admiring the view of the **fortress**★. A rough *(but driveable)* track zigzags along the 2km as far as the fine gateway. The interior, now in ruins, is huge. Tucked away, further down on the seaward side, and shaded by pine trees in places, are a few fields and a hamlet that is completely cut off from the rest of the world.

■ Further south, make sure you stop at the **beach of Mirtós**★★★ *(13km from Ássos, reached by a road on the right descending steeply towards the sea)*, which is undoubtedly the most beautiful beach on the island – indeed in the whole of Greece, according to the Greeks – with its majestic white cliffs towering over the turquoise water.
Beyond Mirtós, the road meanders down the mountainside in a breathtaking **landscape**★★ overlooking the sea, as far as the ay of Argostóli where it meets Bosset's Bridge leading across to the capital of the island *(30km from Mirtós)*.

Making the most of Cephalonia

COMING AND GOING

See also page 300 "Making the most of the northern coast of the Peloponnese".

By boat – There is no longer a direct service to Corfu; the boats stop at Patras, on the mainland. For Ithaca (departing from Fiskárdo), the boat timetables change every year, so get current details from a travel agency (see below the "Address book" for Fiskárdo).

For Zacynthus: note that the boats stop at Pessáda, further south, and not at Ar-

gostóli. 2 daily crossings, at 7.45am and 5.30pm (Zacynthus-Pessáda: 9am and 7pm); tickets €3.50 (80min).

From Sámi, numerous connections to the other islands. A large ferry runs a shuttle service to Patras, and there is a high-speed service that takes only 20min.

By air – From Athens (west terminal), there are 2 daily flights (1hr flight). Estimate about €51. Book as soon as possible, as the plane is tiny! For the return trip, there are also 2 flights a day to Athens (55min flight). There are no buses to Argostóli, only taxis (estimate a maximum of €6).

GETTING AROUND

By bus – *Main bus station* on the outskirts of Argostóli, Odós Ioánnis Metaxá, ☎ (0671) 22 276 and 22 281. A very pretty, old-fashioned terminus, undoubtedly one of the most beautiful reconstructed buildings in town! The office of the *KTEL* agency, which operates the network, is located in the right wing of the building. 8am-1.30pm / 6pm-9.30pm. Ask for their brochure, which contains all the bus timetables and information about possible excursions on the island.

By two-wheeled vehicle – The island is huge and the roads are very winding. So use a car if you want to cover any distance and motorcycles or scooters only for short trips.

By car – The ideal way to get around, given that the bus network is still fairly limited, and the island is a maze of tiny roads (especially in the south). There are plenty of filling stations at Argostóli and on the roads in the south, fewer in the north (if you are going to Fiskárdo, fill up at Sámi).

Vehicle hire – There are several companies with two-wheeled vehicles for hire in Argostóli. Be sure to check the vehicle. *Safe*, Odós Ioánnis Metaxá 21, ☎ (0671) 24 024 and 24 674. Good prices.

For cars, try *Hertz*, which has an office at the airport and another at Lássi, but you will also find a branch in Argostóli itself, on the little street just behind the theatre. Very attractive prices out of season. *Eurodollar*, Argostóli, Odós Rókou Vergóti 3 (the street leading to the theatre).

Another good agency in Argostóli: *Holiday Autos*, Víronos 23, ☎ (0671) 22 338, Fax (0671) 23 014, right next to the Hotel Argostóli. Branches at the airport, at Lourdáta and in Skála.

By boat – Since the coastline is difficult to negotiate by car, a boat is the best way to explore the *Paliki Peninsula*. Ferries run to Lixoúri all day (every 30min in the afternoon) from 8am to 11pm. You pay on board. Embark just beyond the Hotel Star, beyond the large ferries (sign "To Lixoúri", on the quay).

ADDRESS BOOK
In Argostóli

Tourist information – There is a small office on the quay, at the freight harbour, just opposite the police station, ☎ (0671) 22 248. Very friendly welcome. 7am-2.30pm, and also from 5.30pm to 10pm or 11pm in summer. Maps of Argostóli and the island.

Banks / Currency exchange – There are numerous banks with cash dispensers on Odós Ioánnis Metaxá, which runs along next to the harbour.

Post office – Odós Lithóstrotos. 7.30am-2pm; closed at the weekend.

Telephone – Odós Georgíou Vergóti. 2 card phones in front of the door. 7am-2.40pm.

Internet – The *Excellis* Cybercafé, just next door to the post office (sign from the Church of Ágios Spirídonas). 9am-2.30pm / 6pm-10pm; closed Saturday afternoon and Sunday. 3 computers.

Police – Odós Ioánnis Metaxá, ☎ (0671) 22 200.

Medical service – You will find several pharmacies, notably on Odós Ioánnis Metaxá and Odós Lithóstrotos. *Medical Centre*, Odós Lithóstrotos 18, behind the old post office. This is the surgery of Dr Michaelides, ☎ (0671) 23 338, mobile 093 228 7600. Available for consultation daily except Sunday, 9am-2pm and 6pm-8.30pm.

Hospital, on the outskirts of Argostóli, by Odós Devosétou, on the left, ☎ (0671) 23 230 and 22 641.

Airlines – *Olympic Airways*, 8am-3.30pm, closed Saturday and Sunday.

Travel agencies – *Apollo*, Odós Georgíou Vergóti 2, at the beginning of Platía Valiánou. Air and boat tickets and general information. Very warm welcome and efficient service. Open from May to October.

V Shipping & Travel, 21 Maýou 2, ☎ (0671) 22 214. Same services.

Shipping companies – *Minoan*, Ioánnis Metaxá. Tickets for Zacynthus and the other islands. Not very friendly.

Other – *Apyros Bookshop*, Odós Lithóstrotos, opposite the Church of Ágios Spirídonas. International newspapers, books in Greek and English, stationery.

In Sámi

Tourist information – *Sámi Star*, on the seafront, near the jetty, ☎ (0674) 22 813, Fax (0674) 23 110. Acts as a tourist office ("Central Tourist Office" sign). You will find all the services you need here: air tickets, boat tickets, money-changing facilities, car hire, accommodation and excursions to local places of interest. Similar services at *V Shipping & Travel*, on the seafront, ☎ (0674) 22 371.

Post office – Behind the church. 7.30am-2pm.

In Fiskárdo

Tourist information – *Fiskárdo Travel Agency*, below the steps leading down from the car park to the harbour. Located in a small pale-yellow house with blue shutters. 10am-2pm / 5.30pm-9pm. Right next door: *Hertz* car hire, and a bank (changes money). *Pama Travel*, on the first floor of a pink house at the end of the harbour, on the quay. Change, general information about boats for Ithaca and the mainland, cruises, scuba diving, and 3 *Internet* access points. Efficient, thorough service.

Banks / Currency exchange – No cash dispensers in Fiskárdo.

Post office – Right opposite the tourist office. Also changes money. 8am-2pm, from Monday to Friday.

WHERE TO STAY

There are only 2 campsites on the island, at Argostóli and Sámi.

* **Argostóli**

Around €11

Fanari campsite (Argostóli Beach), ☎ (0671) 23 487, Fax (0671) 24 525 – 170 pitches. ✕ ⚲ At the northern end of Argostóli, right next to the katavóthres windmill. Bus 4 times a day to Argostóli and the beach. Very warm welcome from the owner. Small supermarket, ouzo bar, mini-golf and disco (set apart), but the campsite itself could do with an overhaul, particularly the washing facilities.

Between €30 and €41

King Agamemnon, Odós Ioánnis Metaxá 36, ☎ and Fax (0426) 23 915 – 15rm plus studios for up to 3 people. ⍩ ℘ ⌂ Bar and pleasant terrace for

breakfast. All the rooms are well-lit, cool and have a small terrace. Friendly welcome and negotiable prices. €33 in low season, €47 to €62 in summer (August) including breakfast. Good value for money.

Hotel Tourist, Odós Ioánnis Metaxá 109, ☎ (0671) 23 034, Fax (0671) 22 510 – 21rm. ⍩ ⍱ ℘ ⊺� ✕ ⊡ Small, rather uninspiring rooms (shabby carpets), 3 of which have bathrooms along the corridor. This is the cheapest hotel in town, but not as good value for money as the King Agamemnon. Breakfast extra. Unusual restaurant, with rather trendy decor, serves decent food.

Between €45 and €60

Hotel Cephalonia Star, Odós Ioánnis Metaxá 60, ☎ (0671) 23 180 to 183, Fax (0671) 23 180 – 42rm. ⍩⊟ ℘ ⊺⍱ ✕ ⊡ Spacious, bright, clean rooms, with pine furniture and balcony. The upper rooms have small private terraces. Very friendly welcome. Restaurant with pavement terrace. A pity that the building shakes whenever a door closes and, in the evening it's fairly noisy outside.

⊛ ***Hotel Mirabel,*** Platía Valiánou, ☎ (0671) 25 381 to 383, Fax (0671) 25 384, Mirabel@compulink.gr – 33rm. ⍩⊟ ℘ ⊺⍱ ⊡ A pleasant, very well-situated hotel, with spacious, nicely furnished rooms, very clean, each with a terrace. Note that the rooms overlooking the square can be noisy. Bar in the hall and in the courtyard, under a delightful arbour covered with vines. Friendly welcome. Open all year.

⊛ ***Hotel Olga,*** Odós Ioánnis Metaxá 82, ☎ (0671) 24 981 to 984, Fax (0671) 24 985 – 43rm. ⍩⊟ ℘ ⊺⍱ ✕ ⊡ An attractive façade with blue shutters, pleasantly situated facing the palm trees that line the promenade. The owner, Spíros Kougianós, will give you a friendly welcome, and runs his establishment very efficiently. Spotless, spacious rooms with double-glazing and pleasant little balconies. Buffet breakfast, which you can eat on the quay. Bar. Excellent value for a town hotel.

Hotel Mouikis, Odós Víronos 3, ☎ (0671) 23 032 and 23 454, Fax (0671) 24 528 – 42rm. ⍩⊟ ℘ ⊺⍱ ⊡ Mainly British clientele. Pleasant rooms, clean, decent bathrooms. Lovely private terraces from the third floor upwards, a balcony in all the other rooms. Professional welcome. In the same category as the Hotel Olga, but a little more expensive.

Hotel Miramare, Odós Ioánnis Metaxá 2, ☎ (0671) 25 511, 25 513, Fax (0671) 255 512 – 57rm. ⁊ 🗐 ℘ TV On the edge of the town, out towards the katavóthres, in a peaceful setting, facing the sea. Recently built, this elegant hotel has a good reputation, with a mainly Greek clientele. The service is good and the rooms are spotless, spacious and very comfortable, with lovely bathrooms.

• **Skála**

Situated at the southern tip of the island, Skála has long been the domain of British package-tour operators, and it is very difficult to find anywhere to stay. However, out of season, June included, certain hoteliers like to keep a few rooms for private individuals. You can also apply to the **Skalina Tours** agency, ☎ (0671) 83 275, Fax (0671) 83 475, skalina@kef.forthnet.gr, whose owner, Vangélis Spáthis, is the president of an association of independent hotels, who prefer not to deal exclusively with package-tour operators. Opposite the beach, you may be lucky enough to find a room at one of the following:

Between €60 and €68

Paspalis, at the end of the seafront, ☎ (0671) 83 140 and 83 610, Fax (0671) 83 611 (out of season: 83 456) – 30rm. ⁊ 🗐 ℘ ✗ 🔆🔟 ⅗ CC Spacious rooms with balcony or terrace in a number of substantial single-storey buildings. Comfortable, clean and well-lit. Pleasant bar outside on the terrace. Friendly welcome. Good value.

Tara Beach, opposite the beach, right in front of the Paspalis, ☎ (0671) 83 250 and 83 341 to 343, Fax (0671) 83 344. ⁊ 🗐 ℘ ✗ 🔆🔟 ⅗ CC Same category of hotel as the Paspalis, but slightly more expensive. The all-mod-cons accommodation is in attractive, single-storey buildings laid out around a pretty courtyard bright with flowers. Billiard table. Warm welcome.

• **Póros**

Although the town itself has no great charm, the hotels are much cheaper here than in Skála.

Around €23

La Piazza, above the restaurant of the same name, on the side of the square overlooking the seafront, ☎ (0674) 73 019 – 10rm. ⁊ 🛪 ✗ CC Rooms with standard facilities, uninspiring, but clean. Very cheap. English spoken.

Between €30 and €54

🏵 **Hotel Oceanis**, ☎ (0674) 72 581 and 582, Fax (0674) 72 583, oceanis-hl@otenet.gr – 16rm. ⁊ 🗐 ℘ TV 🔆 ⅗ CC 2rm for 4 people and 2 communicating double rooms. Open during the season, but you can also book a room during the winter. Perched on the rocky promontory beyond the ferry port, on the far side of the cape, the hotel has a superb view of Póros and the sea. Rooms with balcony and fridge, very well maintained, spacious and bright. Bar. A few steps and a footpath lead directly down to the harbour below. Breakfast included (buffet).

• **Sámi**

Campsite (around €11)

Karavómilos Beach, on the beach, west of the town, ☎ (0674) 22 480, Fax (0674) 22 932 – 243 pitches. ✗ 🔆 Very well situated, and peaceful despite being close to the town. Each pitch has an electricity point. Small supermarket. Very friendly, professional welcome. Open in high season.

Between €30 and €55

Riviera, in the town centre, on the main street, on the east side of town, ☎ (0674) 22 777 and 23 047 – 14rm to let above the restaurant (cafeteria) of the same name (where you should apply). ⁊ ✗ Small, functional, clean rooms, but a bit stuffy. Try to get one of the rooms at the front, which have balconies looking out to sea. Breakfast is served in the cafeteria.

Hotel Melissáni, ☎ and Fax (0674) 22 464 – 15rm. ⁊ 🛪 ℘ CC Well situated in the centre of Sámi. The rooms are on the small side, but functional, clean and well-lit, with a small balcony. Friendly welcome, family atmosphere. Breakfast included.

Around €54

Hotel Kástro, right in the town centre, overlooking the seafront, ☎ (0674) 22 656 and 22 282, Fax (0674) 23 004 – 55rm. ⁊ 🗐 ℘ CC So well situated that it was even incorporated as part of the scenery for the film "Captain

Corelli's Mandolin" (once its façade had had a facelift to make it look older and much prettier than the original). The film crew also made it their headquarters. Rooms are uninspiring but comfortable, with a balcony looking over the huge inner courtyard or out to sea.

🐚 **Hotel Sámi Beach**, at Karavómilos, the village west of Sámi, the far end of the large beach – 44rm. 🛏️📋 / 🍽️ 🏖️ ✕ (snack-bar) 🏖️ 🏊 🎾 🅲🅲 A lovely place to stay: friendly, professional welcome, and a family atmosphere (TV room) despite the size and luxury of the place. In separate buildings painted in pastel shades, the rooms are comfortable and well-kept, well-lit and attractively furnished, with beautiful bathrooms. Large swimming pool, bar, table-tennis. Breakfast included (buffet).

• **Fiskárdo**

Everywhere above the tavernas and shops there are rooms to let. Look for the signs. They include:

Between €30 and €45

Regína, ☎ (0674) 41 125 and mobile 093 293 2910. A new house at the top of the village (entrance in the car park). 10 rooms, but the house is being extended. Spacious, well-kept rooms, 3 of which have private bathrooms. Try to get a room facing the harbour. Communal kitchen (no breakfast). Family atmosphere.

Erissos, on the harbour, in a fairly quiet corner, ☎ (0674) 41 055 – 2rm with private bathroom, and 2 with shared facilities (on first floor). A real old Fiskárdo house, with yellow roughcast walls. Entrance through the kitchen (available for use of guests), the focal point of the house. Simple comforts and rustic charm in these spacious rooms with high ceilings, furnished with attractive bric-a-brac by Spiridoúla, the owner, who only speaks Greek and Italian. Open from May to October.

Between €55 and €69

Sotiría Tseledi, ☎ (0674) 41 204 and 41 127 – 5rm. 🛏️ Another large, recently built 2-storey house, beautifully kept by Sotiría. Attractive, large, shared, very well-equipped kitchen. 2 rooms with balcony, very pleasant with lovely wooden furnishings. When you arrive, ask at the baker's, below the house, or at Élli's Café (same family). Quite expensive.

🐚 **Fiskárdo Studios**, ☎ (0674) 41 020 and 41 495, mobile 0946 357739 – 6rm. 🛏️ 📋 📺 ✕ 🅲🅲 A small brand-new pink hotel, very well situated at the beginning of the harbour. Well-equipped bedsits for 2 to 5 people, spacious, comfortable and spotlessly clean, all with a large stepped terrace overlooking the harbour. Excellent value for money.

EATING OUT

• **Argostóli**

Numerous restaurants, bars and tavernas – all fairly touristy – line the seafront. The food is good, but unexciting. We recommend you head for the restaurants in the back streets, around Platía Valiánou.

Under €7.50

🐚 **Ellinikó**, Odós Ágios Gerássimos 8. A very pleasant, very simple taverna under an arbour, located in a small street set back from the harbour: try their *skordaliá*, the delicious local garlic-flavoured mashed potatoes, which come with slices of grilled aubergines. Very friendly welcome and tasty food.

Around €9

Portside, Odós Ioánnis Metaxá 58, a busy restaurant with terrace overlooking the harbour. Varied menu.

Mr Grillo, Odós Ioánnis Metaxá 82, near the Hotel Olga, a large taverna with a terrace overlooking the harbour, very busy and popular with the locals. Excellent grilled meat, fish and seafood.

Tzivras, authentic Greek delicacies, simple setting. Only open at lunchtime.

I kalíva – The Cottage, a large covered courtyard, above Platía Valiánou. Simple decor but good service and it serves wonderful Greek food (excellent souvláki, and "Cephalonia Meat Pie".

Around €15

The Indian Queen, Odós Dionissíou Lavragká, next to the British Queen Vic Pub. ☎ (0671) 22 631. Indian food served in a very pleasant courtyard with an arbour, quiet. Tandoori and other tasty dishes, with and without spices. You are advised to book in high season.

• **Lixoúri**

🐚 **Zorbas**, at the corner of Odós Grigoríou Labráki and Odós 25 Martíou. In a large, very attractive shady courtyard, Fános Athanassíou and his family serve very good Greek food.

- **Lourdáta**
Taverna Aléxia, above a small antique shop, ☎ (0671) 31 234. Beautiful terrace overlooking the village square. Arbour covered in vines and crickets. Book ahead.

- **Póros**
Two bays: the beach to the north, the ferry port to the south, behind the small rocky promontory.
Around €9
Along the beach, opposite the ferry port, the **Vanessa** and **Eteki** tavernas have set up their tables under a pretty arbour at the water's edge.
🐾 **Fótis**, near the beach, in a corner of the square on the seafront. A delightful 2-storey terrace, looking right down on the beach and the square. Good home cooking and friendly welcome. They also have rooms to let at the other end of the beach, ☎ (0674) 72 972 / 72 322.
Near the port: **Tzivas**, a simple terrace, blue decor, looking right down over the ferry port. Good fish dishes.
Just up from the Hotel Oceanis, the **unset** and **Lighthouse** tavernas overlook the port (take the road below the one leading to the hotel or the steps leading up from the harbour). The place to dine while watching the sun go down. Varied menus.

- **Sámi**
You will find a plethora of tavernas on the seafront, which are all much the same. Avoid Faros: the owner is obnoxious and the restaurant serves canteen-style food.

- **Fiskárdo**
Around €12
Lagouderá, in a small square set back from the quays, at the corner of the harbour, opposite the tourist office. Grilled dishes are the speciality here, served on a small shady terrace. Good local cooking.
Tselendí, a taverna in one of the most beautiful houses in the village, in a very pleasant little square not far from the harbour. Inside, there is a magnificent dining room with an excellent bar. A pleasant place to have breakfast.
Around €15
Vásso's, right on the harbour, an extensive menu, with a good selection of meze, but very expensive.

Bars

- **Argostóli**
Rock Café, on the quay, just before the palm-tree promenade. Rather contrived modern decor. Better are the cafés in the pedestrian precinct (Lithóstrotos), which are more typical of the area (the **Café K**, the **Metropolis** and the **Antika**), or the Italian-style cafés in Platía Valiánou which come to life in the evening. As for the menu: music, coffee, pizzas, Italian ice cream and pancakes!

- **Fiskárdo**
Veggéra, right next to Vásso's restaurant. Pleasant, tastefully decorated in bricks and wood, plays British music (new and old hits). Attractive terrace looking out on the harbour.

Cake shops, tea rooms
In Argostóli, **Karpatos cake shop**, on Odós Ioánnis Metaxá, good Western-style cakes and baklavas.
Platía Valiánou, delicious ice creams at **Premier**, as well as a Middle-Eastern or Italian cake-shop.
🐾 **Néa Sámi**, on the seafront in Sámi, serves delicious cakes with coffee, and Italian ice creams.

Boat trips – From Argostóli, there are trips in a glass-bottomed boat to see the loggerhead turtles. The trip includes a mud bath, a meal and swimming.

Scuba diving – At Agía Efimía, north of Sámi, **Scuba Diving School**, Odós Marínou Antípa 1, ☎ and Fax (0674) 62 006, info@aquatic.gr A diving club with a very friendly atmosphere. Caters for both beginners and qualified divers. Good equipment (supplied).

Small supermarkets on the quay.

Market – There is a busy market held in the market hall on the quay. Daily in summer, until about 11pm.

Local delicacies – On Odós Lithóstrotos, a small green-fronted shop, opposite the Metropolis Café, has all kinds of local fare: wines (Robola), coffee, honey, etc.
Dionysios, on Odós Lithóstrotos. As the name suggests, it sells wines, but you will also find local confectionery and coffee.

Making the most of Cephalonia

393

ITHACA ★★
(ITHÁKI)

Ionian Islands – District of Cephalonia – 96km² – Regional map page 348
Michelin map 980 fold 27 – Map of the island page 383
Pop 3 100 – Allow 2 or 3 days

Not to be missed
The harbour and bay of Kióni, still unspoilt.

And remember...
In high season, be absolutely sure to book a room.
Watch out for goats on the narrow roads!

"On Ithaca there are neither open plains nor prairies... With its rugged landscape, the island is unsuitable for horses... Although it is narrow, wretched it is not. But ideal for goats..."

Homer, *The Odyssey*.

Lying a stone's throw from Cephalonia, Ithaca's tortuous coast is separated from its larger neighbour by the narrow **Stenó Ithákis** channel. Like two separate islands, two mountainous peninsulas rise up, (Mt Nírito in the north is 809m high), linked by a narrow isthmus barely 620m wide. The island almost looks as if it has been strangled by a giant; perhaps the Cyclops Polyphemus, come to avenge himself for the wound inflicted on him by the King of Ithaca?

Off Cephalonia, the legendary island of Ithaca

B. Chabrol/MICHELIN

The Ionian Islands

But, oddly enough, the island of Odysseus and his first voyage is not so much evocative of the *Odyssey* as of *Don Quixote*, its sail-less windmills conjuring up those picaresque adventures. And after all, what remains of Homer's Ithaca? A few paltry archaeological remains that are difficult for the man or woman in the street to decipher. Clinging to the steep hillsides, the villages still seem to lament the exile of their king, as they peacefully await his unlikely return. The houses, supported by drystone walls, have their windows wide open as if scanning the horizon. But here, myth has made itself invisible, the better to haunt the imagination and the beauty of the landscape. This rugged, serene land, forsaken by the tourists, will appeal to hikers in particular... they have the chance to meet the inhabitants of the island, among the kindest in the world.

Odysseus, an angry man

After more than a century of quarrelling on the part of the experts, archaeologists have finally agreed to identify the modern island of Ithaca as the kingdom of Odysseus, the island "ideal for goats", as described by Homer in the 12 210 verses of his epic poem the Odyssey and from which the hero departed with reluctance to join Agamemnon and deliver Helen from the clutches of King Priam. Under siege for nine years he finally emerged as victor, thanks to the famous ruse of the Trojan Horse. But another ten years were to pass before his return: buffeted between Charybdis and Scylla; locked in epic combat with the Cyclops Polyphemus; resisting the sorceress Circe, the sirens and their evil singing; spending eight years in "sweet captivity" with the nymph, Calypso... the husband of the virtuous Penelope finally returned to discover that his throne had been usurped. Undoubtedly the reason for his name, which means, "in anger".

A deserted island

The history of the island is evident in the evolution of its population, a people with a strong maritime tradition. Continuously occupied from the Mycenaean Period (1400 BC), Ithaca had a population of several thousand until Byzantine times. Its population, decimated in the Middle Ages as a result of incessant harassment from pirates, continued to grow until it reached 14 500 in 1862, the island's commercial fleet prospering under the British Protectorate. Since then, however, emigration has been on the increase: to the Greek mainland and Romania, as well as Australia and the United States. A further exodus was brought about by the violent earthquake of 1953, which destroyed the oldest houses on the island. But this sizeable diaspora was of great significance in the development of Ithaca, since the migrants regularly send money home to their families.

The northern peninsula★

■ **Fríkes**★ — Overlooked by the ruins of two windmills, this tiny port with its clear water could be a stage set, with four or five tavernas, about 15 houses along the quayside, and nothing else — apart from the chattering of the cicadas and the olive trees carpeting the mountainside. Once the tourists have had lunch, they resume their mini-cruises, set sail for other islands and the town takes a deep breath. Apart from Kióni, Fríkes is the most pleasant place to stay on the island, although it is much hotter than Vathí (Itháki) in the high season.

Leave Fríkes by the road hugging the harbour, on the right facing the sea. On the way to Kióni are several lovely **pebble beaches**, which are visible from the road.

■ **Kióni**★★ — *4km south-east of Fríkes.* Heralded by the ruins of the ancient **windmills** which keep watch over its harbour, this delightful little port lies at the foot of three hills, its old houses built on the undulating slopes among the tender green foliage of laurel and eucalyptus trees. It is unbelievably peaceful here: during the day nothing stirs, or virtually nothing, save the yachts bobbing on the waves and, no doubt, the best taverna in town (*see "Making the most of Ithaca"*). In short, a delightful spot to stop: this is a place to discover before mass tourism takes it over.

Leave Kióni by the road that skirts the harbour, to the left facing the sea (it is not possible to go directly from Kióni to Stavrós; you have to go through Fríkes again).

■ **Stavrós** — A large, busy, country town, Stavrós is situated on a hill, at the intersection of the roads in the north of the island. There is nothing particularly charming about Stavrós, but you will find bars and tavernas where you can sit and watch the ordinary comings and goings of everyday life, far away from the chaos of the tourist resorts. In the main square, there is a squat **church** with red domes and in the square opposite, there is a **bust of Odysseus**. From the church, a road leads down towards **Pólis Bay** where a few fishing boats lie dormant, carefully moored alongside the beach of white pebbles. Pólis is supposed to have been the port of Odysseus' capital city. In fact, numerous objects dating from that period have been found in the **cave-shrine of Loizos** (*to the left of the bay; but following the signs to it is a waste of time: the roof of the cave has collapsed and it is currently closed to the public*).

Alternatively, you could have a look at the **Archaeological Museum of Pilikáta** (*1km outside the town, on the road to Fríkes; sign on the right; street parallel to the road; 9.30am-3pm; closed Monday; no charge*). It contains a small collection of figurines and bronze tripods (9C-8C BC) as well as ceramics, small statues, vases and oil lamps from the cave of Pólis and the **hill of Pilikáta** (*1km north of Stavrós*), where excavations have unearthed some important Mycenaean remains, indicating that it may correspond to the acropolis in the Odyssey.

The southern cape*

From Stavrós to Vathí*

From Stavrós, two roads lead to Vathí (Itháki), the capital of the island. Crossing the hinterland, you come across the old village of **Anogí**, famed for the beautiful **Byzantine frescoes*** (18C) in the Church of the Dormition of the Virgin.

You could also stop and take a look at the **Monastery of Panagía Katharón** (*4km further south*) (18C), where there is a splendid **view****.

The other road follows the west coast of the island, and also has splendid **views*** of the sea. It passes the village of **Ágios Ioánnis** and some charming **beaches** – absolutely deserted – particularly the beach of **Áspros Gialós***, overlooked by the ruins of a windmill (*4km south of Stavrós, as you come out of the village of Léfki, take the tarred road on the right, which emerges on a track after 2km; cover the last section on foot – a 10min walk – by the path on the right*).

The two roads join to cross the isthmus, and then plunge into a **landscape**** of astonishing beauty: large grey limestone rocks loom large against the clear blue of the sea and the bright green of the stunted vegetation.

■ **Vathí** (Itháki) – The capital of Ithaca lacks the charm of Kióni, since its houses suffered much greater damage in the 1953 earthquake. But the harbour with all its hustle and bustle, and the tavernas along the quayside make it a pleasant place to stop.

To the left of the OTE (telephone agency), the modern building with a cream façade houses the **Archaeological Museum** (*8.30am-3pm; closed Monday; no charge; photography not permitted*). Here you can see some fine pottery with geometric motifs, including pyxides (tiny round boxes), small statues and miniatures in bronze, dating mainly from the 8C-5C BC, and mostly unearthed during excavations carried out in the 1930s by British archaeologists who were searching – unsuccessfully, as it turned out – for the palace in the Odyssey.

On the left-hand side of the main square (*sign*), is the delightful **Sea and Folk Museum*** (*10am-4pm / 7pm-10pm; closed Sunday; entrance fee*), which opened in 1996. On display are reconstructions of traditional Ithaca interiors, with beautiful objects displayed according to various themes: lace from Anogí, weaving, sailors' garments, musical instruments, pottery, etc.

As you come out of the museum, have a look at the **Church of the Taxiárhes**, which contains an 18C icon attributed to **El Greco**.

West of Vathí, the cave of the nymphs, where Odysseus is supposed to have hidden the treasure confiscated by the Phaeacians, is currently closed while excavations are in progress.

■ **Paleohóra*** – *3.5km south of Vathí, via the Perahóri road (3km). In the village, take the road signposted "Upper Village". When you arrive at a new church with a colourful bell-tower, continue on foot for 50m to a church that is currently being rebuilt; from here, take the path that leads off on the right, behind the building (a 10min walk).* In the Middle Ages, Paleohóra was the most densely populated village on the island. As the capital, it was heavily fortified to protect its inhabitants from pirates. Today, all that remains are a few ruins overlooking the bay of Vathí (pretty **view***), including a church without a roof (*restoration in progress*), housing some fine Byzantine **frescoes***.

■ Four and a half kilometres south of Perahóri, lies the wild **Marathiás Plateau**, which, according to tradition, was the site of the **pig farm of Eumaeus** (where Odysseus was recognised by his faithful swineherd, before regaining his usurped throne). Although quite difficult to reach, it makes a fine destination for keen hikers.

Ithaca

Making the most of Ithaca

COMING AND GOING

By boat – Normally you would travel to Ithaca from Corfu. From the new port of Corfu, a hydrofoil makes the journey in 1hr, landing at Fríkes. There is a daily departure at 3pm; sometimes two, the times of the second are variable; ask at the port (see "Making the most of Corfu", page 364).

Leaving Ithaca: 5 ferries a day leave from Písso Aetós for Sámi (Cephalonia; 1hr crossing) and one for Vassilikí (Leucas; 2hr crossing). From Fríkes, there is a daily connection to Fiskárdo (Cephalonia, 1hr crossing) and Vassilikí (2hr45min). From Vathí, there is a daily connection to Sámi (1hr crossing) and, on the mainland, to Patras (4hr crossing; links up with the bus to Athens) and Astakós (3hr). The timetables change every year. Also, make enquiries in Fríkes, at the **Kikí Travel** agency or at the harbourmaster's office.

GETTING AROUND

By bus – There is a regular bus service to Vathí, Fríkes and Stavrós.

By taxi – On the main square of Vathí, ☎ (0674) 33 030. Around €7 from Fríkes to Stavrós, €15 from Fríkes to Vathí with luggage.

By rental vehicle – You can hire mopeds at the **Kikí Travel** agency in Fríkes and at **Rent a Bike**, in Vathí, ☎ (0674) 33 243. Cars for hire from **Ángelos Koutavás** in Vathí, ☎ (0674) 32 702.

ADDRESS BOOK

Tourist information – Given the fact that there is no tourist office on the island, the **Kikí Travel** agency ☎ (0674) 31 387 / 31 150 – the only travel agency in Fríkes – is an absolute godsend for lost tourists! Friendly welcome and a mine of information, (boat timetables, money-changing facilities, apartments, motorcycle hire, etc).

In Vathí, **Polyctor Tours**, ☎ (0674) 33 130. 8am-12midnight in high season; 9am-1pm / 5pm-8pm in winter. The official agent for Olympic Airways and Stríntzis Lines.

Banks / Currency exchange – You can change money at the travel agencies in Fríkes and Vathí. Visa cash dispenser at the **National Bank of Greece**, on the main square in Vathí. You can also change money at the **Agricultural Bank of Greece**, on the harbour in Vathí (9am-1pm).

Post office / Telephone – Post office in Vathí, on the main square 7.30am-1.30pm; closed Saturday and Sunday. Card phones by the harbours in Fríkes, Kióni and Vathí, and next to the church in Stavrós.

Medical service – Health Centre in Kióni, next to the church (its bell-tower dominates the town).

Chemist in Vathí, to the right of the post office (8.30am-2pm / 5.30am-10.30pm).

Service stations – Avin, above Fríkes, on the Stavrós road, and in Vathí, 100m to the left of the OTE telephone agency.

WHERE TO STAY

Be careful as there are very few proper hotels on the whole island: tourist facilities remain underdeveloped with no more than 300 visitors a year! You will find apartments to let (information at the two travel agencies listed above) – but these are often booked year after year by British package-tour operators – as well as rooms in private houses in the main villages (Fríkes, Vathí, Kióni and Stavrós). Although fairly expensive – there is no competition after all – they are usually inundated with customers in August and September. Booking essential in high season.

● **Vathí (Itháki)**

Between €30 and €60
Hotel Mentor, ☎ (0674) 32 433, Fax (0674) 32 293 – 40rm. ☏ 🛎 TV CC A rather old-fashioned hotel painted white and cream, 200m from the harbour in Vathí. White and pink rooms with balconies and sea views. Clean bathrooms. They also have apartments to let.

Hotel Captain Yiánnis, ☎ (0674) 33 173, Fax (0674) 32 849 – 25rm. ☏ 🍽 ✗ 🛋 ✎ A quiet hotel built in 1996, 900m from the harbour. White, bright rooms with balcony (view over the harbour), in an attractive building up on the hillside, surrounded by cypresses.

- **Fríkes**

Between €30 and €60

Hotel Nostos, 200m above the harbour, ☎ (0674) 31 644 (out of season: 31 476), Fax (0674) 31 716 – 27rm. ⚲ ✎ ✗ ⚓ This large, cream-coloured hotel with red shutters has bright, spacious rooms, all with a balcony. Bathrooms spotlessly clean, even though the hotel is not very new. Family atmosphere and very good restaurant. Nicki and Andreas, the owners, will do everything they can to help you during your stay on the island.

- **Stavrós**

A few rooms in a private house above **Petra's Taverna** (apply at the restaurant). In all cases, basic facilities at a high price.

EATING OUT

- **Kióni**

Under €15

🍴 **Restaurant Calipso**, large terrace on the harbour, ☎ (0674) 31 066. From May to October, 12noon-midnight. A gourmet restaurant not to be missed! Creator of the Ionian pâté (ingredients include three different sorts of cheese, cream, raw and smoked ham), of which you may encounter other paler imitations, this restaurant distinguishes itself for its inventive, freshly prepared, authentic cooking. Fresh fish, tasty artichoke soufflé, and a mouth-watering lamb pie (*kléftiko*), accompanied by olives, cheese and potatoes. Warm welcome.

HAVING A DRINK

Bar – Drakoulis, Vathí, ☎ (0674) 33 435. 7am-3am. On the harbour, a large white colonial-style villa with green shutters. Delightful garden shaded by palms and pine trees, very welcome when trying to escape from the scorching heat.

OTHER THINGS TO DO

Walking – Ithaca is an ideal island for walkers. You will find detailed maps marking the various routes around the island at the **Kikí Travel** agency in Fríkes.

ZACYNTHUS ★★
(ZÁKINTHOS)

Ionian Islands – District of Zacynthus – 406km² – Regional map page 348
Michelin map 980 fold 27 – Pop 35 000 – Allow 3 days

Not to be missed
Shipwreck (Navágio) Bay, with its wreck, and the crystal-clear waters of Gérakas.
Boat trip around the island.
The sunset over the cliffs of Kerí.

And remember...
Hire a two-wheeled vehicle, the ideal way to explore the island at leisure.

The most southerly of the Ionian Islands overlooks the Peloponnese coast. A choice position which, over the centuries, has attracted the attention of many a conqueror. The island's mild climate and fertile soil are equally attractive: from the *Iliessa* (wooded land) of Homer to the *"Fior di Levante"* (flower of the Levant) of the Venetians, all its conquerors have talked of a green island, carpeted with pines and olive trees, lemon trees and vines, where life is sweet. But the *arékia*, the traditional songs that you always hear in the tavernas, also bring to life its unusual physiognomy. Because Zacynthus has two facets: like a plateau that has tipped into the sea, it slopes down to the east

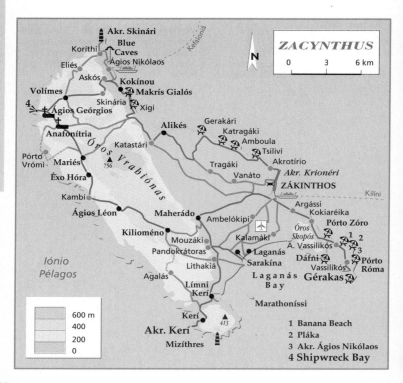

ZACYNTHUS

0   3   6 km

1 Banana Beach
2 Pláka
3 Akr. Ágios Nikólaos
4 Shipwreck Bay

in a huge agricultural plain fringed with beaches, while, in the west, the **Vrahiónas Chain** is a spectacular range of white cliffs, a veritable wall indented with creeks, caves and arches, that can only be reached by boat. In other words, two islands in one: one welcoming and serene, the other wild and rugged; a melting pot of flavours to be savoured on land and at sea...and in the local *Verdéa* wine.

The island of poets

Solomós, or the poetry of the homeland
Having established himself in Italy as an eminent man of letters, Dhionísios Solomós nevertheless took the decision to return to Zacynthus and join the struggle for Greek independence, a struggle which for him also implied the rehabilitation of the Greek language with which he had grown up. The war was also to inspire him to write his first poem, a hymn to freedom (1823), which was to become the Greek national anthem. A great figure of the Ionian School, Solomós is regarded as the father of modern Greek poetry.

When Zacynthus came under the Venetian yoke in 1489, it was the beginning of a long period of economic as well as intellectual prosperity. Fleeing from Ottoman oppression, many Cretan artists sought refuge here (1669), laying the foundations for the **Ionian School of Painting**, a blend of the Byzantine tradition and the Venetian Renaissance. The influence of Venice was also to be seen in its architecture. With streets with porticoes and bell-towers standing apart from the churches, the town of Zákinthos took on an Italian air. At the beginning of the 19C, when the island came under the British Protectorate, its reputation as a literary centre attracted poets, writers and musicians, who succeeded in fusing the Hellenic and Italian cultures. Of these, **Ugo Foscolo** (1778-1827) was to come forward as one of the leading names in Romantic Italian literature, while the Greek poet **Dhionísios Solomós** (1798-1857) was to portray Greek independence, together with the poet and indefatigable traveller **Andréas Kálvos** (1792-1867).

Zákinthos Town★

Pop 10 000. Allow half a day.

Framed by the steep hill of **Sirani**, the inspiration behind some of the verses of the poet Solomós' national anthem, and by the hill of **Bóhali**, topped by a Venetian fortress, is Zákinthos town. Its rather soulless buildings line the **Stráta Marína** (Odós C Lombárdou), overlooking the ferries which come and go in the harbour.

At first glance, with its busy, noisy seafront, the town is unprepossessing. But you don't have to go very far before you reach **Platía Dhionísios Solomós★**, a huge esplanade with palm trees which is tucked away at the north end of the town. On either side are two elegant neo-Classical buildings, framing a statue of the poet and some flower beds. After the terrible earthquake which destroyed the town in 1953, they were rebuilt exactly as they had been. One of them houses the **Byzantine Museum★** *(8.30am-2.30pm; closed Monday; entrance fee)*, which contains an interesting collection of icons and sacred paintings illustrating the post-Byzantine art of the Ionian Islands. Also of note are the wooden **iconostases★★** dating from the 17C to 19C retrieved from churches on the island destroyed in the earthquake.

At right angles to the museum, the other building houses a **library** and a very pleasant **café**, with tables spilling out onto the terrace under the portico of the façade. Nearby is the **Church of Ágios Nikólaos tou Molou★** (St Nicholas of the Mole) (16C), one of the few buildings from the Venetian town that have survived, which is notable for the paleness of its stonework and the simplicity of its architectural features (attractive **bell-tower**).

Between the two buildings, the short Leofóros Vassiléos Georgíou leads off towards the centre of the town, emerging in the hustle and bustle of **Platía Ágios Márcos★★**. An almost identical copy of how it was before the earthquake of 1953, it looks rather like a film set with its Italian façades painted in pastel shades and its perfectly aligned porticoes. At one time a popular meeting place for the local townsfolk, it has now become the favourite haunt of young people and tourists, who flock here to the bars and restaurants in the evening. To the left of the little pointed belfry of the **Roman Catholic church** stands the one belonging to the **Dhionísios Solomós Museum** (9am-2pm; no charge), where the poet lies buried, along with Andréas Kálvos.

Leading off Platía Ágios Márcos, **Odos 21 Maÿou*** is the commercial street of Zákinthos, a real hive of activity (apart from siesta time). Much of it now a pedestrian precinct, it runs the length of the town parallel to the seafront, its bars, souvenir and fashion shops housed under the shady **porticoes**.

Returning to the seafront via the side streets, you come to the other large square in Zákinthos, on the south side of the town, overlooked by the tall **bell-tower** of the **Church of Ágios Dioníssios**. Straight as a die, it is reminiscent of the bell-tower of St Mark's in Venice, keeping watch over the harbour like a lighthouse. The church, which was built in 1925, is not particularly interesting, except for the fact that it contains the relics of the patron saint of the island, kept in a **silver casket** that is the focus of attention when the locals come to worship here (long skirts and trousers required; suitable garments are available to lend to visitors).

More noteworthy perhaps are the beautiful façades of the **Church of Faneroménis*** nearby, another relic of the Venetian town (17C), which stands in the shade of a huge plane tree.

Try to get into the **Church of Kyrías ton Angélon**** (ask for the keys at the Metrópole, the large church nearby), an enchanting Venetian chapel which has remained intact. Behind its **Renaissance façade****, "Our Lady of the Angels" has a magnificent gilt wooden **iconostasis**** dating from the 17C.

To end the day, you could climb up to the **Venetian Citadel** (Kástro) (15min on foot along the shady path winding up the hillside, or along the road, follow the signs), from where there is a splendid **view**. Now the only thing protected by its defensive walls is a pine forest, lovely for a stroll in the cool shade. Or you might prefer to go for a drink on the esplanade near the church below and sit and watch as the lights gradually illuminate the town.

Skopós Point*
Leave the town and head south, passing the church of Ágios Dioníssios, via Argási.
Allow 1 day which includes time for a swim.

Beyond the hill of Sirani, the road winds its way along the side of the mountain, with fine views over the sea and a multitude of small beaches. After the beach of **Pórto Zóro**, which lies below the road (a bit too manicured), you might want to stop at **Banana Beach****. With not too many sunbeds and straw sun-shades here, it's a lovely place for a swim, in a wild setting of dunes, rocks and pine trees (small taverna) in the background.

To the south of Banana Beach lies **Pláka***, a pretty beach which extends as far as the rocks of **Cape Ágios Nikólaos**. On the other side of the promontory, an old white chapel overlooks the **beach** of the same name, which can get very crowded, where there is a water sports centre with facilities for jet-skiing, windsurfing, and other activities.

You are likely to find it more relaxing at **Pórto Róma*** (16km from Zákinthos, on the left as you arrive in Vassilikós), a delightful creek lined with low-lying cliffs, where there is a taverna with tables under straw awnings, and a wonderful **view***.

Beyond Pórto Róma, Skopós Point ends in a narrow rocky ridge which disappears into the sea. On the west coast, it shelters the magnificent **beach of Gérakas*****, a long crescent of sand only part of which has been taken over by rows of sunbeds (only in the middle, and one end is reserved for nudists). After a swim in this calm, limpid water, linger awhile to watch the superb orange glow of the **sunset** behind the curious ridge of tufa. This is also the time to explore the **cirque*** at the western end of the beach (to the left), a strange outcrop of eroded tufa emerging from the sand, dotted with prickly bushes.

Finally, further south, a rough track leads down from the main road to the **beach of Dáfni***, another wild site part of which is protected for the **loggerhead turtles** which come to lay their eggs here.

Heading south: around Laganás Bay**

*About 25km one way. Leave the town by the Maherádo / Kilioméno road
(ignore the first road on the left leading to the airport).
Allow 1 day which includes time for a swim.*

To the south-east of the island lies the huge Bay of Laganás, framed to the west and east by the two **Skopós Points** *(both promontories have the same name!)*. Now a marine national park, its waters have become a sanctuary for the loggerhead turtle, dolphins and the occasional (now very rare) **Monk seal**.

From Zákinthos, the road heads off inland across a vast plateau carpeted with olive trees and vines, with the bluish ridge of the Vrahiónas Mountains (756m) in the distance.

■ Nestling in a small valley below the road, the village of **Maherádo** *(11km)* attracts mainly Greek tourists, who come here to worship in front of the miraculous icon in the **Church of Agía Mavra**** (1873). The church contains a huge gilt wooden iconostasis covered with frescoes – an almost Baroque profusion of gold and other colours. Next to it stands an impressive **bell-tower*** of earlier construction, the bells of which are supposed to be the most tuneful in the whole country (you can hear them being rung during the annual festival of the church, on May 3). Also worth a look is the **church of Ipapándi*** ("of the Purification"), which was devastated by the earthquake. Perched on a knoll just outside the town *(slightly to the left after Agía Mavra)*, it also has a remarkable bell-tower with two broad volutes.

Return to the town centre, go past the apse of Agía Mavra and the car park to join the Lithakiá road, which heads south. At the village of Pandokrátoras (2.5km), take the little road on the left leading down towards the coast.

■ Overlooking a sea of olive and fruit trees, the curious façade of the large **House of Sarakína*** looms up in the middle of nowhere. The only Venetian villa still standing (18C), there is something very romantic about this noble residence, the blue of the sky framed by each window.

From here, there is no point in continuing in the direction of the sea *(except to reach the Laganás campsite)*: the seaside resort of **Laganás** is a place to avoid at all costs. You can only just make out the colour of the sand between the rows and rows of sun-shades and deckchairs, lined up in front of a series of equally regimented hotels, bars, shops and restaurants, all adapted to suit the tastes of the clientele, who come mainly from the UK.

Back on the main road, drive through Lithakiá (2km) and continue south for about 5.5km before turning left down a narrow road that leads down between the olive trees to the harbour of Límni Kerí (1km).

■ A tiny fishing port stranded at the tip of the south coast, **Límni Kerí*** *(6km)* has nothing much to offer except peace and quiet and the temptation to linger for a day or two. Protected by the **island of Marathoníssi***, a large rocky outcrop edged with a strip of white sand, its few houses are clustered around a quiet little harbour full of fishing boats and pleasure craft. There are boat trips along the coastline where the turtles can sometimes be seen, and to the little island which has a beach.

■ At the end of the day, why not head for the hills and the south-west tip of the island taking in the sleepy village of **Kerí***. In the little square, bedecked with flowers, is a *kafenío* with its three tables out on the terrace, a grocery store with a few old ladies chatting outside, and a cluster of old stone houses clinging to the mountainside which stretches down to the bottom of a green valley where there is a dear little **church**.

Zacynthus

The cliffs and beach of magical Shipwreck Bay, Zacynthus

From the village, a narrow road leads along to **Cape Kerí***, a majestic rocky promontory covered with a velvety layer of purple heather, a popular place to watch the **sunset** against the backdrop of the high cliffs of the west coast. Not far away, on the south coast, you can see the impressive "twin" reefs (the meaning of their name in Greek) of the **Mizíthres****, two blades of white stone bordering the cliff, buffeted by the wind and the waves.

A tour around the north of the island**
Leave the town heading north and follow the coast, passing Akrotírio and Cape Krionéri. Allow 1 day which includes time for swimming.

In the north of Zacynthus the great coastal plain is scattered with orchards and salt marshes of grey water. More recently, the land has been colonised by the hotels and resorts which are springing up all over the place. There are countless sandy beaches here, but they are lined with sunbeds and packed in summer .

■ If you drive out beyond **Alikés** *(16.5 km)* and **Katastári** you will find that the terrain is wilder. The coast becomes rockier, with little bays here and there, and the beaches such as **Makrís Gialós*** *(10km from Katastári)*, a lovely beach framed by white rocks, are a mixture of sand and shingle.

■ Soon afterwards, you glimpse the boats of **Kokínou**, a tiny harbour tucked away under a small rocky promontory. A delightful taverna overlooks the blue water, where boats set off, bound for the famous **Blue Caves**** (Galázia Spiliá) *(90min round trip)*. This is a good opportunity to take a boat trip to the northern tip of the island, where there is a remarkable series of arches gouged out of the cliff by the action of the waves. Due to the refraction of the light, the sea turns an astonishing shade of almost phosphorescent turquoise, as if illuminated from below.
By taking one of the boats from Kokínou, you will avoid the long, boring road leading to **Ágios Nikólaos** *(4.5km from Kokínou)*, the port where the ferries set sail for Cephalonia.

V. Voutsas/ON LOCATION

Beyond Ágios Nikólaos, the road loses height as it heads north up the west side of the island, leaving behind **Cape Skinári**★ which overlooks the Blue Caves. The view out to sea from the narrow road that leads to the Cape from the hamlet of **Koríthi** *(on the right; 3km)* is worth the detour. It passes through dry, desolate landscape only to emerge, all of a sudden, on a magnificent **panorama**★★ of Cephalonia.

From Kokínou, you can cut through Askós and Skinária, before Ágios Nikólaos, to avoid the north of the island and a rather tedious section of road.

■ Your arrival at the first (and highest) village of the highlands, **Volímes**★ *(11km from Kokínou)*, the "village in the middle" will be heralded by an array of **carpets** – made locally – spread out over the stone walls beside the road. Against a backdrop of broad, barren hills, its little whitewashed houses line the main street, revealing the occasional shady courtyard brimming with flowers. A small street leads down to the right of the village to the little church of **Agía Paraskeví**★★, situated lower down. Currently under restoration, it is a fine example of 17C Venetian architecture.

■ Continue towards the west coast. There is a road on the right *(after 2.4km)* which opens out onto a breathtaking **view**★★★ over the famous Bay of Ágios Geórgios – a favourite subject of many of the postcards of the island – which has now been renamed **Shipwreck Bay**★★★ (Navágio) (*"Shipwreck" sign*). It is, indeed, a wonderful sight: at the foot of the vertical cliff-face the little bay is lapped by water of a milky turquoise blue. And, washed up on the white sand is the rusty wreck of a ship, the *Panayótis*, which came aground in the 1980s during a violent storm. A small platform has been erected for looking down on the site, but the more adventurous *(proper footwear recommended)* can walk along the edge of the **cliff**★★★ to the narrow promontory where, sitting in the heather and the prickly vegetation, you can take in the whole bay. There is only one way to reach this idyllic spot: by boat. In good weather you can board one of the boats at **Pórto Vrómi**, 55km to the south *(see also "Making the most of Zacynthus")*.

■ Back on the main road, just after the fork leading to the viewpoint, is the charming **Monastery of Ágios Geórgios**★★. Concealed behind a pine wood, it stands in splendid isolation. A serene atmosphere pervades the place, with its impressive **donjon** and courtyard flooded with light, the monks' cells ranged along the sides. There is a pretty **porch**★ in front of the church, a small covered vestibule surrounded by a stone bench.

■ The more famous **Monastery of Anafonítria**★ *(3.5km; in theory 8am-1pm, but, out of season, while there are people still around, it is usually open)* proves, paradoxically, to be rather disappointing: currently undergoing restoration, its walls and frescoes are all masked by scaffolding. Beside it stands a massive **medieval tower**★ which has been converted into a bell-tower. Anafonítria is the oldest monastery on the island. This is where, in 1622, the patron saint of Zacynthus, St Denis (Ágios Dionýsios) died. You can still see his **cell** (uninteresting).

■ Further on, the road passes through several villages: **Mariés**★ *(3km)* with its pretty stone houses, **Éxo Hóra** and **Ágios Léon**, tucked away in the rolling hills surrounded by olive trees and pines, and resounding to the sound of the crickets.

■ Poking through the greenery in the valley below are the red roofs of **Kilioméno** *(7km from Ágios Léon)*. Its large **church** seems to have survived better than the others on the island, and it retains its imposing, delicately carved **bell-tower**★★. The village also has the distinction of having the oldest house on Zacynthus *(the last house at the bottom of the village)*, which dates from 1630. Now a taverna of rustic charm, the **Alitzérinoi** is a good place to stop for a glass of Verdéa.

Zacynthus

COMING AND GOING

See also page 300 "Making the most of the northern coast of the Peloponnese".

By boat – From Kilíni, on the mainland, 1 ferry every hour in summer, 5 a day in winter (1hr crossing). From Cephalonia: 2 ferries daily (1hr15min crossing), leaving from Pessáda, south of Argostóli. You disembark at Ágios Nikólaos, on the northern tip of Zacynthus. The only way to reach the capital is by taxi, which is quite expensive (€35). Otherwise you can take advantage of a tour coach – a fairly common solution – which will drop you off wherever you wish; this will cost you half the taxi fare. Ask at the bar on the ferry during the crossing.

By air – From Athens to Zacynthus: 1 flight daily in each direction, in the morning, and on certain days before 18 June in the evening (45min to 55min flight). Approximately €50. *Zacynthus Airport*, 2km south of Zákinthos, by the road to Lithakiá, ☎ (0695) 23 970 / 23 971. Bus connections.

GETTING AROUND

By bus – In Zákinthos, the main bus station is on the street parallel to the seafront, on the south side of town, in a small shack behind some wasteland. However, it has a snack-bar, open every day. The local bus company is *KTEL*, ☎ (0695) 42 656 / 22 255.

By taxi – *Radio Taxi*, ☎ (0695) 48 400

By two-wheeler – Given that the island is fairly small and the road network in a good condition, a two-wheeler is ideal.

Vehicle hire – You will find rental agencies wherever you go, in Zákinthos (on the quays and in Leofóros Vassiléos Georgíou) and in all the tourist resorts on the island. It's cheap to hire a scooter (less than €38 a week, and prices are negotiable out of season). Avoid Sakis, in Zákinthos, despite its good location in Leofóros Vassiléos Georgíou (opposite the OTE telephone agency): their vehicles are poorly maintained and verge on the dangerous.

Avis, just at the beginning of the commercial thoroughfare Odós 21 Maýou, towards Platía Ágios Márcos, on the right. *Europcar*, on the seafront, to the north of town. *Hertz*, is slightly further

away, opposite the boats which run trips around the island.

ADDRESS BOOK

A number of services are located in Leofóros Vassiléos Georgíou and the streets around Platía Ágios Márcos: scooter hire, banks, as well as restaurants and bars.

Tourist information – There is no tourist office as such, but the travel agencies will supply all the information you need, for example, *Pilot J*, roughly midway along the street running along the seafront (Stráta Marína). Open daily. Money-changing facilities and vehicle hire, cruises, transport, etc. They also sell phone cards with payment by credit card. Another office, at the south end of the harbour, in a small building advertised by a large sign, provides the same services.

Airlines – *Olympic Airways*, Odós 21 Maýou, near the town hall.

Tourist police – On the seafront, ☎ (0695) 27 367. In the absence of any tourist office, this is where you are supposed to obtain information. However, the officers are not very friendly, speak virtually no English and are not very well-informed.

Harbour police – ☎ (0695) 28 117 / 28 118.

Banks / Currency exchange – Platía Ágios Márcos and on the seafront, many of the banks change money and have cash dispensers.

Post office – In Odós Tertseti, one of the streets parallel to Odós 21 Maýou, at the corner of the narrow street that ends in a flight of steps. 7.30am-8pm; closed at weekends. Money-changing facilities.

Telephone – *OTE*, at the beginning of Platía Ágios Márcos, on the right. There are two card phones in front. You can also change money here.

Internet – *Top's Internet Café*, Odós Klavdianoú 34. Behind a strange "Chinese-style" façade that looks like a film set. Above the large, busy billiard room of a bar, with a huge video screen, you will find a quiet room with several computers. Daily, 9.30am-1am.

Medical service – If you suffer from toothache, Zákinthos is the place for you: the town is simply brimming with dental surgeries! Perhaps because there are so many confectioners...

Pharmacy right next door to the town hall, on Odós 21 Maýou.

Hospital, on the hill overlooking the town, ☎ (0695) 42 514 / 515 and 49 111. **Emergencies**, ☎ (0695) 23 166.

International newspapers – There are numerous bookshops in Odós 21 Maýou, on the side of Platía Ágios Márcos.

WHERE TO STAY

Campsites (around €13.50)

Paradise, in Gerakári, on the east coast, 11km north of Zákinthos, ☎ (0695) 61 888. Well situated near the sandy beach of Psarou. ✗ ↯ Launderette, small supermarket, barbecues available, electricity points at each plot. A very well-maintained, quiet, stylish campsite with lots of shade. Warm welcome.

Zante, on the beaches of Katragáki-Amboula, on the east coast, 10min north of Zákinthos, ☎ (0695) 61 710, Fax (0695) 63 030. ✗ ↯ Split into two parts by a valley leading down to the sea, the terrain is more sheltered on one side than the other, the area below the reception being less attractive. New washing block, small supermarket, and a pleasant coffee-bar on the beach. Open from May to October. Several buses per day.

Laganás, Ágios Sostis (just outside Laganás), 8km south-west of Zákinthos via the Lithakiá road, ☎ (0695) 51 585 / 51 708 / 52 285, Fax (0695) 52 284 – 124 pitches. ✗ ↯ A huge campsite set among olive trees, but not very well ventilated (it gets very hot beneath the foliage). It doesn't overlook the sea but has a large swimming pool. Bar, small supermarket, first-aid centre. Clean, well-maintained washing facilities. Slightly more expensive than other campsites.

• **Zákinthos**

All the places we recommend are located in the northern part of town, around Platía Ágios Márcos.

Between €30 and €43

Ⓐ **Geórgios Zourídis**, Odós L Karrer, just opposite the delightful little church of Kyrías ton Angélon, ☎ and Fax (0695) 44 691 – 14rm. ⁿ ⊼ ℘ TV Advertised by a large sign saying "Rooms to let", painted on the façade. To ensure that his guests feel at home, Geórgios has organised everything himself – with good

taste and great flair. On the ground floor, there is a very pleasant split-level lounge, with a mezzanine floor, complete with sofas, armchairs, pedestal tables and bookcases, a mixture of antique and modern furniture. American food is served at meals and at breakfast. On the first floor, the spacious, well-lit rooms are also comfortable (2 have AC). In short, very good value for money. Open all year.

Between €40 and €60

Hotel Alba, Odós L Ziva 38, at the corner of Odós Kapodistríou, ☎ (0695) 26 641 / 642, Fax (0695) 26 642 – 15rm. ⁿ ▤ ℘ TV Behind the porticoes of a rather attractive yellow and white façade, is a charming little hallway where breakfast is served (included). However, the rooms are small and disappointing: despite being nicely furnished, the bathrooms are antiquated and, indeed, not very clean. Open all year.

Between €40 and €63

Strada Marina, on the seafront, ☎ (0695) 42 761-2-3 / 45 501-2-3, Fax (0695) 28 733 – 122rm. ⁿ ▤ ℘ TV ✗ ⌂ ↯ CC Undoubtedly the ugliest building on the seafront. A very large hotel with a superb rooftop terrace with (small) swimming pool and bar-restaurant. The rooms, painted in bright colours, are spacious and comfortable, although some could do with a facelift. The rooms overlooking the harbour have a balcony-terrace. Good value, but go out for breakfast (expensive).

Between €51 and €75

Hotel Diana, Ágios Márcos, right next to the Roman Catholic church, ☎ (0695) 28 547 / 28 604, Fax (0695) 45 047 – 48rm. ⁿ ▤ ℘ TV CC Very well situated, but can be rather noisy (double-glazing). A well-run hotel, with a very friendly welcome. Rooms recently renovated, although the decor is rather gloomy. Large buffet breakfast. 20 % cheaper in winter.

Ⓐ **Hotel Biztaro**, in the north of town, Odós Dionissíou Róma 46, on the corner of Odós L Karrer (it has two entrances: one giving onto the street, the other facing the sea), ☎ (0695) 23 644 / 44 065, Fax (0695) 45 506 – 40rm. ⁿ ▤ ⊼ ℘ TV A very comfortable, well-run hotel, with friendly staff. Pleasant, spacious rooms, with decent bathrooms. The rooms with a sea view have a large balcony, mosquito screens and a mini-bar. Buffet breakfast (included), which you can have on the small terrace looking down over the garden. Open all year. Note that they do not accept credit cards (but intend to shortly). Good value for its category.

Hotel Reparo, Odós Dionissíou Róma, on the corner of Odós Voúltsou, on the north side of town, ☎ (0695) 23 578, Fax (0695) 45 617 – 14rm. ☜ 🖼 🖉 TV CC A hotel with a good reputation, and fine brick and roughcast façade. The rooms are small but comfortable (rather gloomy decor), with pretty balconies overlooking the sea. Mosquito screens. Expensive in high season, 50% less in winter. Breakfast extra.

• Vassilikós-Ágios Nikólaos

A stone's throw from Ágios Nikólaos beach. A large area of the village, consisting of apartments to let and tavernas, seems to belong to the same family, who have set themselves the task of creating a seaside resort of charm. For the time being, they are succeeding, apart from the regimented Pláka beach, which is mainly of interest to tour operators.

Between €30 and €45

Christina's Apartments, not far from the edge of the village, on the left, ☎ (0695) 35 247 – 6rm and 4 studios. ☜ A charming place: a small, attractively decorated building containing some very comfortable imaginatively furnished apartments. Well-equipped kitchen. They accept travellers' cheques.

Virginia, next door to the previous establishment, ☎ (0695) 35 315 / 35 224 and 35 066 – 10rm. ☜ 🍴 ✗ Named after the owner, a jolly Greek lady who speaks English and German. Standard size rooms with 2 or 4 beds, lacking in character. Her husband runs the restaurant on Pláka beach, 5 minutes' walk away, where you can have breakfast (or go to Amos' place; see below). They accept travellers' cheques. Open from May to October.

• Límni Kerí

Between €21 and €45

Seaside, on the harbour, right next to the Rock Café (where you can have breakfast), ☎ and Fax (0695) 43 297, mobile 093 72 50 158, and in Athens (winter): (01) 80 53 384 – 4 apartments for 3 to 5 people and 4 studios for 2. ☜ 🖉 This is a charming place. Olympia,

who is a painter (and speaks English) will give you a warm welcome. She has put her heart and her ideas into furnishing the apartments with taste and comfort in mind. Spacious, spotless and very well thought-out, occupying the whole width of the building, they all have a pleasant terrace. All at an unbeatable price, and even more so in winter.

Villa Fínikes ("Phœnix"), set back from the harbour, a little way up the narrow road leading to Kerí village, ☎ (0695) 49 175 / ☎ and Fax (01) 61 26 513, mobile 093 243 1275 – 10 apartments, 5 of which accommodate 4 people. A real haven of peace: the studios are set in a well-tended garden planted with olive trees. Spacious, well-equipped and very quiet, all with a terrace.

EATING OUT

• Zákinthos

As well as Platía Ágios Márcos, you will find other tavernas near the Church of Ágios Dionýsios, south of the harbour, their terraces in a lovely shady square. Slightly less attractive than Platía Ágios Márcos, but the food is equally good. On Platía Ágios Márcos, avoid The Corner, where the service isn't very good, and The Place, which is awful and too pushy.

Under €11

Arékia, on the north side of town, a small taverna at the roadside, the terrace of which resembles a canteen and is on the other side of the road, overlooking the sea. Protected by bamboo screens, the place is popular with locals and very rarely frequented by tourists. Seated on rather basic benches covered with old fabric, you are served good, simple Greek food, and in the background talented locals have fun singing the "arékia", traditional local ballads – under the stars. Not to be missed.

Around €12

Venetziana, Platía Ágios Márcos. Taste their lamb "kléftiko", cooked in paper with tomatoes and potatoes. The service is friendly and professional, the setting pleasant.

• Límni Kerí

Around €12

To Pósto, just as you enter the village, in the woods. You dine under the trees, in a lovely garden (take precautions against mosquitoes). À la carte menu: tasty traditional dishes from *Zacynthus* and the rest of Greece, cooked with loving care by a young chef who loves his island. Only open in the evening.

• **Kilioméno**

Around €9

Alitzerinoú, at the bottom of the village. The oldest house on the island is now a taverna. Rustic setting, serves simple, very good traditional food, washed down with Verdéa wine. Only open at lunchtime.

• **Vassilikós-Ágios Nikólaos**

Around €12

🍹 **Amos**, on the beach of Ágios Nikólaos, ☎ (0695) 35 000. A fashionable bar under a huge straw canopy, a pleasant place for a drink or lunch, with an excellent selection of Greek and international music, or sometimes jazz. Good food. Prices slightly higher than other places. It caters for people on the beach, so closes in the evening.

HAVING A DRINK

Bars – In Zákinthos, in Platía Ágios Márcos and at the beginning of Odós 21 Maýou there are some very pleasant bars with designer decor. The place to sip iced coffee and listen to music until late into the night.

🍹 **Amos**, in Vassilikós, on the beach of Ágios Nikólaos. See above.

🍹 **Rock Café**, in Límni Kerí, on the harbour, ☎ (0695) 43 226. Right next to the house called Seaside (see "Where to stay"). A modern, stylish building in stone and wood, beautifully furnished. Complete with terrace – great for an iced coffee, an ouzo or fresh orange juice (or breakfast). Good local and international music.

Discos – **Logós Café Bar**, on the Vassilikós-Ágios Nikólaos road, on the left, set deep among the pines. Open every evening from 10pm.

OTHER THINGS TO DO

Boat trips

From Límni Kerí, boats run tours to the surrounding caves (2hr, leaving every hour from 9am to 6pm; €9 per person) and the island of Marathoníssi. Ask for the captain at the harbour (☎ mobile 0932 126403).

Dolphin agency, ☎ (0695) 22 430, Fax (0695) 27 589, organises all sorts of activities: boat trips, trips in 4x4 vehicles, photo-safaris, Greek language and cookery courses, and even hires out motorboats for 2 to 8 people.

Trip around the island – A must. In Zákinthos Town, choose one of the smaller boats, such as the **Dias**, made of wood and not too large (opposite the Pilot J office). The boat follows the east coast north via Cape Skinári, site of the **Blue Caves**, then sails beneath the magnificent cliffs of the west coast. Stops at some of the beaches tucked away in the cliff-face, including the one on **Shipwreck Bay**.

Trip to Shipwreck Bay – Best undertaken in calm weather in one of the little boats leaving from **Pórto Vrómi** (5.5km away from the bay) or **Límni Kerí**, or even **Kokínou** (see below). In this way, you should be able to avoid the "rush hour" of the larger boats from Zákinthos.

Trip to the Blue Caves – On the east coast, north of Zákinthos, the tiny harbour of **Kokínou** is a good point of departure (1hr trip €7.50).

Diving

One centre at Límni Kerí, **Turtle Beach Diving Center**, ☎ (0695) 48 768. To watch loggerhead turtles underwater. Caters for all levels of expertise.

Outdoor pursuits

Water Sport Center on the beach at Ágios Nikólaos. Surfboards for hire at Límni Kerí.

Vassilikós Horse Riding, on the Pórto Róma road, after Ágios Nikólaos (south), ☎ (0695) 35 345 / 35 106, mobile 0937 318131.

SHOPPING GUIDE

In Zákinthos town, in the main street (Odós 21 Maýou), you will find plenty of shops selling gastronomic delicacies, souvenirs, etc.

Local delicacies – On Odós 21 Maýou, foodies will find their heart's desire here: **Zákinthos mandoláto** (soft nougat), crystallised fruits, and all sorts of cakes and biscuits. Wine enthusiasts might want to look out for a bottle of **Verdéa**, one of the local wines.

Ottoman atmosphere: in the streets of Xánthi

MACEDONIA
AND THRACE

At the gates of the Balkans and Turkey, a lesser known Greece, where vast plains alternate with jagged peaks, lies waiting to be explored. Facing both the Balkans and the Aegean Sea, the landscape of the north of Greece is full of contrasts – and therein lies the secret of the region's charm. The land of legend, Macedonia still resounds from the exploits of King Philip II of Macedonia and Alexander the Great. The cradle of Greek civilisation, it was also one of the first centres of Christianity in Europe, and the region contains some of the most important ancient sites in the country including **Vergína**, **Dion**, **Fílipi** (Philippi), as well as the Byzantine jewels of Thessaloníki and impenetrable Mt Athos. Macedonia is the largest province in Greece (34 203km^2), with a population of 2.5 million, including the second-largest town in the country, **Thessaloníki**, a dynamic port backing onto the vast Axiós plain. To the west, **Édessa**, **Véria** and Náoussa lie in the heart of a fertile region carpeted with orchards, vines and fields of cereal crops. Further west still, the mountains provide the backdrop for the superb **Lakes of Prespa** and **Kastoriá**, while, at the other end of the province, mythical **Mt Olympus** rises to a height of 2 917m, watching over the shores of the Aegean and the three-pronged Chalcidice Peninsula.

Beyond the Pangaíon Massif, another world unfolds, where minarets evoke the Greece of Ottoman times. Bordering Turkey, Thrace (8 578km^2) forms the north-eastern corner of Greece. In contrast to the Rhodope Mountains which extend along the Bulgarian border, the shore is flanked by a long fertile plain. The refuge of a wide variety of wildlife (fox, wolf, wild boar, bear), forest still covers almost 30 % of this area, while the rest of the region (with a population of 345 000) is given over to farmland dominated by wheat, maize and livestock farming.

Land of conquerors, land of desires

The legend of Macedonia does not really begin until the 5C BC, with its first great sovereign, **Alexander I Philhellene**, who extended its territory and opened up Macedonia to Greek sympathies by participating in the Olympic Games (496 BC). But it was the accession to the throne (in 360 BC) of **Philip II**, who went on to conquer the whole of Greece, that heralded the dawning of Macedonia, while his son **Alexander the Great** was to go even further by suppressing the Persian Empire, and, in so doing, changed the face of the world (*see also page 22*).

However, Alexander's premature death in 323 BC ushered in a dark age. But it was the arrival of the Romans in the Aegean Sea that tolled the death knell of the kingdom, as Macedonia and Thrace came under the protection of Rome (168 BC). Although the north of Greece remained Greek, the arrival of the colonists and the building of the **Via Egnatia** gave it a new lease of life: as Rome gave way to Byzantium, the region's strategic importance was underpinned by its position at the meeting-point of key land routes, and it soon established itself as one of the first places in Europe to welcome **Christianity**. In the early 4C, the Emperor Galerius decided to transfer his capital to Thessaloníki, which was to become the second-

largest city in the Empire, and the founding of Constantinople (323) moved the centre of gravity of the Greek world to the north of the Aegean.

But this proximity meant that Macedonia too shared in the threat that hung over the great city; even before Constantinople fell to the **Turks** (in 1453), they had taken possession of Thessaloníki (in 1430). While Thrace and Macedonia enjoyed a large amount of autonomy, certain sections of the population adopted **Islam**.

The arrival of the **Jews** who had been expelled from Spain at the end of the 15C brought a new layer to this complex ethnic edifice.

During the second half of the 19C, Macedonia became the main bone of contention between Greeks, Turks and Bulgars, and the **First Balkan War** (1912) set nearly all the nations of the region against the dying Ottoman Empire. As one of the main beneficiaries of the conflict, Greece obtained Thessaloníki and, at the end of the First World War, recovered western Thrace.

The 1990s were to prove years of both a slackening and a renewal of tension for Macedonia in its proximity to a Yugoslavia at war: when the **war in Kosovo** (1999) broke out, the hostile reaction of Greek Macedonians to the movement through the area of the multinational peace force (KFOR) was a reminder that Greece, although allied to the Western democracies, was closely linked to Serbia.

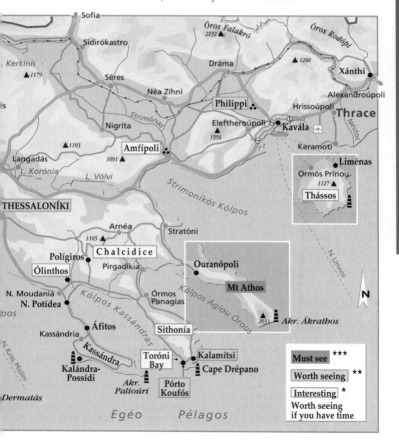

MT OLYMPUS ★★★
DION ★★ (Dío)

Province of Macedonia – District of Piería – 82km from Thessaloníki
Regional map page 412 – Michelin map 980 fold 17

Not to be missed
The site of Dion, particularly the Villa of Dionysus, the Sanctuary
of Isis and the museum.
The ascent of Mt Olympus.

And remember...
If possible, tackle the ascent in July to avoid the rains.

From its beaches of fine sand to the majestic mountains of the gods, the region of Mt Olympus offers a remarkable microcosm of Greece, complete with the ancient ruins of the city of Dion. Although most tourists make a beeline for the resorts on the coast, apparently indifferent to the mythical Greek Pantheon, every year a growing number of walkers set off to conquer the highest peak in the land, **Mt Mítikas**, 2 917m, in search of wildlife, beautiful views... and possibly a taste of eternity as they reach out to the gods. Equally, classical architecture enthusiasts will be just as happy strolling through the marble streets of peaceful Dion, huddled at the foot of the celestial home of Zeus.

Dion, the city of Zeus

The entrance to the site (admission charge) is located in open countryside
to the south of the village of Dion.
Daily, 8am-7pm. Allow 3hr. Cafeteria.

The very name Dion, deriving from *Dios* (Zeus in the genitive), expresses the glorious patronage of the town, which made its entrance into the history books during the reign of **Archelaus**. At the end of the 5C BC, this great king established a festival which, every year, attracted the best athletes and actors of the Greek world for a period of nine days. More than a town, Dion thus became a place of pilgrimage, which was to remain famous throughout Antiquity. The Macedonian kings celebrated their victories here, or came to seek the protection of the gods, as did **Alexander the Great** just before his Asian campaign. Wiped out by the Aetolians under Philip V, Dion was rapidly rebuilt. Then followed the arrival of the Roman consul Philippus, who spared it from pillage (169 BC), marking the beginning of a long period of prosperity. This lasted until the 4C AD, when the Ostrogoths sacked the town, sounding its death knell. Excavations began in 1928, but were not organised systematically until the 1970s. Digging is still in progress.

Among the ruins of the city

The extensive remains lying in the shadow of Mt Olympus continue to evoke the glory of this small city honoured by all the great kings of Macedonia. From the entrance to the site, a path leads to the **ramparts of Kassándra** (4C BC): rebuilt several times, nowadays they protect only a field of ruins.

Once inside the walls, on the left, the large **Roman baths** (about 200 AD) are preceded by a row of **shops**. Enthusiastic about the benefits of bathing and the leisure pursuits which accompanied it, the Macedonians happily devoted whole days to this activity, relaxing or practising some kind of sport, conversing or even praying. The baths, recognisable by the squat **brick piers** which are part of the hypocaust system, were paved in marble, while the other rooms were decorated with rich **mosaics**.

Next to the baths, the little **odeon**, used for concerts and public le[...] ably also used for meetings of the city's administrative council. Th[...] the foundations of a **paleo-Christian basilica** (4C) where there a[...] **mosaic floors**.

Walking back towards the main road, you will come across the[...] **of Euboulos**, which also has fine **mosaic** floors. At the inters[...] on the right, look out for the wall covered with **bas-reliefs,** with bus[...] with shields (4C BC).

But the main attraction of Dion is undoubtedly the luxurious **Villa of Dionysus★** *(when you reach the main road, turn down the path on the left)*, a large complex including several apartments, shops, a banqueting hall, a temple, several *atria*, a library and baths. Built around 200 AD, it was evidently destroyed by an earthquake, but you can still make out the ground plan from what remains of the walls. The villa contained several **statues**, but the most important discovery was the magnificent **mosaic floor★★★** of the banqueting hall: it depicts Dionysus emerging from the waves, riding a chariot pulled by two panthers and two centaurs. Further enhancing the composition are six panels depicting masks, including an unusual satyr.

Gods and games

Outside the walls, further along the main road, stand the ruins of the **Temple of Demeter**, the earliest known sanctuary in Macedonia, which was in use from the 6C BC until the 4C AD. When the sowing season arrived, important nocturnal festivals were held here in honour of the goddess of agriculture and her daughter Persephone.

Now flooded, the **Sanctuary of Isis★** has a rather surreal atmosphere with its columns and altars protruding from the water like reeds of stone. Originally dedicated to Artemis, the goddess of fertility, it was rebuilt under the Severian Emperors (2C AD) to serve the cult of Isis, her Egyptian counterpart, before being destroyed by an earthquake (4C). The site will have to be properly drained before it can be excavated.

A processional way leads first of all to the **Sanctuary of Isis Lochia**, preceded by an altar. Its façade has an elegant colonnade (only the bases of the columns remain), while two secondary temples stand on either side, one dedicated to **Eros** *(on the left)*, the other to **Aphrodite** *(on the right)*, where you can see a copy of the original **statue**, now housed in the museum.

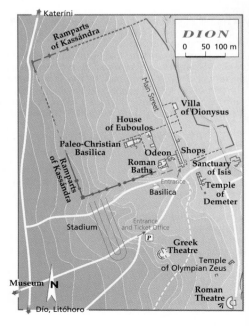

...n sanctuary, standing further forward than the others, *(on the left)*, conceals ...pring placed under the protection of **Isis Tyche**, the goddess of fortune. When ...tatue of the goddess was found it was still standing on its pedestal.

...urn to the Temple of Demeter and continue the tour, walking south.

At the side of the paved way lie the ruins of the **Temple of Olympian Zeus** *(excavations in progress)*, where Alexander the Great paid homage to the god prior to setting off to conquer Asia. Further on, on the edge of a clump of trees, is the little **Roman theatre** (2C AD), currently being restored, which has a beautiful **view★★** of Mt Olympus.

Finally, before you leave the site, have a look at the **Greek theatre** *(on the way back towards the car park)*, of which only one row of stone seating remains (the wooden seating has been added for the Festival of Mt Olympus). According to ancient texts, the spirits of the underworld – Hades – came to the surface by means of "Charon's ladder", an underground passage leading from the stage to the orchestra.

Dion Museum★

In the village. Opening times vary throughout the year: from April to October: open from Tuesday to Sunday 8am-7pm and on Monday, 12.30pm-5pm. From November to March: Tuesday to Saturday 8am-5pm, Sunday 8am-3pm, Monday 12.30pm-5pm. Entrance fee. Allow 1hr.

Displayed on the **ground floor**, are all the treasures from the various sanctuaries and public buildings of the ancient city. Of particular interest are the large baths which contained a rare series of statues depicting the **six children of Asklepios★** (Aesculapius). The statue of Isis stood in the sanctuary dedicated to the goddess, along with the strange plinth featuring a portrait of Cassander – a slab engraved with footprints dedicated to Aphrodite. Finds from the Temple of Demeter include some marble heads of the goddess and of Aphrodite, as well as terracotta figurines, jewellery and a sacred glass vase. Numerous artefacts were found in other sanctuaries on the site – statues of **Hygeia★★**, **Nemesis** and **Medea** – and in the necropolises of Dion, where a stele dating from the 5C BC with a sensitive rendering of a **mother and child★★★** was unearthed.

Two other rooms cover the Early-Christian Period. But devote more time to the **first floor**, where there are **bronzes**, **funerary steles**, **statues** of philosophers and **pottery**, and a very rare bronze **hydraulic organ★★★** dating from the 1C BC.

The tour of the museum ends with the **basement**, which is devoted to items from daily life (coins, amphorae, furniture) and techniques used in sculpture and mosaics, the latter illustrated by some remarkable **Roman mosaics**.

Mt Olympus, the dwelling place of the gods
(Óros Ólimbos)

South of Kateríni, a series of resorts punctuates the coastline as far as **Platamónas** (35km) – the largest of them – which lies in the shadow of a massive **Crusader castle★** (1204).

Dominated by the majestic silhouette of Mt Olympus, the region reveals its charm as you ascend the Enipéas Gorge *(see below)*. Straddling Macedonia and Thessaly, the Olympus massif has no less than nine peaks over 2 600m. Although the lions which populated the forests in Antiquity disappeared a long time ago, the region is still an exceptional natural environment – now protected – which will delight walkers.

B. Kaufmann/MICHELIN

In the land of the gods: Mt Mítikas

Clinging to the south face of the mountain at a height of 300m, is the large town of **Litóhoro**, an excellent place from which to explore the massif. Before beginning the ascent, enjoy a leisurely stroll among its houses of grey stone, from Odós Agíou Nikoláou (the main street), to **Platía Kentrikí**, its busiest square.

The ascent to the home of the gods

Allow a minimum of 2 days for the ascent, with one night in a refuge. The mountain was only climbed for the first time in 1913, but there is nothing technically challenging about this ascent. Nevertheless, you need to be fit. Be prepared for sudden changes in temperature and take warm clothes as well as sunscreen. See also "Making the most of Mt Olympus".
From Litóhoro, there are several possible routes, but the one via **Priona** *(18km from Litóhoro; by car or taxi along a partly tarmacked forestry track)* has several advantages. Two kilometres before you reach the village, a track on the left leads to the **Monastery of Ágios Dionísios** (16C), twice destroyed, first by the Turks (1828), and then by the Germans (1942) who suspected that it was a base for the Resistance movement. It was then rebuilt on both occasions.
The more adventurous might opt for the ascent on foot from the **Enipéas Gorge★★** *(a 4hr walk from Litóhoro; others may choose to get to the starting point of the walk by car)*, hemmed in between two high walls brimming with fir trees.

The home of the gods

Having defeated the Titans, then the Giants and Typhon, the gods chose Mt Olympus as their home, since it was hidden from the view of mortals by the clouds. In this godly eagle's eyrie, Hera, Poseidon, Hades, Athena, Apollo, Aphrodite, Artemis, Ares, Hephaestus, Hermes, Hestia, Demeter and Dionysus held council under the supreme supervision of Zeus. It was here that, between feasts enlivened by the singing of the Muses, they decided the fate of heroes and mortals, like pawns on a celestial chessboard.

When you reach **Priona**, a village perched at 1 100m, on the edge of the national park, you could stop off at the local restaurant before starting the actual ascent. Having filled your water bottle, follow the path to the **Spílios Agapitós Refuge** *(3hr)*, situated at a height of 2 100m. From here, go on to the **Plateau of the Muses** *(3hr)*, where you will find the **Kóstas Zalatás Refuge**. The last section of the climb to the top is more demanding, as the path becomes steeper and more rocky. But you will be well rewarded for your efforts by the wonderful **view★★★** when you get there (clouds permitting).

Making the most of Dion

COMING AND GOING

By train and by bus – From the station in Katerini, which runs regular services, a bus leaves every hour for Dion, 15km further south (a 20min ride).

USEFUL INFORMATION

Telephone – Local code: 0351.

WHERE TO STAY, EATING OUT

Dion has a hotel and several restaurants, but you might be better off finding somewhere to stay on the coast or in Litóhoro (see "Making the most of Mt Olympus"). This way you will be near Mt Olympus and have the advantage of more attractive surroundings.

OTHER THINGS TO DO

Festival – During the *Festival of Mt Olympus* (Festivál Olímbou) (July and August), plays and concerts are staged in Dion, Katerini and in Platamónas Castle.

COMING AND GOING

By train – The station at **Pláka**, on the Thessaloníki-Athens line, is 8km from the village, near the sea, but trains to the station at **Kateríni** (30km) are more frequent. From each of these stations, you then have to take a bus to Litóhoro (a 30min ride).

By bus – From **Litóhoro**, a bus leaves every hour (from Platía Kentrikí), to Kateríni and Thessaloníki (90min). There are three buses daily to Athens (5hr30min).

By taxi – ☎ (0352) 82 333.

ADDRESS BOOK (LITÓHORO)

Municipal tourist office – Odós Agíou Nikoláou16, before the Mirto Hotel, ☎ (0352) 83 100. Daily, 8.15am-8.45pm. The staff, who are efficient and helpful, will look after your luggage free of charge if you want to go for a walk.

Bank – National Bank of Greece, Platía Kentrikí. Cash dispenser.

Post office – On the left of Platía Kentrikí.

Telephone – Local code: 0352. **OTE**, Odós Agíou Nikoláou, near the Mirto Hotel.

Alpine club – EOS, Odós Korovagou 20 (from Odós Agíou Nikoláou, turn left near the Mirto Hotel), ☎ (0352) 84 544. From June to September. This association runs several refuges and has loads of information about Mt Olympus.

WHERE TO STAY

• Litóhoro

Between €30 and €38
Olympos, Odós Agías Paraskevis 30 (from Platía Kentrikí, follow the signs), ☎ and Fax (0352) 81 838 – 17rm. A warm welcome awaits you in this two-storey guesthouse, situated at the upper end of the village. Small, clean, simple apartments with a balcony, ideal for families.

Hotel Aphrodite, Platía Kentrikí, ☎ (0352) 81 415, Fax (0352) 22 123 – 26rm. ♨ ♿ TV Adequate but gloomy rooms (linoleum floors) and indifferent service, however, most rooms have a beautiful view of the mountain. Breakfast included. Booking recommended.

Hotel Enipéas, opposite the Hotel Aphrodite, ☎ (0352) 84 328, Fax (0352) 81 328 – 25rm. ♨ ♿ TV A small, quiet, well-run establishment which also has a wonderful view of Mt Olympus. Breakfast is not included.

Over €38
Mirto Hotel, on the right-hand side of the main road, just before the main square, ☎ (0352) 81 398, Fax (0352) 82 298 – 31rm. ♨ ♿ TV One of the best hotels in town.

♨ **Villa Pantheon**, from Platía Kentrikí, take the street leading to the Mylos restaurant, on the right, and follow the coast road for 1km, ☎ (0352) 83 931 – 12rm. ♨ ♿ TV ▤ A large white building visible from the village, this new hotel has rooms with a balcony, which are comfortable and spotlessly clean. More expensive at the weekend.

• Mt Olympus

Refuge A, Spílios Agapitós, ☎ (0352) 81 800 – 90 beds. ♨ ✗ The refuge run by Kóstas Zalatás is open from May until October, from 6am to 10pm. Booking advisable.

EATING OUT

To Pazari, Odós 28 Oktomvríou. Speciality fish.

Restaurant Erato, Platía Kentrikí. ☕ The food here may not be that exciting but it is served in pleasant surroundings, with a view of the mountain.

OTHER THINGS TO DO

4x4 vehicle hire – Odós Enipéos, above Platía Kentrikí, ☎ (0352) 83 943.

THESSALONÍKI ★★

Capital of the Province of Macedonia – 530km from Athens
Regional map page 412 – Michelin map 980 folds 5-6
Pop 1 000 000

Not to be missed

The Byzantine churches, particularly St Sophia, St George and St Demetrius.
The Galerius complex. The Archaeological Museum and the Byzantine Museum.
A walk along the ramparts.

And remember...

Visit the churches in the morning as opening hours tend to vary in the afternoon.
Avoid the season of international trade fairs (September-October).

After decades of isolation, Thessaloníki, the great and proud city in the north of Greece, is finally drawing on its rich historical past and embracing its links with the emerging regions of Eastern Europe and the Balkans. Only its links with Istanbul remain strained and prevent the city from complete reconciliation with its triple Macedonian, Byzantine and Ottoman legacy. Deprived of its historic district, the city is proud of its modern architecture, but has an exceptional legacy in its museums and Roman and Byzantine buildings, the testimonials of a past as glorious as it was tormented. A dynamic, industrious city, with a serious traffic problem, Thessaloníki lives at a European pace... except at siesta time when it seems to be gripped by an irresistible lethargy. This is the time to set out on foot to explore the avenues lined with chic shops in the lower town, and the winding streets of the citadel. In the evening, head for the open-air cafés and restaurants overlooking the sea.

From Cassander to Galerius

Historians are still arguing about the exact location of Therme, the ancient precursor of Thessaloníki, which some claim is in the Toúmba district. Whatever the truth of the matter, in 315 BC, **Cassander** founded the city which he named after his wife, Thessaloníki, sister of Alexander the Great. As the main commercial port and stronghold of Macedonia, the city attracted large numbers of foreigners and established relations with the great cities of Ancient Greece.

Far from discouraging its development, the **Roman invasion** (168 BC) was to open up a new era for the city. Promoted to capital of the Province of Macedonia, the prosperity of Thessaloníki was assured by its position on the **Via Egnatia**, the main land link between East and West. **Pompey** made it his headquarters before the Battle of Pharsalus, Cicero was exiled here and it was also here that **St Paul** (49-50) established one of the first Christian communities in Europe. In the 3C, the city achieved the status of a metropolis and a Roman colony. The Tetrarch **Galerius**, who erected numerous public buildings all over the city, was to leave behind him a reputation as a great persecutor of Christians and the executor of **Demetrius** (304), the patron saint of Thessaloníki.

Byzantine Thessaloníki

The second city of the Eastern Roman Empire after Constantinople, Thessaloníki was provided with a port by **Constantine**, then defensive walls by **Theodosius I**. An iron fist in a velvet glove, he ordered the massacre of 7 000 of the town's inhabitants, accusing them of rebellion, and established Christianity as the official religion (380). From then on, the town turned its back on its idolatrous past, building many churches, and was soon to shine throughout the Christian world.

But a dark period was to follow, marked by the attacks of the **Ostrogoths** (479), the **Huns** (540) and the **Slavs** (6C-7C) and by the earthquakes of 610 and 630. The pillage of Thessaloníki by the **Saracens** (904), who sold 22 000 of its inhabitants as slaves on the markets of Crete and the East, hit a town busy reviving itself. Then, in the 10C and 11C, it suffered the repeated assaults of the **Bulgars**. Under the **Comnenus emperors** (11C-12C), however, the Macedonian capital rose again from its ashes: the arts and commerce flourished, and the city, which by now had a population of 100 000, had a multitude of churches. But misfortune was to strike again with the invasion of the **Normans** of Sicily (1185), who left the city on its knees after a year of occupation. In 1204, when the Byzantine Empire was divided up after the **Fourth Crusade**, Macedonia ended up with Bernard de Montferrat. Liberated by the Greek Despotate of Epirus (1223), it finally returned to the Byzantine Empire which had been revived by the Paleologues, in 1261. But a new threat hung over the East: the Ottoman Turks, who overran the city in 1387.

Macedonia, a land of conquerors

Macedonia has given the world an extraordinary gallery of prominent figures, conquerors or religious leaders, who have in common the fact that they acquired their glory far from their native land, never to return. Born in Pella, Alexander the Great conquered Phoenicia, Egypt and Persia, crossed the mountains of Afghanistan and reached the Punjab before dying in Babylon more than ten years after his departure. St Cyril, known as the Philosopher, and his brother Methodius, who were born in Thessaloníki (9C), left an immense body of work. Having evangelised the Slavs, they translated the Bible and the Greek liturgy into the Slavonic language using their Cyrillic alphabet. In the 19C, Mehmet Ali, an Albanian born in Kávala, defied the great powers before establishing a dynasty in Egypt that reigned for a century. Finally, nearer our own time, Atatürk, born in Thessaloníki, accomplished his own exceptional destiny by founding modern Turkey on the remains of the Ottoman Empire.

Ottoman times

After a **Venetian** interlude (1423-30), Thessaloníki fell again into the hands of the Ottomans, who pillaged and massacred its population. Under its new masters, the appearance of the city changed: the churches were converted into mosques and baths and markets were erected. The Turks lived in the upper part of the city, while the **Jews** and Greeks lived in the insalubrious downtown areas, each community leading its own life and going to great lengths to avoid the other. In the 18C, a colourful fleet of ships from the four corners of the earth unloaded their cargoes of sugar, pewter, pepper, silk, nutmeg and ivory onto its quays. Caravans of 120 pack animals set off every week for Skopje, Vienna and Sofia, while the French opened a consulate, swiftly followed by the British, the Dutch and the Venetians.

The second Sepharad

Present in Thessaloníki since the 3C BC, for a long time the Jews maintained their traditions before becoming hellenised and taking the name of "Romaniótes" in the Byzantine Period. In 1492, they were joined by 20 000 Sephardic Jews who had fled from Spain, and were welcomed with open arms by Sultan Bayezid II. Wearing kaftans and greatcoats trimmed with fur, they spoke Ladino, a form of Castilian written in the Hebrew script, and specialised in working with wool, silk and precious stones, as well as in commerce. Of the 40 000 people living in the city in 1733, 20 000 were Jews, and they were to continue to form a large proportion of the population until the early 20C. But, during the Second World War, the whole Jewish community was deported by the Nazis. Today there are fewer than 2 000 Jews, and their language is dying out.

Receptive to the ideas of the French Revolution, the region became an important **centre of resistance**, but this was bloodily repressed (1821). However, a new revolution was about to begin: the Industrial Revolution, which was to transform the physiognomy of the city. Avenues were built and the sea walls were razed to the ground. Thessaloníki was connected to the European rail network in 1888, and also

HOTELS

ABC .... ①
Acropol .... ②
Aegeon .... ③
Amalia .... ④
Atlas .... ⑤
Averof .... ⑥
Augoustos .... ⑦
Capsis .... ⑧
City .... ⑨
Electra Palace .... ⑩
Esperia .... ⑪
Louxembourg .... ⑫
Tourist Hotel .... ⑬
Vergina .... ⑭

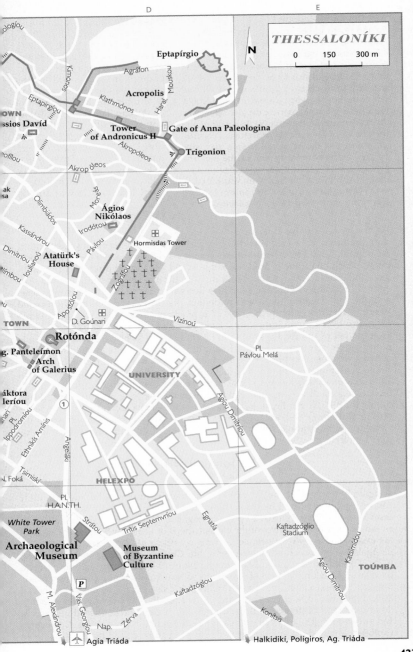

THESSALONÍKI

N

0   150   300 m

Eptapírgio

Agráfon

Acropolis

Klathmónos

Kímonos

Eptapírgiou

ssios Davíd

OWN

Tower
of Andronicus II

Gate of Anna Paleologina

ofílou

Akropóleos

Trigonion

Akropóleos

Moreás

Ágios
Nikólaos

Olimbiádos

Kassándrou

Irodótou

Pávlou

Hormisdas Tower

Dimitríou

Ioulianoú

Atatürk's
House

limbou

Apostólou

† † †
† † †
† † †
† † †

Zografou

u

D. Goúnari

Vizinoú

TOWN

Rotónda

Pl.
Pávlou Melá

g. Panteleímon

Arch
of Galerius

áktora
leríou

UNIVERSITY

nari

Pl.
Ippodrómiou

①

Ethnikís Amínis

Angeláki

Agíou Dimitríou

Tsimiskí

N. Foká

HELEXPO

Pl.
H.AN.TH.

White Tower
Park

Strátou

Tritis Septemvríou

Egnatía

Kaftadzóglio
Stadium

TOÚMBA

Archaeological
Museum

Museum
of Byzantine
Culture

Kaftadzóglou

Agíou Dimitríou

Katsimídou

P

M. Alexándrou

Vas. Georgíou

Zérva

Nap.

Agía Triáda

Konítsis

Halkidikí, Polígiros, Ag. Triáda

423

FYROM or Macedonia?

To the north of the frontier, the Republic of Macedonia, inhabited by Macedonian Slavs and an ethnic Albanian minority, had been one of the constituent republics of Yugoslavia. Its declaration of independence from Yugoslavia (1991) was very badly received by the people on this side of the border, who believed that they would see an attempt to appropriate the glorious Macedonian heritage. During massive demonstrations, the citizens of Thessaloníki protested in particular against the choice of the famous sun with 16 rays as the national symbol of the new republic. Finally, the matter was concluded ambiguously in 1993, when the new state was admitted to the United Nations under the name of FYROM (Former Yugoslav Republic of Macedonia)...

took full advantage of the golden age of steam navigation. However, at the beginning of the 20C, it became one of the flash-points of the fever gripping the Balkans. Claimed by Greeks and Bulgars alike, it was subjected to a wave of terrorist attacks. The revolt of the **Young Turks** (1908), led by a group of officers who were reformers and nationalists, led to a brief lull. For four days, Greeks, Bulgars, Jews and Turks fraternised, but rivalries regained the upper hand and anarchy reigned until Macedonia was finally united with Greece on October 26, 1912.

At the gates of the Balkans

At the outbreak of the First World War, ignoring the opposition of King Constantine, the prime minister **Elefthérios Venizélos** authorised the passage of the Anglo-French troops which had come to lend the Serbs a hand. He formed a provisional government and entered Athens triumphantly in 1917, the same year in which a terrible **fire** ravaged the centre of Thessaloníki, lasting two weeks. But the worst was yet to come, with the deportation of the Jewish community by the Germans during the **Second World War**. Relegated to the rank of a provincial town when the Iron Curtain descended over Eastern Europe, the Macedonian capital had to await its hour.

After the **fall of the Berlin Wall** (1989), Thessaloníki finally re-established its role as the natural maritime outlet of the Balkans. There were plans to build motorways and joint ventures flourished, while the business boom was accompanied by a frantic rise in consumption. As a result of this success, the town became a major centre of attraction for its neighbours in crisis after their separation from the Socialist block (it is estimated that more than 100 000 Albanians came to settle in Thessaloníki during the 1990s). Furthermore, the passage through Macedonia of the Blue Berets sent to **Kosovo** (1999) was unpopular with the people, who were linked to the Orthodox Serbs by a solidarity lasting centuries and always ready to show their anti-American feelings.

The lower town**

Allow half a day

Completely rebuilt after the fire of 1917, the town centre forms the modern, lively part of the city. Bordered by Odós Olimbiádos and the seafront, it is crossed from east to west by Odós Egnatía, a noisy thoroughfare which you will be keen to leave as soon as possible in favour of the elegant shops of Leofóros Tsimiskí, or some of the treasures of Early-Christian architecture, according to your tastes.

Recognisable by its ochre-coloured walls, the **Church of St Sophia**** (Agía Sofía) (C3) (7C) suffered serious damage during a fire in 1890. Its square ground-plan and the choice of vaulting (instead of a wooden roof structure) suggest a transitory phase, between the basilica and the church built on a cross plan. It acted as a cathedral from 1204 until it was converted into a mosque in 1585. Beyond the narthex, decorated with 11C **frescoes**, is the central area of the church, divided into a nave and two side aisles separated by pillars and columns. Note the fine **Corinthian capitals***, where the acanthus leaves almost seem to be ruffled by the wind. Even more notable is the stunning **mosaic★★★** of the Ascension of Christ (9C) on a gold background in the dome. Also look for the beautiful rendering of the **Virgin carrying the Infant Jesus★★** in the apse.

The Galerius complex★ (Anáktora Galeríou) (C3)

The site, open to the sky, must be explored from outside. A group of buildings provides the somewhat unflattering background for the ruins of what was once the ancient political centre of Thessaloníki under Galerius (300 AD). When the complex was built, which included the hippodrome *(south of Odós Egnatía)*, the arch *(on the street)* and the Rotunda *(to the north)*, a large section of the city wall had to be rebuilt further east. The **palace★** stands around a peristyle **courtyard**, with galleries paved with **mosaics** and marble. On the south side was a monumental gateway leading to the harbour. But the main building in the palace is the **octagon★**, the inside of which is decorated with semicircular niches. Its size (30m in diameter) and what remains of the marble decoration suggest that this was a throne room. Close by, archaeologists have uncovered some splendid **mosaic★★** floors. Complete your tour of the palace by visiting the remains of the **hippodrome** *(Platía Ipodromíou)*, a whole hectare in area.

Built after Galerius' victory over the Persians, the monumental **Arch of Galerius★** (Kamára or Apsida Galeríou) (C3) has suffered the ravages of time and from the fact that it is close to Odós Egnatía. Originally, it consisted of two sets of parallel arches 37m long, (only part of the west wall remains), linked by a dome. The Via Regia, which spanned the town from east to west ran through the central arch, while the side arches had porticoes used for pedestrian traffic. Four registers of **bas-reliefs★★** depict the heroic deeds of Galerius. On the second register of the pillar on the side of the street, Diocletian *(on the left)* and Galerius *(on the right)* watch a sacrifice commemorating his victory. The woman on the left symbolises the Universe, on which Peace, on the right, lays her hand. The story of the war is depicted in the bottom

Thessaloníki: a chapel watches over the town

register, while, in the third register, Armenia and Mesopotamia, personified as women, offer their surrender. Finally, in the top register, the citizens of a town welcome Galerius as he arrives on his chariot.

A Byzantine walk

With its sombre façade, the **Church of St George***** (Rotónda) (C3) *(daily, 8.30am-5pm; no charge; the minaret and the frescoes are being restored)* is imbued with a serene aura despite the fact that it is built of brick, a humble building material. But it is in its immense **circular nave****, 30m high and illuminated by the brilliance of its mosaics, that it reveals its true splendour. Conceived as a mausoleum for the sovereign (some interpret it as a temple dedicated to Zeus), it was converted into a church by Theodosius I (end of the 4C). At this time, one of the eight niches was transformed into an apse, the circular wall was extended and a narthex was added. The Turks transformed it into a mosque by adding a minaret. True masterpieces of Early-Christian art (6C), the **mosaics with a gold background***** in the nave belong to the mainstream of the Hellenistic naturalist tradition, evident in the richness of colour, the mobility of the human figures and the expressions of the faces. The seven panels depict the saints. The mosaic in the dome (sadly badly damaged) depicted Christ in a triple mandorla of stars, branches and coloured circles, supported by angels. In the choir there is also a 9C **fresco** of the Ascension in a poor state of repair.

If restoration work has been completed, have a look at the **Church of St Panteleímon** (C3) (13C) *(at the end of the small street leading off at an angle to the Rotónda)*, a charming little building in a mixture of stone and brick (beautiful **frescoes** from the period).

Walk west along Odós Egnatía and turn right after 200m.

Built in 447-48 over some Roman baths, the **mosaic floor** of which can be seen in the north aisle, the **Church of Panagía Ahiropíitos*** (C2) is one of the oldest surviving Christian sanctuaries. Its name refers to the icon of the Virgin *(on the left as you enter)*, executed, according to the legend, "not by a human hand" *(acheiropoíetos)*. Built on a basilical ground-plan, its nave and two side aisles are separated by columns and brightly illuminated. Note the **Corinthian capitals**, created in the best workshops of Constantinople, and the **mosaics*** (5C) which are wonderfully rich in colour *(arches of the galleries and the colonnades, and in the narthex)*. The church also contains some rare **frescoes** (13C) depicting the Forty Martyrs who died in the 4C.

Follow Odós Filípou to Platía Dikastiríon.

Discovered in the 1960s when a new law court was being built, the **Agora** is in fact a Roman forum built (2C AD) over a Greek agora. A large paved square measuring 145m by 90m, it was lined on three sides by a double colonnade with shops. The colonnade on the south side stood over a **cryptoporticus** opening onto the street; an ingenious way of exploiting the slope of the land. In front of the east portico, with its **mosaic pavement**, the **odeon** was altered in the Late Empire to accommodate gladiatorial combats.

The Church of St Demetrius** (Ágios Dimítrios) (C2)

Access to the crypt: Monday 12.30pm-7pm, Thursday-Saturday 8am-8pm, Sunday 10.30am-8pm. No charge. To the north of the agora looms the tall façade of the church of St Demetrius, the last of the numerous sanctuaries to be built on the presumed site of the saint's martyrdom (4C). The modern church, built after the fire of 1917, according to the original plan, has retained features of incomparable historic and artistic interest, although it no longer has the charm endowed by the patina of time. The interior, which is surprisingly large, has a **nave and four side aisles**, each with a corresponding wooden roof. On the north side, the remains of a **minaret** are a reminder that the church was used as a mosque from 1493 until 1912.

To the left of the nave, do not miss the **Florentine sarcophagus*** (15C), set into the wall, and the small adjacent **chapel**. The church contains some **frescoes**, in the right side aisle and on the columns at the entrance to the church (notably a calendar of the movable feasts of the 15C), and in the **Chapel of St Euthymius**★, to the right of the apse (1303). The red, green and white marble **columns**★, come from earlier buildings which explains their difference in height, compensated by **capitals**★, with motifs of wind-ruffled acanthus leaves and rams' heads.

Masterpieces of Byzantine art, some **mosaics**★★★ survived the fire. Dating mostly from the 7C, they are remarkably delicate in structure and colour. The hieratic depiction of the figures already points to the shift in Byzantine art towards a more solemn style. On the right-hand pillar in front of the apse, you will recognise St Demetrius, placed between the founders of the church, St Sergius praying, and St Demetrius accompanied by a deacon bearing the gospel. The left-hand pillar shows Demetrius with two children, as well as the Virgin and a saint who may be St Theodore (9C). To the right of the choir, steps lead down to the **crypt**★★. This ancient Roman bath has an **apse** which probably belonged to the original church (4C). But the holy of holies is the **rotunda**★★ surrounded by small columns and marble basins into which, according to tradition, the sacred oil produced by the body of Demetrius flowed. Pilgrims then collected it from the large **marble basin** on the ground.

Return to the agora and walk along Odós Halkéon to the corner of Odós Egnatía.

Around the central market (B2)

Built in 1028, the **Church of Panagía Halkéon** (Our Lady of the Coppersmiths) follows the conventions of Byzantine art to the letter: it is built on a Greek-cross plan, with a central tower, walls of brick and a tiled roof. Its name derives from the fact that it was formerly the parish church of the coppersmiths who plied their trade nearby. The superb **frescoes** dating from the same period are sadly in a poor state of repair.

There are some fine examples of buildings dating from the Ottoman Period in the town centre. Built in 1467, the **Hamza Bey Mosque** was converted into a cinema when the Turks departed. To the west of the prayer hall, which is surmounted by a dome, is a large portico surrounding an inner courtyard. Further down Odós Venizélou, you can still see the **Bedesten**, a small brick and stone building surmounted by six domes, which housed the textiles bazaar in Ottoman times. Now beautifully restored, it has been converted into shops.

But it is the **central market** (Kendrikí Agorá), on the other side of the road, which has the most oriental atmosphere, its alleyways crowded with stalls selling all sorts of commodities including fish. On the south-west corner, the **Yahudi Hammam** (16C), the old Turkish bath of the Jewish quarter, is now a flower market.

The museums of Thessaloníki★★
Allow half a day (on foot)

A huge esplanade lined with cafés and hotels, **Platía Aristotélous** (B3) is one of the focal points of the city. It opens onto **Leofóros Níkis**, the long avenue running along the seafront which is reminiscent of the Ramblas of Barcelona in the evening when the local teenagers head for the bars overlooking the bay.

But, for the time being, head south-east of the town centre, where most of the museums are concentrated. Isolated from the rest of the ramparts since the sea walls were destroyed (1866), the **White Tower**★ (Lefkós Pírgos) (C4) *(8am-2.30pm; closed Monday)* dominates the seafront with its imposing, austere silhouette. Built by the Turks (15C), it was used as a prison in the 18C and acquired the name of the Tower of Blood after the massacre of the Janissaries at the beginning of the 19C *(see page 26)*. Since most of the collections have been transferred to the Byzantine Museum, with the temporary exception of the icons, it is used for **temporary exhibitions**. There is a wonderful **view**★ from the top.

The Archaeological Museum★★★ (D4)

On the corner of Odós Strátou and Odós Angeláki. From April to October, Tuesday-Sunday 8am-7pm and Monday 12.30pm-7pm; closes at 5pm from November to March. Entrance fee. Even though it has been deprived of the fabulous Vergína treasure, now displayed in situ *(see page 434)*, this museum still has one of the finest collections in Greece. After **Room 1**, on the left of the hall, which contains various remnants of a 6C BC Ionic temple, devote some time to the **sculptures** in **Rooms 2 and 3**, which testify to Macedonia's early prowess as part of the Greek world. Notice also the funerary steles, particularly the delicate bas-relief depicting a **young girl holding a dove★★★** (5C BC). **Room 4** traces the history of the city from Prehistoric times (pottery and jewellery from the Toúmba tumulus), through the Archaic, Classical and Hellenistic Periods (tombs, architectural features). The Roman Period is represented by capitals, mosaics and statues, notably a fine **Harpocrates★★** holding a cornucopia.

Rooms 5 and 6 contain some votive bas-reliefs, glass objects, and two major works: a **marble statue of Augustus★** and a **bronze bust of Alexander Severus★★** (3C). The prize exhibits of the museum are next: an exceptional collection of gold artefacts **(Room 9)** from Macedonian tombs (6C-2C BC). In particular, do not miss the **Dervéni tiara★★**, the **myrtle-leaf crowns** and the **gilt bronze Dervéni crater★★**, also a **stone sarcophagus** decorated with polychrome friezes.

On the floor below, **Room 10** is devoted to the prehistoric settlement around the city (pottery, tools). **Room 7** contains the monumental façade of a **Macedonian tomb★**, reconstructed using original features. The tour concludes with a celebrated exhibit **(Room 8)**, the **Sindos Treasure★★★**, a unique – and superb – example of Macedonian funerary art: weapons, "Illyrian" helmets decorated with gold leaf, gold masks, jewellery, vases, terracottas...

The Museum of Byzantine Culture★★ (M Vizandinoú Politismoú) (D4)

Odós Strátou 2, opposite the Congress Centre; from April to October, Tuesday-Sunday 7pm and Monday 12.30pm-7pm; from November to March, Tuesday-Friday 8am-5pm, weekends 8am-2.30pm and Monday 10.30am-5pm; entrance fee. Reflecting state-of-the-art museum design, this new museum has a wonderful collection of **Early-Christian art** (4C-7C). The first room contains various decorative features from churches in Macedonia: **sculptures**, **mosaics**, **capitals**, while the next room contains objects from everyday life: domestic tools and the **reconstruction of an interior**, with a mosaic floor. The third room illustrates the survival of earlier traditions in the funerary art of the early Christians, with a series of **painted tombs** where the jewellery and personal effects of the dead person were placed. Once complete, the museum should also be able to display the icons from the White Tower. The last room is devoted to temporary exhibitions.

The upper town★★
Around the ramparts
Allow half a day

If you have the time, you could begin your tour with a look at the two churches in the western ramparts; otherwise, start at the Church of the Prophet Elijah. Beyond Odós Olimbiádos, the upper part of the city is a maze of narrow paved streets lined with houses with projecting upper storeys and Byzantine churches.

Tucked away at the foot of the western ramparts, the **Church of the Holy Apostles★** (Dódeka Apostóli) (B1) (14C) is built on a Greek-cross plan. Surmounted by a dome, it is surrounded by a covered gallery on three sides and preceded by a narthex. The fine construction of the outer **brick walls** is balanced by the sumptuous interior decoration. In their realism and dramatic presentation, the **mosaics★★**, which are typical of the Thessalonian style, represent a high point in Early-Christian art. Also notable are the **frescoes★★** in the portico, the choir and the nave, which include scenes of the Life of the Virgin, and the Tree of Jesse, *(eastern end of the south portico).*

Behind the church looms the massive silhouette of the **ramparts*** which cut into the fabric of the modern city. A walk along the remaining 4km (of the original 8km) highlights another facet of Thessaloníki. A unique example of Byzantine fortification, punctuated by about **sixty towers**, the walls are built with layers of stone and mortar alternating with brick. Several ramparts were built after those erected by Cassander, but most of the remains date from the late 4C. They were altered by the Byzantines and then by the Turks, who added two circular towers: the **White Tower** and the **Trigonion** (some attribute them to the Venetians). In the more vulnerable lower part of the town, the walls were further fortified by triangular, crenellated bastions.

In Odós Sahíni, have a look at the charming **Church of St Catherine** (Agía Ekateríni) (B1) (late 13C), with walls of fine brickwork. Dating back to before the Church of the Holy Apostles, it is built on the same Greek-cross plan, but its **frescoes** are in a poor state.

Odós Olimbiádos leads to the **Church of the Prophet Elijah** (Profitis Ilías) (C1), with equally delicate brickwork, a dome and three apses. Built in 1360 to replace an old Byzantine palace, it was converted into a mosque during the Turkish period, but the original **frescoes*** have been preserved.

Hidden away in Odós Agías Sofías in the heart of the upper part of the town, the **Church of Óssios Davíd** (Blessed David)* (C1) (*8am-12noon and 5pm-7pm*) belongs to the ancient monastery of Latomos (late 5C). Its design (difficult to make out because of alterations carried out during the Ottoman Period) is based on the cruciform plan with a dome that was to dominate Byzantine architecture over the centuries. An elderly custodian is responsible for opening the doors to the sanctuary which houses a rare 6C **mosaic*****, showing a young, beardless Christ seated on a rainbow spanning the four rivers of Paradise, surrounded by the symbols of the Evangelists. On the left is the Prophet Ezekiel, in ecstasy, watching a miracle, while, on the right, the Prophet Habakkuk meditates. The sole surviving example of 12C painting in Thessaloníki, the **frescoes**** of the Nativity and the Baptism of Christ herald the artistic explosion that the following two centuries were to bring.

Perched up high, in Odós Eptapirgíou, are the remains of the magnificent **citadel** (D1), the **Tower of Andronicus II Paleologus** and the **Trigonion*** (or Tower of the Chain), which has a superb **view*** over the town. Between them is the **Gate of**

Thessaloníki: below the lofty White Tower

G. de Benoist/MICHELIN

Anna Paleologina which leads into the district occupied by the **Eptapírgio**, which was used as a prison until 1989 (you can still see the visiting room and the exercise area). The complex is to be converted into a museum.

Walk down beside the eastern ramparts, then join Odós Irodótou.

Surrounded by a small garden planted with trees, the **Church of Ágios Nikólaos Orfanós**** (D2) *(8.45am-3pm; closed Monday)* (14C) used to be part of a monastery; these days all that remains of the monastery is the **monumental gateway**. Off to the side of the central area of the church, where there is a marble **templon**, is a pretty doorway divided by a Corinthian column that leads into the gallery. Unusually for Thessaloníki, the church was never converted into a mosque and its remarkable **frescoes***** are virtually intact. The richness of the colour, power of composition and the execution of the facial features all denote an artistic movement that had reached its apogee. Arranged in registers, they cover a wide variety of themes; liturgical festivals, the Passion, Resurrection and miracles of Christ, the Life of the Virgin, the lives of St Nicholas and St Gerasimos, the Annunciation, etc.

If you are interested in modern history, you might like to end your tour by visiting the **Atatürk House Museum** (D2) *(Daily 2pm-5pm; access through the Turkish Consulate, on the corner of Odós Olimbiádos and Odós Apostólou Pávlou, on presentation of identification).* A beautiful 19C house, where Mustafa Kemal, the founder of modern Turkey (1881) was born. Inside this elegant period town house, various personal belongings of the statesman are displayed (including his dinner jacket and top hat).

Making the most of Thessaloníki

COMING AND GOING

By air – *Thessaloníki Airport (Macedonia)*, ☎ (031) 425 011 (16km south of the city). From the bus station, take the 78 bus (about a 45min ride). There are international flights to Paris, London, Brussels, Frankfurt, etc, and local flights to Athens, from Chios, Corfu, Ioánnina, Lesbos, Límnos, Mýkonos, Rhodes, Sámos and Crete.

By train – The *station* (A1) is in Odós Monastiríou, ☎ (031) 517 517. Here you will find a bank, a telephone agency and a left luggage office (6am-9.30pm). Train tickets can be bought on the spot or at the **OSE**, at Platía Aristotélous 18 (B3), ☎ (031) 276 382.

There are numerous services to local destinations: 5 slow trains a day to Athens (an 8hr journey), plus five express trains (a 6hr journey), as well as sleepers with couchettes. To Alexandroúpoli, there are 5 slow trains plus two express trains (a 5hr30min journey), via Kavála, Xánthi and Komotiní. To Lárissa, three slow trains a day with connections to Vólos (a 4hr30min journey).

There are services to several international destinations: to Istanbul, leaving at 7.25am, arriving at 8pm; to Belgrade, leaving at 7.30pm, arriving at 6am; to Budapest, via Sofia and Bucharest, leaving at 10pm.

By ferry – *Harbourmaster's office* (A3), ☎ (031) 531 504. You can also buy tickets at the agencies in Leofóros Tsimiskí and Odós N Koundouriótou, and in Platía Eleftherías.

GA Ferries runs several weekly services in summer to Skiáthos, the Cyclades and Crete, as well as a service to the Dodecanese.

Nel Lines serves Límnos, Lesbos, Chios and Piraeus twice a week in summer.

By hydrofoil – *Minoan Flying Dolphins*, ☎ (031) 547 407. Tickets can be bought from travel agencies or at the port. From June to September, departures at 8am and 4.30pm (except Tuesday and Thursday) to the Sporades. Turn up 30min before boarding (take a jumper as the hydrofoil is air conditioned and can be chilly!).

By bus – As the gateway of Greece, Thessaloníki is connected to the rest of the Balkans. The train company OSE also provides bus connections, but timetables are subject to frequent changes. Tickets are sold at the railway station, from where most of the buses depart. Buses for Sofia leave at 7am, 2pm, 4pm and 10pm (a 6hr journey). Buses leave for Istanbul at 2.30am (daily except Wednesday, a 12hr journey).

There is no separate bus station for domestic bus services but most of them leave from the area around the railway station. Information from *KTEL*, ☎ (031) 528 600 / 924 444.

Buses to Pella (40min), Édessa (1hr45min), Kastoriá (4hr) and Vólos (4hr) leave from Odós Anageníseos 22, south of the railway station.

Buses to Véria (2hr) leave from Odós 28 Oktomvríou 10, between the railway station and the port.

Buses to Athens (a 7hr30min journey) and Tríkala (a 5hr30min journey) leave from Odós Monastiríou 65-67, opposite the railway station. Buses to Ioánnina (a 7hr journey) leave from Odós X Pízou 19, opposite the railway station.

Buses to Kavála (3hr) leave from Odós Langadá 59, north of the railway station.

Buses to Chalcidice leave from Odós Karakási 68, to the east of the railway station (from Odós Egnatía, bus *no* 10).

GETTING AROUND

By bus – The orange buses operate within the town, and the orange and blue buses also operate in the outskirts. Tickets are purchased on the bus.

By taxi – *Alexander the Great*, ☎ (031) 866 866. *Macedonia*, ☎ (031) 517 417.

By car – Perpetual traffic jams and lack of parking make driving here particularly frustrating.

ELPA (Automobile and Touring Club of Greece), Odós Vassilíssis Ólgas 228, ☎ (031) 426 319.

Avis, Leofóros Níkis 3, ☎ (031) 227 126, Fax (031) 224 001.

Hertz, Odós Venizélou 4, ☎ (031) 224 906, Fax (031) 280 388.

ADDRESS BOOK

Tourist information – *EOT*, Platía Aristotélous 8 (B3), ☎ (031) 271 888. Monday-Friday 9am-9pm, Saturday 10am-6pm, Sunday 10am-5pm.

Travel agencies – You will find numerous agencies near the port, in Odós N Koundouriótou and Leofóros Tsimiskí.

Oasis, Odós Mitropóleos 24, ☎ (031) 268 244, Fax (031) 232 541. Booking of plane, ferry and hydrofoil tickets.

Karacharisis, Odós N Koundouriótou 8, ☎ (031) 513 005, Fax (031) 532 289. Booking of ferries and hydrofoils.

Tourist police – Odós Dodekaníssou 4, on the 5th floor, ☎ (031) 554 871.

Banks / Currency exchange – The town centre is brimming with banks and cash dispensers.

National Bank of Greece, Platía Dimokratías (A2) (Monday-Friday 8am-2pm / 6pm-8pm, Saturday 8am-1.30pm, Sunday 9.30am-12.30pm); and Leofóros Tsimiskí 11 (open at weekends). *American Express*, Leofóros Tsimiskí 19. Monday-Thursday 8.30am-2pm, Friday 8am-1.30pm. *Eurocambio*, Odós Egnatía 21 and Odós I Dragoúmi 7 (Monday-Friday 8am-7pm, Saturday 9am-2pm). This bureau de change handles withdrawals by credit card.

Post office – *Main post office*, Leofóros Tsimiskí 45 (B3).

Telephone – Local code: 031. *OTE*, Odós Karoloudíl 27, on the corner of Odós Ermoú (B2-B3). Open 24hr.

Internet – *Ground Floor*, Odós Pávlou Melá 42 (C3). A large modern bar with a games room and Internet access (daily, 11am-1pm).

Abantaz, Odós Agíou Dimitríou 156, near the Turkish Consulate (D2). A bar with games room which also has Internet access (daily, 24hr).

Consulates –

American Consulate General, "Plateia" Commercial Centre, Leofóros Tsimiskí 43, ☎ (031) 242 905 to 907, Fax (031) 242 915, 242 927.

Australian Honorary Consulate, Odós Kifisiás 46, ☎ (031) 482 322, Fax (031) 458 565.

British Consulate, 8th Floor, Odós Venizélou 8, Platía Eleftherías, ☎ (031) 278 006, 269 984, Fax (031) 283 868. *Consulate of Canada*, c/o Bank of Nova Scotia, Leofóros Tsimiskí 17, ☎ (031) 256 350, Fax (031) 236 351. Monday-Friday, 9am-12noon.

Airlines – *Lufthansa*, Odós E Venizélou, on Platía Eleftherías (B2-B3). *Olympic Airways*, Odós N Koundouriótou 3, ☎ (031) 230 240; airport, ☎ (031) 473 720.

WHERE TO STAY

During the international trade-fair season (September-October), prices rise by 30%-50% and finding a room becomes virtually impossible. Most of the hotels are near the railway station (A1), Odós Monastiríou and Odós Egnatía (B2), and in the town centre, near Platía Aristotélous (B3).

Campsites (around €12)

The campsites, which are only open in summer, are concentrated around the airport, at *Agía Triáda*, ☎ (0392) 51 360, bus *no* 67, 72 and 73, and at *Epanomí*, ☎ (0392) 41 358, bus *no* 69.

Under €30

Acropol, Odós Tandalídou 14, ☎ (031) 536 170 – 24rm. Rudimentary rooms, but the prices are unbeatable (bathrooms and toilets along the corridor). Warm welcome and English spoken. Possible to leave luggage for a few days.

Hotel Augustos, Odós Helen Svorónou 4, ☎ (031) 533 550, Fax (031) 522 955 – 24rm. Situated in a narrow street set back from Odós Egnatía, neo-Classical in style, this hotel has simple, well-kept rooms (with or without a bathroom).

Between €30 and €45

Averof, Odós Léondos Sofoú 24 (on the corner of Odós Egnatía), ☎ (031) 538 840, Fax (031) 543 194 – 36rm. Basic facilities (some rooms have a bathroom and TV). Prices soar during the trade fairs. The staff speak English.

Atlas, Odós Egnatía 40, ☎ and Fax (031) 510 038 – 32rm. ⁀ ℓ̷ TV A rather noisy hotel with rudimentary facilities. The rooms with a bathroom on the first floor are better value.

Hotel Louxembourg, Odós Komninón 6, ☎ (031) 278 449 – 29rm. ⁀ ℓ̷ TV Basic facilities and surly staff.

Between €45 and €60

Hotel Aegeon, Odós Egnatía 19, ☎ (031) 522 921, Fax (031) 522 922 – 59rm. ℓ̷ TV CC Recently renovated, this hotel has small, clean, comfortable rooms, mostly with a bathroom. The staff speak English.

🐾 **Tourist Hotel**, Odós Mitropóleos 21, ☎ (031) 270 501, Fax (031) 226 865 – 37rm. ⁀ 🍽 ℓ̷ TV Well situated and very welcoming, the rooms – with high ceilings – are spotlessly clean and comfortable. Breakfast included.

Hotel City, Odós Komninón 11, ☎ (031) 269 421, Fax (031) 274 358 – 104rm. ⁀ ℓ̷ TV CC This luxury hotel in the town centre has very comfortable rooms (most with air conditioning), with balcony. Fixed prices, whatever the season, breakfast included.

Hotel Amalia, Odós Ermoú 33, ☎ (031) 268 321, Fax (031) 233 356 – 66rm. ⁀ 🍽 ℓ̷ TV A 9-storey hotel with excellent facilities, very good value for money. The staff speak English and are very efficient.

Hotel Esperia, Odós Olímbou 58, ☎ (031) 269 321, Fax (031) 269 457 – 70rm. ⁀ ℓ̷ TV Situated near the Ministry for Northern Greece, opposite an archaeological site, this hotel might be unsophisticated but it is comfortable.

Over €75

ABC Hotel, Odós Angeláki 41, ☎ (031) 265 421, Fax (031) 276 542 – 99rm. ⁀ ℓ̷ TV ✗ CC Spotless, comfortable rooms, albeit somewhat lacking in character. Breakfast included.

Hotel Capsis, Odós Monastiríou 18, ☎ (031) 521 321, Fax (031) 510 555 – 428rm. ⁀ 🍽 ℓ̷ TV ✗ CC A vast luxury hotel near the railway station, with a swimming pool on the roof. Wide range of facilities (foreign newspapers, money-changing facilities, car park, satellite TV). Expensive (breakfast included).

Hotel Vergina, Odós Monastiríou 19, ☎ (031) 516 021, Fax (031) 529 308 – 133rm. ⁀ 🍽 ℓ̷ TV CC 100m from the railway station, this vast hotel, which is mainly patronised by businessmen, is often full during the trade fairs. Recently renovated, extremely comfortable, excellent service. Breakfast included.

🐾 **Electra Palace Hotel**, Platía Aristotélous 9, ☎ (031) 232 221, Fax (031) 235 947 – 135rm. ⁀ 🍽 ℓ̷ TV ✗ CC Unique in terms of its situation and elegant neo-Byzantine façade, with its excellent facilities, this hotel has everything! Ask for a room with a view of the square and the seafront, and if possible, with a balcony (from the third floor up). Breakfast is included.

EATING OUT

Thessaloníki has a large number of restaurants of every kind and to suit all budgets: in the little streets around Platía Aristotélous, near the covered market and in the upper part of town. In the early 1990s, the Ta Ladádika district, west of Platía Eleftherías, was made into a pedestrian precinct. The old workshops and warehouses have now been converted into restaurants, pubs and bars. Live music every evening.

Around €12
Taverna Nea Ilyssia, on the corner of Odós Egnatía / Odós Léondos Sofoú (B2). 🍴 Cheap Greek food.

🍴**Nikos**, Odós Komninón 32 (B3). Situated in a busy alleyway of the covered market, this restaurant serves excellent food (calamari stuffed with cheese, spinach with tuna).

Mirovolos Smirni, Odós Komninón 32 (B3), ☎ (031) 274 170. 🍴 Right next door to the previous venue, but bigger and more popular. The Greek clientele and local music add to its attractions. Some tables outside. Seafood, barbecued dishes, kebabs.

Pasar Hamami, Odós Komninón 15A (B3), ☎ (031) 272 894. 🍴 Set in an old Turkish bath converted by Jews who had fled from Spain in the 15C. Pork (!) and excellent seafood.

Taverna Rotonda, Odós Dimitríou Goúnari 47 (D2), ☎ (031) 206 895. 🍴 Located between the Rotunda and the Arch of Galerius, a small Greek restaurant which serves good, cheap food.

Ouzerí Aristotélous, Platía Aristotélous 8 (B3), at the end of a passage on the left-hand side of the square, facing the sea. Open late every evening except Sunday, this bistro-style, friendly restaurant serves excellent meze and kebabs.

Around €23
Zithos, Odós Katoúni 5, Ladádika (B2), ☎ (031) 540 284. 🍴 Elegant brasserie-style restaurant. Try their excellent chocolate gateau.

Palati, Ladádika (B2). 🍴 Varied menu, a good wine list and live music.

🍴**Ta Nisia Restaurant** (B3), Odós Korómila 13, ☎ (031) 285 991. A wonderful place, where they serve refined Greek food.

Salt'N Pepper, Odós Nikifórou Foká 3 (C3), near the White Tower, next to Pizza Hut ☎ (031) 243 219. 🍴 The pasta dishes are excellent, but the service can be frustratingly slow.

Mylos, Odós Andréou Georgíou 56 (off the map, west of the town, bus *no* 31), ☎ (031) 525 968. An old converted mill complex with an art gallery, restaurant, bar and concert hall.

Taverna To Spíti To Piasa, Odós Apostólou Pávlou 35 (D2), ☎ (031) 208 295. Very popular with the locals, this restaurant offers Greek and Western cuisine.

HAVING A DRINK

Thessaloníki comes alive at night, and you will be spoilt for choice as to where to go. In the evening, the local youngsters can be seen strolling along the seafront with its mass of outdoor cafés. Ladádika is also popular with the younger clientele (see above).

Bars, cafés – On the Road, Odós Níkis. Quieter than average, this bar spills out onto a terrace.

Tóttis, Odós Agías Sofías 2 (C2), on the corner of Leofóros Níkis. Large, modern and lively, with a terrace.

Propilaíoni, Odós Eptapirgíou 130 (C1), near the ramparts. It has a terrace with a panoramic view over the town. Live music every evening.

Tzoitzoixléri, Stoá Modianó 19 (B2). The place to go for a coffee, in the middle of the market.

Mylos, (see above).

OTHER THINGS TO DO

Feasts & festivals – The International Fair of Thessaloníki, which is held for two weeks in September and ends with a Greek Music Festival. In October and November this is followed by an international film festival as part of **Demetriosa**, the festival held in honour of the patron saint of the town.

SHOPPING GUIDE

Markets – Kendrikí Agorá (closed Sunday), see above.

Antiques – E&M, Odós Karmpóla 10 (B2), ☎ (031) 283 644. Furniture and lamps, crystal and porcelain. **Antikes**, Odós Karmpóla 8, ☎ (031) 263 284. A selection of clocks, lamps, wooden furniture and coffee mills.

Bookshops – Molho, Leofóros Tsimiskí 10. International magazines and newspapers, and a large choice of books.

Ianos, Platía Aristotélous 7 (B3), ☎ (031) 277 004. Has a wide selection of magazines and books on art and history, also in English. Art gallery upstairs.

VERGÍNA ★★★
VÉRIA AND LEFKÁDIA ★★

Province of Macedonia – District of Imathía – 70km from Thessaloníki
Regional Map page 412 – Michelin map 980 fold 5

Not to be missed
The palace at Vergína and the tomb of Philip II.
The Macedonian tombs at Lefkádia.

And remember...
Combine your tour of Vergína with a trip to the Archaeological Museum
in Thessaloníki.
If you want to stay nearby, opt for Édessa rather than Véria.

On the edge of the Western Macedonian Plain, dominated by the massive silhouette of Mt Vérmio (2 052m), is a broad expanse of vineyards and orchards. But beauty apart, it is the sense of history that makes this region so remarkable: hidden from view for more than two millennia, today, the noble tombs of Vergína and Lefkádia provide an excellent insight into the Macedonian civilisation and its splendour. Although it has many Byzantine churches and old Ottoman houses, the modern town of Véria has little to offer compared with neighbouring Édessa, a much better option if you are looking for a base from which to explore the area, travelling in the footsteps of the great king Philip II of Macedonia and the no less legendary school of Aristotle.

Vergína, ancient Aigai ★★★
Allow half a day

Built on a hillside, at the end of a gorge separating the Pierian Mountains from the Vérmio Massif, ancient Aigai dominates the plain, an expanse of green crossed by the River Aliákmonas. The first Macedonian capital – the exact location of which has aroused the curiosity of generations of archaeologists – has provided a strategic insight into one of the most brilliant kingdoms in Antiquity. After visiting the ruined city, this itinerary takes you out over the plain, to the tomb of the King of Macedonia and its fabulous treasure.

The cradle of Macedonian civilisation

Guided by the oracle at Delphi, **Perdiccas I**, founder of the Macedonian dynasty, decided to establish his capital on this wonderful site. Serving as a springboard for the expansion of the kingdom in the 6C BC, the city retained its prestige even after the capital was transferred to Pella (late 5C BC) and continued to host the great events of the court... with all its tragedies and its splendour: it was to witness the murder of Philip during the wedding of his daughter to the king of Epirus (336 BC) as well as the enthronement of his son, **Alexander the Great**. The city's decline set in following the Roman conquest in the 2C BC and was completed by the barbarian invasions, after which Aigai slipped into oblivion for centuries.

The first excavations, begun in the 19C by the French archaeologist **Léon Heuzey**, were interrupted during the 1920s by the arrival of hordes of Greek immigrants from Turkey, an event that was to have disastrous consequences for the site: the refugees removed huge quantities of material to build the village of Vergína. However, research continued in the 1930s under the leadership of **Konstantínos Rhomaíos**. Then, in 1968, it was the British archaeologist **Nicholas Hammond** who first put forward the theory that the site might be the ancient city of Aigai. But it was **Manólis Andrónikos** who was to have the privilege of discovering – and what a discovery! – the tomb of

Philip II, in 1977. This discovery, along with further excavations around the palace and the agora, have made it possible to reassess the civilisation of the Ancient Macedonians...whom the Ancient Greeks regarded as barbaric! Today the site is a UNESCO World Heritage Site.

The ancient city★

Daily 8am-7pm, entrance fee. All that is left of the **royal palace★** (4C BC) are a few rows of stones perched on a terrace on the hillside, but their vast dimensions are indicative of the magnificence of the Macedonian court. The east wing, pierced by a monumental gateway, was two storeys high and probably housed the royal apartments. Before moving on to the great courtyard surrounded by porticoes, you enter the **tholos**, the most sacred room in the complex, a rotunda which also served as a political forum. On the south side, the rooms paved with splendid **mosaics★★★** with plant motifs (*usually covered in order to protect them*), were the setting of the famous Macedonian libations known as the *symposia*. On the west side, the huge vestibules with fine **pavements★** in

Solid silver oinochoe (Vergína)

opus sectile (marble inlay) were probably used for banquets. Finally, the north wing was preceded by a large **veranda** where the sovereign and his guests could look out over the city and the plain below.

It was at the foot of the palace that archaeologists discovered (1982) the remains of a **theatre**, which must have been one of the largest in the Greek world (4C BC). Badly eroded, the ruins do little to conjure up the performances that were held here (only the bottom row of seating was in stone; the rest, being made of wood, has not survived), but the place is of exceptional historical interest, because it was here that Philip II met his death.

Below lay the **agora**, dominated by the **Eukleia Temple**, consecrated to a Macedonian goddess (*closed to the public*). The site has produced many finds from the time of Alexander the Great: a peristyle, altars, temples, a stoa, etc. The **marble statues** found in the temple (notably a bust which may be the only portrait of Eurydice, mother of Philip II) testify to the influence of Aigai in Macedonian art.

Continue down the road to the **Tomb of Rhomaios★** (3C BC). Sadly, there is nothing left of the painted decoration in the **burial chamber** which is preceded by an attractive portico with semi-engaged Ionic columns. What the archaeologists did discover, however, were some magnificent jewellery and a square marble throne as well as vases and terracotta figurines.

Another throne, of sculpted marble with painted decoration, was found just next door in the **Tomb of Eurydice** (*closed to the public*) (4C BC).

The royal tumulus★★★

Daily 8am-2pm; entrance fee. On the plain below the city is the necropolis of Aigai which takes the form of a large platform containing 300 tumuli. The site, which has yet to be fully explored, contains tombs from several periods, the earliest of which dates from 1000 BC, about which little is known.

Vergína

435

The Vergína Treasure:
the gold burial urn of Philip II

But the main interest of this cemetery is undoubtedly the royal tumulus, situated to the west, which contains the tombs of several important figures. Reconstructed when the excavations were over, this hillock – 13m high and 100m wide – is now a wonderful **museum*****: the actual tombs are closed to the public, but you can see their superb decorated **façades*****, and the extraordinarily rich **treasures***** which were discovered inside them, recently repatriated from the Archaeological Museum in Thessaloníki so that they could be displayed in situ – a rare event indeed – in the corridors between the tombs.

On the left as you enter the tumulus, is **Tomb I**, of which only one **colonnade** remains (dating from c 300 BC).

Next are the ruins of a **small temple**, undoubtedly a *heróon*, dedicated to the glory of dead heroes.

The so-called **Tomb of Persephone*** still guards the secret of the identity of its occupant. The tomb was pillaged in Antiquity and all the archaeologists found was an empty room. However, its superb **frescoes***** (4C BC) have survived, executed with an exquisite delicacy of tone and line, of which you can see reproductions outside. Scenes include Persephone being abducted by Pluto, the King of the Underworld, and Demeter lamenting the disappearance of her daughter. There are also portraits of three women.

Finally, in the heart of the tumulus, the **Tomb of Philip II of Macedonia***** has a tall, majestic **façade**** (5.60m). Decorated at the sides with engaged Doric columns, it is enhanced by a **frieze** depicting a hunting scene with traces of many different pictures in a great variety of colours. Inside, there is a burial chamber and an antechamber, the latter possibly being destined for Cleopatra, the great king's last wife. You can't visit the tomb, but you can have a look at the **treasure*****, which is out of this world. Everything contained in the sarcophagus of the father of Alexander the Great, which lay undisturbed for 24 centuries, is there before your eyes, displayed in cases outside the tomb: his gold and iron breastplate, his silver and gold quiver, gold and bronze dishes, a casket inlaid with a miniature bas-relief in ivory enhanced with gold, gold crowns and tiaras, and the burial urn embossed with a gold sun – the symbol of the dynasty – and even the shroud which was wrapped around the royal bones, a purple fabric embroidered with gold thread.

Do not leave without going to see, on the right, the **Prince's Tomb*** (Tomb III), which has an equally elegant but smaller **façade****, decorated with stone shields which act as columns. The painted frieze, executed on wood or leather, has disappeared, but, inside, archaeologists discovered a **silver burial urn*** topped with a **gold crown**. Everything seems to suggest that this was the tomb of Alexander IV, the son of Alexander the Great and Roxana, who was murdered at the age of 15 along with his mother (311 BC) by Cassander (*see page 420*).

Stop in Véria
Allow 2hr

On the way back from Vergína you have to pass through Véria, the second largest town in the province after Thessaloníki. It is worth stopping to visit three of its beautiful Byzantine churches as well as its wonderful archaeological museum.

The "little Jerusalem"

Véria appears for the first time in ancient chronicles: Thucydides describes how the Athenians tried unsuccessfully to lay siege to it (in 432 BC). Cradle of the Macedonian **Antigonid** dynasty which reigned from the 3C-2C BC, the town enjoyed its first golden age under them, but little evidence of it remains. After the defeat at the battle of **Pydna** (168 BC), its destiny became linked to that of Rome: Pompey made the town his headquarters before the Battle of Pharsalus (48 AD), and, two years later, the Apostle Paul received a warm welcome here. Putting its commercial activity and agricultural wealth to good use, the town achieved the status of a metropolis in 56 AD. The sumptuous festivities organised in honour of the emperors earned it great renown. After the splendour of the 3C, a dark period ensued, marked by the **barbarian invasions** and earthquakes. However, the Byzantine Period was to give the town a significant spiritual boost and, now promoted to the status of a religious metropolis, it saw the construction of many churches. But a new era began with the **Ottoman conquest** (1397), when its sanctuaries were converted into mosques and a Turkish community came to settle here. Finally, at the end of the 15C, Jews expelled from Spain brought with them their weaving skills, ensuring new prosperity for the town. Véria became part of Greece on October 16, 1912.

A Byzantine stroll

More than Antiquity, it was the Byzantine Period which left its mark on Véria: there are no fewer than 50 churches in the town! However, not all of them merit a visit, although the beautiful **Church of the Resurrection of Christ**★★ (Ágios Hristós) is worth seeing (set back from Odós Élla and Odós Mitropóleos; 8.30am-3pm; closed Monday). Built in the 14C, it contains some superb **frescoes**★★ by Geórges Kaliérgis, a great painter of the period.

A stone's throw away, the **Church of Ágios Keríkos**★ is tucked away among some wonderful old **Ottoman houses**. Note the fine patterned masonry on the outside. Its original plan (13C) was altered in the 18C, when a gallery was added, and the original **frescoes** were repainted in the 16C.

Head further south (Odós Pérdika), to the **Church of Ágios Vlássios** (14C), in a simpler style. Here again, various additions have changed the original plan, but you can still see its remarkable original **frescoes**★.

Next on the itinerary is Odós Mitropóleos, the town's main thoroughfare, and the **Church of St Peter and St Paul** (12C), a vast cathedral which once had a nave and two side aisles (the south aisle has been destroyed). Unfortunately closed to the public, it contains **frescoes** dating from the 12C and 14C. From here, you can conclude your tour with a stroll through the **old district**, which lies west of Odós Mitropóleos, and on to the **gorge** created by the waters of the River Tripótamos.

Before entering the **Archaeological Museum** (8.30am-3pm; closed Monday; entrance fee; Odós Anixeos), have a look at the courtyard, where there are some **steles** and **altars** from the Roman Period, and a colossal **Medusa's head**★ (2C BC), features which were later incorporated in the ramparts of the town. The first room contains **pottery**, terracotta **figurines** and burial urns from Archaic and Classical necropolises in the area. In the following room, there are some Hellenistic sculptures and bas-reliefs (note the **torso of Aphrodite**★), and some painted and sculpted **funerary steles**. The last room is devoted to **Roman sculpture**.

Lefkádia★★
Allow 2hr

If you are interested in archaeology and were inspired by the treasures of Vergína, the site of ancient Mieza should not disappoint you. It was a flourishing city in the Hellenistic and Roman Periods, and in addition to the remains of its public buildings (closed to the public), a series of Macedonian tombs of unrivalled historical and artistic interest have been discovered in the surrounding countryside.

Vergína

Funeral banquet

In terms of their architecture, the treasures they contained and their wall-paintings, the Macedonian tombs (hypogea) are some of the most remarkable funerary monuments in Ancient Greece. The structure, which usually resembles a house, a theatre or a temple, is covered with a vault intended to support the weight of the tumulus covering it (unless it is dug out of the rock). In the most important tombs, the façade is decorated with engaged half-columns and frescoes which are exceptionally rich in colour. After the ritual cremation, the ashes were placed in an urn and put into the burial chamber with offerings (including weapons, jewellery and crowns). Conceived as an eternal dwelling place, the tomb also had to be comfortable, indeed luxurious, so that the most eminent dead could decently receive visits from the gods. The burial chamber even took on the appearance of a banqueting hall, with its provisions and kitchen utensils.

The Macedonian tombs★★

Tuesday-Saturday 8.30am-3pm, Sunday and public holidays 9am-2pm. From Véria, take the road leading from Édessa to Kopanós, 12km away. The tombs, marked by signs, are situated close to the road. Begin with the Tomb of Judgement and ask the custodian to show you the others.

A narrow road on the right, after Kopanós, leads to the **Tomb of Judgement**★★ (4C or 3C BC), one of the most beautiful Macedonian burial chambers ever to have been discovered. The structure, built of slabs of poros (limestone), consists of a chamber and an antechamber *(closed; restoration work in progress)*. Take some time to look at its imposing **façade★★★**: 8.60m high, it is superbly decorated with a mixture of Doric and Ionian columns, enhanced by bas-reliefs and frescoes.

Lefkádia: the painted Tomb of Lyson and Kallikles

E. Eliades/T.A.P.

From here, ask the custodian to accompany you to the **Tomb of the Palmettes**★★ (3C BC) nearby. The brightness of the half-columns coated with white lime and the freshness of the painted decoration endow the **façade**★★ with great harmony of colour and line, further enhanced by the three palmettes at the top of the pediment. And here you can see inside the tomb: the ceiling of the antechamber is decorated with a superb **floral fresco**★★★ which has a dream-like quality about it. The antechamber was once separated from the burial chamber by a heavy **marble door**, now lying on the ground.

Return to the main road and head in the direction of Lefkádia. On the right you will notice the **Kinch Tomb** (3C BC). Restored in the 1970s, it is less interesting than the others: the columns of its sombre Doric façade have been removed and most of the **frescoes** which once adorned the burial chamber and the antechamber unfortunately disappeared when the railway was being constructed.

Much more interesting is the **Tomb of Lyson and Kallikles**★ (3C or 2C BC), down a path on the other side of the road, which contains some magnificent **paintings**★★★, executed in vivid colours. As well as the unusual use of perspective (pillars and weapons), the subject matter is also very interesting. There is the motif of the floral garland, for example, which is associated with the cult of Demeter, the goddess of the fertile earth. Also, in the antechamber, note the basin accompanied by a snake entwined around an altar, evoking the ritual of purification and sacrifice associated with death. Above the **niches**, where the burial urns were placed, you can see the names of the dead.

The school of Aristotle★

From Kopanós, take the Náoussa road for 3km. Before you leave, you should try and visit the **Nymphaeum of Mieza**★, better known as the school of Aristotle (4C BC). It was here, in these **caves** beside a stream, that, for three years, the philosopher taught political doctrine to the young Alexander and his fellow students. It is said that King Philip II tried in this way to lure his son away from the influence of his mother. These days all that remains is a **portico**, but it is a lovely place to relax and enjoy the charming setting, picturing the encounters of these two highly exceptional characters.

Making the most of Vergína and Véria

COMING AND GOING

By train – Situated on the Thessaloníki-Kozáni line, Véria is very well served from these two towns. There is also a daily service to Athens.

By bus – From Thessaloníki, take a bus to Véria (a 2hr journey), and then another to Vergína. Buses leave every 2hr to Édessa (a 1hr ride).

ADDRESS BOOK (VÉRIA)

Banks / Currency exchange – *National Bank of Greece*, Odós Mitropóleos, opposite the Church of Ágios Hristós. Cash dispenser.

Post office – Odós Mitropóleos 33, Véria.

Telephone – Local code: 0331. *OTE*, Odós Mitropóleos 45, Véria.

CHALCIDICE★
(HALKIDIKÍ)
Province of Macedonia – District of Chalcidice
Regional Map page 412 – Michelin 980 folds 6-18

Not to be missed
The beaches of Sithonía.

And remember...
Avoid Kassándra and Sithonía at weekends.

Like the sharp points of a trident, doubtless abandoned there by Poseidon after his mythical struggle with the giant Athos, the three peninsulas of Chalcidice protrude deep into the Aegean. A hostile mountainous land covered with forests, the region does not have many ancient remains and it is largely the 500km of coastline, dotted with beaches and seaside resorts, that attracts holidaymakers. In total contrast to its neighbours Kassándra and Sithonía, only the Mt Athos Peninsula is still devoted to the spiritual life. An enclave of monastic living, far removed from the pace and frivolities of the modern world, it is a sanctuary of Byzantine culture *(see following chapter)*.

The beach at Néa Fókea,
on the Kassándra Peninsula

From Thessaloníki to Kassándra

Leave Thessaloníki on the Kassándra road, turn left at Néa Kalikrátia (40km), then continue for 15km on a secondary road.

■ Before heading for the beach, stop off at the **Petrálona Cave** *(daily 9am-9pm; 9am-7pm in winter; entrance fee; guided tour every 30min)*, a yawning cavity of 10 400m² concealing some beautiful concretions *(you can only go 1 500m into the cave)*. In 1960, one of the oldest skulls ever found in Europe – 700 000 years old – was discovered here. Near the entrance, a small **museum** displays fossils of prehistoric wildcats, hyenas, bears, elephants and bison.

■ Perched on a hill overlooking the plain, ancient **Ólinthos*** *(5km east of Néa Moudaniá; daily except Monday, 8am-2.30pm; entrance fee)* will appeal to archaeology enthusiasts. The bases of the **ramparts** and the **houses**, some sections of **pebble mosaics**, all help to trace the outline of the city. Founded by the Boeotians in the 7C BC, Ólinthos headed a coalition against the Athenians in 432 BC and played a key role until it was destroyed by Philip II of Macedonia in 348 BC.

At Gerakiní, take the road north towards Thessaloníki, and continue for 15km.

■ The only feature of interest in the town of **Polígiros** is its **Archaeological Museum** *(daily except Monday, 8.30am-3pm; entrance fee)*, which houses various finds from the sites of Chalcidice. Some of the most beautiful are the polychrome terracottas from Sani, including a magnificent winged statue, vases from the 7C BC, the Akanthos sarcophagus (6C BC) (named after the site where it was discovered), as well as a series of exquisite jewellery from the Archaic, Hellenistic and Roman Periods.

Chalcidice

ON LOCATION

The Kassándra Peninsula
Allow 1 day

A favourite holiday destination for the people of Thessaloníki, Kassándra suffers from being so close to the Macedonian capital (*60km*). Tourism has made its mark along almost 120km of the coast, in the form of marinas, restaurants and luxury hotels. However, in between the beaches, there are a few sites that are worth a detour.

■ After the bridge crossing the Potídea Canal, the road emerges at **Néa Potídea**, built over the ruins of ancient Potidaea (**tower** and remains of the **ramparts**).

■ The road then follows the north coast to **Néa Fókea** (*13km*), a small **beach** guarded by an ancient tower. Then it passes through **Áfitos** (*7km*), a typical little town perched on a cliff overlooking a **beach** where several tavernas have set up shop.

From Kalithéa (4km) onwards, the coast is nothing but a succession of hotels, restaurants and shops, as far as Pefkochóri (16km).

■ Set on a hillside among pine trees, the air perfumed with the scent of resin, **Loutrá** (*on the south coast, 20km*) overlooks one of the loveliest **beaches** on the peninsula. Six kilometres further on, the fishing town of **Néa Skióni** has an equally superb beach of fine sand.

■ The last stop before returning to Néa Potídea, **Kalándra-Possídi** (*8km*) advertises itself as the largest resort on the south coast with its long sandy beach, which lies next to the luxurious complex at **Síviri**.

The Sithonía Peninsula★
Allow 1 day

Less popular than Kassándra, the Sithonía Peninsula offers an excellent alternative with its seaside resorts on a more human scale. A magnificent **coast road**★★ makes it possible to drive right around the peninsula (*110km*), winding up and down over hills covered with pine woods.

■ At the beginning of the peninsula, is **Paralía Nikítas** (*110km from Thessaloníki*), a small, pleasant little town with a **beach** fringed with pines, and with numerous restaurants and houses with rooms to let.

■ There are more beaches along the road heading south, notably **Néos Marmarás** (*20km from Nikitas*), the largest seaside resort on Sithonía, which has several **beaches**. But on the other side of the bay, somewhat incongruously, rise the concrete blocks of **Pórto Carrá** (*5km by road, or by boat: connections every 30min in summer*), a vast holiday complex created by the shipping magnate John C Carras, now in the hands of a banking consortium.

■ Further on, the **Toróni Bay**★ (*20km from Néos Marmarás*) has a long strip of sand which ends at the foot of a small promontory, site of the ruins of an **ancient fortress** and an Early-Christian basilica.

■ After 5km, is the delightful harbour and beach at **Pórto Koufós**★★. The setting is beautiful: the port is located at the head of a bay protected from the sea by a narrow channel which looks as if it has been chopped out of the rocky hills with an axe. The road passes some superb **views**★★ of **Cape Drépano**, a tongue of land covered with scrubland. On a clear day, you can see Mt Athos on the horizon.

■ Finally, **Kalamítsi**★★ (*10km from Pórto Koufós*). A small, romantic resort with a magnificent white sandy **beach** and an end-of-the-world feel.

Although more anonymous, the resort of Sárti (16km) also has some lovely beaches, and you will find others on the road back towards Órmos Panagías (36km).

COMING AND GOING

By bus – In Thessaloníki, the bus terminal is at Odós Karakási 68. Numerous buses go to Kalithéa (90min) and to the resorts of Kassándra, and also to Néos Marmarás (2hr30min) and Sárti (3hr30min) on the Sithonía Peninsula.

GETTING AROUND

Taxi – At Néos Marmarás, taxi rank on the harbour, ☎ (0375) 71 500.

Car hire – See under Thessaloníki (page 430) or, on the spot, in the seaside resorts.

ADDRESS BOOK

Banks / Currency exchange – In Polígiros and in the holiday resorts of Chalcidice, numerous banks change cash and have a cash dispenser.

National Bank of Greece, Néos Marmarás, on the harbour. Money-changing facilities and cash dispenser.

Travel agencies – **Marmarás Tour Agency**, Néos Marmarás, on the harbour, ☎ (0375) 72 110. Numerous services (currency exchange, car hire, apartments to let, ferry tickets), and organises one trip a day to Mt Athos (9.30am-5pm).

WHERE TO STAY

Remember that most places are closed between October and April.

• **Sithonía**

Between €30 and €45
Domátia Eolis, Pórto Koufós, ☎ (0375) 51 421. ⁊ ⌇ A white, freshly painted house facing the sea. The rooms are small but comfortable and have kitchenettes. Significant discount in low season

⌖ **Hotel Marmarás**, Néos Marmarás, 200m from the harbour, ☎ (0375) 72 184, Fax (0375) 72 315 – 15rm. ⁊ ⌇ A small, pleasant, comfortable hotel. Rooms have balconies overlooking the sea (some have air conditioning). Breakfast is not included. Ask for a discount in low season.

Between €45 and €60
Domátia Vraxos, Kalamítsi, ☎ (0375) 41 603 / 41 562 – 12rm. ⁊ ⌇ The

building overlooks the sea with a cafeteria on the ground floor. It has small apartments with two bedrooms and a kitchenette. Significant discount in low season.

Hotel Póntos, Sárti, ☎ and Fax (0375) 94 302 – 56rm. ⁊ ⌇ ✗ ⌖ ⸤cc⸥ Hidden away behind the dunes (swimming pool planned), this pleasant hotel has bicycles and surfboards for hire, and organises excursions in Chalcidice. Note that most of the rooms are booked by a German tour operator. Splendid buffet breakfast.

Hotel Sweet Home, Néos Marmarás, ☎ (0375) 71 664, Fax (0375) 71 828 – 15rm. ⁊ ⌇ ⸤TV⸥ ☰ In a small street at right angles to the harbour. Simple but comfortable rooms. Friendly welcome but only Greek is spoken here. Breakfast extra.

⌖ **Hotel Pórto Koufós**, Pórto Koufós, ☎ (0375) 226 919, Fax (0375) 238 229 – 26rm. ⁊ ⌇ ✗ ⌖ ⸤cc⸥ Standing opposite the entrance to the bay, on the edge of the village, this hotel is perfectly situated. The welcome and service are equally impressive, and the rooms, with balcony, are very comfortable (some have air conditioning). Breakfast is included.

EATING OUT

• **Sithonía**

Between €9 and €15
Chrístos, Néos Marmarás, ☎ (0375) 71 211. On the left of the bay facing the sea (the entrance is difficult to see). ⌂ A vast selection of fish and seafood. Tables inside and on the very pleasant little terrace on stilts (usually packed).

Fáros, **Ta kýmata** and **Thessalonikiá**, Néos Marmarás. ⌂ Three seafood restaurants set on the sandy beach of the little creek north of the town.

Kyaní Aktí, Paralía Nikítas, ☎ (0375) 22 908. ⌂ Another seafood restaurant near the beach, serves fresh fish.

Kafezís estiatoríou, O péfkos, ☎ (0375) 51 206. ⌂ Yet another seafood restaurant... with a pleasant terrace under the pines. Serves excellent fish.

HAVING A DRINK

Cafés, bars – **Dodoni**, Néos Marmarás, near the Chrístos restaurant. ⌂ Claims to have the best ice cream in Greece.

MT ATHOS★★★
(ÁGION ÓROS)

Province of Macedonia – District of Chalcidice – Regional Map page 446
Michelin map 980 folds 7-19 – Mediterranean climate – Allow 4 days

Not to be missed
The monasteries of Símonos Pétras and Great Lavra.

And remember...
Book well ahead to visit the monasteries.
Those who don't have the opportunity of visiting Mt Athos can console themselves by going on a boat trip around the peninsula (see "Making the most of Mt Athos").

Fifty kilometres long and barely 10km wide, the most easterly of the Chalcidice peninsulas is one of the wildest and most mysterious in the whole of the Mediterranean. It is no surprise that the majestic Mt Athos, which rises up 2 030m above the waves, attracted the first ascetics in search of a site suitable for their spiritual rituals. Legend also comes into the story: when the Virgin Mary was caught in a storm on the way to Cyprus, she found refuge on this land, which she then received as a gift of God.

As a result, about 20 monasteries have been built on the slopes of the mountain, practising orthodox monasticism in its purest form. As relics of an empire that is no longer, these timeless strongholds of Byzantine art are also unique (protected as a UNESCO World Heritage Site). However access to Mt Athos remains a male privilege, and even then, only under certain conditions *(see "Useful information", page 451)*.

"Ágion Óros", the Holy Mountain

Mentioned by Homer and Aeschylus, Mt Athos does not appear in the history books until the 7C, when monks from the East, expelled by the Arabs, decided to settle here. Two centuries later, in 885, a decree issued by Emperor Basil I consecrated its vocation as a place of contemplation. However, the main founder of Athonite monasticism was **St Athanasius the Athonite**, confessor of **Nicephorus II Phocas**, who, in 963, founded the monastery of Great Lavra *(see below)*. Breaking with the tradition of strictness and austerity adopted by the ascetics, he proposed a communal life in this vast complex and allowed for a certain amount of munificence. In 1046, Constantine IX Monomachus formalised the rules of coenobitic life and prohibited "any female presence, animal or human, or any eunuch, child or beardless male". Since then, Georgian, Armenian and Latin monks have been accepted here. However, the occupation of Constantinople by the **Latins** (1204-61) was to mark a break with the Roman Catholic Church which maintained a presence here despite the Great Schism of 1054. After the departure of the Franks, the reign of **Andronicus II** (1282-1328) opened up a new golden age, which was interrupted by the bloody incursions of Catalan mercenaries. Thanks to donations from Byzantine emperors and Serbian kings, Mt Athos rose again.

After the Fall of Constantinople (1453), the Holy Mountain kept its privileges in exchange for its submission to the Sublime Porte. But taxes and confiscations led to serious economic difficulties. Anxious to recover the legacy of Byzantium, the princes of the Balkans, Russia and the Ukraine supported the monasteries financially and invited the monks to their court. In this way, Mt Athos gradually established itself as the spiritual and intellectual centre of the Greek revival, which was to end in the insurrection of 1821... and in temporary occupation by the Ottoman Turks. In the 19C, however, the dominant influence of Moscow manifested itself in the arrival of many Russian monks, up until 1912, when the Holy Mountain returned to the Greek fold. Today, despite recent restoration work, it is far from recovering its former glory: the monasteries of Mt Athos house approximately 1 500 monks, compared to 7 000 at the beginning of the 20C.

A theocratic republic

Politically speaking, Mt Athos has always enjoyed an autonomous status, currently defined by the constitution of 1926. As far as the Orthodox Church is concerned, it only refers to the Patriarch in Istanbul about spiritual matters. The depository of administrative power, the **Holy Council**, elected for a year, has 20 delegates and a secretary, while legislative power, in the hands of the Holy Assembly, comprises 20 **igoúmenos** (superiors or abbots of the monasteries). Executive power belongs to the four members of the **Holy Epistasía**, elected for one year, who in turn elect the **prótos**, or head of the confederation. As far as public security is concerned, it relies on the Greek Ministry of Foreign Affairs, which is represented in Kariés by a handful of police officers.

Since the 1990s, all the monasteries have obeyed the same strict regulations of the **coenobitic rule**: the monks live in autarky under the authority of a superior who is elected for life.

In addition to the monasteries, the Holy Mountain is also home to a dozen **skítes** (monasteries of lower rank), hundreds of **kéllions** and **kalýves** (isolated farms with a church) which belong to a monastery, and, finally, a large number of isolated hermitages, sometimes just simple caves with basic facilities. There are also a number of mendicant monks, who form a category all of their own.

G. Guérard

Monks on the march

At the pace of Byzantium

Mt Athos lives literally according to Byzantine time, which begins at sunset (with the exception of the monastery of Ivíron, which has converted to our Chaldean system). Similarly, the Julian calendar, which is thirteen days behind our Gregorian calendar, is still in force. A monk's day is divided into three eight-hour periods, devoted to prayer, rest and work. Communal prayers, announced by the dull sound of a wooden plank, ("símandro") beaten by the "kodonovroústis", are held in the main church or in chapels. Most of them – Vespers, Compline, and Matins – take place at night.

The protector of Byzantine architecture

From the **arsana**, the small harbour, which is sometimes overlooked by a defence tower which also acts as a warehouse, a path leads up to the monastery. With its **defensive wall** it resembles a medieval fortress, an impression reinforced by the **tower** dominating it. In the **main courtyard**, the functional buildings – the hospital, the library and the monks' cells – are surrounded by balconies, which are usually made of wood. The red walls denote the **katholikón** (or main church), which usually has domes and is preceded

by a narthex and an exonarthex. Except for the monasteries of Prótaton and Stavronikíta, they are all based on the monastery of Great Lavra (963). An upward movement, conducive to the uplifting of the soul, permeates the interior space, with the frescoes, icons and iconostases enhancing the sense of spirituality. In front of the entrance stands a marble **phiale** (stoup) protected by a dome and small columns. The **refectory** (*trapeza*), the walls of which are sometimes decorated with frescoes, is often the oldest part of the monastery, together with the *katholikón*.

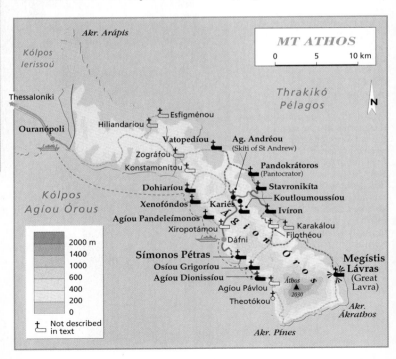

MT ATHOS

0   5   10 km

Akr. Arápis

Kólpos Ierissoú

Thessaloníki

Thrakikó Pélagos

N

Ouranópoli

Esfigménou

Hiliandaríou

Vatopedíou

Ag. Andréou
(Skíti of St Andrew)

Zográfou

Pandokrátoros
(Pantocrator)

Konstamonítou

Dohiaríou

Stavronikíta

Xenofóndos

Kariés

Koutloumoussíou

Agíou Pandeleímonos

Ivíron

Kólpos Agíou Órous

Xiropotámou

Karakálou

Dáfni

Filothéou

2000 m
1400
1000
600
400
200
0

Símonos Pétras

Osíou Grigoríou

Megístis Lávras
(Great Lavra)

Agíou Dionissíou

Áthos
2030

Agíou Pávlou

Theotókou

Akr. Ákrathos

+ Not described in text

Akr. Pínes

Along the west coast

Boat trip departing from Ouranópoli. Stops at Dáfni then you can continue by boat or bus.
See also "Making the most of Mt Athos".

■ **Ouranópoli** – Guarding the entrance to the peninsula, the small resort of Ouranópoli is the port where boats depart for trips around the Mt Athos Peninsula. Before setting off to experience the austerity of monastic life on Mt Athos, spend some time enjoying the pleasant atmosphere that pervades the port in summer and the lovely beaches round about the town. You could also have a look at the Christian-art collections in the **Museum of Byzantine Culture** (*11am-5pm, daily except Monday*), housed in a splendid 14C **tower★** dominating the landing-stage. Then, by all means, board one of the boats heading for Dáfni. From the boat you get a good view of the hillside dotted with monasteries, some of which appear to be clinging to the rocky coastline, looking down on the sea.

The jewels of Byzantine painting

Two schools dominate the art of fresco painting on Mt Athos. The key figure of the Macedonian school, which spread to Thessaloníki and Constantinople in the 13C and 14C, was Pansélinos. The style of this artist is distinctive for its realism, which can be perceived in the mobility of the faces, the dramatic intensity of the composition and the clarity of colour. You will see some beautiful examples in the katholikóns of Prótaton, Hiliandaríou and Vatopedíou. The Cretan school, which appeared in Constantinople during the Ottoman Period, reached its height on Mt Athos in the 16C, (notably in the katholikóns of Great Lavra and Stavronikíta), with the great master Theophanes of Crete and his son Simeon. Characteristics of this school are its sobriety of movement, the hieratic quality of the figures and a temperance of colour.

■ Against a backdrop of wooded hills, a stone's throw from the shore, the **Monastery of Dohiaríou** (10C) looks like a castle with its crenellated tower and its high stone façade. Its **katholikón** (16C) has some fine frescoes of the Cretan school.

■ There is a small **harbour** in front of the **Monastery of Xenofóndos** (of Xenophon), which also stands close to the shoreline. Founded in the 10C, it was rebuilt after a fire in 1817. Its **new katholikón** is the largest on Mt Athos. However, the **old katholikón** is more interesting, with its fine 16C frescoes and a splendid iconostasis.

■ When the boat rounds a cape, the imposing **Monastery of Agíou Pandeleímonos** (St Panteleímon) suddenly sweeps into view, recognisable by its green bulbous domes topped with gold crosses. Founded by Russian monks in the 11C, it operated according to Slav traditions, using very old and intensely spiritual liturgical chants. Below the bell-tower lies the vast **refectory**, which can accommodate 800 diners. The monastery also has the distinction of having one of the richest **libraries** on Mt Athos.

■ A ferry port, **Dáfni** has a restaurant, some shops and a harbour police office. *From here, you can either take a bus to Kariés, inland, or continue along the west coast (our suggestion), by bus or by boat.*

■ The jewel of Athonite architecture, **Símonos Pétras★★★** stands poised on a vertical spur, its high stone walls clinging to the rock like a Tibetan temple. According to tradition, this splendid site was chosen in the 13C by St Simon, who was guided here one Christmas Eve by a divine light. Expanded in the 14C thanks to the donations of a Serb prince, it was destroyed by fire in 1582 and again in 1626, then experienced serious economic hardship from which it did not recover until the 18C. Engulfed by flames yet again in 1891, this time Símonos Pétras benefited from Russian funds which enabled it to build the spectacular **seven-storey**

building★★ we see today, perched high above the sea. Defying the laws of gravity, a multitude of wooden balconies cling to its façade, suspended above a 200m drop. This is the most interesting feature of the monastery, as little remains of the older monasteries (its **katholikón** dates from the late 19C).

■ Another eagle's eyrie is the **Monastery of Osíou Grigoríou★** *(doors closed between 1pm and 5pm)* with its elegant façade and balconies hanging right above the sea. The first courtyard, perfumed by a Virginia creeper, leads to another courtyard containing the **katholikón★** (18C). Decorated with frescoes, it has a magnificent iconostasis decorated with scenes from the Old Testament, as well as some remarkable old icons. But most of its treasures disappeared during the fire of 1761.

■ Built by St Denis and his disciples in the late 14C, the **Monastery of Agíou Dionissíou★** stands on a rocky precipice towering 80m above the waves. In the 16C, some Moldavian princes paid for the complex to be rebuilt and a **tower** was added. The **katholikón★**, which has six domes, contains some 16C frescoes, masterpieces of the Cretan school, as well as a richly decorated iconostasis.

Return to Dáfni by boat.

■ **Kariés** – Huddling in the crook of the hills, the administrative capital of Mt Athos is no more than a large village although the atmosphere is rather oriental. The few shops and craft workshops are run by monks and laymen.
In the centre of the town, the **Church of the Prótaton★** (10C) contains some superb **frescoes★★** (14C) attributed to Manuel Pansélinos, as well as a remarkable marble **iconostasis★★** and a **miraculous icon of the Virgin** (10C), which is supposed to ensure the protection of Mt Athos. The **bell-tower** dates from the 16C.

■ A certain melancholy emanates from the **Skíti of St Andrew** (Agíou Andréou) *(200m north of the town)*, a one-time bastion of Russian monasticism. Dilapidated and overgrown with weeds, this ascetic dwelling is still occupied by four monks. Its large **Baroque church** – the only one on Mt Athos – has an enormous iconostasis.

■ Built on the hillside, the **Monastery of Koutloumoussíou** (10C-11C) *(15min from Kariés, by the path leading to the Monastery of Ivíron)* stands in a pastoral setting. Having fallen into decline after being pillaged by the Catalans, it underwent a revival in the 14C thanks to various Moldavian princes. Several Romanian monks then came to live here. Located in the centre of a courtyard overlooked by balconies, the **katholikón** (1540) contains more fine examples of frescoes of the Cretan school, although sadly these have been repainted. With a bit of luck, you may be able to visit the **treasury★★** (icons, priests' vestments, crosses, etc) and its wonderful **library**.

The monasteries on the east coast
Tour by bus or on foot. See "Making the most of Mt Athos".

■ **Vatopedíou★★** – Probably founded in the 10C, it is the second-largest monastery on Mt Athos. Having suffered from the incursions of pirates and Catalans, Vatopedíou recovered in the 13C thanks to the support of the Paleologus emperors and Serb princes, then, in the 18C, the Russian tsars and Balkan princes. Altered several times (an exonarthex and a bell-tower were added in the 15C), the **katholikón★** is original. Inside, its 14C frescoes were repainted in the 18C, but the **mosaics★★** – the only ones on Mt Athos – and the magnificent **marble pavement★** are original. Opposite, the **refectory** (12C) is decorated with 18C frescoes. But it is to its exceptional **treasury★★★** that Vatopedíou owes its fame: it includes priestly vestments embroidered with gold, portable icons, manuscripts of the Gospels, a piece of the True Cross, the Virgin's Belt... and its precious **library★★** *(can be visited – depending on the goodwill of the monks)*.

■ **Pandokrátoros** (Pantocrator) – Founded in the 13C, this monastery is perched high up on the rocks. Despite several fires and the buffeting of the waves the monastery has retained its impressive **tower*** and a small **katholikón** (14C), the **frescoes** of which were repainted in the 19C.

■ **Stavronikíta** – With its crenellated defence tower and its high walls built on a promontory overhanging the sea, Stavronikíta is reminiscent of a medieval castle. The small **aqueduct** dates from the 17C. Mentioned as early as 1012, the monastery was abandoned in the 13C until the 16C following raids by pirates and the Crusaders. Its **katholikón**, the smallest on the peninsula, has remarkable **frescoes*** by the master Theophanes and his son, including a portrait of the Patriarch Jeremy I. The frescoes in the **refectory** also belong to the Cretan school.

■ **Ivíron**** – Overlooking a little harbour, the monastery presents a curious spectacle: the tall façade of Ivíron is in keeping with its surroundings on the landward side, but this contrasts strongly with the heterogeneous façade that faces out to sea. Founded in the late 10C by a Georgian monk, the monastery is the third-largest on the Mt Athos Peninsula. A sense of complete calm pervades the inner courtyard, which is overlooked by a **tower**. In the centre, note the **phiale** set back against the walls of the **katholikón**. Built in the 11C, it was altered in the 16C. Of the original structure, you can still see the marble paving and the recycled **ancient capitals** decorated with acanthus-leaf and calf-head motifs. The frescoes (16C), however, were repainted in the 19C. Ivíron also has one of the richest **treasuries**** on Mt Athos: there are crosses, mitres, gold-embroidered liturgical vestments, and its **library**** contains some exceptional pieces including manuscripts, early printed books, and chrysobulls (golden bulls) dating from the 10C. As for the monastery's little harbour, it lies under the watchful eye of a well-preserved **tower** dating from 1626.

■ **Megístis Lávras**** (Great Lavra) – This, the cradle of Mt Athos, is the most ancient and largest monastery on the Holy Mountain, positioned right at the top of the Athonite hierarchy. Perched high up in wooded hills on the south-east of the

A red church: the katholikón of Vatopedíou

peninsula, Great Lavra dominates the splendid **view★★** out to sea. Founded by St Athanasius (963), it was home to 700 monks in the 11C, before falling into decline from the 14C to the 17C. At first glance, the monastery resembles a fortified town, guarded by a massive **square tower**. Various buildings several storeys high occupy a space divided up by churches and chapels. Do not miss the huge **katholikón★★**, dedicated to St Athanasius (his remains lie inside): it contains some beautiful **frescoes★★** by Theophanes of Crete (16C), regarded as the painter's greatest works, as well as some portable icons. At the entrance stands a **phiale★** surrounded by a colonnade decorated with sculpted marble and frescoes. Not to be outdone, the **refectory★★** has numerous **frescoes** depicting the Last Supper, Jacob's Ladder and the Life of the Virgin, accompanied by portraits of Greek philosophers. The crowning glory of the monastery is its **treasury★★★**, of a sumptuousness that would outshine the greatest museums in the world. If there is a monk on hand who can open the doors, you will have a chance to see the stunning crown and mantle of Emperor **Nicephorus Phocas**, surrounded by all sorts of precious objects and ecclesiastical robes, including an ancient quiver. Equally breathtaking is the **library★★★**, which contains the Holy Mountain's largest collection of ancient writings, including the **Treasury Missal★★** (said to have belonged to Phocas).

Making the most of Mt Athos

COMING AND GOING

By bus and by boat – From Thessaloníki (Odós Karakási 68), buses leave for Ouranópoli every 2hr between 6am and 6.30pm (2hr30min). Buses return to Thessaloníki between 5.30am and 6.15pm. Ideally, try to sleep in Ouranópoli so as to catch the 9.15am boat to Dáfni, the port of access to the Mt Athos Peninsula (2hr). On the way back, the boat leaves Dáfni at about 12noon.

BOAT TRIP

For anyone not setting foot on the Holy Mountain, the travel agencies in Thessaloníki and Sithonía organise boat trips around the peninsula (1 day). The boat does not stop, but the monasteries are visible from the deck.

GETTING AROUND

For those who have obtained a permit to visit the peninsula.

On foot – Walking is the best way to explore the peninsula and absorb the atmosphere of the place. There is a network of paths linking the monasteries, but it's easy to get lost. So get hold of a good map (on sale in Ouranópoli). The paths along the coast, on the other hand, are easy to follow. The walks between the main sites on the peninsula are as follows:
– Dáfni-Símonos Pétras (2hr), Símonos Pétras-Grigoríou (2hr), Grigoríou-Agíou Dionissíou (2hr).

– Dáfni-Kariés (3hr), Kariés-Ivíron (2hr), Ivíron-Stavronikíta (1hr), Stavronikíta-Pandokrátoros (1hr), Pandokrátoros-Vatopedíou (2hr), Vatopedíou-Kariés (3hr).
– Xiropotámou-Pandeleímonos (1hr).

By minibus – As a concession to modernity, the monks often travel by minibus, but the roads are not tarred and connections are infrequent. In Dáfni, you can take a minibus to Símonos Pétras or Kariés (they leave at around 12noon, or at 10.30am in the other direction, a 45min ride). From Kariés, there is a minibus service to Great Lavra (a 90min ride) via Ivíron, which also goes to the Vatopedíou Monastery. You could try thumbing a lift, but bear in mind that vehicles are few and far between.

By boat – The boat from Ouranópoli to Dáfni stops at Dohiaríou, Xenofóndos and Agíou Pandeleímonos. From Dáfni, a boat goes to all the monasteries along the coast as far as Skíti Theotókou (leaves at about 1pm). On the north coast, services to the monasteries are less regular and depend on the weather.

USEFUL INFORMATION

The pilgrimage office in Thessaloníki now deals with all the applications for permits. Since the number of permits issued to foreigners is limited, you are advised to apply well in advance, and to avoid the summer season. Send a photocopy of your passport and state the date you are intending to arrive. Once you have obtained your permit, book somewhere to stay. Once you have collected (in person) the acknowledgement that your application has been received, take this document and your passport to the office in Ouranópoli (near the fuel station on the outskirts of the village), where they will issue a sleeping voucher (permit), which on average costs around €24. This magical document gives you the right to spend three nights on Mt Athos and you will be asked to show it at some of the monasteries. Arrive early in the morning in order not to miss the boat from Dáfni.

Advice – As a centre of spirituality, Mt Athos calls for respect and reverence, as well as appropriate clothing at all times (arms and legs should be covered, the head uncovered). Your presence at mass will be appreciated and, in some monasteries, they will come to wake you up at 4am! Non-Orthodox visitors may watch from the narthex, without penetrating the sanctuary (remember that, in Orthodox churches, they make the sign of the Cross finishing with the left shoulder). Once mass is over, meals are served in the refectory, the silence broken only by the monk reading from holy scriptures. Since the everyday fare is rather frugal, you are advised to buy food in Ouranópoli, especially if you are thinking of walking.

What to take – A torch, towel, pullover and bottle of water will all come in handy. Note that interior photography and the use of flash are prohibited and some monasteries do not even allow shots to be taken from anywhere within their precincts. Never photograph a monk without his consent (often refused).

Pilgrim office – *Pilgrim Office of Holy Mount Athos*, Odós Konstantínos Karamanlís 14 (formerly New Egnatía), Thessaloníki, ☎ (031) 861 611, Fax (031) 861 811 (Monday – Friday, 8.30am-1pm).

Telephone – Local code: 0377. Take a phone card.

WHERE TO STAY

• Ouranópoli

Between €30 and €45

Hotel Acrogiali, 100m from the bus stop, on the left, by the sea, ☎ (0377)

71 201 – 15rm. ⌂ Comfortable but monastic-style rooms, ideal for preparing oneself for life on Mt Athos... Some have sea views. No breakfast.

Xenios Zeys, in the main street, on the sea side, ☎ (0377) 71 274, Fax (0377) 71 185 – 20rm. ⌂ ▤ ♪ TV This small hotel is good value for money. Try to get a room with a sea view. Breakfast extra.

Over €75

⌂ **Xénia Hotel**, on the outskirts of the village, ☎ (0377) 71 412, Fax (0377) 71 362 – 20rm. ⌂ ♪ TV ✗ ▥ ▨ cc A very pleasant, quiet, comfortable establishment, with a private beach. The service is very professional but prices are high (considerable discount in low season). Breakfast is included and you can stay there on a half-board basis.

• Mt Athos

If you are hoping to get a bed in a monastery, arrive before sunset because the doors remain closed at night. The cells (from 2 to 10 beds) are rather spartan, but accommodation is free (maximum one night). With a few exceptions (notably Great Lavra and Agíou Dionissíou), the monasteries require a reservation: Xenofóndos, ☎ (0377) 23 249 (9am-2pm); Pandeleímonos, ☎ (0377) 23 252 (10am-12noon); Símonos Pétras, ☎ (0377) 23 254 (1pm-3pm); Grigoríou, ☎ (0377) 23 668 (11am-1pm); Koutloumoussíou, ☎ (0377) 23 226 (12noon-2.30pm); Ivíron, ☎ (0377) 23 643 (12noon-2pm); Stavronikíta, ☎ (0377) 23 255 (1pm-3pm); Pandokrátoros, ☎ (0377) 23 253 (12noon-2pm); Vatopedíou, ☎ (0377) 23 219 (10am-4pm).

Hotel Iánni Patní, Kariés, ☎ (0377) 23 243. ✗ Only as a last resort: a small, hotel with communal bathrooms.

EATING OUT

Ouranópoli has a good choice of seafood restaurants.

Karidas, ☎ (0377) 71 180. ⌂ A taverna on the harbour, offering a wide selection of fish at a reasonable price.

SHOPPING GUIDE

Icons – Icons painted by the monks are on sale in Ouranópoli and Kariés.

AMFÍPOLI★

Not to be missed
The Archaeological Museum.
The Acropolis. The "palaestra". The walls.

And remember...
Approach Amfípoli from the Kavála road, preferably in your own vehicle.
Buy the little booklet on sale in the museum: it contains a map of the site.

Before being abandoned for centuries, the jewel that was Amfípoli shone brightly from classical Antiquity until the Byzantine Period, a period that spanned more than one thousand years. Lost in the enchanting setting of the Macedonian countryside, where gently rolling hills stretch as far as the eye can see, its ruins are like a history book open to the sky. As one of the most powerful ancient cities in the north, Amfípoli has left some most revealing remains...

Thucydides, the first historian

As commander-in-chief of the Athenian fleet when Amfípoli was taken by the Spartans, Thucydides (465-395 BC) succeeded in saving the port of Aigion. But since the city had fallen into the hands of its besiegers, Thucydides was held responsible by Athens for this catastrophic defeat. Condemned to exile, Thucydides turned to writing, undertaking to compile a "History of the Peloponnesian War". This brilliant description of the mechanisms of war, where the author refrained from automatically resorting to mythological explanations, is still regarded today as the precursor of historical science.

"Visible from every direction"

The area around the mouth of the River **Strymon** was inhabited at a very early date, but it only enters the history books in 437 BC when the Athenian Hagnon founded the colony of Amphipolis, meaning "visible from every direction". But a mere thirteen years later, the Spartan general **Brasidas** routed the Athenians, who were never to regain their authority despite numerous attempts to do so. It was then that the city, in its position as gateway to the mines and the rich agricultural plains of the hinterland, acquired an important role, which it was to maintain throughout Antiquity, even after the arrival of the **Macedonians** (357 BC). Philip II then Alexander the Great made it the focal point of their battle plans and erected a number of prestigious buildings, while the gold mines of Mt Pangaíon added to the city's good fortune. Upon the death of Alexander, Cassander, his successor, was to send Alexander's son and wife, Roxanne, into exile, before having them executed.

After the **Battle of Pydna** (168 BC), Amfípoli was the last Macedonian city to fall into the hands of the Romans. Seat of one of the four administrative districts created on the ruins of the kingdom, its position on the **Via Egnatia** meant that trade prospered. After the Battle of Pharsalus (48 BC) Pompey sought refuge here in a desperate attempt to pursue his struggle against Julius Caesar, and a few years later, Mark Antony gathered his fleet here before the decisive battle against Octavian, at **Actium**.

Amfípoli, which welcomed the Apostle Paul in 50 AD, underwent a revival in the Early-Christian Period and even became the seat of a bishopric. Battered by the Slav invasions (8C and 9C), it nevertheless played a strategic role in the Byzantine Period before sliding into permanent oblivion with the fall of the Byzantine Empire.

Macedonia and Thrace

Tour of the site

On the Kavála road, turn left in the direction of Séres. 2km further on, turn left again down the narrow road leading to the village of Amfípoli. Allow 3hr.

Stretching from the hill that dominates the banks of the Strymon to the mouth of the river, the site is enormous. Scattered with remains dating from various periods, from Antiquity to the Middle Ages, it is an archaeological paradise! And Amfípoli still has many secrets to reveal: although excavations have unearthed several sanctuaries, most of them have yet to be discovered.

The Archaeological Museum★

8am-2.30pm; closed Monday; entrance fee; notes and maps in English. Before exploring the ruins, visit the museum, situated on the outskirts of the village. Opened in 1995, it contains most of the finds from the site which date back to the Late Neolithic (bronze objects, terracotta tools), the Iron Age (gold jewellery, weapons) as well as the Byzantine Period. Near the entrance is a **silver ossuary★★** crowned with a **tiara decorated with gold-leaf**, closely followed by the **Hellenistic section** which has three remarkable **funerary hydrias★★** (urns with three handles) dating from the 4C BC, in silver, black-painted pottery and polychrome pottery.

The **treasure from a Macedonian tomb★** (tiara decorated in gold leaf, other trinkets, rings, etc) along with various everyday objects (bed, oil lamp, shoe soles, comb) throw interesting light on daily life in Antiquity. You will also see funerary steles, marble statues and terracotta statuettes, notably a bust of the handsome Attis, the god who castrated himself after Cybele struck him with a frenzy to punish him for his infidelity. The **Roman Period** is represented by **sculptures**, glassware, ceramics and **mosaic floors**, while the capitals and steles from the 6C belong to the **Early-Christian Period**.

Turn left 200m after the museum and continue for 1km.

The romantic ruins of Amfípoli

The acropolis*

Perched on a desolate plateau above the village, the melancholy ruins of the basilicas of Amfípoli have been watching over the plain since the 4C or 5C. Most of them incorporated features from earlier buildings but, today, only the first few layers of stone walling are visible, and a few fragments of mosaics (*sometimes covered*).

All that remains of the great **Basilica G** (dating from the second half of the 5C) (*on the left of the entrance*) are the bases of the columns that separated the nave from the side aisles. However, the fine **mosaic floor** of the nave with its geometric and animal motifs, similar to the one in the atrium, has survived.

Another large building, **Basilica A** (dating from the mid-6C) (*just to the right*) also had a nave and two side aisles and an atrium, with a narthex and exonarthex. Here, all that remains of its colonnades are a few **Corinthian capitals**, which are dotted here and there among the remnants of the green marble columns. Look out for the very beautiful **mosaics*** in the south aisle, one of which depicts peacocks while another shows deer drinking, surrounded by swans. More mosaics with animal motifs decorate the adjacent rooms.

To the east of Basilica A, you can see a section of the walls of the huge **bishop's palace**, which was recently excavated. The three compartments at the south-west corner of the building were probably used as a **cistern** during the Early-Christian Period. The palace stands next to **Basilica D** (second half of the 5C) (*further on, on the right*), built on the same plan as the other basilicas, but smaller.

Spend some time in front of the ruins of the **church with a central ground-plan*** (6C) (*to the east*), a rare example of this type of building: reminiscent of a seashell, it is built around a hexagonal structure surrounded by a wide circular gallery interrupted by an apse on the east side. The church, which must have had two storeys, once had an atrium with porticoes. You can still see part of its elegant black and white **marble paving** with geometric motifs.

The last building on the acropolis, **Basilica B** (6C) (*just to the north*) also has some **mosaics**. South-west of its atrium lies the **coping** of a marble well, which was once linked to an underground cistern.

Leave the acropolis and follow a path heading south-west for 200m.

The basilicas are not the only buildings to be adorned with mosaics: in the ruins of a **Roman villa** (*next to the eroded ruins of what was probably a Roman palaestra*), archaeologists discovered three very fine works, the most famous of which, *The Rape of Europa*, has been transferred to the museum in Kavála. The two other **mosaic floors*** (2C-3C AD) depict *The Three Ages of Womanhood* and scenes from Greek mythology. From here, proceed to the imposing **west wall**, which is 80m long, with a **defence tower** at either end. *Then, back at the acropolis, take the path leading down to the sea (south-east) and continue for 300m beyond the ruins of the Hellenistic house (closed to the public).*

The palaestra*

Discovered in 1982 on the east side of the hill, this vast complex was built at the turning-point between the Classical and Hellenistic Periods (4C BC), then renovated at the beginning of the Imperial Period following a fire. With its massive walls built of large tufa blocks, the **palaestra** (47m by 36m) is the main building of the complex, where ephebes (youths) were taught how to become proper men. On the east side, a **monumental staircase** gave access to the various rooms of the sports complex, located around a central courtyard with porticoes where the athletes competed. Finally, in the **water room** (*north-east*), there are some marble pools – still waiting for bathers after all these years.

A large number of objects were found in situ (*on display in the Archaeological Museum*), in particular the **herm**** of a young man (a torso, where the body has been replaced by a pedestal), a masterpiece of the Classical style, together with an **engraved stele**, 2.65m high, which has provided vital information about the lifestyle of the gymnasts. **The north part** of the complex included some **cisterns**, and a **covered track** which has been partially excavated, where the athletes could train in bad weather.

Back at the village, take the road leading north to the river.

The north wall

In the Classical Period, two defensive walls of tufa blocks were erected, around the acropolis (2 200m long) and the town (7 500m). Resembling stone snakes, their towers, gates and bastions made the structure seem particularly vast. You can get some idea of its scale by exploring the foundations of the north wall.

The west section (108m), which includes **Gate B** and a round **tower** built within a square-shaped Hellenistic tower, runs past the ruins of a **building with columns** from an earlier date. Under constant threat of flooding from the River Strymon, the next section (which connects the bridge to the defence system) was crisscrossed with **drainage pipes**. A little further on is **Gate G**, the largest gateway of the ramparts, with walls 2m thick. But the most impressive feature is undoubtedly the superstructure of the **bridge**** discovered on the dry riverbank: resembling the wreck of a ship that has run aground, hundreds of posts are scattered on the ground, covered with silt deposits, the deepest of which date from the Classical Period (5C BC).

To the east, the road runs along beside the river passing below a **Byzantine tower** (1367) decorated with ancient columns and pieces of marble. Built by two brothers who were generals, Alexis and John, the main doorway was located 2m above the ground to make it more secure.

Built on the side of the hill, the **east section of the ramparts** (167m), which is more than 7m high in places, has two gateways, one of which is Hellenistic in style, the other Classical, which have been blocked by debris from the flood water. Narrow trapezoidal passageways in the wall allow the water to escape without providing access for the enemy. Next to it, the **thesmophorion** (a sanctuary dedicated to a female divinity), which is probably older than the enclosure wall, yielded numerous votive vases and clay figurines.

From Gate A, go back to the Séres road and turn right, heading south, then turn right again after the village and continue as far as the river.

The famous **Lion of Amfípoli*** (4C BC) is a magnificent statue which has been mounted on a modern pedestal. It was discovered quite by chance during the Balkan War of 1912 by some soldiers who dug a trench here. Some scholars have interpreted it as a monument dedicated to Laomedon, one of Alexander the Great's generals, while others see the statue as a funerary monument.

Making the most of Amfípoli

COMING AND GOING

By bus – From Thessaloníki, take a bus for Kavála and ask to be let off at Kerdília, which is within walking distance of Amfípoli (3km) or you can find a taxi.

USEFUL INFORMATION

Telephone – Local code: 0322.

EATING OUT

Amfípoli, opposite the museum. 🍴 A small, excellent restaurant, even though the exterior doesn't inspire much confidence .

KAVÁLA

Province of Macedonia – Capital of the district of Kavála
175km from Thessaloníki – Regional Map page 412
Michelin map 980 fold 7 – Pop 60 000

Not to be missed
The Ottoman district and the Archaeological Museum.

And remember...
Explore the town on foot, thereby avoiding the traffic and inconvenience
of having to find a parking space.

The size of Kavála is something of a surprise: the town stretches as far as the eye can see over and away into the hills, their steep sides running down to the blue waters of the Aegean Sea creating a succession of bays and promontories, and making for stunning views. Situated on the edge of eastern Macedonia, Kavála began to develop rapidly in the 20C with the arrival of a large number of Greeks who had been expelled from Asia Minor. Today, this is a dynamic, modern town, relying on fishing and the clothing industry, but also on the production of grapes and honey. You can get a feel of Kavála by strolling along the quayside or up through the steep streets that climb the hills on which it is built; but nowhere more than in the old quarter of Panagía and the citadel will you be able to detect the aromas of years gone by. The town is also the ideal base for trips to Fílipi and the island of Thássos. Unless, that is, you prefer to head straight for the beaches of Kalamítsa, Tósca, Palio, Néa Iraklítsa or Néa Péramos.

A tumultuous history

Ancient Neapolis, which corresponds to the modern district of **Panagía**, was probably founded in the 7C BC by the inhabitants of Thássos and Páros. Situated next to the gold mines of Mt Pangaíon, the town enjoyed great prosperity, a fact borne out by its considerable coin production. But its position between East and West resulted in less fruitful visits by the Persians, then by Philip II of Macedonia, who made the town the port of the town of Fílipi (340 BC). Four centuries later, it was here at Kavála that **St Paul** first set foot on European soil. Renamed Christopolis in the 9C, until the 14C the town was the target of raids by the Slavs, the Catalans and especially the

Mehmet Ali, or the Arab revival

A fascinating fate is that of an Albanian native of Kavála, Mehmet Ali (1769-1849), who defied the great powers of his time and founded a dynasty that was destined to rule over the Nile until 1952. Sent to Egypt at the head of an Albanian contingent to fight Napoleon Bonaparte, he proclaimed himself viceroy after the departure of the French, massacred the Mamelouks, hounded the Wahhabites of Arabia, attacked pirates on the Red Sea and founded Khartoum! In 1827, his fleet put down a Greek rebellion, but it was defeated at Navarino (see page 278). Furious that he had been unable to acquire Syria, Mehmet Ali conquered Palestine. In 1839, he defeated the Turks with the support of France but, under British pressure, he was forced to withdraw to Egypt and the Sudan, territory that he had received in legacy and where he ended his days. Although Egyptians consider him tyrannical, Mehmet Ali is still regarded as the founder of modern Egypt and the precursor of the Arab revival.

Normans of Sicily (1185), before succumbing to the Ottomans in 1391. Kavála then managed to make a living from trading **horses** (hence its name) until the beginning of the 16C, when a number of Jews were transferred here from Hungary by the Ottomans. The town then enjoyed another golden age, during which **Süleyman the Magnificent** built new fortifications and an aqueduct. Thanks to its situation, the town pursued its commercial vocation, establishing trading links with Marseilles. In the 19C, fuelled by the dynamism of the Greek community, it expanded beyond the boundaries of Panagía. But it was not until

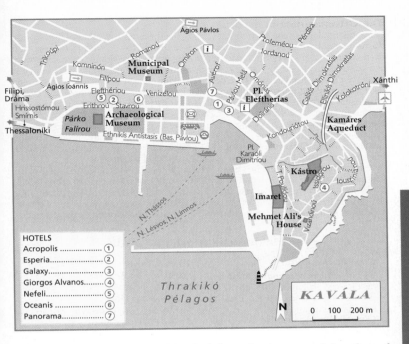

HOTELS
Acropolis .... ①
Esperia....................... ②
Galaxy........................ ③
Giorgos Alvanos......... ④
Nefeli.......................... ⑤
Oceanis .... ⑥
Panorama................... ⑦

KAVÁLA
0   100   200 m

1913, after being briefly occupied by the Bulgars, that it re-entered the sphere of Athens. Then in 1922, the town became a refuge for 25 000 Greeks exiled from Asia Minor as part of the exchange of populations between Greece and Turkey.

Tour of the town
Allow 1 day

The main thoroughfares, Odós Elefthériou Venizélou and Odós Erithroú Stavroú, where the heart of the modern city beats, run parallel to the seafront, ending at **Platía Eleftherías**. From the opposite side of the square, it is easy to reach the old quarter of Panagía, which clings to a rocky promontory overlooking the harbour.
Odós Ethnikís Antístasis is the site of the very inspiring **Archaeological Museum★** (*Tuesday-Friday 8am-7pm, Saturday, Sunday and public holidays 8am-2.30pm; entrance fee*), dedicated to eastern Macedonia, which covers a period ranging from the Neolithic to the Roman Empire. The first courtyard, dotted with various steles and Roman architectural features, leads to the **Neapolis** room, which contains objects from the sanctuary dedicated to the goddess Athena Parthenos, the ruins of which dominate the old town. The corridor opposite the entrance contains a number of marble **sculptures** found at **Amfípoli**, together with various stone and terracotta objects from the Neolithic and the Bronze Age. At the far end, the Amfípoli room conjures up the splendour of this town in the Classical, Hellenistic and Roman Periods with **funerary steles★**, sculptures, vases, terracottas and gold **jewellery★★**. Housed in an elegant neo-Classical building, the **Municipal Museum** (*Odós Filípou 4, Monday-Friday 8am-2pm, Saturday 9am-1pm*) throws light on contemporary Greek art, and, in particular, on the works of the painter and sculptor **Polýgnotos Vagís** (1894-1965). A rather curious staircase adorned with stuffed birds leads to the upper floor where there is an exhibition of **folk art** (costumes, tools, etc.).

457

The Ottoman district (Panagía)

Built under Süleyman the Magnificent (1550), the three tiers of arches of the majestic **Kamáres aqueduct*** dominate the entrance to the old town. With its **houses** with overhanging upper storeys built without any apparent order along stepped alleyways and cobbled streets, Panagía smacks unmistakably of the East. An impression that is reinforced in the **Imaret** (1817), Odós T Poulídou, which resembles a caravanserai with its domes and internal courtyards. The building was once a school and even a hospice for the poor. A less needy clientele now patronises the place, lingering over a drink to admire the **view*** over the town.

Mehmet Ali's house *(10am-2pm and 5pm-7pm; closed Monday and from October to April; donation)*, an imposing building overlooking a small square, provides a rare chance to see an **Ottoman interior** (1720). The original furniture has disappeared, but you can admire the lovely **view** over the town and the harbour.

By continuing to explore the heights of Panagía, you reach the crenellated walls of the **kástro**, a symbol of the town and of its glorious past *(daily 9am-6pm; no charge)*. Built by the Byzantines, this citadel was altered by the Turks and then the Venetians in the 15C. Inside there is an underground **cistern** which was later converted into a prison, a **defence tower** and an **open-air theatre** (beautiful **panorama*** over the town).

Making the most of Kavála

COMING AND GOING

By air – *Mégas Aléxandros Airport* is on the road to Xánthi (30km). KTEL provides a bus shuttle service from the terminal (30min).

Olympic Airways runs two daily flights to Athens, in the morning and the evening, and more in summer.

Aegean Airlines has one flight a day.

By train – The nearest station, at **Dráma** (30km), is on the line to Thessaloníki and Alexandroúpoli.

By bus – The **terminal** is located at the intersection of Odós Metropolítou Hrissostómou and Odós Filikís Eterías. For Athens and Thessaloníki, tickets can be purchased at the ticket office, while tickets for other destinations can be purchased on board. For Fílipi, take a bus for Dráma (every 30min; a 30min ride) and ask to be dropped at the site. For Thessaloníki, buses leave every hour (2hr), as do buses to Keramotí (1hr). Buses to Xánthi leave every 30min (1hr).

By ferry – Tickets to Thássos are on sale at the harbourmaster's office, where you will also find the timetables. In winter, the service is reduced (see page 467).

Níkos Miliádis Shipping Agency, Platía K Dimitríou 36, ☎ (051) 226 147, Fax (051) 838 767. Information and bookings for Límnos (4hr30min) and Lesbos (11hr30min).

Zolotas Travel, near the ferry landing-stage for the Aegean Sea, ☎ (051) 835 671. In summer there are services to Samothrace (4hr).

By hydrofoil – *Aneth*, ☎ (051) 834 464 (see page 467).

GETTING AROUND

By bus – The main bus station is located in Platía K Dimitríou, on the harbour.

By taxi – ☎ (051) 232 001 / 002 / 003.

By rental vehicle – *Europcar*, Odós Elefthériou Venizélou 24d, ☎ (051) 223 615. ***Budget***, Odós Elefthériou Venizélou 35, ☎ (051) 228 785. ***Hertz***, Odós Erithroú Stavroú 32, ☎ (051) 838 310.

ADDRESS BOOK

Tourist information – *EOT*, Platía Eleftherías (west side), ☎ (051) 222 425. In summer, Monday-Friday 7am-8pm, Saturday 8am-1pm; in winter, Monday-Friday 8am-2pm. Maps and information about hotels, transport and local festivals.

Detak, Odós Hrissostómou Smírnis, at the west entrance to the town, ☎ (051) 831 388, Fax (051) 831 378. The municipal tourist office is a mine of information. Monday-Friday 8am-4pm / 5pm-9pm, Saturday 8am-4pm.

Tourist police – Odós Omónias 119, ☎ (051) 222 905.

Banks / Currency exchange – There are plenty of banks and cash dispensers in Odós Stavroú, Odós Venizélou, Odós Omónias and Platía Eleftherías. The **National Bank of Greece**, Platía Eleftherías, has money-changing facilities and a cash dispenser. **Midas Exchange**, Platía Eleftherías, next to the EOT. 8.30am-9pm, Saturday 9am-8pm.

Post office / Telephone – Main post office, Odós Metropolítou Hrissostómou 8, on the corner of Odós Erithroú Stavroú. Monday-Friday 8am-8pm. **OTE**, in the square of the Iróon municipal park, and on the corner of Odós Antístasis and Odós Avérof.

Internet – Cyber Club, at the west end of Odós Elefthériou Venizélou.

Airlines – Olympic Airways, Odós Ethnikís Antístasis 8, ☎ (051) 836 639.

WHERE TO STAY

The town is fairly noisy. Hotels concede a discount of up to 50 % in low season.

Under €30

Giorgos Alvanos, Odós Anthémiou 35, ☎ (051) 228 412 – 8rm. A small, traditional house in the heart of Panagía (parking difficult), with simple, cramped, but cheap and well-kept rooms.

Between €30 and €60

Hotel Panorama, Odós Elefthériou Venizélou 26c, ☎ (051) 224 205, Fax (051) 224 685 – 52rm. The rooms, with or without bathroom, are rather gloomy but well-kept and the welcome is friendly. Good value for money.

Hotel Acropolis, 29 Odós Elefthériou Venizélou, ☎ (051) 223 543, Fax (051) 830 752 – 14rm. A hotel since 1925, this establishment has rooms with or without a bathroom. Upkeep and facilities are basic, but the large room with a terrace has a superb view over the harbour.

Hotel Nefeli, Odós Erithroú Stavroú 50, ☎ (051) 227 441, Fax (051) 227 440 – 99rm. ⌑ ℘ ✗ CC A comfortable hotel, with air conditioning and TV in some rooms, but it's the most expensive in this category. In low season, do not hesitate to bargain for lower rates.

Over €60

Hotel Esperia, Odós Erithroú Stavroú 44, ☎ (051) 229 621, Fax (051) 220 621 – 105rm. ⌑ ▤ ✈ ℘ ✗ CC Parking. On a noisy avenue, a vast hotel with very comfortable if impersonal rooms.

Oceanis Hotel, Odós Erithroú Stavroú 32, ☎ (051) 221 980 – 168rm. ⌑ ℘ ✗ ⌇ CC This luxurious seven-storey hotel resembling an ocean liner has a small swimming pool on the roof with an unbeatable view. A haven of peace amid the hustle and bustle...

Hotel Galaxy, Odós Elefthériou Venizélou 27, ☎ (051) 224 205, Fax (051) 224 685 – 150rm. ⌑ ℘ TV CC A large, slightly run-down hotel with spacious, comfortable rooms, some of which have a balcony overlooking the harbour. Unfortunately very noisy.

EATING OUT

Odós T Poulídou, in the citadel, has a good choice of restaurants.

Around €11

Taverna To Koutoukáki, Odós T Poulídou 29. ⌂ A cheap place serving good grilled fish.

Around €13

Taverna Antonia, Odós T Poulídou. ⌂ A very popular place with the locals. Good for fish.

Estiatório Imaret, in the Imaret, Odós T Poulídou. Greek food served in a very pleasant setting.

Ta Plakákia Restaurant, Odós Doïránis 4, on the harbour. ⌂ This restaurant serves excellent seafood, but try not to turn up at the same time as a tour group!

HAVING A DRINK

Cafés, bars – Imaret, Odós T Poulídou. Ideal for a quiet coffee or a salad.

Café Líthos, Odós T Poulídou. A small, trendy bar where the youngsters meet.

Café Tebelhanío, Odós T Poulídou. A more traditional venue, this café also serves meze.

SHOPPING GUIDE

Market – Every Saturday morning on Odós Ethnikís Antístasis (seafront).

Bookshop – Papadogiánnis Bookshop, Odós Omónias 46, on Platía Eleftherías, sells magazines and newspapers in English.

Making the most of Kavála

459

FÍLIPI ★★
(PHILIPPI)
Province of Macedonia – District of Kavála
16km from Kavála – Regional map page 412 – Michelin map 980 fold 7

Not to be missed
The theatre. The forum. Basilica B. The octagonal basilica.

And remember...
Spend the night in Kavála and visit Fílipi the next morning.

Situated in the outlying region of the great plain of eastern Macedonia, the ancient town of Fílipi has seen the fate of the West played out here on several occasions. It was here that Antony and Octavian defeated the armies of Brutus and Cassius – the prelude to the establishment of the Roman Empire – and that Paul preached the Christian faith for the first time in Europe. In the forum, the screaming and the shouting subsided a long time ago, but the majestic ruins testifying to the town's extraordinary history are still standing, moving testimonials to the great civilisations of the past.

An unusual destiny
Founded in 360 BC by a group of Thasians led by Callistratus, an exiled Athenian, the small town of **Krinídes** did not have time to create itself much of a history: in 356 BC, it came under the yoke of Philip II of Macedonia, from whom it acquired its name. Dominating the route between the interior of Thrace and the coast, the town gained considerable importance, augmented by the exploitation of the gold mines of Mt Pangaíon, which proved to be a providential source of revenue through which to establish its autonomy. Large-scale drainage work soon made it possible to open up the plain to agriculture, and the town expanded.

The "Apostle of the Gentiles"
A Jew born in Tarsus, Cilicia (Asia Minor), Paul grew up in a Greek-inspired environment before going to study in Jerusalem, with Rabban Gamaliel the Elder. A great persecutor of Christians, he was sent to Damascus to subdue some agitators in around 33 AD. But on the way, he was swayed by a vision of Christ which persuaded him that he must be baptised immediately. After that, he travelled widely to establish Christian communities in Asia Minor, Macedonia and Greece. The prototype of a zealous missionary, haranguing the crowd amid jeers, he was stoned and thrown into prison. His influence was decisive at the "Council of Jerusalem" which marked the break with Judaism and its tradition. Paul advocated the abandoning of circumcision, an obstacle to the propagation of the faith among pagans. For fear of creating second-rate Christians, he also rejected the law of purity, which forbade Jews to eat at the same table as non-Jews. A protagonist of the separation from Judaism, Paul still insisted on the Jewish origin of the Christian faith. The fact that he was a Roman citizen meant that he was not crucified, but beheaded, in Rome, in about 66 AD.

A prosperous Roman city – Having passed into the hands the Romans in October 42 BC, Fílipi was the setting for an encounter which was to have immeasurable consequences: the victory of Octavian and Mark Antony over the Republicans Brutus and Cassius sealed the destiny of Rome and precipitated the end of the Republic. After the battle, the veterans settled in the city, which received the status of a Roman colony. Henceforth, its inhabitants were to enjoy the same rights as Roman citizens in Italy, and Latin became the official language. Thanks to its position on the Via Egnatia trade route, Fílipi enjoyed considerable prosperity, which reached its peak in the 2C AD.

The Epistle of St Paul to the Philippians – But another drama was to be acted out. With his first visit in the year 49-50, during which he was imprisoned, Paul paved the way for Christianity in Europe. When he returned to Fílipi six years later, the "Apostle of Nations" had privileged links with the city, as his Epistle to the Philippians (certainly sent from Rome in the year 64) confirms. Assisted by the influence of Constantinople in the 4C, Christianity became established in the region, resulting in a return to Greek culture and the Greek language. Seat of the Metropolitan, who controlled several bishoprics, Fílipi was adorned with a number of basilicas.

Chronicle of a predictable decline – But numerous incursions on the part of the barbarians weakened the town. After the Goths (in the late 4C), it was the turn of the Slavs (7C-8C) and the Bulgars (9C) to ravage Fílipi. In the 10C, the Byzantine Emperor Nicephorus Phocas restored the ramparts and built the towers on the acropolis, giving the town the status of a fortress. It was no longer the religious centre that it had once been, but its position on the Via Egnatia allowed it to carry on its trading activities. However, the arrival of the Franks in the early 13C, marked the beginning of a long decline. After the Turkish conquest in 1387, the town's inhabitants deserted Fílipi and it fell into ruin. And it was not until the excavations conducted by the French School of Archaeology in Athens (1914-37), followed by those of the Greek archaeological services, that the glorious city returned from oblivion.

Tour of the site

Situated near the village of Krinídes, the ancient town is cut in half by the Kavála-Dráma state highway, which follows the route of the Via Egnatia. Daily, 8am-8pm from June to October; 8am-6.30pm in October, April and May, 8am-5pm from November to April. Entrance fee; plan of the site on sale at the ticket office. Allow between 2hr and 3hr to visit the site.

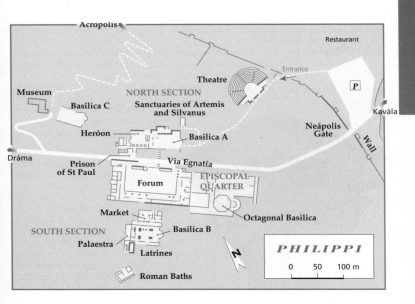

The north section

The site is reached by a passageway through the **defensive wall**, all 3 500m of it, which snakes up the hill. Part of the foundations built by Philip II are still visible, including the **Neápolis Gate** (4C BC), but most of the remains date from the reign of the Emperor Justinian (6C).

Immediately to the right, erected against the ramparts and the slope of the hill, is the **theatre*** with its broad, shell-shaped expanse of white seating. Built by Philip II (4C BC), it was altered during the Roman Period to accommodate performances involving gladiatorial combat and wild animals. Today it provides the setting for less bloodthirsty performances held during Fílipi's annual festival. One of the pillars of the entrance is decorated with **bas-reliefs** depicting Mars and Victory, and a magnificent **bucranium** (sculptured ox-skull).

During the Roman Period, sanctuaries dedicated to various divinities were built on the road leading up the hill to the acropolis, humble recesses dug out of the rock. On the small projection jutting out from the slope, just before Basilica A, appears the bas-relief of the **Sanctuary of Artemis**, which shows the goddess hunting a deer. The three nearby niches probably belonged to the **Sanctuary of Silvanus**, which scholars associate with the **Latin inscriptions** engraved in the rock *(on the right)*, mentioning its benefactors (2C-3C).

Little remains of **Basilica A** (late 5C) the eroded walls of which still give an idea of the extent of the nave and two side aisles, the narthex and the area of the atrium. Only two reconstructed **columns** disturb the melancholy sight of the blocks of marble and fine capitals scattered everywhere.

West of the basilica, you can see the massive foundations of a building consisting of two rooms: a Hellenistic **heróon** (monument to heroes) or a building of Roman date, scholars are divided about its interpretation. One thing is certain: the Byzantines converted it into a **cistern**.

Lower down, near the road, you will see another one, Roman in date this time, which was later transformed into a place of worship. According to tradition, it was here that **St Paul was imprisoned**.

Before crossing the road, head north-west to the nearby **Basilica C**, called outside the walls (late 5C), which has a fine **marble floor**. After it was destroyed, the narthex was converted into a cemetery.

Close by, the **museum** *(temporarily closed for renovation)* contains the finds unearthed by the French School of Archaeology in Athens at Fílipi, but also at Dikili Tash and Sitagri.

Byzantine Fílipi: a capital in Basilica A

On exiting the museum, you can follow the path that climbs up the hill of the **acropolis**: from between the ruins of two **square Byzantine towers**, there is a splendid **view** over the site.

The south section

The tour continues on the other side of the main road. At the bottom of the steps leading to the lower part of the site, you can make out the cart ruts worn into the paving of the ancient **Via Egnatia**, which runs along the side of the **forum***. Once the ancient heart of the city, this vast square paved with marble (100m by 50m) has **steps** and **porticoes** on three sides. Built under Marcus Aurelius in the 2C, the main public buildings were

B. Kaufmann/MICHELIN

concentrated here: the **temple** and the **library**, on the left, and the **curia** (place of assembly), on the right. Next to the Via Egnatia, you can still see the monumental **fountains** and the **tribune** where orators used to harangue the crowd.

Opposite, the few **columns** still standing mark the site of the old **market**, partly covered by Basilica B. Contemporary with the administrative forum, this huge market consisted of a central courtyard with a peristyle where the shops were located.

An impressive paleo-Christian building, **Basilica B★★** (550), called the Pillared Basilica, dominates the whole site. Here again, its ground plan can be clearly made out, the ruined walls delineating the nave, the side aisles and the apse, with the narthex and the atrium at the front. The building was probably never completed: too ambitious a project, the dome designed by the architects collapsed and the narthex was then converted into the main sanctuary, with a small apse. Today, you can still see the beautiful **marble arch** in the wall separating the narthex from the nave and the four enormous **pillars** which once supported the dome. The few **columns** also give an idea of the splendour of the original building: drums of green marble from Thessaly with Byzantine capitals carved with acanthus-leaf motifs.

Beyond the market square, the basilica has also encroached on the area of the **palaestra** (to the west), a vast courtyard used for athletic training (2C), of which only the **latrines** remain. Further south, in the ruins of the **Roman baths** (3C), converted into craft workshops after the arrival of the Goths, there are some fine floor **mosaics**.

The bishop's quarter★

Tour at fixed times. Next to the forum, to the east, the bishop's quarter is one of the best-preserved of all the ancient cities in the Balkans. From the Via Egnatia, on the right, a majestic **stoa** (walkway with porticoes) leads to the **narthex** of the **octagonal basilica★**, the ancient cathedral of Fílipi. Built in about 400 above the primitive basilica of Paul, it was destroyed in the 7C and only the base of the walls remains, showing the original ground-plan: an octagon within a square, surrounded by an ambulatory, once covered by a dome or a sloping roof. The only external projections are the narthex and the apse (to the east), occupied by a **synthronon**. In the 6C, four **exedras**, semicircular niches, were added to the corners. Incredibly, in the basilica you can still see some **mosaic floors★★** and part of its **marble paving★★**.

The Macedonian tomb that has been excavated is still unfortunately closed to the public, together with the residential quarter, just to the east, which is currently under excavation. As you leave the bishop's quarter, you pass the **bishop's palace**.

--- **Making the most of Fílipi** ---

COMING AND GOING

By bus – The buses from Kavála to Dráma stop in front of the site (20min).

WHERE TO STAY

If you don't wish to drive as far as Kavála, head for this comfortable hotel near Fílipi.

€38

Hotel Yánnis, Laspóloutra, on the road from Krinídes to Kavála (22km from Kavála), ☎ and Fax (051) 517 361. ⌷ ♪ ✗ ⌷ ⌷⌷ A place without any special charm, but with clean, bright, spacious rooms with a balcony overlooking the countryside. Not to be missed: a mud bath, renowned for its therapeutic properties. The clientele of the hotel is fairly elderly, since the place is known for its 29°C thermal springs. Open from June to the end of October.

OTHER THINGS TO DO

Feasts & festivals – In July and August, the theatre at Fílipi is the setting for the *Macedonian Festival* of Fílipi-Thássos. Information can be obtained from the EOT in Kavála, ☎ (051) 222 425, or on the spot, ☎ (051) 516 470, 6pm-9pm.

THÁSSOS★

North Aegean Sea – Province of Macedonia – District of Kavála
25km from Kavála – 380km² – Regional map page 412
Michelin map 980 fold 7 – Pop 13 500 – Allow 2 days

Not to be missed
Golden Beach and Paradise Beach.
Alikí Bay.
And remember...
Go for the beaches on the east and south coasts rather than those on the west.

Only a stone's throw away from the coast of Thrace, the mountainous silhouette of the island of Thássos rises above the turquoise waters of the Aegean Sea. Dominated by the pine-covered slopes of Mt Ipsário (1 127m), the coast is dotted with strips of sand and sheltered creeks. A green island with sun-kissed shores and an excellent infrastructure, Thássos has a number of attractions which make it an ideal place to stay. And it has been so since Antiquity. Because before it became a destination for tourists, it was the centre of one of the most enterprising societies in the north of Greece, as testified by the marble ruins of Liménas.

Wine, oil, marble and gold
Settled during the Neolithic Period, Thássos very soon produced a seafaring civilisation, which expanded in the Bronze Age thanks to trade in metals, wool, wine and oil. At a time when navigation was limited to coastal activities, its geographical position, between the Black Sea and the great economic centres further south, was a great asset. In the 7C BC, the first colonists from Páros settled on the site of modern Liménas, taking advantage of the rich agricultural plain, the trading posts established in Thrace and the gold deposits of Mt Pangaíon. The island then became known as a maritime power of the first order. Thássos was to succeed in maintaining its prosperity and in making its many aggressors respect it: Persians, Athenians, Macedonians and Romans, the latter providing a new boost to the trade in wine and marble. But after a brief period of occupation by the Genoese, in the 15C, Thássos finally passed into the hands of the Turks until the beginning of the 20C.

Liménas (Thássos)
Allow 2 days

As soon as you disembark from the ferry, head for the **old harbour** *(on the left)*, treat yourself to a drink on the terrace, and watch the return of the fishing boats. A small **beach** of fine sand awaits you nearby.
Tucked away at the foot of a wooded hillside on which the Ancients built an acropolis, Liménas has conserved numerous ancient remains. This is the only charming feature of this large modern town, now entirely devoted to tourism. But it is a friendly place and worth a visit or at least a stroll along **Odós 28 Oktomvríou**, set slightly back from the seafront, which is brimming with shops, hotels and restaurants.

The ancient city
Allow 2hr to explore on foot. Situated just behind the old harbour, in the middle of the houses, the ancient **agora**★ is now a vast rectangular space overgrown with weeds. Immediately beyond the entrance, on the left, are a few columns: all that remains of its **south-west portico** which dates back to Roman times (the bas-reliefs are displayed at the Louvre in Paris). Continue towards the south corner *(in an anticlockwise direction)* to the vestiges of a **monumental altar**, then make your way back towards the ruins of the **north-east portico**, three columns of which have been reconstructed.

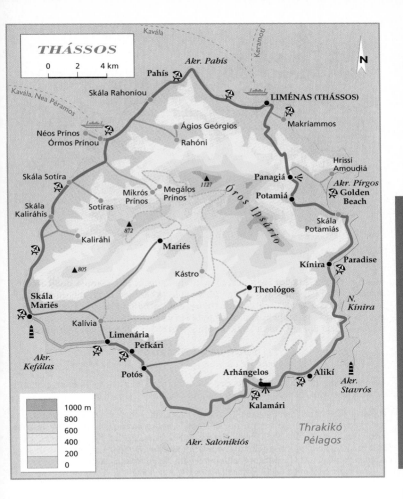

THÁSSOS

0   2   4 km

Kavála

Keramotí

Akr. Pahís

Pahís

Skála Rahoníou

Kavála, Nea Péramos

Néos Prínos
Órmos Prínou

Ágios Geórgios

Rahóni

LIMÉNAS (THÁSSOS)

Makríammos

Hrissí
Amoudiá

Skála Sotíra

Skála
Kaliráhis

Mikrós
Prínos

Megálos
Prínos

1127

Óros Ipsário

Panagiá

Akr. Pírgos
Golden
Beach

Potamiá

Sotíras

Kaliráhi

872

Mariés

Skála
Potamiás

805

Kástro

Skála
Mariés

Kalívia

Akr.
Kefálas

Limenária
Pefkári

Potós

Theológos

Kínira

Paradise

N.
Kínira

Arhángelos

Kalamári

Alikí

Akr.
Stavrós

1000 m
800
600
400
200
0

Thrakikó
Pélagos

Akr. Saloníkiós

Thássos

Go and see the **Archaeological Museum**∗ (*opposite the entrance to the agora*) which will give you a further opportunity to explore the agora (the excavations were conducted by the French School of Archaeology in Athens). When looking at the sculptures, note the impressive 6m-high **kouros**∗ (6C BC) and the very realistic **head of Silenus**∗. The museum also contains finds from the Temple of Artemis (same period), including a **bronze mirror-handle**∗ and an extraordinary **ivory lion's head**∗∗. Notice also the two **heads from the school of Scopas** (4C BC).

Behind the old harbour, a path follows the line of the **walls** along the hillside, directly above the **ancient harbour**, the ruins of which lie under water. Then further along is the **theatre** in its bucolic setting. Dating from the Hellenistic Period, it was altered by the Romans to accommodate performances involving wild animals. At the top of the hill, the path emerges at the triple **acropolis**, surrounded by pines. The first thing you come across is the **citadel**, built by the Genoese using material from the sanc-

The old village of Alikí

tuary of Pythian Apollo. Then you come to the remains of a **temple dedicated to Athena** (5C BC), at the top of the second hill. When you reach the third, a little lower down is a small **rock-cut sanctuary dedicated to Pan**. From it, there is a superb **view★** out to the island of Samothrace which you can see in the distance to the east. Then continue your walk, heading south and following the **ramparts**.

Tour of the island★
Route via the east, 95km. Allow 1 day.

Between the blue sea and the wooded hills, the road follows the winding contours of the coast with its profusion of creeks and beaches.

■ **Panagiá** – *8km from Liménas.* This large town, once the capital of the island, has a certain charm despite the plethora of hotels and souvenir shops. Pretty **houses with stone roofs** line the narrow streets and squares shaded by plane trees. Here and there you will glimpse beautiful **views★** of **Golden Beach★★**, a long strip of sand stretching away into the distance, also lined with hotels and restaurants (*you can reach it via a panoramic road which gradually descends over 4km*).

■ **Potamiá** – *2km from Panagiá.* With fewer tourists, but without the charm of its neighbour, Potamiá does have an interesting **museum** (*Tuesday-Saturday 9.30am-12.30pm and 6pm-9pm, Sunday and public holidays 10am-1pm*) which pays homage to its most famous son, the painter **Polýgnotos Vagís**.

■ Once out of the village, head towards **Skála Potamiás**, then **Kínira** (*8km*). Huddled at the foot of green hills (sadly ravaged by fire in parts), this village has a magnificent **setting★★**, and you will find numerous hotels near the pebble beach. But opt for **Paradise Beach★★**, a very pleasant little sandy beach opposite an **island**.

■ **Alikí★★** – Straddling the peninsula (*11km*) with a **beach** lapped by blue water on either side (the one on the east side is the best), Alikí is a delightful spot. It is hard to resist the charm of the few tavernas with white walls and stone roofs set among pine and olive trees. A short walk brings you to the ruins of an **ancient city** and a disused **marble quarry**, as well as the remains of two **paleo-Christian basilicas**.

■ Beyond Alikí, the south coast of Thássos has some magnificent **scenery****, unfortunately damaged by recent fires. Atop a rock overlooking the sea, the **Monastery of Arhángelos** *(2km)* has an exceptional **view***, looking right down over **Kalamári Bay*** and its delightful **beach** of fine sand.

At Potós, take the road on the right that sets off inland.

■ **Theológos*** *(10km from Potós)* is, without any doubt, the most beautiful village on the island, its narrow streets lined with white, stone-roofed **houses***. Spared the ravages of tourism, it is the perfect place to get away from it all.

■ Before continuing along the west coast, return to **Potós** *(19km from Alikí)*, a large but rather pleasant town with numerous hotels and restaurants by the sea. But even more charming is **Pefkári** *(1km further on)*, a small resort with a few hotels hidden among the pines, opposite a **beach**.

■ Two and a half kilometres further on, there is no point in lingering at **Limenária**, a large seaside resort which is also a fishing port. You might want to take advantage of its small **beach**, but, at all costs, avoid the **Papagiorgíou Museum**, which houses a collection of rather dubious objects: its exhibits include a "flea-killer" plate, an "authentic ancient arrow", a statue of a Siamese goat, a human embryo...
From Limenária you can make another foray inland on the **Kalívia** road *(12km)* to the charming village of **Mariés**.

■ Beyond Limenária, the west coast is dotted with a succession of little harbours *(skála)* and beaches, but they do not have the charm of the beaches in the south of the island. With the exception of the fishing village of **Skála Mariés** *(8km)* which has yet to be discovered by tourists.

The road then heads north, passing Skála Kaliráhis, Skála Sotíra and Skála Prínou, the second-largest port on the island (14km from Liménas), then Skála Rahoníou.

■ Finally, before reaching Liménas, you might want to have lunch at **Pahís**, where there is a pleasant **beach**.

Making the most of Thássos

COMING AND GOING

By ferry – From Kavála to Skála Prínou, twelve daily departures, from 9.15am to 11.15pm (1hr15min). From Keramotí to Liménas, nine daily departures, from 7.45am to 9.45pm (40min).

By hydrofoil – In summer, *Aneth*, ☎ (0593) 322 426, runs six daily return services to Liménas and Kavála (40min). Timetables are displayed at the harbourmaster's office.

GETTING AROUND

By bus – In Liménas, the bus station is opposite the landing-stage. Six times a day a bus drives clockwise around the island (2hr). There are also numerous services to Limenária via the west of the island.

By taxi – Liménas, at the ferry landing-stage, ☎ (0593) 23 391.

By bicycle – In Liménas, *Babi's Bike*, in the little street leading from Odós 28 Oktomvríou to the main square, ☎ (0593) 22 129.

Thomai Tsipou, Liménas. See below.

Motorcycle hire – *Billy's Bike*, Liménas, ☎ (0593) 25 253. *Thomai Tsipou*, Liménas, Odós Theogénous, ☎ (0593) 22 815. *Sakis Bikes*, Skála Potamiás, ☎ (0593) 62 024. *Megas*, Potós, ☎ (0593) 52 777.

Car hire – *Avis*, in Liménas, ☎ (0593) 22 535; at Golden Beach, ☎ (0593) 61 022; at Skála Potamiás, ☎ (0593) 61 735; at Potós, ☎ (0593) 53 070; at Skála Prínou, ☎ (0593) 72 075. *Europcar*, in Liménas, ☎ (0593) 23 387; at Potós, ☎ (0593) 52 970.

Hertz, in Liménas, Odós K Demetriosadi 11, ☎ (0593) 23 952.

ADDRESS BOOK (LIMÉNAS)

Tourist police – Opposite the landing-stage, ☎ (0593) 23 580. Information about Thássos, and it is possible to book hotel rooms here.

Port authority – ☎ (0593) 22 106.

Banks / Currency exchange – **National Bank of Greece**, opposite the landing-stage. Cash dispenser.

Post office – Odós G Alexándrou (from the harbour, follow Odós Theogénous and turn right at the crossroads). Monday-Friday 7.30am-2pm.

Telephone – Local code: 0593. **OTE**, Odós 28 Oktomvríou, near the Amfípolis Hotel.

Internet – **Nicko's**, west of Odós 28 Oktomvríou, near the quay. 10am-3am. At Potós, **Internet Cafe**, in the street which runs at an angle to the beach (8am-1am in summer).

Travel agency – **Mythos Travel**, Odós G Alexándrou, opposite the post office, ☎ and Fax (0593) 23 740. Boat trips and bus tours.

WHERE TO STAY
Most hotels are closed from October to May. In low season (September to June) the ones that do open extend discounts of about 20%. You will find hotels in all the villages on the coast.

• **Liménas**
Under €38
Hotel Vicky, ☎ (0593) 22 314 – 19rm. 📶 ♗ ⸦cc⸧ Comfortable, bright rooms in a small three-storey building. Most rooms have a kitchenette.
Hotel Victoria, Odós K Dimitriádou, next to the Hotel Mironi, ☎ (0593) 22 556, Fax (0593) 22 132 – 11rm. 📶 ♗ ⸦cc⸧ A small building with spacious, comfortable rooms with fridge.
Hotel Acropolis, follow the road leading south out of the main square, ☎ (0593) 22 488, Fax (0593) 22 441 – 11rm. 📶 ♗ ⸦cc⸧ An attractive-looking house dating from the early 20C, distinctive on account of its yellow façade. It has a pleasant lounge and simple but rather noisy rooms. Very friendly welcome.

Between €38 and €60
Timoleon Hotel, on the harbour, near the bus stop, ☎ (0593) 22 177,

Fax (0593) 23 277 – 30rm. 📶 ♗ ⸦TV⸧ ⸦cc⸧ A large building with rather ordinary but comfortable rooms, with a balcony overlooking the harbour. Bus service to the beach of Isteri (3km) and permission to use the swimming pool of the Amfípolis Hotel, next door. Breakfast included.
Hotel Mironi, Odós K Dimitriádou, ☎ (0593) 23 256, Fax (0593) 22 132 – 10rm. 📶 ♗ ⸦cc⸧ Run by the owner of the Hotel Victoria. A vast, marble hall leads to large, spotlessly clean rooms (with fridge). Breakfast is extra and quite expensive.
Hotel Pegasus, at the beginning of Odós K Dimitriádou, ☎ (0593) 22 061, Fax (0593) 22 373 – 27rm. 📶 ♗ ✗ ⸦≋⸧ ⸦cc⸧ A comfortable and excellently run hotel, with a gym, jacuzzi and Turkish bath. Some rooms have TV and air conditioning. Breakfast is included.
Amfípolis Hotel, on the corner of Odós 28 Oktomvríou and Odós Theogénous, ☎ (0593) 23 101, Fax (0593) 22 110 – 42rm. 📶 ♗ ⸦TV⸧ ✗ ⸦≋⸧ ⸦cc⸧ A large establishment built, somewhat surprisingly, in the neo-Gothic style. The rooms are luxurious and well ventilated, but the swimming pool is rather disappointing. Breakfast included.

• **Panagiá**
Under €30
Domátia Emanouíl Kousópoulos, behind the school, near the fountain, ☎ (0593) 61 981 – 10rm. 📶 The rooms, which are clean, quiet and comfortable, offer very good value for money. And from the balcony, the view over the bay is superb.

Between €38 and €45
≋ **Thássos Inn**, ☎ (0593) 61 612, Fax (0593) 61 027 – 15rm. 📶 ♗ ⸦TV⸧ The ideal place to stay in Panagiá, at the top of the village, near a church (follow the signs). The rooms are comfortable, some have a balcony. From the shady terrace where breakfast is served, there is a wonderful view of the village. Take note that prices double in high season.

• **Potós-Pefkári**
Under €38
Hotel Potós, ☎ (0593) 51 416 – 20rm. 📶 ✗ Spotlessly clean rooms, with mini-bar and balcony. Some small flats for families. Breakfast included.

Hotel Esperia, in Pefkári, ☎ (0593) 51 342, Fax (0593) 53 021 – 39rm. 🍴✗🛏 Near the Hotel Akti, and in the same category, this establishment offers half-board.

Hotel Akti, in Pefkári, ☎ (0593) 51 877 – 25rm. 🍴✗🛏 A small white building set among pine trees, with pleasant, well-kept rooms, and a balcony with sea view. Breakfast included.

• **Limenária**

Under €38

Hotel Ralitsa, ☎ (0593) 51 578 – 24rm. 🍴✗🛏 Situated near the Hotel Asterias, this hotel caters mainly for groups. The rooms (some have TV and fridge) are not as attractive but prices are slightly lower.

Hotel Asterias, ☎ (0593) 51 497 – 5rm. 🍴🅿 📺✗🛏 A small seafront hotel. The rooms are comfortable. Breakfast included.

• **Golden Beach**

Campsite (around €12)

Golden Beach campsite, ☎ (0593) 61 472. Next to the beach. Shaded by plane trees, it has a mini-supermarket, and the wash-blocks are very clean.

Between €45 and €60

Fedra Hotel, ☎ (0593) 61 474 – 11rm. 🍴✗🛏 Clean, comfortable rooms with sea view. The clientele consists mainly of British tour groups. Breakfast is extra.

🕯**Dionysos**, ☎ (0593) 61 822, Fax (0593) 61 823 – 33rm. 🍴🅿✗⚓ 💳 Set back slightly from the beach, on the hillside, this stone-roofed building has a superb view of the sea. The rooms are simple, but bright and comfortable. Breakfast included.

• **Skála Potamiás**

Between €55 and €60

Hotel Miramare, go to the end of the quay, then turn right by the harbour, ☎ (0593) 61 040, Fax (0593) 61 043 – 30rm. 🍴🅿 📺✗⚓ Surrounded by pines, in a quiet setting 100m from the beach. Pleasant rooms and very professional staff.

EATING OUT

• **Liménas**

You will find plenty of places to eat, particularly around the old harbour.

Between €9 and €13

Ta Platanákia, by the old harbour. 🍽 Good food and reasonable prices, but the ambience is rather touristy.

I Sími, next door to the restaurant above. 🍽 The fish is good here but the welcome varies, depending on the number of tourists.

Antónis, in the street leading from the main square to Odós G Alexándrou. Excellent barbecued food.

• **Around the island**

Restaurant Vigli, at the north end of Golden Beach. 🍽 Superbly situated on a rocky promontory dominating the bay, here they serve meze, grilled food, pizzas and seafood. It's also a pleasant place to go just for a drink.

Taverna Theagénis, Skála Potamiás, near the small harbour. 🍽 Greek dishes and seafood.

Christos, Ágios Geórgios. 🍽 A pleasant little fish restaurant under a pergola.

Odysse, Pefkári, ☎ (0593) 52 173. 🍽 Pefkári has a whole range of hotel-restaurants overlooking the beach. This one serves good seafood, but the service can take forever.

Pachys, Pahís beach. 🍽 A very pleasant shady terrace, near the beach, where they serve excellent fish.

HAVING A DRINK

Bars, night-clubs – Full Moon, Liménas, Odós 28 Oktomvríou.

Anonymous Café, Liménas, next to the Full Moon. An eclectic choice of music.

OTHER THINGS TO DO

Excursions – The **Eros II** sails round the island once a day, with stops for fishing, swimming and snorkelling off the most beautiful parts of the island. Barbecue lunch. The boat departs from the old harbour of Liménas at 9.45am, and returns at 5.45pm. ☎ (0593) 22 704.

Angetour, berthed in the old harbour of Liménas, organises fishing trips.

Making the most of Thássos

XÁNTHI

Province of Thrace – District of Xánthi – 56km from Kavála
Regional map page 412 – Michelin map 980 fold 8 – Pop 35 000

Not to be missed
The Ottoman quarter.
And remember...
From Kavála, you can visit Xánthi and the surrounding area in a day (with a vehicle).

The gateway to Thrace, Xánthi reveals a little-known facet of Greece, dating from the time before the great upheaval between the two wars, when large numbers of Turkish Muslims still lived in the north of the country. Its Eastern charm is especially poignant in the old Ottoman quarter, one of the few to have survived the earthquakes of 1870 and 1910. Otherwise, the modern town offers the usual array of avenues brimming with shops and café terraces.

The old town, an Ottoman city*
Allow half a day

An unmistakable landmark, **Odós 28 Oktomvríou** crosses Xánthi from south to north (*one way*), via **Platía Eleftherías**, then **Platía Kentrikí**, the main square, dominated by a **bell-tower**.
Just north of Platía Kentrikí lies little **Platía Antíka**, one of the most lovely squares in Xánthi, which comes alive every evening when the terraces of the restaurants fill up. From here, a picturesque cobbled street leads up the hill on which the Ottoman quarter is situated. Very quickly, the noises of the town vanish, to become a distant memory. **Odós Antíka** and **Odós Venizélos** have a very special, old-fashioned charm: old, pastel-coloured, half-timbered houses with corbelled roofs stand next to the neo-Classical residences built at the beginning of the 20C by the tobacco merchants. Outside, you will see women wearing the traditional Muslim headscarves, a reminder that Xánthi is home to a sizeable Turkish-speaking Muslim community.

Minorities in the north of Greece
As a result of the enormous amount of inter-racial mixing over five centuries of Ottoman occupation, the population of Macedonia and Thrace is quite different to that of the rest of Greece. In addition to the Romany-speaking Vlachs and the Bulgarian-speaking Muslim Pomaks, the region is also populated by communities of Slavs and Albanians, all of whom have been absorbed into the Greek population. Victims of the Nazis during the Second World War, the Jews, who constituted more than half the population of Thessaloníki, now number only a few thousand. But the largest minority is undoubtedly that of the 120 000 Muslim Turks of Thrace.

An elegant town house, which once belonged to the Koumtzogli brothers – tobacco traders – has been converted into a **Folk Museum** (*Odós Antíka 7, near the Metrópole, daily 11am-1pm; entrance fee*) housing a fine collection of traditional costumes, fabrics, jewellery, furniture and copper objects.

Around Lake Vistonioda*
60km south-east of Xánthi, by the Porto Lagos road. Allow half a day.

■ On the way to the lake, stop at **Abdera** (*28km south of Xánthi. Turn right at Vafeika, then right again at Abdera, and proceed for 7km. Daily 8am-2.30pm*). Founded in the 6C by inhabitants of Teos (Asia Minor), this ancient city was one of the most important in Thrace. Its past splendour is evoked by the ruins of the **Hellenistic defensive wall**, the **craft workshops**, **shops**, **villas** and **Roman baths**. Perched on the hill, on the other side of the road, the **Byzantine basilica** has a fine **view*** out to sea.

■ Beyond **Porto Lagos** (*24km from Abdera, on the road to Alexandroúpolis*), the road follows a narrow spit of land hugged by two expanses of water: the Aegean Sea and **Lake Vistonioda⋆**. On the right, **St Nicholas' Monastery** seems to rise up out of the marshes bordering the sea while, on the other side, the lake with its reeds and tall grasses is an exceptional **natural habitat⋆**: almost 200 000 birds winter here, including storks, terns, various species of duck, herons, pelicans and flamingos.

— Making the most of Xánthi —

COMING AND GOING

By air – Situated 45km away, on the road to Kavála, **Hrissoúpoli Airport** can be reached by taxi or by taking a bus to Hrissoúpoli, then a taxi for the remaining 11km. **Olympic Airways** operates a flight to Athens in the morning (except Tuesday), and another in the evening.

By train – From the station, situated 2km south of the town, several trains a day leave for Thessaloníki (4hr). The Istanbul train also stops at Xánthi.

By bus – Buses to Komotiní and Thessaloníki, via Kavála, leave the main terminal, located near the fish market, west of Platía Eleftherías.

ADDRESS BOOK

Banks / Currency exchange – **National Bank of Greece**, north of Platía Kentrikí, walk up the pedestrian precinct of Odós I Stavró. Monday-Thursday, 8am-2pm, Friday 8am-1.30pm.

Main post office – Odós Giorgíou 16.

Telephone – Local code: 0541. **OTE**, Odós M Vógdou 2.

Internet – **Speedy net**, Odós Velissaríou 11 (200m south of the Hotel Orphéas).

Airline – **Olympic Airways**, Odós M Vógdou 6A, ☎ (0541) 26 497, Fax (0541) 23 784.

Travel agency – **Pilot Travel**, Odós Thermopílon 2, near Platía Kentrikí, ☎ (0541) 71 120, Fax (0541) 74 019. For booking tickets only.

WHERE TO STAY

At most of the hotels listed below, breakfast is extra.

Between €30 and €45

Hotel Dimocritos, Odós 28 Oktomvríou 41, north of Platía Kentrikí, ☎ (0541) 25 111, Fax (0541) 25 537 – 40rm. ⁂ ℘ The renovation work planned will give a little sparkle to this rather run-down hotel, but the prices (agree in advance) are likely to rise as a result.

Between €45 and €60

Hotel Xanthippion, Odós 28 Oktomvríou 212, south of Platía Kentrikí, ☎ (0541) 77 061, Fax (0541) 77 076 – 53rm. ⁂ ℘ TV CC This large, modern, six-storey hotel has comfortable but characterless rooms. The staff, who are professional, speak English and there is a car park, an unusual luxury.

Hotel Orphéas, Platía K Dimitríou 40, south of Platía Kentrikí, ☎ (0541) 20 121, Fax (0541) 20 998 – 38rm. ⁂ ℘ TV ▤ CC New, comfortable bedrooms, but smaller than the ones at the Xanthippion and at a slightly higher price.

EATING OUT

Platía Kentrikí has a large number of restaurants and cafés with a terrace.

Taverna To Palió Meráki, Platía Antíka. ⁂ An excellent restaurant for Greek food.

HAVING A DRINK

Café Ano-Kato, in the old town, Odós Paleológou 73. A good place for a drink at any time of day.

Café Kipos, by the river (north of the town). The place lives up to its name, which means "garden": a delightful verdant corner, as charming as you could wish, the perfect place to cool off and relax when the heat gets too much. This is also a favourite meeting place for the locals, who congregate here at the end of the day to chat under the pergola.

SHOPPING GUIDE

Markets – The **fish market** is located near Platía Antíka, while the large **covered market** is situated west of Platía Eleftherías.

ÉDESSA★

THE ANCIENT SITE OF PELLA

Province of Macedonia – Capital of the district of Pella – 86km from Thessaloníki
Regional map page 412 – Michelin map 980 folds 4-5
Pop 17 000 – Mild climate

Not to be missed
The Ottoman quarter.
The waterfalls cascading down the cliff.
The thermal springs of Loutra Loutriakiou.

And remember...
Explore the town on foot: this is the best way to soak up the atmosphere.

Perched high up on the edge of a range of high cliffs, Édessa occupies a very unusual position. The town is crisscrossed by streams and every street corner resounds with the echo of these impetuous currents which crash down off the cliffs onto the plain. Although undeniably without major attractions, Édessa is unjustly neglected by tourists, but this small lively town in the Macedonian hinterland is a very pleasant place to stop off and recharge your batteries. If the mild climate, the panorama of the waterfalls and the charm of the old Ottoman quarter are not enough of an incentive, you could supplement these with a visit to the ancient town or an excursion to the nearby thermal springs in the Voras Mountains.

An ancient Macedonian stronghold

Probably inhabited since prehistoric times, the site took on the appearance of a small town during the reign of Philip II (4C BC) and was then fortified by Alexander the Great's successors. At that time, Édessa stretched from the plateau (the acropolis) to the plain (Logos, the lower town). In the 3C AD, to counter assaults from barbarian hordes, the inhabitants hastily erected bastions on the acropolis, and reinforced the walls of the lower town with materials taken from ancient buildings. But Logos was finally abandoned following raids by Slavs and Avars (6C-7C). Only the high town survived. Part of Greece since October 1912, Édessa was briefly occupied by the allied French forces during the First World War.

Tour of the town
Allow half a day

Almost all of the town's activities are concentrated around three main streets: **Odós Filípou**, which leads into the heart of the town, and running parallel to it, **Odós Egnatía**, which leads to the Pella road, not forgetting **Odós Dimokratías**. Allow yourself some time for a stroll here before visiting **Waterfall Park**, situated on the edge of the cliffs. Overlooking the drop, it is one of the best spots to view the **waterfalls★★** and the **panorama** over the plain. A path which runs alongside the waterfalls leads to a **cave**.

Another equally attractive place for a leisurely stroll is the old **Ottoman district of Varosi★★**, where the alleyways are lined with beautiful **houses** with overhanging upper storeys. Opposite a renovated **watermill**, a **lift** in the side of the cliff permits easy access to the **Rope Museum**. It is worth the detour, if only to have a look at the building, its architecture typical of the industrial revolution (1908).

Returning to Varosi, you can visit the **Folk Museum** (*Odós Alexándrou; 10am-6pm; closed Mondays; entrance fee*), which houses a fine collection of **traditional costumes** from Édessa and the villages of the region, as well as various tools and weaving looms.

Right next door, the **Church of the Dormition of the Virgin** (Kímissis tis Panagías) contains some **frescoes** from the 11C-14C (*ask for the key from the Archaeological Office, near the OTE*).

Of the six mosques which Édessa once boasted, three have disappeared, one is used as a cinema, another as a church, and the **Yeni Cami** houses an **archaeological collection** (*closed at present*).

A stroll in the vicinity

Go along the Pella road, and turn left towards Logos Édessas, 2km further on. Nothing survives of old Édessa, which has been swallowed up by the modern town. Only the lower town of **Logos** has managed to preserve a few vestiges of its monumental defensive wall. The most interesting feature, the **Southern Gate**, opens onto the ancient Via Colonnata with a few of the **columns** still standing. From here, you can continue your walk along a country path.

Well worth the effort is a trek up into the **Voras Mountains**, as far as the thermal spa resort of **Loutra Loutrakiou*** (*25km, by bus*), located in an enchanting setting (*numerous hotels*). A dip in the steaming waters of the **stream** – at 37°C! – which winds along the bottom of a narrow wooded gorge, is a moment of pleasure which you will never forget.

Excursion to Pella

49km from Édessa and 37km from Thessaloníki. Allow 90min for the visit.

Adrift in the midst of a charmless and dreary plain, on the road from Édessa to Thessaloníki, Alexander the Great's ancient capital is hardly the most exciting location. For history lovers, however, it is a must.

The capital city of Philip and Alexander

Originally situated on the coast, Pella was relegated to an inland position during the Classical Period due to the build-up of alluvial deposits. It made its entry into the history books at the end of the 5C when **Archelaus** established the capital of

Édessa, a town of water

L. Hapsis/ON LOCATION

Macedonia there. From that time onwards, the town attracted some of the greatest Greek writers and artists, including **Euripides**, who wrote his play *Bacchants* there, and the painter **Zeuxis**. Later, **Philip II** fortified the town and endowed it with a new palace, while the fame of his son **Alexander** would spread throughout the civilised world. Wishing to affirm his power after the death of the valorous king, Cassander had the entire city redesigned. His successors put finishing touches to his work, adorning Pella with prestigious buildings and connecting it to the sea with a canal. An important artistic and political centre, its influence extended over the whole of Greece under Antigonus Gonatas (276-239 BC). But the **Roman conquest** (168 BC) brought Pella's glory to an end. Relegated to the rank of provincial capital, it was then passed over in favour of Thessaloníki and, weakened by a series of invasions, faded into obscurity.

The Archaeological Museum★★

Tuesdays-Sundays 8am-7pm, Mondays 12am-7pm. The ticket also gives access to the archaeological site. Although a long way short of what you would expect given the importance of the site, the museum nonetheless possesses a few treasures. Among the most remarkable statues are a **sitting dog**, a head of **Alexander★**, a statue of the king as the **god Pan★** (4C BC), the funereal stele of a man with his dog (5C BC) and a small bronze **Poseidon**. The museum also has some vases on display, including a **hydria★** depicting the dispute between Athena and Poseidon (c400 BC), along with furniture, architectural pieces, terracotta figurines, gold jewellery, various objects from the Neolithic Period, as well as a **mural** from a house in Pella. In the last room, you will see the mosaics from the house of Dionysus; one depicts a languid **Dionysus★★★** on a slender panther, a composition of great harmony, and the other a **lion hunt★★★**, depicted with dramatic intensity (some archaeologists interpret this as the episode when Alexander the Great, threatened by a lion, is saved by his friend Craterus).

The site

Same visiting times as the museum. The illustrious capital of Philip II and Alexander is now no more than a ruin; its past splendour is, however, successfully evoked by the size of the agora and the beauty of the mosaics. Protected by powerful fortifications, the town was set out like a chessboard around the agora, with the exception of the palace, perched atop a hill to the north, yet still remaining an integral part of the urban fabric. Several necropolises (dating from the 5C BC to the Roman Period) have also been discovered, to the east of the site.

To the right, beyond the entrance, lie the foundations of the **House of Dionysus** (late 4C BC), a vast single-storey mansion, of which one of the peristyles of **Ionic columns** has been partially reconstructed. Most of the mosaics are now to be found in the museum.

To the left is the **house of the abduction of Helen**. Its sumptuous mosaic floors include the amazing **stag-hunting scene★★★**, with its wonderfully delicate hues, the first signed work (Gnosis) in the history of this art. The remarkably expressive **Abduction of Helen★★★** depicts the terrified young woman being hoisted onto a chariot.

A short distance to the north lies a vast chaotic area of stonework invaded by weeds, the site of the **agora** (200m by 182m), the ancient heart of the city. Arranged in colonnades on all four sides were the various buildings: terracotta workshops (east wing), shops (south), studios (west) and administrative buildings (north). The south-west corner was where archives were kept, and the sanctuary (destroyed) dedicated to Aphrodite and to the mother of the gods stood adjacent to the square to the north.

Making the most of Édessa

COMING AND GOING

By train – Nine trains daily connect Édessa with Thessaloníki and Flórina (2hr30min). To Athens, you have the choice of the Intercity (5hr) or the normal train service (8hr). The station is at the eastern end of Odós 28 Oktomvríou.

By bus – From the main bus station, on the corner of Odós Filípou and Odós Pávlou Melá, there is a bus every hour to Thessaloníki (1hr45min), 6 daily to Véria (1hr) and 3 daily to Athens (8hr). Prices are higher than for the train.

From the bus station located on the corner of Odós Egnatía and Odós Pávlou Melá, there are 4 services daily to Flórina (90min) and Kastoriá (2hr30min).

ADDRESS BOOK

Tourist information – Located in one of the kiosks in Waterfall Park, ☎ (0381) 22 300. Open every day 10am-8pm. This office supplies an abundance of practical and tourist information.

Banks / Currency exchange – There are plenty of banks and cash dispensers in the town centre.

National Bank of Greece, Platía Dimokratías 2. Cash dispenser.

Post office – Odós Pávlou Melá, near the bus station.

Telephone – Local code: 0381. **OTE**, Odós Ágiou Dimitríou.

Internet – **Cafe Internet**, Odós Filelínon 17, near the stadium. 9am-2am.

WHERE TO STAY

The prices charged by hotels do not vary much from season to season. Note, however, that breakfast is rarely included in the price.

Between €15 and €30

Domátia Olympia, Odós 28 Oktomvríou 51, ☎ (0381) 23 544 – 6rm. This guesthouse is in a building near the railway station. Rather uninspiring rooms, but clean, and good value for money.

Hotel Pella, Odós Egnatía 26, ☎ and Fax (0381) 23 541 – 25rm.

This hotel offers respectable but gloomy rooms, and the street is noisy.

Between €38 and €60

Hotel Katarrakte, Odós Karánou 4, ☎ (0381) 22 300, Fax (0381) 27 237 – 44rm. Comfortable and very well kept, this reputable establishment is about 100m away from the waterfalls and most of the restaurants.

Hotel Varosi, Odós Arh Meletíou 45, ☎ (0381) 21 865, Fax (0381) 28 872 – 8rm. In a traditional house in the Ottoman quarter, this is a charming new hotel with warm, friendly staff. The rooms are small but comfortable and attractively decorated.

Over €75

Xénia Hotel, on the corner of Odós Filípou and Odós Giannitsón, ☎ (0381) 21 898, Fax (0381) 29 708 – 38rm. Opened in 1998, the most luxurious hotel in town with a cliff-top setting and the advantage of a superb view over the plain. Extremely comfortable, with very professional staff. The swimming pool was under construction at the time of writing.

EATING OUT

Katarrakte, Odós Dimotikós Kípos. Pleasantly situated in the middle of Waterfall Park, this vast municipal establishment serves traditional if predictable fare.

Oi Kukoi, 5km from Édessa, on the Flórina road. Accessible by taxi, this restaurant boasts a magical lakeside setting. Serves Greek dishes and fish. In winter, concerts at weekends.

Faro Taverna Onissis Micháils Mipoilgoíris, Odós 28 Oktomvríou 20. A good place for fish, octopus, meat, snails...

HAVING A DRINK

Cafés, bars – The bars are concentrated around the crossroads of Odós Dimokratías and Odós 28 Oktomvríou, and near Waterfall Park.

Café Enplo, Odós Konstantinoupóleos 43. A pleasant terrace with two streams running alongside.

KASTORIÁ ★★
THE PRESPA LAKES ★★
Province of Macedonia – Capital of the district of Kastoriá
210km from Thessaloníki – Regional map page 412 – Michelin map 980 folds 3-4
Pop 15 000 – Alt 620m – Mild climate, cool in winter

Not to be missed
The Byzantine churches and traditional houses in the town.
The Byzantine Museum.
An excursion to the Prespa Lakes.

And remember...
Avoid driving a car in Kastoriá.
In summer, book your hotel in advance if you want to stay overnight
at the Prespa Lakes.

A land of lakes and mountains, situated on the doorstep of Albania and Macedonia (the former Yugoslav Republic), the natural setting of the western edge of Greek Macedonia has a wild and powerful undercurrent, far removed from the peaceful

Macedonia and Thrace

HOTELS	
Aiolis	①
Anessis	②
Europa	③
Kastoria	④
Orestion	⑤
Xenia	⑥

images of Aegean Greece. Here, even the vestiges of the past reinforce the region's Balkan character, evoking the glory of Byzantium and the Ottoman times, rather than Ancient Greece. Although overlooked by tourists, the region has a lot to offer, and the untamed majesty of the countryside makes you appreciate all the more the charming prettiness of the narrow streets and alleyways of Kastoriá.

"The town of a hundred churches"

Nothing remains of the city which, according to legend,

Beavers and mink

The Jewish inhabitants of Kastoriá are generally considered to be the originators of the trade in furs in the 15C although there are people who believe that it dates back to the Byzantine Era, when local craftsmen would sell furs brought back from Russia to the rich families of Constantinople. Whatever its origins, under the Ottomans the furs and skins from Kastoriá were famous: they were sold throughout the Balkans and Central Europe, and were in great demand at the Leipzig Fair. Nowadays, the tradition persists, but most of the pelts now come from North America and Scandinavia. Nonetheless, mink farming still goes on in Kastoriá, representing 25% of world production. During the 1990s, however, the fur trade was badly affected by negative publicity, and production has halved.

was founded by Orestes. After it was destroyed by the barbarians (4C-5C), Emperor Justinian endowed it with a fortress (6C), only scant remains of which have survived the passage of time. On the other hand, Kastoriá has retained much of its heritage from the Medieval Period, a time of prosperity during which it flaunted itself as one of the richest cities in the Byzantine Empire. Famed for its art, it was to be passed relentlessly backwards and forwards between the Bulgars, the Franks, the Despotate of Epirus, the Serbs and the Albanians. The Ottoman conquest in 1387 brought the Byzantine chapter to a close... leaving in its wake no fewer than 72 churches decorated with frescoes! Under its new masters, the town continued to prosper thanks to links it maintained with the Venetian territories nearby. The arrival of Greek troops in 1912 would bring an end to a Turkish presence which had lasted for 525 years.

Tour of the town
Allow one day

Astride a peninsula in **Lake Orestiás** (Límni Kastoriás), Kastoriá appears like an oasis in the hollow of a magnificent circle of mountains. Far off the tourist track, the town exudes a timeless charm, enhanced by its countless Byzantine churches and sturdy patriarchal houses. To immerse yourself thoroughly in its atmosphere, you can do no better than set off to explore the maze of sloping alleyways which somehow always end up at the lake. In a deep sleep during the siesta, Kastoriá comes to life in the evening, when a lively crowd descends on the terraces of the cafés on Odós Megálou Alexándrou and the steps of the museum.

Before setting off on a tour of the churches, pay a visit to the **Byzantine Museum**★ (*Platía Dexamenís, at the top of the hill; 8am-3pm; closed Mondays; no charge*). On display here is a small but exciting collection of **icons**★★, covering a period from the 12C-17C. Of a very high quality, the items are displayed in chronological and thematic order, contrasting the differences in style between the Byzantine (very expressive) and the post-Byzantine (more formal and hieratic).

A Byzantine stroll...
For a guided tour, enquire at the museum. Allow 3hr.
Begin near Platía Omónia: a short distance away the tiny **Panagía Koubelídiki Church**★★ (11C) stands with its slender, tapering dome... right in the middle of a car park. The church is constructed entirely of brick and stone, on a cruciform plan;

Kastoriá's little Byzantine jewel: the Church of Ágios Stéfanos (detail)

some beautiful 15C **frescoes** can be seen inside the porch. But the main treasure is inside: a magnificent **Dormition of the Virgin★★★** (13C), which is striking for the brightness of its colours and the richness of its composition.

Down from the square, the **Ágios Nikólaos Kasnídzi Church** also contains some remarkable **frescoes★★** (12C), notably a portrait of the benefactor and his wife *(in the narthex)*.

Then go down along Odós Manoláki and turn right into an alleyway. Even older (9C), the **Taxiárhes Mitropóleos★** was without doubt used as a funeral chapel for the eminent people whose portraits hang on the outside walls. The church, formed by a nave and two side aisles separated by colonnades (beautiful Early-Christian **capitals**), has retained its original **frescoes** in the narthex and in the eastern aisle. Others, which date from the 14C, illuminate the high part of the nave (scenes of the Passion, very expressive) and the apse, where there is a beautiful scene of the Virgin Mary surrounded by angels.

Constructed at the end of the 9C, the old Episcopalian church of **Ágios Stéfanos** *(to the north-east of town, Odós Paleológou)* was completed in the 16C with the addition of two side porches. In the upper part of the narthex, part of the original decor can still be seen, while the very high vault of the nave is adorned with some **12C frescoes** depicting the Nativity and the Purification.

Similar to Ágios Stéfanos, but slightly larger, the **Church of Ágii Anárgiri★★** *(Odós Vitsiou, near the previous entry)* (10C) is dedicated to Cosmas and Damian, known for their benevolence ("anárgiri" means "without money") in caring for the sick. The two saints are featured under the porch of the church. Most of the interior **frescoes★**, eroded in parts, date from the 11C-12C. In some places, however, a layer from the 10C still shows through (the heads of St Basil and St Nicholas, on the right-hand side of the narthex) and, in the gallery to the left, you can even discern three different layers. Closer to the nave, you can see the benefactors, the Limniotis couple, framing the Virgin Mary. Most importantly, do not miss the very beautiful **Lamentation★★** on the north wall, which foreshadows the Pietà of Western art.

... and an Ottoman one

Then take a stroll through the districts to the east (*northern bank, and between Odós Orestiádos and Platía Emanouíl*) to see the **archontiká**, the noble, half-timbered houses built by wealthy furriers between the 17C-19C (*see page 85*). Above the storeroom on the ground floor, the middle floor is taken up by the living quarters and the work-shop, while the top floor is kept for the reception rooms and summer lounges.

Some *archontiká* have been renovated and converted into museums. This is the case with the **Nerándzis Aïvazís House★**, now the **Folk Museum** (*Odós Kapetán Lázou, open every day 10am-12noon and 4pm-6pm; entrance fee*). This is a marvellous recre-ation of the living conditions of the Macedonian bourgeoisie in the 17C. A vast paved **hall** connects the **service quarters** (storeroom for spices and food, wine cellar, dough-kneading trough, bread oven, kitchen) and the **fur workshop**. In the **courtyard**, where a boat and some fishing equipment are stored (originally, the house was so close to the lake that a bit of fishing could be done from the balcony), you can also see a well and an alcohol distillery. The tour continues on the next floor... with the lavatories, which have a secret passage for escaping from police raids! In the sumptuous **drawing room★**, guests would either be seated on armchairs or benches, according to their status (diplomats, officers, VIPs), where they could be spied upon by the young females of the house from their **sewing room**, through a grille. The same system allowed them to watch a suitor being received in the **living room★** (note the delicate **frescoes★★**). If the mother liked him, he would be served with a coffee with sugar: no sugar, no marriage!

Continue as far as the **Emanouíl House★** (*Odós Vizandíou, open every day, 10am-12noon and 4pm-6pm; entrance fee*), which has been converted into a **Costume Museum**. It has retained very little of its furnishings, but is a very beautiful example of interior architecture. The outstanding collection of **furs and embroidered garments★★**, with some pieces dating from the 17C, is also worth a look.

To end the day

To the east of town, a narrow road leads off between the lake and the barren **hill** which guards the end of the peninsula. This countryside promenade (*9km*) leads to the **Panagía Mavriótissa Monastery★**. The main building, an attractive katholikón with a tiled roof and whitewashed walls (12C), contains some 12C and 13C **frescoes★**. Those on the outside wall illustrate the Tree of Jesse, with the Virgin Mary sur-rounded by the prophets, while those inside depict the Final Judgement (*east wall of the narthex*), the Passion, Pentecost, and the Dormition of the Virgin Mary (*west wall*), as well as the Virgin Mary surrounded by the Evangelists (*apse*). To the south-east of the church, the **Chapel of Ioánnis Theológou** was added in the 16C.

A land forgotten by man

Suspended at an altitude of 850m, the two lakes straddle three countries, cut off from the Macedo-nian hinterland by the Barnous Mountains which rise to a height of approximately 2 000m. To the north, Megáli Préspa, the larger of the two lakes (288km²), is divided up between Macedonia, Albania and Greece. A narrow strip of land separates it from Lake Mikrí Préspa (43km²), shared between Albania and Greece. The region, which is classed as a na-tional nature reserve, has a remarkable flora and fauna: there are no fewer than 1 500 species of plants and 260 species of birds (herons, egrets, cranes, pelicans and very rare cormorants from Dal-matia), as well as wolves, chamois, and even bears.

On the banks of the Prespa Lakes
(Límnes Préspes)
64km from Kastoriá. Head out of town on the Flórina road. Allow one day.
Take your swimming things if you fancy a dip.

On the border of Greece, Albania and Macedonia, the Prespa Lakes and their moun-tainous bower present a scene of great beauty, albeit wild and austere. This isolated region, where a handful of fishermen and shepherds maintain a semblance of human occupation, is the domain of **pelicans** and **herons**. It also reads like a history textbook with yellowed pages, recalling the Bulgar Tsar Samuel (10C-11C), responsible for the Church of Ágios Ahílios, the Byzantine Emperor Basil II, who erected fortifications throughout the region, Michael VIII Paleologus and his son Andronicus II (13C-14C), who built churches, and the Dragas family, which provided Byzantium with its last emperor, who was killed defending Constantinople (15C) against the Turks.

Ágios Germanós

Turn right as you get to the lakes and continue for 4km. Perched high up in the hills, this picturesque village boasts a wonderful panorama of the lake; but the main point of interest is the tiny **domed church***, which contains some beautiful 11C **frescoes****, as well as the tomb of **St Germanós**, the Patriarch of Constantinople (8C).

Back on the plain, follow the narrow strip of land between the lakes and treat yourself to a short break on **Koula beach**, with its two tavernas.

On the Prespa Lakes: the ruins of the Church of Ágios Ahílios

Psarádes★

Turn right and go on for 5km. Huddled around a little bay which opens out into Lake Megáli Préspa, this charming village has a hotel (recently opened) and several tavernas. The fishermen organise motorboat excursions *(90min)* to nearby Albania, which include a visit to a number of **caves** decorated with **rock paintings**, as well as various hermitages. The main attraction is **Panagía Eleoússa** (early 15C) which is decorated with **frescoes** from that period.

The island of Ágios Ahílios★★

To the left after the strip of land which separates the two lakes. As though cast away off the shore of Lake Mikrí Préspa, with its colonies of birds seeking refuge in the bullrushes, this little island conjures up the most romantic of images. On the bank where the ferry lands, the old stone and cob houses of a long-forgotten village are huddled together in a rather melancholic fashion. At various points on the island, there are magical **views★★** over the lake and the vestiges of its past.

The last residence of Tsar Samuel, the **Basilica of Ágios Ahílios** (11C) (*go left as you leave the village and walk for 500m*) recalls the time when the island was the capital of the ephemeral Bulgarian Empire. Originally a structure with a nave and two side aisles, the only parts which have survived are the apse and the arches of the left gallery, which are silhouetted against the sky, close to the water. Continue to the end of the island, as far as the **Monastery of Panagía Porfíra** (16C), its riverbank location invaded by reeds. Badly damaged by a German bombing raid in 1941, it has however managed to retain its church and **frescoes**.

Making the most of Kastoriá

COMING AND GOING

By air – The **Aristoteles Airport** is 10km to the south, ☎ (0467) 42 515. From May-October, 4 flights weekly to Athens, in the morning.

By bus – The bus station is in Odós A Diákou, to the south of town, ☎ (0467) 83 455.

6 services daily to Thessaloníki (4hr), some via Véria. 5 services daily to Kozáni (2hr); and 2 to Athens (9hr). To get to Ioánnina, catch the 7am bus to Neápoli, where a second bus departs at 9am (4hr). There is no direct service to Flórina either: you have to change at Amíndeo. There are also services to Édessa.

GETTING AROUND

By taxi – ☎ (0467) 42 333.

By boat – A small boat makes the crossing between the north and south banks several times daily, sailing around the peninsula (30min). There are timetables posted on the quayside.

ADDRESS BOOK

Tourist information – **EOT**, Odós Ioustinianoú, in the town hall building, down from Platía Daváki, ☎ (0467) 26 777. Mondays-Fridays, 8.30am-2.30pm.

Bank – **National Bank of Greece**, Odós 11 Noemvríou. Automatic cash dispenser and currency exchange.

Post office – To the north of Odós M Alexándrou.

Telephone – Local code: 0467. **OTE**, Odós Agíou Athanassíou.

Internet – **Aéras café**, Odós Agíou Athanassíou 48. Open 9am till late at night.

Airline company – **Olympic Airways**, Odós M Alexándrou 15, ☎ (0467) 22 275.

WHERE TO STAY

In most places, breakfast is extra.

Between €38 and €45

Anessis, Odós Grámou 10, ☎ (0467) 83 908, Fax (0467) 83 768 – 21rm. ⌐¶ ☞ TV CC Recently renovated and very well-maintained, this hotel has extremely comfortable rooms, with balcony, but the street is a bit noisy and the staff are not that friendly.

Xenia, Platía Dexamenís 11, ☎ (0467) 22 565, Fax (0467) 26 391 – 14rm. ⌐¶ ☞ TV CC Situated in a quiet district a short distance from the Byzantine Museum, this large Soviet-style building houses an old "luxury" hotel. It is a bit run-down, but the rooms are large and comfortable.

Orestion, Platía Daváki 1, ☎ (0467) 22 257, Fax (0467) 22 258 – 20rm. ⌐¶ ☞ TV CC Characterless, rather noisy rooms, but well maintained and comfortable. English-speaking staff.

Europa, Odós Agíou Athanassíou 12, ☎ (0467) 23 826, Fax (0467) 25 154 – 36rm. ⌐¶ ☞ TV CC Another good hotel, near Platía Daváki, as comfortable as the Orestion and at comparable prices. The staff speak English.

Between €60 and €75

Aiolis, Odós Agíou Athanassíou 30, ☎ (0467) 21 070, Fax (0467) 21 080 – 14rm. ⌐¶ ☞ TV CC Housed in a colonnaded building on the corner, this luxury hotel, if rather flashy, is extremely comfortable and the service is very professional. Breakfast is included.

🏨 **Kastoria**, Odós Níkis 122, ☎ (0467) 29 453 – 37rm. ⌐¶ ☞ TV CC Standing some way apart, on the north bank, this recently renovated luxury hotel has rooms decorated in classical style (some with air conditioning). Opt for the rooms on the second floor, which have balconies with a view over the lake.

EATING OUT

Under €12

Swan Restaurant, Odós Thomaídos 1, ☎ (0467) 27 994. 🍴 Warm welcome, inexpensive, serves excellent trout and grilled meats, which you eat under the watchful eye of the swans and cats... although sometimes there can be a slightly unpleasant smell from the lake.

Omonoia, Odós Mitropóleos 97, near Platía Omónia. A small restaurant, simple and not expensive.

Around €15

Nostalgia, Odós Níkis 2, opposite the landing-stage, ☎ (0467) 22 630. 🍴 In

a quiet and pleasant setting, facing the lake. Serves grilled meat and fish dishes.

Restaurant Mavriotissa, near the monastery, at the end of the peninsula, ☎ (0467) 85 234. 🍴 On an attractive terrace shaded by plane trees, fish and beef in sauce are on the menu here. However, the place gets very busy at weekends.

OTHER THINGS TO DO

Festivals – From 6-8 January, a very colourful carnival takes place during the **Ragoutsaria**.

The first weekend in August, the village of **Nestorio** (20km from Kastoriá) organises a series of concerts as part of the River Festival.

Making the most of the Prespa Lakes

COMING AND GOING

By bus – As getting to the Prespa Lakes is difficult, it is better to hire your own vehicle. 2 bus services weekly departing Flórina at 7.45am and 2.30pm (90min). Departures in the other direction at 6.45am and 3.45pm. On Saturdays, only the morning service operates, and there is no service on Sundays. From Kastoriá, you have to travel via Flórina.

GETTING AROUND

By taxi – In Ágios Germanós, ☎ (0385) 51 207. Koula beach, ☎ (0385) 51 247.

By boat – For the island of Ágios Ahílios, barges wait at the landing-stage just down from the road. But during the siesta, you have to telephone: ☎ (0385) 46 112.

ADDRESS BOOK

Information centre – The **Prespa Lakes Information Centre**, on the way into the village of Ágios Germanós, has an exhibition on the natural and historical treasures of the region (in Greek).

The **Psarádes Information Centre** can supply a great deal of information on the flora and fauna.

WHERE TO STAY, EATING OUT

Flórina, the customary departure point for visiting the Prespa Lakes, has little to offer. You would do better to stay at the lakes, or do the trip in one day from Kastoriá.

Under €30

Ágios Germanós Hostel, Ágios Germanós, at the end of the village, ☎ (0385) 51 320 – 10rm. 🍴 A small guesthouse run by the village women's agro-tourism co-operative.

Ágios Ahílios, on the island of Ágios Ahílios, ☎ (0385) 46 601, Fax (0385) 46 112. 🍴✗ This guesthouse is located in one of the more robust traditional houses, and has a pleasant lounge with a fireplace.

Over €30

Hotel Psarádes, Psarádes, ☎ (0385) 46 015 – 16rm. 🍴✗ A comfortable hotel on the far side of the bay, facing the village. Breakfast is not included.

• **Eating out in Psarádes**

The village has several restaurants on the lakeside terrace. They serve excellent fish dishes, but tourists are not always given the friendliest welcome, with the exception of **Taverna Kóstas**, on the way into the village.

NOTES

NOTES

NOTES

NOTES

INDEX

Delphi: sight or place described in the text
Venizélos (Elefthérios): historical figure
Ouzo: practical information or term explained in the text

Maps and plans

Manufacture Française des Pneumatiques Michelin
Société en commandite par actions au capital de 304 000 000 EUR
Place des Carmes-Déchaux – 63000 Clermont-Ferrand (France)
R.C.S. Clermont-Fd B 855 200 507

© Michelin et Cie, Propriétaires-éditeurs, 2002
Dépôt légal janvier 2002 – ISBN 2-06-100063-0– ISSN 0763-1383
No part of this publication may be reproduced in any form without
the prior permission of the publisher.
Printed in France 01-02/1.1
Typesetting: Nord Compo – Villeneuve d'Ascq
Printing: IME – Baume-les-Dames

Cover photography:
Egósthena, on the Gulf of Corinth (B. Kaufmann/MICHELIN)
Detail of a kylix showing Apollo making a libation, Museum of Delphi (T.A.P.)
An Orthodox priest (R. Mattès/MICHELIN)

Please send us your comments and suggestions to help us improve this guide.

Michelin Travel Publications   or   **Michelin Travel Publications**
Hannay House   PO Box 19008
39 Clarendon Road   Greenville
Watford, WD17 1JA   SC 29302-9008
UK   USA

neos@uk.michelin.com

Tell us of your experiences. You may have come across a restaurant or hotel that we haven't mentioned, or a pretty village that we haven't pointed out. Please let us know. Please also indicate any out-of-date information.

■ **Have you bought any other NEOS guides?**

   Yes ☐   No ☐

■ **If so, which title(s)?**

_____

_____

■ **What made you choose this guide?**

	(1 = not important)		*(4 = very important)*	
Cover and layout	☐ 1	☐ 2	☐ 3	☐ 4
Practical information	☐ 1	☐ 2	☐ 3	☐ 4
Information on culture	☐ 1	☐ 2	☐ 3	☐ 4
Contact details for hotels and restaurants	☐ 1	☐ 2	☐ 3	☐ 4
Maps and plans	☐ 1	☐ 2	☐ 3	☐ 4
The Michelin brand	☐ 1	☐ 2	☐ 3	☐ 4
Brand loyalty	☐ 1	☐ 2	☐ 3	☐ 4

■ **How would you rate the following aspects of your NEOS guide?**

	(1 = poor)		*(4 = excellent)*	
Cover design	☐ 1	☐ 2	☐ 3	☐ 4
Illustrations	☐ 1	☐ 2	☐ 3	☐ 4
Information on culture	☐ 1	☐ 2	☐ 3	☐ 4
The "Meeting the people" chapter	☐ 1	☐ 2	☐ 3	☐ 4
The choice of places covered	☐ 1	☐ 2	☐ 3	☐ 4
Touring programmes	☐ 1	☐ 2	☐ 3	☐ 4
Site descriptions (eg style, length, descriptions)	☐ 1	☐ 2	☐ 3	☐ 4
Practical information (eg transport, useful addresses)	☐ 1	☐ 2	☐ 3	☐ 4
Accommodation suggestions	☐ 1	☐ 2	☐ 3	☐ 4
Maps and plans	☐ 1	☐ 2	☐ 3	☐ 4

Comments _____
_____
_____

■ How often did you use the following chapters?

	(1 = never)		(4 = often)	
Setting the scene (red border)	☐ 1	☐ 2	☐ 3	☐ 4
Meeting the people (green border)	☐ 1	☐ 2	☐ 3	☐ 4
Practical information (orange border)	☐ 1	☐ 2	☐ 3	☐ 4
Exploring… (blue border)	☐ 1	☐ 2	☐ 3	☐ 4

Comments _____
_____
_____

■ Were there enough contact addresses?

	Not enough	Enough	Too many
Hotels	☐	☐	☐
Restaurants	☐	☐	☐

Comments _____
_____
_____

■ How many marks out of 10 would you give your NEOS guide?
(1 = poor; 10 = excellent)
_____/10

■ Which other destinations would you like to see covered by the NEOS collection?
_____
_____
_____

■ Personal details

Male ☐   Female ☐

Age: under 24 ☐   25-34 ☐   35-49 ☐   50-64 ☐   over 65 ☐
Name: _____
Address: _____
_____
_____